MILITARY *Living's*™

MILITARY SPACE-A AIR OPPORTUNITIES

ALL NEW SPACE-A RULES

Around the World

• You can save thousands of $$$ with this book!

by

William "Roy" Crawford, Ph.D
President, Military Marketing Services, Inc.
and Military Living Publications

Lela Ann Crawford
Vice-President, Military Marketing Services, Inc.
and Publisher, Military Living Publications

EDITOR: Bryce D. Thompson

COVER DESIGN: Rupprecht & Associates
LAYOUT ARTIST: June Douglas
ASSISTANT LAYOUT ARTISTS: Pamela Greer
Bryce D. Thompson

EDITORIAL ASSISTANTS: Rose C. McLain
Pamela Greer

MARKETING MANAGER: William R. Crawford, Jr.

OFFICE STAFF: Anna Belle Causey, Irene Kearney,
Helen Henderson

Military Living Publications
P.O. Box 2347
Falls Church, Virginia 22042
(703) 237-0203

NOTICE

The information in this book has been compiled and edited either from the activity/facility listed, its superior headquarters, or from other sources that may or may not be noted. All listed facilities, their locations, hours of operation, and telephone numbers could change. Flight schedules, including destinations, routings, frequency of flights, and types of aircraft used, are always subject to change; however, many of the flights listed in this guide have followed the same routes for over 40 years. Though we have published the most up-to-date information available to us, regulations governing Space-A passenger eligibility could change. The "how to travel Space-A" supporting information in the appendices is also subject to change, but the latest changes to these appendices were included at press time. This book should be used as a guide to Space-A travel with all o the above in mind. **Please forward any corrections or additions to the publisher.**

This guide is published by Military Marketing Services, Inc., a private firm in no wa connected with the U.S. Federal or any other governments. The guide is copyrighted by William Roy and Lela Ann Crawford. Opinions expressed by the publisher and writer are not to be considered an official expression by any government agency or official.

The information and statements contained in this book have been compiled from source believed to be reliable and to represent the best current opinion on the subject. N warranty, guarantee, or representation is made by **Military Marketing Services, Inc** as to the absolute correctness or sufficiency of any representation contained in this o other publications and we can assume no responsibility.

Copyright 1988
William Roy and Lela Ann Crawford
MILITARY LIVING PUBLICATIONS
MILITARY MARKETING SERVICES, INC.

First Printing - February 1988
Second Printing - July 1988

All rights reserved under International and Pan-American copyright conventions. No pa of this book may be reproduced in any form without permission in writing from tl publisher, except by a reviewer who wishes to quote briefly from listings in connectic with a review written for inclusion in a magazine or newspaper, with source credit MILITARY LIVING'S MILITARY SPACE-A AIR OPPORTUNITIES AROUND TH WORLD. A copy of the review when published should be sent to Military Marketi Services, Inc., P. O. Box 2347, Falls Church, Virginia 22042.

Library of Congress Cataloging-in-Publication Data

Crawford, William Roy, 1932-
  Military space-A air opportunities
around the world.

  Includes index.
  1. United States--Armed Forces--
Transportation--Directories. 2. United States--
Armed Forces--Facilities--Directories.
3. Air travel--Directories. I. Crawford,
Ann Caddell. II. Thompson, Bryce D.
III. Title.
UC333.C73 1988   355.8'3'02573   88-1231
ISBN 0-914862-15-4

SPACE-A PASSENGERS REGULATION UPDATE

From Military Living's R&R Report, Copyright 1988

1.) Revalidation Change
2.) Family Members Rule Change

Late 1987 brought great news to Space-A travelers. First, Space-A travelers no longer have to revalidate their intention to fly at two-week intervals, but may now sign up just once. Active duty personnel may sign up for a full 30 days, but must be on leave at the time of sign-up and remain on leave while waiting to travel. Retirees may now sign up for the full 45 days. DoD began this policy worldwide on 1 October 1987.

This new "no revalidation" system will also help those flying overseas for their return flights. No longer will they have to keep returning to their departure terminal to revalidate their intention to fly. Once passengers arrive overseas, they should immediately go to the Space-A sign-up desk and register on the list for the return flight - if they plan to return during a 30-day period for active duty or 45 days for retired personnel. They can then go their way, enjoying their vacation while their names move to the top of the list. This plan eliminates a lot of paperwork and frustration for Space-A travelers.

Secondly, family members flying Space-A with their sponsors to or from overseas can now stay on that flight even if it stops somewhere in the continental United States before reaching its final destination. Previously, family members had to get off at the first stateside stop or they were not allowed to board at all.

Some examples from different parts of the country: a family traveling Space-A from Offutt AFB, Nebraska, to Hawaii, could not board a flight that made a stop in California. Now they can. The change in regulation makes the return trip more convenient as well, because the family will not have to leave the flight at the first stop within the continental United States. Another example: family members may now travel on a flight from Plattsburgh AFB, New York, to Hickam AFB, Hawaii, even though an en route stop is made in California. Conversely, family members may travel from RAF Mildenhall, England, to Plattsburgh AFB with an en route stop at Pease AFB, New Hampshire.

Pointers to remember: this new rule change applies only if the family remains on the same airplane for the entire trip. Family members are still not eligible for flights that change airplanes within the United States. Travelers should also be prepared to defray the cost of lodging and meals if the international mission involves an overnight stay at the en route stop. Finally, the intent of this rule change is to provide point-to-point international air transportation when no change of aircraft or mission number is involved.

To receive changes about Space-A information between new editions of Military Living's <u>Military Space-A Air Opportunities Around the World</u>, subscribe to Military Living's R&R Report, an all-ranks travel newsletter giving the latest information about Space-A air travel; temporary military lodging; military RV, camping, and rec areas; plus discounts in civilian hotels, motels, attractions, and transportation.

You can call in your order using a VISA, Master Card, or American Express Card: (703) 237-0203. Or send $12.00 for one year (6 issues), or $20.00 for two years to: Military Living's R&R Report, P. O. Box 2347, Falls Church, Virginia 22042. Our R&R subscribers are "in the know" before anyone else!

INTRODUCTION

Military Living's <u>Military Space-A Air Opportunities Around the World</u> is a comprehensive guide to Space-A air opportunities. This edition has been completely revised, and contains more than 300 Space-A departure locations worldwide. In response to our readers' needs, we have provided information about Space-A air opportunities for active duty, reserve/guard, and retired uniformed services personnel and their families. These opportunities are provided by the active Army, Navy, Marine Corps, Air Force, and Coast Guard, as well as the Reserve and National Guard. You can save thousands of $$$ with this book.

HOW THIS DIRECTORY IS ORGANIZED

This directory is divided into four major sections: Section I - Continental United States (CONUS); Section II - outside the Continental United States (OCONUS); Section III - foreign countries; and Section IV - detailed appendices containing information essential to Space-A travelers.

Listings within each section are alphabetized by state, territory, foreign country, and/or departure location. Some minor departure locations and some large continental geographic areas with changing departure locations and limited Space-A air opportunities have been placed in composite listings. These departure stations are easily identified in the table of contents.

This directory also provides country and state abbreviations, location identifiers, a cross-referenced index to location identifiers, and key Space-A questions and answers. The contents pages serve as the book's index. A sample listing follows which explains in detail how to use this directory.

HOW TO USE THIS DIRECTORY

Departure Location

Three Character Location Identifier

Country/Area Code, Comm Tel Info No
DOD Auto Voice Network(ATVN) Info No
Federal Tel System(FTS) Info No
U S Military Tel System Info No

Mailing Address of Unit Responsible for Space-A Passenger Activities

LOCATION: Here you'll find specific driving instructions to the departure location from local major cities, interstate/country highways and routes. More than one routing may be provided. **RM:** is the Rand McNally Road Atlas reference to the location and **HE:** is the Hallwag Europe Road Atlas reference to the location. **NMC:** is the nearest major city. Distance in miles and **DIRECTIONS FROM THE DEPARTURE LOCATION TO THE NMC ARE PROVIDED.**

FACILITIES	LOCATION	HOURS	PHONE	COMMENTS
PAX TERM INFO	Term Bldg #	Hrs of Operation	Comm & ATVN Tel #'s	
	Driving directions to the hangar and other pertinent information is also provided.			
Recording	Location	Hours	Tel # (s)	When tape is updated
Pax Svc Ofc	Location	Hours	Tel # (s)	Staffing & other pertinent information
Pax Paging	Location	Hours	Tel # (s)	How to request paging svc

PAX LOUNGES	General information about available lounge facilities			
General	Location	Hours	Tel # (s)	Facilities & services
DV/VIP	Location	Hours	Tel # (s)	Fac & svcs. Grades srvd.
Protocol Svc	Location	Hours	Tel # (s)	Fac & svcs. Grades srvd.
Family	Location	Hours	Tel # (s)	Services & restrictions
FOOD SERVICE	General information about available food services			
Cafeteria	Location	Hours	Tel # (s)	Other pertinent information
Dining Hall	Location	Hours	Tel # (s)	In-flight kitchen info
Enl Club	Location	Hours	Tel # (s)	Fac & svcs. Grades srvd.
NCO/CPO Club	Location	Hours	Tel # (s)	Call for service hours.
OFC Club	Location	Hours	Tel # (s)	Call for service hours
Restaurants	Location(s)	Hours	Tel # (s)	Names of restaurant(s)
Snack Bars	Location(s)	Hours	Tel # (s)	Other pertinent information
TRANSPORTATION	General info about available transportion on & off Base			
Air Tickets	Location(s)	Hours	Tel # (s)	Organization providing svc
Bus	Location	Hours	Tel # (s)	Comm, Shuttle, &/or Gov
Car Rentals	Location	Hours	Tel # (s)	Agencies and information
Limo Service	Location	Hours	Tel # (s)	Agencies and information
TAXI	Location	Hours	Tel # (s)	Comm, Shuttle, &/or Gov
Trains	Location	Hours	Tel # (s)	Call for local train info.
Parking	Location(s)	Hours	Tel # (s)	Short & long term info
OTHER SERVICES	General information about availability of other services			
Exchange	Location	Hours	Tel # (s)	Other pertinent information
Bank/Exc	Location	Hours	Tel # (s)	Other pertinent information
Hair Styles	Location	Hours	Tel # (s)	Barber & Beauty shops
Laundry/DryC	Location	Hours	Tel # (s)	Self-served laundry fac
Medical	Location	Hours	Tel # (s)	Emerg care for AD & retired
Postal	Location	Hours	Tel # (s)	US Postal Service facility
TML	Location	Hours	Tel # (s)	All Ranks & DV/VIP info

TRAVELERS AID	General info about agencies on & off Base. Family Services.
ARC	Location Hours Tel # (s) Duty & 24 hr tel #'s
Chaplain	Location Hours Tel # (s) Duty, 24 hr, emerg tel #'s
Emerg Relief	Location Hours Tel # (s) Type of relief organization
Lost/Found	Location Hours Tel # (s) Agency providing service
Sec Police	Location Hours Tel # (s) Other pertinent information
USO	Location Hours Tel # (s) May be off Base. Call.
ATTRACTIONS	Key attractions at the location or in the nearby area

SCHEDULED FLIGHTS

DESTINATION	ROUTING	FREQ	EQ/CMTS
Destination of Flight	Location Identifiers read left to right-originating to terminating	Freq of Flight Days, Months	Types of Equip and Missions See Appendix I

Subsequent destinations are listed in alphabetical sequence

IMPORTANT NOTE: Scheduled Uniformed Services flights by Service owned and operated aircraft and contractor furnished aircraft change often with respect to the key elements of destination, routing, schedules, aircraft equipment, and mission. There are frequent, minor (and sometimes not so minor) adjustments made in these key elements with very limited prior notice. Many of the CONUS, OCONUS, and foreign country routes have been flown for more than 40 years with constant modification of some or all of these key elements to meet the needs of the Uniformed Services. We have provided the most current reported information concerning these key elements for this edition/printing. Subsequent printings will contain the most current information at that time. We encourage you to keep current on changes in Military Space-A Air Opportunities Around the World by subscribing to our travel newsletter "Military Living's R & R Report." Lastly, we encourage you to call or visit your intended Space-A departure location prior to registering for Space-A travel to obtain the latest information regarding the key elements.

UNSCHEDULED FLIGHTS

This section lists destinations of occasional unscheduled flights, types of aircraft, and missions. Sometimes, routings and frequency of flights to general geographic designations (i.e. regions) are provided. Restrictions and limitations are specified.

CONTENTS

CONTINENTAL UNITED STATES (CONUS)

LOCATION IDENTIFIER	INSTALLATION	PAGE
	ALABAMA	
BHM	Birmingham Municipal Airport	1
OZR	Cairns Army Airfield	1
MXF	Maxwell Air Force Base	2
MOB	Mobile Coast Guard Aviation Training Center	4
HUA	Redstone Arsenal	4
	ARIZONA	
DMA	Davis-Monthan Air Force Base	5
LUF	Luke Air Force Base	6
PHX	Sky Harbor International Airport	8
YUM	Yuma Marine Corps Air Station	8
	ARKANSAS	
BYH	Eaker Air Force Base	9
LRF	Little Rock Air Force Base	10
	CALIFORNIA	
NGZ	Alameda Naval Air Station	12
BAB	Beale Air Force Base	13
MER	Castle Air Force Base	15
EDW	Edwards Air Force Base	15
NJK	El Centro Naval Air Facility	16
NZJ	El Toro Marine Corps Air Station	17
OAR	Fritzsche Army Airfield	18
VCV	George Air Force Base	19
NLC	Lemoore Naval Air Station	19
LAX	Los Angeles International Airport	20
RIV	March Air Force Base	22
MHR	Mather Air Force Base	23
MCC	McClellan Air Force Base	25
NKX	Miramar Naval Air Station	27
NUQ	Moffett Field Naval Air Station	28
NZY	North Island Naval Air Station	30
SBD	Norton Air Force Base	32
OAK	Oakland International Airport	34
NTD	Point Mugu Pacific Missile Test Center	36
SAN	San Diego Coast Guard Air Station	37
SUU	Travis Air Force Base	37
VNY	Van Nuys Air National Guard Base	40
VBG	Vandenberg Air Force Base	41
	COLORADO	
BKF	Buckley Air National Guard Base	42
FCS	Butts Army Airfield	43
COS	Peterson Air Force Base	43

CONNECTICUT

BDL	Bradley International Airport...................................	46

DELAWARE

DOV	Dover Air Force Base..	46
ILG	Greater Wilmington Airport......................................	49

DISTRICT OF COLUMBIA

See MARYLAND

FLORIDA

NZC	Cecil Field Naval Air Station...................................	49
PIE	Clearwater Coast Guard Air Station..............................	50
VPS	Eglin Air Force Base..	50
HST	Homestead Air Force Base..	52
NIP	Jacksonville Naval Air Station..................................	53
NQX	Key West Naval Air Station......................................	55
MCF	MacDill Air Force Base..	56
COF	Patrick Air Force Base..	58
NPA	Pensacola Naval Air Station.....................................	60

GEORGIA

MGE	Dobbins Air Force Base..	61
VAD	Moody Air Force Base..	63
WRB	Robins Air Force Base...	64
SAV	Savannah International Airport..................................	64

IDAHO

MUO	Mountain Home Air Force Base....................................	65

ILLINOIS

NBU	Glenview Naval Air Station......................................	67
ORD	O'Hare Air Reserve Forces Facility..............................	68
BLV	Scott Air Force Base..	69

INDIANA

GUS	Grissom Air Force Base..	71

IOWA

NONE

KANSAS

FOE	Forbes Field Air National Guard Base............................	72
FRI	Marshall Army Airfield..	73
IAB	McConnell Air Force Base..	73
FLV	Sherman Army Airfield...	74

KENTUCKY

HOP	Campbell Army Airfield..	75
FTK	Godman Army Airfield..	75
SDF	Standiford Field..	76

LOUISIANA

BAD	Barksdale Air Force Base	76
AEX	England Air Force Base	78
NBG	New Orleans Naval Air Station	78
POE	Polk Army Airfield	80

MAINE

BGR	Bangor Air National Guard Base	81
NHZ	Brunswick Naval Air Station	81
LIZ	Loring Air Force Base	83

MARYLAND

ADW	Andrews Air Force Base	83
MTN	Martin State Airport	86
NHK	Patuxent River Naval Air Station	86
APG	Phillips Army Airfield	88
FME	Tipton Army Airfield	88
NSF	Washington Naval Air Facility	88

MASSACHUSETTS

BED	Hanscom Field	89
AYE	Moore Army Airfield	90
CPD	Otis Air National Guard Base	90
NZW	South Weymouth Naval Air Station	90
CEF	Westover Air Force Base	91

MICHIGAN

SAW	K. I. Sawyer Air Force Base	92
MTC	Selfridge Air National Guard Base	93
OSC	Wurtsmith Air Force Base	94

MINNESOTA

MSP	Minneapolis-St. Paul International Airport	95

MISSISSIPPI

JAN	Jackson Municipal Airport	96
BIX	Keesler Air Force Base	96
NMM	Meridian Naval Air Station	99
VKS	Vicksburg Municipal Airport	100

MISSOURI

TBN	Forney Army Airfield	100
STL	Lambert St. Louis International Airport	101
STJ	Rosecrans Memorial Airport	102

MONTANA

GFA	Malmstrom Air Force Base	103

NEBRASKA

OFF	Offutt Air Force Base	104

NEVADA

NFL	Fallon Naval Air Station...................................	106
LSV	Nellis Air Force Base......................................	107

NEW HAMPSHIRE

PSM	Pease Air Force Base.......................................	108

NEW JERSEY

NEL	Lakehurst Naval Air Engineering Center......................	110
WRI	McGuire Air Force Base.....................................	110
MMU	Morristown Municipal Airport................................	112

NEW MEXICO

ABQ	Kirtland Air Force Base....................................	113

NEW YORK

RME	Griffiss Air Force Base....................................	114
IAG	Niagara Falls International Airport.........................	116
PBG	Plattsburgh Air Force Base..................................	116
SCH	Schenectady County Airport..................................	117
SWF	Stewart International Airport...............................	117
FOK	Suffolk County Air National Guard Base......................	118
GTB	Wheeler-Sack Army Airfield..................................	118

NORTH CAROLINA

CLT	Charlotte/Douglas International Airport.....................	119
NKT	Cherry Point Marine Corps Air Station.......................	119
ECG	Elizabeth City Coast Guard Air Station......................	121
POB	Pope Air Force Base..	122
GSB	Seymour Johnson Air Force Base..............................	123

NORTH DAKOTA

RDR	Grand Forks Air Force Base..................................	124
MIB	Minot Air Force Base.......................................	125

OHIO

MFD	Mansfield Lahm Airport.....................................	126
LCK	Rickenbacker Air National Guard Base........................	127
FFO	Wright-Patterson Air Force Base.............................	128
YNG	Youngstown Municipal Airport................................	130

OKLAHOMA

LTS	Altus Air Force Base.......................................	130
FSI	Henry Post Army Airfield...................................	132
TIK	Tinker Air Force Base......................................	132
OUN	Westheimer Airpark Airport..................................	134
OKC	Will Rogers Air National Guard Base.........................	135

OREGON

PDX	Portland International Airport..............................	135

PENNSYLVANIA

N68	Chambersburg Municipal Airport....................................	136
PIT	Greater Pittsburgh International Airport.........................	136
MDT	Harrisburg International Airport.................................	137
PHL	Philadelphia International Airport...............................	137
NXX	Willow Grove Naval Air Station...................................	139

RHODE ISLAND

OQU	Quonset State Airport..	140

SOUTH CAROLINA

NBC	Beaufort Marine Corps Air Station................................	141
CHS	Charleston Air Force Base..	141
CHS	Charleston International Airport.................................	144
CAE	Columbia Metropolitan Airport....................................	145
SSC	Shaw Air Force Base..	146

SOUTH DAKOTA

RCA	Ellsworth Air Force Base...	146

TENNESSEE

TYS	McGhee Tyson Airport...	147
MEM	Memphis International Airport....................................	148
NQA	Memphis Naval Air Station..	148
BNA	Nashville Metropolitan Airport...................................	150

TEXAS

BSM	Bergstrom Air Force Base...	150
BIF	Biggs Army Airfield..	150
FWH	Carswell Air Force Base..	151
NIR	Chase Field Naval Air Station....................................	152
NGP	Corpus Christi Naval Air Station.................................	153
NBE	Dallas Naval Air Station...	153
DYS	Dyess Air Force Base...	155
EFD	Houston Coast Guard Air Station..................................	156
SKF	Kelly Air Force Base...	156
DLF	Laughlin Air Force Base..	160
TXK	Muni-Webb Field Airport..	160
RND	Randolph Air Force Base..	160
REE	Reese Air Force Base...	162
GRK	Robert Gray Army Airfield..	163
SPS	Sheppard Air Force Base..	163

UTAH

HIF	Hill Air Force Base..	164
SLC	Salt Lake City International Airport.............................	166

VERMONT

NONE

VIRGINIA

DAA	Davison Army Airfield..	166
LFI	Langley Air Force Base...	167
NGU	Norfolk Naval Air Station..	168
NTU	Oceana Naval Air Station...	171

WASHINGTON

SKA	Fairchild Air Force Base...	172
GRF	Gray Army Airfield...	174
TCM	McChord Air Force Base...	174
NUW	Whidbey Island Naval Air Station.......................................	176

WEST VIRGINIA

MRB	Eastern West Virginia Regional Airport.................................	177
CRW	Yeager Airport...	178

WISCONSIN

GMF	General Billy Mitchell Field...	178
VOK	Volk Field Air National Guard Base.....................................	179

WYOMING

CYS	Cheyenne Municipal Airport...	179

OUTSIDE CONTINENTAL UNITED STATES (OCONUS)

ALASKA

ADK	Adak Naval Air Station...	181
AIS	Alaska Isolated Stations...	182
	BIG Allen Army Airfield AKN King Salmon Airport	
	CLF Clear Air Force Station NOU Sitka CG Air Station	
	GAL Galena Airport	
ANC	Anchorage International Airport..	182
EIL	Eielson Air Force Base...	183
EDF	Elmendorf Air Force Base...	185
ADQ	Kodiak Coast Guard Air Station...	187
SYA	Shemya Air Force Base..	188

AMERICAN SAMOA

PPG	Pago Pago International Airport..	189

GUAM

NGM	Agana Naval Air Station..	191
UAM	Andersen Air Force Base..	191

HAWAII

NAX	Barbers Point Naval Air Station..	194
HIK	Hickam Air Force Base..	196

PACIFIC ISLANDS

MDY	Midway Island Naval Air Station....................................	198
PIS	Pacific Islands, TT...	199

ROR Babelthuap Arpt, WCI/TT   PNI Ponape, ECI/TT
JON Johnston Island, JO   SPN Saipan, Mariana Is
KSA Kosrae Airport, WCI/TT   TKK Truk, ECI/TT
KWA Kwajalein, Marshall Is/TT   YAP Yap Island, WCI/TT

AWK	Wake Island Air Force Base..	200

PUERTO RICO

BQN	Borinquen Coast Guard Air Station.................................	201
NRR	Roosevelt Roads Naval Air Station.................................	201

US VIRGIN ISLANDS

STX	Alexander Hamilton Airport..	204

FOREIGN COUNTRIES

AFRICA

AFR	Africa Stations...	207

BBE Berbera Airport, SM   NDJ N'Djamena Intl Arpt, CD
KRT Khartoum Airport, SU   PZU Port Sudan Airport, SU
MGQ Mogadishu Intl Arpt, SM

ANTIGUA & BARBUDA

SJH	Coolidge Airport (St. Johns), AN..................................	207

AUSTRALIA

ASP	Alice Springs Airport...	208
LEA	Learmonth RAAFB...	209
RCM	Richmond RAAFB..	210
UMR	Woomera Airfield..	211

BAHRAIN

BAH	Bahrain International Airport.....................................	212

BELGIUM

CHE	Chievres Air Base...	212
BFS	Florennes Air Base..	213

BERMUDA

BDA	Bermuda Naval Air Station...	214

CANADA

YYR	Goose Bay Air Base (Newfoundland).................................	215
YYT	St. John's Airport (Newfoundland).................................	216

CARIBBEAN, CENTRAL & SOUTH AMERICA

CAB	Caribbean, Central & South America.....................		217
	SCL Arturo Merinobenitez Arpt,CH	LPB JF Kennedy Intl, BO	
	MGA Augusto "C" Sandino Intl, NI	LIM Jorge Chavez Intl, PE	
	BZE Belize Intl, BZ	GUA La Aurora Arpt, GT	
	BSB Brasilia Arpt, BR	UIO Mariscal Sucre Arpt, EC	
	CCS Caracas Arpt, VE	KIN Norman Manley Intl, JM	
	MVD Carrasco Intl, UG	PLA Palmerola Arpt, HO	
	BOG El Dorado Arpt, CL	ASU Pres Stroessner Arpt,PG	
	BUE Ezeiza Arpt, AG	RIO Rio de Janeiro Intl, BR	
	PAP Francois Duvalier Intl, HA	SDQ San Isidro AB, DR	
	GBI Grand Bahama Aux AF, BH	OCO Santamaria Intl, CS	
	BGI Grantley Adams Intl, BB	MIQ Simon Bolivar Intl, VE	
	SAL I Lopango Intl, ES	TGU Toncontin Intl, HO	

CUBA

GAO	Guantanamo Bay Naval Station.........................	219

CYPRUS

AKT	Akrotiri Airport.....................................	220
LCA	Larnaca Airport......................................	221

DENMARK

SFJ	Sondrestrom Air Base (Greenland).....................	221
THU	Thule Air Base (Greenland)...........................	222

EGYPT

CAI	Cairo International Airport..........................	223

GERMANY (WEST) & BERLIN

RMS	Ramstein Air Base....................................		223
FRF	Rhein Main Air Base..................................		226
SEX	Sembach Air Base.....................................		230
THF	Tempelhof Central Airport (Berlin)...................		231
WGS	West Germany Stations................................		233
	LHN Ahlhorn GAFB	NDO Nordholz GAFB	
	STR Echterdingen AAF	NRV Norvenich GAFB	
	FEL Fuerstenfeldbrueck GAFB	NUE Nurnberg Airport	
	LPH Leipheim GAFB		

GREECE

ATH	Athinai Airport......................................	234
VWH	Iraklion Air Station (Crete).........................	237
SOC	Souda Bay Naval Air Facility (Crete).................	238

ICELAND

KEF	Keflavik Airport.....................................	238

INDIAN OCEAN

NKW	Diego Garcia Atoll...................................	240

INDONESIA

DJK	Halim Perdanakusuma International Airport.....................	242

ISRAEL

TLV	Ben Gurion International Airport (Tel Aviv)....................	242

ITALY

AVB	Aviano Air Base..	243
BDS	Brindisi/Casale Airport..	245
NAP	Capodichino Airport (Naples)...................................	246
DCU	Decimomannu Air Base...	248
PSA	San Guisto Airport (Pisa)......................................	250
SIZ	Sigonella Airport (Sicily).....................................	251

JAPAN

NJA	Atsugi Naval Air Facility......................................	253
FUK	Fukuoka Airport..	255
NFO	Futenma Marine Corps Air Station...............................	256
IWA	Iwakuni Marine Corps Air Station...............................	256
JXP	Japan (Mainland) Air Bases & Airports (Hokkaido Island)........	258
	CTS Chitose Airport KUH Kushiro Airport	
JAB	Japan (Pacific Island) Air Bases & Airports....................	259
	IWO Iwo Jima Air Base MUS Minami Torishima Airport	
DNA	Kadena Air Base (Okinawa)......................................	259
MSJ	Misawa Air Base..	262
OKO	Yokota Air Base..	263

JORDAN

AMM	King Abdullah Air Base...	266

KENYA

NBO	Jomo Kenyatta International Airport............................	267

KOREA (SOUTH)

KOE	Korean Stations..	267
	CJU Cheju Do Intl Airport KWJ Kwang Ju ROKAFB	
	KHE Kimhae Intl Airport	
KUZ	Kunsan Air Base..	268
OSN	Osan Air Base..	270
TAE	Taegu Air Base...	272

LIBERIA

ROB	Monrovia Roberts International Airport.........................	274

NEW ZEALAND

CHC	Christchurch International Airport.............................	274

NORWAY

OSL	Fornebu Airport..	276

OMAN

MRH	Masirah Oman Air Force Base.................................	276

PANAMA

HOW	Howard Air Force Base.......................................	277

PHILIPPINES

CRK	Clark Air Base..	279
CUA	Cubi Point Naval Air Station................................	282

PORTUGAL

LGS	Lajes Field (Azores)..	284

SAUDI ARABIA

DHA	Dhahran International Airport...............................	286
JED	Jeddah Airfield...	287

SINGAPORE

SGP	RSAF Paya Lebar...	288

SOUTH AFRICA

JNB	Jan Smuts Airport (Johannesburg)............................	289

SPAIN

RTA	Rota Naval Air Station......................................	290
TOJ	Torrejon de Ardoz Air Base..................................	292
ZAZ	Zaragoza Air Base...	295

THAILAND

BKK	Don Muang Airport...	296

TURKEY

IGL	Cigli Turkey Air Base.......................................	297
ESB	Esenboga Airport..	298
ADA	Incirlik Airport (Adana)....................................	300
TUR	Turkey Air Bases & Airports.................................	302
	BZI Balikesir Airport ERZ Erzurum Airport	
	DIY Diyarbakir Airport ESK Eskisehir Turkey AF	
	EHC Erhac Turkey Air Force SIO Sinop Army Airfield	
YES	Yesilkoy Airport (Istanbul).................................	303

UNITED KINGDOM

ASI	Ascension Auxiliary Air Field...............................	304
BWY	RAF Bentwaters..	305
FFD	RAF Fairford..	306
MZH	RAF Mildenhall..	307
PIK	Prestwick Airport (Scotland)................................	310

ZAIRE

FIH Kinshasa N'Djili Airport.. 311

APPENDICES

APPENDIX A	Space-A Passenger Regulations............................	313
APPENDIX B	Personal Entry Requirements..............................	321
APPENDIX C	Passports and Other Documents............................	332
APPENDIX D	Visa Information...	335
APPENDIX E	Customs and Duty...	340
APPENDIX F	Locations Reporting Limited Space-A......................	343
APPENDIX G	Descriptions of Aircraft.................................	345
APPENDIX H	Country and State Abbreviations..........................	346
APPENDIX I	General Abbreviations....................................	348
APPENDIX J	Location Identifiers and Cross-Referenced Index..........	350
APPENDIX K	Space-A Questions and Answers............................	356
APPENDIX L	Space-A Passenger Booking Card...........................	363
APPENDIX M	Authentication of Reserve Status for Travel Eligibility...	364
APPENDIX N	Special Travel Aids......................................	365
APPENDIX O	LI-ICAO Conversion Table.................................	366
APPENDIX P	Military Airlift Command (MAC) MEDEVAC Flights............	367
APPENDIX Q	Standard Time Conversion Table...........................	369

MOVING TO WASHINGTON? "ONE SHOT" HELP................................. 373
CENTRAL ORDER COUPONS... 375

Info On Military Living

MILITARY LIVING PUBLICATIONS
(MILITARY MARKETING SERVICES, INC.)

Military Living was founded in 1969. The company publishes *Military Living*, a 30,000 circulation monthly magazine distributed on more than twenty military installations in the Washington, D.C. area.

Our travel newsletter, Military Living's *R&R Report*, has been published since 1971 and is available worldwide by subscription.

In addition to five (5) books currently available, Military Living published *U.S. Forces Travel Guide Europe* which is out of print but is under revision at this time. The company is also researching additional titles to improve the "quality of life" of the military and their families. See Central Order Coupon on pages 375 and 377.

HOW TO RECOGNIZE MILITARY LIVING'S BOOKS

All of Military Living's books carry the famous Military Living logo. Military Living is known as "The Morale Booster Publisher." The slogan, "Travel On Less Per Day ... The Military Way" is copyrighted by Military Living.

Ann Crawford, the founder of Military Living, is a well known travel writer whose articles reach military families around the world.

The president of the parent company, Military Marketing Services, Inc., is Wm. "Roy" Crawford, Sr., Ph.D.

Our company offices are located at 137 N. Washington Street, Suite 201, Falls Church, VA 22046. The mailing address, however, is P.O. Box 2347, Falls Church, VA 22042. The telephone number is (703) 237-0203.

This logo appears on all of Military Living's publications.

CONTINENTAL UNITED STATES
ALABAMA

Birmingham Municipal Airport (BHM)
117 TRW, Air National Guard
Birmingham MAP, AL 35217-0198

Comm: 205-841-9200
ATVN: 694-2210

LOCATION: Exit I-59/20 at Tallapoosa St, N 1/2 mi to R on East Lake Blvd to Installation. NMC: located in the NE section of Birmingham. RM: p-5, W/16.

FACILITIES	LOCATION	HOURS	PHONE	COMMENTS
PAX TERM INFO	Base Ops	Hrs=Tng days	C-841-9408	Call for flt info.
PAX LOUNGES	None	See Base Ops	A-694-2408	
FOOD SERVICE	Vending machines	24 hrs dly		(Food services at MAP)
TRANSPORTATION Parking	Comm bus at MAP. Call for hours. C-252-7171 or C-323-1678 Car rentals, Limo & Taxi at MAP. See telephone directory. None on ANG Base.			
TRAVELERS AID Sec Police	Amer Red Cross - 2225 3rd Ave N 0800-1200 dly C-322-5661 Main gate 24 hrs dly C-841-9240			
ATTRACTIONS	Vulcan (iron man statue) on Red Mountain in city, largest shopping mall in southeast, new horse racing track			

UNSCHEDULED FLIGHTS

Flights via transient aircraft to CONUS and OCONUS locations. Call for destinations, routings, and schedules. Limited Space-A from this ANG Base.

Cairns Army Airfield (OZR)
Air Operations
Fort Rucker, AL 36362-5000

Comm: 205-255-6181
ATVN: 558-1110

LOCATION: Ninety mi SE of Montgomery, midway between the capital city and Florida Gulf Coast, and 7 mi S of Ozark, off US-231 on Rt 249. Clearly marked. RM: p-5, Q/13. NMC: Dothan, 26 mi SE.

FACILITIES	LOCATION	HOURS	PHONE	COMMENTS
PAX TERM INFO	Bldg 30101 24 hrs dly C-255-2314/3907, A-558-2314/3907 Fm main gate (Daleville), cont on AL 85 to ATC tower/Base Ops.			
PAX LOUNGES General	Bldg 30101 24 hrs dly C-255-2314/3907, A-558-2314/3907 A/C, Tel C, TV, O/S seats. Also, pilot's lounge.			
DV/VIP	Bldg 30101 24 hrs dly C-255-2314/3907, A-558-2314/3907 A/C, Tel C&A, TV, Rest-rms, O/S seats. Protocol Svc A-558-3100.			

ALABAMA
Cairns AAF, Cont'd

FOOD SERVICE				
Cafeteria	Bldg 30101	0630-2000 M-F	C-598-6384-EX-69	Closed Sa-Su
NCO/CPO Club	Bldg 2908	1100-2100 dly	C-255-5191	Call for svc hrs.
OFC Club	Bldg 113	0630-2100 dly	C-255-5187	Call for svc hrs.
TRANSPORTATION Bus(Comm)	Main gate	Call for hrs.	Ozark GH=C-774-5500,	Fort Rucker TW=C-598-2375
Limo Service	Dothan	24 hrs dly	C-983-4886	$9-Dothan to OZR
TAXI(Comm) (Gov)	Daleville Bldg 701	24 hrs dly 0730-1600 dly	C-598-4464/5 C-255-4188	Duty Pax only
OTHER SERVICES	\multicolumn{4}{l}{Most spt svc avail. PX Bldg 9214 C-598-6384, Emergency med Lyster AR Hosp C-255-4186, ARC Bldg 5315 C-255-6214/6314, Bank C-598-2401,Mil Police (main gate) 24 hrs dly C-255-4175.}
TML	\multicolumn{4}{l}{Biltg Office Bldg 308 24 hrs dly C-205-255-3782/3213, A-558-3782/3213 All Ranks. DV/VIP C-205-255-3100,A-558-3100.}

UNSCHEDULED FLIGHTS

Unscheduled flts only. Most flts are via C-12A and U-21A aircraft. Most freq destinations are: Washington DC/Baltimore MD areas; Davison AAF VA (DAA); and Langley AFB VA (LFI) for Fort Monroe VA. Most missions posted 24 hrs in advance. Call for destinations and seat availability.Baggage limit is 30 lbs. Call ATM Branch   C-255-2127/5587, A-558-2127/5587.

Maxwell Air Force Base (MXF)
3800 ABW/LGTTA
Maxwell AFB, AL 36112-5000

Comm: 205-293-1110
ATVN: 875-1110

LOCATION: In west section of city. Take I-85 to I-65, exit on Day St which leads to main gate of Base. RM: p-5, Y/4. NMC: Montgomery, 1.5 mi SE.

FACILITIES	LOCATION	HOURS	PHONE	COMMENTS
PAX TERM INFO	Bldg 844	0700-1700 M-F	C-293-6454, A-875-6454	Schedule rec'd 24 hrs in advance. Day St to L on Ash St, R on 1st St.
Pax Svc Ofc	Bldg 844	0700-1600 M-F Flight recording 24 hrs dly	C-293-7372 C-293-6760, A-875-6760	
PAX LOUNGES General	Bldg 844	0700-1700 M-F	C-293-6454, A-875-6454	A/C, Tel C&A, TV, Rest-rms, P/C seats
DV/VIP	Bldg 844	0700-2300 dly	C-293-6961, A-875-6961	A/C, Coffee/tea srvd, Tel C&A, TV, Rest-rms, O/S seats (06+,GS15+)
Protocol Svc	Bldg 800	0800-1700 M-F	C-293-2095	Air Univ (06+ or civ eq)

ALABAMA

Maxwell AFB, Cont'd

FOOD SERVICE				
Cafeteria	Bldg 1090	0630-1430 M-F	C-263-6044	Breakfast/Lunch
Dining Hall	Bldg 668/1420	Call for hrs.	C-293-5127, A-875-5127	
NCO Club	Bldg 742	0930-2400 M-F,	1100 Sa-Su	C-262-8364
OFC Club	Bldg 144	0830-2200 M-F,	1100 Sa-Su	C-264-1731
Vending	Bldg 844	0700-2300 dly	C-834-5946	
TRANSPORTATION				
Air Tickets	Car rental, limo svc, & taxi off Base. Tel numbers at Term. Bldg 924 0715-1600 M-F C-264-0076 SATO			
Bus(Comm)	Bldg 927	0500-2400 dly	C-293-5038	MXW-MTG
TAXI(Gov)	Bldg 927	0500-2400 dly	C-293-5038	Duty Pax only
Parking	Bldg 843 (In front & across street - short & long term)			
OTHER SERVICES				
Exchange	Bldg 1090 0900-1800 M-F, 1700 Sa, 1200-1700 Su C-834-5946			
Bank/Exc	Bldg 1081 0900-1300 M-F C-832-8190			
Hair Styles	Bldg 1090 0900-1700 M-F, 1500 Sa C-263-3444 Barber 0800-1700 M-F, 1500 Sa C-263-3010 Beauty			
Laundry/DryC	Bldg 1090 0900-1730 M-F C-263-7826			
Medical	Bldg 50 24 hrs dly C-293-7861			
TML	Bldg 117 24 hrs dly C-293-2430, A-875-2430 Extensive fac. All ranks. DV/VIP C-293-2095, A-875-2095.			
TRAVELERS AID				
ARC	Bldg 18 0730-1630 M-F C-293-5626 After duty hrs C-293-7333			
Chaplain	Bldg 155 0730-1630 M-F C-293-7602 After duty hrs C-293-2862			
Sec Police	Bldg 837 24 hrs dly C-293-7222			
Emerg Relief	Bldg 500 0730-1630 M-F C-293-2353			
ATTRACTIONS	Air Univ, state capital & historical homes in Montgomery			

SCHEDULED FLIGHTS

DESTINATION	ROUTING	FREQ	EQ/CMTS
Andrews AFB MD (ADW)	MXF-ADW	Daily	C-12A/P & C-21A/P
Randolph AFB TX (RND)	MXF-RND	2 ea wk	C-21A/P
Scott AFB IL (BLV)	MXF-BLV	2 ea wk	C-21A/P

ALABAMA
Maxwell AFB, Cont'd

| Wright-Patterson AFB OH (FFO) | MXF-FFO | 1 ea wk | C-21A/P |

Note: Bag limit is 30 lbs on all above executive aircraft.

Mobile Coast Guard Aviation Training Center (MOB)
Commanding Officer
Mobile, AL 36608-5000

Comm: 205-694-6110
FTS: 537-6110
ATVN: 436-3635

LOCATION: Take Airport Blvd exit, W from I-65, 8 mi from Base. Turn right on Schillinger Road, then L on Tanner Williams Road, 1 mi. Clearly marked. RM: p-5, Y/11. NMC: Mobile, 1 mi NW.

FACILITIES	LOCATION	HOURS	PHONE	COMMENTS
PAX TERM INFO	Main hangar 0800-1600 M-F C-694-6428, FTS-537-6428 N side of Bates Municipal Airport. 2nd deck on ramp side. No Pax lounge. Rest-rms, Vending machines available.			
OTHER SERVICES	Many spt fac avail. CG BX C-694-6398, EM Club C-694-6358, Barber C-694-6494, TML C-694-6130, Medical C-694-6400.			

UNSCHEDULED FLIGHTS

Flights to East and Midwest. No overseas or helicopter Space-A.

Redstone Arsenal (HUA)
Flt Ops Div, Attn: AMSMI-RA-FO
Redstone Arsenal, AL 35898-5320

Comm: 205-876-2151
FTS: 876-2151
ATVN: 746-0011

LOCATION: Off US 231 on Martin Rd for main gate with visitor control. For uniformed pers, Gate #8 is on Drake Ave. Take US 72 onto Jordan Lane, then W on Drake Ave. Drake Ave becomes Goss Rd on the Arsenal. RM: p-4, D/15. NMC: Huntsville, adjacent N and E sides.

FACILITIES	LOCATION	HOURS	PHONE	COMMENTS
PAX TERM INFO	Bldg 4809 0630-1730 dly C-876-2186/1916, A-746-2186 Fm Gate 8, take Hale Rd to Arsenal AAF, Base Ops, Bldg 4809.			
PAX LOUNGES	Bldg 4809 0630-1730 dly C-876-2186, A-746-2186 A/C, Read/write rm, Tel C&A, TV, Rest-rms, O/S seats			
Protocol Svc	Bldg 5250 Duty hrs C-876-7135 (06+) MICOM			
FOOD SERVICE	Good on and off Base. Cafeteria C-876-7923, Enl Club C-881-6525, NCO/CPO Club C-837-0750, O'Club C-830-2582, Restaurant C-882-9631, Snack Bar C-881-1591			
TRANSPORTATION	Good on and off Base. Bus(Comm) GH=C-536-5349, TW=C-534-1681 Taxi(Gov) C-876-2261, Car Rentals Avis=C-772-9301, Hertz= C-772-9331, Natl=C-772-9336, Parking short term only at Term.			

ALABAMA

Redstone Arsenal, Cont'd

OTHER SERVICES	All spt fac avail. Emerg med, Fox AR Hosp C-876-8287, PX C-883-6100, ARC C-876-4427, Bank C-883-0173, Chaplain C-876-5707, Sec Police C-876-2222
TML	Billeting Office Bldg 244 0700-1630 C-205-876-5713, A-746-5713 All Ranks. DV/VIP C-205-876-7135, A-746-7135.
ATTRACTIONS	Space & Rocket Center (Hwy 20), Tenn River, and Southern BBQ

UNSCHEDULED FLIGHTS

All flts unscheduled. Missions posted 24 hrs in advance when possible. Most flts are to Wright-Patterson AFB OH (FFO) and Atlanta, GA and to the Midwest, including Lambert St Louis Intl Arpt MO (STL), Kansas City Downtown Arpt MO (MKC), and Kansas City IAP MO (MCI). Call for availability of flights and seats. Baggage limit is 30 lbs.

ARIZONA

Davis-Monthan Air Force Base (DMA)
836 Air Division/LGTT
Davis-Monthan AFB, AZ 85707-5270

Comm: 602-748-3900
ATVN: 361-1110

LOCATION: SE of Tucson. Exit I-10 N Palo Verde, R on 29th St, R on Craycroft Rd to main gate. RM: p-7, P/11. NMC: Tucson, 3 mi NW.

FACILITIES	LOCATION HOURS PHONE COMMENTS
PAX TERM INFO	Bldg 4820 0700-1600 M-F C-748-3641, A-361-3641 Continue on Craycroft Rd to flight line, below ATC tower.
Pax Svc Ofc	Bldg 4820 0700-1600 M-F C-748-3641, A-361-3641
PAX LOUNGES General	No family lounge Bldg 4820 0700-1600 M-F C-748-3641, A-361-3641 A/C, Bag check, Tel C&A, Rest-rms, TV, O/S seats
DV/VIP	Bldg 4820 24 hrs dly C-748-4315, A-361-4315 A/C, TV, Tel C&A, Showers,O/S seats,Rest-rms, Coffee/tea srvd Contact Base/Ops in advance (06+ and VIP).
Protocol Svc	Bldg S-1 0700-1600 M-F C-748-3600 (06+ and VIP) TAC spon'd
FOOD SERVICE	Good on and off Base. Flt Kitchen C-748-3532, NCO Club C-748-3100, O'Club C-748-0660, Vending C-748-7887
TRANSPORTATION	Good on and off Base. SATO C-748-4842, Bus(Comm) C-792-9222 (Shuttle) C-748-3391, Rental Car C-748-4842, Taxi (Comm) Yellow=C-624-6611, Checker=C-623-1133, Taxi(Gov) C-748-3391, Parking C-748-3641 (notify Security Police)
OTHER SERVICES	Good on and off Base. Exchange C-748-7887, Bank C-AZ and FCU, Hair Styles C-748-7887, Laundry/DryC C-748-7887, Medical C-748-7878, Postal/Wire C-748-3900
TML	Bldg 2350 0700-1600 dly C-748-1500, A-361-1500 All Ranks. DV/VIP C-748-3600, A-361-3600.

ARIZONA
Davis-Monthan AFB, Cont'd

TRAVELERS AID	ARC C-748-3205/623-0541, Chaplain C-748-5411, Emerg Relief C-748-4451, Sec Police C-748-3517
ATTRACTIONS	Old movie sets, Pima Air Museum, AZ-Sonora Desert, Zoo

SCHEDULED FLIGHTS

DESTINATION	ROUTING	FREQ	EQ/CMTS
Biggs AAF TX (BIF)	DMA-BIF-SKF-BLV	Tu,F	C009A/ME
Kelly AFB TX (SKF)	DMA-BIF-SKF-BLV	Tu,F	C009A/ME
Luke AFB AZ (LUF)	DMA-LUF-SUU	M,W	C009A/ME
Scott AFB IL (BLV)	DMA-BLV	Tu,F	C009A/ME
Travis AFB CA (SUU)	DMA-LUF-SUU	M,W	C009A/ME

Note: Some flights to East Coast CONUS and infrequently to OCONUS. Call for destinations, routings, and schedules.

Luke Air Force Base (LUF)
832nd Air Division
Luke AFB, AZ 85309-5000

Comm: 602-856-7411
ATVN: 853-0111

LOCATION: From Phoenix, W on I-10 to AZ-85 to Litchfield Rd. N on Litchfield Rd, approx 7 mi. Also, fm Phoenix on US-60 to AZ-89 to Glendale Avenue. West on Glendale Ave to intersection of Glendale Ave and Litchfield Rd, approximately 10 mi. Clearly marked. RM: p-8, K/6. NMC: Phoenix, 20 mi SE.

FACILITIES	LOCATION	HOURS	PHONE	COMMENTS
PAX TERM INFO	Bldg 439	0630-2230 M-F, 0730-1800 Sa, Su, Hol C-856-7131, A-853-7131. Fm main gate W on F St to L on 8th St to Term on flight line.		
Recording	Bldg 439	24 hrs dly	C-856-7016, A-853-7016	
PAX LOUNGES General	Bldg 439	See Pax Term	C-856-6631/7131 A/C, Bag check, Read/write rm, Tel C&A,TV, Rest-rms,P/C seats	
DV/VIP	Bldg 439	See Pax Term	C-856-6087, A-853-6087 Located in rear wing of Terminal	
Protocol Svc	Bldg 11	0730-1630 M-F	A-853-6101 (O6+) TAC	
FOOD SERVICE Dining Hall	Many on and off Base. Please call for dly hrs. Bldg 543	0430-1800 dly	C-856-6420/7097, A-853-6420/7097	
NCO/CPO Club	Bldg 259	1300-2200 M,Tu,Th, 1300-2400 W, 1300-0100 F, 1100-0100 Sa	C-856-7136	

ARIZONA

Luke AFB, Cont'd

OFC Club	Bldg 750	0630-2200 M-Sa	C-932-9311/856-6446
Run-In-Chef Snack Bars	Bldg 1540 1000-1700 M-F,0900-1630 Sa C-935-4029 0600-1400 M-F, 0700-1400 Sa C-935-4661 Dty hrs. C-269-5879, A-853-6549 Other hrs.		
Vending	Bldg 439	24 hrs dly	C-269-5879
TRANSPORTATION Air Tickets	Bldg 28	0730-1630 M-F	C-856-6891 SATO
TAXI(Gov)	Bldg 330	0700-1600 dly	C-856-6866 O/hrs C-856-3702
Parking	Bldg 439	24 hrs dly	C-856-7131, A-853-7131 Unlimited
OTHER SERVICES Exchange	Bldg 1540	1000-1700 M, 1800 Tu-F, 0900-1700 Sa, 1100-1600 Su C-935-2671/2, A-863-6421	
Bank/Exc	1st Natl Bank of AZ 0930-1600 M-Th, 0830-1600 F & pay days C-935-3382 Located directly across fm main gate		
Hair Styles	Bldg 1540 0900-1600 M, 1000-1600 Tu-F, 0800-1600 Sa C-935-3466 Barber, C-935-5850 Beauty		
Laundry/DryC	Bldg 1540	0700-1600 M, 1800 Tu-F, 0900-1600 Sa C-935-9554	
Medical	Bldg 1130	24 hrs dly	C-856-7506, A-853-7506
Postal	Bldg 151	0800-1630 M-F (closed 1300-1330) C-935-1343	
TML	Bldg 666 All Ranks.	24 hrs dly C-856-6336, A-853-6336 DV/VIP C-856-6101, A-853-6101.	
TRAVELERS AID ARC	Bldg 883	0800-1630 M-F	C-856-7823
Chaplain	Bldg 799	0730-1630 dly	C-856-6211
Sec Police	Bldg 179	24 hrs dly	C-856-6322
ATTRACTIONS	Colorful Scottsdale nearby, fairgrounds and coliseum in Phoenix (state capital), AZ State University in Tempe, Sun City - largest retirement center in the world.		

SCHEDULED FLIGHTS

DESTINATION	ROUTING	FREQ	EQ/CMTS
Biggs AAF TX (BIF)	SUU-LUF-DMA-BIF-SKF-BLV	Tu,F	C009A/ME
Davis-Monthan AFB AZ (DMA)	SUU-LUF-DMA-BIF-SKF-BLV	Tu,F	C009A/ME
Kelly AFB TX (SKF)	SUU-LUF-DMA-BIF-SKF-BLV	Tu,F	C009A/ME

ARIZONA

Luke AFB. Cont'd

Nellis AFB NV (LSV)	SBD-LUF-LSV-SBD	2/Su	C-141B/M(R)
Norton AFB CA (SBD)	LSV-LUF-SBD SBD-LUF-LSV-SBD	2/Su 2/Su	C-141B/M(R) C-141B/M(R)
Scott AFB IL (BLV)	SUU-LUF-DMA-BIF-SKF-BLV	Tu,F	C009A/ME
Travis AFB CA (SUU)	SUU-LUF-DMA-BIF-SKF-BLV	Tu,F	C009A/ME

Sky Harbor International Airport (PHX)
161st Air Refueling Group (ANG)
Phoenix, AZ 85034-5000

Comm: 602-244-9841
ATVN: 853-9211

LOCATION: Exit 152 off I-10 or I-17 N. RM: p-7, O/3. NMC: Phoenix, 3 mi NW.

FACILITIES	LOCATION	HOURS	PHONE	COMMENTS
PAX TERM INFO	ANG schedule. Call for hrs/directions C-231-8058, A-853-9058.			
OTHER SERVICES	Facilities of an IAP available.			

UNSCHEDULED FLIGHTS

Space-A flights are available via KC-135E aircraft to CONUS and OCONUS locations. Call prior to arrival for flight info and specific directions.

Yuma Marine Corps Air Station (YUM)
Marine Corps Air Base, Western Area
Yuma MCAS, AZ 85369-5000

Comm: 602-726-2011
ATVN: 951-2011

LOCATION: From I-8 take Ave 3E S, for 1 mi to Base on right, adjacent to Yuma IAP. RM: p-8, M/1. NMC: Yuma, 3 mi NW.

FACILITIES	LOCATION	HOURS	PHONE	COMMENTS
PAX TERM INFO	Bldg 151	0700-1530 dly	C-726-2729, A-951-2729	Fm main gate straight on Quitter St to R on O'Neill St, Pax Term on L.
Pax Svc Ofc	Bldg 151	0700-1530 dly	C-726-2729	NCO on duty
Pax Paging	Bldg 151	0700-1530 dly	C-726-2729	
PAX LOUNGES DV/VIP	No family lounges Bldg 151	0700-1530 dly	C-726-2729	A/C, Rest-rms, P/C seats
Protocol Svc	Bldg 980	0700-1600 dly	C-726-2275	
FOOD SERVICE	Many services on and off Base. Cafeteria C-726-2369, Dining Hall C-726-2143/49, Enl Club C-726-2457/8, NCO/CPO Club C-726-2171/2406, O'Club C-726-2711/12, Snack Bar C-726-2250, Vending C-726-2729			
TRANSPORTATION	Limited on Base. Yuma IAP Air tickets, Car Rentals Avis= C-726-0104, Taxi(Gov) C-726-2381, Parking C-726-2205			

ARIZONA

Yuma MCAS, Cont'd

OTHER SERVICES	Many services on and off Base. Exchange C-726-2432, Bank C-342-7840, Barber C-726-2100, Beauty C-726-2115, Laundry/ DryC C-726-2884, Medical C-726-2111, Postal C-726-2033
TML	Bldg 1020 24 hrs dly C-726-2197/4970, A-951-3094 All Ranks. DV/VIP C-726-2253.
TRAVELERS AID	Good on Base. ARC C-726-2427/726-2325, Chaplain C-726-3454 Family Svcs C-726-3421, Navy Relief C-726-2373/4, Sec Police C-726-2205/2361
ATTRACTIONS	Desert climate, greyhound racing, maj league baseball train'g

UNSCHEDULED FLIGHTS

Flights to: Beaufort MCAS SC (NBC); Cherry Point MCAS NC (NKT); El Toro MCAS CA (NZJ); Twentynine Palms MCAS CA (NXP); and other locations as needed. Call for destinations, routings, and schedules.

ARKANSAS

Eaker Air Force Base (BYH)
97th Bomb Wing (SAC)
Blytheville AFB, AR 72315-5000

Comm: 501-762-7000
ATVN: 637-1110

LOCATION: From I-55 exit to US-61 N through Blytheville to Gosnell to main gate of AFB. RM: p-9, D/12. NMC: Memphis TN, 70 mi S.

FACILITIES	LOCATION	HOURS	PHONE	COMMENTS
PAX TERM INFO	Bldg 201	24 hrs dly	C-762-7272, A-721-7272	
	From main gate straight on Memorial Dr to R on 3rd St, then L on Tennessee Ave to Base Ops on L. Under ATC tower.			
Pax Svc Ofc	Bldg 201	24 hrs dly	C-762-7272	NCO on duty
Pax Paging	Bldg 201	24 hrs dly	C-762-7272	
PAX LOUNGES General	No family lounge Bldg 201 24 hrs dly C-762-7272 A/C, Rest-rms, P/C seats			
DV/VIP	Bldg 201 24 hrs dly C-762-7272 A/C, Bag lks, Coffee/tea srvd, Game rm, Read/write rm, TV, Rest-rms, Showers, Nursery, O/S seats			
Protocol Svc	Bldg 233	0730-1630 M-F	C-762-7765	97th BMW
FOOD SERVICE	Adequate services on and off Base. Cafeteria C-762-7272 Dining Hall C-762-7000, NCO/CPO Club C-762-7110, O'Club C-762-7111			
TRANSPORTATION	Limited on and off Base. SATO C-762-7765, Taxi(Comm) C-763-3334, Taxi(Gov) C-762-7495, Parking C-762-7331			
OTHER SERVICES	Good on Base. Exchange C-532-8534, Bank C-532-5633, Barber C-532-2750, Beauty C-532-2153, Laundry/DryC C-532-8419, Medical C-762-7219/7426, Postal C-762-7201 (Civ) 762-7260 (Mil)			

ARKANSAS

Eaker AFB Cont'd

TML	Bldg 702 24 hrs dly C-762-7461/3, A-637-7461/3 All Ranks. DV/VIP same location, hrs, & phone as All Ranks.
TRAVELERS AID	Many agencies on Base. ARC C-762-7220/988-3429, Chaplain C-762-7365, AF Aid Society C-762-7375, Lost/Found C-762-7331 Sec Police C-762-7331
ATTRACTIONS	Mississippi River and Memphis TN, 70 mi S.

SCHEDULED FLIGHTS

DESTINATION	ROUTING	FREQ	EQ/CMTS
Andersen AFB GU (UAM)	BYH-UAM	3 per yr	KC-135E/M
Elmendorf AFB AK (EDF)	BYH-EDF	4 per yr	KC-135E/M
RAF Fairford UK (FFD)	BYH-PSM-FFD	2 per yr	KC-135E/M
Pease AFB NH (PSM)	BYH-PSM-FFD	2 per yr	KC-135E/M

Little Rock Air Force Base (LRF)
314th TRNNS/TROR
Little Rock AFB, AR 72099-5000

Comm: 501-988-3131
ATVN: 731-1110

LOCATION: Use US-67/167 to Jacksonville, take AFB exit to main gate. RM: p-9, G/7. NMC: Little Rock, 18 mi SW.

FACILITIES	LOCATION	HOURS	PHONE	COMMENTS
PAX TERM INFO	Bldg 120 0400-1630 dly C-988-3684, A-731-3684 Main gate on Vandenberg Blvd for 1.5 mi to L on 1st St, Pax Term - 2nd Bldg on R.			
Recording	Bldg 120	24 hrs dly	C-988-3330	
Pax Svc Ofc	Bldg 120	0730-1630 M-F	C-988-3684	
Pax Paging	Bldg 120	0400-1630 dly	C-988-3684	
PAX LOUNGES DV/VIP	Bldg 120 No general lounge. Lobby, A/C, Couch, Rest-rms. Bldg 120 24 hrs dly C-988-3539/3684 A/C,Rest-rms,O/S seats			
FOOD SERVICE Cafeteria	Bldg 960	0730-1330 Tu-F, 0900-1330 Sa C-988-1139		
Dining Hall	Bldg 864&756	0530-1800 dly	C-988-3131	Call for svc hrs.
Enl Club	Bldg 868	Call for hrs.	C-988-3220	Call for svc hrs.
NCO/CPO Club	Bldg 1080	1000-2200 Su-Th,2300 F-Sa	C-988-4121	C/for svc hrs.
OFC Club	Bldg 1030	1000-2200 M-Sa, 1400 Su	C-988-1111	C/for svc hrs.
Snack Bars	Bldg 120	24 hrs dly	C-988-1148	"Runway Inn"

ARKANSAS

Little Rock AFB, Cont'd

TRANSPORTATION Air Tickets	Worldwide Travel C-982-7551 Bldg 1250 0730-1630 M-F C-988-6568 SATO
Car Rentals	Bldg 120 0600-2300 dly C-378-0777
TAXI(Comm) (Gov)	Off Base 24 hrs dly C-982-1500 Jacksonville Taxi Co. Black & White C-374-0333. $15+ to LIT Bldg 551 24 hrs dly C-988-6086 Duty Pax only
Parking	Bldg 120 24 hrs dly Short term-across from Terminal; long term-contact Security Police C-988-3221.
OTHER SERVICES Exchange	Bldg 940 1000-1800 M-F, 1700 Sa-Su C-988-1150
Bank/Exc	Bldg 970 0830-1600 M-F C-982-4521
Hair Styles	Bldg 959 1000-1800 M-F, 1700 Sa-Su C-988-1150
Laundry/DryC	Bldg 959 0700-1800 dly C-988-1150
Medical	Base Hospital 24 hrs dly C-988-7333
Postal	Bldg 966 0830-1700 M-F, 1200 Sa C-988-3131
TML	Bldg 1024 24 hrs dly C-988-6753, A-731-6753 All Ranks. DV/VIP C-988-3588.
TRAVELERS AID ARC	Bldg 840 0730-1630 M-F C-988-3249 After hrs-operator
Chaplain	Bldg 950 0730-1630 M-F C-988-6014 After hrs-operator
Lost/Found	Bldg 120 0400-1630 dly C-988-3684
Sec Police	Bldg 1260 24 hrs dly C-988-3221
ATTRACTIONS	Little Rock, Arkansas River, and Lake Conway

SCHEDULED FLIGHTS

DESTINATION	ROUTING	FREQ	EQ/CMTS
Charleston AFB Intl SC (CHS)	LRF-CHS	Weekly	C-130E/M
RAF Fairford UK (FFD)	LRF-PSM-FFD	1 per mo	KC-135E/C
Patrick AFB FL (COF)	LRF-COF	Th	C-130E/M
Pease AFB NH (PSM)	LRF-PSM-FFD	1 per mo	KC-135E/C
Travis AFB CA (SUU)	LRF-SUU	Weekly	C-130E/M

ARKANSAS
Little Rock AFB, Cont'd

UNSCHEDULED FLIGHTS

Flights to CONUS, OCONUS, and foreign countries. Weekly schedule is received each Friday for the M-Su flights. Call for destinations, routings, schedules.

CALIFORNIA

Alameda Naval Air Station (NGZ)
Operations Department
Alameda NAS, CA 94501-5000

Comm: 415-869-0111
ATVN: 686-0111

LOCATION: From Nimitz Freeway, I-880 S, take the Broadway/Alameda Exit. I-880 N, take Broadway Exit (880 N does not say Alameda). Directions to NAS are clearly marked. RM: p-11, ND/22. NMC: Oakland, 2 mi NW.

FACILITIES	LOCATION	HOURS	PHONE	COMMENTS
PAX TERM INFO	Bldg 77	0615-2300 dly	C-869-3530, A-686-3530	Call for Space-A register info. South end of Taxiway, 2 blks N of East Gate and 5 blks W of main gate.
Recording	Bldg 77	24 hrs dly	C-869-2727, A-686-2727	Updated dly
Pax Svc Ofc	Bldg 77	0615-2300 dly	C-869-3530	
Pax Paging	Bldg 77	0615-2300	C-869-3530	
PAX LOUNGES General	No family lounge at Air Terminal Bldg 77 0615-2300 dly C-869-3530 Tel L&LD,Rest-rms,P/C seats			
DV/VIP	Bldg 19 0700-2300 dly C-869-2512 ODO Coffee/tea srvd, Read/write rms, Tel L,LD,&ATVN, Rest-rms, O/S seats			
Protocol Svc	Bldg 1	0800-1630 M-F	C-869-2384	(O7+, GS15+)
FOOD SERVICE Cafeteria	Many services on and off Base Bldg 2 0930-1500 Tu-Sa C-869-6306			
AnchorLounge	Bldg 264	1100-2200 dly	C-748-8188	Sandwiches/Bev/Pool
Enl Club	Bldg 4	0600-0100 M-Sa	C-869-2931	Call for svc hrs.
NCO/CPO Club	Bldg 285	1700-2100 dly	C-869-4441	Call for svc hrs.
OFC Club	Bldg 60	1800-2200 dly	C-869-3241	Call for svc hrs.
Restaurants	Bldg 119	0600-2300 dly	C-521-4700	McDonalds
Snack Bars	Bldg 2	0930-2300 dly	C-869-6308	Bowling alley
Vending	Bldg 77	0615-2300 dly	C-869-2345	
TRANSPORTATION Air Tickets	Good on and off Base Bldg 271 0800-1630 M-F C-869-2851 SATO			
Bus(Comm) (Gov)	Bldg 77 NGZ to OAK OAK-IAP	24 hrs M-F, 0650-1250 Sa-Su C-839-2882 GH=C-834-3212, TW=C-444-5600 1350 dly To Travis AFB express		

CALIFORNIA

Alameda NAS, Cont'd

Car Rentals	OAK-IAP	24 hrs dly	All major rentals w/in 6 mi of Base
Limo Service	Bldg 77	24 hrs dly	C-865-1834 Limo service of Alameda
TAXI(Comm)	Bldg 77	24 hrs dly	Goodwill, Veterans, & Yellow
Parking	Bldg 77 (15 spaces); long term-Lot 120, 1 block from Terminal, 10 days. Call Security Police for info/assistance C-869-3053.	24 hrs dly	Short term-Lot 158, S of Bldg 77
OTHER SERVICES Exchange	Many services on and off Base Bldg 118	Call for hrs.	Information C-748-8100
Credit Union	Bldg 62	0900-1700 Tu-Sa C-865-3500	No bank on Base
Hair Styles	Bldg 118	0900-1700 Tu-Sa C-748-8112 C-523-1400	Barber Beauty
Laundry/DryC	Bldg 118	0900-1700 Tu-Sa C-748-8139	
Medical	Bldg 16	24 hrs dly	C-869-4444 Ambulance, C-869-3166 Appoint
Postal	Bldg 18	0930-1600 M-F	C-869-4269
TML	Bldg 101, "D" St 0800-1600 M-F C-869-2032, A-686-2036 Navy Lodge C-869-3206. DV/VIP C-869-2384.		
TRAVELERS AID ARC	Many on Base Bldg 135	24 hrs dly	C-869-4781 Night C-834-6656
Chaplain	Bldg 135	0800-1600 M-F	C-869-4386
Emerg Relief	Bldg 135	0800-1600 M-F	C-869-4002 Navy Relief
Lost/Found	Bldg 77	0615-2300dly	C-869-3530
Sec Police	Bldg 30	24 hrs dly	C-869-3053
USO	OAK-IAP	24 hrs dly	C-415-562-3448
ATTRACTIONS	San Francisco Bay area		

UNSCHEDULED FLIGHTS

Frequent dly flts to: Fallon NAS NV (NFL); Lemoore NAS CA (NLC); McChord AFB WA (TCM); San Diego CGAS CA (SAN); and Whidbey Island NAS WA (NUW). Infrequent flts to: Dallas NAS TX (NBE); Glenview NAS IL (NBU); Jacksonville NAS FL (NIP); Memphis NAS TN (NQA); Norfolk NAS VA (NGU); Salt Lake City IAP UT (SLC); and Willow Grove NAS PA (NXX). There are very few flts & seats available for overseas stations.

Beale Air Force Base (BAB)
9th Strategic Reconnaissance Wing
Beale AFB, CA 95903-5000

Comm: 916-634-2113
ATVN: 368-1110
FTS: 634-XXXX

LOCATION: Fm CA-70 N, exit S of Marysville, to N Beale Rd, continue for 10 mi until Rd deadends at main gate. RM: p-10, NK/10. NMC:Sacramento, 40 mi SW.

CALIFORNIA
Beale AFB, Cont'd

FACILITIES	LOCATION	HOURS	PHONE	COMMENTS
PAX TERM INFO	Bldg 1062	0700-1600 M-F	C-634-2700, A-368-2700. One blk N of ATC tower. Non-dty hrs flt info at B/Ops. Main gate-Beale Rd to L on J St, to L on Doolittle Dr to Pax Term on L.	
Pax Svc Ofc	Bldg 1062	0700-1600 M-F	C-634-2700, A-368-2700	
Pax Paging	Bldg 1062	0700-1600 M-F	C-634-2700, A-368-2700	
PAX LOUNGES	Bldg 1062	0700-1600 M-F	C-634-2700, A-368-2700 Bag check, Tel C&A, TV, Rest-rms	
Protocol Svc	Bldg 1086	0730-1630 M-F	C-634-2050, A-368-2050	SAC sponsored
FOOD SERVICE NCO/CPO Club	Bldg 5800	1700-2000 dly	C-788-0286	(Also EM Club)
OFC Club	Bldg 2340	1130-1300 M-F, 1800-2030 M-Sa	C-788-0292	
Snack Bars	Bldg 1060	0700-1800 M-F	C-788-1550	
TRANSPORTATION Air Tickets	Limited. POV (Privately Owned Vehicle) desirable. Bldg 2432	0730-1600 M-F	C-634-2046	SATO
Bus(Shuttle)	Bldg 1060 across street fm Term	0600-1800 M-F	C-634-2677	
TAXI(Comm) (Gov)	Marysville Bldg 2491	24 hrs dly 24 hrs dly	C-743-4661 C-634-2677	
Parking	Bldg 1060 Short & long term adjacent Terminal. 24 hrs dly		C-634-2700	No reservations necessary.
OTHER SERVICES Bank/Exc	Bldg 2433	0900-1500 M-F	C-634-2251	
Exchange	Bldg 2434	1100-1700 M, 1000-1800 Tu-F, 1000-1700 Sa, 1200-1600 Su,	C-788-0221	
Hair Styles	Bldg 2434	0830-1700 M-Sa	C-788-0053	Barber & Beauty
Laundry/DryC	Bldg 2434	0900-1700 M-Sa	C-788-0192	
Medical	Bldg 5700	24 hrs dly	C-634-4444/2333	Emergency
Postal	Bldg 2483	0700-1630 M-F	C-634-2766	
TML	Bldg 2156	24 hrs dly	C-788-0216, A-368-2084	All Ranks. DV/VIP C-788-0216. Several off Base motels nearby.
TRAVELERS AID ARC	Bldg 2145	24 hrs dly	C-634-2380	After duty hrs call Oper.
Chaplain	Bldg 5700	24 hrs dly	C-634-2992	In Hospital ER
Lost/Found	Bldg 1062	0700-1600 M-F	C-634-2700	
Sec Police	Bldg 2440	24 hrs dly	C-634-2131	

CALIFORNIA

Beale AFB, Cont'd

ATTRACTIONS	Sutter's Fort, zoo, Old Sacramento (rebuilding China Town)

SCHEDULED FLIGHTS

DESTINATION	ROUTING	FREQ	EQ/CMTS
Eielson AFB AK (EIL)	BAB-EIL-DNA	W/every 3 wks (Apr-Sep)	KC-135/M
Hickam AFB HI (HIK)	BAB-HIK-DNA	W/every 3 wks (Oct-Mar)	KC-135/M
Kadena AB JA (DNA)	BAB-EIL-DNA	W/every 3 wks (Apr-Sep)	KC-135/M
	BAB-HIK-DNA	W/every 2 wks (Oct-Mar)	KC-135/M
RAF Mildenhall UK (MHZ)	BAB-MHZ	Tu/3 Monthly	KC-135/M

Note: KC-135 refueling missions may not accept Space-A pax. Infrequent unscheduled CONUS flights. Customs agents were assigned to Beale AFB on 1 April 1987. Space-A Pax may now return non-stop to the West coast from Europe.

Castle Air Force Base (MER)
93rd Bomb Wing (SAC)
Castle AFB, CA 95342-5000

Comm: 209-726-4636
ATVN: 347-1110

LOCATION: From Sacramento, take CA-99 S to Atwater, take Buhach exit to AFB. RM: p-11, NQ/12. NMC: Fresno, 60 mi S.

FACILITIES	LOCATION	HOURS	PHONE	COMMENTS
PAX TERM INFO	Bldg 1340	24 hrs dly	C-726-2611, A-347-2611	
	From main gate straight on 8th St, L of Apron Avenue, R on 7th St to deadend at Base Operations/tower.			
OTHER SERVICES	Full Base support facilities			

UNSCHEDULED FLIGHTS

Flights via KC-135A/R aircraft to CONUS, OCONUS, and foreign countries.

Edwards Air Force Base (EDW)
Air Force Flight Test Center
Edwards AFB, CA 93523-5000

Comm: 805-277-1110
ATVN: 527-1110

LOCATION: Eighteen mi E of Rosamond, and 30 mi NE of Lancaster, off CA-14. Also, 10 mi SW of Boron, off CA-58. RM:p-13,SI/14. NMC:Los Angeles, 90 mi SW.

FACILITIES	LOCATION	HOURS	PHONE	COMMENTS
PAX TERM INFO	Bldg 1200	0600-2200 dly	C-277-2222, A-527-2222	
	Fm W gate, Rosamond Blvd, R on Fitzgerald Blvd, L on Wolfe Ave.			
Pax Svc Ofc	Bldg 1200	0600-2200 dly	C-277-3571, A-527-3571	
Pax Paging	Bldg 1200	0600-2200 dly	C-277-2222	

CALIFORNIA

Edwards AFB, Cont'd

PAX LOUNGES General	No separate family lounge Bldg 1200　　0600-2200 dly　　C-277-2222, A-527-2222 A/C, Bag check, Tel C&A, TV, Rest-rms, Showers, O/S seats
DV/VIP	Bldg 1200　　0600-2200 dly　　C-277-3326, A-527-3326　(06+) A/C, Tel C&A, O/S seats
Protocol Svc	Bldg 2650　　0730-1630 M-F　　C-277-3326, A-527-3326 AFSC
FOOD SERVICE	Good on Base. NCO/CPO Club C-277-3230, O'Club C-277-2830, Snack Bar C-258-5696/5987, Vending C-277-2222
TRANSPORTATION	Limited on Base. SATO C-277-3160, Bus(Shuttle) C-277-2620, Car Rental C-258-8023, Taxi(G) C-277-2620, Parking C-277-2222
OTHER SERVICES	Full Base support facilities available. Exchange C-258-6573, Medical C-277-2330
TML	Bldg 5602　　24 hrs dly　　C-277-3302, A-527-3302 All Ranks.　　　　　　　　　　DV/VIP　C-277-3302 (06+).
TRAVELERS AID	Limited on Base. ARC C-277-2845, Chaplain C-277-6976, Sec Police C-277-3340
ATTRACTIONS	Mojave Desert area, historic mining, and ghost towns

SCHEDULED FLIGHTS

DESTINATION	ROUTING	FREQ	EQ/CMTS
Hill AFB UT (HIF)	EDW-HIF	1 ea mo	KC-135/M
Wright-Patterson AFB OH (FFO)	EDW-FFO	1 ea wk	C-130A/M

Note: Call for other CONUS, OCONUS, and foreign country destinations routings, and schedules.

El Centro Naval Air Facility (NJK)
El Centro, CA 92243-5000

Comm: 619-339-2555
ATVN: 958-8555

LOCATION: Take I-8, 2 mi W of El Centro, to Forrester Rd exit. R on Forrester Rd. Continue 1.5 mi to L on Even Hewes Hwy (W) for 4 mi then R on Bennet Rd to main gate.　RM: p-13, SP/21.　NMC: El Centro, 7 mi E.

FACILITIES	LOCATION	HOURS	PHONE	COMMENTS
PAX TERM INFO	Bldg 519	0700-2300 M-Sa	C-339-2426, A-958-8426	
OTHER SERVICES	Good Pax lounge & full Base support facilities.			

UNSCHEDULED FLIGHTS

Two-three days notice on Space-A flights. Most flights via P-3A aircraft to CONUS and OCONUS locations. Call before going to Base.

CALIFORNIA

El Toro Marine Corps Air Station (NZJ)
Air Freight/Passenger Terminal
Station Ops Maintenance Squad
El Toro MCAS, CA 92709-5000

Comm: 714-651-3736
ATVN: 997-3736

LOCATION: Off I-5, take the Sand Canyon Road exit. Follow signs to the MCAS. RM: p-15, L/15. NMC: Los Angeles, 40 mi NW.

FACILITIES	LOCATION	HOURS	PHONE	COMMENTS
PAX TERM INFO	Bldg 624 3936, A-997-3920/3936	0700-2200 M-F,	0900-1800 Sa-Su C-651-3920/ Main gate straight on Trabuco Road to L on West Marine Way for .25 mi, then R to Pax Term.	
Pax Svc Ofc	Bldg 624	0730-1700 M-F	C-651-3920/3936	
Pax Paging	Bldg 624	0600-2200 dly	C-651-3920/3936	
PAX LOUNGES General	No family lounge Bldg 624 Bag check, Rest-rms, TV, P/C seats	0700-2200 M-F,	0900-1800 Sa-Su C-651-3920	
DV/VIP	Bldg 624 A/C,Rest-rms,TV,O/S seats. Opened per request of Pax Svc OIC.	0700-2200 M-F,	0900-1800 Sa-Su C-651-3920	
Protocol Svc	Bldg 65	0800-1700 M-F	C-651-3736	COMCABWEST
FOOD SERVICE Cafeteria	Many support facilities on and off Base Bldg 649	0700-1800 M-F,	1700 Sa-Su C-651-3340/3438	
Dining Hall	Bldg 364	0500-1800 dly	C-651-3926	Call for svc hrs.
Enl Club	Bldg 718	1100-2100 dly	C-651-2477	Call for svc hrs.
NCO/CPO Club	Bldg 718	1100-2130 dly	C-651-3476/7	Call for svc hrs.
OFC Club	Bldg 39	1100-2130 dly	C-651-2464/5/6	Call for svc hrs.
Restaurants	McDonald's	0600-2400 dly	C-651-3936	Across st from Term
Snack Bars	Ops Tower	0700-2300 dly	C-651-3336	Across st from Term
Vending	Bldg 624	24 hrs dly	C-651-3920	
TRANSPORTATION Air Tickets	Good on and off Base Bldg 58	0800-1600 M-F	C-559-3339/1511	SATO
Bus(Comm)	Bldg 924	0600-1800	C-636-RIDE	Orange County
Car Rentals	Orange County Airport Avis=C-546-9420, Hertz=C-475-1150, Budget=C-540-6511	24 hrs dly		
Limo Service	Bldg 624	On call	C-776-9210	NZJ to LAX $13. Min 5 people.
TAXI(Comm) (Gov)	El Toro C-Pool	24 hrs dly 24 hrs dly	C-770-2828 C-651-2156	Santa Ana C-542-1133
Parking	Bldg 624	24 hrs dly	C-651-3936	30 day limit

CALIFORNIA
El Toro MCAS, Cont'd

OTHER SERVICES			
Exchange	Many support facilities on Base and in Orange County Bldg 649 1000-1800 M-F, 0900-1700 Sa-Su C-651-3340		
Bank/Exc	Bldg 743	0900-1600 M-F	C-651-2564
Hair Styles	Bldg 649	0800-1700 M-Sa 0715-1600 M-Sa	C-651-3356 Barber C-559-1077 Beauty
Laundry/DryC	Bldg 649	0730-1800 M-Sa	C-651-3340
Medical	Bldg 439	24 hrs dly	C-651-3172/2731
Postal	Bldg 273	0800-1600 M-F	C-651-3808
TML	Bldg 276 0730-2130 dly C-651-2484, A-997-2484 All Ranks. Hostess House C-651-2693. DV/VIP C-651-3814.		
TRAVELERS AID ARC	Bldg 58 Bldg 60	0730-1600 M-F 0800-1600 M-F	C-651-3610/2771 Family Svcs C-651-2471/2 O/hrs C-835-5381
Chaplain	Bldg 83	0800-1600 M-F	C-651-3824/5
Emerg Relief	Bldg 60	0800-1600 M-F	C-651-2473 Navy Relief
Lost/Found	Bldg 624	0600-2200 dly	C-651-3936
Sec Police	Main gate	24 hrs dly	C-651-3527/8
USO	LAX, Term 4 24 hrs dly C-213-642-0188 Also, Greyhound Bus Terminal C-213-624-0066		
ATTRACTIONS	Los Angeles, Disneyland, Anaheim Stadium, Crystal Cathedral (Garden Grove)		

SCHEDULED FLIGHTS

DESTINATION	ROUTING	FREQ	EQ/CMTS
Barbers Point NAS HI (NAX)	NZJ-NAX	2 ea wk	C-130/P *
Kadena AB JA (DNA)	NZJ-DNA	Unit rotations	B747/L1011/P/CC
North Island NAS CA (NZY)	NZJ-NZY	As scheduled	C009A/P
Yuma MCAS AZ (YUM)	NZJ-YUM	As scheduled	UC-12B/P *

* Note: No civilian dependents allowed on some USMC aircraft. Call for destinations, routings, and schedules.

Fritzsche Army Airfield (OAR)
Operations, AFZW-AF
Fort Ord, CA 93941-5000

Comm: 408-242-4200
ATVN: 929-4200

LOCATION: From San Francisco, S for 100 mi on US-101, R onto CA-156 for 10 mi to main gate of Post. RM: p-13, SC/11. NMC: Monterey, 7 mi S.

CALIFORNIA

Fritzsche AAF, Cont'd

FACILITIES	LOCATION	HOURS	PHONE	COMMENTS
PAX TERM INFO	Bldg 518 24 hrs dly C-242-6362/2094, A-929-6362/2094 Off Hwy 1, take Reservation Rd 4 mi E, L into airfield. Full support facilities avail at Ft Ord.			

UNSCHEDULED FLIGHTS

Flts via U-21A aircraft to Alamitos AAF CA (SLI); Barstow-Daggett Arpt CA (DAG); San Francisco IAP CA (SFO); and Travis AFB CA (SUU).

George Air Force Base (VCV)
831st Air Division
George AFB, CA 92394-5000

Comm: 619-269-1110
ATVN: 353-1110

LOCATION: Fm I-15 take D St exit and follow signs. Fm US-395 at Adelanto, Exit E on Air Base Rd, 2 mi on L. RM: p-13, SJ/16. NMC: Barstow, 30 mi NE.

FACILITIES	LOCATION	HOURS	PHONE	COMMENTS
PAX TERM INFO	Bldg 707	24 hrs dly	C-269-2700, A-353-2700	
OTHER SERVICES	Full Base support facilities available.			

UNSCHEDULED FLIGHTS

Unscheduled MEDEVAC flights to March AFB CA (RIV) and Travis AFB CA (SUU) via C009A/ME aircraft. Limited Space-A air opportunities from this Base. Flight information available day of departure only.

Lemoore Naval Air Station (NLC)
Base Air Operations, COMLATWINGPAC
Lemoore Naval Air Station, CA 93245-5001

Comm: 209-998-2211
ATVN: 949-2211

LOCATION: On CA-198, 24 mi E of I-5, 30 mi W of CA-99 in the south central part of the state. RM: p-13, SD/9. NMC: Fresno, 40 mi NNE.

FACILITIES	LOCATION	HOURS	PHONE	COMMENTS
PAX TERM INFO	Bldg 180 24 hrs dly C-998-3565, A-949-3565 From main gate straight on Enterprise Ave, L on Franklin Ave for 5 mi to Ops area and Pax Term on right.			
Pax Svc Ofc	Bldg 180	24 hrs dly	C-998-3565	
Pax Paging	Bldg 180	24 hrs dly	C-998-3565	
PAX LOUNGES General	Limited lounge space. No DV/VIP or family lounge. Bldg 180 24 hrs dly C-998-3565 Only for scheduled flights originating at NLC			
Protocol Svc	Hangar 1	0800-1700 M-F	C-998-3360	COMLATWINGPAC
FOOD SERVICE	Good services on and off Base. Cafeteria C-998-3543, Enl Club C-998-3331, NCO/CPO Club C-998-3495, O'Club C-998-3551			

CALIFORNIA
Lemoore NAS, Cont'd

TRANSPORTATION	Ltd on Base. Bus(Shuttle) C-998-3326, Taxi at main gate
OTHER SERVICES	Good services on and off Base. Exchange C-998-3620, Bank C-998-3606, Hair Styles C-998-3400, Laundry/DryC C-998-3611 Medical C-998-3232/3484, Postal C-998-5112
TML	Bldg 843 24 hrs dly C-998-3266, A-949-3266 Navy Lodge C-998-5791. DV/VIP C-998-3121.
TRAVELERS AID	Good on Base. ARC C-998-3674/584-5015, Chaplain C-998-3696 Family Svcs C-998-3450, Navy Relief C-998-3239, Sec Police C-998-3306 (24 hrs at main gate)
ATTRACTIONS	Sequoia National Park, 70 mi E of NASL. Ski areas nearby.

UNSCHEDULED FLIGHTS

Frequent flts to: Alameda NAS CA (NGZ); China Lake NWC CA (NID); Fallon NAS NV (NFL); Miramar NAS CA (NKX); North Island NAS CA (NZY); and Whidbey Island NAS WA (NUW). Call for destinations, routings, and schedules.

Los Angeles International Airport (LAX)   Comm: 213-643-0715
Det 1, 63rd APS (MAC)   ATVN: 833-0715
380 World Way, Room 5111A
Los Angeles, CA 90045-5810

LOCATION: At Los Angeles International Airport, Tom Bradley International Terminal (between Terms 3 & 4) departure level. LAX is one mile W of I-405 S, and is clearly marked. RM: p-14, H/7. NMC: Los Angeles (downtown), 10 mi NE. NMI: LAAFB, 3 mi S of LAX at 200 Douglas Street.

FACILITIES	LOCATION	HOURS	PHONE	COMMENTS
PAX TERM INFO	Tom Bradley International Terminal	0730-2030 dly	C-643-0715, A-833-0715	
Pax Svc Ofc	Tom Bradley International Terminal	0730-1700 dly	C-643-0716, A-833-0716	
Pax Paging	Pax Term	24 hrs dly		
PAX LOUNGES General	No separate DV/VIP or family lounges LAX Pax Term 24 hrs dly All Intl Arpt facilities avail			
Protocol Svc		0730-2230	C-643-0715, A-833-0715	See Pax NCO.
FOOD SERVICE Cafeteria	At LAX, LAAFB and off Base Terms 1-8 24 hrs dly		C-643-0715	See Pax Svc f/assistance.
NCO/CPO Club	LAAFB Area B Bldg 208	1100-2000 dly	C-643-2743/4	
OFC Club	LAAFB Area A Bldg 120	0600-2300 dly	C-643-2230	
Vending	Term 4	24 hrs dly		
TRANSPORTATION Air Tickets	Extensive facilities and means at LAX and LAAFB LAAFB Area B Bldg 243 0800-1600 M-F C-643-1130 SATO			
Bus(Comm)	City bus: RTD=C-626-4455, GH=C-620-1200			

CALIFORNIA

Los Angeles Intl Arpt, Cont'd

Car Rentals	Thrifty=C-645-1880, Hertz=C-646-4861, Avis=C-646-5600, Budget=C-645-4500, Ajax=C-800-367-2529, Tropical=C-216-9130
Limo Service	Arpt Express=C-679-5603 24 hrs dly, Arpt Limo Svc=C-645-4346
TAXI(Comm)	Arpt Taxi Srvc=C-837-7252, A-1 Cab=C-222-1234, United Independent=C-653-5050, Red Top=C-822-4100
Trains	Los Angeles 24 hrs dly C-624-0171 Amtrak
Parking	Near LAX 24 hrs dly Long term-avail w/shuttle svc. Parking may be avail at L.A. Air Force Base-coordinate w/Sec Police.
OTHER SERVICES Exchange	Most support service available at LAX or LAAFB LAAFS Bldg 244 1000-1730 M-F, 1600 Sa-Su C-640-0129
Bank/Exc	Pax Term Hrs posted Check-cashing LAAFB clubs & BX
Hair Styles	Pax and LAAFB Bldg 244 0830-1730 M-F C-640-0379 (unisex)
Laundry/DryC	LAAFB Bldg 244 0900-1700 M-F, 1500 Sa C-615-0441
Medical	LAAFB Bldg 200 0700-1500 dly C-643-0964
Postal/Wire	LAX Term 3 and LAAFB
POV Shipmt	All State Auto Delivery Inc 0800-1700 M-F C-678-5111 or by owner 0800-1600 M-F C-643-1627
TML	Fort MacArthur - 22 miles from LAX 0715-1600 dly C-643-0260 Limited TML for Space-A Pax. Use any of the many local hotels/motels.
TRAVELERS AID ARC	100 World Way Room 330, Los Angeles CA 90045 C-646-2271
Chaplain	LAAFB Bldg 219 Duty hrs C-643-1956 After hrs C-643-0486
Emerg Relief	LAAFB Bldg 219 0800-1600 M-F C-643-1121 AF Aid Society
Lost/Found	Term 4 0730-2230 dly C-417-1603
Sec Police	LAAFB Bldg 241 24 hrs dly C-643-2122/3 Desk Sgt
USO	Term 4 - At American Airlines Hrs vary C-642-0188
ATTRACTIONS	Many in Los Angeles & surrounding areas: Disneyland, Anaheim; Universal Studios, Hollywood; Queen Mary, Long Beach

SCHEDULED FLIGHTS

DESTINATION	ROUTING	FREQ	EQ/CMTS
Andersen AFB GU (UAM)	LAX-HNL-UAM-CRK	F	DC-8/P/CC

CALIFORNIA

Los Angeles Intl Arpt, Cont'd

Clark AB RP (CRK)	LAX-OAK-ANC-DNA-CRK STL-LAX-ANC-DNA-CRK LAX-HNL-UAM-CRK	1/2/4/Sa 1/2/4/W F	B747/P/CC B747/P/CC DC-8P/CC
Honolulu IAP HI (HNL)	LAX-HNL-UAM-CRK	F	DC-8/P/CC
Kadena AB JA (DNA)	LAX-OAK-ANC-DNA-CRK STL-LAX-ANC-DNA-CRK	1/2/4/Su 1/2/4/W	B747/P/CC B747/P/CC
Metro Oakland Intl CA (OAK)	LAX-OAK-ANC-DNA-CRK	1/2/4/Sa	B747/P/CC

March Air Force Base (RIV)
Base Operations, 15th Air Force (SAC)
March AFB, CA 92518-5000

Comm: 714-655-1110
ATVN: 947-1110

LOCATION: Off CA-60 and on I-215 which bisects AFB. RM: p-15, I/23.
NMC: Riverside, 7 mi NW.

FACILITIES	LOCATION	HOURS	PHONE	COMMENTS
PAX TERM INFO	Bldg 265	0730-1630 M-F & during flight processing C-655-2913, A-947-2913 From West Gate, Ellsworth Street to left on Graeber Street to Base Ops on right.		
Pax Svc Ofc	Bldg 265	0730-1630 M-F	C-655-2913	
PAX LOUNGES General	Very limited lounge facilities Bldg 265 0730-1630 M-F C-655-2913 Limit 15-20 people - most wait in snack bar next door.Rest-rms,O/S seats.			
Protocol Svc	Bldg 3403	0800-1700 M-F	C-655-2213	HQ 15th AF
FOOD SERVICE Dining Hall	Bldg 962	0500-0100 dly	C-655-4251	
NCO/CPO Club	Bldg 2706	1100-2300 dly	C-655-3620	Call for svc hrs.
OFC Club	Bldg 110	1000-0100 dly	C-653-2121	Call for svc hrs.
TRANSPORTATION Air Tickets	Bldg 2405	0800-1600 M-F	C-653-3107	
Car Rentals	Riverside	0800-1600 M-Sa	C-787-4840	
TAXI(Comm)	Main gate	24 hrs dly	C-684-1234	Red, Yellow, Riverside
OTHER SERVICES Exchange	Many services on and off Base Bldg 758	1000-1800 M-F, 1600 Sa-Su	C-653-3111	
Bank/Exc	Bldg 659	1000-1500 M-F	C-653-1121	
Hair Styles	Bldg 758	0900-1800 M-F, 1600 Sa	C-653-3650 C-653-4323	Barber Beauty
Laundry/DryC	Bldg 758	0900-1800 M-F, 1600 Sa	C-653-3003	
Medical	Bldg 2990	24 hrs dly	C-655-4266,	Ambulance C-655-2433

CALIFORNIA

March AFB, Cont'd

Postal	Bldg 323	0800-1500 M-F	C-655-3010	
TML	Bldg 100 All Ranks.	24 hrs dly DV/VIP	C-655-5241, A-947-5241 C-655-4764.	
TRAVELERS AID ARC	Bldg 470 Bldg 641	24 hrs dly 0800-1600 M-F	C-655-2244 C-655-4189/4180	Action Line Other hrs C-655-1110
Chaplain	Bldg 2600	0800-1800 M-F	C-655-4751	Other hrs C-655-4689
Sec Police	Bldg 394	24 hrs dly	C-655-4689	
USO	LAX Term 4	24 hrs dly	C-642-0188	
ATTRACTIONS	Greater Los Angeles area, Palm Springs resorts & golf courses			

SCHEDULED FLIGHTS

DESTINATION	ROUTING	FREQ	EQ/CMTS
Anderson AFB GU (UAM)	RIV-UAM	Every other wk	KC-10/135E/M
Hickam AFB HI (HIK)	RIV-HIK	1 ea wk	KC-10/135E/M

UNSCHEDULED FLIGHTS

CONUS, OCONUS, and foreign country locations. Call after 1400 Friday for following week's destinations, routings, and schedules.

Mather Air Force Base (MHR)
323rd Air Base Group/OT
Mather AFB, CA 95655-5000

Comm: 916-364-1110
ATVN: 828-1110

LOCATION: In Rancho Cordova, US-50 to Mather Field Rd direct to main gate.
RM: p-11, NM/10. NMC: Sacramento, 12 mi W.

FACILITIES	LOCATION	HOURS	PHONE	COMMENTS
PAX TERM INFO	Bldg 4579 Fm main gate straight on Eknes St, L on "H" St & Pax Term R.	24 hrs dly	C-364-2506, A-828-2506	
Recording	Bldg 4579	24 hrs dly	C-364-4425	Updated daily
Pax Svc Ofc	Bldg 4579	24 hrs dly	C-364-2506	
PAX LOUNGES General	Modest lounge facilities. No family lounge. Bldg 4579	24 hrs dly	C-364-2506	A/C, Rest-rms, P/C seats
DV/VIP	Bldg 4579 Small room in Base Ops - TV	24 hrs dly	C-364-2506	
Protocol Svc	Bldg 2527	24 hrs dly	C-364-1110	DO-323rd FTW
FOOD SERVICE Cafeteria	Bldg 3547	24 hrs dly	C-362-4796	

CALIFORNIA
Mather AFB, Cont'd

Dining Hall	Bldg 1226	0530-0100 dly	C-364-4905 4th meal
NCO/CPO Club	Bldg 1400	0800-2330 dly	C-362-8030/8122 C/for svc hrs.
OFC Club	Bldg 2774	0730-2300 dly	C-362-7177 Call for svc hrs.
Snack Bars	Golf course	Call for hrs.	C-362-4391
TRANSPORTATION Air Tickets	Bldg 2460	0730-1600 M-F	C-364-3256/4655
Bus (Comm)	Bldg 4579	0800-2100 M-F, 1700 Sa	C-327-2877 Metro area
Car Rentals	SAC	Call for hrs.	Thrifty=C-447-2847, American=C-921-0555, Budget=C-424-5688
TAXI(Gov)	Bldg 3950	24 hrs dly	C-364-4652 Duty Pax only
Trains	SAC	24 hrs dly	AMTRAK (Southern Pacific)
Parking	Bldg 4579	24 hrs dly	C-364-2579 No restrictions
OTHER SERVICES Exchange	Bldg 3636	1000-2000 M-F, 1800 Sa-Su	C-363-7363
Bank/Exc	Bldg 2655	1000-1500 M-Th, 1800 F	C-364-3202
Hair Styles	Bldg 3636	0800-2000 M,Tu,Th,F, 1730 W, 1330 Sa	C-366-9968 Barber, C-362-6316 Beauty
Laundry/DryC	Bldg 3636	0830-1800 M-F	C-362-7788
Medical	Bldg 650	24 hrs dly	C-364-3333
Postal	Bldg 2566	0800-1600 M-F	C-364-4118
TML All Ranks.	Bldg 2750	24 hrs dly DV/VIP	C-364-2932, A-828-2932 C-364-2506.
TRAVELERS AID ARC	Bldg 35750 Bldg 35750	0800-1645 M-F 0800-1630 M-F	C-364-4382 Family Services C-364-2234
Chaplain	Bldg 3510	0800-1700 M-F	C-364-4375
Emerg Relief	Bldg 3306	0800-1645 M-F	C-364-2665
Sec Police	Bldg 1230	24 hrs dly	C-364-2314

SCHEDULED FLIGHTS

DESTINATION	ROUTING	FREQ	EQ/CMTS
Hickam AFB HI (HIK)	MHR-HIK	2 ea mo	T-43/P
Randolph AFB TX (RND)	MHR-RND	M,W,F	T-43/P

CALIFORNIA

Mather AFB, Cont'd

UNSCHEDULED FLIGHTS

Flts to CONUS, OCONUS, & foreign countries. Call for destinations, routings, and schedules. Schedules available one week in advance.

McClellan Air Force Base (MCC)
Sacramento Air Logistics Center
McClellan AFB, CA 95652-5990

Comm: 916-643-2111
ATVN: 633-1110

LOCATION: Off I-80 N. Fm I-80 take Madison Ave exit. Clearly marked. RM: p-11, NK/25. NMC: Sacramento, 10 mi SW.

FACILITIES	LOCATION	HOURS	PHONE	COMMENTS
PAX TERM INFO	Bldg 251	0730-1615 M-F	C-643-4105, A-633-4105	Gate 1 straight on Peacemaker Way to Pax Term on L. Also USCG flt via C-130 aircraft to CONUS and OCONUS locations. Call C-643-2081, F-533-3237, and A-633-2081.
Recording	Bldg 251	24 hrs dly	C-643-4105	Updated 0800 dly
Pax Svc Ofc	Bldg 251	0730-1615 M-F	C-643-3944	Other services
PAX LOUNGES General	No family lounge 24 hrs dly Bldg 251 0600-1615 M-F		C-643-3944	A/C, Bag check, Tel C&A, TV, Rest-rms, P/C seats
DV/VIP	Bldg 251 srvd,Tel C&A,TV,Rest-rms,O/S seats	24 hrs dly	C-643-2845	A/C, Coffee/tea (06+) Active & Retired
Protocol Svc	Bldg 200	0730-1615 M-F	C-643-2845	(06+)Active & Retired
FOOD SERVICE Cafeteria	Bldg 280	0600-2030 M-F	C-927-3829	Call for svc hrs.
Dining Hall	Bldg 1401	0600-0045 dly	C-643-5092	Call for svc hrs.
Enl Club	Bldg 560	1600-0130 M-Sa	C-643-4139	Call for svc hrs.
NCO/CPO Club	Bldg 1425	1100-2100 dly	C-922-9667	Call for svc hrs.
OFC Club	Bldg 150	1100-2130 M-Sa	C-927-5013	Call for svc hrs.
Snack Bars	Bldg 911	0830-1800 M-F	C-920-9394	Call for wknd hrs.
TRANSPORTATION Air Tickets	Bldg 209	0730-1600 M-F	C-643-4410	SATO
Bus(Comm)	Gates 1,3,&4	Hrs vary	C-321-BUSS	Call for rates & hrs.
Limo Service	Presidential	24 hrs dly	C-920-1123	Call for rates & hrs.
TAXI(Comm)	Yellow=C-444-2222, GH=C-444-8294			24 hrs dly
Parking	Behind main cafeteria 24 hrs dly for designated areas (Long term-Bank of America)			
OTHER SERVICES Bank/Exc	Bldg 925	1000-1500 M-F	C-924-6582	Bank of America

CALIFORNIA
McClellan AFB, Cont'd

Exchange	Bldg 911	1000-1730 M-F	C-920-0537 Call for wkend hrs.
Hair Styles	Bldg 911	0800-1800 M-Sa	C-925-3374 Beauty,C-927-7521 Barber
Laundry/DryC	Bldg 911	0730-1730 M-F, 0900-1600 Sa C-922-0389	
Medical	Bldg 41	24 hrs dly	C-643-6736 Ambulance EX-115
Postal	Bldg 960	0830-1600 M-F	C-643-3971 No wire service
TML	Bldg 89 Palm & 30th Sts	24 hrs dly All Ranks.	C-643-6223, A-633-6223 DV/VIP C-643-4311.
TRAVELERS AID ARC	Bldg 334	0830-1600 M-F	C-643-4013 Wkends C-643-1110
Chaplain	Bldg 1420	0800-1600 dly	C-643-3598 Other hrs C-643-2751
Emerg Relief	Bldg 334	0800-1600 dly	C-643-3815 Family Services
Lost/Found	Bldg 948	0800-1600 dly	C-643-3460
Sec Police	Bldg 948	24 hrs dly	C-643-6160 Police Desk
ATTRACTIONS	Lake Tahoe CA and Reno NV nearby (2 hr drive NE) and San Francisco Bay area (1 1/2 hrs drive SW)		

SCHEDULED FLIGHTS **

DESTINATION	ROUTING	FREQ	EQ/CMTS
Hickham AFB HI (HIK)	MCC-HIK	1-2 flts ea mo	C-135 Trans/AC
Hill AFB UT (HIF)	MCC-HIF	2 flts ea mo	C-21A/P*
Norton AFB CA (SBD)	MCC-SBD	4 flts ea mo	C-21A/P*
Offutt AFB NE (OFF)	MCC-OFF	4 flts ea mo	C-21A/P*
Peterson AFB CO (COS)	MCC-COS	4 flts ea mo	C-21A/P*
Scott AFB IL (BLV)	MCC-BLV	4 flts ea mo	C-21A/P*
Tinker AFB OK (TIK)	MCC-TIK	2 flts ea mo	C-21A/P*
Wright-Patterson AFB OH(FFO)	MCC-FFO	4 flts ea mo	C-21A/P*

Note: A schedule is posted ea day at 0830 hrs for flts for the next 24 hrs.
 * Baggage limit for C-21A/P aircraft is 30 lbs.
 ** No regular scheduled flights.

CALIFORNIA

Miramar Naval Air Station (NKX)
Operations Maintenance Division
Miramar Naval Air Station, CA 92145-5000

Comm: 619-537-1011
ATVN: 577-1011

LOCATION: Fifteen miles N of San Diego CA, off I-15. Take Miramar Way exit. RM: p-15, K/23. NMC: San Diego CA, 15 mi SW.

FACILITIES	LOCATION	HOURS	PHONE	COMMENTS
PAX TERM INFO	Bldg 476	0700-2400 dly	C-537-4283, A-577-4283	
	Fm main gate, straight on Miramar Way to L on Mitscher Way, turn R on Regulus Rd and L at fork in road to front of Pax Term. One of the busiest Air Terminals in the Navy.			
Recording	Bldg 475	24 hrs dly	C-537-4996	
Pax Svc Ofc	Bldg 476	0700-2400 dly	C-537-4284	NCO on duty
Pax Paging	Bldg 476		C-537-4283	
PAX LOUNGES General	Limited lounge facilities. No separate family lounge.			
	Bldg 476	0700-2400 dly	C-537-4283	Rest-rms,TV,W&P/C seats
DV/VIP	Bldg K-211	0700-2400 dly	C-537-4277	Rest-rms,TV,O/S seats
Protocol Svc	Bldg 402	24 hrs dly	C-537-1657	OOD COMFITAEWWINGPAC
FOOD SERVICE Cafeteria	Many services on and off Base			
	Bldg 600	0630-1500 dly	C-695-7276	Flight line
Dining Hall	Bldg M-305	0530-1930 dly	C-537-1380/83	
Enl Club	Bldg M-309	1100-2400 dly	C-537-4281/19	
NCO/CPO Club	Bldg M-379	1100-2000 dly	C-537-4800	
OFC Club	Bldg 472	1100-2100 dly	C-537-4816	
Snack Bars	Bldg 525	0900-2400 dly	C-537-6022	Bowling Center
Vending	Bldg M-309	1000-2200 dly	C-537-4825	Pizza Parlor
TRANSPORTATION Air Tickets	Limited on Base			
	Bldg K-175	0800-1700 M-F	C-222-0375	SATO
Bus(Comm) (Shuttle)	Main gate	0600-1800 dly	C-233-3004	
	Bldg K-211	0600-1730 M-F	C-537-1142	Base, every 30 min
Car Rentals	Bldg K-214	0800-1700 M-F	C-695-7291	
Limo Service	San Diego	24 hrs dly	C-291-9002	
TAXI(Base)	Main gate	0700-2400 dly	C-537-1142	
Parking	Bldg K-211	24 hrs dly	C-537-4277	R side, no restrictions
OTHER SERVICES Exchange	Good on and off Base			
	Bldg 660	1000-1800 Sa-W, 2000 Th-F	C-271-8262	
Bank/Exc	Bldg 513	0930-1600 M-F	C-230-4717	California 1st Bank

CALIFORNIA
Miramar NAS, Cont'd

Hair Styles	Bldg 600 Bldg M-257	0900-1800 M-F, 1400 Sa 0900-1800 dly		C-695-2196 Barber C-695-7227 Beauty
Laundry/DryC	Bldg M-273	0700-1700 dly	C-695-7238	
Medical	Bldg 495	24 hrs dly	C-537-4632	
Postal	Bldg 257	0800-1500 M-F, 1145 Sa	C-537-4578	
TML	Bldg 638 (BEQ) C-537-1172, Bldg M-312 (BOQ) C-537-4233 Navy Lodge C-537-4855			
TRAVELERS AID ARC	Many spt fac on and off Base C-537-4099 Family Services Bldg 273 0800-1600 M-F C-291-2620			
Chaplain	Bldg 332	0745-1800 dly	C-537-1333/38	
Navy Relief	Bldg 273	0800-1600 M-F	C-537-1807	
Lost/Found	Bldg 476	0700-2400 dly	C-537-4283	
Sec Police	Bldg M-310	24 hrs dly	C-573-4059	
USO	San Diego	Call for hours.	C-619-235-6503	
ATTRACTIONS	San Diego, beautiful beaches, Sea World, San Diego Zoo			

UNSCHEDULED FLIGHTS

Frequent flights to the following destinations: Alameda NAS CA (NGZ); Andrews AFB (NAF) MD (ADW); Beaufort MCAS SC (NBC);Cecil Field NAS FL (NZC); Charleston AFB SC (CHS); Dallas NAS TX (NBE); Memphis NAS TN (NQA); Patuxent River NAS MD (NHK); Pensacola NAS FL (NPA); Point Mugu NAS CA (NTD); Travis AFB CA (SUU); Whidbey Island NAS WA (NUW); & Willow Grove NAS PA (NXX). Call Pax Term for info on flights that may be scheduled 1-3 days prior to flight.

Moffett Field Naval Air Station (NUQ)
Air Operations, Bldg 158
Moffett NAS, CA 94035-5000

Comm: 415-966-5411
ATVN: 462-5411

LOCATION: On Bayshore Freeway, US-101, 35 mi S of San Francisco. RM: p-11, NK/25. NMC: San Jose, 7 mi S.

FACILITIES	LOCATION	HOURS	PHONE	COMMENTS
PAX TERM INFO	Bldg 158 24 hrs dly C-966-5231, A-462-5231 From main gate on Clark Memorial Blvd to R on Wescoat Rd to R on Cody Rd, Air Ops L. Contact squadron/unit by tel # given to you by Pax Term personnel. No dependents on most flights because of type of in-flight facilities.			
Recording	Bldg 158	24 hrs dly	C-966-5233	Updated daily
Pax Svc Ofc	Bldg 158	24 hrs dly	C-966-5231	NCO on duty
Pax Paging	Bldg 158	24 hrs dly	C-966-5231	

CALIFORNIA
Moffett Field NAS, Cont'd

PAX LOUNGES Protocol Svc	No central lounge facilities. Check with unit sponsoring flt. Bldg 17 0800-1700 M-F C-966-5438/5612 COMPATWINGSPAC			
FOOD SERVICE Cafeteria	Good facilities on and off Base Bldg 476	1000-1800 dly	C-940-6222	Call for svc hrs.
Dining Hall	Bldg 152	0500-1800 dly	C-966-6102	Dial-a-Menu
Enl Club	Bldg 244	1100-2200 dly	C-966-5471	Call for svc hrs.
NCO/CPO Club	Bldg 243	1100-2200 dly	C-966-5181	Call for svc hrs.
OFC Club	Bldg 3	1130-2200 dly	C-966-5306	Call for svc hrs.
Snack Bars	Bldg 234	0700-2100 dly	C-966-5332	Golf course
TRANSPORTATION Air Tickets	Limited facilities on Base Bldg 23	0800-1600 M-F	C-966-5844	
Bus(Comm) (Shuttle)	Bldg 158 Bldg 158	Call for schedule. C-408-287-4210 Connects w/BART 0600-1730 dly C-966-5710 On Base-schedule posted		
Parking	Bldg 146	24 hrs dly	C-966-5456	Call for instructions.
OTHER SERVICES Exchange	Many facilities on and off Base Bldg 476	1000-1900 dly	C-940-6211/6212	
Bank/Exc	Bldg 556	0800-1500 M-F	C-969-6222	
Hair Styles	Bldg 476 Bldg 25	0800-1700 M-Sa 0800-1700 M-Sa	C-940-6231 C-967-6996	Barber Beauty
Laundry	Bldg 88	0800-1700 M-Sa	C-940-6210	
Medical	Bldg 546	24 hrs dly	C-966-5111	
Postal	Bldg 67	0830-1700 M-F	C-966-5382	
TML	Bldg 552 All Ranks.	0800-1600 dly C-966-5911, A-462-5911 Navy Lodge C-800-NAVY-INN. DV/VIP C-966-5411.		
TRAVELERS AID ARC	Bldg 207A Bldg 48	0800-1700 M-F 0900-1200 M-F	C-966-4911 C-966-5933	Other hrs C-415-322-2143
Chaplain	Bldg 48	0800-1630 M-F	C-966-5721/5940	
Emerg Relief	Bldg 48	0800-1630 M-F	C-966-5148	Navy Relief
Sec Police	Bldg 15 & 26	24 hrs dly	C-966-5141	
ATTRACTIONS	"Silicon Valley", San Jose, Santa Cruz, and San Francisco			

UNSCHEDULED FLIGHTS

Frequent flts to CONUS stations:Brunswick NAS ME (NHZ);Glenview NAS IL (NBU); Jacksonville NAS FL (NIP); Memphis NAS TN (NQA); North Island NAS CA (NZY); Patuxent River NAS MD (NHK); Point Mugu NAS CA (NTD); Whidbey Island NAS WA (NUW). OCONUS flts to Barbers Point NAS HI (NAX); Elmendorf AFB AK (EDF); Hickam AFB HI (HIK); and Midway NAF MW (MDY). Foreign country flts are made to the Orient via MDY. Most flights are via P-3A and HC-130 aircraft.

CALIFORNIA

North Island Naval Air Station (NZY)
Air Terminal Officer
North Island NAS, CA 92135-5000

Comm: 619-437-6011
ATVN: 951-0111

LOCATION: From I-5 N or S exit at Coronado Bridge (toll). Also, from CA-75 N to CA-282 to Base. In Coronado. RM: p-15, N/22. NMC: San Diego, 4 mi NE.

FACILITIES	LOCATION	HOURS	PHONE	COMMENTS
PAX TERM INFO	Bldg 700	24 hrs dly	C-437-6936/6489, A-951-6936/6489	
	Main gate on McCain Blvd, L on Roosevelt Blvd, to Pax Term R.			
Recording	Bldg 700	24 hrs dly	C-437-6935	Updated daily
Pax Svc Ofc	Bldg 700	24 hrs dly	C-437-6936/6489	NCO on duty
Pax Paging	Bldg 700	24 hrs dly	C-437-6936/6489	
PAX LOUNGES General	No separate family lounge Bldg 700 24 hrs dly C-437-6936/6489 A/C, Bag check, Rest-rms, Tel L, TV, O/S seats			
DV/VIP	Bldg 516 24 hrs dly C-437-6321 A/C, Bag check, Rest-rms, Tel L&ATVN, TV, O/S seats			
Protocol Svc	Bldg 8	24 hrs dly	C-437-6310	OOD COMNAVAIRPAC
FOOD SERVICE Cafeteria	Many svcs on and off Base. Bldg 502	24 hrs dly	McDonalds C-435-0074 (on Base) C-437-7031	
Dining Hall	Bldg 794	0530-0100 dly	C-437-6011	
Enl Club	Bldg 417	Call for hrs.	C-437-7046	"Windjammer"
NCO/CPO Club	Bldg 864	Call for hrs.	C-437-7372	
OFC Club	Bldg X	Call for hrs.	C-437-7651	
Restaurants	Bldg 243	Call for hrs.	C-435-4451	Civilian cafe
Snack Bars	Bldg 772	0900-2400 dly	C-435-0245	Bowling
Vending	Bldg 700	24 hrs dly	C-437-7033	
TRANSPORTATION Air Tickets	Bldg 515	0800-1630 M-F	C-435-1837 or C-437-5216	
Bus(Comm) (Shuttle)	Bldg 700 Bldg 493	Call for hrs. 0530-1730 dly	C-233-3004 C-437-7731	
TAXI(Comm) (Gov)	Coronado Bldg 493	24 hrs dly 0730-1500 M-F	C-435-6211 C-437-5447	Duty Pax only
Parking	Bldg 700	24 hrs dly		Very limited
Exchange	Bldg 483	1000-1800 dly	C-435-2231	
Bank/Exc	Bldg 318	0900-1500 M-F	C-435-5417/8	Credit Union
Hair Styles	Bldg 483	1000-1800 dly	C-435-2231	Barber and Beauty

CALIFORNIA

North Island NAS, Cont'd

Laundry/DryC	Bldg 483 1000-1800 dly C-435-0313	
Medical	Bldg 600 24 hrs dly C-437-6278/6263	Ambulance C-233-2417
Postal	Bldg 124 0900-1600 M-F, 1200 Sa C-437-7698	
TML	Bldg 1402 24 hrs dly All Ranks. Navy Lodge C-435-7623. DV/VIP C-437-6011.	
TRAVELERS AID	Many agencies in San Diego area. Family Svcs C-437-6693.	
ARC	Bldg 607 0800-1600 M-F C-435-3195	
Chaplain	Bldg 665 Duty hrs C-437-7269 Other hrs call OOD C-437-6204.	
Emerg Relief	Bldg 607 0900-1300 M-F C-437-7649 Navy Relief Society	
Lost/Found	Bldg 700 0700-1500 M-F C-437-5665	
Sec Police	Main gate 24 hrs dly C-437-6383	
USO	433 Harbor Dr Call for hrs. C-619 235-6503	
ATTRACTIONS	Beaches, Old San Diego, Sea World, Mexico nearby	

SCHEDULED FLIGHTS

DESTINATION	ROUTING	FREQ	EQ/CMTS
Alameda NAS CA (NGZ)	NGZ-NZY-NGZ	3 ea wk	C009B/P
Andrews AFB MD (ADW)	ADW-NZY-ADW	2 ea mo	T-39/P
Barbers Point NAS HI (NAX)	NAX-NZY-NUQ-NZY-NAX	Su,F	P-3/M Limited seats
Glenview NAS IL (NBU)	NZY-NBU-NZY	1 ea mo	C009B/P
Jacksonville NAS FL (NIP)	NZY-NIP-NZY	2 ea mo	C009B/P
McChord AFB WA (TCM)	NZY-TCM-NZY	2 ea wk	C009B/P
Moffett Field NAS CA (NUQ)	NAX-NZY-NUQ-NZY-NAX	Su,F	P-3/M
Nellis AFB NV (LSV)	NZY-LSV-NZY	3 ea mo	C009B/P
New Orleans NAS LA (NBG)	NBG-NZY-NBG	2 ea mo	T-39/P
Norfolk NAS VA (NGU)	NZY-NGU-NZY	2 ea mo	C009B/P
Whidbey Island NAS WA (NUW)	NZY-NUW-NZY	2 ea wk	C009B/P

CALIFORNIA
North Island NAS, Cont'd

UNSCHEDULED FLIGHTS

Frequent flights to: China Lake NAS CA (NID); Fallon NAS NV (NFL); Lemoore NAS CA (NLC); Oceana NAS VA (NTU); and Point Mugu NAS CA (NTD). Call for destinations, routings, and schedules.

Norton Air Force Base (SBD)
63rd MAW/PA
Norton AFB, CA 92409-5000

Comm: 714-382-1110
ATVN: 876-1110

LOCATION: From I-10 take Tippecanoe Ave N to Gate #1. From I-15, take Mill St exit, proceed for 3 mi to Tippecanoe Ave. Turn left (N) to Gate #1. RM: p-15, E/24. NMC: San Bernardino, 1 mi NW.

FACILITIES	LOCATION	HOURS	PHONE	COMMENTS
PAX TERM INFO	Bldg 673	24 hrs dly	C-382-5354, A-876-5354	Fm Gate #1 go straight. Take R on C St, then L on 7th St. Pax Term on R.
Recording	Bldg 673	24 hrs dly	Updated 2200 hrs C-382-7230,A-876-7230	
Pax Svc Ofc	Bldg 673	24 hrs dly	C-382-6724	
Pax Paging	Bldg 673	24 hrs dly	C-382-5354, A-876-5354	
PAX LOUNGES General	Bldg 673	24 hrs dly	C-382-5354, A-876-5354	A/C, TV, P/C seats,Rest-rms,Bag chk/lockers,Tel C&A.No sleeping in lounge.
DV/VIP	Upper L side of lounge	24 hrs dly	C-382-7615, A-876-7615	or Pax Svc-24 hrs dly. A/C, Coffee/tea srvd, TV, O/S seats. No host available after 1615.
Protocol Svc	Bldg 673	0730-1615 dly	C-382-7615 or Pax Svc-24 hrs dly	
FOOD SERVICE Cafeteria	Bldg 673	24 hrs dly	C-885-4116	
Dining Hall	Bldg 144	0500-0100 dly	C-382-3695	4 blks fm Terminal
Enl Club	Bldg 48	Call for hrs.	C-382-5769	
NCO/CPO Club	Bldg 48	0800-2100 dly	C-889-0635	
OFC Club	Bldg 6	0630-2100 dly	C-884-8701	
Snack Bars	Bldg 534	0715-1445 M-F	C-885-1210	
Vending	Bldg 673	24 hrs dly	C-884-4807	
TRANSPORTATION Air Tickets	Bldg 512	0800-1630 dly	C-382-3741/6110/3118 SATO	
Bus(Comm)	Omni Bus Lines to downtown twenty minutes to the hour. GH=C-884-4796 and TW=C-888-3271	0640-1840 hrs	From Term at Cost is $.75 exact change.	
Car Rentals	Budget Rent-a-Car=C-889-0076, Thrifty Rent-a-Car=C-884-1896			

CALIFORNIA

Norton AFB, Cont'd

TAXI(Comm)	On call 24 hrs dly C-884-4747,C-884-1111,C-382-6758, or C-884-0777. Cost approximately $6.00 to downtown.
(Gov)	In front of Pax Term 24 hrs dly C-382-4041
Parking	Short term-Bldg 673, 24 hrs dly; long term-available S of Bldg 701. Contact Passenger Service Center.
OTHER SERVICES	
Exchange	Bldg 58 1000-1800 M-F,1000-1700 Sa,1030-1600 Su C-884-4807
Bank/Exc	Bldg 105 0930-1500 M-F C-382-2834
Hair Styles	Bldg 58 0900-1745 M-F (closed 1645 Sa) C-885-3550 Barber Bldg 58 0800-1800 M-F (closed 1600 Sa) C-885-3005 Beauty
Laundry/DryC	Bldg 58 0900-1800 M-F, 1000-1700 Sa C-885-3907
Medical	Bldg 100 C-382-3633 Emergency C-382-7818
Postal	Bldg 455 0900-1700 M-F (closed 1200 Sa) C-382-2601
TML	Bldg 512 24 hrs dly C-382-5531, A-876-5531 All Ranks. DV/VIP C-382-7615.
TRAVELERS AID ARC	Bldg 515 0800-1600 M-F C-382-6102 Other hrs C-382-1110
Chaplain	Bldg 104 Duty hrs C-382-4087
Lost/Found	Bldg 673 24 hrs dly C-382-5354
Sec Police	Bldg 608 24 hrs dly C-382-6606
ATTRACTIONS	Los Angeles, 60 mi W and Palm Springs, 35 mi E

SCHEDULED FLIGHTS

DESTINATION	ROUTING	FREQ	EQ/CMTS
Alice Springs Arpt AU (ASP)	SBD-HIK-PPG-CHC-RCM-ASP	Th	C-141B/C
Andersen AFB GU (UAM)	SBD-SUU-HIK-UAM-CRK-DNA-OKO	Daily	C-141B/M
Christchurch Intl NZ (CHC)	SBD-HIK-PPG-CHC-RCM-ASP	Th	C-141B/M
Hickam AFB HI (HIK)	SBD-SUU-HIK SBD-HIK-PPG-CHC-RCM-ASP SBD-HIK-PPG-RCM-UMR-LEA	Su Th Sa	C-141B/M C-141B/C C-141B/C
Kadena AB JA (DNA)	SBD-SUU-EDF-OKO-CRK-DNA	Daily	C-141B/M
Learmonth RAAFB AU (LEA)	SBD-HIK-PPG-RCM-UMR-LEA	Sa	C-141B/C

CALIFORNIA
Norton AFB, Cont'd

McChord AFB WA (TCM)	SBD-TCM SBD-TCM	Varies Varies	C-141B/C C-141B/M
Pago Pago Intl AS (PPG)	SBD-HIK-PPG-CHC-RCM-ASP SBD-HIK-PPG-RCM-UMR-LEA	Th Sa	C-141B/C C-141B/C
Richmond RAAFB AU (RCM)	SBD-HIK-PPG-CHC-RCM-ASP SBD-HIK-PPG-RCM-UMR-LEA	Th Sa	C-141B/C C-141B/C
Travis AFB CA (SUU)	SBD-SUU-HIK-UAM-CRK-DNA-OKO SBD-SUU-HIK	Daily Su	C-141B/M C-141B/M
Woomera AFLD AU (UMR)	SBD-HIK-PPG-RCM-UMR-LEA	Sa	C-141B/C
Yokota AB JA (OKO)	SBD-SUU-HIK-OKO	Daily	C-141B/M

UNSCHEDULED FLIGHTS

There are many unscheduled flights to destinations in CONUS and overseas. Call C-714-382-7230 or ATVN 876-7230 for 24 hour status after 2200 hrs.

Oakland International Airport (OAK)
Det 1, 60th APS
1 Airport Drive, Box 44
Oakland, CA 94621-5000

Comm: 415-635-8515
ATVN: 837-5789

LOCATION: Take Hegenberger Rd exit fm I-880 (Nimitz Frwy), approx 17 mi S of I-80/I-880 intersection. Clearly marked. RM:p-11,NE/23.NMC:Oakland,11 mi NW.

FACILITIES	LOCATION	HOURS	PHONE	COMMENTS
PAX TERM INFO	OAK lobby	0800-2300 dly	C-635-8515, A-837-5789	Hegenberger Rd becomes Airport Dr which leads to Pax Term. MAC check-in desk is at far N end of main ticket area (Pax asst).
Recording	OAK lobby	24 hrs dly	C-635-8482, A-837-2407	
Pax Svc Ofc	OAK lobby	0800-1700 M-F	C-635-8515, A-837-5789	
Pax Paging	OAK lobby	0500-0300 dly	C-577-4000	
PAX LOUNGES	OAK lobby	24 hrs dly	C-635-8515	All support fac
DV/VIP	Tower lounge	1230-2130 dly	C-635-8515	8th floor
Family	USO 2nd floor	0900-2300 M-Sa	C-562-3448	Nursery, Refreshments
FOOD SERVICE Cafeteria	Main lobby	0600-2130 dly		See arpt manager for svc hrs.
Snack Bars	Main lobby	0630-2100 dly		See arpt manager for svc hrs.
Vending	Main lobby	24 hrs dly		
TRANSPORTATION Bus(Comm) (Shuttle)	Front Term Front Term	7 days a wk 0600-2400 dly		AC Transit to OAK Travis AFB; AIRBART to BART subway Term

CALIFORNIA

Oakland Intl Arpt, Cont'd

Car Rentals	Bag claim area 24 hrs dly	Courtesy phones to Co's	
Limo Service	Main lobby 0800-2000 dly	Brewers Limo Svc=C-569-0660	
TAXI(Comm)	Main lobby 24 hrs dly	C-893-4991 OAK-$14, SFO-$25	
Trains	AMTRAK 24 hrs dly	C-645-4607	
Parking	OAK 24 hrs dly	(Short and long term lots avail)	
OTHER SERVICES Exchange	Main lobby 24 hrs dly	C-577-4906 Gift shops (two)	
Hair Styles	Main lobby 24 hrs dly	C-577-4136 Barber	
Medical	OAK Navy Regional 24 hrs dly	C-633-5190/5440 Emergency	
Postal	Main lobby 24 hrs dly	Mail box/stamps	
Porter	Main lobby 24 hrs dly	C-577-4428 Red Cap service	
POV Proc	Oakland AB Bldg S-4	0800-1630 M-F C-466-3365	
TML	OAK Army Base Bldg 560 24 hrs dly C-466-3113, A-859-3113 All Ranks. DV/VIP C-466-3113, A-859-3113 (AR Base controls Biltg at Ft Mason).Presidio of SF Bldg 42 24 hrs C-561-2096, A-586-2096 All Ranks. DV/VIP C-561-3950/2540,A-586-3950/2540. Marines Memorial Club, 609 Sutter St, SF CA 94102, C-673-6672		
TRAVELERS AID Emerg Relief	ARC Alameda NAS Duty hrs C-869-4781 or C-834-6656 Term 2nd floor 0800-1600 dly C-635-8515		
Lost/Found	Term 2nd floor 24 hrs dly C-577-4095 Contact NCOIC.		
OAK Police	Main lobby 0500-0200 dly C-577-4900		
USO	USO Center - Mezzanine Level C-562-3448		
ATTRACTIONS	SF, Bay area, cable cars, great seafood at Tadich Grill, 240 CA St, 391-2373. Tell Chris(Mgr) you were sent by Mil Living.		

SCHEDULED FLIGHTS

DESTINATION	ROUTING	FREQ	EQ/CMTS
Clark AB RP (CRK)	LAX-OAK-ANC-DNA-CRK	Sa	B747/P/CC
Kadena AB JA (DNA)	LAX-OAK-ANC-DNA-CRK	Sa	B747/P/CC
Lambert-St Louis IAP MO (STL)	OAK-STL	W,F	B747/P/CC
Los Angeles IAP CA (LAX)	OAK-LAX	F	B747/P/CC

CALIFORNIA
Oakland Intl Arpt, Cont'd

Osan AB RK (OSN)	STL-OAK-OKO-OSN	Tu,Th	B747/P/CC
Yokota AB JA (OKO)	STL-OAK-OKO-OSN	Tu,Th	B747/P/CC

Point Mugu Pacific Missile Test Center (NTD)
Air Operations Department, Air Terminal Division
Point Mugu, CA 93042-5000

Comm: 805-989-1110
ATVN: 351-1110

LOCATION: 8 mi S of Oxnard and 40 mi N of Santa Monica, on Coastal Highway, CA-1. RM: p-13, SL/11. NMC: Los Angeles, 50 mi SE.

FACILITIES	LOCATION	HOURS	PHONE	COMMENTS
PAX TERM INFO	Air Terminal 0700-2200 M-F C-989-7731, A-351-7731 - Closed holidays 0930-1800. Reduced hours during Christmas and New Years. Enter gate 2, follow signs to Pacific Missle Test Center Air Terminal on 11th Street, Bldg 339.			
Pax Svc Ofc	Air Terminal	0700-2200 M-F	C-989-7731/7026	
PAX LOUNGES General	Limited lounge facilities. Air Terminal 0700-2200 M-F Bag check, Rest-rms, TV, P/C seats		No DV/VIP lounge. C-989-7731	
Protocol Svc	Bldg 1	24 hrs dly	C-989-7209	Officer of the Day
FOOD SERVICE Cafeteria	Bldg 366	0700-1330 M-F	C-989-7189	
Enl Club	NAS	1100-0200 dly	C-989-8420/8714	
NCO/CPO Club	NAS	1100-2400 dly	C-989-8570	
OFC Club	NAS	1100-2200 dly	C-989-7507	
Snack Bars	Golf course	0800-1700 dly	C-989-4620	
TRANSPORTATION Air Tickets	Bldg 1	0800-1700 M-F	C-989-8378	
Bus(Shuttle)	Air Terminal	0700-0815, 1100-1300, 1500-1630,	C-989-7406	
Car Rentals	Off Base	Budget=483-2326, Avis=487-9429		
TAXI(Comm)	Off Base	C-483-2444		
Parking	Security	24 hrs dly	C-989-7907	

CALIFORNIA

Point Mugu Pac Mis Tst Ctr Cont'd

OTHER SERVICES Exchange	BX Complex has Hair Styles and Laundry/Dry Cleaning. BX Complex 1000-1800 M-F, 1500 Sa C-989-7189		
Bank/Exc	Mugu Road	0900-1500 M-F	C-989-8787 MFCU
Medical	Dispensary	24 hrs dly	C-989-8821/3331
Postal	NAS	0800-1600 M-F	C-989-8253
TML	Bldg 241 24 hrs dly 7317/7378/7510 All Ranks.		C-989-7617/7378, A-351- DV/VIP C-989-8672.
TRAVELERS AID ARC	Port Hueneme 0800-1600 M-F		C-989-4424
Chaplain	NAS	0800-1700 M-F	C-989-7967
Emerg Relief	NAS	0800-1700 M-F	C-989-8918 Navy Relief
Sec Police	Main gate	24 hrs dly	C-989-7907
USO	LAX, Term 4	24 hrs dly	C-213-642-0188
ATTRACTIONS	Beaches, Los Angeles, Disneyland		

UNSCHEDULED FLIGHTS

Flts to: Agana NAS GU (NGM); Andrews AFB MD (ADW); Cubi Point NAS RP (CUA); Kadena AB JA (DNA); Rota NAS SP (RTA); Sigonella Arpt IT (SIZ); and Yokota AB JA (OKO) via various contract aircraft. Also, Antarctic Dev Sqd 6 (VXE-6) and the Naval Construction Battalion Center Support "Operation Deep Freeze" with flts from NTD to Christchurch NZ (CHC) from August through February via C141B and LC-130 aircraft. Dial direct C-805 989-7129/7585 for VXE-6.

San Diego Coast Guard Air Station (SAN)
2710 Harbor Drive
San Diego, CA 92101-1079

Comm: 619-557-5816
FTS: 895-5816

LOCATION: Off I-5. Clearly marked. Ask for directions to the Coast Guard hangar. RM: p-15, N/23. NMC: San Diego, 2 mi E.

FACILITIES	LOCATION	HOURS	PHONE	COMMENTS
PAX TERM INFO	CG hangar 0800-1600 M-F C-557-5816, F-895-5816 East end of Lindburgh Field on Harbor Drive. Barber, BX, Medical & TML. Fixed-wing Space-A opportunities extremely limited. Call for destinations, routings, and schedules.			

Travis Air Force Base (SUU)
60th APS/TROP
Travis AFB, CA 94535-5000

Comm: 707-438-4011
ATVN: 837-1110

LOCATION: 35 miles NE of San Francisco. 7 mi E of Fairfield. From I-80 take Travis AFB Parkway ramp. RM: p-10, NN/8. NMC: San Francisco, 35 mi SE.

CALIFORNIA
Travis AFB, Cont'd

FACILITIES	LOCATION HOURS PHONE COMMENTS
PAX TERM INFO	Bldg P-3 24 hrs dly C-438-2311/2, A-837-2311/2 From main gate take Travis Ave, turn right on 2nd Ave, Pax is 2 1/2 blocks on left, adjacent to control tower (Bldg P-4).
Recording	Bldg P-3 24 hrs dly C-438-2313, A-837-2313 Updated 2200 hrs
Pax Paging	Bldg P-3 24 hrs dly C-438-2311/2, A-837-2311/2
PAX LOUNGES General	Generous and well-appointed lounge facilities for all Pax Bldg P-3 24 hrs dly C-438-2311, A-837-2311 Separate smoking (B) & no smoking (A) Lounges, Showers, P/C seats, Free TV, Bag check/lockers, Rest-rms
DV/VIP	Between Bldgs P-3 and P-4 C-438-3185, A-837-3185 (06+) Staffed 0600-1700 M-F,0600-1300 Sa-Su Ask for Protocol Svc. A/C, O/S seats, Showers, Rest-rms, TV, Coffee/tea served
Family	Bldg P-3 (USO) 0800-2400 dly C-438-3316, A-837-3316 A/C, O/S seats,Crib rm (24 hrs dly),Game rms, Rest-rms, TV
FOOD SERVICE Cafeteria	Many on and off Base Bldg P-3 24 hrs dly C-438-2092 Call for svc hrs.
Dining Hall	Bldg 247 (2 blks fm Pax Term) 0630-1900 M-F, 0600-1930 Sa-Su 4th meal 2230-0200 M-F C-438-2155 No retirees
Enl Club	Bldg 212 0700-0100 dly C-438-5659 Call for svc hrs.
NCO/CPO Club	Bldg 660 0700-0100 dly C-438-5071 Call for svc hrs.
OFC Club	Bldg 480 0700-0100 dly C-438-3368 Call for svc hrs.
Snack Bars	Bldg 836 0600-2200 dly C-437-9597 "Flight Line"
Vending	Bldg P-3 24 hrs dly C-437-4655
TRANSPORTATION Air Tickets	Many means and facilities on and off Base Bldg P-3 24 hrs dly C-437-3386 E&J Travel
Bus(Comm)	Bldg P-3 0430-2330 M-F, 0430-2100 Sa-Su and holidays SUU-OAK-SFO-SF See E&J Travel. $14 1-way C-437-3386/7
(Shuttle)	Bldg P-3 0600-1700 dly (every half hour)
Car Rentals	Budget=C-437-4411, Hertz=C-800-654-3131, Natl=C-437-2529
TAXI(Comm)	Bldg P-3 24 hrs dly C-437-2961 Outside customs area
Parking	Short term-in front of Bldg P-3 (2 hr limit); long term-valid 3 mo permit issued at Pax Svcs when selected for flight. RVs $5 per mo - contact Crosswinds Recreation Center.
OTHER SERVICES Exchange	Many services available on and off Base Bldg 650 M-Su C-437-4633 Call for hours.
Bank/Exc	Bldg 658 Bank of America C-422-1520 Call for hours.
Hair Styles	Bldg P-3 dly C-437-9926 Barber, Bldg 650 C-437-2848 Beauty

Travis AFB, Cont'd CALIFORNIA

Laundry/DryC	Bldg 650 (Main Exc Shopping Ctr Complex) C-437-2733, DryC Bldg 1325 M,W,F C-437-2996, Laundromat Bldg 651 24 hrs dly
Medical	Bldg 383 24 hrs dly C-437-9860 Emergency
Postal	Bldg 542 M-F C-438-2783 Call for hours.
POV Shipment	OAK Army Base C-466-3365 (turn in and pick up yourself) Commercial service at SUU - Union Garage C-437-3394
TML	Bldg 404 24 hrs dly C-438-2987, A-837-2987 All Ranks. DV/VIP C-438-3185, A-837-3185 (O6+).
TRAVELERS AID ARC	Many agencies on and off Base Bldg P-3 0800-1700 M-F C-438-2262 and C-437-3550
Chaplain	Bldg 438 Duty hrs C-438-2652 Other hrs C-438-3293
Emerg Relief	Bldg 246 C-438-2536 Air Force Aid Society
Lost/Found	Bldg P-3 0800-1700 M-F C-438-2180, Wknds/holidays EX-5877
Sec Police	Bldg 850 24 hrs dly C-438-3293
ATTRACTIONS	San Francisco, 35 miles SW; Sacramento, 50 miles NE

SCHEDULED FLIGHTS

DESTINATION	ROUTING	FREQ	EQ/CMTS
Andersen AFB GU (UAM)	SBD-SUU-HIK-UAM	Daily	C-141B/M
	SBD-SUU-HIK-UAM-OKO-DNA	Daily	C-141B/M
	SBD-SUU-HIK-UAM-OKO-DNA	Daily	C-141B/M
	SUU-HIK-UAM-DNA	Daily	C005A/C
	SUU-HIK-UAM-CUA	Daily	C-141B/C
	SUU-HIK-UAM-CRK	Su,1/3/4Tu,W,Sa	C-141B/M
	TIK-SUU-HIK-UAM-CRK	M	C-141B/M
	SUU-HIK-UAM-CUA	1/3/W	C005A/C
	SUU-HIK-UAM-CRK	2/W,4/Th,Sa	C005A/C
	SUU-HIK-UAM-DNA	F	C-141B/C
Clark AB RP (CRK)	SUU-HIK-UAM-CRK	Su,1/3/4Tu,W,Sa	C-141B/M
	TIK-SUU-HIK-UAM-CRK	M	C-141B/M
	SUU-HIK-UAM-CRK	2/W,4/Th,Sa	C005A/C
Cubi Point NAS RP (CUA)	SUU-HIK-UAM-CUA	M,1/3/4/W,Sa	C-141B/M
	SUU-HIK-UAM-CUA	1/3/W	C005A/C
	SUU-HIK-UAM-CUA	Th	C-141B/C
Dover AFB DE (DOV)	SUU-TIK-DOV-RMS-MHZ	W,F	C005A/C
Eielson AFB AK (EIL)	SUU-TCM-EIL-EDF	1/3/Sa	C-141B/M
Elmendorf AFB AK (EDF)	SUU-TCM-EIL-EDF	1/3/Sa	C-141B/M

CALIFORNIA
Travis AFB, Cont'd

Hickam AFB HI (HIK)	SBD-SUU-HIK-UAM-OKO-CRK-DNA SBD-SUU-HIK-UAM SUU-HIK-UAM-CRK TIK-SUU-HIK-UAM-CRK SUU-HIK SUU-HIK-UAM-CUA SUU-HIK-UAM-CUA SUU-HIK-UAM-CUA SUU-HIK-UAM-DNA SUU-HIK-OKO-OSN SUU-HIK-UAM-CRK	Daily Su-F Su,1/3/4Tu,W,Sa M M,Tu M,1/3/4/W,Sa 1/3W Th F F Sa	C-141B/M C-141B/M C-141B/M C-141B/C C-141B/M C-141B/M C005A/C C-141B/M C005A/C C005A/C C005A/C
Kadena AB JA (DNA)	SBD-SUU-HIK-UAM-CRK-OKO-DNA SUU-HIK-UAM-DNA SUU-HIK-UAM-DNA	Daily Th F	C-141B/M C-141B/C C-141B/C
RAF Mildenhall UK (MHZ)	SUU-TIK-DOV-RMS-MHZ	W,F	C005A/C
McChord AFB WA (TCM)	SUU-TCM EDF-SUU-TCM SUU-TCM SUU-TCM-EIL-EDF SUU-TCM-SKA	Su 2/4/Su 3/Tu,W,Sa 1/3/Sa F	C-141B/C C-141B/M C-141B/M C-141B/M C009A/M
Norton AFB CA (SBD)	SUU-SBD	Su,1/3/M,2/4/Sa	C-141B/M
Osan AB RK (OSN)	SUU-HIK-OKO-OSN	F	C005A/C
Ramstein AB GE (RMS)	SUU-TIK-DOV-RMS-MHZ	W,F	C005A/C
Tinker AFB OK (TIK)	SUU-TIK SUU-TIK-DOV-RMS-MHZ SUU-TIK	M W,F Sa	C-141B/C C005A/C C-141B/M
Yokota AB JA (OKO)	SBD-SUU-HIK-UAM-CRK-DNA SUU-HIK-OKO-OSN	Su,Sa F	C-141B/M C005A/C

UNSCHEDULED FLIGHTS

Numerous CONUS, OCONUS and foreign country flights occur daily. MEDEVAC flights to following destinations on days indicated via C009A/ME: Andrews AFB MD (ADW) on Th,Su; Buckley ANGB CO (BKF) on F; Kelly AFB TX (SKF) on Tu; and Scott AFB IL (BLV) on Tu,Th,F,S.

Van Nuys Air National Guard Base (VNY)
146th Tactical Airlift Wing (ANG)
8030 Balboa Blvd
Van Nuys, CA 91406-1195

Comm: 818-909-2200
ATVN: 873-6310

CALIFORNIA

Van Nuys ANGB, Cont'd

LOCATION: Northeast of intersection of San Diego, 405 freeway and Ventura 101 freeway. Exit W fm I-405 N on Roscoe Blvd to airport. RM: p-15, C/5. NMC: Los Angeles CA, 10 mi SE.

FACILITIES	LOCATION	HOURS	PHONE	COMMENTS
PAX TERM INFO	Bldg 104	0800-1630 M-F	C-909-2219, A-873-2219	
	In NW corner of large main hangar.			
Recording	Bldg 100	0800-1630 dly	C-909-2439, A-873-6439	
PAX LOUNGES General	Limited lounge facilities			
	Bldg 104	0800-1630 dly	C-909-2219	
	A/C, Bag chk, Tel L,LD,&ATVN, TV, Rest-rms, P/C & O/S seats			
FOOD SERVICE	Combined Officers' and NCO/CPO Club 1630-2200 M-F C-909-2220			
	No food available.			
Vending	Bldg 104 Base Ops 24 hrs dly C-909-2219			
TRANSPORTATION	Greyhound in North Hollywood, Car rental and Taxi at Term. Limited general parking. Check with Security Police, EX-360.			
OTHER SERVICES	Base Exchange 1000-1700 W-Sa			

UNSCHEDULED FLIGHTS

Flights to: Anchorage IAP AK (ANC); Honolulu IAP HI (HNL); and many CONUS locations via C-130E aircraft. Call for destinations, routings, and scheds.

Vandenberg Air Force Base (VBG)
4392nd AEROSG/LGTT
Vandenberg AFB, CA 93437-5000

Comm: 805-866-1611
ATVN: 276-1611

LOCATION: Fm S on US-101, W on CA-246, N on CA-S20 to AFB. Fm N on US-101, W on US-1 fm Gaviota, N on CA-S20 to AFB. RM: p-7, SJ/7. NMC: Lompoc, 6 mi S.

FACILITIES	LOCATION	HOURS	PHONE	COMMENTS
PAX TERM INFO	Bldg 1749	0800-1700 dly	C-866-7742, A-276-7742	Fm main gate on CA Blvd to R on 13th St,L on Airfield Rd, Pax Term L.
Pax Svc Ofc	Bldg 1749	0800-1700 dly	C-866-7742	NCO on duty
PAX LOUNGES General	Limited lounge facilities			
	Bldg 1749	0800-1700 dly	C-866-7742	
	Game room, Rest-rooms, TV, P/C seats			
DV/VIP	Bldg 1746	0800-1700 dly	C-866-7742	
	Rest-rms, Showers, TV, Coffee/tea svc, O/S seats			
FOOD SERVICE	Limited services off Base. Many facilities on Base. Dining Hall C-866-3894/9571, Enl Club C-866-3153, NCO/CPO Club C-734-4465, O' Club C-734-4411, Restaurants C-734-2153.			
TRANSPORTATION	Good on Base. Air Tickets C-734-4381 SATO, Shuttle Bus C-866-5714, Car Rentals C-734-3664, Limo Service C-736-3636, Government Taxi C-866-5711.			

CALIFORNIA
Vandenberg AFB, Cont'd

OTHER SERVICES	Exchange C-734-1231, Bank/Exc C-734-4351, Hair Styles C-734-1259 Barber, C-734-1264 Beauty, Laundry/DryC C-734-3039 Postal C-866-3223
Medical	Bldg 13850 24 hrs dly C-866-3333 Ambulance
TML	Bldg 13005 24 hrs dly C-866-8913, A-276-8913 All Ranks. DV/VIP C-866-3711. Guest House C-866-3406.
TRAVELERS AID	AF Family Services C-866-4225/5484, ARC C-866-6701, Chaplain C-866-3631, Emerg Relief (AF Aid) C-866-3250
Sec Police	Bldg 13405A 24 hrs dly C-866-3911 Desk Sgt
ATTRACTIONS	Great beaches, historic missions, and Hearst Castle

SCHEDULED FLIGHTS

DESTINATION	ROUTING	FREQ	EQ/CMTS
Travis AFB CA (SUU)	VBG-SUU	Su	C009A/ME

UNSCHEDULED FLIGHTS

Flights to: Los Angeles IAP CA (LAX) and March AFB CA (RIV).

COLORADO

Buckley Air National Guard Base (BKF)
Aircrew Support Section/140RMS/LGTP
Buckley ANGB, CO 80011-9599

Comm: 303-340-9011
ATVN: 877-9011

LOCATION: On E 6th Ave off I-225. RM: p-17, C/26. NMC: Denver CO, 25 mi W.

FACILITIES	LOCATION	HOURS	PHONE	COMMENTS
PAX TERM INFO	Bldg 809	0700-1900 dly	C-340-9662, A-877-9662	
	From main gate S to L at fire station to 3rd Bldg on R. Army Flt Ops Bldg 1500 0600-1600 M-F C-340-9847, A-877-9847			
Pax Svc Ofc	Bldg 809	0700-1900 dly	C-340-9662	Personnel on duty
PAX LOUNGES General	Limited lounge space. No separate DV/VIP or family lounges. Bldg 809 0700-1900 dly C-340-9662 Bag chk,Coffee/tea svc,Tel L,LD,&ATVN, TV, Rest-rms,O/S seats			
OTHER SERVICES	Limited Base support facilities. Barber Bldg 809 0830-1500 duty days. NCO Club and Exchange available.			
TRANSPORTATION	Parking Bldg 806. Check with Security Police C-340-9930.			

SCHEDULED FLIGHTS

DESTINATION	ROUTING	FREQ	EQ/CMTS
Scott AFB IL (BLV)	BKF-BLV BLV-BKF-BLV SUU-BKF-BLV	Tu Tu,Th,F F	C009A/ME C009A/ME C009A/ME

COLORADO

Buckley ANGB, Cont'd

Travis AFB CA (SUU)	BLV-BKF-SUU	W,Sa	C009A/ME

UNSCHEDULED FLIGHTS

Army flts to CONUS locations dly. C/for destinations, routings, & schedules.

Butts Army Airfield (FCS)
Airfield Commander, Bldg 9601
Fort Carson, CO 80913-5000

Comm: 719-579-5811
ATVN: 691-5811

LOCATION: From Colorado Springs, take I-25 or CO-115 S. Clearly marked.
RM: p-17, J/24. NMC: Colorado Springs, 6 mi N.

FACILITIES	LOCATION	HOURS	PHONE	COMMENTS
PAX TERM INFO	Bldg 9601	0730-1630 M-F, 0730-1530 Sa	C-579-5462/3935, A-691-5462/3935.	Ask guard at Gate 1 for map and directions to the airfield.
Pax Svc Ofc	Bldg 9601	0730-1630 M-F	C-579-5462	
PAX LOUNGES	Bldg 9601	0730-1630 M-F, 0730-1530 Sa	C-579-3935	No lounge. Pax wait in Base Ops. Tel L,LD,&ATVN, Rest-rms, P/C seats.
OTHER SERVICES	Full support facilities at Fort Carson main post. Cafeteria C-576-6670, NCO Club C-576-7540, Officers' Club C-576-6646, PX C-576-6313, Medical C-579-7111, Taxi C-634-6601 (24 hrs dly), Security Police C-579-2333.			

UNSCHEDULED FLIGHTS

Frequent flights via C-12A and U-21A aircraft to: Barstow-Daggett Arpt CA (DAG); Biggs AAF TX (BIF); Killeen Municipal Arpt TX (ILE); Robert Gray AAF TX (GRK); Sherman AAF KS (FLV); and Marshall AAF KS (FRI).

Peterson Air Force Base (COS)
1001 Trans Sqdn, TMO Br/LGTTS
Peterson AFB, CO 80914-5000

Comm: 719-554-7321
ATVN: 692-7011

LOCATION: Off US-24 (Platte Ave) E of Colorado Springs. Clearly marked.
RM: p-17, I/26. NMC: Colorado Springs, 6 mi NW.

FACILITIES	LOCATION	HOURS	PHONE	COMMENTS
PAX TERM INFO	Bldg 122	0630-1730 M-F, 0700-1600 Sa-Su	C-554-4707/4521, A-692-4707/4521	Fm main gate, straight on Peterson Blvd to flt line & Pax Term R in old city Term Bldg.
Recording	Bldg 122	24 hrs dly	C-554-4707/4009	
Pax Svc Ofc	Bldg 122	0730-1630 M-F	C-554-4979	NCO on duty
Pax Paging	Bldg 122	Duty hrs M-F, 0700-1700 Sa-Su	C-554-4521	
PAX LOUNGES General	No separate family lounge Bldg 122	0530-1930 M-F, 0700-1700 Sa-Su	C-554-4707/4521	Bag check, Game rm, Tel LD&ATVN, TV, Rest-rms, O/S seats

COLORADO
Peterson AFB, Cont'd

DV/VIP	Bldg 122 0700-1630 M-F, 24 hrs on call C-554-4225 A/C, Coffee/tea svc, TV, Rest-rms, Showers, O/S seats
Protocol Svc	Bldg 122 0700-1630 M-F, 24 hrs on call C-554-4225 (O6+) SPACECOMMAND
FOOD SERVICE Cafeteria	Good services on and off Base Bldg 1425 0930-1730 dly C-554-7769 Call for svc hrs.
Dining Hall	Bldg 1160 0530-1730 dly C-554-4727 In-flight meals
Run-In-Chef	Bldg 122 0700-1600 dly
NCO/CPO Club	Bldg 725 0700-2330 dly C-554-4194/597-7876 C/for svc hrs.
OFC Club	Bldg 1013 0630-2330 dly C-554-4181 Call for svc hrs.
Restaurants	Bowling Bldg 406 0900-2330 dly C-554-4607. Golf C-554-4454.
Snack Bars	Bldg 122 0700-1430 M-F C-554-4707
Vending	Bldg 172 24 hrs dly C-554-4707
TRANSPORTATION Air Tickets	Good systems on and off Base Bldg 122, Rm 1 0730-1630 M-F C-596-4307 SATO
Bus(Comm) (Gov)	Bldg 122 0554-1722 dly C-475-9733 COS to Ft Carson Bldg 1229 24 hrs dly C-554-4717 Call for schedule.
Car Rentals	Bldg 122 24 hrs dly Avis=C-596-2751 Hertz=C-596-1863 Budget=C-574-7400 National=C-596-1519
Limo Service	Bldg 122 24 hrs dly Through Colorado Springs Municipal Arpt
TAXI(Comm) (Gov)	Bldg 122 24 hrs dly Airport=C-596-7300 Yellow=C-634-6601 Bldg 122 24 hrs dly C-554-4307 Duty Pax only
Parking	Short term-Bldg 122 24 hrs max; long term-Bldg 1326, notify Security Police C-554-4000.
OTHER SERVICES Exchange	Good services on Base and in area Bldg 1425 0800-1730 M-Sa C-597-0300
Bank/Exc	Bldg 1485 0900-1500 M-Th, 1700 F C-475-6387
Hair Styles	Bldg 1425 0800-1730 M-Sa C-597-0300 Barber, C-596-0579 Beauty
Laundry/DryC	Bldg 1425 0830-1730 M-Sa C-597-3050
Medical	Bldg 959 24 hrs dly C-554-4333
Postal	Bldg 1466 0830-1630 M-F, 1130 Sa C-554-4596
TML	Bldg 1164 24 hrs dly C-554-7851/4513, A-692- 7851/4513 All Ranks. DV/VIP 554-3011.
TRAVELERS AID ARC	On Base and at Fort Carson Bldg 1470 0800-1600 M-F C-554-7590

COLORADO

Peterson AFB, Cont'd

Chaplain	Bldg 1410	0715-1600 M-F	C-554-4442	
Emerg Relief	Fort Carson	0800-1600 M-F	C-579-2311	
Lost/Found	Bldg 122	0630-1730 dly	C-554-4707	Pax Services
Sec Police	Bldg 1376	24 hrs dly	C-554-4000	
USO	Colorado Springs Municipal Airport		C-303-574-9626	
ATTRACTIONS	Ski resorts, US Olympic Training Center			

SCHEDULED FLIGHTS

DESTINATION	ROUTING	FREQ	EQ/CMTS
Andrews AFB MD (ADW)	COS-ADW	4 ea wk	C-21A/P C-135E/P
Barksdale AFB LA (BAD)	COS-BAD	2 ea mo	T-39/P C-130E/P
Bergstrom AFB TX (BSM)	COS-BSM	1 ea mo	T-39/P
Eglin AFB FL (VPS)	COS-VPS	1 ea mo	T-39/P C-130E/P
Kelly AFB TX (SKF)	COS-SKF	2 ea mo	T-39/P
Kirtland AFB NM (ABQ)	COS-ABQ	1 ea wk	T-39/P
Los Angeles IAP CA (LAX)	COS-LAX	3 ea mo	T-39/43/P C-130E/P
March AFB CA (RIV)	COS-RIV	2 ea mo	T-39/P C-130E/P
Maxwell AFB AL (MXF)	COS-MXF	3 ea mo	T-39/43/P
McChord AFB WA (TCM)	COS-TCM	1 ea mo	T-39/43/P C-130E/P
McClellan AFB CA (MCC)	COS-MCC	1 ea wk	T-39/43/P
Norton AFB CA (SBD)	COS-SBD	2 ea wk	T-39/43/P C-130E/P
Offutt AFB NE (OFF)	COS-OFF	3 ea wk	T-39/43/P C-135E/P
Randolph AFB TX (RND)	COS-RND	1 ea wk	T-39/P C-130E/P

COLORADO
Peterson AFB, Cont'd

Scott AFB IL (BLV)	COS-BLV	2 ea wk	T-39/43/P C-135E/P
Travis AFB CA (SUU)	COS-SUU	1 ea mo	T-39/43/P
Wright- Patterson AFB OH (FFO)	COS-FFO	2 ea wk	T-39/43/P

NOTE: 24 hr notice available on all scheduled and unscheduled flights. 30 lb luggage limit on C-21 and T-39/43 aircraft.

CONNECTICUT

Bradley International Airport (BDL)
Bradley ANG Base/103 TFG
East Gramby, CT 06026-5000

Comm: 203-623-8291
ATVN: 636-8310

LOCATION: From I-91 N or S, Exit #40 W for 5 mi to IAP. RM: p-19, C/11.
NMC: Hartford CT, 12 mi S.

FACILITIES	LOCATION	HOURS	PHONE	COMMENTS
PAX TERM INFO	IAP departures	24 hrs dly	C-623-8291, A-636-8310	In the IAP. Serves New London Naval Submarine Base CT and Newport Naval Education and Training Center RI-activated primarily during exercise periods. All facilities of IAP available. For more info contact 438th APS/TROP, McGuire AFB NJ 08641-5000, C-609-724-2810/2749, A-440-2810/2749.

SCHEDULED FLIGHTS

DESTINATION	ROUTING	FREQ	EQ/CMTS
RAF Mildenhall UK (MHZ)	PHL-BDL-PIK-MHZ	3/Th	DC-863/P/CC
Philadelphia Intl PA (PHL)	MHZ-PIK-BDL-PHL	2/F	DC-863/P/CC
Prestwick Arpt UK (PIK)	PHL-BDL-PIK-MHZ	3/Th	DC-863/P/CC

DELAWARE

Dover Air Force Base (DOV)
436 APS/TROP
Dover AFB, DE 19902-5496

Comm: 302-678-7011
ATVN: 455-6881

LOCATION: Off US-113. Clearly marked. RM: p-41, F/24. NMC: Dover, 3 mi NW.

FACILITIES	LOCATION	HOURS	PHONE	COMMENTS
PAX TERM INFO	Bldg 500	24 hrs dly	C-678-6892/3, A-455-6892/3	Fm main gate on 13th St to L on 18th St, R after Wing Hq Bldg to Pax Term in ATC Bldg 500. In-flt meals avail at check-in.

DELAWARE

Dover AFB, Cont'd

Recording	Bldg 500	24 hrs dly	C-678-6891, A-455-6891	
	Recording updated at 2000 dly.			
Pax Svc Ofc	Bldg 500	0730-1730 M-F	C-678-6998	NCO on duty
Pax Paging	Bldg 500	24 hrs dly	C-678-6892/3	
PAX LOUNGES General	Family lounge 2nd floor Bldg 500 1st floor 24 hrs dly C-678-6892/3 A/C, Bag check/lockers, Tel C,A,&LD, TV, Rest-rms, P/C seats. Non-smoking sec. No sleeping in lounge area.			
DV/VIP	Bldg 501 24 hrs dly C-678-6892/3 Base Ops Not staffed. A/C, Tel C,A,&LD, TV, O/S seats. (O6+)			
Protocol Svc	Bldg 201 0800-1600 M-F C-678-6610/6649, A-455-6610/6649 MAC sponsored.			
FOOD SERVICE Cafeteria	Bldg 501	24 hrs dly (closed 1430-1530 M-F)		C-674-3380
Dining Hall	Bldg 403	0600-0045	C-678-6242	Call for svc hrs.
NCO/CPO Club	Bldg 479	0700-2400 M-F,0800 Sa-Su	C-678-0651	C/for svc hrs.
OFC Club	Bldg 813	1130-2300 M-Sa	C-678-6363	Call for svc hrs.
Snack Bars	Bldg 266	0900-1500 M-Sa	C-678-6304	
Vending	Bldg 500	24 hrs dly	C-674-4862	Lounges/lobby
TRANSPORTATION Air Tickets	Bldg 500	0830-1630 M-F	C-736-1668 SATO	Wkend flt arrivals
Bus(Comm)	Dover	24 hrs dly	GH=C-734-3372, TW=C-734-4648	
Car Rentals	Bldg 500	0800-1700 dly	Natl=C-734-5774, Avis=C-734-5550	
Limo Service	Bldg 500 24 hrs dly B&B Express=C-734-7272 Sea Coast=C-834-7575, JG Exec=C-800-441-8775 and C-697-3173			
TAXI(Comm)	Bldg 500	24 hrs dly	C-734-5968	City Cab
Trains	Wilmington, 45 mi	24 hrs dly	C-1-800-872-7245 AMTRAK	
Parking	Bldg 500 24 hrs dly C-678-6892 Lot in front of Term limited to 12 hrs.Long term marked.Notification not required.			
OTHER SERVICES Exchange	Bldg 266	0900-1800 M-F, 1600 Sa	C-678-6515	
Bank/Exc	Bldg 267	0900-1500 M-F	C-734-0281	Mellon Bank
Hair Styles	Bldg 266	0800-1800 M-F (closed 1400 Sa)	C-674-5717	Barber
	Bldg 266	0830-1700 M-F (closed 1500 Sa)	C-734-1747	Beauty
Medical	Bldg 300	24 hrs dly	C-735-2600	Hospital
Postal	Bldg 442	0730-1630 M-F	C-678-6228	

DELAWARE

Dover AFB, Cont'd

Valet/Dry C	Bldg 266	0800-1800 M-F, 0900-1300 Sa C-674-0794
TML	Bldg 805 Biltg Office 24 hrs dly C-678-6329 All Ranks. DV/VIP C-678-6095.	
TRAVELERS AID ARC	Bldg 439	0730-1630 M-F C-678-6600 After hrs C-678-1555
Chaplain	Bldg 419	0745-1645 M-F C-678-6341 Other hrs 678-1555
Emerg Relief	Bldg 520	0730-1630 M-F C-678-6388 Air Force Aid
Lost/Found	Bldg 500	24 hrs dly C-678-6998 See Pax Term NCO.
Sec Police	Bldg 727	24 hrs dly C-736-6483 See SP to park RVs.
Retired Desk	Bldg 500	Near flt hrs C-678-6893 Unique svc-volunteers
ATTRACTIONS	State capital, great beaches, and the Delaware Bay	

SCHEDULED FLIGHTS

DESTINATION	ROUTING	FREQ	EQ/CMTS
Cairo Intl EG (CAI)	DOV-RMS-CAI	M	C-141B/C
Dhahran Intl SA (DHA)	DOV-RMS-DHA DOV-TOJ-DHA-JDW	Th Th	C-141B/C C-141B/C
Incirlik Arpt TU (ADA)	DOV-RMS-ADA DOV-TOJ-ADA DOV-RMS-ADA	M,Th F Sa	C005A/C C005A/C C-141B/C
King Abdullah AB JR (AMM)	DOV-RMS-SIZ-AMM	Sa	C-141B/M
RAF Mildenhall UK (MHZ)	DOV-MHZ-FRF SUU-TIK-DOV-RMS-MHZ	M Th,F	C005A/C C005A/C
Norfolk NAS VA (NGU)	DOV-NGU	Tu,Th	C005A/M
Ramstein AB GE (RMS)	DOV-RMS DOV-RMS-CAI DOV-RMS-ADA DOV-RMS-DHA DOV-RMS SUU-TIK-DOV-RMS-MHZ DOV-RMS-SIZ-AMM	Su,W,F M M,Th Th 1/2/3/Th Th,Sa Sa	C005A/C C-141B/M C005A/C C-141B/C B747/C/CC C005A/C C-141B/M
Rhein Main AB GE (FRF)	DOV-FRF DOV-FRF	Su,W,F Tu,Th	B747/C/CC C005A/C
Sigonella Arpt IT (SIZ)1	DOV-RMS-SIZ-AMM	Sa	C-141B/M
Tinker AFB OK (TIK)	MHZ-DOV-TIK-SUU DOV-TIK-SUU	Su,Tu 2-4 flts wkly	C005A/C C-141B/M

DELAWARE

Dover AFB, Cont'd

Torrejon de Ardoz AB SP (TOJ)	DOV-TOJ-DHA DOV-TOJ-FRF DOV-TOJ-ADA	Th F Sa	C005A/C C005A/C C-141B/C
Travis AFB CA (SUU)	MHZ-DOV-TIK-SUU SUU-TIK-DOV-RMS DOV-TIK-SUU	Su,Tu Th,Sa 2-4 flts wkly	C005A/C C005A/C C-141B/M

UNSCHEDULED FLIGHTS

Limited flights to Charleston AFB-Intl SC (CHS).

Greater Wilmington Airport (ILG)
Base Ops, 166th Tac Airlift Gp, ANG
New Castle, DE 19720-2495

Comm: 302-323-3525
ATVN: 455-3525

LOCATION: From I-95 N or S, take Exit 5 to DE-41 S for 1 mi to the intersection of DE-37 (Commons Blvd) where entrance to ANGB is well marked. RM: p-41, B-23. NMC: Wilmington DE, 7 mi NE.

FACILITIES	LOCATION	HOURS	PHONE	COMMENTS
PAX TERM INFO	Bldg 2812 Base Ops 0800-1630 M-F and during flt processing C-323-3525, A-455-3525 Entrance off DE-41 and straight to ANG Base Ops. Also, DE ANG Flt Ops Bldg 2812. All fac of a regional airport are available at the Comm Arpt Term.			
Pax Svc Ofc	Bldg 2812	0800-1630 M-F	C-323-3525	
PAX LOUNGES General	Limited lounge facilities. No DV/VIP or family lounges. Bldg 2812 0800-1630 M-F C-323-3525 A/C, Rest-rms, P/C seats			
TRANSPORTATION Car Rentals	Greater Wilmington Airport. Call for hours. Dollar=C-655-7117, Natl=C-328-5636			
Parking	Behind Bldg 2812	24 hrs dly	C-323-3525	No restrictions
ATTRACTIONS	Historic section of Wilmington			

UNSCHEDULED FLIGHTS

Some flights to CONUS and OCONUS locations via C-130H aircraft. Call for destinations, routings, and schedules.

DISTRICT OF COLUMBIA
See Maryland

FLORIDA

Cecil Field Naval Air Station (NZC)
Air Operations Officer
Cecil Field NAS, FL 32215-5000

Comm: 904-778-5675
ATVN: 860-5675

LOCATION: Take Normandy exit W off I-295 and follow Normandy (FL-228) to main gate. RM: p-21, E/11. NMC: Jacksonville, 13 mi E.

FLORIDA
Cecil Field NAS, Cont'd

FACILITIES	LOCATION	HOURS	PHONE	COMMENTS
PAX TERM INFO	Bldg 47	24 hrs dly	C-778-5536/5481, A-860-5536/5481	
	From main gate, straight on "D" Ave to L on 1st St to Air Processing Term on R.			
Pax Svc Ofc	Bldg 47	24 hrs dly	C-778-5536	
PAX LOUNGES	Bldg 47	24 hrs dly	C-778-5536	Limited facilities
FOOD SERVICE	Good on Base. Dining Hall C-778-5317/8, Enl Club C-778-6153/4, NCO/CPO Club C-778-5390/5840, O'Club C-778-5274/5, Snack Bar C-778-5225			
TRANSPORTATION	Limited on Base. SATO C-778-5676, Taxi(Comm) C-778-5381 (Gov) C-778-5487			
OTHER SERVICES	Good on Base. Exchange C-778-3571, Bank C-778-4274, Barber C-778-3198, Beauty C-771-0351, Medical C-778-5213/4			
TML	Bldg 331	24 hrs dly	C-771-0641	Guest House
TRAVELERS AID	ARC C-778-5337, Fam Svcs C-778-5239/5366, Chaplain C-778-5340/9, Navy Relief C-778-6170/1, Sec Police C-778-5381, USO C-778-2821			
ATTRACTIONS	Beaches, Disney World (Orlando area), Cypress Gardens			

UNSCHEDULED FLIGHTS

Weekly flights to: Brunswick NAS ME (NHZ); Charleston AFB IAP SC (CHS); Jacksonville NAS FL (NIP); and Norfolk NAS VA (NGU) via P-3/M and C009A/ME aircraft/missions. The best Space-A in the area is at Jacksonville NAS.

Clearwater Coast Guard Air Station (PIE)
Commanding Officer
Clearwater, FL 33520-5000

Comm: 813-535-1437
FTS: 826-1350
ATVN: 968-4273

LOCATION: At the St Petersburg - Clearwater IAP, take the FL-686 exit from I-275 and go for 1 mile W. RM: p-21, P/3. NMC: St Petersburg, 5 mi S.

FACILITIES	LOCATION	HOURS	PHONE	COMMENTS
PAX TERM INFO	USCG Hangar	0800-1600 M-F	C-535-1437,F-826-1247,A-968-4273	
	Ask Security Police for directions. Parking - west of hangar.			
OTHER SERVICES	Many support facilities available to include: Barber, Exchange, Emergency medical, and TML.			

UNSCHEDULED FLIGHTS

Flights to: CONUS AND OCONUS locations via C-130 aircraft. No Space-A on helicopter aircraft. Call for destinations, routings and schedules.

Eglin Air Force Base (VPS)
Passenger Terminal Officer
Eglin AFB, FL 32542-5000

Comm: 904-881-6668
ATVN: 872-1110

FLORIDA

Eglin AFB, Cont'd

LOCATION: Exit I-10 at Crestview and follow posted direction signs to Niceville and Valparaiso (Eglin AFB). RM:p-21, W/5. NMC:Fort Walton Beach, 7 mi S.

FACILITIES	LOCATION	HOURS	PHONE	COMMENTS
PAX TERM INFO	Bldg 60	0600-1800 M-F, 0800-1600 Sa-Su	C-882-5732/5313, A-872-5732/5313	From west gate straight on Eglin Blvd to L on 7th Street to L on Choctawhatchee Avenue to Pax Term R. Also, check with Base Ops Hurlburt Field, Base Ops Bldg 90730, C-884-7806 for flights.
Pax Svc Ofc	Bldg 60	0600-1800 M-F, 0800-1600 Sa-Su	C-882-5732	NCO on dty
Pax Paging	Bldg 60	0600-1800 M-F, 0800-1600 Sa-Su	C-882-5732	
PAX LOUNGES General	No separate family lounge. Bldg 60 24 hrs dly C-882-5732 A/C, Coffee/tea service, Rest-rms, TV, P/C seats			
DV/VIP	Bldg 60 24 hrs dly C-882-5732 No host A/C, Coffee/tea svc, Rest-rms, Sep read/write rms, O/S seats			
Protocol Svc	Bldg 1	0715-1600 M-F	C-882-3011	Armament Division
FOOD SERVICE Cafeteria	Bldg 1759	0900-1400 M-Sa	C-651-4821	"Run-in-Chef"
Dining Hall	Bldg 18-D	0530-1800 dly 24 hrs dly	C-882-5053 C-882-5014	Call for svc hrs. Flight kitchen
NCO/CPO Club	Bldg 860	0700-2400 dly	C-678-5127	Call for svc hrs.
OFC Club	Bldg 10870	0600-2330 dly	C-651-1010	Call for svc hrs.
Snack Bars	Bldg 100	0700-1500 dly	C-678-5932	
TRANSPORTATION Air Tickets	Good on and off Base. Bldg 350	0730-1630 M-F	C-678-5146	SATO
Bus(Shuttle)	Bldg 509	0700-1600 dly	C-882-5432	
TAXI(Gov)	Bldg 509	24 hrs dly	C-882-3791	Duty Pax only
Parking	Bldg 60	24 hrs dly	C-882-2502	In front of Bldg
OTHER SERVICES Exchange	Bldg 1757	1000-1700 M-Sa	C-651-2512	
Bank/Exc	Bldg Memo Lake	0900-1700 M-F	C-651-1112	
Hair Styles	Bldg 1757	0900-1700 M-Sa 0800-1700 M-Sa	C-651-5122 C-651-5224	Barber Beauty
Laundry/DryC	Bldg 12	1000-1700 M-Sa	C-651-4924	
Medical	Bldg 2825	24 hrs dly	C-885-3337	
Postal	Bldg 10	0900-1600 M-F	C-882-3311	

FLORIDA
Eglin AFB, Cont'd

TML	Bldg 11001 All Ranks.	24 hrs dly DV/VIP	C-882-8761, A-872-8761 C-882-3011.
TRAVELERS AID ARC	Many on Base. Bldg 210	Family Services 0800-1600 M-F	C-882-2981. C-882-5848 Other hrs C-882-2485
Chaplain	Bldg 868	0715-1615 M-F	C-882-2111
Emerg Relief	Bldg 210	0715-1615 M-F	C-882-4395
Lost/Found	Bldg 60	0600-1800 M-F	C-882-5732
Sec Police	Bldg 272	24 hrs dly	C-882-2502
ATTRACTIONS	Beaches, sport fishing, dog races		

SCHEDULED FLIGHTS

DESTINATION	ROUTING	FREQ	EQ/CMTS
Kelly AFB TX (SKF)	VPS-BIX-SKF-BLV	W,Sa	C009A/ME
Keesler AFB MS (BIX)	VPS-BIX-SKF-BLV	W,Sa	C009A/ME
Scott AFB IL (BLV)	VPS-BIX-SKF-BLV	W,Sa	C009A/ME

UNSCHEDULED FLIGHTS

Many unscheduled flights to: Andrews AFB MD (ADW); Langley AFB VA (LFI); Pensacola NAS FL (NPA); and Wright-Patterson AFB OH (FFO).

Homestead Air Force Base (HST)
31st TRANS/LGTT
Homestead AFB, FL 33039-5000

Comm: 305-257-8011
ATVN: 791-0111

LOCATION: Off Florida Turnpike, US-1, take Homestead exit. Clearly marked.
RM: p-21, V/15. NMC: Miami, 40 mi NE.

FACILITIES	LOCATION	HOURS	PHONE	COMMENTS
PAX TERM INFO	Bldg 701 Call for hrs. C-257-7551/7455, A-791-7551/7455 Fm West Gate straight on Bougainville Blvd to R on Coral Sea Road to Pax Term on R.			
Pax Svc Ofc	Bldg 701	Call for hrs.	C-257-7551	NCO on duty
Pax Paging	Bldg 701	Call for hrs.	C-257-7551	
PAX LOUNGES General	No separate family lounge Bldg 701 Call for hrs. C-257-8659 First floor A/C, Bag check, Tel L&ATVN, TV, Rest-rms, P/C seats			
DV/VIP	Bldg 702 24 hrs dly C-257-8659 A/C, Bag check, Tel L&ATVN, TV, Rest-rms, P/C seats			

FLORIDA

Homestead AFB, Cont'd

Protocol Svc	Bldg 931	0730-1630 M-F C-257-7212
FOOD SERVICE	Good on and off Base. Cafeteria C-257-5117, Dining Hall C-257-7667, Enl Club C-257-8949/6186, NCO/CPO Club C-257-5511 O'Club C-257-8791. Call each locaton for service hours.	
TRANSPORTATION	Good on and off Base. Air Tickets C-257-2941, Bus(Gov) C-257-7766, Car Rental C-257-2525, Taxi(Gov) C-257-7766, Parking C-257-7200 (across from Terminal)	
OTHER SERVICES	Good on and off Base. Exchange C-257-5811, Bank C-257-5887 Barber C-258-5133, Beauty C-257-2546, Laundry/DryC C-257-4218 Medical C-257-7668, Postal C-257-7277	
TML	Bldg 945 24 hrs dly C-257-5831, A-791-5831 All Ranks. DV/VIP C-257-7212.	
TRAVELERS AID	Good on and off Base. ARC C-257-4600, Chaplain C-257-7895 AF Aid C-257-8611, Sec Police C-257-7200, USO C-258-0055	
ATTRACTIONS	Biscayne Bay, horse and dog racing, and water sports	

SCHEDULED FLIGHTS

DESTINATION	ROUTING	FREQ	EQ/CMTS
Charleston AFB IAP SC (CHS)	Varies	Su,1/2/3/F	C-141B/M
Jacksonville NAS FL (NIP)	CHS-MCF-HST-NIP	F	C-141B/M
Keesler AFB MS (BIX)	Varies	Tu,F	C009A/ME
MacDill AFB FL (MCF)	CHS-NIP-HST-MCF CHS-MCF-HST-NIP	Su F	C-141B/M C-141B/M

Jacksonville Naval Air Station (NIP)
Box 7, Code 308, Air Terminal
Jacksonville NAS, FL 32212-5000

Comm: 904-772-2338
ATVN: 942-2345

LOCATION: Access from US-17 S (Roosevelt Blvd). On the St Johns River. RM: p-21, E/15. NMC: Jacksonville, 9 mi NE.

FACILITIES	LOCATION	HOURS	PHONE	COMMENTS
PAX TERM INFO	Bldg 118 24 hrs dly C-772-2537/3825, A-942-2537/3825 From main gate, straight on Yorktown Ave to L on Wasp St to R on Albemarie Ave, Term on L.			
Pax Svc Ofc	Bldg 118	24 hrs dly	C-772-2537/3825	
Pax Paging	Bldg 118	24 hrs dly	C-772-2537	
PAX LOUNGES General	General lounge Bldg 118 24 hrs dly C-772-2537 Contact P/O upon entering lounge. A/C, Bag chk, Tel L, Rest-rms, P/C seats.			

FLORIDA
Jacksonville NAS, Cont'd

DV/VIP	Bldg 118 24 hrs dly C-772-2537 (06+) A/C, Bag chk, Tel ATVN, TV, Rest-rms, O/S seats
Protocol Svc	Bldg 1 0800-1700 M-F C-772-2413 COMSEABASEDASWWINGSLANT
FOOD SERVICE Cafeteria	Many facilities on and off Base Bldg 118 24 hrs dly C-772-2519
Dining Hall	Bldg 855 0530-1800 dly C-772-3302/3821 C/for svc hrs.
Enl Club	Bldg 798 1100-0100 dly C-772-3521/2209 C/for svc hrs.
NCO/CPO Club	Bldg 789 1100-0100 dly C-772-3461 Call for svc hrs.
OFC Club	Bldg 10 1100-2200 M-Sa C-772-3041/2 Call for svc hrs.
Snack Bars	Convenience Store 1100-2200 dly C-772-0414 Pizza delivery
Vending	Bldg 118 24 hrs dly C-772-2521
TRANSPORTATION Air Tickets	Good on and off Base Bldg 620 0800-1630 M-Sa C-778-1411/2449 SATO
Bus(Comm) (Gov) (Shuttle)	Bldg 118 To JAX #70 on Base C-633-7330 Call for schedule. Bldg 118 3 times daily to Cecil Field NAS and 2 times daily to Mayport NS C-772-2110 Bldg 118 0630-1830 M-F C-772-2110 Every 45 min on Base
Car Rentals	Bldg 118 0900-1800 M-Sa C-388-1212 Other companies C-778-3821 Navy Exchange
TAXI(Comm)	See local telephone directory in Terminal.
Parking	Bldg 118 Short term-restricted to 8 hrs C-772-2661
OTHER SERVICES Exchange	Many services on and off Base Bldg 27 0900-1730 M-F, 2000 Sa, 1200-1600 Su C-777-7286 or C-778-3040
Bank/Exc	Bldg 816 0800-1600 M-F C-791-7075, C-772-3870 Barnett
Hair Styles	Bldg 3 0900-1730 M-F, 2000 Sa C-777-7228/9 Barber & Beauty
Laundry/DryC	Bldg 27 0700-1700 M-F, 1330 Sa C-778-3040
Medical	Bldg H-2080 24 hrs dly C-777-7340 Ambulance C-772-2423
Postal	Bldg 920 0830-1600 M-F C-772-3495
WIRE	Bldg 620 24 hrs dly C-771-5368
TML	Bldg 803 C-772-6200/2549 or 800-628-9466 A-942-6200/2549 Navy Lodge. All Ranks.
TRAVELERS AID ARC	Many agencies Bldg 8 0800-1600 M-F C-772-2766/7 Fam Svcs Bldg 8 0730-1600 M-F C-772-2426 Other hrs C-772-2338
Chaplain	Bldg 752 0800-1600 dly C-772-3440/3051

FLORIDA

Jacksonville NAS, Cont'd

Emerg Relief	Bldg 8	0900-1500 M-F	C-772-3515	Navy Relief
Lost/Found	Bldg 118	24 hrs dly	C-772-2521	
Sec Police	Bldg 9	24 hrs dly	C-772-2661	
USO	Bldg 8	0800-1600 M-F	C-778-2821	
ATTRACTIONS	Beaches, fishing, St. Augustine, Orlando			

UNSCHEDULED FLIGHTS

Frequent flights to: Bermuda NAS BM (BDA); Brunswick NAS ME (NHZ); Charleston AFB IAP SC (CHS); Guantanamo Bay NS (GAO); Homestead AFB FL (HST); MacDill AFB FL (MCF); Norfolk NAS VA (NGU); Patuxent River NAS (NHK); and Roosevelt Roads NAS PR (NRR).

Note: 2-3 days prior notice on flights. Schedules subject to change. Also, manages flights departing Cecil Field NAS and Mayport NAF. Most flights to East Coast destinations and some to OCONUS and foreign countries. Call for destinations, routings, and schedules.

Key West Naval Air Station (NQX)
Air Operations Officer
Key West NAS, FL 33040-5000

Comm: 305-292-2434
ATVN: 483-2434

LOCATION: Take Florida Turnpike, US-1 S to exit signs for Key West NAS on Boca Chica Key, 7 mi N of Key West. RM: p-21, Z/11. NMC: Miami, 150 mi N.

FACILITIES	LOCATION HOURS PHONE COMMENTS
PAX TERM INFO	NAS ATC tower 0800-1600 dly C-296-3561/2735, A-483-2735 On Boca Chica Key, easily visible.
Pax Svc Ofc	ATC/Ops 0800-1600 dly C-296-3561/2735 NCO on duty
PAX LOUNGES	No Pax Term. All Pax processing handled at ATC/Ops C-296-3561/2735. A/C, Rest-rms, TV, O/S & P/C seats.
FOOD SERVICE	Cafeteria C-292-2687, Dining Hall C-292-2687, Enl Club C-292-2495, NCO/CPO Club C-292-2407, O'Club C-295-5571
TRANSPORTATION	Bus(Shuttle) C-292-2342, Car Rentals, AVIS=C-296-8744, Hertz=C-294-1039, Taxi(Comm) C-292-2342/2268, Parking ATC/OPs
OTHER SERVICES	Also at NB. Exchange C-294-7262, Bank C-294-1796, Hair Styles C-292-7221, Medical C-292-2335, Postal C-292-2406
TML	Bldg 2076 24 hrs dly C-294-2112/5571, A-483-2112/5571 All Ranks. DV/VIP C-292-2178.
TRAVELERS AID	On Base and in Key West. ARC C-296-3651, Fam Svcs C-294-5760, Chaplain C-292-2318, Navy Relief C-294-3561, Sec Police C-292-2455
ATTRACTIONS	Water sports, Ernest Hemingway Home

FLORIDA
Key West NAS, Cont'd

SCHEDULED FLIGHTS

DESTINATION	ROUTING	FREQ	EQ/CMTS
Homestead AFB FL (HST)	NQX-HST	Weekly	C009A/ME
MacDill AFB FL (MCF)	NQX-MCF	Weekly	C009A/ME

Note: Call for other destinations, routings, and schedules.

MacDill Air Force Base (MCF)
56th TTW/LGTT (TAC), Passenger Terminal
MacDill AFB, FL 33608-5000

Comm: 813-830-1110
ATVN: 968-1110

LOCATION: Take I-75 S to I-275 S, exit at Dale Mabry Hwy (US-92) S, 5 mi S to MacDill AFB main gate. RM: p-21, 9/4. NMC: Tampa, 5 mi N.

FACILITIES	LOCATION	HOURS	PHONE	COMMENTS
PAX TERM INFO	Hangar #5	0730-1630 M-Sa,	C-830-2310/2485,	A-968-2310. Enter Dale Mabry gate. Turn L on N Boundry Rd to R on Hangar Loop Road, 5th Hangar on R. Hangar #5 Army Aviation C-830-2808, A-968-2808. Flights on C-12 aircraft to CONUS destinations.
Pax Svc Ofc	Hangar #5	0730-1630 M-Sa	C-830-2485, A-968-2485	No Paging
PAX LOUNGES General	General lounge is also family lounge. Hangar #5	0730-1630 M-Sa	C-830-2310	A/C, Bag chk, Tel L,LD,&ATVN, TV, Rest-rms, P/C seats.
DV/VIP	Hangar #5	0730-1630 M-Sa	C-830-2310	A/C,Coffee/tea srvd, Read/write rms, Tel L,LD,&ATVN,TV,Rest-rms,Showers,O/S seats
Protocol Svc	Bldg 9	0730-1630 M-F	C-830-2056	56th TTW
FOOD SERVICE Cafeteria	Good services on and off Base. Bldg 298	0800-2400 dly	C-830-3808	
Dining Hall	Bldg 259	0500-0100 dly	C-830-1110	4 meals + In-flt
Enl Club	Bldg 499	0700-2100 dly	C-830-3357	Call for svc hrs.
NCO/CPO Club	Bldg 499	0700-2100 dly	C-830-3357	Call for svc hrs.
OFC Club	Bldg 397	0630-2200 M-Sa	C-837-1031	Call for svc hrs.
Snack Bars	Hangar #5	1000-1600 dly	C-840-2077	
Vending	Hangar #3	24 hrs dly	C-830-2100	
TRANSPORTATION Air Tickets	Good on Base and in Tampa. Bldg 528	0730-1630 M-Sa	C-830-4327	SATO
Bus (Comm)	Bldg 926	0530-0730 dly		Heartline Bus
Car Rentals	Bldg 17	0730-1730 dly	C-840-2303	Dayton Andrews

FLORIDA

MacDill AFB, Cont'd

TAXI(Comm)	Gates	24 hrs dly	C-253-0121	Yellow
(Gov)	Bldg 176	24 hrs dly	C-830-5281	Duty Pax only
Parking	Short term-in front of Hangar #3, 1 day limit; long term-across from Hangar #3. Call Sec Police for info C-830-3322.			
OTHER SERVICES				
Exchange	Bldg 926	1000-1800 M-F, 1700 Sa	C-840-0511	
Bank/Exc	Bldg 240	1000-1600 M-F	C-840-0511	
Hair Styles	Bldg 926	0730-1700 M-F, 1600 Sa	C-840-0511	Barber
		0800-1600 M-Sa	C-840-0511	Beauty
Laundry/DryC	Bldg 926	1000-1800 M-Sa	C-840-0511	
Medical	Bldg 711	24 hrs dly	C-839-3344	
Postal	Bldg 344	0800-1700 M-F	C-830-4438	
TML	Bldg 411	24 hrs dly	C-830-4179, A-968-4179	
	All Ranks.	DV/VIP C-830-2056.		
TRAVELERS AID				
ARC	Bldg 27	0830-1630 M-F	C-830-3156	
Chaplain	Bldg 355	0730-1630 M-F	C-830-3621	
Lost/Found	Bldg P-26	24 hrs dly	C-830-3322	
Sec Police	Bldg P-26	24 hrs dly	C-830-3322	
USO	318 Madison, Tampa	Call for hrs.	C-813-229-9401	

SCHEDULED FLIGHTS

DESTINATION	ROUTING	FREQ	EQ/CMTS
Charleston AFB	MCF-CHS	Su	C-141B/M
IAP SC (CHS)	MCF-HST-NIP-CHS	1/2/3/F	C-141B/M
Homestead AFB	CHS-NIP-HST-MCF	Su	C-141B/M
FL (HST)	CHS-NIP-HST-NIP	F	C-141B/M
Jacksonville	CHS-NIP-HST-MCF	Su	C-141B/M
NAS FL (NIP)	CHS-NIP-HST-NIP	F	C-141B/M
Keesler AFB	MCF-BIX	Tu,F	C009A/ME
MS (BIX)			

UNSCHEDULED FLIGHTS

Frequent flights to: Andrews AFB MD (ADW); Dover AFB DE (DOV); Eglin AFB FL (VPS); Langley AFB VA (LFI); Maxwell AFB AL (MXF); McChord AFB WA (TCM); Pope AFB NC (POB); Pease AFB NH (PSM); Scott AFB IL (BLV); and Wright-Patterson AFB OH (FFO). Flights are known one day in advance.

FLORIDA

Patrick Air Force Base (COF)
6550 ABG/LGTAP
Patrick AFB, FL 32925-5000

Comm: 407-494-1110
ATVN: 854-1110

LOCATION: I-95 exit 73 (marked Patrick AFB/Wickham Rd), approx 5 miles S on Wickham Rd, take Hwy 404 east (toll road) to Patrick AFB exit. Base on Hwy A1A, approx 5 mi S of Cocoa Beach. RM: p-20, L/15. NMC: Orlando, 60 mi NW. Melbourne, Cocoa, and Merritt Island - all within 20 miles of Base.

FACILITIES	LOCATION	HOURS	PHONE	COMMENTS
PAX TERM INFO	Bldg 800 0730-1630 M-F C-494-5631, A-854-5631 1 mi N of South Gate on S Patrick Dr. Pax Svc entrance faces S Patrick Dr. Same Bldg as Base Ops and control tower.			
Pax Svc Ofc	Bldg 800 0730-1630 M-F C-494-5631, A-854-5631			
PAX LOUNGES General	No separate family lounge Bldg 800 1st flr 0730-1630 M-F C-494-5631, A-854-5631 A/C, TV, O/S seats, Rest-rms, Tel C&A, Bag check.			
DV/VIP	Bldg 800 0730-1630 dly C-494-5631, A-854-5631 (06+) A/C, TV, O/S seats, Rest-rms, Tel C&A, Bag check.			
FOOD SERVICE Cafeteria	Bldg 546 2nd floor 1030-1500 M-Sa C-494-5523 "Comet Club"			
Enl Club	Bldg 546 1030-1500 M-Sa C-494-5523			
NCO/CPO Club	Bldg 967 0630-2200 M-F, 0800-2000 Sa-Su C-494-7491			
OFC Club	Bldg 250 0630-1930 M-F, 0800-1930 Sa-Su C-494-4001			
Restaurants	Bldg 600 0800-2000 M-Su C-494-2042 "Boat House"			
Snack Bars	Bldg 732 0800-2300 M-Sa C-494-2598 Snack bars also at bowling alley, golf course C-494-6510			
Vending	Bldg 800 0730-2300 dly			
TRANSPORTATION Air Tickets	Bldg 530 0730-1630 M-F C-783-1600 SATO			
Bus(Comm) (Shuttle)	None on Base (Avail in Melbourne/Cocoa 0730-2000 dly) Bldg 800 0730-1700 M-F C-494-7247 On Base routing			
Car Rentals	Bldg 400 0800-1630 M-F C-783-2608			
Limo Service	Bldg 400 (Dly between Orlando Intl/PAFB) C-676-4557 $11			
TAXI(Comm) (Gov)	In Cocoa Beach 24 hrs dly C-783-7200/2500 Bldg 329 0730-2300 M-F, 0730-1500 Sa-Su C-494-7247 (For military personnel on orders only)			
Parking	Short term-N of Bldg 800 (Pax Term) 0730-2300 dly (no overnight); long term-150 yds S of Bldg 800 (unlimited hours).			
OTHER SERVICES Exchange	Off Base 0930-1800 M-F, 1630 Sa-Su C-494-7457			
Bank/Exc	Bldg 720 0900-1700 M-F C-783-3411			

FLORIDA

Patrick AFB, Cont'd

Hair Styles	Bldg 415 C-784-2781 Barber, C-784-1241 Beauty
Laundry/DryC	Bldg 415 0930-1800 M-F, 1630 Sa-Su C-783-3625
Postal	Bldg 424 Call for hrs. C-494-6297
Medical	Bldg 1380 24 hrs dly C-494-813
WIRE	Western Union available in Cocoa Beach
TML	Bldg 400 24 hrs dly C-494-2075, A-854-2075 All Ranks. Coral Lodge (on C St). DV/VIP C-494-4506.
TRAVELERS AID ARC	Bldg 425 0730-1630 M-F C-494-2402
Chaplain	Serving all faiths Duty hrs C-494-4073
Lost/Found	Bldg 800 0730-1630 M-Su C-494-5631
Sec Police	Bldg 405 24 hrs dly C-494-7777
ATTRACTIONS	NASA Space Flight Center, Daytona Beach, Orlando-Disney World

SCHEDULED FLIGHTS

DESTINATION	ROUTING	FREQ	EQ/CMTS
Ascension Aux AF UK (ASI)	COF-SJH-ASI	M,W	C-141B/M
Charleston AFB Intl SC (CHS)	COF-CHS	W,F	C-141B/M
Coolidge Arpt AN (SJH)	COF-SJH-ASI	M,W	C-141B/M
Grand Bahama Aux AF BH (GBI)	COF-GBI	F	C-130E/M
Jacksonville FL (NIP)	COF-NIP-BIX	Tu,F	C009A/ME
Keesler AFB MS (BIX)	COF-NIP-BIX	Tu,F	C009A/ME
McGuire AFB NJ (WRI)	COF-WRI	2/F (usually 2nd full wk)	C-141B/M
Pope AFB NC (POB)	COF-POB	F	C-130E/M

UNSCHEDULED FLIGHTS

Andrews AFB MD (ADW)	COF-ADW	As required	C-21A or C-12A

FLORIDA

Pensacola Naval Air Station (NPA)
Air Operations
Pensacola NAS, FL 32508-5000

Comm: 904-452-2311
ATVN: 922-2311

LOCATION: Off US-98, 4 mi S, and 12 mi S of I-10. Take Navy Blvd from US-98 or US-29 directly to NAS. RM: p-21, X/3. NMC: Pensacola, 8 mi N.

FACILITIES	LOCATION	HOURS	PHONE	COMMENTS
PAX TERM INFO	Bldg 1852	24 hrs dly	C-452-3311/2432, A-922-3311/2432	
	From main gate, straight on Duncan Rd to R on Taylor Rd to R on Radford Rd to Air Ops on R.			
Pax Svc Ofc	Bldg 1852	24 hrs dly	C-452-3311/2432	
Pax Paging	Bldg 1852	24 hrs dly	C-452-2432	
PAX LOUNGES General	No separate family lounge			
	Bldg 1852	24 hrs dly	C-452-2432	
	A/C, Rest-rms, Showers, Tel L&ATVN, O/S seats			
DV/VIP	Bldg 1852	24 hrs dly	C-452-2432	A/C, Rest-rms, O/S seats
Protocol Svc	Bldg 501	0800-1700 M-F	C-452-2311	CNET
FOOD SERVICE Cafeteria	Many facilities on and off Base			
	Bldg 634	0800-1730	C-455-0392	
Enl Club	Bldg 746	Call for hrs.	C-452-3251/4357	"Seabreeze"
NCO/CPO Club	Bldg 3558	Call for hrs.	C-452-3214/3533	
OFC Club	Bldg 253	Call for hrs.	C-455-2276	Mustin Beach
Snack Bars	McDonalds	Call for hrs.	C-452-3311/2432	
Vending	Bldg 1852	24 hrs dly	C-452-2432	
TRANSPORTATION Air Tickets	Good on and off Base			
	Bldg 45	0800-1600 M-F	C-455-5481	SATO
Bus(Comm)	Fairfield Rd	0930-1630 M-F	C-436-9383	
(Shuttle)	Bldg 1852	0600-1700 M-F	C-452-2753	On Base
Car Rentals	Bldg 470	0730-1800 M-Sa, 1430 Su	C-456-5165	NX on Base
TAXI(Comm)	Bldg 1852	24 hrs dly	C-455-8506	Warrington
Parking	Bldg 1852	24 hrs dly	C-452-3453	
OTHER SERVICES Exchange	Many facilities on and off Base			
	Bldg 634 0900-1800 M-Th,Sa,2000 F,1200-1700 Su C-453-5311			
Bank/Exc	Murray Rd	0900-1630 M-F	C-453-3411	1st Navy Bank
Hair Styles	Bldg 634	0900-1800 M-Sa, 1200-1700 Su	C-455-5738	Barber
		0800-1800 M-Sa, 1200-1700 Su	C-455-5224	Beauty
Laundry/DryC	Bldg 634	0900-1630 M-Sa	C-455-5313	
Medical	Naval Hospital	24 hrs dly	C-452-6731	Ambulance C-452-4138

FLORIDA

Pensacola NAS, Cont'd

Postal	Bldg 223	0900-1600 M-F	C-452-2726
TML	Bldg 600 24 hrs dly Navy Lodge C-456-8676		C-452-2255, A-922-2255
TRAVELERS AID ARC	Many agencies Bldg 25 0730-1600 M-F C-452-3393/4 Fam Svcs Bldg 25 0730-1600 M-F C-452-2492 Other hrs C-452-6601		
Chaplain	Bldg 634	0730-1600 M-F	C-452-2341
Emerg Relief	Bldg 16	0900-1600 M-F	C-455-8574 Navy Relief
Lost/Found	Bldg 1852	24 hrs dly	C-452-2432
Sec Police	Main gate	24 hrs dly	C-452-3453
ATTRACTIONS	Sport fishing, dog races, Naval Aviation Museum, Blue Angels		

SCHEDULED FLIGHTS

DESTINATION	ROUTING	FREQ	EQ/CMTS
Corpus Christi NAS TX (NGP)	NPA-NGP	6 ea mo	Adm Acft/P
Dobbins AFB GA (MGE)	NPA-MGE	6 ea mo	Adm Acft/P
Jacksonville NAS FL (NIP)	NPA-NIP	8 ea mo	Adm Acft/P
Memphis NAS TN (NQA)	NPA-NQA	6 ea mo	Adm Acft/P
New Orleans NAS LA (NBG)	NPA-NBG	11 ea mo	Adm Acft/P
Norfolk NAS VA (NGU)	NPA-NGU	7 ea mo	Adm Acft/P
Orlando IAP FL (MCO)	NPA-MCO	6 ea mo	Adm Acft/P
Washington NAF MD (NSF)	NSF-NBG-NPA-NSF	10 ea mo	Adm Acft/P

Note: Flight schedules available 48 hrs prior to departure.

GEORGIA

Dobbins Air Force Base (MGE)
94th Tactical Airlift Wing
Dobbins AFB, GA 30069-5000

Comm: 404-421-5000
ATVN: 925-1110

LOCATION: From I-75 N exit to GA-280 W to AFB. Clearly marked. RM: p-24, B/1. NMC: Atlanta, 16 mi SE.

GEORGIA
Dobbins AFB, Cont'd

FACILITIES	LOCATION	HOURS	PHONE	COMMENTS
PAX TERM INFO	Bldg 737 Base Ops 0700-2300 dly C-421-4903/4904, A-925-4903/4904 From main gate, straight on Mimosa Dr to dead end at Pax Term. NAS Ops 0700-2300 dly C-421-5359, A-925-5359 Atlanta NAS is co-located with Dobbins AFB.				
Pax Svc Ofc	Bldg 737	0700-2300 dly	C-421-4903/4904	
Pax Paging	Bldg 737	0700-2300 dly	C-421-4903/4904	
PAX LOUNGES General	Limited lounge facilities Bldg 737 0700-2300 dly C-421-4903 Capacity 40. A/C, Tel (Pay), Rest-rms, P/C seats			
DV/VIP	Bldg 737 0700-2300 dly Commercial telephone in Pax Term Capacity 5. Key fm Dispatcher. A/C,Tel A,Rest-rms,O/S seats			
Protocol Svc	Bldg 922	0730-1615 M-F	C-421-4873	Base Exec Officer
FOOD SERVICE Dining Hall	Limited services on Base. Good services off Base. Bldg 60 NAS 0615-1730 M-Sa, 1300 Su C-421-5469 C/for svc hrs.			
Consol Club	Atlantic Ave NAS	Call for hrs.	C-421-5551	
EM Club	Bldg 64 NAS	Call for hrs.	C-421-5692	"Tradewinds"
OFC Club	Bldg 53 NAS	1130-0100 dly	C-421-5393	Call for svc hrs.
TRANSPORTATION Air Tickets	Bldg 812	0730-1615 M-F	C-421-4848	SATO
Bus(Comm)	Hwy 41 N	Daily	GH=C-427-3011, TW=C-429-0092	
Car Rentals	ATL IAP	24 hrs dly	Avis=C-530-2700, Hertz=C-530-2900	
TAXI(Gov)	Motor Pool	0800-1600 M-F	C-421-4853	Duty Pax only
Parking	Bldg 827	Long and short term		
OTHER SERVICES Exchange	Bldg 735	1000-1730 M-Sa, 1100-1700 Su	C-428-3054	
Hair Styles	Bldg 735	0900-1700 Tu-F, 1500 Sa	C-421-4869	
Medical	NAS Clinic	24 hrs dly	C-421-5302	
Postal	Bldg 709	0730-1615 M-F	C-421-5049	
TRAVELERS AID Chaplain	Bldg 32 NAS	0730-1600 W-Su	C-421-4955/6	
Sec Police	Main gate	24 hrs dly	C-421-4910	
USO	ATL IAP 0900-2000 M-Th, 2100 F, 1200-1800 Sa, 1400-2000 Su C-761-8061 North Term			
ATTRACTIONS	Stone Mountain, Six Flags			

GEORGIA

Dobbins AFB, Cont'd

SCHEDULED FLIGHTS

DESTINATION	ROUTING	FREQ	EQ/CMTS
Charleston AFB IAP SC (CHS)	CHS-MGE-CHS	Su,F	C-141B/M
Greenville/ Spartanburg Arpt SC (GSP)	CHS-MGE-GSP-POB	F	C-141B/M
Pope AFB NC (POB)	CHS-MGE-GSP-POB	F	C-141B/M

UNSCHEDULED FLIGHTS

Frequent flights to CONUS locations by AFRES C-141B, C-130E, and Navy VR-46 and DC-9 aircraft.

Moody Air Force Base (VAD)
347th Tactical Fighter Wing/Air Ops
Moody AFB, GA 31699-5000

Comm: 912-333-4211
ATVN: 460-1110

LOCATION: On GA-125, 10 mi N of Valdosta. Also, can be reached from I-75, via GA-122. RM: p-23, R/9. NMC: Valdosta, 10 mi S.

FACILITIES	LOCATION HOURS PHONE COMMENTS
PAX TERM INFO	Bldg 622 0700-2300 M-F, 0800-1600 Sa-Su and Holidays C-333-3305, A-460-3510 From main gate, straight on Mitchell Blvd to Austin Ellipse to Bradley Circle. R to Dexter St to R on Savannah St. Pax Term at flight apron. All Pax processed by Base Ops. No lounges. Pax wait in Base Ops. All Base support facilities available. For details see Military Living's "U.S. Forces Travel Guide USA & Caribbean Areas."
Pax Svc Ofc	Bldg 622 Same as Pax Term C-333-3510 NCO on duty
FOOD SERVICE	Flight Line Snack Bar C-333-3101, NCO Club C-333-3792, Ofc Club C-333-3258, Dining Hall C-333-3031. Call for svc hrs.
TRANSPORTATION Parking	Commercial Travel C-333-4278. Taxi C-333-3461. ATC tower Same as Pax Term. No restrictions.
OTHER SERVICES Medical	BX C-333-3431, Hair styles C-244-8541 Bldg 900 24 hrs dly C-333-3232
TML	Bldg 320 24 hrs dly C-333-3893, A-460-3893 All Ranks. DV/VIP C-333-3480.
TRAVELERS AID Sec Police	ARC C-333-3542, Chaplain C-333-3211, Family Svcs C-333-3068 Bldg 617 24 hrs dly C-333-3108
ATTRACTIONS	Historic homes in Valdosta, Okefenokee Swamp - 50 mi E

UNSCHEDULED FLIGHTS

Flts on most W & Sa via C009A/ME to: Eglin AFB FL (VPS); Kelly AFB TX (SKF); Keesler AFB MS (BIX); and Scott AFB IL (BLV). Other CONUS flts infrequent.

GEORGIA

Robins Air Force Base (WRB)
2853rd Air Base Group
Robins AFB, GA 31098-5000

Comm: 912-926-1113
ATVN: 468-1113

LOCATION: Off US-129 on GA-247 at Warner Robins. Access from I-75 S. RM: p-23, K/7. NMC: Macon, 18 mi NW.

FACILITIES	LOCATION	HOURS	PHONE	COMMENTS
PAX TERM INFO	Bldg 111	0700-1700 M-F	C-926-3166, A-468-3166	From Gate 1, straight on 1st St to L after Bldg 125 (on L).
Pax Svc Ofc	Bldg 111	0700-1700 M-F	C-926-3166	
Pax Paging	Bldg 111	0700-1700 M-F	C-926-3166	
PAX LOUNGES General	No separate family lounge			
	Bldg 111	0700-1700 M-F	C-926-3166	A/C, Bag chk, TV, Rest-rms
DV/VIP	Bldg 110	24 hrs dly	C-926-5826	Base Ops A/C, Showers, TV, Read/write rms, O/S seats
Protocol Svc	Bldg 215	24 hrs dly	C-926-2761	
FOOD SERVICE	Good services on and off Base. Cafeteria C-922-8635, Dining Hall C-926-1113, Enl Club C-922-6191, NCO Club C-923-5581, O'Club C-922-3011, Restr C-926-3031, Vending C-926-3166			
TRANSPORTATION	Good on and off Base. Air Tickets C-926-5363, Bus(Shuttle) C-926-3493, Taxi(Comm) C-923-6414 (Gov) C-926-3493, Parking Bldg 111, 2 blks NW, unmarked spaces only			
OTHER SERVICES	Good facilities on Base. Exchange C-922-5538, Barber C-923-5385, Beauty C-923-7027, Laundry/DryC C-922-2332, Medical C-926-3845, Postal C-926-3078			
TML	Bldg 557	24 hrs dly	C-926-2100/4412 or C-923-7146	A-468-2100/4412 All Ranks. DV/VIP C-926-2100.
TRAVELERS AID	Chaplain C-926-2821/2166, Fam Svcs C-926-6648, Lost/Found C-926-3166, Sec Police C-926-2187, USO C-912-922-5885			
ATTRACTIONS	Andersonville Trail, RAFB Museum			

UNSCHEDULED FLIGHTS

Some flights available via C-141B and C-130B/E aircraft to CONUS locations. Base performs depot maintenance on C-141B and C-130B/E aircraft.

Savannah International Airport (SAV)
165th Tactical Airlift Group (ANG)
Savannah IAP, GA 31402-5000

Comm: 912-964-1941
ATVN: 860-8210

LOCATION: From I-95 N or S, Exit 18 to US-80 E to L (N) on GA-307 for 3 mi to IAP. RM: p-23, W/13. NMC: Savannah GA, 4 mi SE.

FACILITIES	LOCATION	HOURS	PHONE	COMMENTS
PAX TERM INFO	ANG area	During flight processing	C-964-1941, A-860-8210	

GEORGIA

Savannah Intl Arpt, Cont'd

| OTHER SERVICES | All services and facilities of an IAP available |

UNSCHEDULED FLIGHTS

Most flts on wkends via C-130E aircraft to CONUS & OCONUS locations. Also chk for Space-A at nearby Hunter AAF (SVN) Army Ops C-912-352-5500, A-971-5500. CGAS (SVN) Ops at HAAF has very limited Space-A C-912-352-2908, A-434-1690.

IDAHO

Mountain Home Air Force Base (MUO)
366th Tactical Fighter Wing/Air Ops
Mountain Home AFB, ID 83648-5000

Comm: 208-828-2111
ATVN: 857-1110

LOCATION: Fm Boise, take I-84 SE, 39 mi to Mountain Home exit. Follow road through town to Airbase Rd, 10 mi to main gate. RM: p-25, N/4. NMC: Boise ID, 51 mi NW.

FACILITIES	LOCATION	HOURS	PHONE	COMMENTS
PAX TERM INFO	Bldg 262	0730-1630 M-F	C-828-2304, A-857-2304	
Pax Svc Ofc	Bldg 262	0730-1630 M-F	C-828-2304, A-857-2304	
PAX LOUNGES General	No separate family lounge Bldg 262 0600-0100 dly C-828-2304 A/C, Bag chk, Tel L&ATVN, Rest-rms, P/C seats			
DV/VIP	Bldg 262 0600-2300 dly C-828-2304 (06+) A/C, Bag check, Coffee/tea srvd, Read/write rms, Tel L&A, TV, Rest-rms, O/S seats			
Protocol Svc	Bldg 1506	0730-1630 M-F	C-828-2366	366th Tac Fighter Wing/XO
FOOD SERVICE Cafeteria	Good services on Base Bldg 2607	1000-1800 dly	C-832-4353	Call for svc hrs.
Dining Hall	Bldg 2316	0500-1800 dly	C-832-2313	Call for svc hrs.
Enl Club	Bldg 195	1100-2300 dly	C-828-6546	Call for svc hrs.
NCO/CPO Club	Bldg 195	1100-2300 dly	C-828-2105	Call for svc hrs.
OFC Club	Bldg 2605	1100-2130 dly	C-828-2597	Call for svc hrs.
Restaurants	Bldg 2618	1000-2200 dly	C-828-6546	Recreation Center
Snack Bars	Bldg 2207	1100-2000 M-F, 2200 Sa-Su	C-832-4424	
Vending	Bldg 262	0600-2300 dly	C-832-2304	
TRANSPORTATION Air Tickets	Bldg 1211	0730-1630 M-F	C-828-2440	SATO

IDAHO
Mountain Home AFB, Cont'd

Bus(Shuttle)	Bldg 1126	0600-1800 dly	C-828-2339 Main Base points
TAXI(Gov)	Bldg 1126	24 hrs dly	C-343-2215/2239
Parking	Bldg 262	0600-0100 dly	C-828-2256
OTHER SERVICES Exchange	Bldg 2607	1000-1700 M-Sa	C-832-4353
Bank/Exc	Bldg 2620	1000-1500 M-F	C-832-4202 Fed Cred Union C-832-46757
Hair Styles	Bldg 2607	0900-1700 M-Sa 0900-1700 M-F, 1500 Sa	C-832-7191 Barber C-832-4090 Beauty
Laundry	Bldg 2607	1000-1700 M-F	C-832-7465
Medical	Bldg 100	24 hrs dly	C-828-6274 Ambulance C-828-2233
Postal	Bldg 111	0900-1600 M-F	C-828-6452
TML	Bldg 2604 All Ranks.	24 hrs dly DV/VIP	C-828-6451, A-857-6451 C-828-6451/2366.
TRAVELERS AID ARC	Bldg 2408 Bldg 2408	0900-1700 M-F 0730-1630 M-F	C-828-2272 Family Services C-828-6622/3
Chaplain	Bldg 2606	0730-1630 M-F	C-828-6417 Other hrs C-828-2111
Emerg Relief	Bldg 278	0900-1700 M-F	C-828-2503/6148
Sec Police	Bldg 1013	24 hrs dly	C-828-2256

SCHEDULED FLIGHTS

DESTINATION	ROUTING	FREQ	EQ/CMTS
Buckley ANGB CO (BKF)	MUO-HIF-BKF-BLV	F	C009A/ME
Fairchild AFB WA (SKA)	MUO-GFA-SKA-TCM-SUU	W	C009A/ME
Hill AFB UT (HIF)	MUO-HIF-BKF-BLV	F	C009A/ME
Malmstrom AFB MT (GFA)	MUO-GFA-SKA-TCM-SUU	W	C009A/ME
McChord AFB WA (TCM)	MUO-GFA-SKA-TCM-SUU	W	C009A/ME
Scott AFB IL (BLV)	MUO-HIF-BKF-BLV	W	C009A/ME
Travis AFB CA (SUU)	MUO-GFA-SKA-TCM-SUU	W	C009A/ME

ILLINOIS

Glenview Naval Air Station (NBU)
Air Operations Department
Glenview NAS, IL 60026-5000

Comm: 312-657-1000
ATVN: 932-0111

LOCATION: Take Willow Rd exit off I-294 to Pfingsten S to West Lake Ave, and proceed E to main gate. RM: p-28, F/8. NMC: Chicago, 20 mi NW.

FACILITIES	LOCATION	HOURS	PHONE	COMMENTS
PAX TERM INFO	Hangar #1	0700-2300 dly	C-657-2324, A-932-2324	
	Fm main gate, straight on ADM Ewen Ave to L on 4th St to Pax Term on R. Fort Sheridan Army Flight Detachment C-657-2188.			
Recording	Hangar #1	24 hrs dly	C-657-2326, A-932-2326	
Pax Svc Ofc	Hangar #1	0700-2300 dly	C-657-2324	NCO on duty
Pax Paging	Hangar #1	0700-2300 dly	C-657-2324	
PAX LOUNGES General	No separate family lounge			
	Hangar #1	0700-2300 dly	C-657-2324	
	A/C, Bag chk, Coffee svc, Rest-rms, TV, P/C seats			
DV/VIP	Hangar #1	0700-2300 dly	C-657-2324	
	Read/write rooms, Showers, TV			
Protocol Svc	Hangar #1	0800-1700 M-F	C-657-2107	NAVRES
FOOD SERVICE Enl Club	Limited services on Base. Good services off Base.			
	Bldg 39	1100-2400 dly	C-657-2396	Call for svc hrs.
OFC Club	Bldg 45	1800-2200 dly	C-657-2339	
Snack Bars	Hangar 106	0730-1500 Tu-Sa	C-657-2643	
TRANSPORTATION Parking	Very limited on Base. Call taxi at main gate.			
	Hangar #1	24 hrs dly	S of Hangar #1	No restrictions
OTHER SERVICES Exchange	Full services at Great Lakes NTC			
	Bldg 23	1000-1700 Tu-Sa, 1500 Su	C-657-2643/729-5244	
Bank/Exc	Bldg 23	0900-1700 Tu-Sa	C-657-2643	
Hair Styles	Bldg 25	0900-1700 Tu-Sa	C-657-2639	Barber
		0900-1700 Tu-Sa	C-657-2422	Beauty
Medical	Bldg 43	0730-1600 Tu-Su	C-657-2157	
TML	Bldg 45	24 hrs dly	C-657-2275, A-932-2275 Officer.	
	Bldg 55 C-657-2453, A-932-2453, Enlisted. DV/VIP C-657-1000.			
TRAVELERS AID ARC	Bldg 46	Great Lakes	C-688-5676	
Chaplain	Bldg 43	0800-1630 dly	C-657-2100/2445	
Sec Police	Main gate	24 hrs dly	C-657-2476/2311	

ILLINOIS
Glenview NAS, Cont'd

USO	Bldg 927	Great Lake NTC	C-688-2274	Call for hrs.
ATTRACTIONS	Museum of Science & Industry, Museum of Natural History, Chicago			

SCHEDULED FLIGHTS

DESTINATION	ROUTING	FREQ	EQ/CMTS
Minneapolis-St Paul IAP MN (MSP)	NBU-MSP	2 ea mo (Su,F)	P-3A/M C009A/M
Scott AFB IL (BLV)	NBU-BLV	Every other day	C009A/ME
Wright-Patterson AFB OH (FFO)	NBU-FFO	1 ea mo	C009A/ME

UNSCHEDULED FLIGHTS

Flights available to CONUS, OCONUS, and foreign countries. Army flights are via C-12 aircraft; USMC Reserve via KC-130; and Navy Reserve via P-3A, VR-51 and C-9 aircraft. Schedules available 24-72 hrs prior to departure.

O'Hare Air Reserve Forces Facility (ORD)   Comm: 312-694-6000
928th Tactical Airlift Group/OTM   ATVN: 930-1110
O'Hare ARFF, IL 60666-5000

LOCATION: NE corner of O'Hare IAP. Main gate 500 ft W of intersection of US-45 (Mannheim Rd) & IL-72 (Higgins Rd). RM: p-28, H/7. NMC: Chicago, 15 mi SE.

FACILITIES	LOCATION	HOURS	PHONE	COMMENTS
PAX TERM INFO	Base Ops 0700-1530 M-F Bldg 19 0730-1600 M-F		C-694-6623, A-930-6623 C-694-6983, A-930-6983	Non-ANG only ANG only
Recording	Non-ANG only 24 hrs dly ANG only 24 hrs dly		C-694-6623, A-930-6623 C-694-6983, A-930-6983	
FOOD SERVICE Cons Club	O'Hare IAP and O'Hare area Bldg 2 1130-1300 M-F		C-694-6448	Call for svc hrs.
Vending	Bldgs 30 & 19			
TRANSPORTATION Air Tickets	No Gov transportation to or from O'Hare IAP Civilian Terminal Bldg 40 0730-1545 M-F		C-694-6505	SATO
Parking	O'Hare ARFF			Short term
TRAVELERS AID Chaplain	O'Hare IAP Terminal 2 0830-1500 dly O'Hare IAP Daily		C-686-7562 C-686-2636	Call for hrs.
USO	O'Hare IAP 0900-2300 Su-F, 1700 Sa		C-686-7396	
ATTRACTIONS	City of Chicago, Art Institution of Chicago, major sports			

ILLINOIS

O'Hare ARF Fac, Cont'd

UNSCHEDULED FLIGHTS

Flts to CONUS, OCONUS (limited), and foreign country destinations (limited) via ANG KC-135E and Reserve C-130A aircraft on cargo or training missions. C-130A missions CONUS only. Call before you go.

Scott Air Force Base (BLV)
375th Trans Sqd/LGT/TROP
Scott AFB, IL 62225-5000

Comm: 618-256-1110
ATVN: 576-1110
FTS: 256-1110

LOCATION: Off I-64 E or W, 19E or 19A W to IL-158, S 2 mi and watch for signs to AFB entry. RM: p-27, S/8. NMC: St Louis MO, 25 mi W.

FACILITIES	LOCATION	HOURS	PHONE	COMMENTS
PAX TERM INFO	Bldg P-8 0445-2400 dly (closed Xmas & New Years)C-256-3017/ 4042, A-576-4042/3017. Main gate, Scott Dr straight to 4-way stop, L on Airlifters Ave, 2.5 blocks to Pax Term on R.			
Pax Svc Ofc	Bldg P-8	0730-1630 M-F	C-256-2014	NCO on duty
Pax Paging	Bldg P-8	0445-2400 dly	C-256-3017/4042	
PAX LOUNGES General	Thru cafeteria door after 2400 hrs dly. No family lounge. Bldg P-8 24 hrs dly C-256-3017/4042 A/C,Bag chk/lks, Game rm, Read/write rms, Tel C&A, TV, Rest-rms, O/S seats			
DV/VIP	Bldg P-8 24 hrs dly C-256-2609/4042 (O6+, Civ eq & MOH) A/C, Coffee svc, Read/write rms,Tel C&A,TV,Rest-rms,O/S seats			
Protocol Svc	Bldg 1600	Duty hrs	C-256-5555/3215	Hq MAC
FOOD SERVICE Cafeteria	Many facilities on Base. P-8 24 hrs dly		Limited off Base. C-746-4199 (closed major hols)	
Dining Hall	Bldg 1907	0530-0030 dly	C-256-4215	"Gateway Inn"
Enl Club	Bldg 1930	1730-2330 dly	C-254-3921	Call for svc hrs.
NCO/CPO Club	Bldg 1948	0630-0100 dly	C-744-0300	Call for svc hrs.
OFC Club	Bldg 1500	1000-2100 dly	C-744-0444	Call for svc hrs.
Snack Bars	Bldg 1650	0930-1700 dly	C-746-2841	"Dog House"
Vending	Bldg P-8	24 hrs dly	C-256-0877	
TRANSPORTATION Air Tickets	Facilities on Base and nearby communities Bldg P-8 0700-1600 M-F C-256-3690 SATO			
Bus (Comm) (Gov)	Bldg P-8 Bldg 530	Call for hrs. 0730-1630 M-F	To Belleville IL & St Louis MO C-256-3201 Duty Pax only	
Car Rentals	Bldg P-8	0800-1700 M-F	Budget=C-233-4143, Enterprise=C-277-8000, Rent-A-Wreck=C-234-7892	
Limo Service	Bldg 350	24 hrs dly	C-256-3066	BLV to STL
TAXI (Comm)	Bldg P-8	24 hrs dly	C-277-1515, C-744-1300/1244	

ILLINOIS
Scott AFB, Cont'd

Parking	Bldg P-8	24 hrs dly	C-256-2223	Short term-W of Pax Term-24 hr limit; long term-W of Pax Term/old gym. Notify SP.
OTHER SERVICES Exchange	Full services on Base. Bldg 1650	1000-1800 dly	Limited off Base. C-744-0888	Call for svc hrs.
Bank/Exc	Bldg 1644	0900-1500 M-F,	1200 Sa C-744-1144	
Hair Styles	Bldg 1650	0800-1800 M-F, 0800-1700 M-Sa,	1400 Sa C-746-2899 2000 Th C-744-1544	Barber Beauty
Laundry/DryC	Bldg 1650	0830-1800 M-F,	1600 Sa C-746-2417	
Medical	Bldg 1530	24 hrs dly	C-256-7595	
Postal	Bldg 1900	0830-1700 M-F,	1200 Sa C-256-5942	
WIRE	Bldg 1650	1000-1800 dly	C-744-0877	
TML	Bldg 1510 All Ranks.	24 hrs dly DV/VIP C-256-6555.	C-744-1200, A-576-3224/2045	
TRAVELERS AID ARC	AF Family Services Bldg 21	0800-1630 M-F	C-256-3936 C-256-7584	Other hrs C-658-2000
Chaplain	Bldg 1620	0730-1600 M-F	C-256-3303	Other hrs C-256-1110
Emerg Relief	Bldg 10	0730-1600	C-256-4210	
Lost/Found	Bldg P-8	0500-2400 dly	C-256-3017	
Sec Police	Bldg 1970	24 hrs dly	C-256-2223	
USO	STL	24 hrs dly	C-314-429-1234	West end Arrival
ATTRACTIONS	St Louis nearby, Mississippi River			

SCHEDULED FLIGHTS

DESTINATION	ROUTING	FREQ	EQ/CMTS
Andrews AFB MD (ADW)	BLV-BIX-ADW BLV-GAO-NRR-ADW BLV-ADW-SUU BLV-ADW	Su,W M Th F,Sa	C009A/ME C009A/ME C009A/ME C009A/ME
Buckley ANGB CO (BKF)	BLV-BKF BLV-BKF-SUU	M-Sa W,Sa	C009A/ME C009A/ME
Charleston AFB SC (CHS)	BLV-BIX-CHS	S,W	C009A/ME
Eglin AFB FL (VPS)	BLV-BIX-VPS	M,F	C009A/ME
Guantanamo Bay NS CU (GAO)	BLV-GAO-NRR-ADW	M	C009A/ME

ILLINOIS
Scott AFB, Cont'd

Keesler AFB MS (BIX)	BLV-BIX-ADW BLV-BIX BLV-BIX-BLV	Su,W M,F Tu	C009A/ME C009A/ME C009A/ME
Kelly AFB TX (SKF)	BLV-SKF-SUU BLV-SKF-BLV BLV-SKF	M,W Tu Th,Sa	C009A/ME C009A/ME C009A/ME
McChord AFB WA (TCM)	BLV-TCM	W,Sa	C009A/ME
McGuire AFB NJ (WRI)	BLV-ADW-WRI	F	C009A/ME
Offutt AFB NE (OFF)	BLV-OFF	Tu,Th	C009A/ME
Roosevelt Rds NAS PR (NRR)	BLV-GAO-NRR-ADW	M	C009A/ME
Travis AFB CA (SUU)	BLV-SKF-SUU BLV-BKF-SUU BLV-ADW-SUU	M,W W,Sa Th,Sa	C009A/ME C009A/ME C009A/ME
Wright-Patterson OH (FFO)	BLV-FFO	M,W,F	C009A/ME

UNSCHEDULED FLIGHTS

Many unscheduled flights to CONUS via C-9, C-12, C-21, C-130, T-39, and T-43 aircraft.

INDIANA

Grissom Air Force Base (GUS)
305th CSG/OTM/Stop 24
Grissom AFB, IN 46971-5000

Comm: 317-689-5211
ATVN: 928-1110

LOCATION: On US-31, 15 mi N of Kokomo and 7 mi S of Peru. RM: p-31, G/10.
NMC: Indianapolis, 72 mi S.

FACILITIES	LOCATION	HOURS	PHONE	COMMENTS
PAX TERM INFO	Bldg S-14	24 hrs dly	C-689-2256, A-928-2254	
	Fm main gate straight on Sabre Dr to Invader St and one half L Base Ops on circle.			
Pax Svc Ofc	Bldg S-14	24 hrs dly	C-689-2254	NCO on duty
Pax Paging	Bldg S-14	24 hrs dly	C-689-2254	
PAX LOUNGES General	No separate family lounge Bldg S-14 24 hrs dly C-689-2254 A/C, Bag check Coffee srvd, TelC&ATVN, TV, Rest-rooms, O/S seats			
DV/VIP	Bldg S-14	24 hrs dly	C-689-2254	(O6+) Separate rm
Protocol Svc	Bldg S-14	24 hrs dly	C-689-2254	SAC

INDIANA
Grissom AFB, Cont'd

FOOD SERVICE	Good services on and off Base. Dining Hall C-689-2414, NCO/CPO Club C-689-9151, O'Club C-689-9134, Snack Bars C-689-2504 (in bowling alley) and C-689-7184
TRANSPORTATION	Limited transportation on Base. Air Tickets C-689-2553, Bus(Comm) C-452-0028, Car Rentals limited, Taxi(Comm) C-472-3359, Parking C-689-3385 (see Security Police)
OTHER SERVICES	Exchange C-689-9436, Bank/Exc C-689-2276/473-6661, Barber C-689-7627, Beauty C-689-7584, Medical C-689-3302/3217, Postal C-689-2100
TML	Bldg 549 24 hrs dly C-689-2618/2146, A-928-2618/2146 All Ranks. DV/VIP C-689-2240.
TRAVELERS AID	Limited on and off Base. Fam Svcs C-689-2476 (other hrs C-689-3032), Chaplain C-689-2191, AF Aid C-689-2476, Sec Police C-689-3385
Sec Police	Bldg 101 24 hrs dly C-689-3385
ATTRACTIONS	City of Peru, Indianapolis Motor Speedway, 72 mi S.

SCHEDULED FLIGHTS

DESTINATION	ROUTING	FREQ	EQ/CMTS
Howard AFB PN (HOW)	GUS-HOW	2 ea mo (Tu)	KC-135E/M

UNSCHEDULED FLIGHTS

Limited flights to CONUS, OCONUS, and foreign country locations via KC-135E aircraft. Call for destinations, routings, and schedules.

IOWA
NONE

KANSAS

Forbes Field Air National Guard Base (FOE)
190th Air Refueling Group (ANG)
Forbes Field, KS 66619-5000

Comm: 913-862-1234
ATVN: 720-4210

LOCATION: Off US-75 S. Also accessible from I-470/70 East/West. RM: p-34, Q/7. NMC: Topeka, 4 mi N.

FACILITIES	LOCATION	HOURS	PHONE	COMMENTS
PAX TERM INFO	Bldg 611			During flight processing C-862-1234, A-720-4210 From main gate straight on South Sreet to dead end at Base Ops. Small BX is the only US military Base support facility.

UNSCHEDULED FLIGHTS

Air National Guard Unit Flying Training Missions to CONUS and OCONUS locations via KC-135E aircraft. Call for flight schedule information.

KANSAS

Marshall Army Airfield (FRI)
Airfield Operations Detachment
Fort Riley, KS 66442-5000

Comm: 913-239-3911
ATVN: 856-1110

LOCATION: On KS-13 and off I-70 in the central part of the state. Junction City, 5 mi SW and Manhattan, 10 mi NE. RM: p-35, E/18. NMC: Topeka, 50 mi E.

FACILITIES	LOCATION	HOURS	PHONE	COMMENTS
PAX TERM INFO	Bldg 743	24 hrs dly	C-239-2530, A-856-2530	Ask for directions and map at main gate. Located at base of Old Tower on AAF. NCO on duty.
OTHER SERVICES	Limited facilities. DV/VIP between Hangars 1 and 2 (06+) on request from Pax Svc NCO. Full Base facilities available. See Military Living's "US Forces Travel Guide USA & Caribbean Areas" for details.			

UNSCHEDULED FLIGHTS

Space-A is via C-12A/U-21 aircraft to Midwest and East Coast destinations. Call for destinations, routings, and schedules.

McConnell Air Force Base (IAB)
384th CSG/OTM
McConnell AFB, KS 67221-5000

Comm: 316-652-6100
ATVN: 743-1110

LOCATION: Take I-35 to Wichita, exit at Kellogg St (US-54) W to Rock Rd S and McConnell AFB. RM: p-35, Q/4. NMC: Wichita, 6 mi NW.

FACILITIES	LOCATION	HOURS	PHONE	COMMENTS
PAX TERM INFO	Bldg 1112	24 hrs dly	C-652-3701/2, A-743-3701/2	Fm E gate straight on Kansas St for 1.5 mi to Base Ops on R.
Pax Svc Ofc	Bldg 1112	24 hrs dly	C-652-3701/2	NCO on duty
PAX LOUNGES General	General lounge used by families Bldg 1112 24 hrs dly C-652-3701 A/C, Tel L,LD&ATVN, Rest-rooms, P/C seats			
DV/VIP	Bldg 1112	24 hrs dly	C-652-3701	Tel L&ATVN
Protocol Svc	Bldg 1112	24 hrs dly	C-652-3701	384th
FOOD SERVICE	Dining Hall C-652-4183, NCO/CPO Club C-652-4164, O'Club C-652-4147, Snack Bar C-652-4019 (in bowling alley), Vending C-681-5271			
TRANSPORTATION	Very limited transportation on Base. Air Tickets C-652-4002, Taxi(Comm) C-652-5479 (Gov) C-652-4047, Parking C-681-5201			
OTHER SERVICES	Good services on Base and in Wichita. Exchange C-685-0231, Bank/Exc C-652-5450, Barber C-686-9971, Beauty C-689-8716, Laundry C-684-1881, Medical C-652-5027, Postal C-652-3554			
TML	Bldg 193 24 hrs dly C-652-5193, A-743-5193 All Ranks. DV/VIP C-652-6100			

KANSAS
McConnell ARB, Cont'd

TRAVELERS AID	Many agencies. Fam Svcs C-652-3740, ARC C-652-3562, Chaplain C-652-3562, AF Aid C-681-5224, Sec Police C-652-3976
ATTRACTIONS	Wichita (new downtown), zoo, Museum of Art and History

UNSCHEDULED FLIGHTS

Two flights per month via KC-135R/M aircraft to: Pease AFB NH (PSM) or RAF Mildenhall UK (MHZ). Also other CONUS and OCONUS locations, but very infrequent. Call for destinations, routings, and schedules.

Sherman Army Airfield (FLV)
Attn: ATZN-GOP-AV, Bldg 132
Fort Leavenworth, KS 66027-5071

Comm: 913-684-4021
ATVN: 552-4021
FTS: 753-4021

LOCATION: Fm I-70 W exit US-73 N to Leavenworth. Fort is adjacent to city of Leavenworth. RM: p-35, D/23. NMC: Kansas City, 30 mi SE.

FACILITIES	LOCATION	HOURS	PHONE	COMMENTS
PAX TERM INFO	Bldg 132	0730-1630 M-F	C-684-2396, A-552-2396	Fm main gate straight on Grant Ave for 2 mi to four way stop at USDB, R on Riverside Ave to AAF on R.
Pax Svc Ofc	Bldg 132	0730-1630 M-F	C-684-2396	NCO on duty
PAX LOUNGES General	Bldg 132 S side of Hangar #2	0730-1630 M-F	C-684-2396	A/C, Tel L, LD, & ATVN, TV. No seats.
DV/VIP	Bldg 132 E side of Hangar #2	0730-1630 M-F	C-684-2396 (O6+)	A/C, Bag chk, Coffee/tea, Tel L,LD,&ATVN,TV,Rest-rms,Wood seats
Protocol Svc	Bldg 22	0730-1630 M-F	C-684-4062	Pope Ave, CAC
FOOD SERVICE				Good services on Base. Dining Hall C-651-6573, NCO/CPO Club C-651-6852, O'Club C-651-7013, Snack Bar C-651-6586, Vending in Crew Lounge in Bldg 132
TRANSPORTATION				Good on and off Base. Air Tickets C-651-5071, Bus(Gov) C-684-3496 (Shuttle) C-682-0517, Car Rentals C-727-2333, Limo Service C-651-4649, Taxi(Comm) C-684-3496 (Gov) C-682-1229, Parking C-684-2396
OTHER SERVICES				Good services on Base. Exchange C-651-7270, Bank/Exc C-682-9090, Hair Styles C-651-7270, Laundry/DryC C-651-7270, Medical C-684-3570/2171, Postal C-682-0052
TML	Bldg 225 All Ranks.	24 hrs dly	C-684-4931, A-552-4931 DV/VIP C-684-4064.	
TRAVELERS AID	Many agencies available. ARC C-684-4383, Chaplain C-684-2148, Emerg Relief C-684-4154/4357, Lost/Found C-684-2461, Security Police C-684-2461/2111			
ATTRACTIONS	Fort Leavenworth Museum, Harry S. Truman Library & Museum			

KANSAS

Sherman AAF, Cont'd

SCHEDULED FLIGHTS

DESTINATION	ROUTING	FREQ	EQ/CMTS
Biggs AAF TX (BIF)	FLV-BIF	2 ea mo	C-12A/P
Davison AAF VA (DAA)	FLV-DAA	6 ea mo	C-12A/P
Godman AAF KY (FTK)	FLV-FTK	1 ea mo	C-12A/P
Langley AFB VA (LFI)	FLV-LFI	6 ea mo	C-12A/P
San Antonio TX (SAT)	FLV-SAT	1 ea mo	C-12A/P

Note: Call for other destinations, routings, and schedules.

KENTUCKY

Campbell Army Airfield (HOP)
Base Air Operations
Fort Campbell, KY 42223-5000

Comm: 502-798-2151
ATVN: 635-1110

LOCATION: In the SW part of KY, 4 mi S of intersection of US-41A and I-24. Ten mi NW of Clarksville TN. RM: p-37, P/4. NMC: Hopkinsville, 15 mi N.

FACILITIES	LOCATION	HOURS	PHONE	COMMENTS
PAX TERM INFO	Zone H/I	24 hrs dly	C-789-2151, A-635-2151 Fm Gate 6 on US Alt 41 straight on Morgan Road to AAF right.	
OTHER SERVICES	Full large Base support facilities available. See Military Living's "US Forces Travel Guide USA & Caribbean Areas" for full details.			

UNSCHEDULED FLIGHTS

Flights via Army executive aircraft, C-12A and C-21A, to CONUS East Coast and Midwest locations. Call for destinations, routings, and schedules.

Godman Army Airfield (FTK)
Base Air Operations
Fort Knox, KY 40121

Comm: 502-624-1181
ATVN: 464-0111

LOCATION: Fm I-65 N in Louisville, exit Jefferson Freeway 841W to 31W, go S to Fort Knox. Fm I-64, exit I-264W (Waterson) to I-65S, to Jefferson Freeway to US-31W, N to Fort Knox. Fm I-71, exit I-65S to exit Jefferson Freeway 841W, to 31W then S to Fort Knox. RM:p-37, J/10. NMC:Louisville, 25 mi N.

FACILITIES	LOCATION	HOURS	PHONE	COMMENTS
PAX TERM INFO	Bldg 5220	24 hrs dly	C-624-1181, A-464-1181 Fm US-31W enter Fort on Chaffee Ave to L on Pilot St. Air Ops on L.	

KENTUCKY

Godman AAF, Cont'd

OTHER SERVICES	Full large Base support facilities available. See Military Living's "US Forces Travel Guide USA & Caribbean Areas" for full details.

UNSCHEDULED FLIGHTS

Flights via Army executive aircraft, C-12A and C-21A to CONUS East Coast and Midwest locations. Call for destinations, routings, and schedules.

Standiford Field (SDF)
123rd TRW/TMO/Pax TRVL (ANG)
Louisville, KY 40213-2678

Comm: 502-364-9400
ATVN: 989-4400

LOCATION: Take I-65 N or S, exit Preston Street, W for 1 mi to L Grade Lane and entrance sign R for 1 block to ANG Base Ops. RM: p-36, D/9. NMC: Louisville, Standiford Field in city.

FACILITIES	LOCATION	HOURS	PHONE	COMMENTS
PAX TERM INFO	ANG Base Ops No Pax Term.	0730-1600 M-F	C-364-9433, A-989-4433	All Space-A managed by ANG Air Operations.
OTHER SERVICES	Full support of a metropolitan airport available.			

UNSCHEDULED FLIGHTS

Flights to CONUS, OCONUS, and foreign countries via ANG C-130, C-131, and C-141B aircraft. Call for destinations, routings, and schedules.

LOUISIANA

Barksdale Air Force Base (BAD)
2nd Bomb Wing, Air Operations
Barksdale AFB, LA 71110-5000

Comm: 318-456-2252
ATVN: 781-1110

LOCATION: Exit I-20 at Airline Drive, go S to Old Minden Road (.25 mi), L on Old Minden Road (1 block), then R on North Gate Drive (1 mi) to North Gate of AFB. RM: p-38, A/13. NMC: Shreveport, 1 mi W. Co-located with Bossier City in Shreveport.

FACILITIES	LOCATION	HOURS	PHONE	COMMENTS
PAX TERM INFO	Bldg 6404	0630-1630 M-F	C-456-3738, A-781-3738	From West Gate straight on Barksdale Blvd Pax Term R at Hangar Line Road.
Pax Svc Ofc	Bldg 6404	0630-1630 M-F	C-456-3738	NCO on duty
PAX LOUNGES General	Bldg 6404	24 hrs dly	C-456-3738	No separate family lounge A/C, Rest-rms, Tel L&ATVN, P/C seats
DV/VIP	Bldg 6402	Hrs per request on Base Ops	C-456-3738	A/C, Rest-rms, TV, Coffee/Tea svc, O/S seats
Protocol Svc	Bldg 6402	24 hrs dly	C-456-2151	2nd Bomb Wing

LOUISIANA

Barksdale AFB, Cont'd

FOOD SERVICE				
Dining Hall	Limited on Base. Flight kitchen Bldg 6402. Bldg 4631 0530-1830 dly C-456-2252 Call for svc hrs.			
NCO/CPO Club	Bldg 1955	1000-2200 dly	C-746-3366	Call for svc hrs.
OFC Club	Bldg 2945	1030-2200 dly	C-746-2203	Call for svc hrs.
Vending	Bldg 6402	24 hrs dly	C-456-3594	
TRANSPORTATION				
Air Tickets	Bldg 4161	0730-1630 M-F	C-456-4575	
TAXI(Gov)	Bldg 4173	24 hrs dly	C-456-2208	Duty Pax only
Parking	Bldg 6402	24 hrs limit	C-456-2551	Base Ops lot
OTHER SERVICES				
Exchange	Bldg 4265	1000-1800 M-F, 1500 Sa	C-746-2554	
Bank/Exc	Bldg 5435	0900-1500 M-F	C-456-2252	
Hair Styles	Bldg 4265	1000-1800 M-F, 1500 Sa	C-746-2554	Barber & Beauty
Laundry/DryC	Bldg 4265	1000-1800 M-Sa	C-742-0133	
Medical	Bldg 4543	24 hrs dly	C-456-4051	
Postal	Bldg 5376	0800-1700 M-F	C-456-2276	
TML	Bldg 5155 All Ranks.	24 hrs dly DV/VIP	C-456-3091, A-781-3091 C-456-2161.	
TRAVELERS AID				
ARC	Bldg 5485	0800-1700 M-F	C-456-5485	
Chaplain	Bldg 3578	0800-1700 M-F	C-456-2111	O/hrs C-456-2151
Emerg Relief	Bldg 5345	0800-1700 M-F	C-456-3520/4480	Air Force Aid
Sec Police	Bldg 5676	24 hrs dly	C-456-2551	Desk Sgt
ATTRACTIONS	Water sports, horse racing (LA Downs)			

SCHEDULED FLIGHTS

DESTINATION	ROUTING	FREQ	EQ/CMTS
RAF Fairford UK (FFD)	BAD-PSM-FFD	1 ea mo	KC-135E/10/M
Pease AFB NH (PSM)	BAD-PSM-FFD	1 ea mo	KC-135E/10/M

UNSCHEDULED FLIGHTS

Flights to CONUS, OCONUS, and foreign countries. Call for destinations, routings, and schedules.

LOUISIANA

England Air Force Base (AEX)
23rd Combat Support Group/OTM
England AFB, LA 71311-5004

Comm: 318-488-2100
ATVN: 683-1110

LOCATION: From Alexandria, take LA-1 to Airbase Road and enter main gate or take LA-28 to Vandenberg Drive (LA-3054) and enter back gate. RM: p-38, F/5. NMC: Alexandria, 5 mi E.

FACILITIES	LOCATION	HOURS	PHONE	COMMENTS
PAX TERM INFO	Bldg 107 0700-2200 M-F, 0900-1100 Sa-Su C-448-5721/2460, A-683-5721/2460 Fm main gate on Oliver Drive to R on Mitchell Blvd to Pax Term L. Check with Base Ops for flt processing.			
PAX LOUNGES DV/VIP	No general lounge. Bldg 1107 0700-2200 M-F, 0900-1100 Sa-Su EX-5721 Coffee and refreshments served upon request.			
FOOD SERVICE Cafeteria	Call for service hours for cafeteria and clubs. Bldg 1107 0700-2200 M-F, 0900-1100 Sa-Su EX-5580			
NCO/CPO Club	Bldg 904 0700-2200 M-F, 0900-1100 Sa-Su EX-2525			
OFC Club	Bldg 1150 0700-2200 M-F, 0900-1100 Sa-Su EX-2421			
Vending	Bldg 107 24 hours daily			
TRANSPORTATION Air Tickets	Bldg 900 0730-1600 M-F C-445-8053			
TAXI(Gov)	Bldg 1708 0700-2000 dly EX-5313 Call for non-duty hours.			
OTHER SERVICES	Full Base support facilities. See Military Living's "US Forces Travel Guide USA & Caribbean Areas" for details.			
TML	Billeting Office Bldg 1102 Lighting St 24 hrs dly C-448-5313 All Ranks. DV/VIP EX-5181.			

UNSCHEDULED FLIGHTS

Frequent flights via C009A/ME to: Barksdale AFB LA (BAD); Carswell AFB TX (FWH); Robert Gray AAF TX (GRK); Kelly AFB TX (SKF); Scott AFB IL (BLV); Sheppard AFB TX (SPS); and Tinker AFB OK (TIK). Call for destinations, routings, and schedules.

New Orleans Naval Air Station (NBG)
Operations Department
New Orleans NAS, LA 70143-5000

Comm: 504-393-3011
ATVN: 363-3011
FTS: 680-3011

LOCATION: Off LA-23 in Belle Chasse. Clearly marked. RM: p-38, J/11. NMC: New Orleans, 10 mi N.

FACILITIES	LOCATION	HOURS	PHONE	COMMENTS
PAX TERM INFO	Bldg 1 0700-2300 dly C-393-3100/3101, A-363-3100/3101, From main gate on Russell Ave to L on RADM Fowler Drive to R on Coast Guard Road to Air Ops.			
Recording	Bldg 1 24 hrs dly C-393-3103, A-363-3103 Updated daily			

LOUISIANA

New Orleans NAS, Cont'd

Pax Svc Ofc	Bldg 1	0700-2300 dly	C-393-3100
Pax Paging	Bldg 1	0700-2300 dly	C-393-3100
PAX LOUNGES General	No separate family lounge Bldg 1 0700-2300 dly C-393-3100 A/C, Tel L&ATVN, TV, Rest-rms, P/C seats		
DV/VIP	Bldg 1 0700-2300 dly C-393-3100 A/C, Coffee, Read/write rms, Tel L&ATVN, TV, Rest-rms, Showers, O/S seats		
Protocol Svc	Bldg PAO	0730-1000 Tu-Sa C-393-3260	(O6+)
FOOD SERVICE Dining Hall	Good services on and off Base Bldg 23 0500-0100 dly C-393-3421 Call for svc hrs.		
Enl Club	Bldg 410	1000-2100 dly C-393-3508	Call for svc hrs.
NCO/CPO Club	Bldg 300	1100-2300 Tu-Su C-393-3512	Call for svc hrs.
OFC Club	Bldg 40	1100-0100 W-Su C-393-3841	Call for svc hrs.
Vending	Bldg 1	0700-2300 dly	
TRANSPORTATION Bus(Gov)	Bldg 1	24 hrs dly C-393-3253	Official & pre-arranged
Car Rentals	Bldg 1	Various car rental agencies off Base	
TAXI(Comm)	Bldg 1	24 hrs dly Various cab companies service Base	
Parking	Bldg 1 0700-2300 dly Short term-no overnight; long term-Fowler Drive.		
OTHER SERVICES	Exchange Bldg 300 1000-1700 Tu-Su C-393-3510		
Bank/Exc	Bldg 300	0900-1300 Tu-Sa C-393-3527	
Hair Styles	Bldg 300	0730-1600 Tu-Su C-393-3511	Barber
Laundry/DryC	Bldg 300	1000-1700 Tu-Su C-393-3510	
Medical	Bldg 41	24 hrs dly	C-393-3660
Postal	Bldg 46	1000-1300 Tu-Sa C-393-3204	
TML	Bldg 40 24 hrs dly C-393-3841/2, A-363-3841/2 All Ranks. DV/VIP C-393-3201.		
TRAVELERS AID ARC	Many agencies at NAS and NSA Gretna LA 24 hrs dly C-504-366-4178		
Chaplain	Bldg 403	0730-1600 Tu-Su C-393-3525	
Emerg Relief	NSA, Algiers 0900-1200 M-F C-362-0752 Navy Relief		
Lost/Found	Bldg 1	0700-2300 dly	C-393-3101
Sec Police	Bldg 70	24 hrs dly	C-393-3461

LOUISIANA
New Orleans NAS, Cont'd

SCHEDULED FLIGHTS

DESTINATION	ROUTING	FREQ	EQ/CMTS
Alameda NAS CA (NGZ)	NBG-NGZ-NBG	1 ea mo	P-3/M
Andrews AFB MD (ADW)	NBG-ADW	Varies	C-131/M
Atlanta NAS GA (NCQ)	NBG-NCQ	2-3 ea mo	C009B/P
Dallas NAS TX (NBE)	NBG-NBE-NBG	Varies	C009B/P
Ellington Fld Arpt TX (EFD)	NBG-NBE-NBG	Varies	C009B/P
Glenview NAS IL (NBU)	NBG-NBU	2-3 ea mo	P-3/M
Jacksonville NAS FL (NIP)	NBG-NBE-NBG	Varies	C009B/P
Memphis NAS TN (NQA)	NBG-NQA	2-3 ea mo	C-131/M
Norfolk NAS VA (NGU)	NBG-NGU	1 ea wk	C-131/M
North Island NAS CA (NZY)	NBG-NZY	1-2 ea mo	P-3/M
Pensacola NAS FL (NPA)	NBG-NPA	1 ea wk	C009B/P

UNSCHEDULED FLIGHTS

Ten-fifteen flights daily to CONUS, OCONUS, and foreign areas. Passenger, cargo, and mixed missions via T-39, C-12A, P-3, C-9 and C-131 aircraft.

Polk Army Airfield (POE)
Base Air Operations
Fort Polk, LA 71459-5000

Comm: 318-535-2911
ATVN: 863-1110
FTS: 528-1110

LOCATION: Off US-171, at LA-10, 9 mi S of Leesville. RM: p-38, G/4.
NMC: Alexandria, 45 mi NE.

FACILITIES	LOCATION HOURS PHONE COMMENTS
PAX TERM INFO	AAF Base Ops 0600-2400 M-F, 0800-1600 Sa-Su Fixed wing C-535-4831/7328, A-863-4831/7328 Rotary wing C-535-2722/2044, A-863-2722/2044.
OTHER SERVICES	Full large Base support facilities available. See Military Living's "US Forces Travel Guide USA & Caribbean Areas."

LOUISIANA

Polk AAF, Cont'd

SCHEDULED FLIGHTS
Provided by Royale Airlines. Call 318-537-0063 for details.

UNSCHEDULED FLIGHTS
Limited flts via U-21 aircraft. Call for destinations, routings, & schedules.

MAINE

Bangor Air National Guard Base (BGR)
101st Air Refueling Wing (ANG)
Bangor, ME 04401-4393

Comm: 207-941-2211/2215
ATVN: 698-6700
476-6211/6215

LOCATION: N fm I-95 exit on Ohio St, drive two blocks turn L, go one block turn R on Union St (State Rte 222), pass Bangor IAP, turn L on Griffin Rd, entrance is 300 yds on R. RM: p-39, L/7. NMC: Bangor, Base in city limits.

FACILITIES	LOCATION	HOURS	PHONE	COMMENTS
PAX TERM INFO	Bldg 491	0730-1600 M-F	C-941-2211/2215, A-476-6211/6215	Ask SP for directions.
OTHER SERVICES	Facs of an IAP avail. Other fac off Base. BX C-941-2233.			
TRANSPORTATION Parking	Taxi to Bangor ($4) 5-10 min. City bus 0730-1740 dly (.50) every 30 min. Car rental at IAP. Bldg 489 Security Police 24 hrs dly A-476-6311			
TML	22 Cleveland Avenue at BGR 24 hrs dly C-942-2081, A-698-6700 "Pine Tree Inn"			
TRAVELERS AID	Bldg 489 24 hrs dly A-476-6311 Security Police			
ATTRACTIONS	Lobster and other seafood, Bar Harbor, beaches and boating			

SCHEDULED FLIGHTS

DESTINATION	ROUTING	FREQ	EQ/CMTS
Diego Garcia Atoll IO (NKW)	NGU-BGR-SIZ-NBO-NKW	1/2/3/Tu	DC-862/M/CC
Jomo Kenyatta Intl KE (NBO)	NGU-BGR-SIZ-NBO-NKW	1/2/3/Tu	DC-862/M/CC
Sigonella Arpt IT (SIZ)	NGU-BGR-SIZ-NBO-NKW	1/2/3/Tu	DC-862/M/CC

UNSCHEDULED FLIGHTS
Flts to: CONUS (SAC Bases), OCONUS (Europe & Pacific areas), & foreign countries via KC-135E ANG aircraft. Call for destinations, routings, and scheds.

Brunswick Naval Air Station (NHZ)
Air Operations
Brunswick NAS, ME 04011-5000

Comm: 207-921-2214
ATVN: 476-2214

LOCATION: Fm I-95 N exit US-1 N to Brunswick, Old Bath Rd to main gate of Brunswick NAS. RM: p-39, I/4. NMC: Portland, 30 mi SW.

MAINE
Brunswick NAS, Cont'd

FACILITIES	LOCATION	HOURS	PHONE	COMMENTS
PAX TERM INFO	Bldg 200	24 hrs dly	C-921-2689/2682, A-476-2689/2682	
	Fm Security straight on Fitch Ave, R on Orion St, Air Ops L.			
Pax Svc Ofc	Bldg 200	24 hrs dly	C-921-2689/2682/2256 NCO on duty	
PAX LOUNGES General	Limited lounge facilities. No DV/VIP or family lounges. Bldg 200 Main Lobby 24 hrs dly Rest-rms, Tel L & ATVN, O/S seats			
Protocol Svc	Bldg 4	0800-1700 M-F	C-921-2648	COMPATWINGSLANT
FOOD SERVICE Cafeteria	Good services on and off Base Bldg 11 0630-1700 M-F, 1500 Sa C-921-2455			
Dining Hall	Bldg 211	0600-2400 dly	C-921-2214	"Neptune Hall"
Enl Club	Bldg 516	1100-2400 M-Th, 1300 F-Sa, 2200 Su C-921-2121		
NCO/CPO Club	Bldg 201	1100-2030 Tu-Sa	C-921-2291	Call for svc hrs.
OFC Club	Bldg 38	1100-2400 M-Sa	C-921-2589	Call for svc hrs.
Snack Bars	Bldg 11	0930-1700 M-F, 1500 Sa-Su C-921-2378 Deli/Bakery		
TRANSPORTATION Bus(Comm)	Very limited transportation on Base Bldg 200 0425-2200 dly C-729-1577 NHZ-Portland IAP .50			
Limo Service	Bldg 200	0650-0050 dly	C-729-0221	ATC, Inc
Parking	Bldg 200	24 hrs dly	C-921-2457	Long term
OTHER SERVICES Exchange	Bldg 11	0900-1700 M-F, 1500 Sa C-921-2378		
Bank/Exc	Bldg 18	0900-1500 M-F	C-921-2732/2677	Credit Union
Hair Styles	Bldg 11	0800-1700 M-F, 1500 Sa 0900-1800 M-F, 1630 Sa	C-921-2346 Barber C-921-2248 Beauty	
Laundry/DryC	Bldg 11	0800-1700 M-F, 1500 Sa C-921-2576		
Medical	Bldg 645	24 hrs dly	C-921-2992/2222	
Postal	Bldg 20	0800-1500 M-F	C-921-2518	
TML	Bldg 512	24 hrs dly	C-921-2386/2568, A-476-2386/2568	
	All Ranks. DV/VIP C-921-2323. Navy Lodge C-921-2206.			
TRAVELERS AID ARC	Good on Base Bldg 18	0800-1700 M-F	C-921-2777	
Chaplain	Bldg 585	0800-1700 M-F	C-921-2231/2	
Emerg Relief	Bldg 27	0800-1700 M-F	C-921-2679/2414	Navy Relief
Sec Police	Bldg 37	24 hrs dly	C-921-2457	
ATTRACTIONS	Snow skiing area, lobster/seafood, Maine Maritime Museum			

MAINE

Brunswick NAS, Cont'd

UNSCHEDULED FLIGHTS

Frequent flights via P-3A/M to: Andrews AFB MD (ADW); Bermuda NAS BM (BDA), Jacksonville NAS FL (NIP); Norfolk NAS VA (NGU); Patuxent River NAS MD (NHK); and other CONUS locations. Call for destinations, routings, and schedules.

Loring Air Force Base (LIZ)
42nd Bomb Wing, Air Operations
Loring AFB, ME 04751-5000

Comm: 207-999-1110
ATVN: 920-1110

LOCATION: Take I-95 to Houlton, exit to US-1 N to Caribou (50 mi). The AFB is 1 mi N of ME-89 & ME-223 intersection. Clearly marked. RM: p-39, B/17. NMC: Caribou, 3 mi SW.

FACILITIES	LOCATION	HOURS	PHONE	COMMENTS
PAX TERM INFO	Base Ops	24 hrs dly	C-999-2227, A-920-2227	
	Enter East Gate fm ME-89/ME-223 and ask gate guard for directions to Base Ops. No Pax Term. All flts handled by Base Ops.			
OTHER SERVICES	Full Base support. See details in Military Living's "US Forces Travel Guide USA & Caribbean Areas."			

UNSCHEDULED FLIGHTS

Flights via KC-135E/KC-10 to CONUS, OCONUS, and foreign countries (Europe). Call for destinations, routings and schedules.

MARYLAND

Andrews Air Force Base (ADW)
93rd Aerial Port Squadron/TRPO
Andrews AFB, MD 20331-5000

Comm: 301-981-9111
ATVN: 858-9111

LOCATION: From I-95 (east part of Capital Beltway, I-495) N or S, Exit 9. First traffic light after leaving exit ramp, turn R into main gate of AFB. Also, from I-395 N, exit S Capital St, cross Anacostia River on S Capital St, bear left to Suitland Parkway E. Exit Parkway at Morningside on Suitland Rd E to main gate of AFB. Clearly marked. RM: p-42,J/11. NMC: Washington, 6 mi NW.

FACILITIES	LOCATION	HOURS	PHONE	COMMENTS
PAX TERM INFO	Bldg 1245	0600-2200 dly	C-981-3528, A-858-3528.	R of B/Ops and ATC tower. Main gate, L cross Perimeter Rd. Continue .25 mi, R on Arnold Ave to 1st stop. L to new Pax Term. Term open after hrs for later flts. Navy Ops in Bldg 3198 24 hrs dly C-981-2740/4, A-858-2740/4, (E side of AAFB). No ground trans provided to Navy Ops. See Washington Naval Air Fac MD (NSF) listing in this book. Also, D.C. National Guard C-981-5004.
Recording	Bldg 1245	24 hrs dly	C-981-3527, A-858-3527	Updated 1330, 1800, 0600 dly
Pax Svc Ofc	Bldg 1245	0730-1630 M-F	C-981-6198, A-858-6198	Not for flight information. Call Pax Term or Recording.
Pax Paging	Bldg 1245	0600-2200 dly	C-981-3604, A-858-3604	

MARYLAND
Andrews AFB, Cont'd

PAX LOUNGES		
General	Bldg 1245	0600-2200 dly C-981-3528, A-858-3528 A/C, Bag check, Game rm, Tel C,A,&LD, TV, Rest-rms,P/C seats
DV/VIP	Bldg 1245	24 hrs dly C-981-2100, A-858-2100 A/C, Coffee/Tea srvd, Tel C,A,&LD, TV, Rest-rms, O/S seats. Hostess. (O6+) Active & Retired.
Protocol Svc	Bldg 1245	0600-1630 M-F C-981-2100, A-858-2100 (O6+) Active & Retired. MAC sponsored.
FOOD SERVICE		
Cafeteria	Bldg 1245	0630-1800 M-F, 0800-1400 Sa-Su C-568-2357
Dining Hall	Arnold Ave #1	24 hrs dly C-981-6516
NCO/CPO Club	Bldg 1889	0900-2200 M-Th,Su 1000-2300 F-Sa C-568-3100
OFC Club	Bldg 1352	0700-2300 M-Th, 0700-0130 F-Sa C-420-4744
Snack Bars	Bldg 1672	0700-2300 M,Tu,F 1000-2300 Sa-Su C-981-6452
Vending	Bldg 1245	0600-2200 dly
TRANSPORTATION		
Air Tickets	Bldgs 1245/1535	0800-1630 M-F C-981-2867 SATO
Bus(Comm) (Shuttle) (PTG Shu)		Departs North Gate to Washington D.C. Dly C-981-4092 Bldg 1245 20 min after hr, 25 min before hr C-981-2867 Bldg 1245 0805-1405 M-F C-981-2867 (AFSC, BAFB, PTG)
Car Rentals	Bldg 1245	0730-2000 M-F, 0900-1700 Sa, 1200-2000 Su Value Rent-A-Car=C-420-7766
Limo Service	Bldg 1245	0900-1600 dly C-800-441-8775 Dover Limo
TAXI(Comm) (Gov)	Bldg 1245 Bldg 1568	24 hrs dly C-420-3000 At Pax Term 24 hrs dly C-981-2526 For official duty
Trains	AMTRAK	24 hrs dly C-484-7540 Call for schedule.
Parking	Bldg 1245	24 hrs dly C-981-3528 Short term-100 yds W of Pax Term, Menoher Dr; long term-600 yds W of Term.
OTHER SERVICES		
Bank/Exc	Bldg 1677	0900-1700 M-F, 0800-1200 Sa C-735-8100
Exchange	Bldg 1683	1000-1900 dly C-568-1500
Hair Styles	Bldg 1245 Bldg 1683	0800-1700 M-F C-420-9383 Barber 0800-1800 M-F, 0800-1700 Sa C-735-1988 Beauty
Laundry/DryC	Bldg 1668	0830-2030 M-Sa, 0900-1700 Su C-568-2546
Medical	Bldg 1050	24 hrs dly C-981-2333 Hosp emergency
Postal	Bldg 1668	0800-1615 M-F C-981-3539 No wire svc (AFB)
Valet/Dry C	Bldg 1642	0900-1800 M-Sa C-736-3246 No porter svc

MARYLAND

Andrews AFB, Cont'd

TML	Bldg 1375 All Ranks.	24 hrs dly DV/VIP (06+)	C-981-4614, A-858-4614 C-981-4525, A-858-4525.	
TRAVELERS AID ARC	Bldg 1050	0800-1530 M-F	C-981-6008	Hospital
Chaplain	Bldg 1345	24 hrs dly	C-981-2111	Chapel #1
Lost/Found	Bldg 1245	0600-2200 dly	C-981-3526	Pax Term, NCO
Sec Police	Bldg 1845	24 hrs dly	C-981-2001	Main gate
USO	Bldg 1245	0600-1730 M-F	C-981-2525	
ATTRACTIONS	Aerial gateway to Wash D.C., home of "Air Force One" (the President's aircraft), monuments, White House, parks & more			

SCHEDULED FLIGHTS

DESTINATION	ROUTING	FREQ	EQ/CMTS
Brunswick NAS ME (NHZ)	ADW-PSM-NHZ-LIZ-RME-WRI	Tu,W,F,Sa	C009A/ME
Bush Field Arpt GA (AGS)	ADW-NGU-POB-SSC-CHS-AGS-LSF-BIX-BLV	M,Th	C009A/ME
Charleston AFB SC (CHS)	ADW-NGU-POB-SSC-CHS-AGS-LSF-BIX-BLV	M,Th	C009A/ME
Griffiss AFB NY (RME)	ADW-PSM-NHZ-LIZ-RME-WRI	Tu,W,F,Sa	C009A/ME
Keesler AFB MS (BIX)	ADW-NGU-POB-SSC-CHS-AGS-LSF-BIX-BLV	M,Th	C009A/ME
Kelley AFB TX (SKF)	ADW-SKF-NKX-SUU	Th,Sa	C009A/ME
Lawson AAF GA (LSF)	ADW-NGU-POB-SSC-CHS-AGS-LSF-BIX-BLV	M,Th	C009A/ME
Loring AFB ME (LIZ)	ADW-PSM-NHZ-LIZ-RME-WRI	Tu,W,F,Sa	C009A/ME
McGuire AFB NJ (WRI)	ADW-PSM-NHZ-LIZ-RME-WRI	Tu,W,F,Sa	C009A/ME
Miramar NAS CA (NKX)	ADW-SKF-NKX-SUU	Th,Sa	C009A/ME
Norfolk NAS VA (NGU)	ADW-NGU-POB-SSC-CHS-AGS-LSF-BIX-BLV	M,Th	C009A/ME
Pease AFB NH (PSM)	ADW-PSM-NHZ-LIZ-RME-WRI	Tu,W,F,Sa	C009A/ME
Pope AFB NC (POB)	ADW-NGU-POB-SSC-CHS-AGS-LSF-BIX-BLV	M,Th	C009A/ME

MARYLAND
Andrews AFB, Cont'd

Scott AFB IL (BLV)	ADW-NGU-POB-SSC-CHS-AGS-LSF- BIX-BLV ADW-BLV	M,Th W,Th,Sa	C009A/ME C009A/ME
Shaw AFB SC (SSC)	ADW-NGU-POB-SSC-CHS-AGS-LSF- BIX-BLV	M,Th	C009A/ME
Travis AFB CA (SUU)	ADW-SKF-NKX-SUU	Th,Sa	C009A/ME

UNSCHEDULED FLIGHTS

All unscheduled flts oper with 24 hr notice. Destinations vary widely. Equip is C-12 or C-21 in most cases. Baggage on these aircraft limited to two pieces-NMT 30 lbs combined. Some special missions and other flts to overseas destinations.Consult the recording or Pax Svc for information on all flights.

Martin State Airport (MTN)
135th Tactical Airlift Group (ANG)
2701 Eastern Blvd
Baltimore, MD 21220-2899

Comm: 301-687-6270
ATVN: 235-9210

LOCATION: From US 40E exit to MD-700 E and continue E to MD-150. Enter ANG Base at airport. RM: p-40, M/7. NMC: Baltimore, 8 mi SW.

FACILITIES	LOCATION	HOURS	PHONE	COMMENTS
PAX TERM INFO	ANG Base Ops	During flt processing	24 hrs dly	Ask for directions at gate to ANG Base.
Parking	Park next to ANG Base Operations. Short term only.			

UNSCHEDULED FLIGHTS

Flights via C-130 aircraft to CONUS, OCONUS, and foreign country locations. Call for destinations, routings, and schedules.

Note: This organization is not staffed to process requests for Space-A travel on a regular basis.

Patuxent River Naval Air Station (NHK)
Air Operations Department
Patuxent River NAS, MD 20670-5409

Comm: 301-863-3000
ATVN: 356-3000

LOCATION: Fm I-95 (east portion of Capital Beltway, I-495) exit 7A to Branch Ave (MD-5) S. Follow MD-5 until it turns into MD-235 near Oraville, on to Lexington Park, and the NAS. Main gate is on MD-235 and MD-246 (Cedar Point Rd). RM: p-41, L/18. NMC: Washington DC, 65 mi NW.

FACILITIES	LOCATION	HOURS	PHONE	COMMENTS
PAX TERM INFO	Bldg 103	24 hrs dly	C-863-3836/7, A-356-3836/7	Fm main gate straight on Cedar Pt Rd-2.5 mi R, Air Ops sign.
Pax Svc Ofc	Bldg 103	24 hrs dly	C-863-3836/7	NCO on duty
Pax Paging	Bldg 103	24 hrs dly	C-863-3836	P/A System

MARYLAND

Patuxent River NAS, Cont'd

PAX LOUNGES General	No separate family lounge Bldg 103 2nd Deck 0700-2300 dly C-863-3836 A/C, Bag chk, Tel L & ATVN, Showers, O/S seats	
DV/VIP	Bldg 103 2nd Deck 0700-2300 dly C-863-3836 (06+) Advance notice to PPR. A/C, Bag chk, Tel L&ATVN, Rest-rms, O/S seats.	
FOOD SERVICE Cafeteria	Good services on Base Bldg 460 0700-1430 M-Sa C-863-8855	
Enl Club	Bldg 1454 1700-0100 M-F C-863-3643 Call for svc hrs.	
NCO/CPO Club	Bldg 441 1100-0100 M-F C-863-3657 Call for svc hrs.	
OFC Club	Golf Club 1130-2000 Tu-Sa C-863-3656 Call for svc hrs.	
Restaurants	Cedar Pt Rd 0600-2300 dly C-862-3833 "McDnalds"	
Snack Bars	Bldg 103 0700-1300 M-F C-863-8987	
Vending	Bldg 103 24 hrs dly C-863-3836	
TRANSPORTATION Air Tickets	Good on Base. Limited off Base. Bldg 409 0700-1500 M-F C-863-1078/1071	
Bus(Shuttle)	Bldg 103 0700-1000 dly C-863-4088 See Air Ops for schedule. Pax Shuttle Bus DCA to NHK 2 buses dly C-863-3737.	
Car Rentals	Bldg 460 0700-1800 M-F National=C-862-1090, Aldridge=C-863-8111	
TAXI(Comm)	Bldg 103 24 hrs dly Friendly=C-863-8141	
Parking	Bldg 103 24 hrs dly Short term-unmarked spaces only; long term-North side of Bldg C-863-3836.	
OTHER SERVICES Exchange	Good services on Base Bldg 460 1000-1700 M-F, 1600 Sa C-863-8814	
Bank/Exc	1st Natl 0900-1800 M-Th C-475-8081	
Hair Styles	Bldg 460 0830-1700 M-F, 1600 Sa C-863-8733 Barber C-863-5686 Beauty	
Laundry/DryC	Bldg 460 0800-2100 M-Sa C-863-6410	
Medical	Bldg 1370 24 hrs dly C-863-1418/1422	
Postal	Bldg 409 0800-1700 M-F, 1200 Sa C-863-3674	
TML	Bldg 423 0730-1600 dly C-863-3244, A-356-3848	
TRAVELERS AID ARC	Bldg 409 0930-1500 M-F C-863-4100	
Chaplain	Bldg 401 24 hrs on call C-863-3812	
Sec Police	Main gate 24 hrs dly C-863-3208 Desk Sgt	

MARYLAND
Patuxent River NAS, Cont'd

| ATTRACTIONS | Calvert Cliffs Nuclear Power Plant Museum, Naval Aviation Test & Evaluation Museum, Cecil's Mill |

UNSCHEDULED FLIGHTS

Frequent flights via P-3A/M and administrative aircraft to: Brunswick NAS ME (NHZ); Dallas NAS TX (NBE); Jacksonville NAS FL (NIP); Norfolk NAS VA (NGU); South Weymouth NAS MA (NZW); and Willow Grove NAS PA (NXX). Other CONUS destinations. Call for destinations, routings, and schedules.

Phillips Army Airfield (APG)
Base Air Operations, ATTN: STEAP-PF-V
Aberdeen Proving Ground, MD 21005-5001

Comm: 301-278-5201
ATVN: 298-1110

LOCATION: Take Exit 5 E from I-95 N on MD-22 E for 2 mi to main gate.
RM: p-41, D/20. NMC: Baltimore, 23 mi SW.

FACILITIES	LOCATION	HOURS	PHONE	COMMENTS
PAX TERM INFO	Bldg 1060	24 hrs dly	C-278-3483/4019, A-298-3483/4019	
	From Aberdeen Blvd W to L (S) on Maryland Blvd to L on Deer Creek to Army Airfield.			
OTHER SERVICES	Full large Base spt fac avail. See Military Living's "US Forces Travel Guide USA & Caribbean Areas" for full details.			

UNSCHEDULED FLIGHTS

Flights via Army executive aircraft C-12A and C-21A to East Coast and other locations. Call for destinations, routings, and schedules.

Tipton Army Airfield (FME)
Base Air Operations
Fort George G. Meade, MD 20755-5000

Comm: 300-677-6261
ATVN: 923-6261

LOCATION: Off Baltimore-Washington Parkway, I-295, exit MD-198 E which is Fort Meade Rd. Clearly marked. RM: p-42, C/12. NMC: Baltimore MD and Washington DC, 30 mi from each city.

FACILITIES	LOCATION	HOURS	PHONE	COMMENTS
PAX TERM INFO	Bldg 90 Base Ops	24 hrs dly	C-677-6261, A-923-6291	
	Fm MD-175 exit to Rock Ave, R to O'Brien Rd, L to AAF on R.			
OTHER SERVICES	Full large Base support facilities available. See Military Living's "US Forces Travel Guide USA & Caribbean Areas" for full details.			

UNSCHEDULED FLIGHTS

Flights via Army executive aircraft C-12A and C-21A to East Coast locations. Call for destinations, routings, and schedules.

Washington Naval Air Facility (NSF)
Washington, DC 20396-5130

Comm: 301-981-9111
ATVN: 858-9111

LOCATION: From I-95 (east part of Capital Beltway, I-495) N or S, Exit 9. At

MARYLAND

Washington NAF, Cont'd

first traffic light after leaving exit ramp, turn right into main gate of AFB. Also, from I-395 N, exit S Capital St, cross Anacostia River on S Capital St, bear left to Suitland Parkway E, exit Parkway at Morningside on Suitland Rd E to main gate of AFB. Follow signs to E side of Andrews AFB, Bldg 3198, N of Hangar 12. Clearly marked. RM: p-42, J/11. NMC: Washington DC, 6 mi NW.

FACILITIES	LOCATION	HOURS	PHONE	COMMENTS
PAX TERM INFO	Bldg 3198	24 hrs dly	C-981-2740/2744, A-858-2740/2744. Report to ATC desk, 1st fl S end of Bldg. No recording.	
PAX LOUNGES	Bldg 3198	0600-2300 dly	C-981-2740, A-858-2744	No overnight use by Pax. Lounge in Bldg lobby. A/C, Bag check, Tel C, Rest-rms, P/C seats, TV.
DV/VIP	Bldg 3198 Off lobby	24 hrs dly	C-981-2740, A-858-2740 (06+)	A/C, Tel C&A, Rest-rms, O/S seats
Protocol Svc	Bldg 3198	24 hrs dly	C-981-2740, A-858-2740 (CDO)	
FOOD SERVICE	Bldg 3198 Vending See Andrews AFB listing for complete svcs.			
TRANSPORTATION	Bldg 3198 See Andrews AFB listing for complete services.			
Parking	Bldg 3198	24 hrs dly	Short & long term available. Contact NAF SP C-981-4796/4648. No parking in lot next to Bldg 3198.	
OTHER SERVICES	Bldg 3198 Post Office 0900-1600 M-F, NAF Security Police C-981-4796/4648. See Andrews AFB listing for other services.			

UNSCHEDULED FLIGHTS

There are no scheduled flts from the Washington NAF. Most flts are planned 24 hrs prior to departure. Call for info. There are frequent unscheduled flts to the following destinations: Brunswick NAS ME (NHZ); Cherry Point MCAS NC (NKT); Dallas NAS TX (NBE); Glenview NAS IL (NBU); Jacksonville NAS FL (NIP); Memphis NAS TN (NQA); Moffett Fld NAS CA (NUQ); New Orleans NAS LA (NBG); New River MCAS NC (NCA); Pensacola NAS FL (NPA); South Weymouth NAS MA (NZW); Willow Grove NAS PA (NXX); Norfolk NAS VA (NGU). Equipment flown varies with flts and distances. Most aircraft are C-9, C-12, C-130, CV-58, P-3, and T-39.

MASSACHUSETTS

Hanscom Field (BED) Comm: 617-377-4441
3245th ABG/Pax Operations ATVN: 478-4441
Hanscom AFB, MA 01731-5000

LOCATION: Fm I-95 N take Exit 45 NW, MA-2A W for 2 mi to R on Hartwell Rd which bisects the AFB. RM: p-43, E/2. NMC: Boston, 17 mi SE.

FACILITIES	LOCATION	HOURS	PHONE	COMMENTS
PAX TERM INFO	Bldg 1714	24 hrs dly	C-861-4441, A-478-4441	Uses runways of Laurence G. Hanscom Field, state-operated airfield adjoining base.
OTHER SERVICES	Full large Base supt fac avail. For details see Military Living's "US Forces Travel Guide USA & Caribbean Areas"			

MASSACHUSETTS
Hanscom Field, Cont'd

UNSCHEDULED FLIGHTS

Many flights to Andrews AFB MD (ADW). Transient aircraft to East Coast locations. Call for destinations, routings, and schedules.

Moore Army Airfield (AYE)
ATTN: Dispatch
Fort Devens, MA 01433-5090

Comm: 508-796-3911
ATVN: 256-3911

LOCATION: Fm Boston follow MA-2 W and exit at Fort Devens, about 5 mi W of I-495. In Ayer. RM: p-45, D/14. NMC: Boston, 35 mi SE.

FACILITIES	LOCATION	HOURS	PHONE	COMMENTS
PAX TERM INFO	Bldg 3822 0800-1600 dly C-796-3130/2982, A-256-3130/2982 Located 3 mi N of main post on MA-2A.			
OTHER SERVICES	All Pax processed by Base Ops. Full large Base support facilities available.			

UNSCHEDULED FLIGHTS

Flights via C-12A and C-21A aircraft to New England and East Coast locations. Call for destinations, routings, and schedules.

Otis Air National Guard Base (CPD)
Cape Cod Coast Guard Air Station
Otis ANGB, MA 02542-5000

Comm: 508-968-5300
ATVN: 557-5300
FTS: 829-5300

LOCATION: Off MA-28 at the Massachussetts Military Reservation on Cape Cod (Otis ANGB) on former Otis AFB. RM: p-45, M/22. NMC: Boston, 50 mi NW.

FACILITIES	LOCATION	HOURS	PHONE	COMMENTS
PAX TERM INFO	Base Ops/CG Hangar 0800-1600 M-F Wkend hrs vary C-968-5361, A-557-5361, F-829-5361. No Pax Term. Pax processed by CG Ops.			
OTHER SERVICES	No lounge facilities. No comm bus on Base. Comm taxi avail in Providence RI. Parking in BOQ lot, walk to hangar. Small Exchange, Barber, Emergency medical, and TML.			

UNSCHEDULED FLIGHTS

Some Space-A. Call for destinations, routings, and schedules.

South Weymouth Naval Air Station (NZW)
Air Operations
South Weymouth NAS, MA 02190-5000

Comm: 617-786-2500
ATVN: 478-5980

LOCATION: Fm MA-3 (Pilgrims Hwy) Exit 16 to MA-18 (Main St) S to 3rd traffic light, turn left, follow Union St to White St, turn right. NAS at end of White St. Located in residential area. RM: p-45, H/19. NMC: Boston, 15 mi NW.

FACILITIES	LOCATION	HOURS	PHONE	COMMENTS
PAX TERM INFO	Hangar #1 0700-2300 dly C-786-2713, A-955-2713 From main gate straight on Shea Memorial Drive to Hangar #1, left around hangar to South entrance.			

MASSACHUSETTS

South Weymouth NAS, Cont'd

Pax Svc Ofc	Hangar #1 0700-2300 dly C-786-2713 NCO on duty
PAX LOUNGES General	No separate family lounge Hangar #1 0700-2300 dly C-786-2713 Bag check, Tel L,LD,&ATVN, TV, Rest-rms, O/S seats
DV/VIP	Hangar #1 0700-2300 dly C-786-2713 A/C, Tel L,LD,&ATVN, TV, Rest-rms, O/S seats
Protocol Svc	Bldg 17 24 hrs dly C-786-2500 (06+) See OOD.
FOOD SERVICE Dining Hall	Good services on and off Base Bldg 9 Galley 0530-0700, 1130-1300, 1530-1700 dly C-786-2653
Enl Club	Bldg 112 1100-2300 Tu-Su C-786-2766 Call for svc hrs.
NCO/CPO Club	Bldg 5 1100-2300 Tu-Su C-786-2741 Call for svc hrs.
OFC Club	O'Club 1000-2300 Tu-Su C-786-2983 Call for svc hrs.
Snack Bars	Bldg 12 1100-1630 Tu-Su C-786-2980
TRANSPORTATION Car Rentals	Bldg 102 1000-1700 Tu-Su C-786-2950 NEX
Trains	Braintree MBTA Station Trains to Boston
Parking	Hangar #1 0700-2300 dly C-786-2713 Short term-no overnight; long term-NE of Terminal.
OTHER SERVICES Exchange	Bldg 102 1000-1700 Tu-Su C-786-2952
Hair Styles	Bldg 102 0730-1630 W-Sa C-786-2809 Appointment required
Laundry/DryC	Bldg 102 1000-1700 Tu-Sa C-786-2673
Medical	Bldg 24 24 hrs dly C-786-2674
TRAVELERS AID Chaplain	Bldg 17 1000-1600 M-F C-786-2748 Navy Family Services Bldg 97 0800-1700 M-F C-786-2604
Sec Police	Bldg 32 24 hrs dly C-786-2610/2605
ATTRACTIONS	Historic Quincy, Boston, Massachusetts Bay

UNSCHEDULED FLIGHTS

Flights are to various CONUS locations including: Brunswick NAS ME (NHZ); Jacksonville NAS FL (NIP); Norfolk NAS VA (NGU); Washington NAF MD (NSF); and Willow Grove NAS PA (NXX) via C009B/M, C-12A/P, P-3A/M, and/or other aircraft and missions. Call for destinations, routings, and schedules.

Westover Air Force Base (CEF)
439th Tactical Air Lift Wing
Westover AFB, MA 01022-5000

Comm: 413-557-1110
ATVN: 589-1110

LOCATION: Take exit 5 off I-90 (MA Trnpk) in Chicopee. Westover is on Rt 33, N of I-90; signs mark way to Base. RM: p-45, H/7. NMC: Springfield, 8 mi S.

MASSACHUSETTS
Westover AFB, Cont'd

FACILITIES	LOCATION	HOURS	PHONE	COMMENTS
PAX TERM INFO	Bldg 7091	0700-2300 dly	C-557-2951, A-589-2951	From Holyoke Gate straight on Central Ave, R on Ellipse Dr to Woodward St, Base Ops L.
Pax Svc Ofc	Bldg 7091	0700-2300 dly	C-557-2951	NCO on duty
PAX LOUNGES DV/VIP	Bldg 7091	0700-2300 dly	C-557-2951	No general Pax lounge. Pax processed thru lobby of Base Ops. (O6+) A/C, Bag lks, Read/write rm, Tel L,LD&ATVN, TV, Rest-rms, Showers, O/S seats
FOOD SERVICE				Limited on Base. Good off Base. Dining Hall C-557-2994, Cons Club C-593-5531, Snack Bar C-557-3390, USO C-557-2951
TRANSPORTATION				Bus(Comm) C-781-3320 (Shuttle) C-557-3855, Car Rentals C-732-5191 or C-533-4888, Taxi(Comm) C-534-3333 or C-536-1400 Parking adjacent to Base Ops. No restrictions.
OTHER SERVICES				Exchange C-593-5941, Barber C-593-5941, Medical C-557-3557
TML	Bldg 2200 All Ranks.	0745-2245 dly	C-557-3032, A-589-3032 DV/VIP C-557-1110.	
TRAVELERS AID				ARC Springfield, MA C-737-4306 or 737-4781, Lost/Found C-557-2951, Sec Police C-557-3557
ATTRACTIONS				Springfield, Mt. Tom Snow Ski Resort

UNSCHEDULED FLIGHTS

Flights to CONUS & OCONUS locations via C-130A aircraft. Most departures on Friday. Not a foreign clearance Base for returning foreign flights.

MICHIGAN

K. I. Sawyer Air Force Base (SAW)
410th BMW/Air Ops
K I Sawyer AFB, MI 49843-5000

Comm: 906-346-6511
ATVN: 472-1110

LOCATION: In the MI upper peninsula. Fm US-41 S of Marquette, take MI 460 W to Gate 2. RM: p-47, F/2. NMC: Marquette, 23 mi NW.

FACILITIES	LOCATION	HOURS	PHONE	COMMENTS
PAX TERM INFO	Bldg 427	24 hrs dly	C-346-2345/2663, A-472-2345/2663	Fm Gate 2 straight on Fifth St to L on C Ave to R on Third St direct to Base Ops.
Pax Svc Ofc	Bldg 427	24 hrs dly	C-346-2345/2663	Dispatch on duty
PAX LOUNGES General	Bldg 427	24 hrs dly	C-346-2345	No separate family lounge Bag chk, Tel L, TV, Rest-rms, O/S seats
DV/VIP	Bldg 247	24 hrs dly	C-346-2345	Bag chk, Tel L, TV, Rest-rms, O/S seats

MICHIGAN

K.I. Sawyer AFB, Cont'd

Protocol Svc	Wing HQ Map #1 0730-1630 M-F C-346-2763
FOOD SERVICE	Good on and off Base. Cafeteria C-346-3518, Dining Hall C-346-2288, NCO/CPO Club C-346-2842, O'Club C-346-2480, Restaurant C-346-4011, Snack Bar C-346-2184, Vending C-346-2345
TRANSPORTATION	Good off Base. Air Tickets C-346-1418, Bus(Comm) C-346-6585 (Shuttle) C-225-1112, Greyhound=C-485-5140, Car Rental C-475-4177, Taxi(Comm) C-226-2521, Parking Bldg 427
OTHER SERVICES	Good on and off Base. Exchange C-346-6313, Bank C-346-9266, Barber C-346-9183, Beauty C-346-5015, Laundry/DryC C-346-5679 Medical C-346-2233, Postal C-346-2605
TML	Bldg 801 24 hrs dly C-346-2145, A-472-2145 All Ranks. DV/VIP C-346-6511.
TRAVELERS AID	Many agencies on and off Base. ARC C-346-2622, Chaplain C-346-2922, AF Aid C-346-2323, Sec Police C-346-2131
ATTRACTIONS	Lake Superior, Keweenaw Peninsula, outdoor sports

SCHEDULED FLIGHTS

DESTINATION	ROUTING	FREQ	EQ/CMTS
Scott AFB IL (BLV)	SAW-BLV	M,W	C009A/ME

Flights via KC-135E/M to CONUS, OCONUS, and foreign countries. Two or three flights per quarter.

Selfridge Air National Guard Base (MTC)
Det 1, HQ Michigan Air National Guard
Selfridge ANGB, MI 48045-5004

Comm: 313-466-4011
ATVN: 273-0111

LOCATION: Take I-94 N from Detroit, to Selfridge exit, then E on MI-59 to main gate of Base. RM: p-48, D/12. NMC: Detroit, 25 mi SW.

FACILITIES	LOCATION HOURS PHONE COMMENTS
PAX TERM INFO	Base Ops Bldg 50 0715-2315 dly, 1515 Holidays C-466-5322, A-273-5322 ANG. Base Ops location approx 1.25 mi fr main gate on Wilbur Wright Drive. Naval Air Facility Ops R fm main gate on Perimeter Rd C-466-4420/5821, A-273-4420/5821. Location ID (NOI) has own clearance authority. ANG & NAF flts are cleared by ANG.
Recording	C-313-466-5884, A-273-5884 for dly/wkly schedules
PAX LOUNGES	No lounges. Flights are processed by ANG.
FOOD SERVICE	Limited services on Base. NCO/CPO Club C-466-4786, O'Club C-466-4785, Snack Bars C-469-3660
TRANSPORTATION	Limited transportation on Base. Air Tickets C-466-4931, Parking C-466-4222 (check with Security Police)
OTHER SERVICES	Good services on Base. Exchange C-466-4614, Bank/Exc C-465-2400, Hair Styles C-468-8009, Laundry/DryC C-466-0610, Medical C-466-4650, Postal C-466-4123

MICHIGAN
Selfridge ANGB, Cont'd

TML	Bldg 410 0700-2245 C-466-4435, A-273-4435
	All Ranks. DV/VIP C-466-5444.
TRAVELERS AID	Chaplain C-466-4761/3, Emerg Relief C-466-5903/4514, AF Aid C-517-739-6558, Navy Relief C-466-4763
ATTRACTIONS	City of Detroit, Lake St Clair

UNSCHEDULED FLIGHTS

No regularly scheduled flights. Frequent flights via C-130A, C009A, and other aircraft within CONUS. Very infrequent overseas flights. Call recording for destinations, routings, and schedules.

Wurtsmith Air Force Base (OSC)
379th CSG/OTM
Wurtsmith AFB, MI 48753-5000

Comm: 517-739-2011
ATVN: 623-1110

LOCATION: Off US-23, 2 mi NW of Oscoda. On F-41. Clearly marked. RM: p-47, N/14. NMC: Bay City, 65 mi SW.

FACILITIES	LOCATION	HOURS	PHONE	COMMENTS
PAX TERM INFO	Bldg 14	24 hrs dly	C-747-6263, A-623-6263	
	From main gate straight on Skeel Ave to L on Missile St to R on Operations St and Base Ops. Flt info recording C-747-5099.			
Pax Svc Ofc	Bldg 14	24 hrs dly	C-747-6263	NCO on duty
PAX LOUNGES	No separate family lounge. General & DV/VIP C-747-6263, Protocol Service C-747-5013			
FOOD SERVICE	Good services on Base. Dining Hall C-747-6382, NCO/CPO Club C-747-6493, O'Club C-747-6353, Snack Bars C-747-6100, Vending C-747-6263			
TRANSPORTATION	Very limited on and off Base. POV essential. Bus(Comm) C-739-3491 (Greyhound), Parking C-747-6251 (one week limit)			
OTHER SERVICES	Exchange C-739-7466, Barber C-739-5589, Beauty C-739-3808, Medical C-747-6423, Postal C-739-3939			
TML	Bldg 1600 24 hrs dly C-747-6692/6033, A-623-6692/6033 All Ranks. DV/VIP-C-739-8252			
TRAVELERS AID	Good on Base. ARC C-747-6726 (other hrs C-739-2011), Chaplain C-747-6113 (other hrs C-739-2011), AF Aid C-747-6558, Security Police C-747-6023			
ATTRACTIONS	Lake Huron, outdoor and water sports			

SCHEDULED FLIGHTS

DESTINATION	ROUTING	FREQ	EQ/CMTS
Eglin AFB FL (VPS)	OSC-VPS	1 ea mo	KC-135E/M

MICHIGAN

Wurtsmith AFB, Cont'd

RAF Fairford UK (FFD)	OSC-PSM-FFD	1 ea mo	KC-135E/M
Homestead AFB FL (HST)	OSC-HST	1 ea mo	KC-135E/M
MacDill AFB FL (MCF)	OSC-MCF	1 ea mo	KC-135E/M
RAF Mildenhall UK (MHZ)	OSC-MHZ	1 ea mo	KC-135E/M
Pease AFB NH (PSM)	OSC-PSM-FFD	1 ea mo	KC-135E/M
Scott AFB IL (BLV)	OSC-BLV	M,W,F	C009A/ME

MINNESOTA

Minneapolis-St. Paul International Airport (MSP)
133rd Tactical Air Lift Wing (ANG)
934th Tactical Air Lift Group (AFRES)
Minneapolis-St Paul IAP, MN 55450-5000

Comm: 612-725-5011
ATVN: 825-5681 (ANG)
825-5100 (AFRES)

LOCATION: From I-35 E to crosstown MN-62, exit at 34th Ave and entrance. Also, MN-55 S to crosstown MN-62, exit to 34th Ave and entrance. RM: p-49, J/6. NMC: Minneapolis-St Paul, in city limits.

FACILITIES	LOCATION HOURS PHONE COMMENTS
PAX TERM INFO	Bldg 821 Base Ops 0730-1600 dly C-725-8018/5552, A-825-8018/5552 From main gate straight on main rd to Base Ops. Separate facilities maintained by ANG and AFRES.
PAX LOUNGES	No lounges. All Pax processed by Base Ops.
OTHER SERVICES	Limited support facilities available. BX Bldg 751 C-726-9023, NCO Club C-726-5390, O'Club C-726-5402
TML	Bldg 711 0700-1800 M-Th, 2100 F, 1300 Sa-Su C-725-5320, A-825-5320. All Ranks. DV/VIP C-725-5320.
TRAVELERS AID Sec Police	Main gate 24 hrs dly C-725-5400
ATTRACTIONS	On the Mississippi and Minnesota Rivers

UNSCHEDULED FLIGHTS

Flights to CONUS locations via C-130A aircraft. Most flights on weekends. Call for destinations, routings, and schedules.

MISSISSIPPI

Jackson Municipal Airport (JAN)
172nd Tactical Airlift Group (ANG)
Jackson, MS 39208-0810

Comm: 601-932-8309
ATVN: 731-9309

LOCATION: Off I-20 E or W & US-49 N or S. RM:p-52, I/7. NMC:Jackson, 5 mi W.

FACILITIES	LOCATION	HOURS	PHONE	COMMENTS
PAX TERM INFO	Base Ops 0730-1600 dly C-932-8387, A-731-9387 No separate Pax Term. No military spt facilities. All spt of a commercial airport provided.			

UNSCHEDULED FLIGHTS

Flights to overseas & CONUS locations via C-141/B aircraft. Call for destinations, routings, and schedules. Most flights on training weekends.

Keesler Air Force Base (BIX)
3380th ABG/DOOB
Keesler AFB, MS 39534-5000

Comm: 601-377-1110
ATVN: 868-1110

LOCATION: From I-10 Exit 46, follow signs to Base. From US-90, N on White Ave to main gate. RM: p-52, P/4. NMC: Biloxi, in the city.

FACILITIES	LOCATION	HOURS	PHONE	COMMENTS
PAX TERM INFO	Bldg 4205 0600-2300 dly C-377-2120, A-868-2120 Fm main gate straight on Larcher Blvd, L on Meadows Dr, L on Hangar Rd, 1st hangar on R. Enter Term at rear away fm road.			
PAX LOUNGES General	Located on flight line side of hangar Bldg 4205 0600-2300 M-F C-377-2120 rooms, Tel L&A, TV, Rest-rooms, P/C & O/S seats			A/C, Read/write
DV/VIP	Bldg 4205	0600-2300 M-F	C-377-2215	Coffee/tea, Tel LD
Protocol Svc	Bldg 2816	0630-1630 M-F	(07+)	Air Training Command
FOOD SERVICE Cafeteria	Good on and off Base Bldg 2301 0630-1400 M, 0630-1500 Tu-F, 0800-1600 Sa C-435-5284 "Gulf Breeze"			
Dining Hall	Bldg 4812	0500-2400 dly	C-377-1110	
Enl Club	Bldg 7502	1700-2000 M-F, 2400 Sa-Su	C-377-2424	
NCO/CPO Club	Bldg 2221	0630-2400 M-F, 0800-0200 Sa, 2400 Su	C-377-3439	
OFC Club	Bldg 3910	0600-2200 M-F, 2400 Sa-Su	C-377-2791	
Snack Bars	Bldg B4120	0630-1500 M-F	C-436-3124	
Vending	Bldg 0468	24 hrs dly	C-377-2215	Bill changer

MISSISSIPPI

Keesler AFB, Cont'd

TRANSPORTATION				
Air Tickets	Good on Base			
	Bldg 0701	0715-1600 M-F	C-377-2503	SATO
Bus(Gov)	Bldg 4430	24 hrs dly	C-377-2430	
(Shuttle)	Bldg 4430	0630-1940 dly	C-377-2430	Call for Sa-Su sched.
Car Rentals	Biloxi, and Gulfport Municipal Airport. AAFES car rental 0900-1700 M-F, 0900-1600 Sa, 1400-1700 Su, C-435-2325.			
Limo Service	Bldg 7303	0800-1700 M-F	C-432-2649	"Coastliner"
TAXI(Comm)	Main gate	24 hrs dly	C-377-3720	
(Gov)	Bldg 4430	24 hrs dly	C-377-2430	
Parking	Bldg 4205	24 hrs dly	C-377-3040	Short & long term
	with no restrictions. Notify Security Police.			
OTHER SERVICES				
Exchange	Good on and off Base			
	Bldg 2303	1000-1800 M-F, 1700 Sa-Su	C-435-2216	
Bank/Exc	Bldg 1550	0830-1500 M-F	C-374-1740	1st Mississippi
Hair Styles	Bldg 2303	0900-1700 M-Sa	C-436-4181	Barber Shop
Laundry/DryC	Bldg 2303	0900-1800 M-F, 1700 Sa	C-432-0772	
Medical	Bldg 0468	24 hrs dly	C-377-6555/6556	
Postal	Bldg 4818	0800-1630 M-F, 1200 Sa	C-377-1110	
Weather	Bldg 4205	24 hrs dly	C-377-4175	Recording
TML	Bldg 2101	24 hrs dly	C-377-2631/3224, A-868-2631	
	All Ranks.		DV/VIP C-377-3663/3774.	
TRAVELERS AID	Many agencies on and off Base. ARC C-377-6172 (other hrs C-377-1110), Chaplain C-377-2110, Emerg Relief C-377-2340 (other hrs C-377-4330), Lost/Found C-377-3040, Sec Police C-377-3040			
ATTRACTIONS	Beaches, seafood, New Orleans and Mobile easy drives			

SCHEDULED FLIGHTS

DESTINATION	ROUTING	FREQ	EQ/CMTS
Andrews AFB MD (ADW)	BIX-LSF-AGS-CHS-SSC-POB-NGU-NKT-ADW	Su,W	C009A/ME
	BIX-ADW-BLV	Su,Th	C009A/ME
Birmingham Munic Arpt AL (BHM)	BIX-NIP-AGS-MGE-BHM-HSV-BLV	F	C009A/ME
Bush Fld Arpt GA (AGS)	BIX-LSF-AGS-CHS-SSC-POB-NGU-NKT-ADW	Su,W	C009A/ME
	BIX-NIP-AGS-MGE-BHM-HSV-BLV	F	C009A/ME

MISSISSIPPI
Keesler AFB, Cont'd

Charleston AFB Intl SC (CHS)	BIX-LSF-AGS-CHS-SSC-POB-NGU-NKT-ADW	Su,W	C009A/ME
Cherry Point MCAS NC (NKT)	BIX-LSF-AGS-CHS-SSC-POB-NGU-	Su,W	C009A/ME
Dobbins AFB GA (MGE)	BIX-NIP-AGS-MGE-BHM-HSV-BLV	F	C009A/ME
Eglin AFB FL (VPS)	BIX-MXF-VAD-WRB-PAM-VPS-BIX BIX-MXF-VAD-WRB-VPS-PAM-BIX	W Sa	C009A/ME C009A/ME
Homestead AFB FL (HST)	BIX-NIP-MCF-HST-NQX-MCO-BIX BIX-MCO-COF-HST-NQX-MCF-NIP-BIX	Tu F	C009A/ME C009A/ME
Huntsville-Madison County Arpt FL (HSV)	BIX-NIP-AGS-MGE-BHM-HSV-BLV	F	C009A/ME
Jacksonville NAS FL (NIP)	BIX-NIP-MCF-HST-NQX-MCO-BIX BIX-MCO-COF-HST-NQX-MCF-NIP-BIX BIX-NIP-AGS-MGE-BHM-HSV-BLV	Tu F F	C009A/ME C009A/ME C009A/ME
Kelly AFB TX (SKF)	BIX-SKF-BLV	W,Sa	C009A/ME
Key West NAS FL (NQX)	BIX-NIP-MCF-HST-NQX-MCO-BIX BIX-MCO-COF-HST-NQX-MCF-NIP-BIX	Tu F	C009A/ME C009A/ME
Lawson AAF GA (LSF)	BIX-LSF-AGS-CHS-SSC-POB-NGU-NKT-ADW	Su,W	C009A/ME
MacDill AFB FL (MCF)	BIX-NIP-MCF-HST-NQX-MCO-BIX BIX-MCO-COF-HST-NQX-MCF-NIP-BIX	Tu F	C009A/ME C009A/ME
Maxwell AFB AL (MXF)	BIX-MXF-VAD-WRB-PAM-VPS-BIX BIX-MXF-VAD-WRB-VPS-PAM-BIX	W Sa	C009A/ME C009A/ME
Moody AFB GA (VAD)	BIX-MXF-VAD-WRB-PAM-VPS-BIX BIX-MXF-VAD-WRB-VPS-PAM-BIX	W Sa	C009A/ME C009A/ME
Norfolk NAS VA (NGU)	BIX-LSF-AGS-CHS-SSC-POB-NGU-NKT-ADW	Su,W	C009A/ME
Orlando Exec Arpt FL (MCO)	BIX-NIP-MCF-HST-NQX-MCO-BIX BIX-MCO-COF-HST-NQX-MCF-NIP-BIX	Tu F	C009A/ME C009A/ME
Patrick AFB FL (COF)	BIX-MCO-COF-HST-NQX-MCF-NIP-BIX	F	C009A/ME
Pope AFB NC (POB)	BIX-LSF-AGS-CHS-SSC-POB-NGU-NKT-ADW	Su,W	C009A/ME
Robins AFB GA (WRB)	BIX-MXF-VAD-WRB-PAM-VPS-BIX BIX-MXF-VAD-WRB-VPS-PAM-BIX	W Sa	C009A/ME C009A/ME

MISSISSIPPI

Keesler AFB, Cont'd

Scott AFB IL (BLV)	BIX-ADW-BLV BIX-BLV BIX-SKF-BLV BIX-NIP-AGS-MGE-BHM-HSV-BLV	Su,Th M,Th W,Sa F	C009A/ME C009A/ME C009A/ME C009A/ME
Shaw AFB SC (SSC)	BIX-LSF-AGS-CHS-SSC-POB-NGU-NKT-ADW	Su,W	C009A/ME
Tyndall AFB FL (PAM)	BIX-MXF-VAD-WRB-PAM-VPS-BIX BIX-MXF-VAD-WRB-VPS-PAM-BIX	W Sa	C009A/ME C009A/ME

Meridian Naval Air Station (NMM)
Air Operations
Meridian NAS, MS 39309-5000

Comm: 601-679-2211
ATVN: 446-2211

LOCATION: Take MS-39 N from Meridian, for 12 mi to 4-lane access road. Clearly marked. Right for 3 mi to NAS main gate. RM: p-52, I/11. NMC: Meridian, 15 mi SW.

FACILITIES	LOCATION HOURS PHONE COMMENTS
PAX TERM INFO	Map #61 1400-0300 M-Th, 2200 F-Su C-679-2454, A-446-2454. From main gate straight on Whitaker Blvd to R on Fuller Rd for 2.5 mi to Base Ops on left.
Pax Svc Ofc	Base Ops 1400-0300 M-Th, 2200 F-Su C-679-2454 NCO on duty
PAX LOUNGES General	Limited lounge facilities Base Ops 24 hrs dly C-679-2454 A/C, Rest-rms, P/C seats
DV/VIP	Base Ops 1400-0300 M-Th, 2200 F-Su C-679-2454 (O6+) On request
FOOD SERVICE	Good on and off base. Cafeteria C-679-2681, Dining Hall C-679-2211, Enl Club C-679-2636, NCO/CPO Club C-679-2650, O'Club C-679-2667, Snack Bar C-679-2531
TRANSPORTATION	Limited on & off Base. Bus(Shuttle) to Meridian 1700-2400 F, 0900-2400 Sa-Su, Taxi(GOV) C-679-2645, Parking C-679-2454
OTHER SERVICES	Good on Base. Exchange C-679-2725, Bank C-679-2501, Barber C-679-2569, Beauty C-679-8411, Laundry C-679-2632 Medical C-679-2444, Postal C-679-2211
TML	Bldg 208 24 hrs dly C-679-2414/2616, A-446-2414/2616 All Ranks. DV/VIP C-679-2211.
TRAVELERS AID	ARC C-679-2679, Chaplain C-679-2475, Navy Relief C-679-2504, Sec Police C-679-2361. Attractions at Lake Okatibbee.

SCHEDULED FLIGHTS

DESTINATION	ROUTING	FREQ	EQ/CMTS
Pensacola NAS FL (NPA)	NMM-NPA-NMM	Tu,W	Adm Acft/P

Note: Flts to CONUS destinations. Call for destinations, routings, and schedules.

MISSISSIPPI

Vicksburg Municipal Airport (VKS)
121st ARCOM ASF (ISG)
Route 2, Box 86E
Vicksburg, MS 39180-9616

Comm: 601-638-6550
ATVN: 782-5011
Ask for EX

LOCATION: Take US-61 S from I-20 E or W for 6 mi, exit W (R) to airport.
RM: p-52, J/5. NMC: Vicksburg, 6 mi N.

FACILITIES	LOCATION	HOURS	PHONE	COMMENTS
PAX TERM INFO	ARRES 0730-1600 dly C-638-6550, A-782-5011-EX-6550 ARRES Hangar is largest hangar on south end of field. No Pax Terminal. All Pax processed through Base Ops. Commercial facilities available at Commercial Pax Terminal.			

UNSCHEDULED FLIGHTS

Flights via UH-1H aircraft to: Birmingham Municipal Airport AL (BHM); Cairns AAF AL (OZR); Kansas City IAP MO (MCI); Lawson AAF GA (LSF); Monroe County Airport AL (MVC); and Tuscaloosa Municipal Airport AL (TCL). Call for other destinations, routings, and schedules.

MISSOURI

Forney Army Airfield (TBN)
Air Operations
Fort Leonard Wood, MO 65473-5000

Comm: 314-368-0113
ATVN: 581-0110
FTS: 270-0110

LOCATION: Two mi S of I-44, adjacent to St Robert & Waynesville, at Ft Leonard Wood exit. RM: p-55, L/16. NMC: Springfield, 85 mi SW.

FACILITIES	LOCATION	HOURS	PHONE	COMMENTS
PAX TERM INFO	Base Ops 24 hrs dly C-368-2166 or 329-2400, A-581-2166/2400 From south gate straight on Iowa Ave to L exit to AAF. Comm Pax Term and comm flts at the AAF. All the support of a large fort available at nearby Fort Leonard Wood			

SCHEDULED FLIGHTS

DESTINATION	ROUTING	FREQ	EQ/CMTS
Buckley ANGB CO (BKF)	TBN-BKF-BLV	Tu,Th	C009A/ME
Scott AFB IL (BLV)	TBN-BKF-BLV	Tu,Th	C009A/ME

UNSCHEDULED FLIGHTS

Flts to E and SE CONUS via C-12A and C-21A aircraft. Call for destinations, routings, and schedules.

MISSOURI

Lambert St. Louis International Airport (STL)

Det 2, 60 APS
PO Box 10305
St Louis, MO 63145-0305

Comm: 314-263-6269
ATVN: 693-6269

LOCATION: Twelve miles NW of St Louis, on I-70. Airport is also accessible from I-170. RM: p-53, D/6. NMC: St Louis, 12 mi SE.

FACILITIES	LOCATION	HOURS	PHONE	COMMENTS
PAX TERM INFO	MAC counter is on upper level of main terminal near exit 5. 0800-2400 dly C-263-6269, A-693-6270			
Recording	MAC Center	24 hrs dly	C-263-6262, A-693-6262	
Pax Paging	MAC Center	0800-2400 dly	C-263-6269	
PAX LOUNGES General	Lambert IAP Pax Svc A/C, TV, O/S seats, Rest-rms, Lockers, Game rm, Read/write rm (USO), Coffee/tea srvd (USO), Nursery (USO)			
DV/VIP	Lambert IAP	Limited hrs	C-263-6269	Check with Pax Svc.
Protocol Svc	Scott AFB IL C-618-744-1200, A-7-638-4313 (fm STL)			
Family	Nursery avail at USO, west end of arrival level C-429-1234			
FOOD SERVICE Cafeteria	Located in west end, upper level, of Lambert IAP 24 hrs dly			
Restaurants	Located at west end, upper level, of main Term			
Snack Bars	Located on all levels of the main Term			
TRANSPORTATION Air Tickets	SE end, upper-level, main Term, near Exit 5 C-263-6269			
Bus(Comm) (Shuttle)	Service counter on arrival level, Exit 13 To & fm Scott AFB-no charge C-256-4042,A-7-638-3066 (fm STL)			
Car Rentals	Arrival level, near Exit 11 24 hrs dly			
Limo Service	Lower level, near Exit 6. Departs approx every 15 mins for hotels & downtown. Call for rates C-256-3066, A-638-3066.			
TAXI(Comm)	Lower level 24 hrs dly C-427-9348			
Parking	Short term-across from Term 24 hrs dly; long term-marked. .5 mi W (bus to Term). Valet parking upper level C-426-8070.			
OTHER SERVICES Hair Styles	Arrival level 0800-1700 dly C-423-3222 Near Concourse B			
Medical	Lower level, west end		First Aid	
Postal	Lower level, west end, near Exit 6			
WIRE	Western Union avail on "will-call" basis C-429-4999			

MISSOURI
Lambert St. Louis Intl Arpt, Cont'd

TML	38 mi E of airport. Shuttle avail to Scott AFB Bldg 1510 0800-2400 dly C-618-215-2045, A-576-2045 (From STL) All Ranks A-576-3224. DV/VIP A-576-6555.
TRAVELERS AID ARC	STL C-658-2061 Scott AFB C-256-3291, A-576-3291
Lost/Found	MAC counter 0800-1600 dly C-263-6404 1-800-367-5458
USO	Arrival level, west end, main Term 24 hrs dly C-429-1234
ATTRACTIONS	St Louis (nearby) and Mississippi River

SCHEDULED FLIGHTS

DESTINATION	ROUTING	FREQ	EQ/CMTS
Clark AB RP (CRK)	STL-LAX-ANC-DNA-CRK	Tu	B747/P/CC
Kadena AB JA (DNA)	STL-LAX-ANC-DNA-CRK	Tu	B747/P/CC
Los Angeles Intl CA (LAX)	STL-LAX-ANC-DNA-CRK	Tu	B747/P/CC
Metro Oakland Intl CA (OAK)	STL-OAK-OKO-OSN	M,W	B747/P/CC
Osan AB RK (OSN)	STL-OAK-OKO-OSN	M,W	B747/P/CC
Philadelphia Intl PA (PHL)	STL-PHL-FRF	F	B747/P/CC
Rhein Main AB GE (FRF)	STL-FRF STL-PHL-FRF	Tu F	DC-10/B747/P/CC DC-10/B747/P/CC
Yokota AB JA (OKO)	STL-OAK-OKO-OSN	M,W	B747/P/CC

Rosecrans Memorial Airport (STJ)
139th TAG/DO (ANG)
Pony Express Station
St Joseph, MO 64503-3247

Comm: 816-271-1300
ATVN: 720-9210

LOCATION: From US-36 E or W exit N on KS-238. Straight 1.5 mi to airport entrance. RM: p-54, B/1. NMC: St Joseph, 3 mi SE.

FACILITIES	LOCATION HOURS PHONE COMMENTS
PAX TERM INFO	Bldg 017 Squadron Operations 0730-1600 dly C-271-1260, A-720-9260. Ask SP for ANG facility. All support facilities of a regional airport. Main gate open 24 hrs dly C-271-9315.

MISSOURI

Rosecrans Memorial Arpt, Cont'd

UNSCHEDULED FLIGHTS

Flts via C-130H aircraft to CONUS stations. Call for destinations, routings, and schedules.

MONTANA

Malmstrom Air Force Base (GFA)
341st CSG/OTM
Malmstrom AFB, MT 59402-5000

Comm: 406-731-9990
ATVN: 632-1110

LOCATION: From I-15 N or S take 10th Ave S exit to AFB. From E take Malmstrom exit off US-87/89 to AFB. Clearly marked. RM: p-57, P/22. NMC: Great Falls, 1 mi W.

FACILITIES	LOCATION	HOURS	PHONE	COMMENTS
PAX TERM INFO	Bldg 360 Base Ops 24 hrs dly C-731-2290/2445, A-632-2290/2445 From main gate straight on Goddard Ave to R on Ave D to Base Operations. Right at flight line.			
Pax Svc Ofc	Bldg 360	24 hrs dly	C-731-2290	NCO on duty
PAX LOUNGES General	Limited lounge facilities in Base Operations Bldg 360 24 hrs dly C-731-2290 Bag check, Tel L&ATVN, Rest-rooms, Overstuffed seats			
Protocol Svc	Bldg 160	Duty hrs	C-731-9990	
FOOD SERVICE	Good on Base. Dining Hall C-731-9990, NCO/CPO C-761-4155, O'Club C-761-6431, Snack Bar C-727-0671, C-731-2494			
TRANSPORTATION	Limited on Base. Air Tickets C-731-2934, Bus(Comm) C-727-0382, Car Rental C-761-7610, Taxi(Comm) C-453-3241 (Gov) C-731-3763, Parking at Base Ops (no restrictions)			
OTHER SERVICES	Good on Base. Exchange C-454-1301, Barber C-761-8131, Beauty C-452-2552, Laundry/DryC C-453-1031, Medical C-731-3483, Postal C-761-4980.			
TML	Bldg 1680 24 hrs dly C-731-3394, A-632-3394 All Ranks. DV/VIP C-731-9990.			
TRAVELERS AID	Good on Base. ARC C-727-2212, Chaplain C-731-3721/22, Emerg Relief C-731-3132, Sec Police C-731-3892			
ATTRACTIONS	Snow skiing, Yellowstone & Glacier National Parks			

SCHEDULED FLIGHTS

DESTINATION	ROUTING	FREQ	EQ/CMTS
Scott AFB IL (BLV)	GFA-MUO-BKF-BLV	F	C009A/ME
Travis AFB CA (SUU)	GFA-SKA-TCM-SUU	W	C009A/ME

NEBRASKA

Offutt Air Force Base (OFF)
55th TRANS/LGTTAP
Offutt AFB, NE 68113-5000

Comm: 402-294-1110
ATVN: 271-1110

LOCATION: From I-80 exit to US-73/75 S to AFB exit, 6.5 mi S of I-80/US-73/75 interchange. RM: p-59, L/24. NMC: Omaha, 98 mi N.

FACILITIES	LOCATION	HOURS	PHONE	COMMENTS
PAX TERM INFO	Bldg T-47	0500-2100 M-F, 0700-1900 Sa-Su	C-294-3757/6235, A-271-3757/6235	There are 5 gates. Ask SP for directions. From SAC gate, straight on Lincoln Highway to Pax Term on R.
Pax Svc Ofc	Bldg T-47	See Pax Term	C-294-3757/6235	NCO on duty
PAX LOUNGES General	No separate family lounge Bldg T-47	See Pax Term	C-294-3757	A/C, Tel L&LD, TV, Read/write rooms, Rest-rooms, P/C seats
DV/VIP	Base Ops	See Pax Term	C-294-3207	
Protocol Svc	Bldg 500	0730-1630 M-F	C-294-2212	(07+) SAC
FOOD SERVICE Cafeteria	Good on and off Base Bldg 165	1000-1800 M-F, 1700 Sa-Su	C-291-9596	
Dining Hall	Bldg 404	0500-0100 dly	C-294-3980	Will serve retirees.
Enl Club	Bldg 418	1000-2200 Su-Th, 0100 F-Sa	C-291-6785	
NCO/CPO Club	Bldg 132	1100-2100 dly	C-292-1600	
OFC Club	Bldg 462	1100-2100 dly	C-292-1560	
In-Flight	Bldg 404	24 hrs dly	C-294-5755	Meal only with boarding pass
Snack Bars	Bldg 64	24 hrs dly	C-291-9596	
Vending	Bldg T-47	See Pax Term	C-294-3757	
TRANSPORTATION Air Tickets	Good on and off Base Bldg 500, Rm 188 Bldg T-47	0730-1730 M-F 0745-1645 M-F	C-294-3333 C-294-5045	SATO
Bus(Comm) (Shuttle)	Bldg T-47 Bldg T-47	0800-1700 dly 0530-1730 M-F	C-294-3757 C-294-4375	2 trips daily
Car Rentals	Bldg 165	1000-1800 M-F, 1700 Sa-Su	C-292-9676	BX
Limo Service	Bldg T-47	24 hrs dly	C-342-8000	Airport limo
TAXI(Comm) (Gov)	Bldg T-47 Bldg T-47	24 hrs dly 24 hrs dly	Checker=C-342-8000 Yellow=C-341-9000 C-294-4375/6 Duty Pax only	
Parking	Bldg T-45 24 hrs dly.	Short term-15 minutes at Term; long term- Security Police C-294-6110.		

NEBRASKA

Offutt AFB, Cont'd

OTHER SERVICES			
Exchange	Good on and off Base Bldg 165 1000-2100 M-F, 1700 Sa-Su C-291-9100		
Bank/Exc	BX area 0900-1600 M-F, 1200 Sa C-291-1400 Bellevue		
Hair Styles	Bldg 165 0730-1800 M-F, 1700 Sa C-291-8521 Barber C-292-1520 Beauty		
Laundry/DryC	Bldg 162 0730-1800 M-F, 1700 Sa C-292-1232		
Medical	Bldg 4000 24 hrs dly C-294-3000		
Postal	Bldg 137 0830-1630 M-F, 1200 Sa C-294-3523		
TML	Bldg 44 24 hrs dly C-294-3671/9000, A-271-3671/9000 All Ranks. DV/VIP C-294-4461.		
TRAVELERS AID			
ARC	Many agencies available Bldg C 24 hrs dly C-294-3600		
Chaplain	SAC chapel 0730-1730 M-F C-294-6244 Other hrs C-294-1110		
Emerg Relief	Bldg C 0730-1730 M-F C-294-3600 Air Force Aid		
Lost/Found	Bldg T-47 See Pax Term C-294-3757		
Sec Police	Main gate 24 hrs dly C-294-6110		
ATTRACTIONS	City of Omaha, steaks, zoo, art and music		

SCHEDULED FLIGHTS

DESTINATION	ROUTING	FREQ	EQ/CMTS
Andrews AFB MD (ADW)	OFF-ADW	3 daily	C-21A/ C-135/P
Barksdale AFB LA (BAD)	OFF-BAD	1 weekly	C-21A
Kelly AFB FL (VPS)	OFF-SKF	1 weekly	C-21A
McClellan AFB CA (MCC)	OFF-MCC	2 weekly	C-21A
Norton AFB CA (SBD)	OFF-SBD	2 weekly	C-21A
Peterson CO (COS)	OFF-COS	2 weekly	C-21A
Randolph AFB TX (RND)	OFF-RND	1 weekly	C-21A
Scott AFB IL (BLV)	OFF-BLV	2 weekly	C-21A

NEBRASKA
Offutt AFB, Cont'd

Wright-Pattrsn AFB OH (FFO)	OFF-FFO	2 weekly	C-21A

Note: New flt schedules received daily. Flts confirmed 24 hrs in adv. Flts to other CONUS & OCONUS destinations. Call for destns, routings, & schedules.

NEVADA

Fallon Naval Air Station (NFL)
Field Services
Fallon NAS, NV 89406-5000

Comm: 702-426-5161
ATVN: 830-2110

LOCATION: From US-50 exit to US-95 S at Fallon, for 5 mi to left on Union St to NAS. RM: p-60, G/4. NMC: Reno, 72 mi W.

FACILITIES	LOCATION	HOURS	PHONE	COMMENTS
PAX TERM INFO	Hangar 400	0630-2245 M-F, 0800-1800 Sa, 1200-1700 Su C-426-3415, A-830-3415 From main gate to 4-way stop, R for 2 miles to L at Navy Lodge.		
Pax Svc Ofc	Hangar 400	See Pax Term for hrs	C-426-3415	
Pax Paging	Hangar 400	See Pax Term for hrs	C-426-3415	
PAX LOUNGES General	No separate family or DV/VIP lounges Hangar 400 See Pax Term for hrs C-426-3415 A/C, Bag Ck coffee/tea svd, Tel L, LD, ATVN, TV, Rest-rms, shws, O/S sts			
Protocol Svc	Hangar 400	See Pax Term for hrs	C-426-3415	See Master Chief P/O
FOOD SERVICE	Good on and off Base. Cafeteria C-426-2501, Enl Club C-426-2482, NCO/CPO Club C-426-2453, O'Club C-426-2454, Restaurant C-426-2449, Snack Bars C-426-2818, Vending C-426-3415			
TRANSPORTATION	Limited on and off Base. Car Rentals C-426-2583, Taxi(Comm) C-426-5317, Parking C-426-3415			
OTHER SERVICES	Good on Base. Exchange C-426-2818, Bank/Exc C-426-2500, Hair Styles C-426-2547, Laundry/DryC C-426-2818, Medical C-426-3100, Postal C-426-2738			
TML	Navy Lodge 0800-1600 dly C-426-2817, A-830-2817 All Ranks. DV/VIP C-426-5161/2520			
TRAVELERS AID	Good on Base. ARC C-426-2813, Chaplain C-426-2813, Emerg Relief C-426-2739, Lost/Found C-426-3415, Sec Pol C-426-2803			
ATTRACTIONS	Reno and Lake Tahoe nearby			

SCHEDULED FLIGHTS

DESTINATION	ROUTING	FREQ	EQ/CMTS
Alameda NAS CA (NGZ)	NGZ-NFL-NGZ	1/Th	C009A/M

NEVADA

Fallon NAS, Cont'd

UNSCHEDULED FLIGHTS

Freq flts to: Alameda NAS CA (NGZ); Barbers Point NAS HI (NAX); Cecil Field NAS FL (NZC); Chase Field NAS TX (NIR); Cherry Point MCAS NC (NKT); China Lake NWC Arpt CA (NID); Dover AFB DE (DOV); El Toro MCAS CA (NZJ); Jacksonville NAS FL (NIP); Lemoore NAS CA (NLC); McChord AFB WA (TCM); Meridian NAS MS (NMM); Miramar NAS CA (NKX); Nellis AFB NV (LSV); New Orleans NAS LA (NBG); Norfolk NAS VA (NGU); North Island NAS CA (NZY); Oceana NAS VA (NTU); Pensacola NAS FL (NPA); Point Mugu NAS CA (NTD); Travis AFB CA (SUU); Whidbey NAS WA (NUW); Yuma MCAS AZ (YUM). Flts are via C-5A/B, C-9B, C-12A, C-141B, and P-13A. Call for destinations, routings, and schedules.

Nellis Air Force Base (LSV)
Air Ops, USAF TFWC
Nellis AFB, NV 89191-5000

Comm: 702-652-1110
ATVN: 682-1110

LOCATION: Off I-15. Also accessible from US-91/93. Clearly marked. RM: p-60, N/10. NMC: Las Vegas, 8 mi SW.

FACILITIES	LOCATION	HOURS	PHONE	COMMENTS
PAX TERM INFO	Bldg 1044	0730-1630 dly	C-652-1854/1860	
	From Main gate straight on Fitzgerald Blvd to L on "D" St, R on Depot Rd to Pax Term on L.			
Pax Svc Ofc	Bldg 1044	0730-1630 dly	C-652-1854	NCO on duty
Pax Paging	Bldg 1044	0730-1630 dly	C-652-1854	
PAX LOUNGES	Limited lounge facilities.			No separate family lounge.
	Bldg 1044	0730-1630 dly	C-652-1854	General/DV/VIP
Protocol Svc	Bldg 166	0800-1700 M-F	C-652-2987	
FOOD SERVICE	Good on and off Base. Dining Hall C-652-2800, Enl Club C-652-9732, O'Club C-652-2582			
TRANSPORTATION	Limited on Base. Air Tickets C-644-5400, Taxi(Comm) C-643-1041 (Gov) C-652-1843, Parking C-652-1844 (across from Term)			
OTHER SERVICES	Good on and off Base. Exchange C-644-2062, Bank/Exc C-385-8150, Medical C-652-1847, Postal C-652-2769			
TML	Bldg 502	24 hrs dly	C-652-2710	
TRAVELERS AID	Good on and off Base. ARC C-643-2106, Chaplain C-652-2950, AF Aid C-652-9430, Lost/Found C-652-2311, Sec Pol C-652-2311			
ATTRACTIONS	Las Vegas, Lake Mead, Thunderbirds			

SCHEDULED FLIGHTS

DESTINATION	ROUTING	FREQ	EQ/CMTS
Luke AFB AZ (LUF)	LSV-LUF-SBD	2/F	C-141B/M
Norton AFB CA (SBD)	LSV-SBD	2/Su	C-141B/M
	LSV-LUF-SBD	2/F	C-141B/M

NEVADA
Nellis AFB, Cont'd

| Travis AFB CA (SUU) | LSV-SUU | Th | C-141B/M |

UNSCHEDULED FLIGHTS

Numerous unscheduled flights, especially during exercise weekends, to various locations throughout CONUS. Call for destinations, routings, and schedules.

NEW HAMPSHIRE

Pease Air Force Base (PSM)
509TH LGT/LGTT
Pease AFB, NH 03803-5000

Comm: 603-430-0100
ATVN: 852-1110

LOCATION: From I-95 N to Spaulding Turnpike (exit #4). N on Spaulding Trpk to Exit #1. Left to AFB. RM: P-61, O/12. NMC: Portsmouth, 3 mi NE.

FACILITIES	LOCATION	HOURS	PHONE	COMMENTS
PAX TERM INFO	Bldg 237 0800-1700 M-F C-430-2103, A-852-2103 From main gate straight on Newington Rd to L on Franklin Ave to Pax Term on R between control towers (after fire station) Pax reps open Terminal for after-hours flights.			
Recording	Bldg 237 1700-0800 M-F, wknds 24 hrs C-430-2103, A-852-2103. Weekly flight schedule available after 1600 F.			
Pax Svc Ofc	Bldg 237	0800-1700 dly	C-430-2103	NCO on duty
PAX LOUNGES General	No separate family lounge Bldg 237 0800-1700 dly C-430-2103 Small facility Rest-rms, TV, P/C seats, O/S couches, Magazine rack			
Protocol Svc	Bldg 47	Duty hrs	C-852-0100	Chief of Staff
FOOD SERVICE In-flight	Many off Base. Limited on Base. Bldg 60 24 hrs dly C-430-2670 In-flight meals must be ordered and picked up prior to Space-A show time.			
Dining Hall	Bldg 46 0600-0100 dly C-430-2670 4th meal Call for svc hrs.			
NCO/CPO Club	Bldg 26	1100-2100 dly	C-430-3559	Call for svc hrs.
OFC Club	Bldg 99	1130-2130 dly	C-430-2558	Call for svc hrs.
Snack Bars	Bldg 238 (Base Ops), Bldg 28 (Bowling Center), Bldg 115 (BX). Call for hours.			
Vending	Bldg 238	24 hrs dly		Sodas only
TRANSPORTATION Air Tickets	Bldg 31	0800-1430 M-F	C-430-3229	SATO
Bus (Comm)	Portsmouth NH. Greyhound & Trailways to all locations & from Park Square Bus Terminal in Boston MA.			
Car Rentals	Portsmouth, Manchester, and Boston			
Limo Service	Front gate 24 hrs dly C-964-7111 Local Svc to Logan IAP, Boston ($16 one way, $26 round trip)			

NEW HAMPSHIRE
Pease AFB, Cont'd

TAXI(Gov)	Bldg 79 Off Base	24 hrs dly 24 hrs dly	C-430-3588 C-436-7500/0008/7111/7777
Parking	Short term-in front of Pax Term; long term-billeting office parking lot (bldg #96). Pick up parking form at Pax Term.		
OTHER SERVICES Exchange	Many support facilities on and off Base Bldg 115	0900-2100 M-Sa, 1200-1700 Su	C-436-0302
Bank/Exc	Bldg 115	0900-2100 M-F, 1200-1700 Sa	C-436-0537/7592
Hair Styles	Bldg 115	0800-1800 Tu-F C-436-2903 0900-1600 M-Sa C-431-5660	Barber Beauty
Laundry/DryC	Bldg 31	0830-1700 M-F, 1400-1700 Sa	C-436-4057
Medical	Bldg 93	24 hrs dly	C-430-3752, C-430-2333 (Emerg)
Postal	Bldg 4	0800-1600 M-F	C-430-2628
TML	Bldg 96	24 hrs dly C-430-3385, A-852-3385 DV/VIP C-430-3385/3426.	
TRAVELERS AID ARC	Many agencies Bldg 5 Bldg 79 1000-1400 M-F	C-430-3330 Family Services C-436-7716	
Chaplain	Bldg 25	Duty hrs	C-430-2343
Lost/Found	Bldg 79	24 hrs dly	C-430-2747
Sec Police	Bldg 79	24 hrs dly	C-430-2747/48 or CB-Channel 9
USO	Logan IAP (BOS) ground level C-617-567-9330		
ATTRACTIONS	Portsmouth, sea coast, snow skiing, camping, fishing		

SCHEDULED FLIGHTS

DESTINATION	ROUTING	FREQ	EQ/CMTS
Andrews AFB MD (ADW)	ADW-BLV-PSM-ADW	Tu,F	C009A/ME
RAF Fairford UK (FFD)	PSM-FFD	1-2 flts ea wk	KC-135E/M *
RAF Mildenhall UK (MHZ)	PSM-MHZ	1-2 flts ea wk	KC-135E/M **

Note: * No retirees into Fairford.
     ** May be weeks with no overseas flights.

UNSCHEDULED FLIGHTS

Many flights to CONUS, OCONUS, and foreign countries via AF KC-135E/KC-10A acft and ANG/AFRES acft to both active AF and ANG/AFRES bases. Call for other destinations, routings, and schedules.

NEW JERSEY

Lakehurst Naval Air Engineering Center (NEL)
Air Department, ATC Code 3022
Lakehurst NAEC, NJ 08733-5085

Comm: 201-323-2011
ATVN: 624-1110

LOCATION: From Garden State Parkway take NJ-70 W to junction of NJ-547. Turn R and go 1 mi to Base. RM: p-63, 0/11. NMC: Trenton, 30 mi NW.

FACILITIES	LOCATION	HOURS	PHONE	COMMENTS
PAX TERM INFO	Bldg 307 0700-1700 M-F C-323-2316, A-624-2316 From main gate straight to first stop sign, turn R then L on next street to stop sign, L to Pax Term. Full Base support. Also ERADCOM Army Aviation C-323-2112, A-624-2112			
PAX LOUNGES General	Limited lounge facilities Bldg 307, 2nd deck 0700-1700 M-F C-323-2316 A/C, Tel L&A, Rest-rms, Showers, P/C seats			
DV/VIP	Bldg 307, 2nd deck 0700-1700 M-F C-323-2316 A/C, Coffee/tea srvd, Tel L&A, Rest-rms, Showers, P/C seats			

UNSCHEDULED FLIGHTS

Flights via Navy administrative aircraft and Army C-12A and C-21A aircraft to CONUS East Coast locations. Call for destinations, routings, and schedules.

McGuire Air Force Base (WRI)
438th Aerial Port Squadron/TROP
McGuire Air Force Base, NJ 08641-5000

Comm: 609-724-1110
ATVN: 440-0111

LOCATION: From NJ Turnpike, Exit 7 to NJ-68 SE to AFB. Adjacent to Fort Dix. Clearly marked. RM: p-63, 0/9. NMC: Trenton, 18 mi NW.

FACILITIES	LOCATION	HOURS	PHONE	COMMENTS
PAX TERM INFO	Bldg 1706 0600-2400 dly C-724-2526, A-440-2526. Fm main gate straight through 1st & 2nd circle. Pax Term in front of 2nd circle. Space-A desk, 1st floor, manned 0600-2400 hrs.			
Recording	Bldg 1706 24 hrs dly C-724-3671, A-440-3671 Updated 0800			
Pax Svc Ofc	Bldg 1706 0600-2400 dly C-724-2810, A-440-2810 SP-A desk			
Pax Paging	Bldg 1706 24 hrs dly C-724-2864, A-440-2864 SP-A desk			
PAX LOUNGES General	Bldg 1706 1st floor 0600-2400 dly C-724-3078 A/C, Bag lks, Game Rm, Tel C&A, TV, Rest-rms, Showers, P/C seats			
DV/VIP	Bldg 1706 1st floor 0600-2400 dly C-724-2749, A-440-2749 A/C, Bag lks, Coffee/tea srvd,R/W rms, Tel C&A, TV, Rest-rms, O/S seats.Check w/counter #1 f/access to lounge/Protocol svc.			
Family	Bldg 1706 1st floor 0600-2400 dly C-724-3078 Unmanned A/C, Bag lks, Tel C&A, Rest-rms, P/C seats, Play rm			

NEW JERSEY

McGuire AFB, Cont'd

FOOD SERVICE				
Cafeteria	Bldg 1706	24 hrs dly	C-723-5056	1st floor
Dining Hall	Bldg 2501	24 hrs dly	C-724-2450	Active Duty only
Enl Club	Bldg 2508	Call for hrs.	C-724-3737	
NCO/CPO Club	Bldg 2508	Call for hrs.	C-724-3188/2396	
OFC Club	Bldg 2705	Call for hrs.	C-724-3296	
Golf Course	Bldg 2003	Call for hrs.	C-724-2169	
TRANSPORTATION				
Auto Ship	Wrightstown	Call for hrs.	C-723-3632	Bell Trans
Air Tickets	Bldg 1706	0800-2100 M-F	C-723-1323	SATO
Bus(Comm)	Bldg 1706	Call for hrs.	C-723-3833	To PHL, NY, NJ
(Shuttle)	Bldg 1706	0600-1800 dly	C-724-2864, 0700-1700 every 1/2 hr to most locations on Base	
Car Rentals	Bldg 1706	0600-2400 dly	Some agencies on Base	
Limo Service	Bldg 1706	24 hrs dly	C-723-3220	
TAXI(Comm)	Bldg 1706	0600-2400 dly	C-723-2000	At Pax Term
Trains	Newark NJ	Call for hrs.	C-800-523-5700	AMTRAK
Parking	Bldg 1706	24 hrs dly	C-724-2001	Short and long term
OTHER SERVICES				
Bank/Exc	Bldg 2605	0900-1500 M-F	C-723-7770	
Exchange	Bldg 3452	1000-2100 M-Sa, 1730 Su	C-723-5190	
Hair Styles	Bldg 1706/3453	0900-1600 M-F, 1545 Su	C-723-4449 Barber C-723-7377 Beauty	
Medical	Bldg 2411	0730-1630 dly	C-724-3950, C-723-4000 Ambulance	
Postal	Bldg 2603	0900-1700 M-F, 1100 Sa	C-724-4687	
WIRE	On Fort Dix			
Valet/Dry C	Bldg 3453	1000-1700 M-Sa	C-723-6446	
TRAVELERS AID				
ARC	Bldg 2588	Call for hrs.	C-724-3086	
Chaplain	Bldg 2503	Duty hrs C-724-3811	After duty hrs EX-2000	
Emerg Relief	Bldg 2916	0800-1700 M-F	C-724-4353	
Lost/Found	Bldg 1706	0600-2400 dly	C-724-2526	
Retired Aff	Bldg 2916	Duty hrs	C-724-3388	
Sec Police	Bldg 1814	24 hrs dly	C-724-2001	

NEW JERSEY
McGuire AFB, Cont'd

ATTRACTIONS	Atlantic City NJ (short drive), Philadelphia PA, or CT

SCHEDULED FLIGHTS

DESTINATION	ROUTING	FREQ	EQ/CMTS
Goose Bay AB CN (YYR)	WRI-YYR-SFJ-THU	W	C-141B/M
Keflavik Arpt IC (KEF)	WRI-KEF-LGS WRI-KEF	Every other F Every other F	C-141B/C C-141B/M
Lajes Fld PO (LGS)	WRI-LGS	Su-W,F	C-141B/M
Norfolk NAS VA (NGU)	WRI-NGU WRI-NGU	3 ea wk 3 ea wk	C-141B/C C-141B/M
Pope AFB NC (POB)	WRI-POB	2 ea wk	C-130E/C
Rhein Main AB GE (FRF)	WRI-LGS-FRF-TOJ-ATH WRI-LGS-FRF WRI-LGS-FRF-TOJ-SIZ-ATH-ESB-ADA WRI-LGS-FRF-TOJ-SIZ-ATH-IGL-ADA WRI-FRF	Su-W,Th Su-W,Th Su-W,Th Su-W,Th Su-W,Th	C-141B/M C-141B/M C-141B/M C-141B/M C-141B/M
Sondrestrom AB DN (SFJ)	WRI-SFJ-THU WRI-YYR-SFJ-THU	M W	C-141B/C C-141B/M
Thule AB DN (THU)	WRI-YYT-THU WRI-YYR-SFJ-THU	M W	C-141B/M C-141B/M

UNSCHEDULED FLIGHTS

Unscheduled flights via C-141 aircraft to: Charleston AFB SC (CHS); Dover AFB DE (DOV); Patrick AFB FL (COF); Pope AFB NC (POB); and St John's Arpt CN (YYT).

Morristown Municipal Airport (MMU)
AMCCOM Aviation Detachment
Morristown, NJ 07960-5000

Comm: 201-724-4021
ATVN: 880-4021

LOCATION: From I-80 E or W to I-287 S, take Exit 35-B to NJ-10 E to 1st light. Turn R to end of road. Turn L, go to 3rd light, go L to Columbia Pike, airport entrance .25 mi L. RM: P-62, F/10. NMC: Morristown, 3 mi SE.

FACILITIES	LOCATION	HOURS	PHONE	COMMENTS
PAX TERM INFO	Aero Svc Term	0730-1600 M-F	C-538-6066, A-880-2493/4	After entering airport, first R, cross taxi-way, follow signs to Term on R. Full services of a regional airport. Complete Military Base spt at nearby Picatinny Arsenal, Dover, NJ.
PAX LOUNGES	Limited			

NEW JERSEY

Morristown Munic Arpt, Cont'd

General	Aero Term 0600-2400 dly C-538-8505 A/C, Tel L&LD, Restrooms, Showers, O/S seats
Protocol Svc	AMCCOM 0730-1600 M-F C-724-7025

UNSCHEDULED FLIGHTS

Flts via U-21A and UH-1H aircraft to: Davison AAF VA (DAA); Quad-City Arpt IL (MLI); and other CONUS locations. Call for destinations, routings, and schedules.

NEW MEXICO

Kirtland Air Force Base (ABQ) Comm: 505-844-0011
1606th ABW/MAC OTMB   ATVN: 244-0011
Kirtland AFB, NM 87117-5000

LOCATION: From I-40 E, exit on Wyoming Blvd, S for 2 mi to Wyoming gate to AFB. RM: p-70, P/10. NMC: Albuquerque, 1 mi NE.

FACILITIES	LOCATION	HOURS	PHONE	COMMENTS
PAX TERM INFO	Bldg 333	0600-1800 M-F, 0800-1700 Sa-Su, C-844-0889, A-244-0889. From Carlisle gate straight on Carlisle Ave to R on Clark Ave to Pax Term on R. Carlisle gate 0600-1700. Truman gate after 1700. Ask for directions.		
Pax Svc Ofc	Bldg 333	See Pax Term	C-844-0889	NCO on duty
Pax Paging	Bldg 333	See Pax Term	C-844-9070	Base Ops
PAX LOUNGES DV/VIP	Adequate lounge facilities. General lounge available. Bldg 333 0600-2200 dly C-844-9070 Next to Base Ops desk A/C, coffee/tea srvd, Sep R/W rms, Rest-rms, TV, O/S seats			
Protocol Svc	Bldg 333	0600-2200 dly	C-844-9070	(O6+) MAC
FOOD SERVICE Cafeteria	Good on and off Base Bldg 20206	0630-1300 Tu-Sa	C-265-4304	
Dining Hall	Bldg 923W	0500-0100 dly	C-844-0011	
Enl Club	Bldg 20255	0600-2400 dly	C-844-5611	
NCO/CPO Club	Bldg 20255 Bldg 201	0600-2400 dly 0600-2400 dly	C-844-7512 C-844-3488	Call for svc hrs. Call for svc hrs.
OFC Club	Bldg 202000 Bldg 1900	0600-2400 dly 0600-2400 dly	C-844-7512 C-844-3488	Call for svc hrs. Call for svc hrs.
Snack Bars	Bldg 20170	1000-1800 dly	C-265-3679/7301	
Vending	Bldg 333	0600-2200 dly	C-265-3679/7301	
TRANSPORTATION Air Tickets	Very limited on Base Bldg 333	0715-1600 M-F	C-844-0511	SATO

NEW MEXICO
Kirtland AFB, Cont'd

Bus(Comm)	Albuquerque-Greyhound
Trains	Albuquerque is a major AMTRAK stop.
Parking	Bldg 333 24 hrs dly C-844-4618 West side of Term
OTHER SERVICES Exchange	Many available in areas 1, 2, and 3 Bldg 20170 1000-1800 dly C-265-3679
Bank/Exc	Bldg 426 0800-1500 M-F C-844-0011 KFCU
Hair Styles	Bldg 20170 1000-1800 dly C-265-3679
Laundry/DryC	Bldg 20170 1000-1800 dly C-265-3679
Medical	Bldg 20140 24 hrs dly C-844-4611
Postal	Bldg 926 0800-1445 M-F C-844-6688
TML	Bldg 22010 24 hrs dly C-844-2936/0561 A-244-2936/0561 All Ranks. DV/VIP C-844-1606.
TRAVELERS AID	Bldg 20685 Rm 114 0900-1500 M-F C-844-0011 Family Services
Chaplain	Bldg 589 0800-1700 M-F C-844-2011
Emerg Relief	Bldg 20201 Rm 112 0800-1700 M-F C-844-0011 Air Force Aid
Sec Police	Bldg 20219 24 hrs dly C-844-4618
ATTRACTIONS	National Atomic Museum, Albuquerque

UNSCHEDULED FLIGHTS

Freq flts to: Andrews AFB MD (ADW); Davis-Monthan AFB AZ (DMA); Hill AFB UT (HIF); Kelly AFB TX (SKF); Norton AFB CA (SBD); Offutt AFB NE (OFF); Randolph AFB TX (RND); Scott AFB IL (BLV); Travis AFB CA (SUU), Wright-Patterson AFB OH (FFO). Several flts weekly to each location. Other flts to CONUS locations. A MAC training base. Call for destinations, routings, and schedules.

NEW YORK

Griffiss Air Force Base (RME)
416th Bomb Wing, Air Operations
Griffiss AFB, NY 13441-5000

Comm: 315-330-1110
ATVN: 587-1110

LOCATION: Off NY-49 in Rome. Entrance off NY-49 and from Chestnut St, Floyd St, and E Dominick St. RM: p-67, EK/8. NMC: Utica, 17 mi SE.

FACILITIES	LOCATION	HOURS	PHONE	COMMENTS
PAX TERM INFO	Base Ops Bldg 100.	24 hrs dly	C-330-7400/7450, A-587-7400/7450	
	Ask for directions at main gate.			
Recording	Bldg 100	24 hrs dly	330-2089	

NEW YORK

Griffiss AFB, Cont'd

Pax Svc Ofc	Base Ops	24 hrs dly	C-330-7400/7450	NCO on duty
PAX LOUNGES	Pax lounge. All Pax processed by Base Ops.			
FOOD SERVICE Cafeteria	Limited on Base Bldg 1	0700-1530 M-F	C-330-0700	
Dining Hall	Bldg 400	0800-2300 dly	C-330-7097	
NCO/CPO Club	Bldg 272	1100-2100 M-F,	0100 Sa-Su	C-330-5075
OFC Club	Bldg 724	1130-2230 M-F,	2400 Sa-Su	C-330-7915
Restaurants	Ask at gate. 1100-2200 dly		C-330-7945	
TRANSPORTATION Air Tickets	Limited on Base Depot 1	0800-1700 M-F	C-330-7183	SATO
TAXI(Comm) (Gov)	IAP & Oneida County Airport Bldg T-9	24 hrs dly	C-330-1110 C-330-3541	
Parking	Bldg 100	24 hrs dly	No restrictions	
OTHER SERVICES Exchange	Bldg 1	1000-1730 M-F,	1600 Sa-Su	C-330-0700
Bank/Exc	Bldg 311	0900-1600 M-F	C-339-0300	
Hair Styles	Bldg 1	0800-1700 M-F,	1500 Sa-Su	C-330-0700
Laundry/DryC	Bldg 1	0800-1700 M-F,	1500 Sa	C-339-2259
Medical	USAF Hospital	24 hrs dly	C-330-4108	
Postal	Bldg 310	0800-1700 M-F	C-330-1110	
TML	Bldg 704 All Ranks.	24 hrs dly DV/VIP	C-330-4391, A-587-4391 C-330-4391.	
TRAVELERS AID ARC	Bldg 428 Bldg 14	0900-1500 M-F 0930-1430 M-F	C-330-2031 Family Services C-330-2942	
Chaplain	Chapel Center 0800-1600 M-F C-330-3017			
Emerg Relief	Bldg 14	0800-1600 M-F	C-330-4488 AF Aid	
Sec Police	Bldg 308	24 hrs dly	C-330-7174/4455	
ATTRACTIONS	Erie Canal Village, Sports Hall of Fame			

SCHEDULED FLIGHTS

DESTINATION	ROUTING	FREQ	EQ/CMTS
Andrews AFB MD (ADW)	RME-ADW-FFO	Tu or W	C009A/ME
RAF Fairford UK (FFD)	RME-PSM-FFD	1 ea mo	KC-135E/M

NEW YORK

Griffiss AFB, Cont'd

Pease AFB NH (PSM)	RME-PSM-FFD RME-ADW-FFO	1 ea mo Tu or W	KC-135E/M C009A/ME
Wright- Patterson AFB OH (FFO)	RME-ADW-FFO	Tu or W	C009A/ME

Note: Call for other destinations, routings, and schedules. One to two days notice prior to flights.

Niagara Falls International Airport (IAG)   Comm: 716-236-2000
914th Tactical Airlift Group/OTM   ATVN: 489-3011
Niagara Falls IAP, NY 14304-5000

LOCATION: From I-190 N or S exit to NY-182 E to IAP entrance off Lockport Rd. RM: p-68, WB/4. NMC: Niagara Falls, 5 mi W.

FACILITIES	LOCATION	HOURS	PHONE	COMMENTS
PAX TERM INFO	Bldg 800	0800-1600 M-F	C-236-2174/2161, A-489-2174/2161. From main gate, L on Kirkbridge Dr to Bldg 800.	
PAX LOUNGES	No Pax lounges. All Pax processed in Ops (East wing) of HQ Bldg 800. Minimum essential. Rest-rooms.			
Protocol Svc	Bldg 800	0800-1600 M-F	C-236-2138	PAO
FOOD SERVICE Snack Bars	Limited on Base Bldg 314 Bldg 206	1130-2100 dly 0800-1900 M-F	C-297-6604/5 C-236-2329	Cons'd Open Mess In Recreation Ctr
Vending	Bldg 800	0800-1600 M-F	Beverages only	
TRANSPORTATION Parking	Full transportation facilities at commercial side of IAP Limited - by arrangement with Security Police			
OTHER SERVICES Exchange	Limited on Base Bldg 805	1030-1700 Tu-F, 0930-1700 Sa	C-236-2100	
TML	Bldg 312	0730-2300 dly	C-236-2014, A-489-2014	
TRAVELERS AID Sec Police	Main gate	24 hrs dly	C-236-2279	
ATTRACTIONS	Beautiful Niagara Falls, Lake Erie, Lake Ontario			

UNSCHEDULED FLIGHTS

Frequent flts via C-130E aircraft to CONUS locations and less frequent flts to Europe & Panama locations. Call for destinations, routings, & schedules.

Plattsburgh Air Force Base (PBG)   Comm: 518-565-5000
380th CSG/OTM   ATVN: 689-5000
Plattsburgh AFB, NY 12903-5000

LOCATION: From I-87 take exit 36. Directions to AFB are clearly marked. RM: p-67, EC/15. NMC: Burlington, 20 mi SE.

NEW YORK

Plattsburgh AFB, Cont'd

FACILITIES	LOCATION	HOURS	PHONE	COMMENTS
PAX TERM INFO	Bldg 2712	24 hr dly	C-565-5441/2, A-689-5441/2	
	From main gate straight on New York Rd to L on Idaho Ave to ATC tower/Base Ops on R.			
Pax Svc Ofc	Bldg 2712	24 hrs dly	C-565-5441/5521	NCO on duty
PAX LOUNGES	Limited. Adjacent to Base Ops dispatch counter. General and DV/VIP C-565-5441, Protocol Service C-565-5173			
FOOD SERVICE	Good on and off Base. Dining Hall C-565-7204, NCO/CPO Club C-563-3956, O'Club C-563-4780, Snack Bars C-565-5558			
TRANSPORTATION	Greyhound Bus and Amtrak in Plattsburg. Bus(Gov) C-565-5444, Taxi(Comm) C-561-2424/563-2121 (Gov) C-565-7555, Parking C-565-7191 (check with Security Police)			
OTHER SERVICES	Good on and off Base. Exchange C-561-6622/5219, Bank/Exc C-563-5667, Barber C-561-1160, Beauty C-561-4287, Laundry/DryC C-561-9659, Medical C-565-7223, Postal C-565-5554			
TML	Bldg 381	24 hrs dly	C-565-7614, A-689-7614 DV/VIP-C-565-5171	
TRAVELERS AID	AF Family Svcs C-565-7608, ARC C-565-7608 (other hrs C-561-7280), Chaplain C-565-5211 (other hrs C-565-7233), Lost/Found C-565-7191, Security Police C-565-7191			
ATTRACTIONS	Lake Champlain, snow-ski areas, Canada a short drive away			

UNSCHEDULED FLIGHTS

Frequent flts via KC-135E/M, C009A/ME aircraft to CONUS, OCONUS and foreign country locations. Flights known 30 days in advance. Call for destinations, routings, and schedules.

Schenectady County Airport (SCH)
109th Tactical Airlift Group (ANG)
Scotia, NY 12302-9752

Comm: 518-381-7420
ATVN: 974-9420

LOCATION: From I-87 N exit to NY-146 W. Continue on Lenridge Rd to Maple Ave. L to ANG Rd. RM: p-67, ET/2. NMC: Schenectady, 3 mi S.

FACILITIES	LOCATION	HOURS	PHONE	COMMENTS
PAX TERM INFO	ANG Hangar	0800-1600 M-F	C-381-7420, A-974-9420	
	Ask gate guard for directions. All the support facilities of a regional airport. Limited military spt facilities.			

UNSCHEDULED FLIGHTS

Flights to CONUS locations via C-130H aircraft. Call for destinations, routings, and schedules.

Stewart International Airport (SWF)
105th Military Airlift Group (ANG)
Newburgh, NY 12550-0031

Comm: 914-563-2000
ATVN: 247-2000

NEW YORK
Stewart Intl Arpt, Cont'd

LOCATION: From I-87 take Newburgh exit to Rt 17-K W. Follow signs to Stewart ANG Base. RM: p-67, EU/13. NMC: New York City, 60 mi S.

FACILITIES	LOCATION	HOURS	PHONE	COMMENTS
PAX TERM INFO	Base Ops 24 hrs dly C-563-2286/2285, A-247-2286/2285 (ANG Ops). C-563-3298/3359/3478, A-247-3298 (Army Ops). Full Base support at the adjacent Stewart Army Sub-post. Limited Pax facilities. Is a United States IAP of entry. See Military Living's "US Forces Travel Guide USA & Caribbean Areas" for complete details. For general mil info call C-563-3552.			

UNSCHEDULED FLIGHTS

Some flights via Army C-12A aircraft. ANG flights via C-5A scheduled to begin in 1988. Call for destinations, routings, and schedules.

Suffolk County Air National Guard Base (FOK)
106th ARRG/Suffolk County Airport (ANG)
Westhampton Beach, NY 11978-1294

Comm: 516-288-4200
ATVN: 456-7216

LOCATION: On Long Island. One mi S of NY-27 (Sunrise Hwy), Exit 63 onto Old Riverhead Rd. RM: p-69, WO/20. NMC: Southhampton, 12 mi E.

FACILITIES	LOCATION	HOURS	PHONE	COMMENTS
PAX TERM INFO	Bldg 362 0730-1600 M-F C-288-4200, A-456-7216 Between large hangars, 1/8 mi fm main gate. All facilities of a regional airport. Ltd military support facilities. BX Bldg 348 1100-1400 M-Th C-288-4200-EX-357. Park near Bldg 362.			

UNSCHEDULED FLIGHTS

Flts via HC-130 aircraft to CONUS locations. Call for destinations, routings, and schedules.

Wheeler-Sack Army Airfield (GTB)
ATTN: AFZS-PTS
Fort Drum, NY 13602-5000

Comm: 315-785-5647
ATVN: 341-5647

LOCATION: From Syracuse, take I-81 N to exit 48, past Watertown, and follow signs to Fort Drum. RM: p-67, EG/6. NMC: Watertown, 8 mi SW.

FACILITIES	LOCATION	HOURS	PHONE	COMMENTS
PAX TERM INFO	Bldg P-2059 0700-1700 C-785-5681, A-341-5681 One mi E of main post. All Pax processed by Base Ops. DV/VIP lounge. All the facilities of a large post.			

UNSCHEDULED FLIGHTS

Flights to NE CONUS via U-21A and UH-1H aircraft. Call for destinations, routings, and schedules. Limited space-A.

NORTH CAROLINA

Charlotte/Douglas International Airport (CLT)

145th Tactical Airlift Group (ANG)
Charlotte, NC 28208-5000

Comm: 704-399-6363
ATVN: 583-9210

LOCATION: From I-77 N or S exit 6 A/B to Graham Parkway (US-521) N to IAP entrance L. RM: p-72, 0/9. NMC: Charlotte, 3 mi E.

FACILITIES	LOCATION	HOURS	PHONE	COMMENTS
PAX TERM INFO	ANG 24 hrs dly C-399-6363, A-583-9210 Ask SP for directions. No Pax facilities. All Pax processed by Base Ops. Full support of an IAP available. Limited military Base spt.			

UNSCHEDULED FLIGHTS

Flights via C-130A aircraft to CONUS and OCONUS locations on training missions. Call for destinations, routings, and schedules.

Cherry Point Marine Corps Air Station (NKT)

Transient Services Division
Airfield Operations Department
Cherry Point, NC 28533-5000

Comm: 919-466-4232
ATVN: 582-4232

LOCATION: On NC-101 between New Bern and Morehead City. US-70 connects with NC-101 at Havelock. RM: p-73, I/21. NMC: Jacksonville, 30 mi SW.

FACILITIES	LOCATION	HOURS	PHONE	COMMENTS
PAX TERM INFO	Bldg 199	0600-2300 dly	C-466-3225/3232/2379, A-582-3225	From main gate take Roosevelt Blvd to R on "A" St to end. Pax Service in ATC tower Bldg. Also, New River MCAS C-451-6197 helicopters only - very limited Space-A.
Pax Svc Ofc	Bldg 199	0730-1630 dly	C-466-3225, A-582-3225/2379	
Pax Paging	Bldg 199	0600-2300 dly	C-466-3225	Pax Svc NCO on duty
PAX LOUNGES General	No separate family lounge Bldg 199 0600-2300 dly C-466-3225 A/C, Bag check, Tel L&LD, Rest-rms, P/C seats			
DV/VIP	Bldg 199 0600-2300 dly C-466-3225 (06+) A/C, Bag check, Tel ATVN, Rest-rms, O/S seats			
Protocol Svc	Bldg 2	24 hrs dly	C-466-4232	Hq 2nd MC Airwing
FOOD SERVICE Cafeteria	Many facilities on and off Base Bldg 1691	0700-1830 M-F	C-466-4381	Soda fountain
Dining Hall	Map #17	0500-0100 dly	C-466-4232	4th meal Call for svc hrs.
Enl Club	Bldg 3542	1100-2400 dly	C-466-2997	(E5-) C/for svc hrs.
NCO/CPO Club	Bldg 499	1100-0100 dly	C-447-3430	(E6+) C/for svc hrs.

NORTH CAROLINA
Cherry Point MCAS, Cont'd

OFC Club	Bldg 491	0630-0100 dly	C-447-2303	Call for svc hrs.
Restaurants	Bldg 3918	1000-1630 dly	C-447-7041	"CP's Cafe"
Snack Bars	Bldg 199	0600-1800 M-F	C-466-3225	Top side of Pax Term
Vending	Bldg 199	0600-2300 dly	C-466-3225	Soda and snacks
TRANSPORTATION Air Tickets	Good on and off Base Bldg 298	0800-1600 M-F	C-466-2106	SATO
Bus(Comm)	Main gate	0900-1750 M-F, 1300 Sa	C-447-2391	Off Base
Car Rentals	In Havelock NC and major companies at New Bern Airport			
Limo Service	Bldg 199	On call from NKT to New Bern Airport $14		
TAXI(Comm)	Main gate 24 hrs dly Cherry Cab=C-447-3101 Union=C-447-0444 $2-4 on Sta and Havelock			
(Gov)	Bldg 160	24 hrs dly	C-466-2808	Duty Pax only
Parking	No parking in Terminal area due to flight line security. See Security Police for long term parking.			
OTHER SERVICES Exchange	Good on and off Base Bldg 3918	1000-1800 M-F, 1700 Sa-Su	C-447-7041	
Bank/Exc	Bldg 91	0900-1300 & 1500-1700 M-Th, 1700 F	C-447-2077	
Hair Styles	Bldg 3918	0900-1800 M-F, 1700 Sa 0830-1700 M-Sa	C-447-7041 C-447-7041	Barber Beauty
Laundry/DryC	Bldg 3918	1000-1800 M-F, 1700 Sa-Su	C-447-1947	
Medical	Bldg 296	24 hrs dly	C-466-4410/4419	
Postal	Bldg 153	0800-1630 M-F, 1200 Sa	C-466-2496	
Porter/WIRE	Havelock	0900-1800 M-F, 1730 Sa	C-447-3925	
TML	Bldgs 487/214 24 hrs dly C-466-3601, A-582-3601 All Ranks. Hostess House C-466-3569. DV/VIP C-466-5169.			
TRAVELERS AID ARC	Bldg 298 Family Svc C-466-4470/4401 Many agencies on Base Bldg 298 0800-1500 M-F C-466-3613/3641			
Chaplain	Bldg 100	0800-1700 M-F	C-466-2585	
Emerg Relief	Bldg 298	0800-1500	C-447-2074/2031	Navy Relief
Lost/Found	Bldg 294	24 hrs dly	C-466-3445	
Sec Police	Bldg 294	24 hrs dly	C-466-3445	
USO	9 Tallman St, Jacksonville NC C-455-3411 Call for svc hrs.			
ATTRACTIONS	Great Outer Banks of NC, New Bern-1st colonial capital of NC			

NORTH CAROLINA

Cherry Point MCAS, Cont'd

UNSCHEDULED FLIGHTS

Frequent CONUS flights to: Beaufort MCAS SC (NBC); El Toro MCAS CA (NZJ); Norfolk NAS VA (NGU); and Washington NAF (NSF) (Andrews AFB MD) via C009A, T-39, and C-12 aircraft on passenger missions. OCONUS flights to: Kadena AFB JA (DNA) and Iwakuni MCAS JA (IWA) via B747, DC-863, C-141B, and C005A aircraft on passenger/cargo missions.

Elizabeth City Coast Guard Air Station (ECG)
Commander/Base Operations
Elizabeth City CGAS, NC 27909-5000

Comm: 919-338-3941
FTS: 931-0001

LOCATION: Take I-64 E to VA-104S to US-17 S to Elizabeth City, L on Halstead Blvd, 3 mi to main gate of Ctr. RM: p-73, C/23. NMC: Elizabeth City, in the city.

FACILITIES	LOCATION	HOURS	PHONE	COMMENTS
PAX TERM INFO	Air Ops Ctr	0800-1600 M-F	C-335-6332, A-723-1540, F-931-0332	Ask gate guard for directions.
Pax Svc Ofc	Air Ops Ctr	0800-1600 M-F	C-335-6332	Duty Officer
PAX LOUNGES	No Pax lounges. Pax assemble at Air Ops Center located at base of ATC tower for processing			
FOOD SERVICE OFC Club	Limited on Base EMC C-335-6388, NCOC C-335-6301 Bldg 35 1100-2200 dly C-335-6226 Noon meal only M-F			
Snack Bars	Hangar area	24 hrs dly		
TRANSPORTATION TAXI(Comm) (Gov)	Very limited on Base Main gate Main gate	24 hrs dly 24 hrs dly	C-335-4333 C-335-7180	
Parking	ATC tower	24 hrs dly		Limited/some reserved spaces
OTHER SERVICES Exchange	BX C-335-6269, Barber C-335-6403, Beauty C-335-6382, Chaplain C-335-6202			
Medical	Dispensary	24 hrs dly	C-338-6460	
TML	Bldg 5	0800-1630 dly	C-338-3941, A-723-3390	
Sec Police	Main gate	24 hrs dly	C-335-6398	
ATTRACTIONS	North Carolina Outer Banks, fresh seafood, beaches			

UNSCHEDULED FLIGHTS

Freq flts via C-130H aircraft to: Bermuda NAS BM (BDA); Borinquen CGAS PR (BQN); Clearwater Air Park Arpt (CLW); Gander Intl Fld CN (YQX); Guantanamo Bay NS CU (GAO); Norfolk NAS (NGU); St Johns Arpt CN (YYT). Call for destinations, routings, and schedules.

NORTH CAROLINA

Pope Air Force Base (POB)
317th Tactical Airlift Wing/LGTT
Pope AFB, NC 28308-5000

Comm: 919-394-0111
ATVN: 486-0111

LOCATION: Take I-95, exit to NC-87/24 W. Signs point the direction to AFB and Fort Bragg. RM: p-73, H/14. NMC: Fayetteville, 12 mi SE.

FACILITIES	LOCATION	HOURS	PHONE	COMMENTS
PAX TERM INFO	Bldg 708	24 hrs dly	C-394-4429/2701, A-486-4429/2803	From gate 3, straight on Manchester Rd to R on Surveyor St to Pax Term L. Signs at all gates give directions to Pax Term. Also check for flts via Army C-12A and C-21A aircraft fm Simmons AAF (FBG) at nearby Fort Bragg: C-396-0011. Limited flight availability.
Pax Svc Ofc	Bldg 703	24 hrs dly	C-394-4429	NCO on duty
PAX LOUNGES General	No separate family lounge Bldg 708 A/C, Rest-rms, TV, P/C seats	24 hrs dly	C-394-4429	
DV/VIP	Bldg 708 A/C, Bag check/lockers, coffee/tea srvd, TV, O/S seats	24 hrs dly	C-394-4429	
Protocol Svc	Bldg 309	0800-1700 M-F	C-394-0111	317th TAW
FOOD SERVICE Cafeteria	Good on and off Base Bldg 704	24 hrs dly	C-497-6670	
Dining Hall	Bldg 717	0530-0100 dly	C-394-1110	
Enl Club	Bldg 232	Call for hrs	C-394-2779	
NCO/CPO Club	Bldg 430	0730-2100 dly	C-497-4051/2641	
OFC Club	Bldg 236	1100-2100 dly	C-497-4031/2154	
Vending	Bldg 708	24 hrs dly	C-394-4429	
TRANSPORTATION Air Tickets	Good on and off Base Bldg 306, 3rd fl	0800-1600 Tu,W,F	C-394-4493/4135	
Bus(Comm)	Greyhound=C-483-0491-POB TW=C-483-5127-POB Greyhound=C-497-3117-Ft Bragg TW=C-497-8746-Ft Bragg			
(Shuttle)	Bldg 704	0630-1830	C-394-4429	Main St side
Car Rentals	PX-Ft Bragg	1100-1800 M-F, 1600 Sa		
Limo Service	Grannis Field Airport	0600-2300 dly	C-484-2121	
TAXI(Comm) (Gov)	Bldg 708 Bldg 708	24 hrs dly 24 hrs dly	C-483-5151-POB, C-436-3900-Ft Bragg C-394-2674-POB, C-396-1191-Ft Bragg	
Trains	Fayetteville		C-483-2658	
Parking	Bldg 708	24 hrs dly	Next to Pax Term.	No restrictions.
OTHER SERVICES Exchange	Good on and off Base. Also nearby Fort Bragg. Bldg 355	1030-1730 M-F, 1300 Sa	C-497-2111	

Pope AFB, Cont'd
NORTH CAROLINA

Bank/Exc	Bldg 346	0900-1700 M-F	C-497-6161
Hair Styles	Bldg 355	1000-1800 M-F	C-497-2111 Barber & Beauty
Laundry/DryC	Bldg 355	0900-1700 M-F, 1500 Sa	C-497-2111
Medical	Bldg 307	24 hrs dly	C-394-2327/2232
Postal	Bldg 381	0715-1630 M-F, 1000 Sa	C-394-2828
TML	Bldg 235 All Ranks.	24 hrs dly	C-394-4404, A-486-4404 DV/VIP-C-394-4739.
TRAVELERS AID ARC	Good on and off Base Bldg 1-1139	0800-1630 M-F C-396-1234 Other hrs C-394-0111	
Chaplain	Bldg 317	0800-1700 M-F	C-394-2676, Other hrs C-394-0111
Emerg Relief	Bldg 308	0715-1615 M-F	C-394-2470 AF Aid
Lost/Found	Bldg 378	24 hrs dly	C-394-2800
Sec Police	Bldg 378	24 hrs dly	C-394-2800/1
USO	333 Ray Ave, Fayetteville	Call for hrs	C-919-483-3179
ATTRACTIONS	Raleigh, Durham, Chapel Hill Triangle		

UNSCHEDULED FLIGHTS

Frequent flts via C005, C-12A, C-21, C-130/M and C-141B/M series aircraft to the following CONUS and OCONUS locations: Andrews AFB MD (ADW); Charleston AFB-Intl SC (CHS); Dobbins AFB GA (MGE); Dover AFB DE (DOV); Dyess AFB TX (DYS); Greenville/Spartanburg Arpt SC (GSP); Little Rock AFB AR (LRF); MacDill AFB FL (MCF); McChord AFB WA (TCM); McGuire AFB NJ (WRI); Norton AFB CA (SBD); Patrick AFB FL (COF); Scott AFB IL (BLV); and Travis AFB CA (SUU). Call for other destinations, routings, and schedules.

Seymour Johnson Air Force Base (GSB)
4th Tactical Fighter Wing/LGTTP
Seymour Johnson AFB, NC 27531-5270

Comm: 919-736-0000
ATVN: 488-1110

LOCATION: From US-70 take Seymour Johnson AFB exit onto Berkeley Blvd which leads to main gate. Clearly marked. RM: p-73, G/17. NMC: Raleigh, 50 mi W.

FACILITIES	LOCATION	HOURS	PHONE	COMMENTS
PAX TERM INFO	Bldg 4507	24 hrs dly	C-736-6163/6161, A-488-6163/6161	Fm gate 1 straight on Wright Ave to L on Humphrey St to R on Curtiss Ave. Pax Term on left.
Pax Svc Ofc	Bldg 4507	24 hrs dly	C-736-6163/6161	NCO on duty
PAX LOUNGES	Limited. No DV/VIP or separate family lounges. General C-736-6163, Protocol Service C-736-0000			
FOOD SERVICE	Good on Base. NCO/CPO Club C-734-2993/2753, O'Club C-735-8546, Restaurants C-736-5574, Snack Bars C-735-8514			

NORTH CAROLINA
Seymour Johnson AFB, Cont'd

TRANSPORTATION	Limited on Base. Air Tickets C-736-6559/6359, Taxi(Gov) C-736-6635, Parking at Bldg 4507 (no restrictions)
OTHER SERVICES	Exchange C-735-8511/9801, Bank/Exc C-735-4680, Barber C-735-9332, Beauty C-734-7504, Laundry/DryC C-734-7436, Medical C-736-5577, Postal C-736-6270
TML	Bldg 3804 24 hrs dly C-736-6705/6168, A-488-6705/6168
TRAVELERS AID	Good on base. ARC C-736-6423, Chaplain C-736-5211, Security Police C-736-6413/5522
ATTRACTIONS	NC research triangle of Raleigh, Durham, and Chapel Hill

SCHEDULED FLIGHTS

DESTINATION	ROUTING	FREQ	EQ/CMTS
RAF Fairford UK (FFD)	GSB-PSM-FFD	Monthly	KC-135E/M
RAF Mildenhall UK (MHZ)	GSB-PSM-MHZ	Monthly	KC-135E/M
Pease AFB NH (PSM)	GSB-PSM-FFD GSB-PSM-MHZ	Monthly Monthly	KC-135E/M KC-135E/M

NORTH DAKOTA

Grand Forks Air Force Base (RDR)
321st CSG/OTM
Grand Forks AFB, ND 58205-5000

Comm: 701-747-3000
ATVN: 362-1110

LOCATION: Fm I-29 take US-2 W exit for 14 mi to Grand Forks, County Rd B-3 (Emerado/Air Base) 1 mi to AFB. RM: p-71, D/15. NMC: Grand Forks, 15 mi E.

FACILITIES	LOCATION	HOURS	PHONE	COMMENTS
PAX TERM INFO	Bldg 528 24 hrs dly C-747-4409/4410, A-362-4409/4410 From main gate straight on Steen Blvd for 1 mi to Base Ops on left under old ATC tower.			
Pax Svc Ofc	Bldg 528 24 hrs dly C-747-4409/4410 NCO on duty			
PAX LOUNGES	General and fam lounge combined. General & DV/VIP C-747-4409			
FOOD SERVICE	Good services on Base. Burger King C-594-8581, Dining Hall C-747-3276, NCO/CPO Club C-747-3392, O'Club C-747-3054, Snack Bar C-594-2695 (Bowling Alley), Vending C-747-4409			
TRANSPORTATION	Limited on and off Base. Air Tickets C-594-5507, Bus(Shuttle) C-747-4409, Car Rentals at Grand Forks IAP 9 mi E of Base, Taxi(Gov) C-747-3976, Parking C-747-4283			
OTHER SERVICES	Exchange C-594-5542, Bank/Exc C-795-3355, Barber C-594-2124, Beauty C-594-4531, Laundry/DryC C-594-2331, Medical C-747-5601, Postal C-747-3841			

NORTH DAKOTA
Grand Forks AFB, Cont'd

TML	Bldg 117 24 hrs dly All Ranks.	C-747-3844, A-362-3844 DV/VIP C-747-4523
TRAVELERS AID	AF Family Svcs C-747-3240, ARC C-747-3855, Chaplain C-747-3076, AF Aid C-747-4904, Security Police C-747-5351	
ATTRACTIONS	Outdoor sports and recreation, Canada easy drive N via I-29	

SCHEDULED FLIGHTS

DESTINATION	ROUTING	FREQ	EQ/CMTS
Buckley ANGB CO (BKF)	RDR-MIB-RCA-HIF-BKF-BLV RDR-MIB-RCA-BKF-OFF-BLV	Tu Sa	C009A/ME C009A/ME
Ellsworth AFB SD (RCA)	RDR-MIB-RCA-HIF-BKF-BLV RDR-MIB-RCA-BKF-OFF-BLV	Tu Sa	C009A/ME C009A/ME
Hill AFB UT (HIF)	RDR-MIB-RCA-HIF-BKF-BLV	Sa	C009A/ME
Minot AFB ND (MIB)	RDR-MIB-RCA-HIF-BKF-BLV RDR-MIB-RCA-BKF-OFF-BLV	Tu Sa	C009A/ME C009A/ME
Offutt AFB NE (OFF)	RDR-RCA-BKF-OFF-BLV	Tu	C009A/ME
Scott AFB IL (BLV)	RDR-MIB-RCA-HIF-BKF-BLV RDR-MIB-RCA-BKF-OFF-BLV	Tu Sa	C009A/ME C009A/ME

Note: Frequent KC-135/R flights to CONUS, OCONUS and foreign country locations. Call for destinations, routings, and schedules.

Minot Air Force Base (MIB)
91st SMW/OT
Minot AFB, ND 58705-5000

Comm: 701-727-4761
ATVN: 344-1110

LOCATION: On US-83, N of Minot. RM: p-71, B/7. NMC: Minot, 15 mi S.

FACILITIES	LOCATION	HOURS	PHONE	COMMENTS
PAX TERM INFO	Bldg 746 Base Ops 24 hrs dly C-723-2348, A-344-2348 From main gate straight on Rd #1 to L on Rd B to Base Ops L.			
Pax Svc Ofc	Bldg 746 24 hrs dly C-727-2348 NCO on duty			
PAX LOUNGES	Limited lounge facilities. General C-727-2348, Protocol Service C-723-3818			
FOOD SERVICE	Good services on Base. Cafeteria C-727-9401/4625, Dining Hall C-723-4695, NCO/CPO Club C-727-3721/6756, O'Club C-727-3721/3731, Snack Bars C-727-4104, Vending C-727-4627			
TRANSPORTATION	Very limited. Air Tickets C-727-4747/2108, Taxi(Gov) C-723-3121/2208, Parking C-727-3096			
OTHER SERVICES	Good services on Base. Exchange C-727-4717, Bank/Exc C-727-6228, Hair Styles C-727-9799, Medical C-727-5304			

NORTH DAKOTA
Minot AFB, Cont'd

TML	Bldg 173 24 hrs dly C-727-2184/6161, A-344-2184/6161 All Ranks. DV/VIP C-727-3818.
TRAVELERS AID	Limited on Base. ARC C-727-2477 (other hrs C-852-2828), Chaplain C-723-3633, Security Police C-723-3096
ATTRACTIONS	Snow ski areas, Canada easy drive N via US-83

SCHEDULED FLIGHTS

DESTINATION	ROUTING	FREQ	EQ/CMTS
Buckley ANGB CO (BKF)	MIB-RCA-BKF-BLV	Tu,F	C009A/ME
Ellsworth AFB SD (RCA)	MIB-RCA-BKF-BLV	Tu,F	C009A/ME
RAF Fairford UK (FFD)	MIB-FFD MIB-PSM-FFD	1 ea mo 1 ea mo	KC-135E/M KC-135E/M
MacDill AFB FL (MCF)	MIB-MCF	Every 3 mo	KC-135E/M
March AFB CA (RIV)	MIB-RIV	Every 3 mo	KC-135E/M
Pease AFB NH (PSM)	MIB-PSM-FFD	1 ea mo	KC-135E/M
Scott AFB IL (BLV)	MIB-BLV	Tu,Sa	C009A/ME

Note: Flights via KC-135E/M to CONUS, OCONUS and foreign country locations. Call for destinations, routings, and schedules.

OHIO

Mansfield Lahm Airport (MFD)
179th Tactical Airlift Group (ANG)
Mansfield Lahm Airport, OH 44901-5000

Comm: 419-522-8948
ATVN: 696-6124

LOCATION: Fm US-30 E or W exit to OH-13 N for 1 mi on L.   RM: p-75, NL/14.
NMC: Mansfield, 5 mi S.

FACILITIES	LOCATION	HOURS	PHONE	COMMENTS
PAX TERM INFO	Bldg 101 0745-1630 M-F C-522-8948, A-696-6124 Main gate straight, on R. Full spt at Comm Term. Ltd mil spt.			
Pax Svc Ofc	Bldg 101 0745-1630 M-F C-522-8948 NCO on duty			
PAX LOUNGES General	General lounge only Bldg 101 0745-1630 M-F C-522-6124 A/C, Coffee/tea srvd, Tel C,LD&ATVN, TV, Rest-rms, O/S seats			

OHIO

Mansfield Lahm Arpt, Cont'd

UNSCHEDULED FLIGHTS

Flights via C-130A/M aircraft to CONUS, OCONUS and foreign country locations. Frequent destinations in AK, HI, PR, VI, PN, BM, GE, and UK. Call for destinations, routings, and schedules up to 30 days in advance.

Rickenbacker Air National Guard Base (LCK)
Det 1, OHANG/OTM
Rickenbacker ANGB, OH 43217-5000

Comm: 614-492-8211
ATVN: 950-1110

LOCATION: Fm I-270 take Alum Creek exit S to ANGB. Also accessible off US-23 onto OH-317. Clearly marked. RM: p-77, SC/12. NMC: Columbus, 13 mi NW.

FACILITIES	LOCATION	HOURS	PHONE	COMMENTS
PAX TERM INFO	Bldg 500 Base Ops 0800-1600 Su-M, 0730-2330 Tu-F, 0730-1930 Sa C-492-4595, A-950-4595 Fm inter of Alum Creek & OH-317 south on 5th St to L on Hangar Ave to 1st R at base of Control Tower.				
Pax Svc Ofc	Bldg 500	0800-1600 Su-M, 0730-2330 Tu-F, 0730-1930 Sa C-492-4595 NCO on duty			
Pax Paging	Bldg 500	0800-1600 Su-M, 0730-2330 Tu-F, 0730-1930 Sa C-492-4595			
PAX LOUNGES	General and family lounges combined. General & DV/VIP C-492-4595, Protocol Service C-492-3400				
FOOD SERVICE	Limited services on Base. Dining Hall C-492-8211, Cons Club C-492-4438, Vending C-492-4595				
TRANSPORTATION	Very limited on Base. Car Rentals (all major companies).				
OTHER SERVICES	Good services on Base. Exchange C-492-4493, Barber C-492-4443, Laundry C-497-9987, Medical C-492-4542/238-2227				
TML	Bldg 92 24 hrs dly C-492-4545/6, A-950-4545/6 All Ranks. DV/VIP C-492-8211.				
TRAVELERS AID	Limited on Base. Good in Columbus C-252-0711, ARC C-253-7981, Chaplain C-492-4404, AF Aid (W-PAFB) C-513-257-4811, Security Police C-492-4727/3333, USO C-267-3131				
ATTRACTIONS	Columbus, The Ohio State University, DOD Aerial Spray Unit				

SCHEDULED FLIGHTS

DESTINATION	ROUTING	FREQ	EQ/CMTS
Dobbins AFB GA (MGE)	LCK-MGE	2-3 per mo	C-130A/M
Hickam AFB HI (HIK)	LCK-HIK	1 ea mo	KC-135E/M
MacDill AFB FL (MCF)	LCK-MCF	2-3 per mo	C-130A/M

OHIO
Rickenbacker ANGB, Cont'd

Patrick AFB FL (COF)	LCK-COF	3-4 per mo	C-130A/M & KC-135E/M
Robins AFB GA (WRB)	LCK-WRB	2-3 per mo	C-130A/M

UNSCHEDULED FLIGHTS

Flights to CONUS, OCONUS and foreign country locations via C-130A/M and KC-135E/M aircraft. Call for destinations, routings, and schedules.

Wright-Patterson Air Force Base (FFO)
2750 Air Base Wing/DMTAP
Wright-Patterson AFB, OH 45433-5000

Comm: 513-257-1110
ATVN: 787-1110 (Area A&C)
       785-1110 (Area B)

LOCATION: S of I-70, off I-675 at Fairborn. Also access from OH-4. AFB clearly marked. RM: p-77, SN/12. NMC: Dayton, 10 mi SW.

FACILITIES	LOCATION	HOURS	PHONE	COMMENTS
PAX TERM INFO	Bldg 206 Area C 0530-2200 M-F, 0800-1600 weekends & holidays C-257-7741, A-787-7741 Enter Gate 8C, right on Skeel Avenue, Pax Terminal on left.			
Pax Svc Ofc	Bldg 206	0730-1630 M-F	C-257-7741	NCO on duty
Pax Paging	Bldg 206 0530-2000 M-F, 0800-1600 wkends/holidays C-257-4366			
PAX LOUNGES General	No separate family lounge Bldg 206 0530-2000 M-F, 0800-1600 weekends/holidays C-257-7741 A/C, Rest-rms, TV, Card tables, Plush seating			
DV/VIP	Bldg 206 24 hrs dly C-257-6202 (07+) A/C, Coffee/tea srvd, Read/write rms,Tel C,LD,&ATVN, TV, Rest-rms,Showers,O/S seats			
Protocol Svc	Arnold House 0800-1600 M-F		C-257-3118	2750 Air Base Wing
FOOD SERVICE Cafeteria	Good services on and off Base Bldg 206 24 hrs dly		C-257-4825	
Dining Hall	Bldg 1214 0530-0100 dly C-257-2117.24 hrs dly In-flt kitchen			
Enl Club	Bldg 1226	1100-2300 dly	C-878-8712	Call for svc hrs.
NCO/CPO Club	Bldg 1214	0630-0100 dly	C-257-3767	Call for svc hrs.
OFC Club	Bldg 800	0700-0100 dly	C-879-4450	Call for svc hrs.
Restaurants	Bldg 1	0630-1315 dly	C-257-4902	
Snack Bars	Bldg 22	0530-1400 dly	C-257-4728	
Vending	Bldg 10	0830-2330 dly	C-257-4616	
TRANSPORTATION Air Tickets	Good on and off Base Bldg 11A & 262 0800-1630 dly C-257-6611 SATO			
Bus(Gov)	Bldg 262	0800-1630 M-F	C-257-3755	On Base

OHIO

Wright-Patterson AFB, Cont'd

Car Rentals	Dayton Arpt 24 hrs dly All major companies
Limo Service	Bldg 146 0605-2005 M-F, Sa-Su On-call C-898-7171
TAXI(Gov)	Bldg 262 24 hrs dly C-257-3755 Area not covered by bus
Parking	Bldg 262 24 hrs dly Short term-1 hr in front of Term; long term-overnight parking at north end of Bldg (marked).
OTHER SERVICES Exchange	Good services on and off Base Bldg 1250 1000-1800 M-F, 1600 Sa-Su C-879-5730
Bank/Exc	Bldg 1250 0900-1600 M-F, 1230 Sa C-449-8990
Hair Styles	Bldg 1250 0830-1800 M-F, 1700 Sa C-879-5171 Barber C-879-5281 Beauty
Laundry/DryC	Bldg 1250 1000-1800 M-Sa C-879-5790
Medical	Bldg 830 24 hrs dly C-257-2968
Postal	Bldg 1044 0730-1700 M-F C-257-6523
TML	Bldg 825 24 hrs dly C-257-3810, A-787-3451 All Ranks. DV/VIP C-257-3810.
TRAVELERS AID ARC	Bldg 2 0800-1700 M-F C-257-3592 AF Family Services Bldg 830 24 hrs dly C-257-7062 or 222-6711
Chaplain	Bldg 150 0800-1700 M-F C-257-7427
Emerg Relief	Bldg 2 0800-1700 M-F C-257-6405 AF Aid
Sec Police	Gate 8C 24 hrs dly C-257-6516
USO	Port Columbus IAP, Room 102 C-231-7300 Call for svc hrs.
ATTRACTIONS	Air Force Museum, Wright Brothers Memorial in Dayton

SCHEDULED FLIGHTS

DESTINATION	ROUTING	FREQ	EQ/CMTS
Andrews AFB MD (ADW)	FFO-ADW	Daily	Adm Acft/P
Barksdale AFB LA (BAD)	FFO-BAD	1-2 ea wk	Adm Acft/P
Bergstrom AFB TX (BSM)	FFO-BSM	1-2 ea wk	Adm Acft/P
Dobbins AFB GA (MGE)	FFO-MGE	2 ea mo	Adm Acft/P
Eglin AFB FL (VPS)	FFO-VPS	2 ea wk	Adm Acft/P

OHIO
Wright-Patterson AFB, Cont'd

Homestead AFB FL (HST)	FFO-HST	1 ea mo	Adm Acft/P
Kelly AFB TX (SKF)	FFO-SKF	3 ea wk	C009A/ME
Langley AFB VA (LFI)	FFO-LFI	1-2 ea wk	Adm Acft/P
Offutt AFB NE (OFF)	FFO-OFF	2 ea wk	Adm Acft/P
Peterson AFB CO (COS)	FFO-COS	1-2 ea wk	Adm Acft/P
Randolph AFB TX (RND)	FFO-RND	1-2 per wk	Adm Acft/P
Scott AFB IL (BLV)	FFO-BLV	3 ea wk	C009A/ME
Shaw AFB SC (SSC)	FFO-SSC	1-2 ea wk	Adm Acft/P
Tinker AFB OK (TIK)	FFO-TIK	2 ea mo	Adm Acft/P

UNSCHEDULED FLIGHTS

Flts to CONUS & OCONUS locations. Call for destinations, routings & schedules.

Youngstown Municipal Airport (YNG)
910th Tactical Airlift Group (AFRES)
Youngstown, OH 44473-5000

Comm: 216-392-1000
ATVN: 346-1000

LOCATION: From OH-193 N or S, exit to King Graves Rd W and into airport.
RM: p-75, NA/17. NMC: Youngstown, 8 mi S.

FACILITIES	LOCATION	HOURS	PHONE	COMMENTS
PAX TERM INFO	AFRES Base Ops	24 hrs dly	C-392-1000, A-346-1000	Ask SP for directions. All spt of regional arpt. Ltd mil spt.

UNSCHEDULED FLIGHTS

Flights via C-130B/M aircraft to CONUS and OCONUS locations. Call for destinations, routings, and schedules.

OKLAHOMA

Altus Air Force Base (LTS)
443rd MAW/TROP
Altus AFB, OK 73523-5270

Comm: 405-482-8100
ATVN: 866-1110

OKLAHOMA

Altus AFB, Cont'd

LOCATION: Off US-62 S of I-40 and W of I-44. From US-62 traveling W from Lawton, turn R at 1st traffic light in Altus and follow road to main gate NE of Falcon Rd. RM: p-79, J/12. NMC: Lawton, 56 mi E.

FACILITIES	LOCATION	HOURS	PHONE	COMMENTS
PAX TERM INFO	Bldg 185	0730-1630 M-F	C-481-6350/6428, A-866-6350/6428	
	Fm main gate L on 1st St, R on East Ave to Pax Term on L.			
Pax Svc Ofc	Bldg 185	0730-1630 M-F	C-481-6428/6350	
PAX LOUNGES General	Limited. No separate DV/VIP or family lounges. Bldg 185 0730-1630 M-F C-482-6350 A/C, Bag chk, Tel C,LD&ATVN, TV, Rest-rms, O/S seats			
Protocol Svc	Bldg 1	0800-1700 M-F	C-481-7554	443rd MAW
FOOD SERVICE Dining Hall	Good services on and off Base Bldg 317	0600-0100 dly	C-481-7797	
Enl Club	Bldg 307	0600-2400 dly	C-481-6295	Call for svc hrs.
Rec Center	Bldg 116	1100-2200 dly	C-481-6600	Call for svc hrs.
OFC Club	Bldg 39	0700-2200 dly	C-481-6224	Call for svc hrs.
Snack Bars	Bldg 106	24 hrs dly	C-481-6300	Bowling Alley
TRANSPORTATION Air Tickets	Limited on Base Altus=C-477-4554		SATO EX-6466	
Bus(Comm)	Altus	C-482-0639	$7-28 Altus to Lawton-2 ea day	
TAXI(Comm) (Gov)	Bldg 352	24 hrs dly 24 hrs dly	C-482-0383 C-481-7273	$3-Altus $40-Lawton Duty Pax only
Parking	Bldg 185	24 hrs dly	Long term-designated areas 24+ hrs.	
OTHER SERVICES Exchange	Good services on Base Bldg 18	1000-1700 Tu-Sa	C-481-7309	
Hair Styles	Bldg 18	0730-1800 Tu-Sa	C-482-8221 C-482-4051	Barber Beauty
Laundry/DryC	Bldg 18	0800-1800 M-Sa	C-482-7344	
Medical	Bldg 46	24 hrs dly	C-481-5222	
Postal	Bldg 129	0700-1500 M-F	C-481-6403	
TML	Bldg 82 All Ranks.	24 hrs dly DV/VIP	C-481-7356/7556, A-866-7356 C-481-7554.	
TRAVELERS AID ARC	Bldg 45	0730-1630 M-F	C-481-6526	

OKLAHOMA
Altus AFB, Cont'd

Chaplain	Bldg 301	0730-1630 M-F	C-481-7485
Lost/Found	Bldg 185	0730-1630 M-F	C-481-6350/6428
Sec Police	Bldg 130	24 hrs dly	C-481-7444
ATTRACTIONS	Western prairie country, outdoor sports		

UNSCHEDULED FLIGHTS

Infrequent flights to: Charleston AFB Intl SC (CHS); Dover AFB DE (DOV); RAF Fairford UK (FFD); Little Rock AFB AR (LRF); McChord AFB WA (TCM); McGuire AFB NJ (WRI); Norton AFB NJ (SBD); Offutt AFB NE (OFF); & Pease AFB NH (PSM).

Note: Flight schedules are received on a week to week basis. Call for destinations, routings, and schedules.

Henry Post Army Airfield (FSI)
Aviation Div/ATZR-TF, USAFACFS
Fort Sill, OK 73503-5100

Comm: 405-351-7090
ATVN: 639-7090

LOCATION: Fm I-44 at Lawton, take US-62/277, 4 mi NW to Post. Clearly marked. RM: p-79, J/14. NMC: Wichita Falls, TX, 50 mi S.

FACILITIES	LOCATION	HOURS	PHONE	COMMENTS
PAX TERM INFO	Bldg 4907 0700-1800 M-F C-351-3508/6160, A-639-3508/6160 I-44 N to Gate Z exit, in ATC bldg.			
OTHER SERVICES	Full Base spt available. Snack bar Bldg 5045 1000-1300 dly			

UNSCHEDULED FLIGHTS

Flights via C-12A/P and C-21A/P aircraft to Midwest and East Coast locations. Call for destinations, routings, and schedules.

Tinker Air Force Base (TIK)
OC-ALC/DSTTHC
Tinker AFB, OK 73145-5270

Comm: 405-732-7321
ATVN: 884-1110

LOCATION: Southeast of Oklahoma City, off I-40. Use Gate 1 off Air Depot Blvd. Clearly marked. RM: p-79, O/6. NMC: Oklahoma City, 12 mi NW.

FACILITIES	LOCATION	HOURS	PHONE	COMMENTS
PAX TERM INFO	Bldg 244 24 hrs dly C-739-4339/4360, A-339-4339/4360 Gate 1 to L at 1st light, 2 more lights to R on "B" St to Pax Term. 24 hrs notice on flights.			
Pax Svc Ofc	Bldg 1	24 hrs dly	C-734-5682	NCO on duty
Pax Paging	Bldg 244	24 hrs dly	C-739-4339/4360	
PAX LOUNGES General	Family and General lounge combined Bldg 244 - 24 hrs dly C-739-4339/4360 A/C, Bag check, Read/write rms, Tel C&ATVN, TV, Rest-rms, P/C seats, Nursery, Child care			

OKLAHOMA
Tinker AFB, Cont'd

DV/VIP	Bldg 240	24 hrs dly	C-734-2191 A/C, Bag check, Read/write rms, Tel C&ATVN, TV, Rest-rms, O/S seats
Protocol Svc	Bldg 460	24 hrs dly	C-739-3900 HQ 2854th ABG
FOOD SERVICE Cafeteria	Many facilities on and off Base Bldg 5905	24 hrs dly	C-734-3037 Flight line
Dining Hall	Bldg 5905 Bldg 5905	0530-0100 dly 24 hrs dly	C-734-MENU Call for svc hrs. C-734-3795 In-flt kitchen box lunches
NCO/CPO Club	Bldg 6001	0600-2200 dly	C-734-3435 Call for svc hrs.
OFC Club	Bldg 5603	1100-2100 dly	C-734-3418 Call for svc hrs.
Snack Bars	Bldg 240	24 hrs dly	C-734-3037
Vending	Bldg 244	24 hrs dly	C-739-4360
TRANSPORTATION Air Tickets	Many facilities and means on Base and in Oklahoma City Bldg 244	0715-1600 M-F	C-739-5057 SATO
Bus(Comm) (Shuttle)	Bldg 244 Bldg 244	24 hrs dly 0530-1730 M-F,	C-235-6425 To Oklahoma City 1000-1500 Sa C-734-3803 On Base
Car Rentals	OKC Arpt	24 hrs dly	C-732-0366 HERTZ
Postal	OKC Arpt	24 hrs dly	C-681-3311 20 mi, $14 TIK-OKC
TAXI(Comm) (Gov)	Gate 1 Bldg 2101	24 hrs dly 24 hrs dly	C-235-1431 SAFEWAY C-734-3803 On Base only
Parking	Short term-Bldg 244; long term-Bldg 650 3 mos limit, C-734-3737. Register with Security Police.		
OTHER SERVICES Exchange	Many support facilities on and off Base Bldg 478	1000-1800 M-F,	0900-1600 Sa-Su C-734-3035
Bank/Exc	Bldg 478	0900-1500 M-F	C-736-2717
Hair Styles	Bldg 478	0800-1700 M-F,	1600 Sa C-732-5032 Barber C-732-6509 Beauty
Laundry/DryC	Bldg 478	0900-1730 M-F	C-734-5225
Medical	Bldg 581	24 hrs dly	C-734-8249 Ambulance C-734-8223
Postal	Bldg 758	0845-1600 M-F,	1045 Sa C-734-3611
TML	Bldg 5604 All Ranks.	24 hrs dly DV/VIP C-734-5511.	C-734-5095, A-884-5095
TRAVELERS AID ARC	Many agencies. AF Family Services C-739-2505. Bldg 3067	0800-1630 M-F	C-232-7121
Chaplain	Bldg 5701	Duty hrs	C-734-2111
Lost/Found	Bldg 244	24 hrs dly	C-739-4360

OKLAHOMA

Tinker AFB, Cont'd

Sec Police	Bldg 650	24 hrs dly	C-734-2000/3737
ATTRACTIONS	Oklahoma City, National Cowboy Hall of Fame		

SCHEDULED FLIGHTS

DESTINATION	ROUTING	FREQ	EQ/CMTS
Charleston AFB SC (CHS)	TIK-CHS	Th	C-141B/C
Dallas NAS TX (NBE)	TIK-NBE	1/F	C009A/ME
Dover AFB DE (DOV)	SUU-TIK-DOV-RMS-MHZ	W	C005A/C C005A/C
RAF Mildenhall UK (MHZ)	SUU-TIK-DOV-RMS-MHZ	W	C005A/C
Ramstein AB GE (RMS)	SUU-TIK-DOV-RMS-MHZ SUU-TIK-DOV-RMS	W Sa	C005A/C C005A/C
Rhein Main AB GE (FRF)	TIK-FRF 1	Tu	C-141B/C
Travis AFB CA (SUU)	RMS-DOV-TIK-SUU TIK-SUU MHZ-DOV-TIK-SUU	M 1/M,Th,F Su	C005A/C C-141B/C C005A/C

UNSCHEDULED FLIGHTS

Frequent flts to: Andrews AFB MD (ADW); Barksdale AFB LA (BAD); Kelly AFB TX (SKF); Kirtland AFB NM (ABQ); Norton AFB CA (SBD); Offutt AFB NE (OFF); Peterson AFB CO (COS); Randolph AFB TX (RND); Scott AFB IL (BLV); Wright-Patterson AFB OH (FFO).

Westheimer Airpark Airport (OUN)
122nd ARCOM ASF (10), 1616 Westheimer Drive
Norman, OK 73069-8495

Comm: 405-321-3170
ATVN: None

LOCATION: Fm I-35 N or S to exit #110 E (Robinson St to airport). RM: p-78, P/9. NMC: Oklahoma City, 15 mi N.

FACILITIES	LOCATION	HOURS	PHONE	COMMENTS
PAX TERM INFO	Bldg 301 main Term.	0730-1600 M-F	C-321-3170	One block S of Report to supervisor for flight sign-in and info.
Pax Svc Ofc	Bldg 301	0730-1600 M-F	C-321-3170	Supv or rep on duty
PAX LOUNGES General	General lounge only Bldg 301 0730-1600 M-F C-321-3170 A/C, Bag chk, Tel C, Rest-rms, O/S and Wood seats. See supv for protocol svc.			
FOOD SERVICE Snack Bars	Limited at ARCOM. Full services at airport Pax Term. Bldg 301 0730-1600 M-F C-321-3170			

OKLAHOMA

Westheimer Airpark Arpt, Cont'd

UNSCHEDULED FLIGHTS

Flights via UH-1F, UH-1H, and OH-58A aircraft to CONUS locations on training and mixed missions. Most flights are on Tu and Th (0730-2300 hrs). Call for destinations, routings, and schedules.

Will Rogers Air National Guard Base (OKC)
137th Tactical Airlift Wing/DOO (ANG)
Will Rogers ANGB, OK 73169-5000

Comm: 405-686-5210
ATVN: 956-8210

LOCATION: Fm I-40 W, exit 144 or 145 S to airport. RM: p-78, O/2. NMC: Oklahoma City, 10 mi NE.

FACILITIES	LOCATION	HOURS	PHONE	COMMENTS
PAX TERM INFO	Bldg 1011	0630-1700 M-Th	C-686-5251, A-956-8251	Main gate straight 4 blocks S. Full services of a regional arpt.
PAX LOUNGES General	Small. Next to Base Ops. No DV/VIP or family lounges. Bldg 1011 0630-1700 M-Th C-686-5251 A/C, Tel C&ATVN, Rest-rms, P/C seats			
OTHER SERVICES	Snack Bar Bldg 1011 0600-1700 M-Th C-685-9054 Security Police Bldg 1029 0630-1700 M-Th C-686-5210			

UNSCHEDULED FLIGHTS

Flts to CONUS and OCONUS via ANG C-130A/M aircraft. Call for destinations, routings, and schedules.

OREGON

Portland International Airport (PDX)
939th Aerospace Rescue and Recovery Sqdn (AFRES)
Portland, OR 97218-2797

Comm: 503-288-5611
ATVN: 891-1701

LOCATION: From I-205 N or S exit to OR-213 for .5 mi to IAP. RM: p-81, M/24. NMC: Portland, 3 mi SW.

FACILITIES	LOCATION	HOURS	PHONE	COMMENTS
PAX TERM INFO	ANG/AFRES Ops 24 hrs dly C-288-5611, A-891-1701 Ask Security Police for directions. All the support of an IAP. Limited military support facilities.			

UNSCHEDULED FLIGHTS

Flights via HC-130H/M and UH-1H/P and H-3 aircraft on training missions. Call EX-201 for destinations, routings, and schedules.

PENNSYLVANIA

Chambersburg Municipal Airport (N68) **Comm:** 717-267-8788/8882
HQDESCOM, NE Flt Det/AMSDS-RE-N **ATVN:** 570-8788/8882
Chambersburg, PA 17201-4170

LOCATION: From I-81 E or W, Exit 6, PA-30 through Chambersburg to R on Franklin St for 1.5 mi to R on Salem Road for .25 mi to Airport Road then left to airport. RM: p-83, WT/17. NMC: Hagerstown MD, 25 mi S.

FACILITIES	LOCATION	HOURS	PHONE	COMMENTS
PAX TERM INFO	Bldg S-8500 0730-1600 M-F C-267-8788/8882, A-570-8788/8882 Ask gate guard for directions.			
PAX LOUNGES General	General lounge only Bldg S-8500 0730-1600 M-F C-267-8788/8882 A/C, Tel L&ATVN, TV, Rest-rms, P/C seats			
Protocol Svc	Letterkenny Army Depot (LEAD) 0730-1600 M-F C-267-7465 HQDESCOM			
OTHER SERVICES	Full large Base support facilities available at Letterkenny Army Depot. See Military Living's "US Forces Travel Guide USA & Caribbean Areas" for specific details.			

UNSCHEDULED FLIGHTS

Flts to the following destinations via C-12A/P & U-21A/P aircraft 1-4 times ea mo: Calhoun County Arpt AL (ANB); Cambridge NY (CAM), Clinton Munic Arpt IA (CWI); Corpus Christi Intl Arpt TX (CRP); Davison AAF VA (DAA); Detroit City Arpt MI (DET); Huntsville-Madison County Arpt AL (HSV); Lambert-St Louis IAP MO (STL); Muni-Webb Fld AR (TXK); Pocono Mountain Munic Arpt PA (MPO); Quad City Arpt IL (MLI); and Seneca Army Airfield NY (SSN). Call for destinations, routings, and schedules.

Greater Pittsburgh International Airport (PIT) **Comm:** 412-269-8000
911th Tactical Airlift Group (AFRES) **ATVN:** 277-8000
Pittsburgh, PA 15231-5000

LOCATION: Take I-279 W which merges into PA-60 (Airport Parkway) into IAP. RM: p-86, E/5. NMC: Pittsburg, 15 mi SE.

FACILITIES	LOCATION	HOURS	PHONE	COMMENTS
PAX TERM INFO	AFRES Base Ops, 0800-1700 M-F & flight times C-269-8000, A-277-8000 (ask for AFRES Ops). ANG Base Ops, 0800-1700 M-F & flight times, C-269-8350, A-277-8350 (ask for ANG Ops). All the support of an IAP. Limited military support.			

UNSCHEDULED FLIGHTS

Frequent flts via AFRES C-130A/M and ANG KC-135E/M aircraft to CONUS, OCONUS, and foreign country locations. Call for destinations, routings, and scheds.

PENNSYLVANIA

Harrisburg International Airport (MDT)
193rd Special Operations Group (ANG)
Middletown, PA 17057-5000

Comm: 717-948-2201
ATVN: 454-9201

LOCATION: Fm I-76 E or W, exit #19 S on PA-230 (2nd St) S to IAP on R.
RM: p-85, EZ/5. NMC: Harrisburg, 5 mi NW.

FACILITIES	LOCATION	HOURS	PHONE	COMMENTS
PAX TERM INFO	ANG Area	0730-1630 M-F	C-948-2201, A454-9201	Ask Security Police for directions. All the support of an IAP. No military facility support.

UNSCHEDULED FLIGHTS

Flights to CONUS and OCONUS locations by ANG EC-130E/M aircraft. Call for destinations, routings, and schedules.

Philadelphia International Airport (PHL)
DET 1, 438TH APS (MAC)
Philadelphia IAP, Terminal D
Philadelphia, PA 19153-5000

Comm: 215-897-5644
ATVN: 443-5644

LOCATION: Seven miles SW of Philadelphia, off I-95 and Rt 291. Clearly marked. RM: p-87, J/5. NMC: Philadelphia, 7 mi NE.

FACILITIES	LOCATION	HOURS	PHONE	COMMENTS
PAX TERM INFO	Term D	0600-2400 dly	C-897-5644, A-443-5644	
Recording	Term D	24 hrs dly	C-897-5645, A-443-5645	Updated 3 X wkly
Pax Svc Ofc	Term D	0800-1700 M-F	C-897-5640, A-443-5640	
Pax Paging	Term D	During flt processing	C-897-5640, A-897-5640	
PAX LOUNGES General	Term D	24 hrs dly	A/C,Tel,TV, Rest-rms,Bag chk/lks	
Protocol Svc	Provided by McGuire AFB		C-609-724-440-2470 (06+)	
Family	USO - Term D 0800-2400 dly		C-365-8889	A/C, Bag chk/lks, TV,Refreshments,Rd/write rm,Rest-rm,Showers,O/S seats,Ch care
FOOD SERVICE Restaurants	2 Restaurants-both in Term B, Ice cream parlor-Concourse C Term B 1100-2000 dly 0600-2200 dly			
Snack Bars	All Terminals 0600-2000 dly			
Vending	All Terminals 24 hrs dly			
TRANSPORTATION Bus(Comm) (Shuttle)	Train - airport line to downtown Southeast PA Trans Authority-at all Terminals 24 hrs dly Airport shuttle to Terminals & parking lots 24 hrs dly			
Car Rentals	Major companies' counters located in baggage claim areas			
Limo Service	Salem Trans 0600-2300 dly to McGuire AFB C-492-2116 J & G Limo Scheduled dly to Dover AFB C-800-441-8775			

PENNSYLVANIA
Philadelphia Intl Arpt, Cont'd

TAXI(Comm)	Available at all Terminals 24 hrs dly
Parking	Short term-Term D arrivals (expensive). Garage D $10 dly. Remote lot approximately $5 dly.
OTHER SERVICES	Gift shops, Video arcade, Bookstore, Florist, Postal Svc Ctr These fac and services are avail within the arpt-Concourse C.
Bank/Exc	Term C Machine 24 hrs dly
Hair Styles	Term B Barber
Medical	Naval Base/Hospital 24 hrs dly C-465-6838 Emergency
TML	Limited-avail at Phil Naval Base C-897-5160, A-443-5160 Comm hotels/motels in arpt area (reduced rates for MAC Pax)
TRAVELERS AID ARC	Term D 7 days as required C-897-5649 (temporary)
Chaplain	Chapel Phil Naval Base Duty hrs C-465-3054-2896
USO	Term D 0800-2400 dly C-365-8889
ATTRACTIONS	Liberty Bell historic exhibits and museums in Philadelphia

SCHEDULED FLIGHTS

DESTINATION	ROUTING	FREQ	EQ/CMTS
Athinai Arpt GR (ATH)	PHL-FRF-AVB-ATH PHL-NAP-ATH-BAH-NKW	M F	L-1011/P/CC DC-862/P/CC
Aviano AB IT (AVB)	PHL-FRF-AVB	M	DC-863/P/CC
Bahrain IAP BA (BAH)	PHL-SIZ-BAH PHL-NAP-ATH-BAH-NKW	M F	L-1011/P/CC DC-863/P/CC
Capodichino Arpt IT (NAP)	PHL-RTA-NAP-SIZ PHL-NAP-ATH-BAH-NKW	W F	DC-863/P/CC DC-863/P/CC
Charleston AFB Intl SC (CHS)	FRF-PHL-CHS	Su	DC-10/P/CC
Diego Garcia Atoll (NKW)	PHL-NAP-ATH-BAH-NKW	F	DC/863/P/CC
Keflavik Arpt IC (KEF)	NGU-PHL-KEF	Tu	DC-862/P/CC
Lambert St Louis IAP MO (STL)	FRF-PHL-STL	Th,Sa	DC-10/B747/P/CC
RAF Mildenhall UK (MHZ)	PHL-MHZ-FRF	M	DC-10/P/CC
Norfolk NAS VA (NGU)	PHL-NGU	M,W	DC-862/P/CC

PENNSYLVANIA
Philadelphia Intl Arpt, Cont'd

Rhein Main AB GE (FRF)	PHL-MHZ-FRF PHL-FRF-AVB-ATH PHL-FRF	M M W,Sa	DC-10/P/CC L-1011/P/CC DC-10B747/P/CC
Rota NAS SP (RTA)	PHL-RTA-NAP-SIZ	W	L-1011/P/CC
Sigonella Arpt IT (SIZ)	PHL-SIZ-BAH PHL-RTA-NAP-SIZ	M W	L-1011/P/CC DC-863/P/CC

Willow Grove Naval Air Station (NXX)
Air Operations Department
Willow Grove NAS, PA 19090-5010

Comm: 215-443-1000
ATVN: 991-1000

LOCATION: Take PA Turnpike (I-276), exit 27 N to PA-611, 5 mi to NAS. RM: p-85, ES/15. NMC: Philadelphia, 21 mi S.

FACILITIES	LOCATION	HOURS	PHONE	COMMENTS
PAX TERM INFO	Hangar #80	0730-1600 W-Su	C-443-6216, A-991-6216	
	From main gate straight to Air Ops Tower on L.			
Recording	Hangar #80	24 hrs dly	C-443-6216, A-991-6216	
Pax Svc Ofc	Hangar #80	0730-1600 W-Su	C-443-6217	
PAX LOUNGES General	No separate family lounge			
	Hangar #80	0730-1600 W-Su	C-443-6216	
	A/C, Bag chk, Tel L&ATVN, Rest-rms, P/C seats			
DV/VIP	Hangar #80	0730-1600 W-Su	C-443-6216	A/C, Bag chk,
	Tel L&ATVN, TV, Read/write rms, Rest-rms, P/C seats			
Protocol Svc	Hangar #80	0800-1700 M-F	C-443-1000	Cmdr NAS
FOOD SERVICE NCO/CPO Club	Limited services on Base			
	Bldg 174	1130-1300 W-Su	C-443-6089	Call for svc hrs.
OFC Club	Bldg 5	1130-0100 Tu-Sa, 2300 Su	C-443-6081	
Snack Bars	Flt Line Inn	0730-1430 Tu-Su	C-672-3040	
Vending	Hangar #80	0730-1600 W-Su	C-443-6216	
TRANSPORTATION Bus(Comm)	Limited on Base			
	Main gate	Call for hrs.	C-443-6048/6454	
Car Rentals	C & C Ford	US-611		Near NAS
Limo Service	PHL to George Washington Lodge, Willow Grove $12.00			
Parking	Adjacent to main gate		C-443-6067	Notify Sec Police
OTHER SERVICES Exchange	Good on Base			
	Bldg 605	1000-1700 Tu-Su	C-443-6029	

PENNSYLVANIA
Willow Grove NAS, Cont'd

Bank/Exc	Bldg 605	0715-1600 Tu-Sa C-443-6013
Hair Styles	Bldg 2	1000-1700 Tu-Su C-443-6029 Barber
Laundry	Bldg 2	1000-1700 Tu-Su C-443-6029
Medical	Bldg 37	24 hrs dly C-443-1600
Postal	Bldg 2	0900-1700 Tu-Sa C-443-6055
TML	Bldg 5 60/76	24 hrs dly All Ranks. C-443-6059/60/76, A-991-6059/ DV/VIP C-443-6060.
TRAVELERS AID Chaplain	Limited on Base Bldg 38	0730-1600 Tu-Su C-443-6002/3/4
Emerg Relief	Bldg 1	1000-1400 W,F C-443-6002 Navy Relief
Sec Police	Bldg 1	24 hrs dly C-443-6067
USO	Naval Base PHL	Call for hrs. C-215-336-0908
ATTRACTIONS	Philadelphia, New Jersey beaches, and Pocono Mountain area	

UNSCHEDULED FLIGHTS

Frequent flights via Navy C-9/R, C-12A and P-3A/M, and AFRES C-130E/P aircraft to: Andrews AFB MD (ADW); Bermuda NAS BM (BDA); Brunswick NAS ME (NHZ); Jacksonville NAS FL (NIP); Lajes Fld PO (LGS); New Orleans NAS LA (NBG); Norfolk NAS VA (NGU); and Rota NAS SP (RTA). Call for destinations, routings, and schedules.

RHODE ISLAND

Quonset State Airport (OQU)
143rd Tactical Airlift Group (ANG)
North Kingston, RI 02852-0794

Comm: 401-885-3960
ATVN: 476-3210

LOCATION: From US-1 N or S exit to RI-403 South. Follow signs to airport. RM: p-19, G/23. NMC: Providence, 20 mi N.

FACILITIES	LOCATION	HOURS	PHONE	COMMENTS
PAX TERM INFO	ANG area 0800-1600 M-F C-885-3960, A-476-3210 Ask Security Police for directions. Facilities of a regional airport available. No military support facilities.			

UNSCHEDULED FLIGHTS

Flights via ANG C-130A/M aircraft to CONUS and OCONUS locations. Call for destinations, routings, and schedules.

SOUTH CAROLINA

Beaufort Marine Corps Air Station (NBC)   Comm: 803-846-2111
Airfield Operations   ATVN: 832-2111
Beaufort MCAS, SC 29904-5010

LOCATION: Fm I-95, exit at Pocataligo to SC-21, 4 mi to MCAS. Clearly marked. RM: p-88, K/10. NMC: Savannah GA, 40 mi S.

FACILITIES	LOCATION HOURS PHONE COMMENTS
PAX TERM INFO	Bldg 860 0700-2300 M-F, 1000-1800 Sa, 1200-2000 Su C-846-7110, A-832-7110 Fm main gate straight on Geiger Blvd to L on Drayton St to Pax Term on L.
Pax Svc Ofc	Bldg 860 0700-2300 M-F, 1000-1800 Sa, 1200-2000 Su C-846-7110 NCO on Duty
PAX LOUNGES General	Combined general and family lounge Bldg 860 0700-2300 M-F, 1000-1800 Sa, 1200-2000 Su C-846-7110 A/C, Bag/chk, Tel L,LD&ATVN, Rest-rms, P/C seats
DV/VIP	Bldg 600 0700-2300 M-F, 1000-1800 Sa, 1200-2000 Su C-846-7301 A/C, Bag/chk, Coffee/tea svc, Tel L,LD&ATVN, TV, TV, Rest-rms, Showers, O/S seats
Protocol Svc	Bldg 1 0800-1700 M-F C-846-2111 Cmdr MCAS
FOOD SERVICE	Good services on and off Base. Cafeteria C-846-7106, Enl Club C-846-7541, O'Club C-846-7541, Snack Bar C-846-2497
TRANSPORTATION	Limited on Base. Bus(Comm) C-524-4646, Taxi(Comm) C-524-4940 (Gov) C-846-7550, Parking C-846-7373 H&HS lot
OTHER SERVICES	Good services on Base. Exchange C-846-2252, Bank C-846-2252, Barber C-846-9293, Beauty C-846-2257, Laundry/DryC C-846-2248, Medical C-846-7530/7311, Postal C-846-7220
TML	Bldg 431 24 hrs dly C-846-7674, A-832-7674 All Ranks. DV/VIP C-846-7121.
TRAVELERS AID	Limited on Base. ARC C-846-7252, Chaplain C-846-7775, Sec Police C-846-7373
ATTRACTIONS	Beaches, seafood, period homes, Savannah, 40 mi S.

UNSCHEDULED FLIGHTS

Frequent admin and school flights via C009A/P and other aircraft to CONUS and OCONUS locations. Call for destinations, routings, and schedules.

Charleston Air Force Base (CHS)   Comm: 803-554-0230
437th APS/TROP   ATVN: 583-0111
Charleston AFB, SC 29404-5466

LOCATION: From I-26 E exit (211A) to W Aviation Ave to 2nd traffic light R. Follow road around end of runway to Gate 2 (River Gate). RM: p-88, I/12. NMC: Charleston, 5 mi SE.

SOUTH CAROLINA
Charleston AFB, Cont'd

FACILITIES	LOCATION	HOURS	PHONE	COMMENTS
PAX TERM INFO	Bldg 164	0500-2300 dly	C-554-2348/2347, A-583-2348/2348 West side across from commercial arpt & ATC tower. Check-in manned 0500-2300 dly.	
Pax Svc Ofc	Bldg 164	0730-1630 M-F	C-554-2310, A-583-2310	
Pax Paging	Bldg 164	0500-2300 dly	C-554-3711/2, A-583-3711/2	
PAX LOUNGES General	Dependents lounge & nursery. See Pax Shift Supervisor. Bldg 164 0500-2300 dly A/C, Bag check/lockers, Tel C,A,&LD, TV lounge, Rest-rms, P/C seats			
DV/VIP	Bldg 164 0500-2300 dly C-554-2348/3471, A-583-2348/3471 Flt line end of Bldg (unmanned). See Pax Svc Shift Supervisor. A/C, Tel C,A,&LD, TV, Rest-rms, O/S seats			
Protocol Svc	Bldg 103	0730-1630 M-F	C-554-2303, A-583-2303	MAC
FOOD SERVICE Dining Hall	Bldg 250&446	4 meals dly	C-554-2395/2336 Call for svc hrs.	
NCO/CPO Club	Bldg 325	0630-2300 dly	C-554-3514 (Closed till 11/89)	
OFC Club	Bldg 355	0830-2300 (closed Su)	C-554-3587 Lunch/Dinner	
Snack Bars	Bldg 221 Bldg 1990 BX	1100-2200 M-F 1000-1800 dly	C-554-2600 Sandwiches/Salad/Pizza C-552-9415 Snack bar/Ice cream	
Golf Course	Bldg 370	0800-1600 dly	C-554-2396 Breakfast/Sandwiches	
Vending	Bldg 164	0500-2300 dly	C-554-2348 Snacks/Sodas	
TRANSPORTATION Air Tickets	Bldg 164 C-544-3246	0800-2000 M-F, 0930-1700 Sa, 1100-1800 Su Services all airlines.		
Bus(Comm)	Charleston	0630-1000 hrs dly	GH=744-4245, TW=723-8649	
Car Rentals	At CHS/IAP	24 hrs dly	Many companies	
TAXI(Comm) (Gov)	Bldg 164 Bldg 408	24 hrs dly 24 hrs dly	C-554-7575 On & off Base C-554-3361 Duty only	
Parking	Bldg 164	Short- and long-term across fm Term.		
OTHER SERVICES Exchange	Bldg 1990	0900-1800 M-F, 1900 Th,Sa, 1100-1700 Su	C-552-1463	
Bank/Exc	Bldg 306	0900-1630 M-F Closed 1300-1500	C-724-5055 SC National	
Hair Styles	Bldg 1990 Bldg 1990 Bldg 237	0800-1800 M-Sa, 1100-1700 Su 0800-1800 M-Sa, 1100-1700 Su 1000-1800 dly	C-552-4880 Barber C-552-0812 Beauty C-760-2315 Barber/Beauty	

SOUTH CAROLINA

Charleston AFB, Cont'd

Laundry/DryC	Bldg 1990	1000-1800 M-Sa (closed Su) C-552-4883 Valet
Medical	Bldg 1000	24 hrs dly C-554-3821 Emergency
Postal/WIRE	Bldg 306	0800-1600 M-F C-554-2370 Wstrn Union in town
Porter	Comm Term	During comm contract mission processing only
POV Shipmt	Chs Auto Proc=C-552-3030, T&D Auto Proc=C-747-0499, Caro Auto Proc=C-552-2592, Owner Proc=C-747-5470 0800-1600 M-F
TML	Bldg 362 24 hrs dly C-554-2640, A-583-2640 From Pax Term dial 60. DV/VIP 0800-1700 dly C-554-3145.
TRAVELERS AID ARC	Bldg 112 Near Term 0730-1630 M-F C-554-3377/8, Emergency C-554-3552. After hours C-744-3552.
Chaplain	Bldg 217 0730-1630 M-F C-554-2541 On call after hrs Bldg 1005 0730-1630 M-F C-554-2536 On call after hrs
Emerg Relief	Bldg 503 0730-1630 M-F C-554-2457
Lost/Found	Bldg 164 0730-1630 M-F C-554-2369. Aft hrs C-554-2348.
Sec Police	Bldg 263 24 hrs dly C-554-2213 Crime Stop C-554-2677
USO	CHS-IAP Call for hrs. C-767-3963
ATTRACTIONS	Charleston Naval Base, 5 mi NW of Charleston off I-26. Take Naval Base exit C-743-4111, A-794-4111. Beaches, period homes.

SCHEDULED FLIGHTS

DESTINATION	ROUTING	FREQ	EQ/CMTS
Caribbean/Cen--tral & South America (CAB)	CHS-HOW-RIO-BUE-SEL-LIM CHS-HOW-LIM-SCL-BUE-RIO CHS-HOW-ASU-MVD-LPB	2/M 3/M 4/Tu	C-141B/M C-141B/M C-141B/M
Dobbins AFB GA (MGE)	CHS-POB-GSP-MGE CHS-MGE-GSP-POB	Su F	C-141B/M C-141B/M
Greenville/ Spartanburg Arpt SC (GSP)	CHS-POB-GSP-MGS CHS-MGE-GSP-POB	Su F	C-141B/M C-141B/M
Homestead AFB FL (HST)	CHS-NIP-HST-MCF CHS-MCF-HST-NIP	Su F	C-141B/M C-141B/M
Howard AB PN (HOW)	CHS-HOW CHS-NRR-HOW CHS-PLA-HOW CHS-HOW-PLA	1/2/M,1/4/Sa 1/3/F Th,Su Th,F	C-141B/M C-141B/M C-141B/M C-141B/M

SOUTH CAROLINA

Charleston AFB, Cont'd

Jacksonville NAS FL (NIP)	CHS-NIP-HST-MCF CHS-MCF-HST-NIP	Su F	C-141B/M C-141B/M
Kinshasa Ndjili ZA(FIH)	CHS-LGS-ROB-FIH	2/4/M	C-141B/M
Lajes Fld PO (LGS)	CHS-LGS-ROB-FIH	2/4/M	C-141B/M
MacDill AF FL (MCF)	CHS-NIP-HST-MCF CHS-MCF-HST-NIP	Su F	C-141B/M C-141B/M
McGuire AFB NJ (WRI)	CHS-WRI	Sa	C-141B/M
RAF Mildenhall UK (MHZ)	CHS-MHZ CHS-PIK-MHZ	Sa Every other day	C-141B/M C-141B/M
Monrovia Robts Intl LI (ROB)	CHS-LGS-ROB-FIH	2/4/M	C-141B/C
Norfolk NAS VA (NGU)	CHS-NGU	Su-Th,Sa	C-141B/M
Palmerola Arpt HO (PLA)	CHS-PLA-HOW	Su,Th	C-141B/M
Patrick AFB FL (COF)	CHS-COF	M,W	C-141B/M
Pope AFB NC (POB)	CHS-POB-GSP-MGE CHS-MGE-GSP-POB	Su F	C-141B/M C-141B/M
Prestwick Arpt UK (PIK)	CHS-PIK-MHZ	Every other day	C-141B/M
Roosevelt Rds NAS PR (NRR)	CHS-NRR-HOW	1/3/W	C-141B/M
Scott AFB IL (BLV)	CHS-BLV	Su,F	C-141B/M

UNSCHEDULED FLIGHTS

Flights to: Dobbins AFB GA (MGE); Greenville/Spartanburg Arpt SC (GSP); Homestead AFB FL (HST); Jacksonville NAS FL (NIP); MacDill AFB FL (MCF); Pope AFB NC (POB); and Scott AFB IL (BLV).

Charleston International Airport (CHS)
Det 1, 437th APS
P.O. Box 124
Charleston IAP, SC 29418-5000

Comm: 803-767-0588/0448
ATVN: 583-2751/2

LOCATION: From I-26 E take Exit 211A to W Aviation Ave, follow sign to new Terminal. RM: p-88, I/12. NMC: Charleston, 5 Mi SE.

SOUTH CAROLINA

Charleston Intl Arpt, Cont'd

FACILITIES	LOCATION HOURS PHONE COMMENTS
PAX TERM INFO	Military Assistance Counter - "B" Concourse 0700-2200 Su, 0100-2200 M, 0700-2200 Tu-F, 0700-1700 Sa C-767-0588/0488, A-583-2751/2 "B" Concourse ticket lobby
Recording	"B" Concourse During non-operational hrs C-554-2751
Pax Svc Ofc	"B" Concourse Same as Pax Term C-554-2751/2 NCO on duty
Pax Paging	"B" Concourse Same as Pax Term C-767-0588
PAX LOUNGES General	No separate DV/VIP or family lounges Comm facilities in IAP. See Charleston AFB listing.
TRANSPORTATION Car Rentals	See Charleston AFB listing. No shuttle bus to AFB. Bag claim area Avis=C-747-1333, Hertz=C-554-6311, Budget=C-554-8070, National=C-744-4278
Limo Service	Bag claim area C-767-1100
TAXI(Comm)	Bag claim area 24 hrs dly Term (front)/Trans Mgmt Counter J
OTHER SERVICES	See Charleston AFB listing for full military facilities spt.
TML	See Charleston AFB listing for hot-line telephone to commercial hotels in the area. Located in baggage claim area.
TRAVELERS AID Lost/Found	See Charleston AFB listing. Domestic baggage claim area
USO	IAP ground floor under domestic baggage claim area C-767-3963
ATTRACTIONS	Beaches, historic homes

SCHEDULED FLIGHTS

DESTINATION	ROUTING	FREQ	EQ/CMTS
Howard AFB PN (HOW)	CHS-HOW	M,1/4Th	B727/P/CC *
Philadelphia IAP PA (PHL)	CHS-PHL-FRF	Sa	DC-10/P/CC **
Rhein Main AB GE (FRF)	CHS-FRF CHS-PHL-FRF	Su,W Sa	DC-10/P/CC DC-10/P/CC **

Notes: * This flight operates only during peak summer months.
      ** Seats on this flight are very limited.

Columbia Metropolitan Airport (CAE)
Jimmie Doolittle Flight Facility, 2625-A Arpt Blvd
West Columbia, SC 29169-2144

Comm: 803-751-7511
ATVN: 734-1110

LOCATION: Fm I-26, exit 113 S on SC-302 (Airport Blvd) to airport. RM: p-88, L/1. NMC: Columbia, 5 mi NE.

SOUTH CAROLINA
Columbia Metro Arpt, Cont'd

FACILITIES	LOCATION HOURS PHONE	COMMENTS
PAX TERM INFO	Jimmie Doolittle Flight Facility C-796-4431/2, C-751-5815 Ask Security Police for directions. All support of regional airport. Full large post support at nearby Fort Jackson.	

UNSCHEDULED FLIGHTS

Very ltd flts via C-21A/P acf. Call for destinations, routings, & schedules.

Shaw Air Force Base (SSC)
363rd TFW/Air Operations
Shaw AFB, SC 29152-5000

Comm: 803-668-8110
ATVN: 965-1110

LOCATION: Off US-76/378, 8 mi W of Sumter. Clearly marked. RM: p-88, E/10. NMC: Columbia, 35 mi W.

FACILITIES	LOCATION HOURS PHONE	COMMENTS
PAX TERM INFO	Bldg 615 Base Ops 24 hrs dly C-668-3468, A-965-3468 Fm South gate on Shaw Dr to R on Killian Ave to Base Ops on R	
OTHER SERVICES	No formal Pax lounges. All Space-A Pax processed by Base Ops. Full lg Base spt available. See Military Living's "US Forces Travel Guide USA & Caribbean Areas" for details.	

UNSCHEDULED FLIGHTS

Flights via T-39/P, C-12A/P and C-21A/P aircraft to CONUS destinations. Call for destinations, routings, and schedules.

SOUTH DAKOTA

Ellsworth Air Force Base (RCA)
44th SMW (SAC), Airfield Mgmt Section
Ellsworth AFB, SD 57706-5000

Comm: 605-385-1000
ATVN: 685-1000

LOCATION: Off I-90, 10 mi E of Rapid City. Clearly marked. RM: p-89, F/4. NMC: Rapid City, 10 mi W.

FACILITIES	LOCATION HOURS PHONE	COMMENTS
PAX TERM INFO	Bldg 7506 24 hrs dly C-385-1052, A-685-1052 From main gate straight on Rushmore Dr to R on Sixth St. L on Ave B to L on Center Dr to dead end at Pax Term (Base Ops).	
Pax Svc Ofc	Bldg 7506 0800-1700 M-F C-385-1052	NCO on duty
PAX LOUNGES	No separate family lounge. General & DV/VIP	C-385-1052
FOOD SERVICE	Good on and off Base. Cafeteria C-923-1455, Dining Hall C-385-1622, NCO/CPO Club C-923-1442, O'Club C-385-1764 Snack Bars C-923-1474, Vending C-385-1052	
TRANSPORTATION	Very ltd on Base. Taxi(Gov) C-385-2907, Parking C-385-1052	

SOUTH DAKOTA

Ellsworth AFB, Cont'd

OTHER SERVICES	Good on Base. Exchange C-923-5821, Bank/Exc C-923-1405, Medical C-385-3430, Postal C-385-1000
TML	Bldg 1103 24 hrs dly C-923-5861 or 385-2844 A-685-2844. All Ranks. DV/VIP C-923-5861.
TRAVELERS AID	Limited on and off base. ARC C-385-1381, Chaplain C-385-1597, Lost/Found C-385-4001, Security Police C-385-4001
ATTRACTIONS	Black Hills and Mt Rushmore nearby, S.D. Aerospace Museum

SCHEDULED FLIGHTS

DESTINATION	ROUTING	FREQ	EQ/CMTS
Buckley ANGB CO (BKF)	RCA-RDR-MIB-HIF-BKF-BLV	Tu,Sa	C009A/ME
Grand Forks AFB ND (RDR)	RCA-RDR-MIB-HIF-BKF-BLV	Tu,Sa	C009A/ME
Hill AFB UT (HIF)	RCA-RDR-MIB-HIF-BKF-BLV	Tu,Sa	C009A/ME
Minot AFB SD (MIB)	RCA-RDR-MIB-HIF-BKF-BLV	Tu,Sa	C009A/ME
Scott AFB IL (BLV)	RCA-RDR-MIB-HIF-BKF-BLV	Tu,Sa	C009A/ME

UNSCHEDULED FLIGHTS

Flts to CONUS, OCONUS, and foreign countries. Call for destinations, scheds.

TENNESSEE

McGhee Tyson Airport (TYS)
134th Air Refueling Group (ANG)
Knoxville, TN 37950-5000

Comm: 615-970-8000
ATVN: 697-8000

LOCATION: Exit N or S from US-129 to Airport. RM: p-91, E/24. NMC: Knoxville, 10 mi N.

FACILITIES	LOCATION	HOURS	PHONE	COMMENTS
PAX TERM INFO	ANG area	0800-1700 M-F	C-970-8403, A-697-8403	
	Ask SP for directions. All the facilities of a regional airport. No military support facilities.			
Recording		24 hrs dly	C-970-8611, A-697-8611	

UNSCHEDULED FLIGHTS

Flts to CONUS, OCONUS, and foreign countries via ANG KC-135E/M aircraft. Call for destinations, routings, and schedules.

TENNESSEE

Memphis International Airport (MEM)
164th Tactical Airlift Group (ANG)
Memphis IAP, TN 38181-0026

Comm: 901-369-4111
ATVN: 966-8210

LOCATION: From I-55 N or S, exit 5A (Brooks Rd) E 2 mi to IAP. RM: p-90, Q/13. NMC: Memphis, 3 mi

FACILITIES	LOCATION	HOURS	PHONE	COMMENTS
PAX TERM INFO	ANG area	0800-1700 M-F	C-369-4111, A-966-8210	
	Ask Sec Police for directions. All the facilities of an IAP. No military support facilities available.			

UNSCHEDULED FLIGHTS

Flts to CONUS and OCONUS locations via ANG C-130A/M aircraft. Call for destinations, routings, and schedules.

Memphis Naval Air Station (NQA)
Air Operations
Millington, TN 38054-5060

Comm: 901-872-5111
ATVN: 966-5111

LOCATION: From US-51 N at Millington, exit to Navy Rd, R to first gate on R, main gate. RM: p-90, G/3. NMC: Memphis, 20 mi SW.

FACILITIES	LOCATION	HOURS	PHONE	COMMENTS
PAX TERM INFO	Bldg N-2	0700-2300 dly	C-872-5331, A-966-5331	
	Fm Gate #2, straight on 5th Ave to dead end at Air Term. Duty desk - 1st floor.			
Recording	Bldg N-2	24 hrs dly	C-872-5332, A-966-5332	
	Updated at least two times daily			
Pax Svc Ofc	Bldg N-2	0700-2300 dly	C-872-5331	NCO on duty
PAX LOUNGES General	Limited lounge facilities. General lounge seats 26.			
	Bldg N-2	0700-2300 dly	C-872-5331	
	A/C, Tel L&LD, TV, Rest-rms, P/C seats			
DV/VIP	Bldg N-2	0700-2300 dly	C-872-5331	(07+)
	A/C, Coffee srvd, Tel L&A, O/S seats			
Protocol Svc	Bldg S-1	24 hrs dly	C-872-5500	See NAS Duty Ofc.
FOOD SERVICE Cafeteria	Good on and off Base			
	Bldg S-752	0530-1800 M-Sa, 1500 Su	C-872-1170	
Dining Hall	Ellison	0430-1915 dly	C-872-5111	
Enl Club	Bldg S-760	1600-2300 M-Sa	C-872-5980	
NCO/CPO Club	Bldg S-191	1100-2330 dly	C-872-5442	
OFC Club	Bldg S-89	1100-2200 dly	C-872-8154	
Snack Bars	Bldg S-56	0930-1730 dly	C-872-7762	
Vending	Bldg N-2	0700-2300 dly	C-872-5331	

TENNESSEE

Memphis NAS, Cont'd

TRANSPORTATION Air Tickets	Limited on Base Bldg S-52 0830-1700 M-F C-872-0142 OMEGA
Bus(Shuttle)	Bldg S-155 0500-2300 M-F C-346-1300 $8.00 to Memphis
Car Rentals	Bldg N-2 24 hrs dly Rayburn=C-872-8181, Natl=873-0900
TAXI(Comm)	Bldg N-2 24 hrs dly C-872-3321 Bldg N-2 24 hrs M-F C-872-5752/5509
Parking	Bldg N-2 0700-2300 dly C-872-5331 Short term-24 hrs in front; long term-30 days if approved by Ops Duty Officer.
OTHER SERVICES Exchange	Good on and off base Bldg S-752 0930-1730 M-F, 1700 Sa, 1600 Su C-872-7716
Hair Styles	Bldg S-752 Same as BX C-872-2191 Barber C-872-2197 Beauty
Laundry/DryC	Bldg S-79 Same as BX C-872-2427
Medical	Bldg H-100 24 hrs dly C-872-5921/5444
Postal	Bldg S-4 0830-1630 M-F C-872-5577
TML	Bldg S-1 24 hrs dly C-872-5500, A-966-5500 All Ranks. DV/VIP C-872-5500.
TRAVELERS AID ARC	Good on Base Bldg S-55 0800-1630 M-F C-872-5607 O/hrs C-872-5509
Chaplain	Bldg S-777 0800-1700 M-F C-872-5344
Emerg Relief	Bldg S-777 0800-1630 M-F C-872-7266 Navy Relief
Sec Police	Bldg S-2 24 hrs dly C-872-5533
USO	7918 Church St, Millington Call for hours. C-872-7722

UNSCHEDULED FLIGHTS

Frequent flts to the following destinations via Navy C009A/ME/P, C-12A/P, and P-3A/M aircraft. Call for routings and schedules which are updated every 12 hours: Alameda NAS CA (NGZ); Birmingham Municipal Arpt AL (BHM); Brunswick NAS ME (NHZ); Buckley ANGB CO (BKF); Cecil Field NAS FL (NZC); Chase Field NAS FL (NIR); Cherry Point MCAS NC (NKT); Columbia Metro Arpt SC (CAE); Columbus AFB MS (CBM); Dallas NAS TX (NBE); Davis-Monthan AFB AZ (DMA); Dobbins AFB/Atlanta NAS GA (MGE); Elmendorf AFB AK (EDF); England AFB LA (AEX); Glenview NAS IL (NBU); Jacksonville NAS FL (NIP); Keesler AFB MS (BIX); Key West NAS TX (NQX); Kingsville NAS TX (NQI); Lemoore NAS CA (NLC); Miramar NAS CA (NKX); Moffett Field NAS CA (NUQ); New Orleans NAS LA (NBG); Norfolk NAS VA (NGU); North Island NAS CA (NZY); Oceana NAS VA (NTU); Orlando Executive Arpt FL (ORL); Patuxent River NAS MD (NHK); Pensacola NAS FL (NPA); Point Mugu NAS CA (NTD); Richards-Gebaur AFB MO (GVW); Rickenbacker AFB OH (LCK); Scott AFB IL (BLV); Selfridge ANGB MI (MTC); Washington NAF MD (NSF); and Whidbey Island NAS WA (NUW).

TENNESSEE

Nashville Metropolitan Airport (BNA)
118th Tactical Airlift Wing (ANG)
Nashville, TN 37217-0267

Comm: 615-361-4600
ATVN: 446-6210

LOCATION: From I-40 E or W, Exit 214, Briley Pkwy S to airport on L. RM: p-90, P/9. NMC: Nashville, 4 mi NW.

FACILITIES	LOCATION	HOURS	PHONE	COMMENTS
PAX TERM INFO	ANG area Ask SP for directions. All the support facilities of a regional airport. No military support facilities.	0800-1700 M-F	C-361-4600, A-446-6210	

UNSCHEDULED FLIGHTS

Flts to CONUS and OCONUS locations via ANG C-130A/M aircraft. Call for destinations, routings, and schedules.

TEXAS

Bergstrom Air Force Base (BSM)
67th TRW/DOB
Bergstrom AFB, TX 78743-5000

Comm: 512-369-4100
ATVN: 685-1110

LOCATION: From US-183 or TX-71. Clearly marked. RM: p-93, WZ/10. NMC: Austin, 7 mi NW.

FACILITIES	LOCATION	HOURS	PHONE	COMMENTS
PAX TERM INFO	Bldg 207	24 hrs dly	C-369-2611, A-685-2611	From main gate straight on Presidential Blvd to Pax Term on L at flight line. Full large Base support. See Military Living's "US Forces Travel Guide USA & Caribbean Areas" for details.

UNSCHEDULED FLIGHTS

Call maximum of one day in advance for destinations, routings, and schedules.

Biggs Army Airfield (BIF)
Air Operations
Fort Bliss, TX 79916-5000

Comm: 915-568-8088
ATVN: 978-8088

LOCATION: Accessible from I-10 or US-54 N or S. Rm: p-93, WW/4. NMC: El Paso, within NE section of the city limits.

FACILITIES	LOCATION	HOURS	PHONE	COMMENTS
PAX TERM INFO	Bldg 11210	0600-2200 M-F, 0800-1600 Sa-Su	C-568-8097, A-978-8097.	NE of main post off Wilson Rd. Ltd facilities.

SCHEDULED FLIGHTS

DESTINATION	ROUTING	FREQ	EQ/CMTS
Scott AFB IL (BLV)	SUU-BIF-SKF-BLV	Tu,F	C009A/ME

TEXAS

Biggs AAF, Cont'd

| Travis AFB
CA (SUU) | BLV-SKF-BIF-SUU | M,W | C009A/ME |

UNSCHEDULED FLIGHTS

Limited flts via C-12A/P and C-21A/P aircraft. Some transient aircraft activity via C-141 and C005A. Call for destinations, routings, and schedules.

Carswell Air Force Base (FWH)
7th Transportation Squadron/LGTT
Carswell AFB, TX 76127-5000

Comm: 817-735-5000
ATVN: 739-1110

LOCATION: Off TX-183. Fm Fort Worth, W on I-30, exit at Carswell AFB on Horne St. Follow signs to main gate. RM: p-96/ D/2. NMC: Fort Worth, 7 mi E.

FACILITIES	LOCATION	HOURS	PHONE	COMMENTS
PAX TERM INFO	Bldg 1423	0730-1630 M-F	C-735-5649/7861, A-739-5649/7861	
	Fm East Gate straight on Jenning Dr to Pax Term on R.			
Pax Svc Ofc	Bldg 1561	0730-1630 M-F	C-735-7222	TMO on duty
PAX LOUNGES General	No separate family lounge			
	Bldg 1423	0730-1630 M-F	C-735-7861	
FOOD SERVICE Dining Hall	Good on and off Base			
	Bldg 1550	0600-1800 dly	C-735-7462	
Enl Club	Bldg 2570	Call for hrs.	C-735-5293	
NCO/CPO Club	Bldg 2570	Call for hrs.	C-735-5293	
OFC Club	Bldg 3102	Call for hrs.	C-731-2774	
Snack Bars	Bldg 1425	24 hrs dly	C-735-7531	Base Operations
Vending	Bldg 1425	24 hrs dly	C-735-7531	Base Operations
TRANSPORTATION	Limited on Base. Air Tickets (SATO) C-735-5579, Bus(Comm) C-782-4000 (Gov) C-735-7142, TAXI(Gov) C-735-7311, Parking C-735-5200 (notify Sec Pol for long term)			
OTHER SERVICES	Good on and off Base. Exchange C-738-1943, Barber C-731-2651, Beauty C-738-8051, Laundry C-763-8093, Medical C-782-4000, Postal C-735-7659			
TML	Bldg 3140	24 hrs dly	C-735-5274/5449, A-739-5274/5449	
	All Ranks.	DV/VIP C-735-5449.		
TRAVELERS AID ARC	Good on and off Base			
	Bldg 1525, Rm 220	Duty hrs C-735-7956	O/hrs C-735-9011	

TEXAS
Carswell AFB, Cont'd

Chaplain	Bldg 1838	0730-1630 M-F	C-735-7301
Emerg Relief	Bldg 1525	Duty hrs	C-735-7956 AF Relief
Lost/Found	Bldg 1423	0730-1630 M-F	C-735-5649
Sec Police	Bldg 1504	24 hrs dly	C-735-5200
ATTRACTIONS	Dallas, Dallas Cowboys, symphony, art, and rodeo		

SCHEDULED FLIGHTS

DESTINATION	ROUTING	FREQ	EQ/CMTS
RAF Fairford UK (FFD)	FWH-PSM-FFD	1 ea mo	KC-135E/M
Hickam AFB HI (HIK)	FWH-RIV-HIK	1 ea 3-6 mo	KC-135E/M
Kelley AFB TX (SKF)	BLV-SKF-FWH-BLV	Tu,Th	C009A/ME
RAF Mildenhall UK (MHZ)	FWH-PSM-MHZ	1 ea 3-6 mo	KC-135E/M
Pease AFB NH (PSM)	FWH-PSM-MHZ	1 ea mo	KC-135E/M
Scott AFB IL (BLV)	BLV-SKF-FWH-BLV	Tu,Th	C009A/ME

UNSCHEDULED FLIGHTS

Flights to: Barksdale AFB LA (BAD); Eielson AFB AK (EIL); and March AFB CA (RIV). Call for other CONUS, OCONUS, and foreign country destinations, routings, and schedules.

Chase Field Naval Air Station (NIR)
Box 12/Air Operations
Chase Field NAS, TX 78103-5000

Comm: 512-354-5011
ATVN: 861-1110

LOCATION: Off US-181, 5 mi SE of Beeville. Clearly marked. RM: p-95, ER/7.
NMC: Corpus Christi, 45 mi SE.

FACILITIES	LOCATION	HOURS	PHONE	COMMENTS
PAX TERM INFO	Base Ops 24 hrs dly C-354-5276/5377, A-861-5276/5377 Ask SP for directions. Full large base support. See Military Living's "US Forces Travel Guide USA & Caribbean Areas" for details.			

UNSCHEDULED FLIGHTS

Flts via C009A/P and other administrative aircraft to CONUS locations. Call for destinations, routings, and schedules.

TEXAS

Corpus Christi Naval Air Station (NGP)
Air Operations Dept/Operations Maintenance Division
Corpus Christi NAS, TX 78419-5000

Comm: 512-939-2811
ATVN: 861-1110

LOCATION: On TX-358, SE side of Corpus Christi. The South Gate is on NAS Drive. RM: p-95, ET/8. NMC: Corpus Christi, 10 mi W.

FACILITIES	LOCATION	HOURS	PHONE	COMMENTS
PAX TERM INFO	Hangar 58, 1st fl	0800-1700 M-F	C-939-2505, A-861-2505	Fm South Gate straight on Lexington Blvd to L on 1st St to L on Ave D to Pax Term on L.
Recording	Hangar 41	0800-1600 M-F	C-939-3385, A-861-3385	Air Ops USCG Air Station, Corpus Christi
Pax Svc Ofc	Hangar 58, 1st fl	0800-1700 M-F	C-939-2505	NCO on duty
PAX LOUNGES General	Hangar 58, 1st fl	0800-1700 M-F	C-939-2505	Limited facilities. No separate DV/VIP or family lounges. A/C, Rest-rms, TV, P/C seats
Protocol Svc	Bldg 1	0800-1600 M-F	C-939-2284	CNATRA
FOOD SERVICE	Good on and off Base. Enlisted Dining Hall C-939-3768, Enl Club C-939-3867, NCO/CPO Club C-939-2240, O'Club C-939-2541, Restaurant C-937-6202 (fast food)			
TRANSPORTATION	Limited on and off Base. Bus(Comm) C-882-1732 (Shuttle) C-939-3841, Limo Svc C-882-1722, Parking at Hangar 58 (must have tag from Sec Police)			
OTHER SERVICES	Good on and off Base. Exchange C-939-2033, Bank/Exc C-939-3113, Barber C-939-8880, Beauty C-939-8901, Laundry/ Dry/C C-939-9142, Medical C-939-2688, Postal C-939-2984			
TML	Bldg 1281, Lodge Bldg 101 0800-1700 M-F C-937-6361, A-861-6361 All Ranks. DV/VIP C-939-2380/2389.			
TRAVELERS AID	Good on Base. ARC C-939-3751, Chaplain C-939-3751, Navy Relief C-939-2560, Sec Police C-939-2480, USO C-939-2391			
ATTRACTIONS	Bay and gulf water sports, historic homes			

UNSCHEDULED FLIGHTS

Flts to CONUS, Midwest, West Coast, and OCONUS locations via USN T-44A/P, USCG HU-25/P, and transient aircraft. Call for destinations, routings and schedules.

Dallas Naval Air Station (NBE)
Air Operations Dept/Pax Terminal
Dallas NAS, TX 75211-5000

Comm: 214-266-6111
ATVN: 874-6111

LOCATION: Exit from I-30 at loop 12, W of Dallas, go S on loop 12 to Jefferson Ave exit, NAS on left or S side of Ave. Near Grand Prairie. RM: p-96, E/7. NMC: Dallas, 15 mi NE.

TEXAS
Dallas NAS, Cont'd

FACILITIES	LOCATION	HOURS	PHONE	COMMENTS
PAX TERM INFO	Bldg 20	0700-2200 dly	C-266-6651, A-874-6651	
	Main hangar is on SW corner of Base bldg complex.			
Recording		24 hrs dly	C-266-6651	
Pax Svc Ofc	Bldg 802	0800-1700 M-F	C-263-0670/0924, A-874-6556/7	
	US Army Reserve Aviation Support Facility			
PAX LOUNGES General	Ltd lounge facilities. Separate DV/VIP lounge.			
	Bldg 20	0700-2300 dly	C-266-6374	A/C, Rest-rms, P/C seats
FOOD SERVICE Cafeteria	Good on and off Base			
	Bldg 12	0630-1730 Tu-Su, 0700-1700 M	C-266-6405	
Dining Hall	Map # 10	0600-1800 dly	C-266-6111	
Enl Club	Bldg 12	1100-2400 dly	C-266-6413	
OFC Club	Bldg 12	0700-2300 dly	C-266-6134	
Snack Bars	Bldg 20	1030-1700 W-Su	C-266-6134	Also vending
TRANSPORTATION Car Rentals	Limited on Base			
	Bldg 20	0800-1600 Tu-Su	Arendale Rent-a-Car=C-261-4261	
			Mid-Cities Auto=C-265-1134	
TAXI(Comm)	Bldg 20	24 hrs dly	City=C-261-7551, State=C-823-2161,	
			Yellow=C-426-6262	
Parking	Bldg 20	24 hrs dly	Short term. Long term outside Term.	
Exchange	Bldg 12	1000-1700 W-Su	C-266-6400	
Hair Styles	Bldg 12	0900-1700 W-Su	C-266-6400	Barber
Laundry/DryC	Bldg 12	1000-1700 W-Su	C-266-6400	
Medical	Map # 9	24 hrs dly	C-266-6283	
TML	Bldg 209	24 hrs dly	C-266-6468/6134, A-874-6468/	
	6134	All Ranks.	DV/VIP C-266-6140.	
TRAVELERS AID Chaplain	Limited on Base			
	Map # 74	0800-1700 M-F	C-266-6132	
Sec Police	Main gate	24 hrs dly	C-266-6132	
ATTRACTIONS	Great city of Dallas nearby			

UNSCHEDULED FLIGHTS

Frequent flts via Navy administrative aircraft, ANG C-130A/P aircraft, and transient aircraft to: Albuquerque (also Kirtland AFB) NM (ABQ); Buckley ANGB CO (BKF); El Paso Intl Arpt TX (ELP); Houston CGAS TX (EFD); Kelly AFB TX (SKF); Kingsville NAS TX (NQI); Miramar NAS CA (NKX); New Orleans NAS LA (NBG); North Island NAS CA (NZY); Pensacola NAS FL (NPA); Tinker AFB OK (TIK); Tulsa Intl Arpt OK (TUL); and Whidbey Island NAS WA (NUW).

TEXAS

Dyess Air Force Base (DYS)
1st Mobile Aerial Port Squadron
Dyess AFB, TX 79607-5000

Comm: 915-696-0212
ATVN: 461-1110

LOCATION: Six mi SW of Abilene. Main gate is 3 mi E of I-20. Also from I-20 & US-277. RM: p-94, EG/2. NMC: Abilene, 6 mi NE.

FACILITIES	LOCATION	HOURS	PHONE	COMMENTS
PAX TERM INFO	Bldg 9001	24 hrs dly	C-696-3108/2237, A-461-2237/3108	Fm N Gate straight on 3rd St to R on Ave A to Base Ops on R.
Pax Svc Ofc	Bldg 9001	24 hrs dly	C-696-3108/2237	NCO on duty
PAX LOUNGES General	Limited lounge facilities. DV/VIP see Pax Svc NCO. Bldg 9001	24 hrs dly	C-696-3108	A/C, Rest-rms, P/C seats
FOOD SERVICE Dining Hall	Good on Base SAC alert	24 hrs dly	C-696-0212	
Enl Club	Bldg 6122	1900-2400 dly	C-692-3220	
NCO/CPO Club	Bldg 7106	1100-2400 dly	C-692-9540	
OFC Club	Bldg 7402	Call for hrs.	C-692-9577	
Snack Bars	Plainview (flight line)	0600-2000 M-F	C-692-5656	
TRANSPORTATION TAXI(Gov)	Very limited. Comm bus and taxi service in Abilene. Bldg 9001	24 hrs dly	C-696-4728	
Parking	Bldg 9001	24 hrs dly	C-696-3108	No restrictions
OTHER SERVICES Exchange	Good on Base Bldg 6142	1000-1800 Tu-Sa, 1700 Su	C-692-5656	
Bank/Exc	Bldg 7331	0900-1430 M-F	C-692-2662	
Hair Styles	Bldg 7333	Same as BX	C-692-5656	
Laundry/DryC	Bldg 7327	Same as BX	C-692-5656	
Medical	Bldg 9201	24 hrs dly	C-696-2333/4	
Postal	Bldg 7333	0800-1600 M-F	C-696-2655	
TML	Bldg 7409 All Ranks.	24 hrs dly	C-696-2467, A-461-2467 DV/VIP C-696-4275.	
TRAVELERS AID ARC	Bldg 7405 Taylor City	0800-1700 M-F 24 hrs dly	C-696-2405 C-677-2622	Family Services
Chaplain	Bldg 6219	0800-1700 M-F	C-696-4224	
Emerg Relief	Ask the Commander		C-696-3355	
Sec Police	Bldg 7216	24 hrs dly	C-696-3352/2131	
ATTRACTIONS	Abilene and outdoor sports			

TEXAS
Dyess AFB, Cont'd

SCHEDULED FLIGHTS

DESTINATION	ROUTING	FREQ	EQ/CMTS
RAF Fairford UK (FFD)	DYS-PSM-FFD	1 ea mo	KC-135E/M
Little Rock AFB AR (LRF)	DYS-LRF	3 ea mo	C-130H/M
Pease AFB NH (PSM)	DYS-PSM-FFD	1 ea mo	KC-135E/M
Pope AFB NC (POB)	DYS-POB	1 ea wk	C-130H/M
Travis AFB CA (SUU)	DYS-SUU	2 ea mo	C-130H/M

UNSCHEDULED FLIGHTS

Flts to CONUS, OCONUS, and foreign country locations. Call for destinations, routings, and schedules.

Houston Coast Guard Air Station (EFD)
Air Operations/Ellington Fld
Houston, TX 77209-5599

Comm: 713-481-0025
ATVN: 954-2316/2637
FTS: 526-7609/7610

LOCATION: From I-45 N or S to Exit 3, E to Ellington Fld. RM: p-95, EN/14. NMC: Houston, 15 mi NW.

FACILITIES	LOCATION	HOURS	PHONE	COMMENTS
PAX TERM INFO	Bldg 1178 0800-1600 M-F C-481-0025, A-954-2316 Ask SP for directions. No Pax lounge. Base Ops processes all Pax. Barber shop available.			

UNSCHEDULED FLIGHTS

Houston CGAS no longer reports unscheduled Space-A flights; however, Space-A flights operated by contract carrier Southwest Services occasionally transit Ellington Field. Also, check with Army RES in Bldg 1173, C-484-6111/2, A-954-2332/3/5, for possible helo aircraft flights.

Kelly Air Force Base (SKF)
San Antonio Air Logistics Center
Kelly AFB, TX 78241-5000

Comm: 512-925-1110
ATVN: 945-1110

LOCATION: All of the following, I-10, I-35, I-37, and I-410 intersect with US-90. From US-90 take either the Gen Hudnell or Gen McMullen exit and go S to AFB. RM: p-95, EY/13. NMC: San Antonio, 7 mi NE.

FACILITIES	LOCATION	HOURS	PHONE	COMMENTS
PAX TERM INFO	Bldg 1614 0700-1800 M-F, 0800-1600 Sa-Su C-925-8714/5, A-945-8714/5 From Gate #1 straight on Duncan Dr to R on Luke Dr to Pax Term on L.			

TEXAS

Kelly AFB, Cont'd

Recording	Bldg 1614	24 hrs dly	C-925-5706	Updated 0700 dly
Pax Svc Ofc	Bldg 1614	Same as Pax Term	C-925-8714/5	NCO on duty
Pax Paging	Bldg 1614	Same as Pax Term	C-925-8714/5	
PAX LOUNGES General	No separate family lounges Bldg 1614 Same as Pax Term C-925-5706 A/C, Tel L&A, TV, Rest-rms, P/C seats			
DV/VIP	Bldg 1610	As needed. See Pax Svc NCO.	C-925-8714/5	
Protocol Svc	Post Commander	24 hrs dly	C-925-6906	SA-Air Logistics Ctr
FOOD SERVICE Cafeteria	Good on and off Base Bldg 1614 24 hrs dly C-925-3875			
Dining Hall	Bldg 1650	0500-0100 dly	C-925-5791 C-925-8350	In-flight meals
NCO/CPO Club	Bldg 3135	0800-2300 dly	C-924-4511	
OFC Club	Bldg 1676	1000-2300 dly	C-924-7341	
Restaurants	Bldg 1437	1100-2300 dly	C-925-4990	
Vending	Bldg 1614	24 hrs dly	C-925-8714	
TRANSPORTATION Air Tickets	Good on and off Base Bldg 1614 0800-1645 M-F C-925-7371 SATO			
Bus(Comm) (Shuttle)	San Antonio GH=C-227-8351, TW=C-226-6136 Bldg 1614 City Bus (VIA) C-227-2020 Bldg 1614 0700-0130 dly C-925-6372 Base area			
Limo Service	Bldg 1614	24 hrs dly	C-671-3555	Lackland Taxi
TAXI(Comm) (Gov)	Bldg 1614 24 hrs dly Yellow=C-226-4242, Checker=C-222-2151 Motor Pool 0600-2345 dly C-925-6372			
Trains	AMTRAK	24 hrs dly	C-223-3226	
Parking	Bldg 1614 24 hrs dly Short term-lot 718, across from Pax Term, 15 days max; long term-lot 105 near main gate.			
OTHER SERVICES Exchange	Good on and off Base Bldg 1637 1030-1730 M-F, 1600 Sa C-924-9247			
Hair Styles	Bldg 1637	1630-1730 M-F, 1600 Sa	C-924-9247	
Laundry/DryC	Bldg 1637	Same as above		
Medical	Bldg 1740	24 hrs dly	C-925-4544	
Postal	Bldg 1650	1000-1400 M-F	C-925-8255	
Weather	Bldg 1650	24 hrs dly	C-925-1115	

TEXAS
Kelly AFB, Cont'd

TML	Bldg 1676 A-945-8931	24 hrs dly All Ranks.	C-925-8931/924-7201, DV/VIP C-925-7678.
TRAVELERS AID ARC	Bldg 147 Bldg 9016	0800-1700 M-F 0800-1630 M-F	C-925-4181 Family Services C-671-3381 O/hrs C-671-4225
Chaplain	Bldg 1669	0800-1700 M-F	C-925-7874
Emerg Relief	Bldg 1650	0800-1700 M-F	C-925-7114/6 AF Aid
Sec Police	Bldg 105	24 hrs dly	C-925-6811
USO	410 South Alamo, San Antonio C-227-9373 Call for hours.		
ATTRACTIONS	Alamo, River Walk, Tower of the Americas		

SCHEDULED FLIGHTS

DESTINATION	ROUTING	FREQ	EQ/CMTS
Barksdale AFB MS (BAD)	SKF-SPS-AEX-BAD-BLV SKF-TIK-LAW-FWH-AEX-BAD	Tu Th	C009A/ME C009A/ME
Carswell AFB TX (FWH)	SKF-TIK-LAW-FWH-AEX-BAD	Th	C009A/ME
Davis-Monthan AFB AZ (DMA)	SKF-ELP-DMA-LUF-NKX-SUU SKF-ELP-DMA-LUF-SUU	M W	C009A/ME C009A/ME
Dyess AFB TX (DYS)	SKF-DYS-LRF-BLV	Su	C009A/ME
El Paso IAP TX (ELP)	SKF-ELP-DMA-LUF-NKX-SUU SKF-ELP-DMA-LUF-SUU SKF-ELP-SUU	M W Sa	C009A/ME C009A/ME C009A/ME
England AFB LA (AEX)	SKF-SPS-BAD-AEX-BAD-BLV SKF-TIK-LAW-FW-AEX-BAD	Tu Th	C009A/ME C009A/ME
Howard AFB PN (HOW)	SKF-HOW	F	C005A/M
Huntsville AL (HSV)	SKF-BIX-MGE-HSV-BHM-BLV	F	C009A/ME
Keesler AFB MS (BIX)	SKF-BIX-MGE-HSV-BHM-BLV	F	C009A/ME
Lawton Municipal Arpt OK (LAW)	SKF-TIK-LAW-FWH-AEX-BAD SKF-TIK-LAW-AEX	Th Sa	C009A/ME C009A/ME
Luke AFB AZ (LUF)	SKF-ELP-DMA-LUF-NKX-SUU SKF-ELP-DMA-LUF-SUU	M W	C009A/ME C009A/ME

TEXAS

Kelly AFB, Cont'd

Miramar NAS CA (NKX)	SKF-ELP-DMA-LUF-NKX-SUU	M	C009A/ME
Scott AFB IL (BLV)	SKF-DYS-LRF-BLV SKF-BLV SKF-SPS-AEX-BAD-BLV SKF-BLV SKF-BLV SKF-BIX-MGE-HSV-BHM-BLV SKF-BLV SKF-BLV	Su Su Tu Tu W F F Sa	C009A/ME C009A/ME C009A/ME C009A/ME C009A/ME C009A/ME C009A/ME C009A/ME
Sheppard AFB TX (SPS)	SKF-SPS-AEX-BAD-BLV	Tu	C009A/ME
Tinker AFB OK (TIK)	SKF-TIK-LAW-FWH-AEX-BAD SKF-TIK-LAW-AEX	Th Sa	C009A/ME C009A/ME
Travis AFB CA (SUU)	SKF-ELP-DMA-LUF-NKX-SUU SKF-ELP-DMA-LUF-SUU SKF-SUU SKF-ELP-SUU	M W Th Sa	C009A/ME C009A/ME C009A/ME C009A/ME

UNSCHEDULED FLIGHTS

Flights via C005A aircraft to the following locations: Charleston AFB SC (CHS); Dover AFB DE (DOV); Eglin AFB FL (VPS); Hickam AFB HI (HIK); Hill AFB UT (HIF); Howard AB PN (HOW); Kadena AB JA (DNA); Lajes AF PO (LGS); McClellan AFB CA (MCC); Mildenhall AB UK (MHZ); New Orleans NAS LA (NBG); Norton AFB CA (SBD); Osan AB RK (OSN); Ramstein AB GE (RMS); Roosevelt Roads NAS PR (NRR); Travis AFB CA (SUU); Tyndall AFB FL (PAM); Wright-Patterson AFB OH (FFO);

NOTES

TEXAS

Laughlin Air Force Base (DLF)
47th Flying Training Wing/Air Operations
Laughlin AFB, TX 78843-5000

Comm: 512-298-3511
ATVN: 732-1110

LOCATION: Take US-90 W from San Antonio, 150 mi or US-277 S from San Angelo, 150 mi to Del Rio area. The AFB is clearly marked off US-90. RM: p-93, WU/15. NMC: Del Rio, 6 mi NW.

FACILITIES	LOCATION	HOURS	PHONE	COMMENTS
PAX TERM INFO	Bldg 317 24 hrs dly C-298-5308/5262, A-732-5308/5262 From main gate straight on Liberty Dr to L on Florida Ave to Base Ops on R. Full large Base support. See Military Living's "US Forces Travel Guide USA and Caribbean Areas" f/details.			
	UNSCHEDULED FLIGHTS			
Occasional flights to CONUS locations via AF administrative aircraft.				

Muni-Webb Field Airport (TXK)
Red River Army Depot Air Operations/SDSRR-AD
Texarkana, TX 75507-5000

Comm: 214-838-2141
ATVN: 829-2141

LOCATION: Off I-30 E or W, take Red River Army Depot exit. Route clearly marked. RM: P-94, ED/14. NMC: Texarkana, 20 mi E

FACILITIES	LOCATION	HOURS	PHONE	COMMENTS
PAX TERM INFO	Depot Aviation Section C-772-9786, A-829-4110-EX-Avn Sec On comm airport, follow signs to Depot Aviation Sec. Full post support at Depot. Regional airport support at airport.			
	UNSCHEDULED FLIGHTS			
Flts via U-21G/P aircraft to CONUS locations. Call for destinations, routings, and schedules.				

Randolph Air Force Base (RND)
12th Trans Sqdn/LGTTPT
Randolph AFB, TX 78150-5000

Comm: 512-652-1110
ATVN: 487-1110

LOCATION: Take Exit 172 off I-35, Pat Booker Rd. Off I-10 take Exit 587, TX FM-1604. RM: p-95, EO/6. NMC: San Antonio, 20 mi SW.

FACILITIES	LOCATION	HOURS	PHONE	COMMENTS
PAX TERM INFO	Hangar 7 east side 0600-1800 M-F, Sa-Su as required C-652-1854/3725, A-487-1854/3725 Fm main gate L on 1st Ave E to R on 5th St E for .75 mi to Pax Term on L.			
Pax Svc Ofc	Hangar 7 0730-1615 M-F C-652-1854/3725 NCO on duty			
PAX LOUNGES General	Limited lounge facilities. No separate family lounge. Hangar 7 0600-1800 M-F C-652-1854 A/C, Tel L,LD&ATVN, TV, Rest-rms, O/S seats			

TEXAS

Randolph AFB Cont'd

DV/VIP	Bldg 8	0600-2200 M-F	C-652-3416	A/C, Coffee/tea srvd, Tel L,LD&ATVN, TV, Rest-rms, O/S seats. No host.
Protocol Svc	Bldg 100	0800-1700 M-F	C-652-1110	12th FTW
FOOD SERVICE Cafeteria	Good services on and off Base Bldg 11 0600-2000 M-F, 1900 Sa-Su C-658-411			
Dining Hall	Bldg 860	0500-1800 dly	C-652-1110	Call for svc hrs.
NCO/CPO Club	Bldg 598	Call for hrs.	C-658-3557	
OFC Club	Bldg 500	Call for hrs.	C-658-7445	
Snack Bars	Bldg 1071	0900-2200 dly	C-658-1440	
Vending	Hangar 7	24 hrs dly	C-652-1854	
TRANSPORTATION Air Tickets	Limited on Base Bldg 152 0730-1615 M-F C-652-2650			
TAXI(Gov)	Bldg 175	24 hrs dly	C-652-3475	
Parking	Hangar 7	24 hrs dly	C-652-5700	SP for long term
OTHER SERVICES Exchange	Good services on Base Bldg 1073 0930-1730 M-Sa, 1600 Su C-658-7471/2681			
Bank/Exc	Bldg 1074	0800-1600 M-F	C-658-727	
Hair Styles	Bldg 1073	0800-1730 M-F, 1600 Sa	C-658-0581 Barber C-658-7755 Beauty	
Laundry	Bldg 1073	0800-1730 M-F	C-659-4260	
Medical	Bldg 675	24 hrs dly	C-652-2666	
Postal	Bldg 220	0830-1630 M-F	C-652-2606	
TML	Bldg 118 All Ranks.	24 hrs dly DV/VIP C-658-4621.	C-652-1844, A-487-1844	
TRAVELERS AID ARC	Bldg 662	0830-1600 M-F	C-652-1855	Other hrs C-652-1859
Chaplain	Bldg 103	0730-1615 M-F	C-652-6121	
Sec Police	Bldg 235	24 hrs dly	C-652-5700	
USO	410 S Alamo, San Antonio		C-512-227-9373	Call for hrs.
ATTRACTIONS	San Antonio, Canyon Lake Recreation Area			

SCHEDULED FLIGHTS

DESTINATION	ROUTING	FREQ	EQ/CMTS
Andrews AFB MD (ADW)	RND-ADW	4-5 ea wk	C-21A

TEXAS
Randolph AFB Cont'd

Mather AFB CA (MHR)	RND-MHR	M,F	T-43/P
Maxwell AFB AL (MXF)	RND-MXF	3-4 ea wk	C-21/A
Scott AFB IL (BLV)	RND-BLV	2-3 ea wk	C-21A
Wright- Patterson AFB OH (FFO)	RND-FFO	2-3 ea wk	C-21A

Reese Air Force Base (REE)
64th Flying Training Wing
Reese AFB, TX 79489-5000

Comm: 806-885-4511
ATVN: 838-4511

LOCATION: Fm I-289 (Loop) take 4th St, 6 mi W. The road terminates at AFB, main gate is one block N. RM: p-92, WJ/12. NMC: Lubbock, 6 mi E.

FACILITIES	LOCATION HOURS PHONE COMMENTS
PAX TERM INFO	Bldg 79 Base Ops 0700-1900 M-Th, 2100 F, 0900-1600 Sa, 1000-1700 Su C-885-3105/6, A-838-3105/6 Fm main gate straight on Main St, cross Hangar Line Rd, Base Ops on R. Pax Svc Ofc, Bldg 79, Base Ops hrs. NCO on duty.
PAX LOUNGES General	Very limited Bldg 79 See Pax Term C-885-3105/6 A/C, Bag chk, Rest-rms, O/S seats
DV/VIP	Bldg 79 See Pax Term C-885-3105/6 A/C, Bag chk, Coffee/tea srvd, Rest-rms, O/S seats
OTHER SERVICES	Full large Base support. For details see Military Living's "US Forces Travel Guide USA & Caribbean Areas."

UNSCHEDULED FLIGHTS

Occasional flights via C009A aircraft. Call for destinations, routings, and schedules.

−NOTES−

TEXAS

Robert Gray Army Airfield (GRK)
Air Operations
Fort Hood, TX 76544-5000

Comm: 817-288-9200/9209
ATVN: 738-1110

LOCATION: From I-35 take US-190 W 12 mi to West Fort Hood exit. Turn left, under US-190, and proceed S on Base Road to West Fort Hood and AAF. RM: p-94, ED/7. NMC: Killeen, at main Post entrance.

FACILITIES	LOCATION	HOURS	PHONE	COMMENTS
PAX TERM INFO	Bldg 90049	1800-2400 M-F	C-288-9718, A-738-9718	Pax Svc is not available.

UNSCHEDULED FLIGHTS

Infrequent flights to CONUS locations via transient AF C-141B/M and C-5A/M aircraft. Commercial ground transportation only.

Sheppard Air Force Base (SPS)
Hq Sheppard Tech Tng Ctr/Air Ops
Sheppard AFB, TX 76311-5000

Comm: 817-851-2511
ATVN: 736-1001

LOCATION: Take US-281 N from Wichita Falls, exit to TX-325 which leads to main gate. Clearly marked. RM: p-92, WA/6. NMC: Wichita Falls, 5 mi SW.

FACILITIES	LOCATION	HOURS	PHONE	COMMENTS
PAX TERM INFO	Bldg 1360	0800-2000 dly	C-851-6474/2180, A-736-6474/2180	Main gate R on 1st St to L on Ave J to Base Ops on R.
Pax Svc Ofc	Bldg 1360	0800-2000 dly	C-851-6474/2180	NCO on duty
PAX LOUNGES General	Limited lounge facilities. No separate family lounge. Bldg 1360 0800-2000 dly C-851-6474 A/C, Bag chk, Tel L&ATVN, Rest-rms, P/C seats			
DV/VIP	Bldg 1360 0800-2000 dly C-851-6474 (O6+) A/C, Bag chk, Coffee/tea srvd, Read/write rms, Tel L&ATVN, Rest-rms, O/S seats			
Protocol Svc	Bldg 400	0730-1630 M-F	C-851-2930	
OTHER SERVICES	Full large Base spt fac avail. For details see Military Living's "US Forces Travel Guide USA & Caribbean Areas."			

SCHEDULED FLIGHTS

DESTINATION	ROUTING	FREQ	EQ/CMTS
Kelley AFB TX (SKF)	SPS-SKF-BLV	2-3 per wk	C009A/ME
Scott AFB IL (BLV)	SPS-SKF-BLV	2-3 per wk	C009A/ME

UNSCHEDULED FLIGHTS

Flights of 2-3 per week via C-21A/P and CT-39/P aircraft to CONUS locations. Call for destinations, routings, and schedules.

UTAH

Hill Air Force Base (HIF)
2849th Air Base Group/DSTTHL
Hill AFB, UT 84056-5000

Comm: 801-777-7221
ATVN: 458-1110

LOCATION: Adjacent to I-15 between Ogden and Salt Lake City. Take Exit 336 E on UT-193 to south gate. RM: p-96, P/7. NMC: Ogden, 8 mi N.

FACILITIES	LOCATION	HOURS	PHONE	COMMENTS
PAX TERM INFO	Bldg 405 Area 1	0600-2200 dly	C-777-1854/2887, A-458-1854/2887	From west area, E on 2nd Street, to Bldg 405 on South Gate Drive, then west to Bldg 405.
Pax Svc Ofc	Bldg 405	0730-1600 dly	C-777-1854	
PAX LOUNGES General	Bldg 1	0600-2200 dly	C-777-1854	Good facilities A/C, Rest-rms, TV, P/C seats
DV/VIP	Bldg 1	24 hrs dly	C-777-5565	(O6+) A/C, Rest-rms, Read/write rms, Coffee/tea srvd, TV, O/S seats
Protocol Svc	Bldg 180 Area 2	0800-1700 M-F	C-777-7221	Ogden Air Logis Ctr
FOOD SERVICE Cafeteria	Bldg 402	24 hrs dly	C-825-7577	Good services on Base Call for svc hrs.
Dining Hall	Bldg 519	0515-0130 dly	C-777-3428	Call for svc hrs.
NCO/CPO Club	Bldg 450	0630-2130 M-Th, 2200 F-Su	C-777-3841	
OFC Club	Bldg 150	1800-2130 Su-Th, 2200 F-Sa	C-773-4924	
Restaurants	Bldg 230	0600-1400 M-F	C-825-1675	
Snack Bars	Bldg 402	24 hrs dly	C-825-7577	
Vending	Bldg 1	24 hrs dly	C-777-1854	
TRANSPORTATION Air Tickets	Bldg 1238	0730-1600 M-F	C-777-4677	
Bus(Shuttle)	Bldg 1	0700-1540 dly	C-777-7221	20 min schedule on Base
Limo Service	Ogden Salt Lake		Key Limo=C-394-7743 Bonneville Limo=C-364-6520	
TAXI(Comm)	Bldg 1138	24 hrs dly	C-777-1843	Yellow=C-394-9411
Parking	Bldg 405	24 hrs dly	C-777-3056	Short term and long term, see Security Police. Pick up and discharge only.
OTHER SERVICES Exchange	Bldg 430	1000-1730 M-F, 1700 Sa-Su	C-773-1207	
Bank/Exc	Bldg 442	0930-1700 M-F, 1500 Sa	C-773-8000	
Hair Styles	Bldg 430	1000-1730 M-F, 1700 Sa-Su	C-773-4602 C-773-4076	Barber Beauty

UTAH
Hill AFB, Cont'd

Laundry	Bldg 430	1000-1730 M-F, 1700 Sa-Su	C-773-3823
Medical	Bldg 570	24 hrs dly	C-777-5285/1847
Postal	Bldg 332	0900-1630 M-F	C-777-2509
TML	Bldg 146 All Ranks.	24 hrs dly DV/VIP C-777-1844.	C-777-1844/2601, A-458-1844/2601
TRAVELERS AID ARC	Bldg 308	0800-1700 M-F	C-777-1855 Other hrs C-927-3533
Chaplain	Bldg 475	0730-1600 M-F	C-777-2106 Other hrs C-777-3007
Emerg Relief	Bldg 308	0800-1700 M-F	C-777-4681 AF Aid
Sec Police	Bldg 1219	24 hrs dly	C-777-3056 Desk Sgt
ATTRACTIONS	Salt Lake City, snow skiing, Park City, Temple Square		

SCHEDULED FLIGHTS

DESTINATION	ROUTING	FREQ	EQ/CMTS
Buckley ANGB CO (BKF)	SUU-TCM-SKA-GFA-MUO-HIF-BKF-BLV	F	C009A/ME
	BLV-BKF-HIF-MUO-GFA-SKA-TCM-SUU	Sa	C009A/ME
Fairchild AFB WA (SKA)	SUU-TCM-SKA-GFA-MUO-HIF-BKF-BLV	F	C009A/ME
	BLV-BKF-HIF-MUO-GFA-SKA-TCM-SUU	Sa	C009A/ME
Malmstrom AFB MT (GFA)	SUU-TCM-SKA-GFA-MUO-HIF-BKF-BLV	F	C009A/ME
	BLV-BKF-HIF-MUO-GFA-SKA-TCM-SUU	Sa	C009A/ME
McChord AFB WA (TCM)	SUU-TCM-SKA-GFA-MUO-HIF-BKF-BLV	F	C009A/ME
	BLV-BKF-HIF-MUO-GFA-SKA-TCM-SUU	Sa	C009A/ME
Mountain Home AFB ID (MUO)	SUU-TCM-SKA-GFA-MUO-HIF-BKF-BLV	F	C009A/ME
	BLV-BKF-HIF-MUO-GFA-SKA-TCM-SUU	Sa	C009A/ME
Scott AFB IL (BLV)	SUU-TCM-SKA-GFA-MUO-HIF-BKF-BLV	F	C009A/ME
	BLV-BKF-HIF-MUO-GFA-SKA-TCM-SUU	Sa	C009A/ME
Travis AFB IA (SUU)	SUU-TCM-SKA-GFA-MUO-HIF-BKF-BLV	F	C009A/ME
	BLV-BKF-HIF-MUO-GFA-SKA-TCM-SUU	Sa	C009A/ME

UTAH

Hill AFB, Cont'd

UNSCHEDULED FLIGHTS

Flights via C-141B/M AFRES to CONUS west and southwest and return to HIF largely on weekends. Call for destinations, routings, and schedules.

Salt Lake City International Airport (SLC)   Comm: 801-521-7070
151st Air Refueling Group (ANG)   ATVN: 790-9210
Salt Lake IAP, UT 84116-5000

LOCATION: From I-215 N or S exit 26 W and follow signs to IAP. RM: p-96, H/9. NMC: Salt Lake City, 5 mi SE.

FACILITIES	LOCATION	HOURS	PHONE	COMMENTS
PAX TERM INFO	ANG area Ask Security Police for directions.	0800-1700 M-F	C-521-7070, A-790-9210	
OTHER SERVICES	Full support of IAP. No military support facilities avail.			

UNSCHEDULED FLIGHTS

Flights via KC-135E/M ANG aircraft to CONUS and OCONUS locations. Call for destinations, routings, and schedules.

VERMONT
NONE

VIRGINIA

Davison Army Airfield (DAA)   Comm: 703-664-6071
Air Operations   ATVN: 354-6071
Fort Belvoir, VA 22060-5726

LOCATION: Fm I-95 S or US-1 take Fort Belvoir exits. Signs clearly mark support facilities. RM: p-99, I/21. NMC: Washington DC, 10 mi NE.

FACILITIES	LOCATION	HOURS	PHONE	COMMENTS
PAX TERM INFO	Bldg 1327 On main road inside Hwy 1, gate sign points to DAAF.	0730-1600 dly	C-664-6565, A-354-6565	
Pax Svc Ofc	Bldg 1327	0730-1600 dly	C-664-6565	NCO on duty
PAX LOUNGES General	General lounge with DV/VIP in separate room Bldg 1327 0730-1600 dly C-664-6565 A/C, Read/write rms, Tel L,LD&ATVN, TV, Rest-rms, P/C and O/S seats			
FOOD SERVICE Snack Bars	Bldg 1333	0600-1400 M-F	C-781-7068	
OTHER SERVICES	Full large Base support. See Military Living's "Assignment: Washington, A Guide to Washington Area Military Installations" for full details on more than 35 military installations in the Washington DC area.			

VIRGINIA

Davison AAF, Cont'd
UNSCHEDULED FLIGHTS

Frequent flts via C-12A/P & C-21A/P aircraft to CONUS East Coast, Southeast, and Midwest locations. Call for destinations, routings, and schedules.

Langley Air Force Base (LFI)
1st TFW/LGTT
Langley AFB, VA 23665-5000

Comm: 804-764-9990
ATVN: 574-1110

LOCATION: Fm I-64 E in Hampton take Armistead Ave exit, R to stop light; R onto LaSalle Ave and enter AFB. RM: p-98, A/2. NMC: Hampton, 1 mi W.

FACILITIES	LOCATION	HOURS	PHONE	COMMENTS
PAX TERM INFO	Bldg 754B 0600-1800 M-F Stand-by other times C-764-4698, A-574-4698 From LaSalle gate (I-64) R on Nealy Ave to L on Danforth St to Pax Term on L.			
Recording	Bldg 754B 24 hrs dly C-764-5807, A-574-5807 Updated 1800			
Pax Svc Ofc	TRADOC Det (Army) Bldg 371 0730-1700 M-F C-727-3707 A-680-3707			
PAX LOUNGES General	General and family lounge combined Bldg 754B 0600-1800 M-F C-764-4311/4698 A/C, Tel L,LD&ATVN, TV, Rest-rms, P/C seats			
DV/VIP	Bdg 754 As required C-764-2504 (06+) A/C, Bag chk, Read/write rms, Tel L,LD&ATVN, TV, Rest-rms, O/S seats			
Protocol Svc	Bldg 693 0800-1700 M-F C-764-5044 (07+) Hq TAC			
FOOD SERVICE	Good services on and off Base. Cafeteria C-766-1225, Dining Hall C-764-5144, NCO/CPO Club C-766-2950, O'Club C-766-1361, Restaurant C-851-7837, Snack Bar C-766-1237, Vending C-764-4698			
TRANSPORTATION	Limited on Base. Air Tickets in Bldg 15, Bus(Shuttle) C-764-5712, Car Rentals, Budget=C-599-3152, Hertz=C-877-9229, Limo Svc C-877-9477, Taxi(Comm) C-723-3377 (Gov) C-764-5712, Parking at Bldg 754B. Short & long term near Pax Term.			
OTHER SERVICES	Good services on Base. Exchange C-766-1282, Bank/Exc C-827-7200, Barber C-766-1805, Beauty C-766-1283, Laundry/DryC C-766-1287, Medical C-764-6800, Postal C-764-3136			
TML	Bldg 75 24 hrs dly C-764-4051, A-574-4051 All Ranks. DV/VIP C-764-3467.			
TRAVELERS AID	Good on Base. ARC C-764-2652/4 (other hrs C-838-7320), Chaplain C-764-7847 (other hrs C-764-9990), AF Aid C-764-2060, Lost/Found C-764-2000, Sec Police C-764-2000, USO C-838-4182/827-1063			
ATTRACTIONS	VA tidewater area, Norfolk nearby, beaches & water sports			

VIRGINIA
Langley AFB, Cont'd

UNSCHEDULED FLIGHTS

Frequent Air Force flts via C-12A/P and C-21A/P aircraft to: Andrews AFB MD (ADW); Davison AAF VA (DAA); Eglin AFB FL (VPS); Hanscom Field Arpt MA (BED); Maxwell AFB AL (MXF); Randolph AFB TX (RND); Scott AFB IL (BLV); and Wright-Patterson AFB OH (FFO). Call for destinations, routings, and schedules. TRADOC Army Det. Also flts to: Cairns AAF AL (OZR); Columbia Metro Arpt SC (CAE); Fulton Co Arpt GA (FTY); Godman AAF KY (FTK); Phillips AAF MD (APG); Redstone AAF AL (HUA); and Simmons AAF SC (FBG).

Norfolk Naval Air Station (NGU)
Air Terminal, Bldg LP-84
Norfolk Naval Air Station, VA 23511-5000

Comm: 804-444-0111
ATVN: 564-0111
FTS: 954-0111

LOCATION: Fm N take I-64 W, take Naval Base exit, follow signs. Fm S take I-64 exit to I-564 into Gate 3. RM: p-98, C/3. NMC: Norfolk, in city limits.

FACILITIES	LOCATION	HOURS	PHONE	COMMENTS
PAX TERM INFO	Bldg LP-84	24 hrs dly	C-444-4118/4148, A-564-4118/4148	MAC Term 3 mi fm Gate 4 off Patrol Rd on A-Term Rd.
Pax Svc Offc	Bldg LP-84	24 hrs dly	C-444-4118/4517, A-690-4118/4517	Dty NCO
Pax Paging	Bldg LP-84	24 hrs dly	C-444-4118, A-690-4118	Space-A desk
PAX LOUNGES General	Bldg LP-84 Bldg LP-84	No separate family lounge 24 hrs dly	C-444-4118, A-690-4118/4148	A/C, Nursery, Free TV, O/S & P/C seats, Rest-rms, Lockers
DV/VIP	Bldg LP-84	24 hrs dly	C-444-4118/4148, A-690-4118/4148	A/C, Showers, Read/write rm, TV, Rest-rms, Lks, Game rm. No hostess.
Protocol Svc	Bldg LP-1	24 hrs dly	C-444-2780(Base Ops), C-444-2442(SDO)	
FOOD SERVICE Cafeteria	Many clubs, messes,& dining halls on Nav Base complex Bldg LP-84	24 hrs dly	C-444-4118	MAC Term grill
Dining Hall	Bldg 1-AA(NS) Bldg U-16(NAS)	0600-1730 wkdys 0700-1730 wkdys	C-444-7024 C-444-3744	Call for meal hrs. Call for meal hrs.
Enl Club	Bldg X-360	0600-2400 dly	C-444-4576	Call for food hrs.
NCO/CPO Club	Bldg U-93 Bldg P-87	0600-2400 dly 0600-2400 dly	C-444-2125 C-444-4033	CPO Club C/for svc hrs. PO Club
OFC Club	Bldg SP-45 (NAS) Bldg SC-400(AFSC)	0600-2400 dly 0600-2400 dly	C-423-8450 C-423-4713	Call for food hrs.
Snack Bars	Bldg LP-84	24 hrs dly	C-440-2282/4118	
Vending	Bldg LP-84	24 hrs dly	C-440-2282	Also pay-telephone

Norfolk NAS, Cont'd VIRGINIA

TRANSPORTATION	
Air Tickets	Facilities and means throughout Naval Base complex Bldg A-48 0830-1700 M-F C-444-2514 SATO
Bus(Comm)	Bldg LP-84 24 hrs dly C-444-3830 Greyhound=C-423-8471, Trailways=C-622-7181
Bus Shuttle	Bldg LP-84 0800-1600 M-F C-444-2514 Fm Term to maj points
Car Rentals	Bldg LP-84 24 hrs dly Avis=855-1944, Budget=855-1038, Dollar=480-1500, Hertz=855-1961, National=855-2037
Limo Service	Bldg LP-84 24 hrs dly C-857-1231 To Norfolk IAP-fare $4.75
TAXI(Comm)	Bldg LP-84 24 hrs dly Ace=543-3333, B&W=489-7777, Norview= 855-3333, Yellow=622-3232. Call for svc. Front of Bldg LP-84.
Trains	Norfolk 24 hrs dly C-444-0111 AMTRAK
Parking	Bldg LP-84 24 hrs dly C-444-4118 Short term-2 hrs; long term-no limit.
OTHER SERVICES	
Exchange	Throughout Naval Base complex Bldg U-40(NAS) Hrs vary C-440-2000, Bldg LP-84 0800-1600 dly
Bank/Exc	NASFCU C-497-9631, NFCU C-480-1777 Call for hrs.
Medical	Bldg CD-2 24 hrs dly C-444-1531 Portsmouth NavHosp C-398-5413
Postal	Bldg U-20
WIRE	Pier 7 24 hrs dly C-440-2254, C-622-4311 Western Union
TML	Bldg J-53 Carter Hall 0730-1615 dly C-444-2839/4294, A-564- 2839/4294. Navy Lodge C-489-2656 All Ranks. BOQ C-444-3250.
TRAVELERS AID ARC	7920 Hampton Blvd 24 hrs dly C-622-3111 Personal Svcs Center Bldg A-67 24 hrs dly C-423-4610 Norfolk 24 hrs dly C-446-7700
Chaplain	Bldg U-53/SP-108 24 hrs dly C-444-7156/7157 All faiths
Emerg Relief	7920 Hampton Blvd 24 hrs dly C-444-6289,Nav Relief C-423-8830
Lost/Found	Bldg LP-84 24 hrs dly C-444-4377 and Pax Svc office
Sec Police	Bldg CEP-161 24 hrs dly C-444-2361 Desk Sgt
USO	Coliseum Mall (Entrance-A) Hampton C-838-8767, C-827-1063
ATTRACTIONS	MacArthur Memorial, Norfolk NS tour, Colonial Williamsburg

SCHEDULED FLIGHTS

DESTINATION	ROUTING	FREQ	EQ/CMTS
Alex Hamilton Arpt VI (STX)	NGU-NRR-STX-BGI-GAO	Tu	L-100/C/CC
Bangor IAP ME (BGR)	NGU-BGR-SIZ-NBO-NKW	Tu	DC-862/M/CC

VIRGINIA
Norfolk NAS, Cont'd

Location	Route	Days	Aircraft
Bahrain Intl BA (BAH)	NGU-RTA-BAH NGU-RTA-BAH	1/2/3/M Th	C-141B/C C005A/M
Charleston AFB IAP SC (CHS)	NGU-CHS NGU-CHS	M,W,F,Su 1/2/3/Th,F	C-141B/M C-141B/C
Diego Garcia Atoll IO (NKW)	NGU-TOJ-SIZ-NBO-NKW NGU-BGR-SIZ-NBO-NKW NGU-TOJ-SIZ-NBO-NKW NGU-TOJ-SIZ-KRT-NBO-NKW	M,W Tu 1/2/4/F 3/F	C-141B/C DC-862/M/CC C-141B/C C-141B/C
Grantley Adams Intl BB (BGI)	NGU-NRR-STX-BGI-GAO	3/Tu	L-100/C/CC
Guantanamo Bay NS CU (GAO)	NGU-NRR-GAO NGU-GAO-NRR NGU-GAO-NRR NGU-NRR-STX-BGI-GAO NGU-NRR-STX-GAO NGU-GAO-NRR NGU-NRR-GAO	4/M,Sa M,Th 3/M,Th 3/Tu 1/2/4/Tu 1/2/3/W F	C-141B/C L-100/C/C C-141B/M L-100/C/CC L-100/C/CC C-141B/C L-100/C/CC
Jomo Kenyatta Intl KE (NBO)	NGU-TOJ-SIZ-NBO-NKW NGU-BGR-SIZ-NBO-NKW NGU-TOJ-SIZ-KRT-NBO-NKW	M,W,1/2/4/F Tu 3/F	C-141B/C DC-862/M/CC C-141B/C
Keflavik Arpt IC (KEF)	NGU-KEF	4/M,1/2/3/W,F	C-141B/
Khartoum Arpt SU (KRT)	NGU-TOJ-SIZ-KRT-NBO-NKW	3/F	C-141B/C
McGuire AFB NJ (WRI)	NGU-WRI NGU-WRI	Su,2/W,3/4/Th,F 3/W,4/Sa	C-141B/C C-141B/M
RAF Mildenhall UK (MHZ)	NGU-SIZ-FRF-MHZ	2/Th	KC-010/M
Rhein Main AB GE (FRF)	NGU-SIZ-FRF-MHZ	2/Th	KC-010/M
Rota NAS SP (RTA)	NGU-RTA NGU-RTA-BAH NGU-RTA-SIG NGU-RTA-BAH	Su,Tu,Th,F 1/2/3/M Tu Th	C-141B/M C-141B/C C-141B/M C005A/M
Roosevelt Roads NAS PR (NRR)	NGU-GAO-NRR NGU-GAO-NRR NGU-NRR-GAO NGU-NRR-STX-GAO NGU-NRR-STX-BGI-GAO NGU-GAO-NRR NGU-NRR-GAO	M,Th 3/M,Th 4/M,Sa 1/2/4/Tu 3/Tu 1/2/3/W F	L-100/C/CC C-141B/M C-141B/C L-100/C/CC L-100/C/CC C-141B/C L-100/C/CC
Sigonella Arpt IT (SIZ)	NGU-TOJ-SIZ-NBO-NKW NGU-BGR-SIZ-NBO-NKW NGU-RTA-SIZ NGU-SIZ-FRF-MHZ NGU-TOJ-SIZ-KRT-NBO-NKW NGU-SIZ	M,W,1/2/4/F Tu Tu 2/Th 3/F 1/3/Sa	C-141B/C DC-862/M/CC C-141B/M KC-010/M C-141B/C KC-010/M

VIRGINIA

Norfolk NAS, Cont'd

Torrejon de Ardoz AB SP (TOJ)	NGU-TOJ-SIZ-NBO-NKW NGU-TOJ-SIZ-KRT-NBO-NKW	M,W,1/2/4/F 3/F	C-141B/C C-141B/C

Oceana Naval Air Station (NTU)
Air Operations
Oceana NAS, VA 23460-5120

Comm: 804-433-2000
ATVN: 433-2000

LOCATION: Fm I-64 exit to Norfolk-Virginia Beach Expressway (VA-44E), east on Virginia Beach Blvd. Bordered by Oceana Blvd (VA-615) and London Bridge Rd. Also, bordered by Potters Rd and Harpers Rd. RM: p-98, F-7. NMC: Virginia Beach, in city limits.

FACILITIES	LOCATION HOURS PHONE COMMENTS
PAX TERM INFO	Bldg 100 24 hrs dly C-433-2260/2162, A-433-2260/2162 From main gate straight on Princess Anne Rd to R on London Bridge Rd and Pax Term at circle dead end.
Pax Svc Ofc	Bldg 100 24 hrs dly C-433-2260/2162 NCO on duty
PAX LOUNGES General	No separate family lounge Bldg 100 24 hrs dly C-433-2260 A/C, Rest-rms, P/C seats
DV/VIP	Bldg 100 Rm 119 As required C-433-2260 A/C, Rest-rms, TV, O/S seats
FOOD SERVICE	Cafeteria C-491-4210, Enl Club C-433-2122/2453, NCO/CPO Club C-433-2637, O'Club C-428-0036
TRANSPORTATION	Very limited on Base. Car Rentals C-855-1921, No Parking at Bldg 100 (notify Sec Police on C-433-3123 for long term)
OTHER SERVICES	Exchange C-491-4210, Bank/Exc C-486-0720, Hair Styles C-491-4210, Laundry/DryC C-491-4210, Medical C-433-2221, Postal in Bldg 531
TML	Bldg 460 24 hrs dly C-433-3293/4, A-433-3293/4 All Ranks. DV/VIP C-433-3293.
TRAVELERS AID	ARC C-433-2666, Chaplain C-433-2871, Navy Relief C-433-5789, Sec Police C-433-3123, USO C-838-4182

UNSCHEDULED FLIGHTS

Frequent flts via Navy UC-12B/P and other admin aircraft to: Charleston AFB Intl SC (CHS); Fallon NAS NV (NFL); Guantanamo Bay NS CU (GAO); Jacksonville NAS FL (NIP); Key West NAS FL (NQX); Los Angeles IAP CA (LAX); North Island NAS CA (NZY); Pensacola NAS FL (NPA); Roosevelt Roads NAS PR (NRR); and Yuma MCAS AZ (YUM). Call for destinations, routings, and schedules.

WASHINGTON

Fairchild Air Force Base (SKA)
92nd CSG/OTM
Fairchild AFB, WA 99011-5000

Comm: 509-247-1212
ATVN: 352-1110

LOCATION: Take US-2 exit from I-90 W of Spokane. Follow US-2 through Airway Heights, after 2 mi L to Base main gate and visitors' control center. RM: p-101, G/23. NMC: Spokane, 12 mi E.

FACILITIES	LOCATION	HOURS	PHONE	COMMENTS
PAX TERM INFO	Bldg 1 Base Ops 24 hrs dly C-247-5435, A-352-5435 Fm main gate straight on Mitchell Ave to R to Bone St to L on Seattle Ave to R on Arnold St to L on Castle St to Pax Term on R.			
Pax Svc Ofc	Bldg 1	24 hrs dly	C-247-5435	NCO on duty (Days)
PAX LOUNGES General	Limited Lounge facilities Bldg 1 24 hrs dly C-247-5435 Bag chk, Tel L&ATVN, Rest-rms, O/S seats			
DV/VIP	Bldg 1 24 hrs dly C-247-5435 Coffee/tea srvd, Tel C, TV, Rest-rms, O/S seats			
Protocol Svc	Hq Bldg	0730-1630 M-F	C-247-2127	
FOOD SERVICE Cafeteria	Good services on Base Bldg 2000 0700-1500 M-Sa, 1600 Su C-244-2022			
Dining Hall	Bldg 620 0530-0100 dly C-247-5348 In-flt Kit C-247-5146			
Enl Club	Bldg 2452	1100-2300 M-Sa	C-244-3622	Call for svc hrs.
NCO/CPO Club	Bldg 2452	1100-2300 M-Sa	C-244-3622	Call for svc hrs.
OFC Club	Bldg 2299	1100-2300 M-Sa	C-244-3644	Call for svc hrs.
Snack Bars	Bldg 2248E	0700-1500 M-Sa, 1600 Su	C-247-2422	
Vending	Bldg 1	24 hrs dly	C-247-5435	
TRANSPORTATION Air Tickets	Good on and off Base Bldg 2249A 0730-1630 M-F C-247-2212			
Bus(Comm)	Main gate	Spokane Transit System	C-328-9336	
Car Rentals	Spokane 24 hrs dly Budget=C-838-1434 Avis=C-747-8081, National=C-624-8995, Thrifty=C-838-8223			
TAXI(Comm) (Gov)	Bldg 1 24 hrs dly Checker=C-624-4741, Yellow=C-624-4321, Motor Pool 24 hrs dly C-247-2244			
Parking	BX Lot facing fence 24 hrs dly C-247-5493-long term			
OTHER SERVICES Exchange	Good services on Base Bldg 2000 1000-1800 Sa, 1600 Su C-244-2832			

WASHINGTON

Fairchild AFB, Cont'd

Bank/Exc	Bldg 2000	1000-1500 M-Sa	C-456-6710	
Hair Styles	Bldg 2000	0900-1700 M-F, 1330 Sa 0900-1700 M-F, 1600 Sa	C-244-2848 Barber C-244-2832 Beauty	
Laundry	Bldg 2000	0930-1700 M-F, 1300 Sa	C-244-9786	
Medical	Bldg 9000	24 hrs dly	C-247-5661	
Postal	Bldg 644	0830-1630 M-F	C-247-2479	
TML	Bldg 2392 All Ranks.	24 hrs dly	C-247-5737/5519, A-352-5737/5519 DV/VIP C-247-2127.	
TRAVELERS AID ARC	Good on and off Base Bldg 2245	0730-1630 M-F	C-247-5650	Other hrs C-326-3330
Chaplain	Bldg 4200	0730-1630 M-F	C-247-2264	
Emerg Relief	Bldg 3505	0730-1630 M-F	C-247-5081	AF Aid
Lost/Found	Bldg 325	24 hrs dly	C-247-5496	
Sec Police	Bldg 4325	24 hrs dly	C-247-5493	
ATTRACTIONS	Spokane, Expo Site, parks			

SCHEDULED FLIGHTS

DESTINATION	ROUTING	FREQ	EQ/CMTS
Buckley ANGB CO (BKF)	SKA-GFA-MUO-HIF-BKF-BLV	F	1C009A/MI
Eielson AFB AK (EIL)	SKA-EIL	1 ea mo	1KC-135E/M
RAF Fairford UK (FFD)	SKA-FFD	1-2 ea mo	1KC-135E/M
Hill AFB UT (HIF)	SKA-GFA-MUO-HIF-BKF-BLV	F	1C009A/ME
Malmstrom AFB MT (GFA)	SKA-GFA-MUO-HIF-BKF-BLV	F	1C009A/ME
March AFB CA (RIV)	SKA-RIV	1 ea mo	1KC-135E/M
McChord AFB WA (TCM)	SKA-TCM-SUU SKA-TCM	W 2 ea mo	1C009A/ME 1KC-135E/M
RAF Mildenhall AFB UK (MHZ)	SKA-MHZ	1-2 ea mo	1KC-135E/M
Mountain Home AFB ID (MUO)	SKA-GFA-MUO-HIF-BKF-BLV	F	1C009A/ME

WASHINGTON
Fairchild AFB, Cont'd

Scott AFB IL (BLV)	SKA-GFA-MUO-HIF-BKF-BLV	F	1C009A/ME
Travis AFB CA (SUU)	SKA-TCM-SUU	W	1C009A/ME

Gray Army Airfield (GRF)
Air Operations
Fort Lewis, WA 98433-5000

Comm: 206-967-6628
ATVN: 357-6628

LOCATION: On I-5 in Puget Sound area, 14 mi N of Olympia. Exits clearly marked. RM: p-100, J/10. NMC: Tacoma, 12 mi N.

FACILITIES	LOCATION	HOURS	PHONE	COMMENTS
PAX TERM INFO	Bldg 3082	0730-1700 M-F	C-967-6628/5998, A-357-6628/5998. Enter main gate on 41st Division Dr, go L on Stricker Ave, then L on 18th St straight to Bldg 3082.	
Pax Svc Ofc	Bldg 3082	0730-1700 M-F	Phone as above	NCO on duty
OTHER SERVICES	Full large Base support. See Military Living's "US Forces Travel Guide USA & Caribbean Areas" for full details.			

UNSCHEDULED FLIGHTS

Flts via Army C-12A/P, C-21A/P and CH-47/M aircraft to CONUS West Coast and Midwest locations. Call for destinations, routings, and schedules.

McChord Air Force Base (TCM)
62nd APS/TROP
McChord AFB, WA 98438-5000

Comm: 206-984-1910
ATVN: 976-1110

LOCATION: Nine miles S of Tacoma WA. Fm I-5 Exit 125 onto Bridgeport Way. One mile to main gate. RM: p-100, I/10. NMC: Tacoma, 9 mi N.

FACILITIES	LOCATION	HOURS	PHONE	COMMENTS
PAX TERM INFO	Bldg 1179	24 hrs dly	C-984-2657, A-976-5944	From main gate, left on Battery Rd, one block to A St, left at gas station, one mile to Pax Term.
Recording	Bldg 1179	24 hrs dly	C-984-2659, A-976-2659	1-day forecast
Pax Svc Ofc	Bldg 1179	Duty hrs	C-984-2658, A-976-2658	
Pax Paging	Bldg 1179	24 hrs dly	C-984-2657, A-976-2657	
PAX LOUNGES General	Bldg 1179	24 hrs dly	C-984-2657, A-976-2657	No family lounge. USO lounge - with Cribs and Rest-rms. Free TV, Rest-rms, Bag chk/lks, Game rm, P/C seats, Telephones

McChord AFB, Cont'd WASHINGTON

DV/VIP	Bldg 1179 24 hrs dly C-984-5944, A-976-2657 Rear of Terminal behind Pax Svc office A/C, Separate reading room, Free TV, Rest-rooms, O/S seats		
Protocol Svc	Bldg 1179	24 hrs dly	C-984-2657, A-976-2658
FOOD SERVICE			
Cafeteria	Bldg 1183	0600-1930 dly	C-582-2092 Call for svc hrs.
Dining Hall	Bldg 1156	0600-0100 dly	C-584-2711 4th meal
Enl Club	Bldg 746	1000-1600 dly	C-984-2918 "Skylark"
NCO/CPO Club	Bldg 700	0700-2300 dly	C-984-5134 Call for svc hrs.
OFC Club	Bldg 171	1000-2300 dly	C-984-5581 Call for svc hrs.
Snack Bars	Bldg 1179	0600-1900 dly	C-582-2092 and C-984-5954
Vending	Bldg 1179	24 hrs dly	C-582-9450
TRANSPORTATION			
Air Tickets	Bldg 1179	0730-1700 M-F	C-984-3521 SATO
Bus(Comm)	Leaves fm Pax Term to area cities and military installations 0540-2240 M-F Leaves 40 min after the hour		
(Shuttle)	From Pax Term every 30 min on half hour 0600-1800 M-F		
Car Rentals	U-SAVE Hot line in Term Bldg M-5 0800-1800 M-F		
TAXI(Comm)	Bldg 1179	24 hrs dly	C-984-3331
Parking	Short term-in front of Pax Term (Bldg 1179) 24 hr limit; long term-behind 1100 area near Arms Qual Training area. No charge or time limit. Security Police C-984-5624.		
OTHER SERVICES			
Exchange	Bldg 1179	Mini Exchange 0600-1900 dly	Main BX 582-9450
Bank/Exc	Bldg 550	1000-1730 M-F	C-584-1010
Hair Styles	Bldg 574 Bldg 573	On "A" St On "A" St	C-582-0056 Barber C-581-0317 Beauty
Laundry/DryC	Bldg 741	0730-1730 M-F, 1300 Sa	C-584-3061
Medical	Center of Base	24 hrs dly	C-984-5601/3 Dispensary
Postal	Bldg 735	0830-1730 M-F	C-984-5198
TML	Bldg 166 On Main St 24 hr dly C-594-1471, A-976-5613 All Ranks. DV/VIP C-984-2621.		
TRAVELERS AID			
ARC	Bldg 521	0800-1600 dly	C-984-5577 After hrs C-984-1910
Chaplain	Bldg 180	0800-1700 M-F	C-984-5556/7
Lost/Found	Bldg 1179	0730-1700 dly	C-984-2657

WASHINGTON
McChord AFB, Cont'd

Sec Police	Main gate	24 hrs dly	C-984-5624	
USO	SEA-TAC Intl Arpt	24 hrs M-Sa	C-433-5438	
	McChord Terminal	24 hrs M-Sa	C-984-2400	
ATTRACTIONS	Seattle (30 mi N), Cascade Mts (Mt Rainier)			

SCHEDULED FLIGHTS

DESTINATION	ROUTING	FREQ	EQ/CMTS
Adak NAS AK (ADK)	TCM-ADK	Tu	C-141B/C
	TCM-EDF-ADK	4/Sa	C-141B/C
Eielson AFB AK (EIL)	TCM-EDF-EIL	M	C-141B/C
	SUU-TCM-EIL-EDF	1/3/Sa	C-141B/M
	TCM-EIL-EDF	1/3/Sa	C-141B/M
Elmendorf AFB AK (EDF)	TCM-EDF-OKO	Su	C-141B/C
	TCM-EDF-EIL	M	C-141B/C
	TCM-EDF-OKO	Th	C-141B/M
	TCM-EDF	Th,2/F	C-141B/C
	TCM-EDF	1/2/3/F	C-141B/M
	TCM-EIL-EDF	1/3/Sa	C-141B/M
	SUU-TCM-EIL-EDF	1/3/Sa	C-141B/M
	TCM-EDF-ADK	3/4/Sa	C-141B/C
Norton AFB CA (SBD)	TCM-SBD	M	C-141B/M
	TCM-SBD	Th,Sa	C-141B/C
Travis AFB CA (SUU)	EDF-TCM-SUU	1/3/Su	C-141B/M
	TCM-SUU	Tu	C-141B/M
Yokota AB JA (OKO)	TCM-EDF-OKO-CRK	Su	C-141B/C
	TCM-OKO	M	C-141B/C
	TCM-OKO	W	C-141B/C
	TCM-EDF-OKO	Th	C-141B/M

UNSCHEDULED FLIGHTS

Frequent CONUS flights available but scheduled on a day-to-day basis as needed. Call C-206-984-2659 or A-976-2659 for status information. TCM also services: Osan AB RK and Shemya AFS AK. Flight schedules change month to month. Call for schedules.

Whidbey Island Naval Air Station (NUW)
Air Operations Division
Oak Harbor, WA 98278-5000

Comm: 206-257-2211
ATVN: 820-0111

LOCATION: Take WA-20 to Whidbey Island, 3 mi W of WA-20 on Ault Field Road. RM: p-100, E/10. NMC: Seattle, 60 mi SE.

FACILITIES	LOCATION	HOURS	PHONE	COMMENTS
PAX TERM INFO	Hangar 2 Bldg 139	24 hrs dly	C-257-2604, A-820-2604	
	Fm main gate straight on Charles Porter Ave to R on Lexington St to Pax Term on L.			

WASHINGTON

Whidbey Island NAS, Cont'd

Pax Svc Ofc	Bldg 139	24 hrs dly	C-257-2604	NCO on duty
PAX LOUNGES General	General lounge only. No DV/VIP or family lounges. Bldg 139 24 hrs dly C-257-2604 Coffee/tea srvd, Showers, TV, Rest-rms, O/S seats			
Protocol Svc	Bldg 113	0730-1630 M-F	C-257-2211	Base Commander
FOOD SERVICE	Good services on Base. Cafeteria C-657-5981, Dining Hall C-257-2211, Enl Club C-257-3308, NCO/CPO Club C-257-2505, O'Club C-257-2521, Snack Bar C-675-8598, Vending C-257-2604			
TRANSPORTATION	Limited on Base. Air Tickets C-675-6652, Car Rentals C-675-1244, Taxi(Comm) C-675-1244 (Gov) C-257-3133, Parking C-257-3121 (limited parking)			
OTHER SERVICES	Exchange C-679-5200, Bank/Exc C-675-0763, Hair Styles C-679-5200, Laundry/DryC C-679-5200, Medical C-679-5353			
TML	Bldg 973 0730-1630 dly C-257-2529/2076, A-820-2529/2076 All Ranks. DV/VIP C-257-2529.			
TRAVELERS AID	Family Svcs C-257-5902, ARC C-675-2559 (other hrs C-257-2631), Chaplain C-257-2414, Navy Relief C-657-5177/2728, Sec Police C-257-3121, YMCA C-675-2771, ARC C-675-2559			

UNSCHEDULED FLIGHTS

Frequent flights via Navy C009B/P, P-3A/M and other aircraft to: Alameda NAS CA (NGZ); Fallon NAS NV (NFL); Fairchild AFB WA (SKA); Glenview NAS IL (NBU); Lemoore NAS CA (NLC); McChord AFB WA (TCM); North Island NAS CA (NZY); and Portland IAP OR (PDX). Call for destinations, routings, and schedules.

WEST VIRGINIA

Eastern West Virginia Regional Airport (MRB)
167th Tactical Airlift Group (ANG)
Martinsburg, WV 25401-5000

Comm: 304-267-5100
ATVN: 242-9210

LOCATION: From US-11, 3 mi S of Martinsburg L on Paynes Ford Rd, 1 mi to sign for ANGB.   RM: p-99, F/18. NMC: Martinsburg, 3 mi N.

FACILITIES	LOCATION	HOURS	PHONE	COMMENTS
PAX TERM INFO	Bldg 120 2nd Floor 0730-1600 M-F C-267-5250, A-242-9250 Ask Security Police for directions.			
Pax Svc Ofc	Bldg 120	0730-1600 M-F	C-267-5311	Scheduling NCO
PAX LOUNGES General	Limited Bldg 120 0730-1600 M-F C-267-5250 A/C, Rest-rms, Showers, P/C seats			

WEST VIRGINIA
Eastern WV Regional Arpt, Cont'd

SCHEDULED FLIGHTS

DESTINATION	ROUTING	FREQ	EQ/CMTS
Charlotte/ Douglas Intl Arpt NC (CLT)	MRB-CLT	1-2 ea mo	C-130A/M

UNSCHEDULED FLIGHTS

Flts to other CONUS & OCONUS locations. Call for destinations, routings, and schedules.

Yeager Airport (CRW)
130th Tactical Airlift Group (ANG)
Charleston, WV 25311-5000

Comm: 304-357-5100
ATVN: 366-9210

LOCATION: Off I-79 N or S, exit 102, follow signs to airport. RM: p-98, J/14. NMC: Charleston, 4 mi SW.

FACILITIES	LOCATION	HOURS	PHONE	COMMENTS
PAX TERM INFO	ANG area	0800-1700 M-F	C-357-5100, A-366-9210 Ask Sec Police for directions. All spt of regional airport.	

UNSCHEDULED FLIGHTS

Flights via ANG C-130A/M aircraft to CONUS and OCONUS locations. Call for destinations, routings, and schedules.

WISCONSIN

General Billy Mitchell Field (GMF)
128th Air Refueling Group (ANG)
Gen Billy Mitchell Field, WI 53207-5000

Comm: 414-747-2532 (ANG)
414-481-6400 (AFRES)
ATVN: 580-8532 (ANG)
786-9110 (AFRES)

LOCATION: From I-94 N or S, exit #318 E to airport. RM: p-103, Z/5. NMC: Milwaukee, 3 mi N.

FACILITIES	LOCATION	HOURS	PHONE	COMMENTS
PAX TERM INFO	Ops Hangar	0800-1700 M-F	C-747-2532 (ANG), C-481-6400-EX-370 (AFRES), A-580-8532 (ANG), A-786-9110 (AFRES)	East side of building. Ask at gate. ANG/AFRES Base. Limited military Base support.

UNSCHEDULED FLIGHTS

Flights via ANG KC-135E/M and AFRES C-130A/M aircraft to CONUS, OCONUS, and foreign country locations. Call for destinations, routings, and schedules.

WISCONSIN

Volk Field Air National Guard Base (VOK)
Air Operations
Camp Douglas, WI 54618-5001

Comm: 608-427-1210
ATVN: 798-3210

LOCATION: Take I-90/94 N or S. Take Exit 55 W to Camp Douglas. Clearly marked. RM: p-103, O/8. NMC: La Crosse, 50 mi W.

FACILITIES	LOCATION	HOURS	PHONE	COMMENTS
PAX TERM INFO	Bldg 508 Base Ops	0800-1700 M-F	C-427-1210, A-798-3210 Fm W gate straight to Base Ops on L.	
Pax Svc Ofc	Bldg 508	0800-1700 M-F	C-427-1210	NCO/Civ on duty
PAX LOUNGES General	Limited Bldg 508	0800-1700 M-F		A/C, Coffee/tea srvd, Tel L,LD&ATVN, Rest-rms, Showers, O/S seats
Protocol Svc	Bldg 100	0730-1600 M-F	C-427-1203, A-798-3203	
FOOD SERVICE	Cons Club C-427-1210-EX-276/389, Vending C-427-1210			
TRANSPORTATION	Air Tickets C-427-1256, Parking at Bldg 408 (no restrictions)			
OTHER SERVICES	Exchange C-427-1210-EX-275, Medical C-427-1210-EX-444			
TRAVELERS AID	Sec Police C-247-1210-EX-212/236			

UNSCHEDULED FLIGHTS

Air National Guard Training Site. Flights via transient ANG aircraft. Call for destinations, routings, and schedules.

WYOMING

Cheyenne Municipal Airport (CYS)
153rd Tactical Airlift Group (ANG)
P.O. Box 2268
Cheynne, WY 82003-5000

Comm: 307-772-6201
ATVN: 943-6201

LOCATION: Fm I-25 N or S, exit on Central Ave E to airport. RM: p-104, K/2. NMC: Cheyenne, 1 mi S.

FACILITIES	LOCATION	HOURS	PHONE	COMMENTS
PAX TERM INFO	Bldg 115	0730-1630 M-F	C-772-6347, A-943-6347	Ops area 3rd floor, NE corner of airport
OTHER SERVICES	Full support of a regional airport. No military facilities.			

SCHEDULED FLIGHTS

DESTINATION	ROUTING	FREQ	EQ/CMTS
Buckley ANGB CO (BKF)	CYS-BKF	W, 2 ea mo	C-130A/M

WYOMING
Cheyenne Munic Arpt, Cont'd

| Van Nuys ANGB CA (VNY) | CYS-VNY | 2 ea mo | C-130A/M |

UNSCHEDULED FLIGHTS

Flights to CONUS locations via ANG C-130A/M aircraft. Call for destinations, routings, and schedules.

NOTES

OUTSIDE CONTINENTAL UNITED STATES (OCONUS)

ALASKA

Adak Naval Air Station (ADK)
PO Box 42
FPO Seattle 98791-5000

Comm: 907-592-8001
ATVN: 317-592-8001

LOCATION: On Adak Island of the Aleutian Island chain, accessible only by air or ship. RM: p-6, K/7. NMC: Anchorage, 1200 air mi NE.

FACILITIES	LOCATION	HOURS	PHONE	COMMENTS
PAX TERM INFO	Bldg 30003 A-592-4196	0800-1700 M-F (O/hrs as req) On main road at flight line. Prior approval from Commander required for entry.		C-592/692-4196, Isolated station.
Pax Svc Ofc	Bldg 30003	0800-1700 M-F	C-592-8026	NCO on duty
Pax Paging	Bldg 30003	0800-1700 M-F	C-592-4196	
PAX LOUNGES General	Bldg 30003 0800-1700 M-F		C-592-4196	General & DV/VIP lounges. No family lounge. Tel C&A, Rest-rms, P/C seats
DV/VIP	Bldg 30003 A/C, Bag check, TV, Rest-rms, Showers	0800-1700 M-F	C-592-4196	
Protocol Svc	Bldg 30003	0800-1700 M-F	C-592-4196	
FOOD SERVICE	Enl Club C-592-8104, NCO/CPO Club C-592-8393, O'Club C-592-8354, Restaurant C-592-8104, Vending C-592-8089			
TRANSPORTATION	Air Tickets C-592-3466, Bus(Shuttle) C-592-8345, Car Rentals 592-4154, Taxi(Gov) C-592-8376 (must be in uniform), Parking C-592-4196 (no overnight)			
OTHER SERVICES	Navy Exchange C-592-8467, Medical C-592-8382			
TML	Biltg Office 0800-1700 dly C-592-8287 Navy Lodge C-592-8287. DV/VIP C-592-8287.			
TRAVELERS AID	Family Svcs C-592-4291, Chaplain C-592-4169/8203, Lost/Found C-592-8287, Sec Police C-592-8051			
ATTRACTIONS	Hunting, fishing, and other outdoor sports			

ALASKA
Adak NAS, Cont'd

SCHEDULED FLIGHTS			
DESTINATION	ROUTING	FREQ	EQ/CMTS
Elmendorf AFB AK (EDF)	ADK-SYA-EDF	1/2/3/W,1/3/Sa	C-141B/C
McChord AFB WA (TCM)	ADK-EDF-TCM	Tu,Th	C-141B/M
Shemya AFB AK (SYA)	EDF-ADK-SYA	F	C-141B/C

Alaska Isolated Stations (AIS)
(Not listed separately in this book)

The stations listed below have Space-A air opportunities. Base support facilities are very limited. Lodging is not available except at Fort Greely. Camping, fishing, hiking, hunting and all outdoor recreation are outstanding. Permission of the station Commander is required for all visitors except for Fort Greely.

ALLEN ARMY AIRFIELD, AK (BIG)
Base Operations
Fort Greely, AK 98733-5000
Comm: 907-872-4220
ATVN: 317-872-4220
RM: Page 6, F/7

CLEAR AIR FORCE STATION, AK (CLF)
Base Operations, AFSPACECOM
APO Seattle 98704-5000
Comm: 907-585-6413
ATVN: 317-585-6413
RM: Page 6, E/6

GALENA AIRPORT, AK (GAL)
OL-D 616th APS/TRO
APO Seattle 98723-5000
Comm: 907-446-3346
ATVN: 317-446-3311
RM: Page 6, E/4

KING SALMON AIRPORT, AK (AKN)
5071st CSS/DO
APO Seattle 98713-5000
Comm: 907-721-3553
ATVN: 317-721-3553
RM: Page 6, H/4

SITKA CG AIR STATION, AK (NOU)
PO Box 6-5000
Sitka, AK 99835-5000
Comm: 907-966-5420
ATVN: None
RM: Page 6, I/10

UNSCHEDULED FLIGHTS

Flights to: Adak NAS AK (ADK); Anchorage IAP AK (ANC); Elmendorf AFB AK (EDF); McChord AFB WA (TCM); and Shemya AFB AK (SYA).

Anchorage International Airport (ANC)
OL-A, 616TH APS
Elmendorf AFB, AK 99506-5000

Comm: 907-243-1950
ATVN: 317-752-3111

LOCATION: Fm Elmendorf AFB S on Post Rd to L (S) on Minnesota Dr to R (W) on IAP Rd to Satellite Dr & Intl Term. RM: p-6, B/10. NMC: Anchorage, 5 mi NE.

ALASKA

Anchorage Intl Arpt, Cont'd

FACILITIES	LOCATION	HOURS	PHONE	COMMENTS
PAX TERM INFO	Intl Term Rm 202	24 hrs dly	C-552-3111	All MAC Space-A seat assignments made fm Elmendorf AFB Term. Also contact 176th TAG (ANG), Kulis ANG Base at Anchorage IAP AK 99502 C-907-243-1145, A-626-1444 for ANG C-130 flights.
Record				
PAX LOUN	Passenger Service Operations at Anchorage IAP have closed down. Passengers are no longer allowed to board or disembark from MAC flights transiting Anchorage. It is a refueling stop only. However, limited flights within CONUS and OCONUS to and from Anchorage are still available via Alaska Air National Guard aircraft operating out of Kulis Air National Guard Base on the south side of Anchorage IAP. Call 907-243-0839 for recorded flight information. Dependents are not eligible for Guard flights out of Kulis.			arpt
FOOD SER				lities
TRANSPOR				
Bus (C				hol svc.
Limo S				hotels
TAXI (Comm)	Intl Term 24 hrs dly From the International Airport to downtown Anchorage - $10, add'l riders free, 15 min			
OTHER SERVICES	Complete support services at Elmendorf AFB & Ft Richardson			

SCHEDULED FLIGHTS

DESTINATION	ROUTING	FREQ	EQ/CMTS
Clark AB RP (CRK)	LAX-OAK-ANC-DNA-CRK STL-LAX-ANC-DNA-CRK	1/2/3/Su W	B747/P/CC B747/P/CC
Kadena AB JA (DNA)	LAX-OAK-ANC-DNA-CRK LAX-OAK-ANC-DNA-CRK	1/2/3/Su W	B747/P/CC B747/P/CC
Lambert St Louis Intl MO (STL)	CRK-DNA-ANC-OAK-STL	1/2/4/M	B747/P/CC
Los Angeles Intl CA (LAX)	CRK-DNA-ANC-OAK-LAX	1/2/4/F	B747/P/CC
Yokota AB JA (OKO)	SUU-TCN-ANC-OKO-OSN	Th	B747/P/CC

Eielson Air Force Base (EIL)
343rd TRNSPS/LGTTA
Eielson AFB, AK 99702-5000

Comm: 907-377-1110
ATVN: 317-377-1110

LOCATION: On the Richardson Hwy (AK-2), AFB is clearly marked. RM: p-6, E/7. NMC: Fairbanks AK, 26 mi NW.

FACILITIES	LOCATION	HOURS	PHONE	COMMENTS
PAX TERM INFO	Bldg 4112	0730-1600 dly (Other hrs as required)	C-377-1854, A-377-1854	Fm main gate to Flight Line Ave. Across from Airfield Management Office (Base Ops).

ALASKA
Eielson AFB, Cont'd

Pax Svc Ofc	Bldg 2216	0730-1600 dly	C-377-1854	
PAX LOUNGES General	Bldg 4112 Bldg 4112 Tel ATVN, TV, Rest-rms, P/C seats	No separate DV/VIP or family lounges 0730-1600 dly C-377-1854		
Protocol Svc	Bldg 3112	Duty hrs	C-377-6101 Ask for Wing Exec Officer.	
FOOD SERVICE Cafeteria	Many facilities on Base and in Fairbanks Bldg 2216 1100-2100 M-Th, 2200 F-Sa, 1200-2000 Su C-377-1126			
Dining Hall	Bldg 3124	0600-1800 dly	C-377-5286	Call for svc hrs.
NCO Club	Bldg 2225	1000-2300 dly	C-372-2162	Call for svc hrs.
OFC Club	Bldg 5223	1000-2300 dly	C-377-1121	Call for svc hrs.
Snack Bars	Bldg 3301	0630-2300 dly	C-377-5145	Bowling alley
Vending	Bldg 3305	24 hrs dly	C-377-2450	"Sourdough Inn"
TRANSPORTATION Air Tickets	Many facilities and means on and off Base Bldg 3112 0800-1700 M-F C-377-1168 SATO			
TAXI(Gov)	Bldg 2351	24 hrs dly	C-377-1843	Duty Pax only
OTHER SERVICES Exchange	Many support services on and off Base Bldg 3310 1000-1800 M-F, Sa 1700 C-372-2139			
Hair Styles	Bldg 3310	1000-1800 M-F, Sa 1700	C-372-3265	
Medical	Bldg 3349	24 hrs dly	C-377-2259	
TML	Bldg 5219 24 hrs dly C-377-1844 Ltd space. DV/VIP C-377-6101.			
TRAVELERS AID ARC	Many facilities on Base Bldg 3348 0800-1700 M-F C-377-1855 Other hrs C-377-1500			
Chaplain	Bldg 3307	24 hrs dly	C-377-2130	
Emerg Relief	Bldg 2266	0800-1700 M-F	C-377-4231	AF Aid
Sec Police	Bldg 2222	24 hrs dly	C-377-5130	
ATTRACTIONS	Fairbanks, North Pole, outdoor sports & recreation			

SCHEDULED FLIGHTS

DESTINATION	ROUTING	FREQ	EQ/CMTS
Elmendorf AFB AK (EDF)	EIL-EDF EIL-EDF-TCM EIL-EDF-TCM-SUU-SBD	1 ea wk W Every other Sa	C-12A/P C-141B/M C-141B/ME
McChord AFB WA (TCM)	EIL-EDF-TCM EIL-EDF-TCM-SUU-SBD	W Every other Sa	C-141B/M C-141B/ME

ALASKA

Eielson AFB, Cont'd

McClellan AFB CA (MCC)	EIL-MCC	Tu	WC-135/P
Norton AFB CA (SBD)	EIL-EDF-TCM-SUU-SBD	Every other Sa	C-141B/ME
Travis AFB CA (SUU)	EIL-EDF-TCM-SUU-SBD	Every other Sa	C-141B/ME

UNSCHEDULED FLIGHTS

Flights via KC-135E/M every W from SAC Bases in CONUS to EIL. Flights every Th from EIL to SAC Bases in CONUS. From April through September, the following flight is scheduled for every 3 W: BAB-EIL-DNA.

Elmendorf Air Force Base (EDF)
616th APS/TROP
Elmendorf AFB, AK 99506-5000

Comm: 907-552-1110
ATVN: 317-552-1110

LOCATION: Off Glenn highway (AK-1). Take Muldoon, Boniface, Post Road or Government Hill exits. The AFB is adjacent to Fort Richardson. RM: p-6, A/11. NMC: Anchorage AK, 2 mi SW.

FACILITIES	LOCATION	HOURS	PHONE	COMMENTS
PAX TERM INFO	Bldg 32-233	0600-2200 dly	C-552-5589, A-317-552-5589	Provides Space-A seating for Anchorage IAP(ANC) C-243-1145 AK NG flts. Fm Post Rd gate to L on 6th St to dead end at Pax Term.
Recording	Bldg 32-233	0600-2200	C-552-1114, A-317-552-1114	(Base 114)
Pax Svc Ofc	Bldg 32-233	0600-2200	C-552-5589/5330, A-317-552-5589/5330	
Pax Paging	Bldg 32-233	0600-2200	C-552-5589, A-317-552-5589	
PAX LOUNGES General	Bldg 32-233	0600-2200	C-552-5589	Family lounge restricted to families w/infants only. Bag check/lockers, Game rm, Tel L&LD, Rest-rms, P/C & O/S seats, TV, Child care
DV/VIP	Bldg 32-233	0600-2200	C-552-5589/3781	(O6+) Bag check, Tel L&LD, Rest-rms, O/S seats, TV
Family	Bldg 32-233	0600-2200	C-552-5589	Rest-rms, TV, O/S seats
FOOD SERVICE Cafeteria	Bldg 32-233	24 hrs dly	C-753-6146	Many facilities on Base and at Fort Richardson. Next to Pax Term
Dining Hall	Bldg 1-86	0530-1830 dly	C-552-2253,	Dial-a-Menu C-552-3993
NCO/CPO Club	Bldg 31-145	1100-2100 dly	C-753-6131	Call for svc hrs.
OFC Club	Bldg 9-580	1130-2000 dly	C-753-3131	Call for svc hrs.
Snack Bars	Bldg 31-147 Bldg 31-148	0600-2100 Tu-Sa 0900-2330 dly	C-552-5191 C-552-3669	Pizza Shack Polar Bowl
Vending	Bldg 31-233	0600-2200	C-552-5589	Pay-tel in Term

ALASKA
Elmendorf AFB, Cont'd

TRANSPORTATION Air Tickets	Local ground transportation also available at Fort Richardson Bldg 2-900 0900-1700 dly C-552-2209 SATO	
Bus(Comm) (Shuttle)	Bldg 32-233 0600-2100 dly C-264-6543 $.75 Base + ANC Bldg 32-233 0600-1830 dly C-552-2107 Schedule-Billeting	
Car Rentals	Bldg 32-233 0700-1800 dly C-752-2178 Maj Co's Limo ANC	
TAXI(Comm) (Gov)	2301 Spenard Rd 24 hrs dly C-272-2422 Anchorage (ANC) Bldg 31-260 24 hrs dly C-552-2792/3 Duty Pax only	
Parking	Bldg 32-233 24 hrs dly C-552-3421 Notify Sec Police.	
OTHER SERVICES Exchange	Full range of support available at EDF and Fort Richardson Bldg 4-932 1000-1800 M-F, 1000-1700 Wkends C-753-4260	
Bank/Exc	Bldg 3-850 1000-1500 Wkdys C-753-1179 1st Natl Bank	
Hair Styles	Bldg 31-145 0800-1900 M-Sa C-753-6131 Barber Bldg 4-936 0900-1800 M-Sa C-753-1215 Beauty	
Laundry/DryC	Bldg 31-160 24 hrs dly C-552-2215 DryC 0800-1730 M-F	
Medical	Bldg 24-800 24 hrs dly C-552-5555 Emerg, C-552-2748 Appoint	
Postal	Bldg 9-854 0930-1530 M-F C-552-1110	
TML	Bldg 31-250 24 hrs dly C-552-2454/4701 All Ranks. DV/VIP C-552-4860.	
TRAVELERS AID ARC	Bldg 2-900 1000-1400 M-F C-552-2694 AF Family Svc Bldg 2-900 0730-1630 M-F C-552-4824 Other hrs C-552-1110	
Chaplain	Bldg 9-824 Duty hrs C-552-4422 Other hrs C-552-1110	
Lost/Found	Bldg 32-233 24 hrs dly C-522-5589 Pax Svc	
Sec Police	Bldg 2-900 24 hrs dly C-552-3421 Desk Sgt	
ATTRACTIONS	Anchorage and outdoor sports (hunting, fishing, etc.)	

SCHEDULED FLIGHTS

DESTINATION	ROUTING	FREQ	EQ/CMTS
Adak NAS AK (ADK)	EDF-ADK-SYA TCM-EDF-ADK	W,Sa M	B737/M C-130/M
Eielson AFB AK (EIL)	TCM-EDF-EIL	As required	Varies
McChord AFB WA (TCM)	EDF-TCM-SUU EDF-TCM EDF-SUU-TCM SYA-EDF-TCM ADK-EDF-TCM EIL-EDF-TCM OSN-OKO-EDF-TCM EDF-TCM	1/3/Su 2/3/4/Su 2/4/Su Su,1/2/3/Th 3/4/Su Tu,W,Sa W 2/4/Sa	C-141B/M C-141B/M C-141B/M C-141B/C C-141B/C C-141B/C C-141B/C C-141B/C

ALASKA

Elmendorf AFB, Cont'd

Shemya AFB AK (SYA)	EDF-ADK-SYA	W,Sa	B737/M
Travis AFB CA (SUU)	EDF-SUU-TCM	2/4/Su	C-141B/M
Yokota AB JA (OKO)	SUU-EDF-OKO	Daily	C-141B/C

UNSCHEDULED FLIGHTS

Unscheduled flights in AK and overseas. Check C-552-4896 for Army C-12A flts.

Kodiak Coast Guard Air Station (ADQ)
Box 33
Kodiak, AK 99619-5000

Comm: 907-487-5158
ATVN: 317-5158

LOCATION: From Kodiak take main road (Rezanof Drive West) SW for 9 mi. Base is on left side. RM: p-6, I/5. NMC: Kodiak, 9 mi NE.

FACILITIES	LOCATION	HOURS	PHONE	COMMENTS
PAX TERM INFO	Hangar #1	0800-1600 M-F	C-487-5158, A-317-5158	
	From Rezanof Drive W take Airport Rd to Pax Term on L.			
Pax Svc Ofc	Hangar #1	0800-1600 M-F	C-487-5158	NCO on duty
PAX LOUNGES	No Pax lounge. All Space-A managed by Ops/Flt Services.			
FOOD SERVICE	Limited on Base and in Kodiak			
Cafeteria	Spt Ctr	1100-2200 dly	C-487-5748	Call for svc hrs.
Enl Club	"Kings Inn"	1630-0100 dly	C-487-5110	Call for svc hrs.
NCO/CPO Club	"Golden Anchor"	1130-2400 dly	C-487-5440	(E6+) C/for svc hrs.
TRANSPORTATION	Limited on and off Base			
Air Tickets	Kodiak Arpt	24 hrs dly		See Directory f/Major airlines.
Bus(Shuttle)	Hangar #1	0800-0100 dly	C-487-5471	On Base & $1 to city
Car Rentals	Kodiak Arpt	0730-1800 dly		See Directory. Avis, Hertz
TAXI(Comm)	Ace Mecca	24 hrs dly	C-486-3211	
Parking	Hangar #1	24 hrs dly	C-487-5149	Across street
OTHER SERVICES	Limited on CG Support Center (closed M-Tu)			
Exchange	Spt Ctr	1000-1800 dly		
	Provides most support (Hair Styles, Laundry/DryC, etc.)			
Medical	Spt Ctr	24 hrs dly	C-487-5757	
TML	Guest House All Ranks.	0745-1630 dly	C-487-5446, A-487-5310/5446 DV/VIP C-487-5265.	

ALASKA
Kodiak CGAS, Cont'd

TRAVELERS AID ARC	Spt Ctr Spt Ctr	Duty hours 0700-1100 M-F	C-487-5481/5402 C-487-5200	Family Services
Chaplain	Spt Ctr	Duty hours	C-487-5730/5731	
Lost/Found	Hangar #1	0800-1600 M-F	C-487-5149	
Sec Police	Main Gate	24 hrs dly	C-487-5267	
ATTRACTIONS	Hunting and fishing paradise			

SCHEDULED FLIGHTS

DESTINATION	ROUTING	FREQ	EQ/CMTS
Attu CGS AK (ATU)	ADQ-SYA-ATU-SYA	2 monthly	C-130H/M
Cordova CGS AK (CDV)	ADQ-CDV-VDZ-JNU-SIT-KTN-SIT	2 monthly	C-130H/M
Elmendorf AFB AK (EDF)	ADQ-EDF-ADQ	Weekly	C-130H/M
Juneau CGS AK (JNU)	ADQ-CDV-VDZ-JNU-SIT-KTN-SIT	2 monthly	C-130H/M
Ketchikan Intl AK (KTN)	ADQ-CDV-VDZ-JNU-SIT-KTN-SIT	2 monthly	C-130H/M
Port Clarence CGS AK (KPC)	ADQ-KPC-NOJ	2 monthly	C-130H/M
St Paul Island CGS AK (SNP)	ADQ-SNP-NOJ	2 monthly	C-130H/M
Shemya AFB AK (SYA)	ADQ-SYA-ATU-SYA	2 monthly	C-130H/M
Sitka CGAS AK (NOU)	ADQ-CDV-VDZ-JNU-SIT-KTN-SIT	2 monthly	C-130H/M

Note: Only military personnel may travel to ATU, KPC and SNP. Prior permission required for non-assigned personnel to travel to ADK.

Shemya Air Force Base (SYA)
OL-E, 616th APS/TRO
APO Seattle 98736-5000

Comm: 907-392-3000
ATVN: 317-392-3000

LOCATION: At W tip of Aleutian Island chain, midway between Anchorage & Tokyo accessible via air only. RM:p-6,J/5. NMC: Anchorage AK, 1800 air mi NE.

FACILITIES	LOCATION	HOURS	PHONE	COMMENTS
PAX TERM INFO	Base Ops Bldg	Duty hrs or during flt processing 1200 Arrival and departure via air. AD mil or civ on orders only. Prior permission from Cmdr required for all others.	C-392-	

ALASKA

Shemya AFB, Cont'd

Pax Svc Ofc	Base Ops Duty hrs C-393-1200
PAX LOUNGES	No Pax lounge. All processing through Base Ops.
FOOD SERVICE NCO/CPO Club	Limited. No off Base facilities. Sep Bldg 0600-2400 dly C-382-3362 Consolidated Mess
Snack Bars	Comp Bldg 0800-1800 dly C-382-3364
TRANSPORTATION Air Tickets	Base Ops Bldg Duty hrs C-392-1200 Reeve Aleutian
OTHER SERVICES Medical	Exchange, Hair styles, Laundry/DryC. Other Base spt avail. Dispensary 24 hrs dly C-382-3550
TML	Billeting Ofc 24 hrs dly C-382-3000 Ask for Billeting.
TRAVELERS AID Chaplain	Chapel Duty hrs C-382-3366
ATTRACTIONS	Summer fishing. No hunting on these islands.

SCHEDULED FLIGHTS

DESTINATION	ROUTING	FREQ	EQ/CMTS
Adak NAS AK (ADK)	SYA-ADK-EDF	1/3/Sa	C-141B/M
Attn CGS AK (ATU)	SYA-ATU-NOJ NOJ-SYA-ATU-SYA	2 ea mo 2 ea mo	C-130H/M C-130H/M
Elmendorf AFB AK (EDF)	SYA-EDF-TCM SYA-EDF	Su,1/2/3/Th Sa	C-141B/C C-141B/C
Kodiak CGAS AK (ADQ)	SYA-ATU-ADQ	2 ea mo	C-130H/M
McChord AFB WA (TCM)	SYA-EDF-TCM	Su,1/2/3/Th	C-141B/C

AMERICAN SAMOA

Pago Pago International Airport (PPG)　　　　Comm: (684) 699-1515
MAC Rep, PO Box 36　　　　　　　　　　　　　　　ATVN: None
Pago Pago, AS 96799-5000

LOCATION: On the S coast of the Island of Tutuila in American Samoa. Approx 3,500 miles SW of Honolulu HI, and 3,000 miles NE of Christchurch NZ. NMC: Village of Utulei, main US Government offices, 9 miles from IAP.

FACILITIES	LOCATION	HOURS	PHONE	COMMENTS
PAX TERM INFO	Pax Term	24 hrs dly	C-699-1515	At IAP. One gate for departures. Contact MAC rep C-699-1945. Basic refuel station.

AMERICAN SAMOA
Pago Pago Intl Arpt, Cont'd

Pax Svc Ofc	Pax Term 24 hrs dly C-639-9107 MAC control-Air Svc Samoa
Pax Paging	Pax Term 24 hrs dly C-699-1515 P.A. system
PAX LOUNGES General	Pax Term 24 hrs dly Comm IAP lounges avail for Space-A Pax Pax Term 24 hrs dly C-699-1515 Bag check/lockers, Rest-rms, Wood seats
DV/VIP	Pax Term 24 hrs dly C-699-1515 A/C, Rest-rms, O/S seats. No hostess.
FOOD SERVICE Enl Club	Svc at IAP, Rainmaker hotel & American Samoa Exchange Rsv Ctr 4 blks fm PPG 1600-0100 dly Vet's Club open to Space-A Pax
Restaurants	Pax Term 0600-2000 dly C-699-9981 Open for MAC flts
Snack Bars	Rainmaker hotel 24 hrs dly C-633-4241
TRANSPORTATION Air Tickets	Pax Term 0800-1700 dly C-699-4222 Air Svc Samoa
Bus (Comm) (Gov)	Pax Term 0800-1700 dly C-699-1515 Pax Term 0600-1700 dly C-699-1515 MAC rep
Car Rentals	PPG/hotels 0800-1600 dly C-633-4323/5520 Hertz, Morris
TAXI(Comm)	Pax Term 24 hrs dly C-639-9270 PPG to hotels $7
Parking	Pax Term 24 hrs dly No restrictions
Medical	LBJ Med Ctr 24 hrs dly C-633-2222 Emergency
TML	No mil TML 24 hrs dly C-633-4241 Rainmaker hotel $50-$60
TRAVELERS AID ARC	LBJ Med Ctr 0800-1600 M-Sa C-633-5222
Sec Police	Pax Term 24 hrs dly C-699-9101
ATTRACTIONS	Beautiful tropical islands, beaches, and fishing

SCHEDULED FLIGHTS

DESTINATION	ROUTING	FREQ	EQ/CMTS
Alice Springs Arpt AU (ASP)	SBD-HIK-PPG-CHC-RCM-ASP	Sa	C-141B/C
Christchurch Intl NZ (CHC)	SBD-HIK-PPG-CHC-RCM-ASP	Sa	C-141B/C
Hickam AFB HI (HIK)	ASP-RCM-PPG-HIK-SBD LEA-RCM-CHC-PPG-HIK-SBD	Tu F	C-141B/C C-141B/C
Learmonth RAAFB AU (LEA)	SBD-HIK-PPG-RCM-UMR-RCM-LEA	M	C-141B/C
Norton AFB CA (SBD)	ASP-RCM-PPG-HIK-SBD LEA-RCM-CHC-PPG-HIK-SBD	Tu F	C-141B/C C-141B/C

AMERICAN SAMOA
Pago Pago Intl Arpt, Cont'd

Richmond RAAFB AU (RCM)	SBD-HIK-PPG-RCM-UMR-RCM-LEA SBD-HIK-PPG-CHC-RCM-ASP	M Sa		C-141B/C C-141B/C
Wommera Afield AU (UMR)	SBD-HIK-PPG-RCM-UMR-RCM-LEA	M		C-141B/C

GUAM

Agana Naval Air Station (NGM)
Air Operations Officer
FPO San Francisco 96637-5000

Comm: 671-344-8103/5
ATVN: 344-8103/5

LOCATION: In the middle of the island of Guam. Main gate is off Route 8. Clearly marked. NMC: Agana GU, 3 mi SW.

FACILITIES	LOCATION	HOURS	PHONE	COMMENTS
PAX TERM INFO	Term	24 hrs dly	C-344-7127, A-344-7127	
	From main gate R on Perimeter Rd to 3rd street on L. Term left before ATC tower. Shares runways with Guam IAP.			
PAX LOUNGES	Term	24 hrs dly	C-344-7127	-
FOOD SERVICE	Cafeteria C-342-1256, Enl Club C-342-2274, NCO/CPO Club C-342-2269			
TRANSPORTATION	Car Rentals C-344-1288, Taxi(Comm) C-646-1155/1034/7957, Parking C-344-7127/7254			
OTHER SERVICES	Exchange C-342-2104, Barber C-342-1204, Beauty C-342-1213, Medical C-344-8201			
TML	Bldg 1300/15 24 hrs dly BOQ C-344-5221. BEQ C-344-5227. DV/VIP C-344-8103.			
TRAVELERS AID	Chaplain C-344-4117/6119 (other hrs C-344-8103), Sec Police C-344-6114, USO C-366-4246/7246			
ATTRACTIONS	Water sports, beaches, tours of island			

UNSCHEDULED FLIGHTS

Many flts to: Barbers Point NAS HI (NAX); Cubi Point NAS RP (CUA); Kadena AB JA (DNA); Midway Island NAS MW (MDY); and Yap Island WCI TT (YAP). Full scheduled services at Andersen AFB GU (UAM).

Andersen Air Force Base (UAM)
605 MASS/TROP
APO San Francisco 96334-5000

Comm: 671-366-1110
ATVN: 366-1110

LOCATION: On the N end of the island, access from Marine Drive (GU-1) which extends the entire length of the island of Guam. NMC: Agana GU, 15 miles S.

FACILITIES	LOCATION	HOURS	PHONE	COMMENTS
PAX TERM INFO	Bldg 17002	24 hrs dly	C-366-5165/5162, A-366-5165/5162	
	Follow Perimeter Rd from main gate to Term on left.			

GUAM
Andersen AFB, Cont'd

Pax Svc Ofc	Bldg 17002	0730-1630 M-F	C-366-4169	NAVY 366-2185
Pax Paging	Bldg 17002	24 hrs dly	C-366-5165/62 See Pax Svc Rep	
PAX LOUNGES General	Bldg 17002 24 hrs dly See Pax NCO for services. Bldg 17002 24 hrs dly C-366-5162 A/C, Bag lks, Game rm, Tel A, L&LD, Rest-rms, Showers, P/C seats			
DV/VIP	Bldg 17002 24 hrs dly C-366-5162 No hostess A/C, Bag lks, Coffee/tea srvd, Rest-rms, TV, Showers, O/S seats			
Protocol Svc	Bldg 23003	Duty hrs	C-366-4228	See Commander/UAM.
Family	Bldg 17002 24 hrs dly C-366-5162 (off Gen Pax lounge) A/C, T/V, O/S seats, Play room, Cribs, Refrigerator			
FOOD SERVICE Cafeteria	Many fac on and off Base See USO recommended restaurants. Bldg 17002 24 hrs dly C-366-8283			
Dining Hall	Hall "B"	0530-1800 M-F, 0600-1300 & 1530-1730 Sa-Su C-366-2195 Call for svc hrs.		
NCO Club	Bldg 26006	0800-2400 M-F, 0800-0400 Sa-Su C-362-3173/3247 Call for svc hrs.		
OFC Club	Bldg 1091	0700-0100 dly	C-362-2991/2 Call for svc hrs.	
Snack Bars	Bldg 27030	0600-2200 dly	C-362-3149 "Latte Stone"drive-in	
Vending	Bldg 17002	24 hrs dly	Departure lounge area	
TRANSPORTATION Air Tickets	Many facilities and means Bldg 22002 0730-1630 M-F C-362-3172 SATO			
Bus(Shuttle)	Bldg 17002	0600-1800 dly	C-366-2239 UAM area every 20 min	
Car Rentals	Bldg 17002	0800-1700 dly	C-362-2181	
TAXI(Gov)	Bldg 1800	24 hrs dly	C-366-2239 Duty Pax only	
Parking	Bldg 17002 24 hrs dly Sht term avail/Long term 30 days max			
OTHER SERVICES Exchange	Full spt svc at UAM and Navy Base/island mil facilities Bldg 22026 1000-1800 dly C-362-1136			
Bank/Exc	Bldg 21000 0900-1500 M-F, C-363-2984/5 Ft Sam Houston Bldg 17002 Automatic Teller Machine 24 hrs dly			
Hair Styles	Bldg 25005	0800-1730 M-F, Sa-1600 C-362-2187 Barber C-362-5164 Beauty		
Laundry/DryC	Bldg 05005	0800-1800 M-F, Sa-1600 C-362-3120		
Medical	Bldg 26000	0700-1630 dly C-366-2978 Appointment 1700-2130 dly C-366-4276 Urgent Care		
Postal	Bldg 21001	0800-1600 M-F, Sa-1200 C-366-3243		
RCA(Comm)	Bldg 17002	0800-1700 dly	C-646-8886/9 Other hrs/collect	

GUAM

Andersen AFB, Cont'd

TML	Bldg 27006 24 hrs dly C-366-8144 All Ranks. DV/VIP C-366-4228
TRAVELERS AID ARC	Many agencies USAF and USN Bldg 21000 Duty hrs C-366-6270 O/hrs C-366-8144
Chaplain	Bldg 22024 Duty hrs C-366-6139 O/hrs C-366-8144
Emerg Relief	Bldg 21000 0730-1630 C-366-4295 "Helpline" C-363-2913 After duty hours
Lost/Found	Bldg 17002 24 hrs dly C-366-5162 See Pax Svc NCO.
Sec Police	Bldg 21000 24 hrs dly C-366-2913 Desk Sgt/Law Enforcement
USO	Bldg 17002 24 hrs dly C-366-4246 Call for desk hrs.
ATTRACTIONS	US Naval Base, WWII battle areas, beaches

SCHEDULED FLIGHTS

DESTINATION	ROUTING	FREQ	EQ/CMTS
Babelthuap WCI/TT (ROR)	UAM-ROR-YAP	2/Tu	C-130E/C
Clark AB RP (CRK)	SUU-HIK-UAM-CRK UAM-CRK TIK-SUU-HIK-UAM-CRK UAM-CRK	Su,W,Sa M-Sa M 2/F,4/Sa	C-141B/M C-141B/M C-141B/C C-130E/C
Cubi Point NAS RP (CUA)	SUU-HIK-UAM-CUA SUU-HIK-UAM-CUA	M,W,Sa 1/3/W,Th	C-141B/M C-141B/C
Hickam AFB HI (HIK)	UAM-HIK-SBD CRK-UAM-HIK-SUU	Daily Tu,W,Th,Sa	C-141B/M C-141B/M
Kadena AB JA (DNA)	SUU-HIK-UAM-DNA SBD-SUU-HIK-UAM-CRK-DNA-OKO	F Daily	C-141B/C C-141B/M
Kosrae Arpt (WCI) TT(KSA)	UAM-KSA	4/Th	C-130E/C
Norton AFB CA (SBD)	UAM-HIK-SBD	Daily	C-141B/M
Ponape ECI/ TT (PNI)	UAM-TKK-PNI	4/W	C-130E/C
Travis AFB CA (SUU)	CRK-UAM-HIK-SUU	Tu,W,Th,Sa	C-141B/ME
Truk IAP ECI/TT (TKK)	UAM-TKK-PNI	4/W	C-130E/C
Yap Intl WCI/TT (YAP)	UAM-ROR-YAP UAM-YAP	2/Tu 2/Th,4/F	C-130E/C C-130E/C
Yokota AB JA (OKO)	SBD-SUU-HIK-UAM-CRK-DNA-OKO	Daily	C-141B/M

HAWAII

Barbers Point Naval Air Station (NAX)　　Comm: 808-684-6266
Ops Dept/ATC Div　　　　　　　　　　　　　　　　ATVN: 430-1111
NAS Barbers Point, HI 96862-5050

LOCATION: Take H-1 W (toward Waianae) to Barbers Point NAS/Makakilo exit,
S for 2.5 mi to main gate. RM: p-7, I/3. NMC: Honolulu, 12 mi E.

FACILITIES	LOCATION	HOURS	PHONE	COMMENTS
PAX TERM INFO	Bldg 4　　　　24 hrs dly　　C-684-2174, A-484-2174 Main gate, straight on Enterprise, L on Midway, R at air Term sign. First floor.			
CG Air Sta	Bldg 1790	0800-1600 M-F	C-682-2621	Ltd flts to MDY & CONUS
Pax Svc Ofc	Bldg 4	24 hrs dly	C-684-2174	Attendant on duty
Pax Paging	Bldg 4	24 hrs dly	C-684-2174	
PAX LOUNGES General	Bldg 4 Bldg 4	Right side from parking lot C-684-2174　Bag chk,Rest-rms,Showers,P/C seats		
DV/VIP	Bldg 4　　　　C-684-2174　　See attendant for key to lounge. Coffee/tea served, Rest-rms, O/S seats			
Protocol Svc	Bldg 4	Duty hours	C-684-6266	Cmdr Patrol Wing
FOOD SERVICE Cafeteria	Many facilities on and off Base Bldg 1744　　0630-1400 dly　C-684-6271　Call for svc hrs.			
Enl Club	Bldg 1702	1100-2200 dly	C-684-7133	Call for svc hrs.
NCO/CPO Club	Bldg 929	1100-2200 dly	C-684-5222	Call for svc hrs.
OFC Club	Bldg 78	0600-1900 dly	C-684-4108	Call for svc hrs.
Snack Bars	"Snack Alley"	Duty hours	C-684-6271	Call for svc hrs.
Vending	Bldg 4	24 hrs dly	C-684-2190	Back of Pax Term
TRANSPORTATION Air Tickets	Limited on Base. Commercial systems off Base. Bldg 50　　　　Duty hours　　C-684-6266　SATO			
Car Rentals	Shangrila	0800-1700 dly	C-682-5677	
TAXI(Comm)	Main Gate	24 hrs dly	C-684-6266	
Parking	Bldg 4	24 hrs dly	C-684-6222	No restrictions
OTHER SERVICES Exchange	Full range of support facilities Bldg 1659　　0930-1700 dly　C-684-6271			
Bank/Exc	Bldg 965	0830-1500 M-F	C-681-3116	Bank of Hawaii
Hair Styles	Bldg 1659	0900-1600 M-Sa	C-684-7191 C-684-6271	Barber Beauty
Laundry/DryC	Bldg 1659	0930-1700 dly	C-684-6271	
Medical	Clinic Saratoga	24 hrs dly	C-684-3133/6241	

HAWAII

Barbers Point NAS, Cont'd

Postal	Bldg 1659	0900-1500 M-Sa	C-684-6266	
TML	Bldg 1788 All Ranks.	24 hrs dly	C-684-2248/2290 DV/VIP C-684-1181.	
TRAVELERS AID ARC	Bldg 50 Bldg 50	Duty hours 0800-1600 M-F	C-684-7198 C-684-5215	Family Services O/hrs C-474-7100
Chaplain	Bldg 52	24 hrs dly	C-684-3111	
Emerg Relief	Bldg 57	Duty hours	C-682-4422	Navy Relief
Lost/Found	Bldg 4	24 hrs dly	C-684-2190	Pax Svc NCO
Sec Police	Bldg 1	24 hrs dly	C-684-6222	Desk Sgt
USO	HIK	24 hrs dly	C-449-2887	Term lounge
ATTRACTIONS	Honolulu, beaches, island tours			

SCHEDULED FLIGHTS

DESTINATION	ROUTING	FREQ	EQ/CMTS *
Agana NAS GU (NGM)	NAX-NGM	5 flts ea wk	
Alameda NAS CA (NGZ)	NAX-NGZ	1 flt ea wk	
Atsugi NAF JA (NJA)	NAX-NJA	10 flts ea mo	
Cubi Point NAS RP (CUA)	NAX-CUA	9 flts ea mo	
Dallas NAS TX (NBE)	NAX-NBE	1 flt ea mo	
Elmendorf AFB AK (EDF)	NAX-EDF	2 flts ea mo	
El Toro MCAS CA (NZJ)	NAX-NZJ	Many flts dly	
Glenview NAS IL (NBU)	NAX-NBU	3 flts ea mo	
Jacksonville NAS FL (NIP)	NAX-NIP	3 flts ea mo	
Kadena NAF JA (NDI)	NAX-NDI	10 flts ea mo	
Midway Is NAS TT (MDY)	NAX-MDW	2 flts ea mo	C-130H/M
Moffett Field NAS CA (NUQ)	NAX-NUQ	Many flts dly	

HAWAII
Barbers Point NAS, Cont'd

North Island NAS CA (NZY)	NAX-NZY	F
Point Mugu NAS CA (NTD)	NAX-NTD	2-3 flts ea mo
Whidbey Island NAS WA (NUW)	NAX-NUW	1-2 flts ea mo
Yokota AB JA (OKO)	NAX-OKO	10 flts ea mo

* Note: Most flights are by C009A/P/ME, C-130A/M, P-3A/M, and Navy administrative aircraft. Call for other destinations, routings, and schedules.

Hickam Air Force Base (HIK)
619th MASS/TROP
Hickam Air Force Base, HI 96853-5000

Comm: 808-422-0531
ATVN: 430-0111

LOCATION: Adjacent to the Honolulu IAP. Accessible from H-1 or HI-92. Clearly marked. RM: p-7, L/7. NMC: Honolulu HI, 6 miles East.

FACILITIES	LOCATION	HOURS	PHONE	COMMENTS
PAX TERM INFO	Bldg 2028	24 hrs dly	C-449-2807, A-449-2807	
	From main gate on O'Malley Blvd, then left before Base Ops Bldg to Pax Term.			
Pax Svc Ofc	Bldg 2028	0730-1700 dly	C-449-1270, A-449-1581	
Pax Paging	Bldg 2028	24 hrs dly	C-449-6833/2807, A-449-6833/2807	
PAX LOUNGES General	Bldg 2028		USO lounge converts to family lounge at closing	
	Bldg 2028	24 hrs dly	C-449-2887	
	A/C, Free TV, Rest-rms, Bag chk/lks, Game rm, Coin TV, Cribs. Pay-tel. No food in lounge.			
DV/VIP	Bldg 2028	24 hrs dly	C-449-1153. C-449-5884 Hostess	
	A/C, Free TV, O/S seats, Rest-rms, Bag chk/lks, Game rm			
Protocol Svc	Bldg 1102	Duty hrs	C-449-1781	Hq PACAF on E St
FOOD SERVICE Cafeteria	Many facilities on and off Base			
	Bldg 2028	24 hrs dly	C-422-8000	"Aloha Inn"
Dining Hall	Bldg 1860	0530-1800 dly	C-449-1555	Call for svc hrs.
NCO/CPO Club	Bldg 422	0630-2100 dly	C-449-1092	"Tradewinds"
OFC Club	Bldg 901	1115-2100 dly	C-449-1998	Call for svc hrs.
Restaurants	HIK Harbor	1100-2100 Tu-Su	C-449-9909	"Sea Breeze"
Snack Bars	Bldg 1113	0700-2230 dly	C-422-5335	"Sub Stop"
Vending	Bldg 2028	24 hrs dly	C-422-8000	Also, pay-telephone

HAWAII

Hickam AFB, Cont'd

TRANSPORTATION Air Tickets	Many means & fac avail. Honolulu city bus info C-531-1611. Bldg 1113 0800-1700 dly C-422-0548 SATO, Term C-422-2729			
Bus(Comm) (Shuttle)	Bldg 2028 0600-0100 M-F-20 min C-531-1611 Bus #19 HIK Term $.60 exact amt.0635-2315 wkends-30 min.NO LARGE LUGGAGE. Bldg 2028 0600-1800 M-F-15 min C-449-1742 Key Base points			
Car Rentals	Bldg 2028	0730-2100 dly	C-423-1369	Rainbow/AAFES
TAXI(Comm) (Gov)	Bldg 2028 Motor Pool	24 hrs dly 24 hrs dly	C-949-4990 C-449-1742	Front door of lobby Duty Pax only
Parking	NW of Term	24 hrs dly	C-449-2222	Lic # to SP, 6+ hrs
OTHER SERVICES Exchange	Full support services available throughout the Base Bldg 2028 24 hrs dly C-422-8400 Main BX, Bldg 1232 C-423-1304			
Bank/Exc	Bldg 1242	0800-1500 M-Th	C-422-2781 F-1800	1st HI Bank
Hair Styles	Bldg 1232 Bldg 1232	0930-1800 M-F 0930-1700 M-Sa	C-422-4045 C-422-6121	Barber Beauty
Laundry/DryC	Bldg 1232	0930-1800 M-F, 0930-1700 Sa C-422-5821/5555		
Medical	Bldg 559	24 hrs dly	C-449-5248	Tripler AMC C
Postal	Bldg 2097	0830-1500 M-F	C-449-9480	
TML	Bldg 1153 24 hrs dly C-423-5511 Hale Koa C-955-0555, A-430-5511 & C-800-367-6027, 0800-1600 hrs HI local time			
TRAVELERS AID ARC	Bldg 1105 Bldg 509	0900-1300 dly 24 hrs dly	C-449-1550 C-449-1488	Air Force Family Svc Other hrs C-449-1648
Chaplain	Bldg 1750	0730-1640 dly	C-449-1754	All faiths
Emerg Relief	Bldg 1102 Bldg 1514	24 hrs dly 24 hrs dly	C-449-5987 C-423-1314	Air Force Aid Nav Relief-Pearl Har
Lost/Found	Bldg 2028	24 hrs dly	C-449-5353	
Sec Police	Bldg 1004	24 hrs dly	C-449-6372	Desk Sgt
USO	Bldg 2028	24 hrs dly	C-449-2887	
ATTRACTIONS	Honolulu, Waikiki beach, and Pearl Harbor			

SCHEDULED FLIGHTS

DESTINATION	ROUTING	FREQ	EQ/CMTS
Alice Springs Arpt AU (ASP)	SDB-HIK-PPG-CHC-RCM-ASP	Sa	C-141B/C
Andersen AFB GU (UAM)	SBD-SUU-HIK-UAM-CRK-DNA-OKO SBD-SUU-HIK-UAM-OKO-DNA SUU-HIK-UAM-CRK SUU-HIK-UAM-CRK SUU-HIK-UAM-CRK SUU-HIK-UAM-CUA	Dly Dly Su Every other W 1/3/W,4/F Th,F	C-141B/M C-141B/M C-141B/M C-141B/M C005A/C C-141B/C

HAWAII
Hickam AFB, Cont'd

Christchurch Intl NZ (CHC)	SBD-HIK-PPG-CHC-RCM-ASP	Sa	C-141B/C
Clark AB RP (CRK)	SUU-HIK-UAM-CRK TIK-SUU-HIK-CRK SUU-HIK-UAM-CR	Su,W,1/2/4/Th M 4/Th	C-141B/M C-141B/C C005A/C
Cubi Point NAS RP (CUA)	SUU-HIK-UAM-CUA SUU-HIK-UAM-CUA SUU-HIK-UAM-CUA	M,W,Sa 1/3/W 4/Th	C-141B/M C005A/C C-141B/C
Kadena AB JA (DNA)	SUU-HIK-UAM-DNA SUU-HIK-UAM-DNA SBD-SUU-HIK-UAM-OKO-DNA	F F Sa	C005A/C C-141B/C C-141B/M
Learmonth RAAFB AU (LEA)	SBD-HIK-PPG-RCM-UMR-LEA	M	C-141B/C
Norton AFB CA (SBD)	UAM-HIK-SBD LEA-RCM-CHC-PPG-HIK-SBD	Daily Su	C-141B/M C-141B/C
Osan AB RK (OSN)	SUU-HIK-OKO-OSN	Sa	C005A/C
Pago Pago Intl AS (PPG)	SBD-HIK-PPG-RCM-UMR-LEA SBD-HIK-PPG-CHC-RCM-ASP	M Sa	C-141B/C C-141B/C
Richmond RAAFB AU (RCM)	SBD-HIK-PPG-RCM-UMR-LEA SBD-HIK-PPG-CHC-RCM-ASP	M Sa	C-141B/C C-141B/C
Travis AFB CA (SUU)	HIK-SUU DNA-HIK-SUU	Daily M	C-141B/M C-141B/C
Woomera Afield AU (UMR)	SBD-HIK-PPG-RCM-UMR-LEA	M	C-141B/C
Yokota AB JA (OKO)	SBD-SUU-HIK-UAM-OKO-DNA SUU-HIK-OKO-OSN	Daily Sa	C-141B/M C005R/C

PACIFIC ISLANDS

Midway Island
Naval Air Station (MDY)
USNAF/MAC Rep, Box 4
FPO San Francisco, CA 96114-1200

Comm: Call Small Island Oper. Ask for Midway Island EX-415/400/814.
ATVN: 430-0111 (Pearl Harbor) EX-415/400/814

LOCATION: On Midway Island in the Pacific Ocean, 1300 air miles NW of HI.
NMC: Honolulu, 1300 mi SE.

FACILITIES	LOCATION	HOURS	PHONE	COMMENTS
PAX TERM INFO	Base Ops	During flt hrs	EX-381/437	Entry approval from Commandant, 14th Nav District, Honolulu 45 days in advance. Space-A Pax handled through Base Ops. No lounge.
FOOD SERVICE	CPO Club EX-864, Officers' Club EX-864, Snack bar EX-415			

PACIFIC ISLANDS

Midway Island NAS, Cont'd

OTHER SERVICES	BX, Pkg Store, Theater EX-541/400, Security Police EX-555
Medical	Dispensary 24 hrs dly EX-666
TML	Bldg 8 24 hrs dly EX-648 Prior approval by Commandant, 14th Naval District, Honolulu
ATTRACTIONS	Water sports, fishing, and beaches

SCHEDULED FLIGHTS

DESTINATION	ROUTING	FREQ	EQ/CMTS
Hickam AFB HI (HIK)	MDY-HIK	F	C-141B/M

UNSCHEDULED FLIGHTS

Freq flts to: Hickam AFB HI (HIK); Barbers Point NAS HI (NAX); and Kadena AB JA (DNA).

Pacific Islands, TT (PIS)
(Not listed separately in this book)

The stations listed below have Space-A air opportunities. Base support facilities are very limited. Billeting and mess arrangements for extended visits should be made and confirmed in advance of your planned visit. All islands are United States Trust Territories except Johnston Island and Saipan, Mariana Islands, which are US.

BABELTHUAP ARPT, WCI, TT (ROR)
OIC Civic Action Team, Koror
PO Box 6005
Koror, Palaua WCI 96940-5000
Contact through NAVY MARS.

JOHNSTON ISLAND, JO (JON)
MAC Rep FCDNA Term Ops
APO San Francisco 96305-5000
ATVN: 315-441-3330-EX-2252/2343

KOSRAE ARPT, WCI, TT (KSA)
OIC Civic Action Team, Kosrae
Kosrae, Kosrae WCI 96944-5000
Contact through NAVY MARS.

KWAJALEIN, MARSHALL IS, TT (KWA)
Kwajalein Missile Range
ATTN: BMDSC-RKL/MAC Rep
PO Box 26
APO San Francisco 96555-5000
Comm: 805-238-7994-EX-3770/3421
ATVN: 254-3770/3421

PONAPE, ECI, TT (PNI)
OIC Civil Action Team
PO Box 507
Kolonia, Ponape ECI 99441-5000
Contact through NAVY MARS.

SAIPAN, MARIANA IS, (SPN)
MAC Rep
USCG Loran Station Saipan
PO Box 337
Saipan, CM 96950-5000
Comm: 6101/6107-EX-7

TRUK, ECI, TT (TKK)
OIC CAT TRUK
PO Box 28
Moen, Truk, ECI 96942-5000
Contact 30NCR MARS STA "A",
322-1110. Ask for 339-1195.

YAP ISLAND, WCI, TT (YAP)
OIC Civic Action Team Yap
PO Box 9
Yap, WCI 96943-5000
Contact through NAVY MARS EX-2189.

SCHEDULED FLIGHTS

DESTINATION and ROUTING	FREQ	EQ/CMTS
JON-HIK	Su	C-141B/M
HIK-KWA-AWK	Tu	C-141B/M

PACIFIC ISLANDS

Pacific Islands, Cont'd

Routing	Freq	Eq
UAM-ROR-YAP	2/Tu	C-130E/M
AWK-KWA-HIK	W	C-141B/M
YAP-UAM	2/W	C-130E/M
KSA-UAM	4/W	C-130E/C
UAM-TKK-PNI	4/W	C-130E/C
PNI-UAM	4/Th	C-130E/C
MDY-HIK	F	C-141B/M
JON-HIK	F	C-141B/M
YAK-UAM	4/F	C-130E/C
KWA-HIK	Sa	C-141B/M
AWK-HIK	1/3/4/Sa	C-141B/M
AWK-CRK	1/Sa	C-130E/M

Wake Island
Air Force Base (AWK)
Det 4 15th ABW/PACAF
APO San Francisco 96501-5000

Comm: Small-Island Oper in Honolulu
ATVN: 430-0111 Ask for Wake Island.

LOCATION: A US island in the Pacific, 2100 air mi NW of Hawaii. NMC: Honolulu, 2100 air mi SE.

FACILITIES	LOCATION	HOURS	PHONE	COMMENTS
PAX TERM INFO	Base Ops	0800-1700 M-Sa	EX-210	All arrivals via air. Letter approval fm CMD, Det 4, 15th ABW, Hickam AFB may be required for all non-Active Duty visitors. All Space-A Pax processed by Base Ops.
Pax Svc Ofc	Base Ops	0800-1700 M-Sa	EX-224	
PAX LOUNGES	Base Ops	0800-1700 M-Sa	EX-210	1st floor. A/C, Tel C, Rest-rms, P/C seats. General lounge only.
FOOD SERVICE Bar	Limited Bldg 1109	0600-1900 dly 1730-2330 M-Sa	EX-486 EX-545	"Drifters Reef"
TRANSPORTATION Bus(Gov)	Base Ops	0800-1700 M-Sa	EX-210	Term to spt facs
OTHER SERVICES	BX EX-395, Barber EX-345, Laundry EX-341, Post Office EX-259			
Medical	Bldg 443	0800-1700 dly	EX-455	
TML	Biltg Office	24 hrs dly	EX-222	Very limited
ATTRACTIONS	Tropical climate and nice beaches			

SCHEDULED FLIGHTS

DESTINATION	ROUTING	FREQ	EQ/CMTS
Clark AFB RP (CRK)	AWK-CRK	1/Sa	C-130E/M
Hickam AFB HI (HIK)	AWK-KWA-HIK AWK-HIK	W 1/3/4/Sa	C-141B/M C-141B/M

PACIFIC ISLANDS

Wake Island AFB, Cont'd

| Kwajalein TT (KWA) | AWK-KWA-HIK | W | C-141B/M |

UNSCHEDULED FLIGHTS

Some flights available from Wake Island AFB (AWK) to: Barbers Point NAS (NAX) and Cubi Point NAS RP (CUA).

PUERTO RICO

Borinquen Coast Guard Air Station (BQN)
CGAS Borinquen
Aquadilla, PR 00604-5000

Comm: 809-890-5201
FTS: 890-5201/7109
ATVN: None

LOCATION: At the old Ramey AFB, W of Aquadilla PR. Take PR-2 W from San Juan or N from Mayaguez to PR-110 N to CGAS. RM:p-119, B/18. NMC: San Juan PR, 65 mi E.

FACILITIES	LOCATION	HOURS	PHONE	COMMENTS
PAX TERM INFO	CG hangar 0800-1600 M-F C-890-7276/5201, F-890-7276/5201 SW corner of CG hangar. Eastern-most corner of large concrete hangars on N side of field. No Pax Terminal.			
PAX LOUNGES	CG hangar 0800-1530 M-F C-890-5201/7276 No Pax lounge. All Pax handled by CG Ops personnel at hangar.			
FOOD SERVICE	Limited on Base. Good off Base. Cafeteria C-890-7109, Cons Club C-890-2581			
TRANSPORTATION	Jitney svc avail fm San Juan. Taxi in Aquadilla & San Juan.			
OTHER SERVICES	Limited support services. Exchange C-890-3127, Hair Styles C-890-3127, Medical C-890-7203, Postal C-890-5201			
TML	Housing area 0800-1700 M-F, 1200 Sa C-890-3137/2581. All ranks. Note: transient housing ltd. Call ahead for info.			
TRAVELERS AID	ARC C-890-5201, Sec Police C-890-2671			
ATTRACTIONS	Local beaches (excellent surfing in winter) & restaurants			

UNSCHEDULED FLIGHTS

From Borinquen CGAS PR (BQN) to: Miami IAP FL (MIA); Mobile CGATC AL (MOB); Elizabeth City CGAS NC (ECG); Roosevelt Roads NAS PR (NRR); Clearwater CGAS FL (PIE); Opa Locka Arpt FL (Miami) (OPF). Flights are mixed missions via HU-25A and HC-130 aircraft. Some missions are for law enforcement and do not take Space-A Pax. No Space-A flights via helicopter.

Roosevelt Roads Naval Air Station (NRR)
Supply Dept, US Naval Station
FPO Miami 34051-5000

Comm: 809-865-2000
ATVN: 831-2000/4311

LOCATION: From San Juan, E on PR-3 for 45 mi. Sign on R indicating exit to Naval Station. RM: p-119, C/26. NMC: San Juan, 50 mi NW.

PUERTO RICO
Roosevelt Roads NAS, Cont'd

FACILITIES	LOCATION	HOURS	PHONE	COMMENTS
PAX TERM INFO	Air Ops Bldg STOP 23 0700-1600 M-Sa, Su for flts only C-865-5208/4263/4374, A-831-5208/4263/4374 From main gate straight to first right to Air Ops on left.			
Pax Svc Ofc	Air Ops Bldg 0700-1600 M/Sa C-865-5208/4263/4374/5414			
Pax Paging	Air Ops Bldg 0700-1600 M-Sa C-865-5208			
PAX LOUNGES	Air Ops Bldg			DV/VIP lounge available
General	Air Ops Bldg 0700-1600 M-Sa C-865-5208/4374 A/C, Rest-rms, P/C seats			
Protocol Svc	Hq CNFC	Duty hrs	C-865-4301/4323	
FOOD SERVICE Cafeteria	Many facilities on and off Base STOP 17 0730-2200 dly C-865-5285			
Dining Hall	STOP 5	0545-0130 dly	C-865-4138/9	"Anchor Inn"
Enl Club	STOP 7	1930-2330 M,W,Th,Su	C-865-4142	
NCO/CPO Club	STOP 8 1100-2400 dly C-865-5279 "Acey-Deucey" C/for svc hrs.			
OFC Club	STOP 3	1100-2400 dly	C-865-7200/5211	C/for svc hrs.
Restaurants	"Seabreeze" 1800-2400 dly C-865-5641			
Snack Bars	STOP 18	1000-1700 Tu-F,1500 Sa C-865-5285 Deli/Bake Shop		
Vending	Air Ops Bldg 0630-1800 M-Sa C-865-4374			
TRANSPORTATION Air Tickets	Many facilities and means on and off Base SATO Bldg 0800-1800 M-Sa C-865-1570			
Bus(Comm) (Shuttle)	Gates 1 & 3 Gate 1	24 hrs dly 24 hrs dly	C-865-4123 C-865-4263	NRR to entire island 26 stops on Base
Car Rentals	NEX garage	0800-1700 M-Sa	C-865-5734	
TAXI(Comm)	Air Ops Bldg	24 hrs dly	C-865-4374	
Parking	Air Ops Bldg	24 hrs dly	C-865-4123	See Security Police.
OTHER SERVICES Exchange	Many support facilities on and off Base STOP 21 1000-1700 M-F, 1600 Sa C-865-5202/5243			
Bank/Exc	STOP 18	0900-1700 Tu-F, 1400 Sa	C-865-8360 NFCU	
Hair Styles	STOP 21	0830-1700 M-F,1630 Sa C-865-5531 Barber & Beauty		
Laundry/DryC	STOP 21	1000-1700 M-Sa	C-865-5202/5243	
Medical	Naval Hosp	24 hrs dly C-865-4144 Emerg, C-865-4133 Appoint		
Postal	STOP 6	0900-1500 M-F	C-865-4335	

PUERTO RICO

Roosevelt Roads NAS, Cont'd

TML	Bldg 1708 24 hrs dly DV/VIP C-865-5434 (07+).	C-865-4145/4147 All Ranks.
TRAVELERS AID ARC	Many agencies Family STOP 19 0800-1600 M-F	Services C-865-4377/5377 C-865-5134 Other hrs C-865-2000
Chaplain	STOP 17 Duty hrs	C-865-4326/8
Emerg Relief	STOP 12 0800-1600 M-F	C-865-4397 Navy Relief
Lost/Found	Air Ops Bldg 0630-1800 M-Sa	C-865-4374 Pax Svc NCO
Sec Police	Gate 1 24 hrs dly	C-865-4123/4311 Desk Sgt
USO	STOP 6 0800-2300 dly	C-865-7350/7275 Near Pier 3
ATTRACTIONS	El Yuunque (L-UN-KEE) rain forest, waterfalls, hiking, restaurants	

SCHEDULED FLIGHTS

DESTINATION	ROUTING	FREQ	EQ/CMTS
Alexander Hamilton Arpt VI (STX)	NRR-STX HOW-PAP-SDQ-NRR-STX	M,Tu,W,Th,F 3/Th	US-2B&H-3/P C-130E/C
Charleston AFB Intl SC (CHS)	NRR-CHS	Every other Sa	C-141B/M
Coolidge Arpt AN (SJH)	NRR-SJH	3/W,3/F	C-141B/M
Francois Duvalier Intl HA (PAP)	STX-NRR-SDQ-PAP-KIN-HOW	3/Th	C-130E/M
Guantanamo Bay NS CU (GAO)	NGU-NRR-GAO	Su	C-141B/C
Howard AB PN (HOW)	STX-NRR-SDQ-PAP-KIN-HOW CHS-NRR-HOW	3/Th Every other F	C-130E/C C-141B/M
Norfolk NAS VA (NGU)	NRR-NGU NRR-NGU	3/Th,3/Sa Su	C-141B/M C-141B/C
Norman Manley Intl JM (KIN)	STX-NRR-SDQ-PAP-KIN-HOW	3/Th	C-130E/M
San Isidro AB DR (SDQ)	STX-NRR-SDQ-PAP-KIN-HOW	3/Th	C-130E/C
StThomas Helip VI (VIO2)	NRR-VIO2	M,Tu,W,Th,F	US-2B&H-3/P

US VIRGIN ISLANDS

Alexander Hamilton Airport (STX)
Army Avn Ops Fac, VI Natl Guard
PO Box 2270, Kingshill
St Croix, VI 00850-5000

Comm: 809-778-3299/2165
ATVN: None

LOCATION: On the S central coast of the island of St Croix. ⋆NMC: Christiansted VI, 8 mi NE.

FACILITIES	LOCATION	HOURS	PHONE	COMMENTS
PAX TERM INFO	VI Natl Guard Hangar	0800-1700 M-F	C-778-3299/2165	W end/ramp
PAX LOUNGES	Commercial Pax Term All support facilities can be used. No sep mil lounges. All flts handled through Ops Div. Emerg, call office of the Adjutant General C-778-2200. There are no US mil facilities available for Space-A Pax.			

SCHEDULED FLIGHTS *

DESTINATION	ROUTING	FREQ	EQ/CMTS
Francois Du-valier Intl HA (PAP)	STX-NRR-SDQ-PAP-KIN-HOM	3/Tu	C-130E/C
Grantley Adams Intl BB (BGI)	NGU-NRR-STX-BGI-GAO	3/Tu	L-100/C/CC
Guantanamo Bay NS CU (GAO)	NGU-NRR-STX-GAO NGU-NRR-STX-BGI-GAO	Tu 3/Tu	L-100/C/CC L-100/C/CC
Howard AB PN (HOW)	STX-NRR-SDQ-PAP-KIN-HOW	3/Tu	C-130E/C
Norman Manley JM (KIN)	STX-NRR-SDQ-PAP-KIN-HOW	3/Tu	C-130E/C
Roosevelt Rds NAS PR (NRR)	STX-NRR-SDQ-PAP-KIN-HOW	3/Tu	C-130E/C
San Isidro AB DR (SDQ)	STX-NRR-SDQ-PAP-KIN-HOW	3/Tu	C-130E/C

* Note: These flights are manifested by Roosevelt Roads Naval Air Station, Puerto Rico C-809-865-2000-EX-5208 (Air Terminal officer).

UNSCHEDULED FLIGHTS

Frequent flights to: Roosevelt Roads NAS PR (NRR); Isla Grande Arpt San Juan PR (SIG); and Cyril E. King Arpt VI (STT) via UH-1H and U-8F aircraft. Flts are mixed missions.

NOTES

Space-A Travel Newsletter
(Space-A Air ... Space-A RV & Camping
... Space-A Temporary Military Lodging)

FREE COPIES FOR PURCHASERS of THIS BOOK

"TRAVEL ON LESS PER DAY....THE MILITARY WAY"

We'd like to acquaint you with our travel newsletter, Military Living's R&R Report. It gives late breaking info on Space-A air travel, new info on military camping and rec areas, and temporary military lodging plus informative and helpful reader trip reports.

We'll send you two free copies (a $4.00 value) if you will send $1.00 to cover the cost of postage and handling.

To get your copies, send your name and address and $1.00 to:
Military Living R&R (Dept. SA)
Box 2347
Falls Church, VA 22042

Note: We regret that this must be a one-time offer and may not be used to extend a current R&R Report subscription or combined with any other discount.

FOREIGN COUNTRIES
AFRICA
AFRICA STATIONS (AFR)
(Not listed separately in this book)

The stations listed below have Space-A air opportunities. Base support facilities are provided by United States Embassies and are very limited.

BERBERA AIRPORT, SM (BBE)
US Embassy
Corso Primo Luglio
Mogadishu, Somalia
Location: East coast of Africa on the Gulf of Aden.
Tel: 28011

KHARTOUM AIRPORT, SU (KRT)
US Embassy
PO Box 699, Sharia Ali Abdel Latif
Khartoum, Sudan
Location: Northeast Africa on the Nile River, 400 mi W of the Red Sea.
Tel: 74700

MOGADISHU IAP, SM (MGQ)
US Embassy
Corso Primo Luglio
Mogadishu, Somalia
Location: East coast of Africa on the Indian Ocean.
Tel: 28011

N'DJAMENA IAP, CD (NDJ)
US Embassy B.P.
413 Rue Felix Eboue
Ndjamena, Chad
Location: In central Africa, 75 mi South of Lake Chad.
Tel: 32-69

PORT SUDAN AIRPORT, SU (PZU)
US Embassy
PO Box 699, Sharia Ali Abdel Latif
Khartoum, Sudan
Location: Northeast Africa on the Red Sea.
Tel: 74700

SCHEDULED FLIGHTS

DESTINATION and ROUTING	FREQ	EQ/CMTS
NKW-BBE-NBO-SIZ-TOJ-NGU	3/M	C-141B/C
NKW-MGQ-NBO-SIZ-TOJ-NGU	4/M	C-141B/C
NKW-NBO-KRT-SIZ-TOJ-NGU	4/M	C-141B/C
FRF-ATH-PZU-DHA	1/W	C-130E/C
NDJ-FIH	2/Th 6 per yr	C-141B/C
NGU-TOJ-SIZ-KRT-NBO-NKW	3/F	C-141B/C

ANTIGUA & BARBUDA

Coolidge Airport (St. Johns), AN (SJH)
Antigua Air Station, Naval Facility
FPO Miami 34054-5000

Comm: 305-494-1110
809-46-23171
ATVN: 854-1110 Ask for Antigua.

LOCATION: One mi from Coolidge Airport, on NE side of island of Antigua.
NMC: St John's AN, 9 mi W.

ANTIGUA & BARBUDA
Coolidge Arpt, Cont'd

FACILITIES	LOCATION HOURS PHONE COMMENTS
PAX TERM INFO	Antigua Term 0730-1630 dly C-46-23223, A-854-1110/234 All Pax info through Patrick AFB FL C-494-5631. Term spt contractor is Pan Am C-46-23223. Term 1 mi fm Coolidge Arpt, AN.
PAX LOUNGES General	Limited facilities Antigua Term 0730-1630 dly C-46-23223 A/C,Rest-rms,O/S seats
FOOD SERVICE OFC Club	Limited at Naval support facility. Many off Base. Map #21 1000-2200 dly C-494-5631-EX-356
Snack Bars	Map #7 1630-2230 dly C-46-23223, A-854-1110-EX-269
TRANSPORTATION Air Tickets	Coolidge Arpt 24 hrs dly C-46-20323/24892 Eastern & Pan Am
Car Rentals	Coolidge Arpt 24 hrs dly Avis=C-46-21815, Dollar=C-46-20362
TAXI(Comm)	Coolidge Arpt 24 hrs dly C-462-4600
OTHER SERVICES	Limited facilities. Active duty on leave are restricted to $20 day purchases except at snack bar & clubs. Retirees may use only club and medical facilities due to SOFA.
Medical	Admin Bldg Map #2 24 hrs dly C-46-23171 Ask for Sick Bay.
TML	Admin Bldg Map #2 24 hrs dly C-46-23171, A-854-1110-EX-398. Limited temporary military lodging.
ATTRACTIONS	Great beaches, forts, museums, casino gambling

SCHEDULED FLIGHTS

DESTINATION	ROUTING	FREQ	EQ/CMTS
Ascension Aux AF UK (ASI)	COF-SJH-ASI	M,W,4/F	C-141B/M
Patrick AFB FL (COF)	ASI-SJH-COF	3/4/Su,W,F	C-141B/M
Roosevelt Rds NAS PR (NRR)	SJH-NRR	3/W,3/Sa	C-141B/M

AUSTRALIA

Alice Springs Airport (ASP)
Det 421, MAC Represenative
APO San Francisco 96369-5000

Comm: (61) 089-522044
           089-522289
ATVN: None

LOCATION: In the northern territory of AU, 1250 air mi W of Sydney AU and 800 air mi S of Darwin AU. NMC: Alice Springs AU, 15 km.

AUSTRALIA

Alice Springs Airport, Cont'd

FACILITIES	LOCATION	HOURS	PHONE	COMMENTS
PAX TERM INFO	Pax Term 24 hrs dly C-089-522044 Limited spt fac available at Arpt. Contact MAC rep for all required support.			
PAX LOUNGES	Very limited lounge facilities - essentials only			
FOOD SERVICE	Restaurants, Snack bars, Coffee houses, and Pubs in ASP			
TRANSPORTATION TAXI(Comm)	ASP has Comm Air, Train, and Motor Coach services Pax Term 24 hrs dly C-089-52201 9 mi to ASP			
TML	No US Gov Billeting. Hotels in AU ($20 +).			
ATTRACTIONS	Royal Flying Doctors Base, Ayers Rock (200 air mi SW)			

SCHEDULED FLIGHTS

DESTINATION	ROUTING	FREQ	EQ/CMTS
Hickam AFB HI (HIK)	ASP-RCM-PPG-HIK-SBD	M	C-141B/C
Norton AFB CA (SBD)	ASP-RCM-PPG-HIK-SBD	M	C-141B/C
Pago Pago Intl AS (PPG)	ASP-RCM-PPG-HIK-SBD	M	C-141B/C C-141B/C
Richmond RAAFB AU (RCM)	ASP-RCM-PPG-HIK-SBD	M	C-141B/C

Learmonth RAAFB (LEA)
NAVCOMMSTA, MAC Rep, Box 32
FPO San Francisco 96680-5000

Comm: (61) 099/49-3216/3444
ATVN: 315-821-1945/3216/3444

LOCATION: In western AU, 700 air mi N of Perth AU, on the Northwest Cape.
NMC: Carnarvon AU, 200 air mi S.

FACILITIES	LOCATION	HOURS	PHONE	COMMENTS
PAX TERM INFO	Pax term 24 hrs dly C-099/49-3216/3444 Limited spt facilities avail on RAAFB. Contact MAC rep for spt svcs.			
PAX LOUNGES	Very limited lounge facilities - essentials only			
FOOD SERVICE	NAVCOMMSTA: Mess Hall, Officers' & EM Clubs, Snack bar			
TRANSPORTATION	Very limited. Comm taxi at LEA.			
Bus(Comm) (Gov)	Pax Term During flt hrs LEA to Exmonth $10.00 AU Pax Term During flt hrs LEA to NAVCOMMSTA			
OTHER SERVICES	No BX or commissary privileges for personnel not assigned in AU due to SOFA. Rec & medical avail. Commonwealth pass obtained fm Civil Commissioner of Exmouth & required to enter Base.			

AUSTRALIA
Learmonth RAAFB, Cont'd

TML	BEQ 0730-1600 dly C-099-49-3587 Very limited TML. Local lodging - "no frills" & expensive.
ATTRACTIONS	Australia bush country, Indian Ocean, and warm climate

SCHEDULED FLIGHTS

DESTINATION	ROUTING	FREQ	EQ/CMTS
Christchurch Intl NZ (CHC)	LEA-RCM-CHC-PPG-HIK-SBD	Th	C-141B/C
Hickam AFB HI (HIK)	LEA-RCM-CHC-PPG-HIK-SBD	Th	C-141B/C
Norton AFB CA (SBD)	LEA-RCM-CHC-PPG-HIK-SBD	Th	C-141B/C
Pago Pago Intl AS (PPG)	LEA-RCM-CHC-PPG-HIK-SBD	Th	C-141B/C
Richmond RAAFB AU (RCM)	LEA-RCM-CHC-PPG-HIK-SBD	Th	C-141B/C

Richmond RAAFB (RCM)
Detachment #1, 619th MASS
APO San Francisco 96209-5000

Comm: (61) 045-70-2341
ATVN: None

LOCATION: Two miles west of Windsor AU and 45 miles northwest of Sydney AU. NMC: Sydney, 45 miles southeast.

FACILITIES	LOCATION	HOURS	PHONE	COMMENTS
PAX TERM INFO	Pax Term 0900-1500 M-F C-045-70-2341 One hundred and fifty yards from rear of flight line. Twenty dollars AU departure tax (all Pax 12 yrs +) and ten dollars US MAC fee. US Pax Svcs by MAC Pax rep personnel ONLY, not RAAFB personnel. Tel for seat avail.Enter Base for sign-up or revalidation only at above hrs or during flight processing.			
Pax Svc Ofc	Bldg 308 0900-1500 M-F C-045-70-2341 See NCO for flt info.			
Pax Paging	Pax Term During flt processing C-045-70-2341			
PAX LOUNGES General	RAAFB Pax Term Bldg Pax Term 1st floor 0800-1700 dly C-045-70-2341 A/C, Rest-rms, P/C seats			
DV/VIP	Pax Term 2nd floor 0800-1700 dly C-045-70-2341 A/C, Rest-rms, Wood seats			
FOOD SERVICE Snack Bars	In-flt meals $2.00 AU C-045-70-2341 Pax Term As required for RAAF flts C-045-70-2341			
Vending	Pax Term 0800-1900 dly C-045-70-2341 RAAFB facility			
TRANSPORTATION Air Tickets	Train and comm taxi only available at RAAFB RCM Sydney 24 hrs dly Maj airlines-Kingsford Smith Arpt			

AUSTRALIA

Richmond RAAFB, Cont'd

TAXI(Comm)	Pax Term 24 hrs dly C-02-622-2200 Svc local area/Sydney
Trains	Station 0500-2400 dly C-02-29-7614 SDY to RCM $6 AU and change trains in Riverstone. Sta to RCM via taxi $5 AU.
Parking	Svc Pol area 24 hrs dly Contact MAC Pax rep for approval.
OTHER SERVICES	No svc at RAAFB RCM. No US BX or banking. Money exchange at banks in Richmond or Windsor. All svc available in Sydney.
TML	No TML on RAAF Base. Several motels in Richmond/Windsor area.
TRAVELERS AID	Bldg 308 0900-1500 Su-F C-045-70-2341 See MAC Pax NCO.
ATTRACTIONS	Sydney (population of 4 million), Great Barrier Reef, Ayers Rock, Tasmania Island. Continent as large as USA.

SCHEDULED FLIGHTS

DESTINATION	ROUTING	FREQ	EQ/CMTS
Alice Springs Arpt AU (ASP)	SBD-HIK-PPG-CHC-RCM-ASP	F	C-141B/C
Christchurch Intl NZ (CHC)	LEA-RCM-CHC-PPG-HIK-SBD	Th	C-141B/C
Hickam AFB HI (HIK)	ASP-RCM-PPG-HIK-SBD LEA-RCM-CHC-PPG-HIK-SBD	M Th	C-141B/C C-141B/C
Learmonth RAAFB AU (LEA)	SBD-HIK-PPG-RCM-UMR-LEA	Su	C-141B/C
Norton AFB CA (SBD)	ASP-RCM-PPG-HIK-SBD LEA-RCM-CHC-PPG-HIK-SBD	M Th	C-141B/C C-141B/C
Pago Pago Intl AS (PPG)	ASP-RCM-CHC-PPG-HIK-SBD LEA-RCM-CHC-PPG-HIK-SBD	M Th	C-141B/C C-141B/C
Woomera Afld AU (UMR)	SBD-HIK-PPG-RCM-UMR-LEA	W	C-141B/C

Woomera Air Field (UMR)
5th Det, SCS/LGTC
APO San Francisco 96287-5000

Comm: (61) 086738-438
ATVN: 312-730-1350
312-629-1636

LOCATION: On the Trans Australian Railway, 1500 air km NW of Sydney in South Australia. NMC: Port Austin, 100 air km SE.

FACILITIES	LOCATION	HOURS	PHONE	COMMENTS
PAX TERM INFO	Pax Term	8 hrs dly	C-086738-438, A-730-1350	Limited spt fac avail at UMR. Contact MAC rep for spt svcs.
PAX LOUNGES	Very limited lounge facility - essentials only			
FOOD SERVICE	Restaurant and Snack bars in UMR			

AUSTRALIA
Woomera Air Field, Cont'd

TRANSPORTATION	Train, motor coach, and taxi service
ATTRACTIONS	Adelaide 490 air km SE - modern city

SCHEDULED FLIGHTS

DESTINATION	ROUTING	FREQ	EQ/CMTS
Learmonth RAAFB AU (LEA)	SBD-HIK-PPG-RCM-UMR-RCM-LEA	W	C-141B/C
Richmond RAAFB AU (RCM)	SBD-HIK-PPG-RCM-UMR-RCM-LEA	W	C-141B/C

BAHRAIN

Bahrain International Airport (BAH)
Bahrain Naval Support Unit
FPO New York 09526-5000

Comm: 973-243-277
ATVN: 237-1110

LOCATION: An island off the coast of Saudi Arabia in the Persian Gulf. NMC: Dhahran SA, 30 mi NW.

FACILITIES	LOCATION	HOURS	PHONE	COMMENTS
PAX TERM INFO	Pax Term	During flt processing	C-243-277-EX-22	Check with Navy Pax Svc desk at IAP for assistance.
OTHER SERVICES	Naval spt unit has NEX, Officers'/CPO Clubs, TML, and Emergency medical. Commercial fac also available. Taxi svc 24 hrs dly (no meters). A/C taxi to city - $3 US.			

SCHEDULED FLIGHTS

DESTINATION	ROUTING	FREQ	EQ/CMTS
Dover AFB DE (DOV)	BAH-RTA-DOV	Sa	C005A/M
Norfolk NAS VA (NGU)	BAH-RTA-NGU	W	C-141B/C
Rota NAS SP (RTA)	BAH-RTA-NGU BAH-RTA-DOV	W Sa	C-141B/C C005A/M

UNSCHEDULED FLIGHTS

To: Dhahran IAP SA (DHA) and Incirlik Arpt TU (ADA).

BELGIUM

Chievres Air Base (CHE)
Det 1, 52nd Tactical Fighter Wing (TFW)
APO New York 09088-5000

Comm: (32) 68-223171
ATVN: 393-2234

LOCATION: Off BE-56 in village of Chievres. HE: p-35,E/3. NMC:Mons, 8 mi SE.

BELGIUM

Chievres AB, Cont'd

PAX TERM INFO	Base Ops 0800-1700 dly and during flight processing C-68-223171, A-393-2234 Ask for Base Ops.
Recording	Gate #2 to industrial area. Base Ops marked. Support Base for US NATO staff at Supreme Hq Allied Powers Europe (SHAPE).
PAX LOUNGES	No lounges. All Space-A Pax processed through Base Ops.
FOOD SERVICE	Limited. Full club svc at SHAPE. Cafeteria C-68-57499
TRANSPORTATION	Bus(Gov) C-68-8-4514 (Shuttle) SHAPE TO Brussels IAP
OTHER SERVICES	Exchange C-68-23512

UNSCHEDULED FLIGHTS

To Ramstein AB GE (RMS). Heavy traffic to CONUS and Europe stations during NATO training exercises.

Florennes Air Base (BFS)
485th Tactical Missile Wing/USAFE
APO New York, 09188-5000

Comm: (32) 71-655560
ATVN: 791-3255

LOCATION: East on BE-36 from Philippeville (in direction of Dinant), 10 mi on L is Base entrance. Also, S of Namar, L at Florennes, follow signs to AB. HE: p-35, F/3. NMC: Brussels, 50 mi N.

PAX TERM INFO	Base Ops During flt processing C-71-655136, A-791-3255 No Pax Term. No USAF fac available for travelers. ID card required for entry. Located on Belgium AB. All Space-A Pax processed by USAF Base Ops.
FOOD SERVICE	Enl Club C-71-655560-EX-506, Snack Bars C-71-655560-EX-363
TRANSPORTATION	Air Tickets C-71-655560-EX-411 (no Gov or Comm trans)
OTHER SERVICES	Exchange EX-442, Bank/Exc EX-337, Hair Styles EX-490, Post Office EX-220, ARC EX-2434, Chaplain EX-207. No TML, Laundry, or Medical. All other support provided by Belgium AB.

SCHEDULED FLIGHTS

DESTINATION	ROUTING	FREQ	EQ/CMTS
RAF Mildenhall UK (MHZ)	BFS-MHZ	M,W	C-23/M
Ramstein AB GE (RMS)	BFS-RMS	Tu	C-23/M

BERMUDA

Bermuda Naval Air Station (BDA) Comm: 809-293-5131
Air Operations Officer   ATVN: 938-5131
FPO New York 09560-5002

LOCATION: Bermuda is 600 mi E of Cape Hatteras NC, in the Atlantic Ocean. The NAS is on the N end of St David's Island near St George City. NMC: Hamilton BM, 6 mi SW.

FACILITIES	LOCATION	HOURS	PHONE	COMMENTS
PAX TERM INFO	Bldg 1079	0800-1600 dly	C-293-5539, A-938-5539	
	From Gate 1 on Corregidor Dr toward beach, Air Ops is on L. Provides runways & service for Bermuda IAP.			
Recording	Bldg 1079	24 hrs dly	C-293-5050	
Pax Svc Ofc	Bldg 1079	0800-1600 M-F	C-293-5539	
Pax Paging	Bldg 1079	0800-1600 dly	C-293-5539	
PAX LOUNGES General	No family lounge Bldg 1079	0800-1600 dly	C-293-5539	A/C, Bag chk/lks, P/C seats
DV/VIP	Bldg 1079	0800-1600 dly	C-293-5539	A/C, Coffee/tea srvd, Nursery, Rest-rms, Read/write rm, TV, O/S seats
Protocol Svc	Bldg 101	Duty hours	C-293-5111	
FOOD SERVICE Cafeteria	Adequate on Base. Good off Base. McDonalds	0700-2300 dly	C-293-6100	
Enl Club	Bldg M-28	Call for hours.	C-293-6137	
NCO/CPO Club	Bldg M-48	Call for hours.	C-293-5292	
OFC Club	Bldg 511	Call for hours.	C-293-5202	"Tradewinds"
Vending	Bldg 1079	0800-1600 dly	C-293-6520	
TRANSPORTATION Air Tickets	Limited on and off Base Bermuda IAP	0900-2200 dly	C-295-8822	Pan American
Bus(Comm)	Front Gate	0630-2300	C-292-3854	To St George & Hamilton
Limo Service	Bermuda IAP	0830-1600 dly	C-293-2500	
Moped Rntls	Bldg P-3	0800-1700 dly	C-293-6437	
TAXI(Comm)	Bermuda IAP	24 hrs dly	C-297-5414	
Parking	Bldg 1079	24 hrs dly	C-293-7231/2	No reserved spaces
OTHER SERVICES Exchange	Many on and off Base Bldg 1564	1030-1730 Tu,W,F, 1200-2000 Th, 0900-1400 Sa	C-293-3106/3267	
Bank/Exc	Bldg M-32	0930-1630 Tu-Sa	C-293-6438	Navy Fed Credit Union
Hair Styles	Bldg 1564	0830-1700 M-F, 1230 Sa	C-293-5496 Barber C-293-6189 Beauty	

BERMUDA

Bermuda NAS, Cont'd

Laundry	Bldg 1564	0800-2100 dly	C-293-6108	
Medical	Bldg M-43	24 hrs dly	C-293-6514	
Postal	Bldg M-35	0800-1600 M-F	C-293-5324	Telephone office
TML	Bldg 550 DV/VIP (06+)	24 hrs dly C-293-6635.	C-293-6635	All Ranks.
TRAVELERS AID ARC	Limited on and off Base Bldg M-32	Duty hours	C-293-5684	
Chaplain	Bldg M-29	Duty hours	C-293-5311	Other hrs C-293-5512
Lost/Found	Bldg 1079	0800-1600 dly	C-293-5539	
Sec Police	Main Gate	24 hrs dly	C-293-5501	
ATTRACTIONS	Great beaches, deep-sea fishing, boating			

SCHEDULED FLIGHTS

DESTINATION	ROUTING	FREQ	EQ/CMTS
Charleston AFB IAP SC (CHS)	HOW-BDA-ADW-CHS	As needed	C-141B/M

UNSCHEDULED FLIGHTS

Flts to: Jacksonville NAS FL (NIP); Norfolk NAS VA (NGU); and Howard AFB RP (HOW). Call for destinations, routings, and schedules.

CANADA

Goose Bay Air Base (Newfoundland) (YYR)
Det 1, 438th MAW
PO Box 160, Station "A"
Goose Bay Airport, Labrador
Newfoundland, CN AOP-ISO

Comm: 709-896-2463
ATVN: 622-9011

LOCATION: In the Canadian Atlantic Providence of Newfoundland on Goose Bay. RM: p-117, B/26. NMC: Happy Valley, 6 mi SE.

FACILITIES	LOCATION	HOURS	PHONE	COMMENTS
PAX TERM INFO	Bldg 248 24 hrs dly C-896-2463,A-622-9011-EX-221 Near Hangar #7. Circle Term at ATC tower."Mole Hole" is Pax holding area.			
Recording	Bldg 248	24 hrs dly	A-622-9011-EX-256	
Pax Svc Ofc	Bldg 248	0800-1700 dly	A-622-9011-EX-221	
Pax Paging	Bldg 248	24 hrs dly	A-622-9011-EX-311	Lounges
PAX LOUNGES General	Families can use Gen Pax lounge (across hall from Snack bar). Bldg 248 24 hrs dly A-622-9011-EX-411 A/C, Game rm, Tel C&A, TV, Rest-rms			

CANADA
Goose Bay AB, Cont'd

DV/VIP	Bldg 248	24 hrs dly A-622-9011-EX-411 See Pax NCO f/key.
Protocol Svc	Bldg 248	24 hrs dly A-622-9011-EX-221
FOOD SERVICE	\multicolumn{2}{l}{Good on and off Base. For Cafeteria, Enl Club, NCO/CPO Club, and O'Club call C-896-OPER. For Snack Bars and Vending call A-622-9011-EX-311.}
TRANSPORTATION	\multicolumn{2}{l}{Limited on and off Base. Car Rentals C-896-OPER, Taxi(Comm) C-896-3311 (Gov) C-896-OPER, Parking C-896-5263 (short term) C-896-5263 (long term)}
OTHER SERVICES	\multicolumn{2}{l}{Limited off Base services. For Exchange, Hair Styles, Medical, and Postal call C-896-OPER.}
TML	Bldg S-485 24 hrs dly	C-896-Oper
TRAVELERS AID	\multicolumn{2}{l}{Chaplain C-896-OPER, Sec Police C-896-5263}
ATTRACTIONS	\multicolumn{2}{l}{Hunting, fishing, and other outdoor sports}

SCHEDULED FLIGHTS

DESTINATION	ROUTING	FREQ	EQ/CMTS
Charleston AFB Intl SC (CHS)	JDW-RMS-MHZ-YYR-CHS PIK-MHZ-YYR-CHS	Su 1/3/4/Su,2/4/M, 2/4/Tu,1/3/4W, 2/Th,1/3/4/F, 2/Sa	C-141B/C C-141B/C
	RMS-YYR-CHS	W,Th	C-141B/M
	MHZ-YYR-CHS	1/2/3/F	C-141B/C
	AVB-RMS-YYR-CHS	1/2/3/F	C-141B/C
McGuire AFB NJ (WRI)	THU-SFJ-YYR-WRI	Tu	C-141B/M
Sondrestrom AB DN (SFJ)	WRI-YYR-SFJ-THU	W	C-141B/M
Thule AB DN (THU)	WRI-YYR-SFJ-THU	W	C-141B/M

St. John's Airport (Newfoundland) (YYT)
Argentia Naval Facility
PERSUPPDET, PO Box 17
FPO New York 09597-5000

Comm: 709-227-8533
ATVN: 568-8533

LOCATION: At terminus of North Sydney (Nova Scotia) to Argentia (Newfoundland Ferry Service. There is access to Trans Canadian Highway (TCH)-1, via CN-101, 25 mi NE. The Naval facilities are in Argentia and are clearly marked. RM: p-117, G/24. NMC: St John's, 100 mi NE.

FACILITIES	LOCATION	HOURS	PHONE	COMMENTS
PAX TERM INFO	Argentia	0730-1630 dly	A-568-8382	Call ATVN number for Pax info. Visitors are restricted fm BX and commissary.

CANADA

St. John's Arpt, Cont'd

Pax Svc Ofc	PSD Argentia 0730-1630 M-F C-227-8533
PAX LOUNGES General	No family lounge. Limited lounge facilities. Hudson General 0700-2300 dly C-576-4981 Bag check, Tel, Rest-rms, P/C seats
DV/VIP	Hudson General 0700-2300 dly C-576-4981 Bag check, Tel, Rest-rms, TV, O/S seats
Protocol Svc	USN 24 hrs dly C-227-8555
FOOD SERVICE	NAV fac has dining hall C-227-8625. O' Club C-227-8731.
TRANSPORTATION	Navy bus meets all aircraft. Comm taxi St John's-expensive.
OTHER SERVICES Medical	BX C-227-5841 Limited spt at NAV fac (more in St John's). Bldg 848 24 hrs dly C-227-8444 Emergency
TML	Bldg 848M 24 hrs dly C-227-8663. DV/VIP C-227-8661.
TRAVELERS AID Chaplain	Chapel Duty hours C-227-8502
ATTRACTIONS	Outstanding hunting & fishing area, nine-cabin Navy rec area

SCHEDULED FLIGHTS

DESTINATION	ROUTING	FREQ	EQ/CMTS
Lajes Fld PO (LGS)	PHL-YYT-LGS	Th	B727/P/CC
Philadelphia IAP PA (PHL)	LGS-YYT-PHL	F	B727/P/CC

CARIBBEAN, CENTRAL & SOUTH AMERICA

Caribbean, Central & South America (CAB)
(Not listed separately in this book)

The stations listed below have Space-A air opportunities. Base support facilities are provided by United States Embassies in each foreign country and are very limited. Passenger management is accomplished by US Embassy, military or contractor personnel. Procedures for processing passengers at each station are the result of local conditions and services available. Stations in most cases are located at International Airports which have all essential facilities and services for international travelers. ATVN service is not available at these stations unless indicated in their listing. Stations are listed in alphabetical order. See the appendix "Personal Entry Requirements."

ARTURO MERINOBENITEZ ARPT, CH (SCL)
USMILGP, US Embassy (Santiago)
APO Miami 34033-5000
Comm: (56) 2-82811 & 710133/90

AUGUSTO "C" SANDINO INTL, NI (MGA)
USADO, US Embassy (Managua)
APO Miami 34021-5000
Comm: (505) 2-23061 & 23881-7

CARIBBEAN, CENTRAL & SOUTH AMERICA

Caribbean, Central & S America, Cont'd

BELIZE INTL, BZ (BZE)
USDAO, US Embassy (Belize City)
Belize City, Belize
Comm: (501) 02-7161

BRASILIA ARPT, BR (BSB)
US Mil Liai Office, BR Sec, USEMB
Brasilia, Brazil
Comm: (55) 021-292-7117

CARACAS ARPT, VE (CCS)
USDAO, US Embassy (Caracas)
APO Miami 34037-0008
Comm: (58) 2-61-43-01 & 2-284-6111/7111

CARRASCO INTL, UG (MVD)
USDAO, US Embassy (Montevideo)
APO Miami 34035-5000
Comm: (598) 2-40-90-51-EX-332/333

EL DORADO ARPT, CL (BOG)
USDAO, US Embassy (Bogota)
APO Miami 34038-5000
Comm: (57) 285-1300/1688

EZEIZA ARPT, AG (BUE)
USMILGP, US Embassy (Buenos Aires)
APO Miami 34034-5000
Comm: (54) 1-774-7611-EX-287 &774-3802

FRANCOIS DUVALIER INTL, HA (PAP)
USDAO, US Embassy (Port-Au-Prince)
Port-Au-Prince, Haiti
Comm: (509) 1-2-0200 & 2-0407

GRAND BAHAMA AUX AF, BH (GBI)
US Mil Liai Office, US Embassy (Nassau)
Nassau, Bahamas
Comm: 809-322-1181/1700

GRANTLEY ADAMS INTL, BB (BGI)
US Embassy, PO Box 302 (Bridgetown)
Bridgetown, Barbados
Comm: 809-426-3574

I LOPANGO INTL, ES (SAL)
USDAO, US Embassy (El Salvador)
APO Miami 34023-5000
Comm: (503) 26-7172 & 26-7100

J F KENNEDY INTL, BO (LPB)
USDAO, US Embassy (La Paz)
APO Miami 34032-5000
Comm: (591) 2-350251-EX-260

JORGE CHAVEZ INTL, PE (LIM)
USMAAG, US Embassy (Lima)
APO Miami 34031-5000
Comm: (51) 14-523765 & 286000

LA AURORA ARPT, GT (GUA)
USDAO, US Embassy (Guatemala City)
APO Miami 34024-5000
Comm: (502) 2-31-15-41

MARISCAL SUCRE ARPT, EC (UIO)
USDAO, US Embassy (Quito)
APO Miami 34039-5000
Comm: (593) 2-520-146

NORMAN MANLEY INTL, JM (KIN)
Mil Liai Office, US Embassy (Kingston)
Kingston 5, Jamaica
Comm: 809-929-4850-9

PALMEROLA ARPT, HO (PLA)
USDAO, US Embassy (Tegucigalpa)
APO Miami 34022-5000
Comm: (504) 33-4618 & 32-3120-9

PRES STROESSNER ARPT, PG (ASU)
USDAO, US Embassy (Asuncion)
APO Miami 34036-5000
Comm: (595) 21-65612-EX-426/422

RIO DE JANEIRO INTL, BR (RIO)
Mil Liai Office, Rio Sec, US Embassy
APO Miami 34030-5000
Comm: (55) 21-262-9978 & 292-7117

SAN ISIDRO AIR BASE, DR (SDQ)
USMILGP, US Embassy (Santo Domingo)
APO Miami 34041-5000
Comm: 809-682-2171-EX-487

SANTAMARIA INTL, CS (OCO)
USDAO, US Embassy (San Jose)
APO Miami 34020-5000
Comm: (506) 255-566-EX-319/338

SIMON BOLIVAR INTL, VE (MIQ)
USMILGP, US Embassy (Maiquetia)
APO Miami 34037-0008
Comm: (58) 2-62-05-63

TONCONTIN INTL, HO (TGU)
USDAO, US Embassy (Tegucigalpa)
APO Miami 34022-5000
Comm: (504) 33-4618 & 32-3120-9

SCHEDULED FLIGHTS

DESTINATION and ROUTING	FREQ	EQ/CMTS
HOW-PLA-CHS	M	C-141B/C
CHS-PLA-HOW	M,W,F	L-100/C/CC

CARIBBEAN

Caribbean, Central & S America, Cont'd

HOW-PLA-CHS	M,W,F	L-100/C/CC
HOW-BOG	1/3/M	C-130H/C
BOG-HOW	1/3/M	C-130H/C
HOW-UIO	4/M	C-130H/C
UIO-HOW	4/M	C-130H/C
SAL-TGU-HOW	Tu	C-130H/C
HOW-SAL	Tu	C-130H/C
SAL-TGU-HOW	Tu	C-130H/C
SAL-HOW	Tu	C-130H/C
HOW-BSB-RIO-BUE-SCL-LIM-HOW	1/Tu	C-141B/M (Note)
HOW-LIM-SCL-BUE-RIO-BSB-HOW	3/Tu	C-141B/M (Note)
NGU-NRR-STX-BGI-GAO	3/Tu	L-100/C/CC
HOW-PAP-SDQ-NRR-STX	3/Tu	C-130E/C
HOW-TGU	1/W	C-130H/M
TGU-OCO-HOW	1/W	C-130H/M
HOW-ASU-MVD-LPB-HOW	2/W	C-141B/M
STX-NRR-SDQ-PAP-KIN-HOW	3/W	C-130E/C
BZE-GUA-OCO-HOW	4/W	C-130H/C
HOW-BZE	4/W	C-130H/C
HOW-LPB-MVD-ASU-HOW	4/W	C-141B/M
CHS-PLA-HOW	Th	C-141B/C
HOW-MGA	3/Th	C-130H/C
MGA-HOW	3/Th	C-130H/C
HOW-MIQ	3/Th	C-130H/C
MIQ-HOW	Th	C-130H/C
HOW-PLA-CHS	F	C-141B/C
HOW-TGU-PLA-HOW	F	C-130H/M

Note: Two scheduled flts to and from HOW monthly. 1/Tu (fol 1/M) HOW-BSB-RIO (remains overnight)-BUE-SCL(remains overnight)-LIM-HOW. 3/Tu (fol 3/Su) HOW-LIM-SCL(remains overnight)-BUE-RIO(remains overnight)-BSB-HOW.

CUBA

Guantanamo Bay Naval Station (GAO)
Passenger Transportation Officer
FBPO Norfolk 23593-5000

Comm: 011-53-99-XXXXX
ATVN: 723-3690 or
564-4063

LOCATION: In the SW corner of the Republic of Cuba. Accessible only by air.
NMC: Miami, 525 air miles NW.

FACILITIES	LOCATION	HOURS	PHONE	COMMENTS
PAX TERM INFO	Map B/2	Flt processing C-996-4204/5, A-723-8850/8523 All arrivals and departures via air. Prior approval required for non-AD personnel to visit or transfer through station. See appendix for personal entry requirements.		
Pax Svc Ofc	Map E/3	Duty hrs	C-996-8523	NCO on duty
PAX LOUNGES		Limited, but adequate facilities Map B/2 Avail during flt processing C-996-8850 See Pax NCO.		
FOOD SERVICE		BX C-996-4115, EM Club C-996-2304, CPO Club C-996-2501, O'Club C-996-2132		
TRANSPORTATION	TAXI(Comm) C-996-2517			

CUBA
Guantanamo Bay NS, Cont'd

OTHER SERVICES	MCX C-996-2682, NEX C-996-4461, Medical C-996-7201/4424
TML	Bldg 1670 24 hrs dly C-996-2406/3826 All Ranks. DV/VIP C-996-4063.
TRAVELERS AID	Chaplain C-996-4550, Sec Police C-996-4105
ATTRACTIONS	Beaches, fishing, and warm climate

SCHEDULED FLIGHTS

DESTINATION	ROUTING	FREQ	EQ/CMTS
Andrews AFB MD (ADW)	BLV-GAO-NRR-ADW	M	C009A/ME
Charleston AFB Intl SC (CHS)	GAO-CHS GAO-CHS	4/M Sa	C-141B/C C-141B/C
Miami IAP FL (MIA)	GAO-MIA-NGU	Tu	L-100/C/CC
Nassau IAP BH (NAS)	NAS-GAO-KIN-GAO-NAS	F	C727/P/CC
Norfolk NAS VA (NGU)	KIN-GAO-NGU GAO-MIA-NGU GAO-NGU GAO-NGU	Tu Tu 3/W F	C-141B/M L-100/C/CC L-100/C/CC L-100/C/CC
Norman Manley Intl JM (KIN)	CHS-NGU-GAO-KIN NAS-GAO-KIN-GAO-NAS	M F	C-141B/M B727/P/CC
Roosevelt Rds NAS PR (NRR)	NGU-GAO-NRR NGU-GAO-NRR NGU-GAO-NRR	M,Th 3/M,3Th 1/2/3/W	L-100/C C-141B/M C-141B/M

CYPRUS

Akrotiri Airport (AKT)
MAC Representative
Akrotiri, Cyprus

Comm: (357)-51 Ask for MAC Rep, RAF Akrotiri or USDAO (357)-21-65151
ATVN: None

LOCATION: On Cape Gata, Southern Coast, Island of Cyprus. At a UK RAF Base. NMC: Limassol, CY, 5 mi NE.

FACILITIES	LOCATION	HOURS	PHONE	COMMENTS
PAX TERM INFO	Pax Term During flt processing (357)-51 Ask for MAC rep. LIMITED ACCESS. See appendix for personal entry requirements. All major support is in Nicosia, CY, 55 mi NE.			

CYPRUS

Akrotiri Arpt, Cont'd

SCHEDULED FLIGHTS

DESTINATION	ROUTING	FREQ	EQ/CMTS
Athinai Arpt GR (ATH)	AKT-VWH-ATH AKT-ATH	Tu F	C-130E/C C-130E/C
Iraklion AS GR (VWH)	AKT-VWH-ATH	Tu	C-130E/C

UNSCHEDULED FLIGHTS

To: Brindisi/Casale Arpt, IT (BDS).

Larnaca Airport (LCA)
MAC Representative
Larnaca, Cyprus

Comm: (357) 41 Ask for MAC Rep Larnaca or USDAO 357-21-65151
ATVN: None

LOCATION: On the south coast of island of Cyprus. NMC: Nicosia, 15 mi NW.

FACILITIES	LOCATION	HOURS	PHONE	COMMENTS
PAX TERM INFO	Pax Term	Flight processing C-(357)-41 Ask for MAC rep. LIMITED ACCESS. See appendix for personal entry requirements.		
Recording	All major support is in Nicosia, CY.			

SCHEDULED FLIGHTS

DESTINATION	ROUTING	FREQ	EQ/CMTS
Sigonella Arpt IT (SIZ)	LCA-SIZ	Th,Su	C-141B/M

DENMARK

Sondrestrom Air Base (Greenland) (SJF)
4684th ABGP (SAC)
APO New York 09121-5000

Comm: None
ATVN: 834-1211-EX-513/246

LOCATION: On the SW coast of the island of Greenland, 3 mi above the Arctic Circle, 7 mi inland on a long fjord. NMC: Holsteinbourg, 100 mi NW.

FACILITIES	LOCATION	HOURS	PHONE	COMMENTS
PAX TERM INFO	Base Ops Bldg	During flight processing	A-834-1212-EX-519	At Base of ATC tower. All Space-A Pax processed by Base Ops. ACCESS LIMITED. See appendix for personal entry requirements. Also used as IAP for Scandanavian Airlines.
PAX LOUNGES General	Limited lounge facilities Base Ops Bldg	As required	A-834-1212-EX-519	A/C, Bag check, Coffee/tea srvd, Game rm, Rest-rms, TV

DENMARK
Sondrestrom AB, Cont'd

FOOD SERVICE Cafeteria	Limited on Base. None off Base. IAP Bldg 0630-1800 dly Oper by Royal Greenland Trade Dept Also Dining Hall available, NCO Club EX-661 and O'Club EX-497
TRANSPORTATION Air Tickets	Limited on and off Base IAP Bldg 0800-1700 dly Scandanavian Airlines
Bus(Gov)	Base Ops On Base dly
TAXI(Gov)	Base Ops 24 hrs dly EX-601 Duty Pax only
OTHER SERVICES	Medical EX-644, Chaplain EX-508, BX EX-283

SCHEDULED FLIGHTS

DESTINATION	ROUTING	FREQ	EQ/CMTS
Goose AB CN (YYR)	THU-SFJ-YYR-WRI	Tu	C-141B/M
McGuire AFB NJ (WRI)	THU-SFJ-YYR-WRI THU-SFJ-WRI	Tu Th,Sa	C-141B/M C-141B/C
Thule AB DN (THU)	WRI-SFJ-THU WRI-YYR-SFJ-THU	M W	C-141B/C C-141B/M

Thule Air Base (Greenland) (THU)
112th ABG, Base Ops
APO New York 09023-5000

Comm: None
ATVN: 834-1211-EX-2155

LOCATION: NW coast of island of Greenland DN; 800 mi S of North Pole; 7 mi N of Arctic Circle; 2500 mi N of McGuire AFB NJ. Closer to Seattle, WA than New York City, NY by 5 mi.

FACILITIES	LOCATION HOURS PHONE COMMENTS
PAX TERM INFO	Bldg 623 0800-1700 M-F, 0800-as needed Sa EX-2155 ACCESS LIMITED. See appendix for personal entry requirements.
PAX LOUNGES	Limited but adequate lounge facilities
FOOD SERVICE Dining Hall	Good on Base. None off Base. Bldg 707 0500-0115 dly EX-2614 Call for service hours.
NCO/CPO Club	Bldg 236 1100-1300,1830-2100 M-F, 1100-1300,1900-2200 Sa 1200-1400,1830-2100 Su Call for service hours.
TRANSPORTATION Bus(Shuttle)	Limited on Base On Base 0600-2000 dly Bus does not service Pax Term.
TAXI(Gov)	Bldg 623 24 hrs dly EX-2022
OTHER SERVICES	BX EX-2732, Bank EX-2586, Hair styles EX-3127, Laundry EX-2249, Medical EX-2696, Postal EX-2615, Chaplain EX-2211, Security Police EX-3234
TML	Bldg 97 24 hrs dly EX-3276 No TML Jun-Sep

DENMARK

Thule AB, Cont'd

SCHEDULED FLIGHTS

DESTINATION	ROUTING	FREQ	EQ/CMTS
McGuire AFB NJ (WRI)	THU-SFJ-WRI	Tu,1/2/3/Th,Sa	C-141B/M
Sondrestrom AB DN (SFJ)	THU-SFJ-WRI	Tu,1/2/3/Th,Sa	C-141B/M

EGYPT

Cairo International Airport (CAI) Comm: (20) 3548211-EX-3212
OL-W, 322ALD ATVN: 895-1456-EX-3212
AMEMB, Box 43
FPO New York 09527-0051

LOCATION: The Cairo IAP is 9 mi NE of Cairo on the E side of the Nile River and approximately 75 mi W of the Gulf of Suez. NMC: Cairo, 9 mi SW.

FACILITIES	LOCATION	HOURS	PHONE	COMMENTS
PAX TERM INFO	Pax Term	0800-1630 Sa-Th	C-3548211-EX-3212, A-895-1456-EX-3212. Flights managed by US Embassy Cairo. No military installations in United Arab Republic of Egypt. See appendix for personal entry requirements.	
PAX LOUNGES	Pax Term	0800-1630 Sa-Th	Phone as above. Seats 10. A/C.	
TRANSPORTATION TAXI(Comm)	Limited Pax Term	24 hrs dly	Average $5.00 to all points Cairo	
OTHER SERVICES	This is a small terminal located on an Egyptian AFB. There are no provisions for food service, car rentals, bank or other normal services. Many hotels provide all services.			
ATTRACTIONS	Pyramids, museums, bazaars, Nile River			

SCHEDULED FLIGHTS

DESTINATION	ROUTING	FREQ	EQ/CMTS
Ramstein AB GE (RMS)	CAI-RMS	W	C-141B/M

GERMANY (WEST) & BERLIN

Ramstein Air Base (RMS) Comm: (49) 06371-47-XXXX
608th APS (MAC) ATVN: 480-1110
APO New York 09012-5000

LOCATION: Adjacent to Autobahn 6 (Saarbruken-Mannheim). Take the Flugplatz Ramstein exit. E and W gates are within 2 miles of exit. HE: p-39, G/2. NMC: Kaiserlautern, 12 mi E.

GERMANY (WEST) & BERLIN
Ramstein AB, Cont'd

FACILITIES	LOCATION	HOURS	PHONE	COMMENTS
PAX TERM INFO	Bldg 2202	0500-2200 dly	C-06371-47-5363/4, A-480-5363/5364 From E or W gate follow signs to S side of Base, behind 316 Air Div Bldg and across from Base Ops on flight line.	
Recording	Bldg 2202	0500-2200 dly	C-06371-47-5364, A-480-5363	
Pax Svc Ofc	Bldg 2202	0500-2200 dly	C-06371-47-2120, A-480-5364	
Pax Paging	Bldg 2202	0500-2200 dly	C-06371-47-2120, A-480-5364	
PAX LOUNGES				
General	Bldg 2202	0500-2200 dly	EX-5363/5364 Bag check/lockers, TV, Rest-rms, P/C seats, Tel C,A&Base	
DV/VIP	Bldg 2202 Front area	0500-2200 dly	EX-2120	TV, Rest-rms
Protocol Svc	Bldg 201	0500-2200 dly	EX-6854	USAFE sponsored (06+)
FOOD SERVICE				
Cafeteria	Bldg 1101	0700-2400 dly	C-06371-42407-EX-6061	
Dining Hall	Bldg 2107	Breakfast 0600-0800 dly, Lunch 1030-1300 dly, Dinner 1515-1800 dly	EX-5750	Call for svc hrs.
Enl Club	Bldg 2411	24 hrs dly	EX-5637	Call for svc hrs.
NCO/CPO Club	Bldg 2411	24 hrs dly	EX-5637	Call for svc hrs.
OFC Club	Bldg 302	0700-2400 dly	EX-6066	Call for svc hrs.
Restaurants	Bldg 2411	1700-2300 dly	EX-5637	
Snack Bar	Bldg 2202	0630-1900 dly		
Vending	Bldg 2202	0500-2200 dly	EX-5364	
TRANSPORTATION				
Air Tickets	Bldg 2406	0700-1700 M-F	EX-5374	SATO
Bus(Comm)	Bldg 2113	Call for schedule.	EX-2411	
(Gov)	Bldg 2202	0600-2300 dly	EX-5961	Off Base routes
(Shuttle)	Bldg 2202	0600-2400 dly	Every 40 mins on Base route Also, Gov contract bus svc from RMS-FRF - fm Pax Term,3 X dly	
Car Rentals	Bldg 1202	24 hrs dly	C-06371-43978 AAFES Avis=C-06371-51705, Euro Car=C-06371-43587,Hertz=C-06371-5419	
TAXI(Comm)	Bldg 2113	24 hrs dly	C-06371-50510/Hot line in Bldg 2202	
Trains	Excellent train service throughout Europe. Check with TMO counter for sched or call train sta (Bahnhof) KC-0631-204361.			
Parking	Short term-24 hr parking in front of Term; long term-parking across from Pax Term on flight line. No limits.			
OTHER SERVICES				
Exchange	Bldg 1101	1000-1800 dly	EX-7110	

GERMANY (WEST) & BERLIN

Ramstein AB, Cont'd

Bank/Exc	Bldg 2163	0900-1600 M-F	EX-2390	AMEXCO	Closes for lunch
Hair Styles	Bldg 2162 Bldg 1101	0800-1600 dly 0800-1600 dly	EX-5673 EX-6040	Barber Beauty	
Laundry/DryC	Bldg 2187	0900-1700 M-F	EX-2412	Valet C-42069	
Medical	Bldg 2114	24 hrs dly	EX-5225	Clinic	Emergency EX-116
Postal	Bldg 426	0900-1600 M-F	EX-7206		
WIRE	Bldg 1101	1000-1800 M-F	EX-7110	BX	
TML	Bldg 305 24 hrs dly 0730-1630, EX-7345/6080 After hrs EX-6652 All Ranks. DV/VIP EX-6854 Protocol Office				
TRAVELERS AID ARC	Bldg 2118	24 hrs dly	EX-5464	After hrs EX-2050	
Chaplain	Bldg 2403	24 hrs dly	EX-5753		
Emerg Relief	Bldg 2402	24 hrs dly	EX-5539		
Lost/Found	Bldg 2202	0500-2200 dly	EX-5364/2364		
Sec Police	Bldg 2409	24 hrs dly	EX-2050	Desk Sgt	
USO	Bldg 412	0800-1800 dly	EX-6326		
ATTRACTIONS	Frankfurt, 78 mi NE (fairs and retail centers); Kaiserslautern, 10 mi E (wine strasse); and Mannheim-40 mi E (industry)				

SCHEDULED FLIGHTS

DESTINATION	ROUTING	FREQ	EQ/CMTS
Aviano AB IT (AVB)	MHZ-RMS-AVB-TOJ	W	C-141B/M
Cairo Intl EG (CAI)	DOV-RMS-CAI	1/3/W	C-141B/M
Charleston AFB Intl SC (CHS)	RMS-YYR-CHS	M,1/3/W,Th	C-141B/M
Decimomannu AB IT (DCU)	MHZ-RMS-DCU-TOJ	F	C-130E/M
Dhahran Intl SA (DHA)	DHA-RMS-YYR-CHS DOV-RMS-DHA	M Sa	C005A/M C005A/M
Dover AFB DE (DOV)	RMS-MHZ-DOV-TIK-SUU RMS-DOV	Su,F M,Tu	C005A/C C005A/C
Goose AB CN (YYR)	RMS-YYR-CHS	M,1/3/W,TH	C-141B/M
Incirlik Arpt TU (ADA)	DOV-RMS-ADA	Tu,F	C005A/C

GERMANY (WEST) & BERLIN
Ramstein AB, Cont'd

King Abdullah AB JR (AMM)	RMS-SIZ-AMM	M	C-141B/M
McGuire AFB NJ (WRI)	RMS-WRI	2/4/W	C-141B/M
RAF Mildenhall UK (MHZ)	RMS-MHZ SUU-TIK-DOV-RMS-MHZ TOJ-ZAZ-RMS-MHZ TOJ-AVB-RMS-MHZ TOJ-DCU-RMS-MHZ	Su Su,F Tu Th Sa	C-130E/C C005A/C C-141B/M C-141B/M C-130E/M
Fornebu Arpt NO (OSL)	RMS-OSL	W	C-130E/C
Rhein Main AB GE (FRF)	SIZ-RMS-FRF NAP-RMS-FRF TOJ-RMS-FRF ATH-RMS-FRF	Su,M M,Tu Tu Th	C009A/ME C009A/ME C009A/ME C009A/ME
Sigonella Arpt IT (SIZ)	DOV-RMS-SIZ-AMM	M	C-141B/M
Souda Bay NAF GR (SOC)	RMS-SOC	Sa	C-130E/C
Tinker AFB OK (TIK)	RMS-DOV-TIK-SUU	Su,F	C005A/C
Torrejon de Ardoz AB SP (TOJ)	MHZ-RMS-ZAZ-TOJ MHZ-RMS-AVB-TOJ MHZ-RMS-DCU-TOJ	M W F	C-141B/M C-141B/M C-130E/M
Travis AFB CA (SUU)	RMS-DOV-TIK-SUU	Su,F	C005A/C
Zaragoza AB SP (ZAZ)	MHZ-RMS-ZAZ-TOJ	M	C-141B/M

Rhein Main Air Base (FRF)
435th APS
APO New York 09057-5000

Comm: (49) 069-699-1110
MIL: RMM-2305-XXXX
ATVN: 330-1110

LOCATION: Adjacent to Frankfurt IAP 10 mi S of Frankfurt GE. Take the Rhein Main exit from Autobahn A-5 which runs N to Frankfurt, and Bremerhaven GE, and S to Darmstadt GE, and the Black Forest GE, area. HE: p-40, B/11. NMC: Frankfurt, 10 mi N.

FACILITIES	LOCATION	HOURS	PHONE	COMMENTS
PAX TERM INFO	Bldg 400	24 hrs dly	C-699-7015/16, A-330-7015/16	
	From main gate go straight to Vaughn Rd, right to Springer Rd, left to Pax Term on right.			
Recording	Bldg 400	24 hrs dly	C-699-7813, A-330-7813	
Pax Svc Ofc	Bldg 400	0730-1630 hrs	C-699-7477, A-330-7477	

GERMANY (WEST) & BERLIN
Rhein Main AB, Cont'd

Pax Paging	Bldg 400	24 hrs dly	C-699-7188, A-330-7188
PAX LOUNGES General	Bldg 400	24 hrs dly	C-699-7015, A-330-7015 Entire upper level. Enter fm front of Term. Use up escalator. AC, Bag lockers, Game rm, Tel C&A, TV, Rest-rms, O/S seats
DV/VIP	Bldg 400	0600-2200 dly	C-699-6345/7475 Hostess Center of upper level next to cafeteria (O6+,GS-15+ eligible) AC,Coffee/tea svc,Read/write rm,Tel C&A,TV,Rest-rms,O/S seats
Protocol Svc	USAFEUR		C-699-6264
Family	Bldg 400	0700-2000 M-F,	0700-1200 Sa/Su C-699-6424
FOOD SERVICE Cafeteria	Bldg 400	24 hrs dly	C-699-7212, A-97-69-2107
Dining Hall	Bldg 131	Call for hrs.	C-699-7367 Call for svc hrs.
Enl Club	Bldg 150	1100-2200 dly	C-699-7727 Call for svc hrs.
NCO/CPO Club	Bldg 125	0630-2300 dly	C-699-7116 Call for svc hrs.
OFC Club	Bldg 125	1100-2300 dly	C-699-7105 Call for svc hrs.
Restaurants	Bldg 110	0800-2000 dly	C-699-1181
Snack Bars	Bldg 400 Bldg 345	0600-1800 dly 0645-2000 M-F,	C-699-2107 0900-2000 Sa-Su C-699-3076
Vending	Bldg 400	24 hrs dly	C-699-7015
TRANSPORTATION Air Tickets	Bldg 400 Bldg 150	0830-1630 M-Sa 1100-2400 dly	C-120-5447 AMEXCO C-699-6201 At Rec Center
Bus(Comm) (Shuttle)	Bldg 400 Bldg 400	Schedule available at TMO counter 0500-2200 dly Every half hour On Base Check w/Pax Term for bus to RMS & other AR,AF Installations.	
Car Rentals	Bldg 110	1000-1700 dly 1030-1800 dly	C-699-2188 C-699-1091 AFFEX Car Rental Avis=A-120-3263, Hertz=A-120-5011
Limo Service	Bldg 400	24 hrs dly	C-06374/1805 Rhein Main/Ramstein only
TAXI(Comm) (Gov)	Bldg 110 Bldg 244	24 hrs dly 24 hrs dly	C-699-7528 C-699-7051
Trains	Excellent service from Frankfurt to all of Europe. Must have tickets in advance-automatic ticket machines. Schedule available at TMO counter.		
Parking	Short term-parking is limited. If you must leave vehicle on Base, 30 day parking is adjacent to Pax Term at Bldg 400. Long term, over 30 days, contact Security Police C-699-7177.		

GERMANY (WEST) & BERLIN
Rhein Main AB, Cont'd

OTHER SERVICES				
Exchange	Bldg 400	Mini exchange open during flights		
	Bldg 100	Main exchange	C-699-7456	Call for hrs.
Bank/Exc	Bldg 400	1000-1400 M-Sa C-699-1687 AMEXCO Money exchange at comm bank Bldg 168, duty hrs,& Consolidated Open Mess Bldg 125 if AD or Retired with any club membership.		
Hair Styles	Bldg 100	0900-1730 M-F,	0900-1545 Sa C-699-7214	Barber
	Bldg 100	0830-1730 M-F,	0830-1600 Sa C-699-7245	Beauty
Laundry/DryC	Bldg 349			
Medical	Bldg 170	Emerg Clinic	C-699-6246	Ambulance-116
Postal	Bldg 142			
WIRE	Bldg 110	Rm 142	Operated by Deutsch Bundepost	
TML	Bldg 110	24 hrs dly C-699-6416/7266, A-330-6416/7266 Limited space avail used mostly for AD. Hotel list avail.		
TRAVELERS AID ARC	Bldg 110	Duty hrs	C-699-6225	After hrs EX-7765
Chaplain	Bldg 155	Duty hrs	C-699-7765	Any time
Lost/Found	Bldg 400	24 hrs dly	C-699-7592	
Sec Police	Bldg 343	Crime stop M-2305-7171,	Emerg M-2305-114	
USO	Bldg 400 2nd floor	M-2305-6424, A-330-6424		
ATTRACTIONS	Frankfurt, trade fairs, zoo			

SCHEDULED FLIGHTS

DESTINATION	ROUTING	FREQ	EQ/CMTS
Andrews AFB MD (ADW)	FRF-ADW-WRI	W,F	C141B/M
Athinai Arpt GR (ATH)	FRF-TOJ-ATH-IGL-ADA	Su	C-141B/M
	WRI-LGS-FRF-TOJ-ATH	M	C-141B/M
	LGS-FRF-ATH-SIZ-ATH	M	C-141B/M
	FRF-ATH-PZU-DHA	1/W	C-130E/C
	FRF-AVB-ATH-VWA-ADA	1/2/3/W	C009A/ME
	WRI-LGS-FRF-TOJ-SIZ-ATH-ESB-ADA	1/2/3/W	C-141B/M
	FRF-TOJ-ATH-ESB-ADA	Th	C-141B/M
	FRF-ATH-IGL-ESB-ADA	Sa	C009A/ME
	WRI-LSG-FRF-TOJ-SIZ-ATH-IGL-ADA	Sa	C-141B/M
Aviano AB IT (AVB)	FRF-PSA-VEN-AVB	M	C009A/ME
	FRF-AVB-ATH-VWH-ADA	1/2/3W	C009A/ME

GERMANY (WEST) & BERLIN

Rhein Main AB, Cont'd

Brindisi/ Casale Arpt IT (BDS)	FRF-BDS-SIZ	Tu	C009A/ME
Capodichino Arpt IT (NAP)	FRF-RMS-VEN-NAP-SIZ	F	C009A/ME
Charleston AFB Intl SC (CHS)	FRF-CHS FRF-PHL-CHS	Tu,Sa Th	DC-10/P/CC DC-10/P/C
Cigli TAB TU (IGL)	FRF-TOJ-ATH-IGL-ADA FRF-ATH-IGL-ESB-ADA WRI-LGS-FRF-TOJ-SIZ-ATH-IGL-ADA	Su Sa Sa	C-141B/M C009A/ME C-141B/M
Dhahran Intl SA (DHA)	FRF-ATH-PZU-DHA	1/W	C-130E/C
Dover AFB DE (DOV)	ADA-FRF-DOV FRF-DOV FRF-DOV	Su,W Tu,Th W,F	C005A/C C005A/C B747C/CC
Esenboga Arpt TU (ESB)	WRI-LGS-FRF-TOJ-SIZ-ATH-ESB-ADA FRF-TOJ-ATH-ESB-ADA FRF-ATH-IGL-ESB-ADA	1/2/3/W Th Sa	C-141B/M C-141B/M C009A/ME
Incirlik Arpt TU (ADA)	FRF-TOJ-ATH-IGL-ADA FRF-ADA FRF-AVB-ATH-VWA-ADA WRI-LGS-FRF-TOJ-SIZ-ATH-ESB-ADA FRF-TOJ-ATH-ESB-ADA FRF-ATH-IGL-ESB-ADA WRI-LGS-FRF-TOJ-SIZ-ATH-IGL-ADA	Su M,W,F,Sa 1/2/3/W 1/2/3/W Th Sa Sa	C-141B/M C-141B/M C009A/ME C-141B/M1 C-141B/M C009A/ME C-141B/M
Iraklion AS GR (VWH)	FRF-VWH FRF-AVB-ATH-VWA-ADA	M 1/2/3/W	C009A/ME C009A/ME
Lambert St Louis Intl MO (STL)	FRF-PHL-STL FRF-STL	W,3/Sa 1/F,1/2/Sa	B747P/CC B747P/CC
Lajes Fld PO (LGS)	ADA-FRF-LGS-WRI ATH-FRF-LGS-WRI FRF-LGS-WRI	Su,Th Tu W	C-141B/M C-141B/M C-141B/M
McGuire AFB NJ (WRI)	ADA-FRF-LGS-WRI FRF-WRI ATH-FRF-LGS-WRI FRF-LGS-WRI FRF-ADW-WRI FRF-WRI	Su,1/2/3/Th Su,4/M,Tu,Th,Sa Tu W,Th W,F Sa	C-141B/M C-141B/M C-141B/M C-141B/M C-141B/M C-141B/C
RAF Mildenhall UK (MHZ)	FRF-MHZ FRF-MHZ	Su Th	C-130E/M C009A/ME

GERMANY (WEST) & BERLIN

Rhein Main AB, Cont'd

Philadelphia IAP PA (PHL)	FRF-PHL FRF-PHL-STL FRF-PHL-CHS	Tu W,3/Sa Th	B747P/CC B747P/CC DC-10P/CC
Port Sudan Arpt SU (PZU)	FRF-ATH-PZU-DHA	1/W	C-130E/C
Ramstein AB GE (RMS)	FRF-RMS FRF-RMS-TOJ-RTA FRF-RMS-VEN-NAP-SIZ	1/2/3/W F F	C-130E/C C009A/ME C009A/ME
Rota NAS SP (RTA)	FRF-ZAZ-RTA FRF-RMS-TOJ-RTA	Tu F	C009A/ME C009A/ME
San Guisto Arpt IT (PSA)	FRF-PSA-VEN-AVB	M	C009A/ME
Sigonella Arpt IT (SIZ)	LGS-FRF-ATH-SIZ-ATH FRF-BDS-SIZ WRI-LGS-FRF-TOJ-SIZ-ATH-ESB-ADA FRF-RMS-VEN-NAP-SIZ WRI-LGS-FRF-TOJ-SIZ-ATH-IGL-ADA	M Tu 1/2/3/W F Sa	C-141B/M C009A/ME C-141B/M C009A/ME C-141B/M
Tempelhof Arpt GE (THF)	FRF-THF	Tu,Th	C-130E/M
Torrejon de Ardoz AB SP (TOJ)	FRF-TOJ-ATH-IGL-ADA WRI-LGS-FRF-TOJ-ATH FRF-TOJ-ATH-ESB-ADA FRF-RMS-TOJ-RTA WRI-LGS-FRF-TOJ-SIZ-ATH-ESB-ADA WRF-LGS-FRF-TOJ-SIZ-ATH-IGL-ADA	Su M Th F 1/2/3/W Sa	C-141B/M C-141B/M C-141B/M C009A/ME C-141B/M C-141B/M
Venezia/ Tessera Arpt IT (VEN)	FRF-PSA-VEN-AVB FRF-RMS-VEN-NAP-SIZ	M F	C009A/ME C009A/ME
Zaragoza AB SP (ZAZ)	FRF-ZAZ-RTA	Tu	C009A/ME

Sembach Air Base (SEX)
66th ECW/PA
APO New York 09130-5000

Comm: (49) 06302-67-1110
ATVN: 496-1110

LOCATION: Fm E-12 Autobahn, Exit 1-6 marked Enkenbach-Alsenborn. Follow B-48 in the direction of Bad Kreuznach. Immediately past town of Munchweiller take R turn-off to Sembach AB. HE: p-40,A/2. NMC: Kaiserslautern GE, 9 mi W.

FACILITIES	LOCATION	HOURS	PHONE	COMMENTS
PAX TERM INFO	Bldg 322 (Flight line side)	0730-1630 M-F	C-6302-67-7081, A-496-7081/7572 Gate 6 to Base Ops - Pax Term 1st fl	

GERMANY (WEST) & BERLIN

Sembach AB, Cont'd

Pax Svc Ofc	Bldg 322 0730-1630 M-F C-6302-67-7081/7572
PAX LOUNGES General	Bldg 322 0730-1630 M-F C-6302-67-7081/7572 Bag check, Tel C&A, Read/write rms, TV, Rest-rms, O/S seats
DV/VIP	Bldg 322 0730-1630 M-F C-6302-67-7081 Rm 105 (06+) Coffee/tea served, Read/write rms, Tel C&A, TV, O/S seats
Protocol Svc	Bldg 111 0800-1700 M-F C-6302-67-7606
FOOD SERVICE	Many on and off Base. Cafeteria C-6302-67-7741, NCO/CPO Club C-6302-67-7719, O'Club C-6302-67-7611, Snack Bar C-6302-67-7696, Vending C-6302-67-7198
TRANSPORTATION	Many means and facilities on and off Base. Air Tickets C-6302-67-6585, Bus(Comm) to Kaiserslautern-Vogelweh, (Gov) C-6302-67-7658, Car Rentals C-6302-67-7658, Taxi(Comm) C-0631-62800 & C-0631-69800 (Gov) C-6302-67-7658, Parking C-6302-67-7171
OTHER SERVICES	Many services on and off Base. Exchange C-6302-67-7198, Bank/Exc C-6302-67-7198, Barber C-6302-67-7442, Beauty C-6302-67-2398, Laundry/DryC C-6302-67-6170, Medical C-6302-67-7495, Postal C-6302-67-7748
TML	Bldg 216 24 hrs dly C-6302-67-7588/7149 All Ranks. DV/VIP C-6302-67-7991.
TRAVELERS AID	ARC C-6302-67-7464, Chaplain C-6302-67-7577, Emerg Relief C-6302-67-7848, Lost/Found C-6302-67-7171, Sec Police C-6302-67-7171, USO C-6301-54570
ATTRACTIONS	Wine strasse, Harry's gift shop C-0631-67081

SCHEDULED FLIGHTS

DESTINATION	ROUTING	FREQ	EQ/CMTS
Ahlhorn GAFB GE (LHN)	SEX-LHN-BWY	M	C-130E/C
RAF BentWaters UK (BWY)	SEX-LHN-BWY	M,Tu,Th	C-130E/C

Tempelhof Central Airport (Berlin) (THF)
7350TH ABG/LGTT
APO New York 09611-5000

Comm: (49) 030-819-92
ATVN: 332-5586/5517

LOCATION: At Platz der Luftbrucke, intersection of Columbia Damm and Tempelhofer Damm Streets. HE: city map 6, Berlin (West). NMC: W Berlin, in the city.

FACILITIES	LOCATION	HOURS	PHONE	COMMENTS
PAX TERM INFO	TCA Bldg A-2 0730-1630 M-F C-819-5586/5517, A-332-5586/5514			

GERMANY (WEST) & BERLIN

Tempelhof Cen Arpt Cont'd

Pax Svc Ofc	TCA Bldg A-2 0730-1630 M-F	C-819-5586 NCO on duty
Pax Paging	TCA Bldg A-2 0730-1630 M-F	C-819-5586 See Pax Svc.
PAX LOUNGES General	TCA Bldg A-2 0730-1630 M-F	C-819-5586 Rest-rms, O/S seats
DV/VIP	TCA Bldg A-2 0730-1630 M-F	C-819-5151 (O6+)
FOOD SERVICE Cafeteria	On Base and at Hq Berlin Brigade. Also, food svc at Bowling Alley Bldg C-2 6th floor 0700-2300 dly C-819-5580. Truman Plaza 0600-1800 M-F, 1500 Sa C-819-4632	
Dining Hall	TCA 0600-0100 dly	C-819-5696 Luftbrucke Hall
NCO/CPO Club	Check Point 1130-2200 dly	C-819-7117, TCA Club C-819-5560
OFC Club	Harnack House 0630-2100 dly	C-819-6252, TCA Club C-819-5391
Vending	TCA 24 hrs dly	C-819-5211
TRANSPORTATION Air Tickets	Military and commercial means TCA Bldg A-2 0900-1600 M-Th, 1500 F C-819-5258 SATO	
Bus(Gov)	TCA "B" Bus Stop 0720-2100 dly C-819-3418 Every 60 min to Berlin Brigade and Truman Plaza. TCA express bus every 2 hrs fm 0700-1500 to Hospital & Truman Plaza.	
"U" Bahn	Platz der Luftbrucke subway/train svc to West Berlin	
Car Rentals	Truman Plaza 1000-1800 M-Sa C-813-5074	
TAXI(Comm) (Gov)	TCA 24 hrs dly TCA 24 hrs dly	C-819-6902 C-819-5150 Duty Pax only
Trains(Duty)	RTO Duty hours	C-819-6381 US duty train/resv
Parking	TCA 24 hrs dly C-819-5314	200 yd walk to Pax Term
OTHER SERVICES Exchange	Services at TCA & HQ Berlin Command TCA 1000-1800 M-F, 1700 Sa, 1400 Su C-819-5211	
Bank/Exc	Truman Plaza 0930-1530 M-F C-819-6542 Services FCU TCA 0930-1530 M-F C-819-5512 Merchant's Natl	
Hair Styles	TCA 1000-1800 M-Sa C-819-5603	
Laundry/DryC	TCA 1000-1800 M-F, 1500 Sa C-819-5211	
Medical	Army Hosp 24 hrs dly C-819-116 Ambulance,C-819-4130/1 Emerg	
Postal	TCA 1100-1715 M-F C-819-5535/3389	
TML	TCA 24 hrs dly C-819-5374 VAQ; Dahlem C-819-6654 EM; Berlin Brigade C-819-5591 VOQ; Harnack C-819-6690 Ofc	
TRAVELERS AID ARC	TCA 1000-1300 M-F C-819-5191 AF Family Svcs	

GERMANY (WEST) & BERLIN

Tempelhof Cen Arpt, Cont'd

Lost/Found	TCA Bldg A-2 0730-1630 M-F C-819-5586
Sec Police	TCA 24 hrs dly C-819-5314/5852 Desk Sgt
ATTRACTIONS	Great zoo, East & West Berlin tours, The Wall, shopping

SCHEDULED FLIGHTS

DESTINATION	ROUTING	FREQ	EQ/CMTS
Charleston AFB Intl SC (CHS)	THF-MHZ-CHS	1 ea mo	C-141B/M
RAF Mildenhall UK (MHZ)	THF-MHZ	1 ea mo	C-141B/M
Nurnberg Arpt GE (NUE)	MHZ-NDO-THF-NUE-RMS-FRF	Th	C009A/ME
Ramstein AB GE (RMS)	MHZ-NDO-THF-NUE-RMS-FRF	Th	C009A/ME
Rhein Main AB GE (FRF)	THF-FRF MHZ-NDO-THF-NUE-RMS-FRF	Tu,F Th	C-130E/M C009A/ME

West Germany Stations (WGS)
(Not listed separately in this book)

The following stations have Space-A air opportunities. United States Base support at these stations is very limited. Most stations are located on and serve West German Air Force Bases. Proper identification will be required for entry to these stations. For specific or detailed information, contact: Passenger Services Officer, 435th APS/TRO (Rhein Main AB), APO New York 09057-5000. Comm: (49) 611-7477/7475, ATVN: 330-7477/7475.

AHLHORN GAFB, GE (LHN)
Det 3, 81st Tactical Fighter Wing
On GE-213. Fm E-72 or E-3 Autobahns.
NMC: Bremen, 28 mi NE.

ECHTERDINGEN AAF, GE (STR)
On GE-312, off the E-11 Autobahn.
NMC: Stuttgart, 8 mi N.

FUERSTENFELDBRUECK GAFB, GE (FEL)
Off GE-2. Access fm E-11 and E-61
Autobahns. NMC: Munchen, 27 mi E.

LEIPHEIM GAFB, GE (LPH)
Det 2, 81st Tactical Fighter Wing
Off E-11 Autobahn on GE-19 N.
NMC: Ulm, 11 mi SW.

NORDHOLZ GAFB, GE (NDO)
Cannot identify location.

NORVENICH GAFB, GE (NRV)
Det 4, 81st Tactical Fighter Wing
From E-5 Autobahn, exit to Duren S,
8 mi, to GAFB. NMC: Koln, 12 mi NE.

NURNBERG AIRPORT, GE (NUE)
Access fm E-5 Autobahn and GE-4 N.
NMC: Nurnberg, 4 mi S.

SCHEDULED FLIGHTS

DESTINATION and ROUTING	FREQ	EQ/CMTS
AVB-FEL-STR-RMS-FRF	M	C009A/ME
MHZ-BWY-LPH-SEX	M	C-130E/C
SEX-LHN-BWY	M	C-130E/C

GERMANY (WEST) & BERLIN

West Germany Sta's, Cont'd

BWY-LPH-NRV-SEX	M	C-130E/C
MHZ-NDO-THF-NUE-RMS-FRF	Th	C009A/ME
MHZ-BWY-NRV-SEX	Th	C-130E/C
SEX-LHN-BWY	Th	C-130E/C
BWY-LPH	F	C-130E/C
LPH-LHN-NRV-BWY-MHZ	F	C-130E/C

UNSCHEDULED FLIGHTS

Flights via Army Exec Acft fm Illeshiem AAF, GE (ILH) & Stuttgart AAF, GE (STR).

GREECE

Athinai Airport (ATH) (Hellenikon AB)   Comm: (30) 1-989-5513
Det 3, 625th MASG   ATVN: 662-1110
APO New York 09223-5000

LOCATION: At the Hellenikon AB, adjacent to the IAP on Vouliagmenis Avenue, on the Saronikos Gulf off coast road to Pireaus and Voula. HE map: p-83, G/2. NMC: Athens GR, 10 mi NE.

FACILITIES	LOCATION	HOURS	PHONE	COMMENTS
PAX TERM INFO	Bldg 500	24 hrs dly	C-989-5474/5405, A-662-5474/5405	
	Fm main gate through Base to Pax Term on R at flight line.			
Pax Svc Ofc	Bldg 500	0730-1600 dly	C-989-5474/5603	NCO on duty
Pax Paging	Bldg 500	24 hrs dly	C-989-5474/5405	
PAX LOUNGES General	Bldg 500	24 hrs dly	C-989-5474	A/C,Bag chk,Rest-rms,P/C seats
Protocol Svc	Bldg 339	Duty hrs	C-989-5373	(06+) C/S 7206th ABG
FOOD SERVICE Cafeteria	Many facilities on and off Base Bldg 215	0600-2100 dly	C-989-5665	"Crossroads"
Dining Hall	Bldg 223	0600-1800 dly	C-989-5513	Call for svc hrs.
NCO/CPO Club	Apollon Palace Hotel	0600-2300 dly	C-989-5393	
OFC Club	Apollon Palace Hotel	0600-2300 dly	C-989-5393	
Snack Bars	Bldg 155	0900-2300 dly	C-989-5534	Bowling Alley
Vending	Bldg 500	24 hrs dly	C-989-5474	Departure lounge
TRANSPORTATION Air Tickets	Many facilities and means IAP	24 hrs dly	C-975-6811	Maj Airlines-Intl Term
Bus(Comm) (Shuttle)	IAP Bldg 500	0600-0100 dly 0530-2315 dly	W arpt to Athens C-989-5262	No lug space Departure times from Base listed. 20 min to Officers'/NCO clubs.
Car Rentals	Olympic & Intl Terms 24 hrs dly Hertz=973-3484, Budget=975-5800, Interent=982-4982, Avis=322-4951			

GREECE

Athinai Arpt, Cont'd

Limo Service	Intl Term	0600-2400 dly-every 20 min, IAP to ATH Const Sq
TAXI(Comm)	IAP	24 hrs dly IAP to ATH $5-$7 35 min
Parking	Bldg 500	24 hrs dly C-989-5676 Short term and long term available. See Security Police.
OTHER SERVICES Exchange	Many support facilities on & off Base Bldg 108 1000-1800 dly C-989-5338 No DAVs. Retired members must show proof of permanent residence in Greece.	
Bank/Exc	Bldg 120 0830-1500 M-F, 1200 Sa C-989-5631 No DAVs. Retired members must show proof of residence in GR.	
Hair Styles	Apollon Palace Hotel C-989-5393 Call for hrs.	
Laundry/DryC	Bldg 132 0730-1600 M-F C-981-1685	
Medical	Bldg 216 24 hrs dly C-981-2740, Appoint C-989-5362	
Postal	Bldg 209 0730-1600 M-F C-989-5234	
TML	Apollon Palace Hotel 24 hrs dly C-989-5393/5532 Limited	
TRAVELERS AID ARC	Many agencies Bldg 262 0730-1600 M-F C-989-5417 Other hrs C-989-5414	
Chaplain	Bldg 127 0730-1600 M-F C-989-5293	
Emerg Relief	Bldg 232 0730-1600 M-F C-989-5495 AF aid	
Lost/Found	Bldg 500 24 hrs dly C-989-5474/5603 Pax Svc NCO	
Retiree Info	Bldg 197 1000-1400 M-Sa C-989-5481 Next to Chapel	
Sec Police	Bldg 203 24 hrs dly C-989-5676 Desk Sgt	
ATTRACTIONS	Acropolis, Parthenon, city of Athens, Greek islands	

SCHEDULED FLIGHTS

DESTINATION	ROUTING	FREQ	EQ/CMTS
Akrotiri Arpt CY (AKT)	ATH-AKT ATH-AKT	Tu F	C-130E/M C-130E/M
Aviano AB IT (AVB)	ATH-SOC-BDS-AVB-NAP ATH-AVB ATH-AVB-SIZ-PHL	M Tu Sa	C-130E/M L-1011/CC DC-8/CC
Ben Gurion Arpt IS (TLV)	ATH-TLV	W	C-130E/M
Brindisi/ Casale Arpt IT (BDS)	ATH-SOC-BDS-AVB-NAP	M	C-130E/M
Capodichino Arpt IT (NAP)	ATH-SOC-BDS-AVB-NAP ATH-NAP-SIZ-PHL-NGU ATH-NAP ATH-NAP	M M Th Sa	C-130E/M DC-8/CC C-130E/M C-130E/M

GREECE
Athinai Arpt, Cont'd

Cigli TAB TU (IGL)	ATH-ADA-IGL-FRF ATH-IGL-ESB-ADA	Su Sa	C-141B/M C-9/ME
Diego Garcia IO (NKW)	ATH-NKW	W	DC-8/CC
Esenboga Arpt TU (ESB)	ATH-ADA-ESB-FRF-LGS-WRI ATH-IGL-ESB-ADA	Th Sa	C-141B/M C-9/ME
Incirlik Arpt TU (ADA)	ATH-ADA-IGL-FRF ATH-ADA ATH-VWH-ADA ATH-ADA-ESB-FRF-LGS-WRI ATH-IGL-ESB-ADA ATH-ADA	Su Tu W Th Sa Sa	C-141B/M C-141B/M C-9/ME C-141B/M C-9/ME C-130E/M
Iraklion Arpt GR (VWH)	ATH-VWH ATH-VWH-ADA ATH-VWH	Tu W F	C-130E/M C-9/ME C-130E/M
Lajes Fld PO (LGS)	ATH-FRF-LGS-WRI ATH-ADA-ESB-FRF-LGS-WRI	Tu Th	C-141B/M C-141B/M
McGuire AFB NJ (WRI)	ATH-FRF-LGS-WRI ATH-ADA-ESB-FRF-LGS-WRI	Tu Th	C-141B/M C-141B/M
Norfolk NAS VA (NGU)	ATH-NAP-SIZ-PHL-NGU	M	DC-8/CC
Philadelphia Intl Arpt PA (PHL)	ATH-NAP-SIZ-PHL-NGU ATH-AVB-SIZ-PHL	M Sa	DC-8/CC DC-8/CC
Ramstein AB GE (RMS)	ATH-SIZ-RMS-FRF ATH-RMS-FRF	M Th	C-9/ME C-9/ME
Rhein Main AB GE (FRF)	ATH-ADA-IGL-FRF ATH-SIZ-RMS-FRF ATH-TOJ-FRF ATH-FRF-LGS-WRI ATH-TOJ-FRF ATH-ADA-ESB-FRF-LGS-WRI ATH-RMS-FRF ATH-TOJ-FRF ATH-TOJ-FRF	Su M M Tu W Th Th F Sa	C-141B/M C-9/ME C-141B/M C-141B/M C-141B/M C-141B/M C-9/ME C-141B/M C-141B/M
Sigonella Arpt IT (SIZ)	ATH-SIZ-RMS-FRF ATH-NAP-SIZ-PHL-NGU ATH-SIZ-YQX-PHL-NGU ATH-AVB-SIZ-PHL	M M Th Sa	C-9/ME DC-8/CC DC-8/CC DC-8/CC
Souda Bay NAF GR (SOC)	ATH-SOC-BDS-AVB-NAP	M	C-130E/M
Torrejon de Ardoz AB SP (TOJ)	ATH-TOJ-FRF ATH-TOJ-FRF ATH-TOJ-FRF ATH-TOJ-FRF	M W F Sa	C-141B/M C-141B/M C-141B/M C-141B/M

GREECE

Iraklion Air Station (Crete) (VWH)
7276th ABG/LGT
APO New York 09291-5000

Comm: (30) 81-761281
ATVN: 668-1110

LOCATION: On the N central coast of Island of Crete. Near the village of Gournes. HE: p-85, 3/B. NMC: Iraklion, GR, 12 mi W.

FACILITIES	LOCATION	HOURS	PHONE	COMMENTS
PAX TERM INFO	TMO Bldg 509 0730-1630 M,Th, 0530-1430 Tu,F, 0900-1800 W C-761281-3920, A-668-3835 All Space-A Pax are processed by Transportation Mgmt Office (TMO).			
Pax Svc Ofc	TMO Bldg 509	0730-1630 M-F	C-761281-3920/3835	
PAX LOUNGES	Limited lounge facilities			
FOOD SERVICE Cafeteria	Bldg 220	1100-2100 dly	C-761281-3278	
Dining Hall	Bldg 413	0600-2000 dly	C-761281	4th meal
Cons Club	Bldg 210	1600-2000 dly	C-761281-3206	
Snack Bars	Bldg 202	0700-2000 M-Sa, 1530 Su	C-761281-3215	
TRANSPORTATION	Local commercial bus and taxi service at main gate.			
OTHER SERVICES Exchange	Other general Base support available Bldg 217	1000-1600 Tu-Sa	C-761281-3217	
Medical	Bldg 306	24 hrs dly	Emerg C-761281-116, Other EX-3528	
TML	Bldg 208	0730-2330 dly	C-761281-3942	All Ranks. DV/VIP Call Operator.
TRAVELERS AID Chaplain	Bldg 154	0800-1600 M-F	C761281-3887	
Emerg Relief	Bldg 301	0800-1600 M-F	C-761281-3561	AF Fam Services
Sec Police	Bldg 301	24 hrs dly	C-761281-3426	
ATTRACTIONS	Knossos Palace, archeological sites			

SCHEDULED FLIGHTS

DESTINATION	ROUTING	FREQ	EQ/CMTS
Athinai Arpt GR (ATH)	FRF-VWH-ATH-SIS-RMS-FRF ATH-VWH-ATH	M Tu,F	C009A/ME C-130E/C
Incirlik Arpt TU (ADA)	FRF-AVB-ATH-VWH-ADA	W	C009A/ME
Ramstein AB GE (RMS)	VWH-ATH-SIG-RMS-FRF	M	C009A/ME
Rhein Main AB GE (FRF)	VWH-ATH-SIG-RMS-FRF	M	C009A/ME

GREECE

Souda Bay Naval Air Facility (Crete) (SOC)
Naval Det, Souda, Crete, GR
FPO New York 09528-5000

Comm: (30) 76-1391
ATVN: 399-9489

LOCATION: On the NW end of the island of Crete on Souda Bay. The NATO Missile Firing Installation (NAMFI) is 5 mi N of Souda, GR. HE: p-85, B/5. NMC: Chania, GR, 10 mi W.

FACILITIES	LOCATION	HOURS	PHONE	COMMENTS
PAX TERM INFO	Air Ops During flt processing C-76-1391-EX-228 Air Ops process all Space-A Pax. Chania, GR Arpt co-located with Souda Bay NAF.			
PAX LOUNGES	New lounge facility in Hangar 5			
FOOD SERVICE	NCO & Officer's Clubs EX-268. Dining Hall, NAMFI, 0530-2030 dly. Local food establishments.			
TRANSPORTATION Air Tickets	Chania Term	0730-2130 dly	Olympic Airlines	
Bus Shuttle	Air Ops	0600-0015 dly	NAMFI-Chania	
TAXI(Comm)	Chania Term	24 hrs dly	Local area to Iraklion, GR	
OTHER SERVICES	BX and Emergency medical at NAMFI			
ATTRACTIONS	Great beaches			

SCHEDULED FLIGHTS

DESTINATION	ROUTING	FREQ	EQ/CMTS
Athinai Arpt GR (ATH)	SOC-ATH	M	C-130E/C
Aviano AB IT (AVB)	ATH-SOC-BDS-AVB-NAP	M	C-130E/C
Brindisi/Casale Arpt IT (BDS)	ATH-SOC-BDS-AVB-NAP	M	C-130E/C
Capodichino Arpt IT (NAP)	ATH-SOC-BDS-AVB-NAP	M	C-130E/C
Ramstein AB GE (RMS)	SOC-RMS	Su	C-130E/C

ICELAND

Keflavik Airport (KEF)
Air Terminal Officer, Box 27, Code 404
US Naval Station
FPO New York 09571-5000

Comm: (354) 25-2000
ATVN: 450-0111

LOCATION: In N Atlantic, 2300 mi NE of NY City and 1000 mi NW of Oslo NO. On the SW coast of the island. NMC: Reykjavik, 45 mi NE.

ICELAND

Keflavik Arpt, Cont'd

FACILITIES	LOCATION	HOURS	PHONE	COMMENTS
PAX TERM INFO	Bldg 810	24 hrs dly	C-354-25-2000-EX-6139/2218, A-450-6139/2280 Main gate straight to dead end at Pax Term Red Bldg to the right of the Navy Lodge.	
Pax Svc Ofc	Bldg 810	24 hrs dly	C-354-25-2000-EX-6139/2218	
Pax Paging	Bldg 810	24 hrs dly	C-354-25-2000-EX-6139/2218	
PAX LOUNGES General	Bldg 810 Bldg 810	24 hrs dly C-354-25-2000-EX-6139	Next to arrival/departure area Rest-rms, TV, P/C seats	
DV/VIP	Bldg 810	24 hrs dly	C-354-25-2000-EX-6139 Private area, Coffee/tea svc, Rest-rms. Host as required.	
Protocol Svc	Bldg 810	Duty hrs	C-354-25-2000-EX-4494	COMICEDEFOR
FOOD SERVICE Cafeteria	Many on and off Base Viking Mall	0800-2100 M-Th, 0900-2200 F-Sa, 0900-2100 Su EX-2149	Viking Restaurant.	
Dining Hall	Bldg 747	0600-2330 dly	EX-2220/7505	4th meal
Enl Club	Bldg 700	0630-2100 dly	EX-6126/4661	"Top of the Rock"
NCO/CPO Club	Bldg 1000	0630-2100 dly	EX-5186	"Windbreaker"
OFC Club	Bldg 619	0630-0100 dly	EX-7004/5	Call for svc hrs.
Vending	Bldg 782	24 hrs dly	EX-4575	Trouble desk
TRANSPORTATION Air Tickets	Intl Term	24 hrs dly	EX-9-50200	Iceland Air
Bus(Comm)	Keflavik	0645-2300 M-F	Keflavik to Reykjavik Proceed out main gate L to bus station. Also at Intl Terminal. $4 for 45 min ride to Reykjavik hotels.	
(Shuttle)	Bldg 782 (STOP #34) 0700-2140 M-F Bus #1. 1400-1700 M-F Bus #2. All on Base locations.			
Car Rentals	Bldg 782	24 hrs dly	EX-6162	Shell C-92410, main gate
TAXI(Gov)	Bldg 782	24 hrs dly	EX-2525/4141	
Parking	Bldg 810	24 hrs dly	EX-2280	Limited spaces. No restrict.
OTHER SERVICES Exchange	Bldg 890	1000-1800 Tu-Th, 1700 W-F, 1600 Sa	EX-4105	
Bank/Exc	Bldg 645	0900-1300 M-F, 1400-1600 Sa	EX-4625/4270	NFCU
Hair Styles	Viking Mall	0800-1630 M-Sa 0800-1700 M-F, Sa 1500	EX-7932 EX-6211	Barber Beauty
Laundry/DryC	Bldg 632	0830-1730 Tu-Sa	EX-6298	
Medical	Bldg 710	24 hrs dly	EX-3300	
Postal	Bldg 771	0900-1500 Tu-F, 0800-1400 Sa	EX-2203	

ICELAND
Keflavik Arpt, Cont'd

TML	Bldg 761 Bldg 786	24 hrs dly Navy Lodge	EX-2182/4333 EX-2210.	All Ranks. DV/VIP EX-4414.
TRAVELERS AID ARC	Bldg 755 Bldg 755	0800-1800 M-F 0800-1700 M-F	EX-4401 EX-6210	Family Services
Chaplain	Chapel	0800-1700 dly	EX-6206/4211	
Emerg Relief	Bldg 755	1000-1800 M-F	EX-4602	Navy Relief
Lost/Found	Bldg 810	24 hrs dly	EX-6139/2280	
Sec Police	Main gate	24 hrs dly	EX-2000	
USO	Bldg 758 0800-2400 M-F, 0900-0230 Sa-Su EX-6113/7980/ 6124. Full service including grill and free coffee			
ATTRACTIONS	Nature (wildlife), glaciers, and ice-caps			

SCHEDULED FLIGHTS

DESTINATION	ROUTING	FREQ	EQ/CMTS
Andrews AFB MD (ADW)	KEF-LGS-BDA-ADW	Every other Sa	C-141B/M
Bermuda NAS BM (BDA)	KEF-LGS-BDA-ADW	Every other Sa	C-141B/M
McGuire AFB NJ (WRI)	KEF-WRI	Th,Sa	C-141B/C
RAF Mildenhall UK (MHZ)	KEF-MHZ	W	KC-135
Norfolk NAS VA (NGU)	KEF-PHL-NGU	W	DC-862/P/CC
Philadelphia Intl PA (PHL)	KEF-PHL-NGU	W	DC-862/P/CC

INDIAN OCEAN

Diego Garcia Atoll (NKW)
Operating Location A
374th TAW/MAC-LO
FPO San Francisco 96685-1200

Comm: Ask O/S Oper for British
       Indian Ocean Territory
ATVN: 870-0111 EX 2297/4128
                4132/4353

LOCATION: In the Chagos Archipelago, approx 1000 mi off the southern tip of India in the Indian Ocean. NMC: Colombo, Sri Lanka, 900 air miles NE.

FACILITIES	LOCATION	HOURS	PHONE	COMMENTS
PAX TERM INFO	Pax Term 24 hrs dly A-870-0111 EX-2297/4330/2433 Center of island near main pier. Space-A Pax must have written approval prior to visit or transit from NAVSUPPFAC Diego Garcia, FPO San Francisco 96685-5000. See appendix for personal entry requirements.			
Pax Svc Ofc	Pax Term	24 hrs dly	EX-2407	NCO on duty

INDIAN OCEAN

Diego Garcia Atoll, Cont'd

PAX LOUNGES	Pax Term 24 hrs dly Also, DV/VIP lounge (05+)
FOOD SERVICE Cafeteria	Limited, but good Pax Term 0600-220 dly EX-2297
Dining Hall	Base 0430-1900 dly EX-2290
Enl Club	Base 1130-2300 dly EX-3384
NCO/CPO Club	Base 1130-2300 dly EX-2207
OFC Club	Base 1130-2300 dly EX-4424
TRANSPORTATION TAXI(Gov)	Official bus & taxi for duty Pax only. NO COMMERCIAL TRANS. Pax Term 24 hrs dly EX-4148
OTHER SERVICES	Ship store, Emergency medical, ARC EX-4170, Communications Tel and Cable service EX-4107, Chaplain EX-3318
TML	Billeting Office (NO COMMERCIAL FACILITIES) EX-3396-Very ltd TML for men. EX-2210-Very ltd TML for women.

SCHEDULED FLIGHTS

DESTINATION	ROUTING	FREQ	EQ/CMTS
Berbera Arpt SM (BBE)	NKW-BBE-NBO-SIZ-TOJ-NGU	3/M	C-141B/C
Clark AB RP (CRK)	NKW-CRK NKW-CRK NKW-SGP-CRK	Su,M,W,F Tu,Th,Sa 1/2/3/W	C-141B/M DC-855/M/CC C-141B/M
Jomo Kenyatta Intl KE (NBO)	NKW-NBO-SIZ-TOJ-NGU NKW-BBE-NBO-SIZ-TOJ-NGU NKW-MGQ-NBO-SIZ-TOJ-NGU NKW-NBO-KRT-SIZ-TOJ-NGU NKW-NBO-SIZ-SNN-NGU	2/Su,W,F 3/M 4/M 4/M Th	C-141B/C C-141B/C C-141B/C C-141B/C DC-862/P/CC
Khartoum Arpt SU (KRT)	NKW-NBO-KRT-SIZ-TOJ-NGU	4/M	C-141B/
Masirah OAFB OM (MRH)	NKW-MRH-NKW	Tu,Sa	C-141B/M
Mogadishu Intl SM (MGQ)	NKW-MGQ-NBO-SIZ-TOJ-NGU	4/M	C-141B/C
Norfolk NAS VA (NGU)	NKW-NBO-SIZ-TOJ-NGU NKW-BBE-NBO-SIZ-TOJ-NGU NKW-MGQ-NBO-SIZ-TOJ-NGU NKW-NBO-KRT-SIZ-TOJ-NGU NKW-NBO-SIZ-SNN-NGU	2/Su,W,F 3/M 4/M 4/M Th	C-141B/C C-141B/C C-141B/C C-141B/C DC-862/P/CC
Shannon Arpt IR (SNN)	NKW-NBO-SIZ-SNN-NGU	Th	DC-862/P/CC

INDIAN OCEAN
Diego Garcia Atoll, Cont'd

Sigonella Arpt IT (SIZ)	NKW-NBO-SIZ-TOJ-NGU NKW-BBE-NBO-SIZ-TOJ-NGU NKW-MGQ-NBO-SIZ-TOJ-NGU NKW-NBO-KRT-SIZ-TOJ-NGU NKW-NBO-SIZ-SNN-NGU	2/Su,W,F 3/M 4/M 4/M Th	C-141B/C C-141B/C C-141B/C C-141B/C DC-862/P/CC
RSAF Paya Lebar SG (SGP)	NKW-SGP-CRK	1/2/3/W	C-141B/M
Torrejon de Ardoz AB SP (TOJ)	NKW-NBO-SIZ-TOJ-NGU NKW-BBE-NBO-SIZ-TOJ-NGU NKW-MGQ-NBO-SIZ-TOJ-NGU NKW-NBO-KRT-SIZ-TOJ-NGU	2/Su,W,F 3/M 4/M 4/M	C-141B/C C-141B/C C-141B/C C-141B/C

INDONESIA

Halim Perdanakusuma
International Airport (DJK)
Military Attache for Defense Programs Box 2
APO San Francisco 96356-5000

Comm: (62) 21-360360-EX-2620
ATVN: None

LOCATION: On NW end of the island of Java. The IAP is 8 mi SE of Jakarta.
NMC: Jakarta, 8 mi NW.

FACILITIES	LOCATION	HOURS	PHONE	COMMENTS
PAX TERM INFO	Pax Term-DJK 0730-1600 M-F C-360260-EX-2620, C-801108-EX-352 Enter mil gate 500 yds fm IAP. No US Base support fac. All support fac at IAP. Cab fm DJK to Jakarta approx $8 US.			
PAX LOUNGES	Base Ops 24 hrs dly C-801108-EX-352 General and DV/VIP lounges A/C, Tel L, Rest-rms, Wood seats			

SCHEDULED FLIGHTS

DESTINATION	ROUTING	FREQ	EQ/CMTS
Clark AB RP (CRK)	DJK-CRK	1/3/W	C-130E/M

ISRAEL

Ben Gurion International Airport (TLV)
Det 32, AFCMC/QAB
APO New York 09672-0008

Comm: 972-3-971-3822
ATVN: None

LOCATION: In the Eastern Mediterranean. The airport is 9 mi E of the city.
NMC: Tel Aviv Yafo, 9 mi W.

FACILITIES	LOCATION	HOURS	PHONE	COMMENTS
PAX TERM INFO	Pax Term 0800-1500 Su-Th C-971-7222/3822 Near Gate 3 Pax processed by contractor, Bedek Aviation. Full services of IAP. No US military facilities available.			

ISRAEL

Ben Gurion Intl Arpt, Cont'd

TRANSPORTATION				
Limo Service	Pax Term	0400-2400 dly	United Tours #222 TLV to city,$1 US
TAXI(Comm)	Pax Term	24 hrs dly	"Sherut" 7 people TLV to city,$4 US
	Pax Term	24 hrs dly	TLV to city, $10 US. 15-20 min ride.

SCHEDULED FLIGHTS

DESTINATION	ROUTING	FREQ	EQ/CMTS
Athinai Arpt GR (ATH)	TLV-ATH	W	C-130E/C

UNSCHEDULED FLIGHTS

Flights to: Athinai Arpt GR (ATH); Ramstein AB GE (RMS); Rhein Main AB GE (FRF); and Sigonella Arpt IT (SIZ).

ITALY

Aviano Air Base (AVB)
Det 5, 625th MASG (MAC)
APO New York 09293-5000

Comm: (39) 434-65-1141
EX-
ATVN: 632-1110

LOCATION: From A-28 N exit Pordenone to IT-159 N for 8 mi to Aviano AB. HE: p-93, C/4. NMC: Udine IT, 30 mi E.

FACILITIES	LOCATION	HOURS	PHONE	COMMENTS
PAX TERM INFO	Bldg 933	0800-1700 dly	C-65-2520, A-632-2520	
	In area F, S of Aviano on R of Pordenone.			
Pax Svc Ofc	Bldg 933	0800-1700 dly	C-65-2520	NCO on duty
Pax Paging	Bldg 933	0800-1700 dly	C-65-2520	
PAX LOUNGES General	Bldg 933	Family lounges available		
	Bldg 933	0800-1700 dly	C-651-2520	A/C,Rest-rms,P/C seats
Protocol Svc	Hq 40th TACG	Duty hrs	C-65-2604	Ask for Chief of Staff.
FOOD SERVICE Cafeteria	Adequate on Base. Good off Base restaurants.			
	Bldg 102	0700-1930 M-Sa, Su 1500	C-65-1141-2348	
CONS Club	Bldg 147	Closed	C-65-1141	Temporarily closed
Dining Hall	Bldg 244	0730-1800 dly	C-65-1141	Call for svc hrs.
Snack Bars	Bldg 914	0730-1500 M-F	C-65-2376	Call for svc hrs.
Vending	Bldg 933	0800-1700 dly	C-65-1123	
TRANSPORTATION Air Tickets	Limited on Base. Many means in AVB & Pordenone.			
	Bldg 109 1200-1600 Tu-F C-65-2385 (Rec Ctr). SATO C-65-2791.			
Bus(Comm) (Shuttle)	Town Square Aviano. Svc to Pordenone and Venice.			
	Bldg 933	0800-1700 M-F (only)		Hrly area 1 and 2

ITALY
Aviano AB, Cont'd

Car Rentals	Bldg 106	1300-1500 M-F	C-65-2385	
TAXI(Comm)	Bldg 933	24 hrs dly	C-65-1073/019/268	Expensive
Trains	Pordenone	24 hrs dly	Venice-50 mi SW, 1 Hr, $7 roundtrip	
Parking	Bldg 933	24 hrs dly C-65-2200	Short & long term. Chk/w SP.	
OTHER SERVICES Exchange	Limited on Base Bldg 179	1000-1800 dly	C-65-2571	
Bank/Exc	Bldg 140	0900-1330 M-F	C-65-2637	
Hair Styles	Bldg 105	0900-1800 Tu-Sa	C-65-2737 Barber,	C-65-1303 Beauty
Laundry/DryC	Bldg 257	24 hrs dly		Coin operated
Medical	Bldg 120	24 hrs dly	C-65-2692	Emergency
Postal	Bldg 142	0900-1600 M-F	C-65-2735	Call for svc hrs.
TML	Bldg 256 All Ranks.	24 hrs dly DV/VIP	C-65-2262 C-65-1141.	Area 2-limited Ask for 40th TACG.
TRAVELERS AID ARC	Limited on Base Bldg 600	0800-1200 M-F	C-65-7089	Other hrs C-65-1141
Chaplain	Bldg 172	Duty hrs	C-65-2211/2577	
Lost/Found	Bldg 933	0800-1700 dly	C-65-2520	
Sec Police	Main gate	24 hrs dly	C-65-2200	Desk Sgt
ATTRACTIONS	Excellent snow skiing in nearby Piancavallo			

SCHEDULED FLIGHTS

DESTINATION	ROUTING	FREQ	EQ/CMTS
Athinai Arpt GR (ATH)	AVB-SIZ-ATH-AVB-SIZ-PHL AVB-NAP-ATH-VWH-ADA AVB-ATH	Tu W Th	DC-10 C009A/ME C-130E/C
Brindisi Casale Arpt IT (BDS)	AVB-BDS	W	C-130E/C
Capodichino Arpt IT (NAP)	AVB-NAP	M	C-130E/M
Charleston AFB Intl SC (CHS)	AVB-PSA-TOJ	M	C-141B/C
Decimomannu ITAB IT (DCU)	AVB-DCU	Tu,Th	C-130E/C
Echterdingen AAF GE (STR)	AVB-FEL-STR-RMS-FRF	M	C009A/ME

ITALY

Aviano AB, Cont'd

Fuerstenfeld-brueck GE(FEL)	AVB-FEL-STR-RMS-FRF	M	C009A/ME
RAF Mildenhall UK (MHZ)	TOJ-AVB-RMS-MHZ	Th	C-141B/M
Philadelphia Intl PA (PHL)	AVB-SIZ-ATH-AUB-SIZ-PHL	Tu	DC-10/P/CC
Ramstein AB GE (RMS)	AVB-FEL-STR-RMS-FRF TOJ-AVB-RMS-MHZ	M	C009A/ME C-141B/M
Rhein Main AB GE (FRF)	AVB-FEL-STR-RMS-FRF	M	C009A/ME
San Guisto Arpt IT (PSA)	AVB-PSA-TOJ-WRI	M Th	C-141B/C
Torrejon de Ardoz AB SP (TOJ)	AVB-PSA-TOJ MHZ-RMS-AVB-TOJ MHZ-RMS-AVB-TOJ	M 1/2/3/W 1/2/3/W	C-141B/C C-141B/M C-141B/M

SCHEDULED FLIGHTS FROM VENEZIA/TESSERA *

DESTINATION	ROUTING	FREQ	EQ/CMTS
Venezia/Tessera Arpt IT (VEN)	FRF-PSA-VEN-AVB FRF-RMS-VEN-NAP-SIZ	M F	C009A/ME C009A/ME

* Note: THIS FLIGHT DOES NOT TRANSIT AVB. Venezia/Tessera Arpt IT (VEN) is located 8 miles north of Venezia. HE: p-49, D/5.

Brindisi/Casale Airport (BDS)
7275th ABG/LGTT
APO New York 09240-5270

Comm: (39) 831-423395
ATVN: 622-3395

LOCATION: On heel of Italy's boot midway between port city of Brindisi and town of San Vito dei Normanni. AS is on SS-379. Follow signs to "US Base." HE: p-52, G/2. NMC: Brindisi, 5 mi S.

FACILITIES	LOCATION	HOURS	PHONE	COMMENTS
PAX TERM INFO	Bldg 733	0730-1630 dly		From main gate, straight to 2nd L. Pax Term is on L in Traffic Management Office Bldg.
Pax Svc Ofc	Bldg 733			NCO available
PAX LOUNGES	Bldg 733			Limited facilities.
FOOD SERVICE CON Club	Bldg 531/723	1100-2030 dly	C-EX-3620/3691	Call for svc hrs.
TRANSPORTATION	Limited on Base. Adequate in Brindisi.			
Car Rentals	Bldg 419	0800-1600 M-F	C-EX-3750	

ITALY
Brindisi/Casale Arpt, Cont'd

OTHER SERVICES	Bldg 542	1000-1700 M-Sa	C-EX-3689	
	BX, Laundry/DryC, Hair styles, and other support services			
Medical	Bldg 612	24 hrs dly	C-EX-3511	Dispensary
Postal	Bldg 533	0900-1530 M-F	C-EX-3955	
TML	Bldg 455	24 hrs dly	C-EX-3906	
TRAVELERS AID Chaplain	Bldg 616	0800-1600 M-F	C-EX-3404	Other hrs-Base Oper
Sec Police	Main gate	24 hrs dly	C-EX-3429	

SCHEDULED FLIGHTS

DESTINATION	ROUTING	FREQ	EQ/CMTS
Athinai Arpt GR (ATH)	NAP-BDS-ATH	Tu	C-130E/M
Aviano AB IT (AVB)	ATH-SOC-BDS-AVB-NAP	M	C-130E/M
Capodichino Arpt IT (NAP)	ATH-SOC-BDS-AVB-NAP	M	C-130E/M
Reggio Calabria ITAF IT (REG)	AVB-BDS-REG-AVB * Note: REG near Potenz. HE: p-52, C/2.	W	C-130E/C *
Rhein Main AB GE (FRF)	FRF-NAP-SIZ-BDS-RMS-FRF	F	C009A/ME
Sigonella Arpt IT (SIZ)	FRF-BDS-SIZ-NAP-RMS-FRF	Tu	C009A/ME

Capodichino Airport (Naples) (NAP)
Det 4, 625th MAC/TROP
FPO New York 09520-5000

Comm: (39) 81-724-1110
ATVN: 625-6011

LOCATION: On the Gulf of Naples. Take Capodichino exit off Naples, Tangenziale (local highway by-passing city). Route to airport is marked. HE: p-23 city map. NMC: Naples, 3 mi SW.

FACILITIES	LOCATION	HOURS	PHONE		COMMENTS
PAX TERM INFO	Bldg 405	0700-1900 M-Sa	C-724-5214/5283, A-625-5214/5283		
	Between the two existing hangars at NSA				
Pax Svc Ofc	Bldg 405	0700-1900 M-Sa	C-724-5256/5259		
	MAC Liaison	C-724-5240/5266			
Pax Paging	Bldg 405	0700-1900 M-Sa	C-724-5214/5283		
PAX LOUNGES General	No family lounge				
	Bldg 405	0700-1900 M-Sa	C-724-5214/5283		
	A/C, Nursery, Rest-rms, TV, P/C seats				

ITALY

Capodichino Arpt, Cont'd

DV/VIP	Across fm Pax Term 0700-1900 M-Sa C-724-5214/5283 A/C, Rest-rms, TV, O/S seats. No host.
Protocol Svc	Map #8 0700-1900 M-Sa C-724-5224/6
FOOD SERVICE Cafeteria	Food service facilities at airport, NSA, AFSOUTH, and GAETA NSA #2 0630-2200 dly C-724-4386 Basement
Dining Hall	AFSOUTH Bldg D 0630-1745 dly C-721-2792 Also at NAP Map #13
Enl Club	AFSOUTH Bldg B 0800-0030 dly C-721-2240 "Flamingo Club"
NCO/CPO Club	NSA #12 1100-2400 dly C-721-4673 Call for svc hrs.
OFC Club	AFSOUTH Bldg T 1100-2400 dly C-721-2801 "Allied Club"
Restaurants	NSA #2 1700-2300 dly C-724-1110 Basement-Dinner only
Snack Bars	NSA #2 1100-1700 dly C-724-1110 Superdog/Pizza-NAP Map #14
Vending	Bldg 405 0700-1900 M-Sa C-724-5214
TRANSPORTATION Air Tickets	Many services on and off Base NSA #2 0800-1600 M-F, 1200 Sa C-724-4253 SATO
Bus(Comm) (Shuttle)	NAP 24 hrs dly Ask for schedule (500 lire per ride) Bldg 405 0600-0105 dly Every 90 min NAP-NSA-HOSP-AFSOUTH (to fleet landing). Every 30 min when fleet is in.
Car Rentals	NAP Arpt 24 hrs dly Avis=C-780-5790,Hertz=C-780-2971 Inter-Car=C-780-2963, Eurocar (BX)=C-780-3082
TAXI(Comm) (Gov)	Comm arpt 24 hrs dly Serves on and off Bases GAETA 24 hrs dly C-724-4797 Duty Pax only
Trains	Naples Central Station 24 hrs dly
Parking	Bldg 405 24 hrs dly 1.5 blks fm Term. Check with SP.
OTHER SERVICES Exchange	Services at NSA, AFSOUTH Post, and GAETA NSA #2 1000-1730 Tu-F, 1600 Sa C-724-4386
Bank/Exc	NSA #10 0800-1600 M-F C-724-4774 AMEXCO
Hair Styles	NSA #2 0900-1700 Tu-F, 1600 Sa C-724-5267 Barber 0830-1730 Tu-F, 1530 Sa C-724-4349 Beauty
Laundry/DryC	NSA #2 0800-1800 Tu-F, 1600 Sa C-724-4386
Medical	Naval Hosp 24 hrs dly C-724-4110 Amb, C-724-3333 Emerg
Postal	NSA #4 0900-1600 M-F C-724-1110
TML	NSA #2 24 hrs dly C-724-4550/4549 Very limited. TML for E-6 and below. Hotel references given.
TRAVELERS AID ARC	NSA #25 Duty hrs C-724-4808 NSA #30 Duty hrs C-724-4788/9 After hrs C-724-4546

ITALY
Capodichino Arpt, Cont'd

Chaplain	NSA #30	24 hrs dly	C-724-4546/4786
Emerg Relief	NSA #30	Duty hrs	C-724-4139 Navy Relief
Lost/Found	Bldg 405	0700-1900 M-F	C-724-5214/5283
Sec Police	NSA #9	24 hrs dly	C-724-4109/4530
USO	NSA #10	0800-1630 M-F	C-724-4664
	Also, near fleet landing	0815-2200 dly	C-724-4142
ATTRACTIONS	Flea markets, Pompeii, Island of Capri and tne people		

SCHEDULED FLIGHTS

DESTINATION	ROUTING	FREQ	EQ/CMTS
Brindisi/Casale Arpt IT (BDS)	NAP-BDS	Tu	C-130E/M
RAF Mildenhall UK (MHZ)	NAP-MHZ	Th	C-130E/M
Olbia/Costa Smeralda IT (OLB)	NAP-OLB	Tu/Th/Sa	C-130E/M
Ramstein AB GE (RMS)	VHW-ATH-NAP-RMS-FRF SIZ-NAP-RMS-FRF	M Tu	CO09A/ME CO09A/ME
Rhein Main AB GE (FRF)	VWH-ATH-NAP-RMS-FRF SIZ-NAP-RMS-FRF NAP-FRF	M Tu Sa	CO09A/ME CO09A/ME C-130E/M
Rota NAS SP (RTA)	NAP-SIZ-RTA	M,W,F,Sa	C-141B/M
Sigonella Arpt IT (SIZ)	NAP-SIZ-RTA PHL-RTA-NAP-SIZ FRF-RMS-VEN-NAP-SIZ	M, W, F, Sa Tu F	C-141B/M DC-863/P/C CO09A/ME
Souda Bay NAF GR (SOC)	NAP-SOC	M	C-130E/C

Decimomannu Air Base (DCU)
Det 4, 40th TAC GP
APO New York 09161-5000

Comm: (39) 70-66-89-71-EX-289
ATVN: 621-9267-EX-289

LOCATION: On Southern Coast of Island of Sardinia. Off IT-130 W.
HE: p-54, B/5. NMC: Cagliari, 10 mi SE.

FACILITIES	LOCATION	HOURS	PHONE	COMMENTS
PAX TERM INFO	Bldg 153 EX-289	0730-1630 M-F	C-66-89-71-EX-289, A-621-9267-EX-289. In the US area of the Italian AB.	

ITALY

Decimomannu AB, Cont'd

Pax Svc Ofc	Bldg 153 0730-1630 M-F C-66-89-71-EX-289 NCO on duty
PAX LOUNGES General	No DV/VIP or family lounge Bldg 153 0730-1630 M-F C-66-89-71-EX-289 A/C, Rest-rms, Magazine racks, Patio, P/C seats
FOOD SERVICE Club Med	Limited on Base. Good off Base. Bldg 163 1800-2200 M-F, 1400-2400 Sa-Su Light food/bev
Restaurants	German Canteen 1200-2300 dly
Snack Bars	Across fm UK Pax Term 1000-1400 M-F
Vending	Bldg 153 0730-1630 M-F EX-289
TRANSPORTATION Air Tickets	IT Travel Agency 0830-1230 M-F, 1400-1530 Sa EX-594
Car Rentals	Elmas Arpt Cagliari 24 hrs dly
TAXI(Comm) (Gov)	Cagliari 24 hrs dly Bldg 153 24 hrs dly EX-568 Duty Pax only
OTHER SERVICES Exchange	Bldg 1 1000-1800 M-F, 0900-1200 Sa EX-570
Hair Styles	Bldg 2 0800-1500 M-F EX-570
Postal	Bldg 2 0900-1500 M-F, 1100 Sa
TML	Bldg 162 0730-1630 dly EX-723 Limited on Base. Two contract hotels off Base.
ATTRACTIONS	Cagliari - a beautiful historic city

SCHEDULED FLIGHTS

DESTINATION	ROUTING	FREQ	EQ/CMTS
Aviano AB IT (AVB)	DCU-AVB	Tu,Th	C-130E/C
Capodichino Arpt IT (NAP)	OLB-NAP	Tu,Th,Sa	C-130E/M *
Torrejon de Ardoz AB SP (TOJ)	MHZ-RMS-DCU-TOJ	F	C-130E/M

UNSCHEDULED FLIGHTS

Frequent C-130 flts to: RAF Alconbury UK (AYH); Bitburg AB GE (BBJ); Camp New Amsterdam NT (CNA); and Ramstein AB GE (RMS).

* Note: Olbia Costa Smeralda IT (OLB) is located on the NE corner of the Island of Sardinia. HE: p-54, D/2.

ITALY

San Guisto Airport (Pisa) (PSA)
OLI, 625th MASG/TROP
APO New York 09019-5000

Comm: (39) 586-94-3001-EX-7773
Direct dial 586-94-7773
ATVN: 633-1110-EX-7773

LOCATION: Arpt is 1 mi E of intersection SS1 & via San Guisto, Italian AB. Camp Darby is 6 mi SW of Pisa. HE: p-50, A/3. NMC: Pisa, 8 mi NE.

FACILITIES	LOCATION	HOURS	PHONE	COMMENTS
PAX TERM INFO	Warehouse 84	0800-1600 M-F	C-586-94-3001-EX-7773,A-633-7773	Main gate R on Perimeter Road to Pax Term.
Pax Svc Ofc	Warehouse 84	0800-1600 M-F	C-586-94-7773, A-633-7773	
Pax Paging	Warehouse 84	0800-1600 M-F	C-586-94-7773, A-633-7773	
PAX LOUNGES General	Small facility in back of Warehouse 84, 3rd door left. Warehouse 84 0800-1600 M-F C-586-94-7773 Rest-rms,Coffee/tea srvd,O/S seats. DV/VIP, see Pax Svc NCO.			
FOOD SERVICE Cafeteria	Camp Darby and off Base Camp Darby	0700-1500 dly	A-633-7464	
NCO/CPO Club	Camp Darby	1700-0100 dly	A-633-7662	
OFC Club	Camp Darby Bldg 204	0700-2200 dly	A-633-7662	
Restaurants	Camp Darby	1100-2100 dly	A-633-7662	
Snack Bars	Camp Darby	1400-2300 dly	A-633-7456	
TRANSPORTATION Air Tickets	Camp Darby	0800-1600 M-F	A-633-7589	ITT
Bus(Shuttle)	Camp Darby	0630-2330 dly		Fm Camp Darby to Terrenia, Leghorn, and return each hour.
Car Rentals	G. Galilei Arpt	24 hrs dly		Check w/Pax Svc NCO for tel #'s.
Parking	Warehouse 84	0800-1600 M-F		For arrival & depart of Pax ONLY
OTHER SERVICES	Full services avail at Camp Darby: Bank EX-7678; Hair Styles EX-7169; Chaplain EX-7267; Postal EX-7325; Exchange EX-7468; Medical EX-97; Laundry/DryC EX-7460; Sec Police EX-7575/10.			
TML	Camp Darby Bldg 303 24 hrs dly C-568-7225 All Ranks. DV/VIP (O6+), see Commander. Also, many fine hotels locally.			
TRAVELERS AID ARC	Camp Darby Bldg 302 Duty hrs C-633-7584			
ATTRACTIONS	Pisa, Leaning Tower of Pisa, beaches, Florence (70 kms)			

SCHEDULED FLIGHTS

DESTINATION	ROUTING	FREQ	EQ/CMTS
Capodichino Arpt IT (NAP)	RFR-AVB-VEN-PSA-NAP-RMS-FRF	M	C009A/ME

ITALY

San Guisto Arpt, Cont'd

Ramstein AB GE (RMS)	FRF-AVB-VEN-PSA-NAP-RMS-FRF	M	C009A/ME
Rhein Main AB GE (FRF)	FRF-AVB-VEN-PSA-NAP-RMS-FRF	M	C009A/ME*
Torrejon de Ardoz AB SP (TOJ)	AVB-PSA-TOJ-CHS	M	C-141B/C

* Note: Occasionally flight stops at Fuerstenfeldbrueck AB GE (FEL) or Echterdingen AAF GE (STR).

Sigonella Airport (Sicily) (SIZ)
Det 2, 625th MASG/TRP
FPO New York 09623-5000

Comm: (39) 95-86-EX-(NAS II)
        95-56-EX-(NAS I)
ATVN: 624-1110

LOCATION: On the island of Sicily. Accessible from A-19 or IT-417.
HE map: p-53, E/4. NMC: Catania IT, 10 mi NE.

FACILITIES	LOCATION	HOURS	PHONE	COMMENTS
PAX TERM INFO	Bldg 436 24 hrs dly C-86-5576, A-624-5576 Main gate NAS II straight to Pax Term.			
Pax Svc Ofc	Bldg 436	0730-1600 dly	C-86-5576	MAC and Navy on duty
Pax Paging	Bldg 436	24 hrs dly	C-86-5576	See Pax Services.
PAX LOUNGES General	Bldg 436 All categories Bldg 436 24 hrs dly C-86-5576 A/C, Bag lks, Game rm, Tel L&ATVN, TV, Rest-rms, P/C seats			
DV/VIP	Bldg 436 24 hrs dly C-86-5575/6 (06+) A/C and other facilities in Terminal			
Protocol Svc	Bldg 436	0730-1600 dly	C-86-5575	See Pax Svc NCO.
Family	Bldg 436 24 hrs dly C-86-5575 A/C, Nursery, and other facs in Terminal			
FOOD SERVICE Cafeteria	Many facilities on and off Base Bldg 436 24 hrs dly C-86-5469			
Dining Hall	Bldg 564	0600-1830 dly	C-86-1110	Call for svc hrs.
Enl Club	Bldg 151	1100-2330 Th-Su	C-56-4263	Call for svc hrs.
NCO/CPO Club	NAS II Pavilion	Sa	C-86-5245	Call for svc hrs.
OFC Club	NAS I Santos	1600-2300 M-F	C-56-4335	Call for svc hrs.
Restaurants	NAS I	1700-2200 W-Su	C-56-4272	Call for svc hrs.
Snack Bars	NAS I	1100-2230 Th-Su, 2330 F-Sa	C-56-4302	Bowling
Vending	Bldg 436	24 hrs dly	C-86-5576	

ITALY

Sigonella Arpt, Cont'd

TRANSPORTATION Air Tickets	Many facilities and means on and off Base Bldg 436	0830-1630 M-F	C-86-5428	SATO
Bus(Comm) (Shuttle)	Bldg 200 Bldg 436	0600-2400 0600-1700-30 mi	C-56-4201/2 1800-2400-1 hr	C-86-5576
Car Rentals	Bldg 436	0830-1700 M-F	C-86-5468	
TAXI(Comm)	Bldg 200	24 hrs dly	C-56-4201/2 To Catania $16-20	
Parking	Bldg 436	24 hrs dly	C-56-4201/2 See Sec Police.	
OTHER SERVICES Exchange	Many support facilities on and off Base Bldg 549 Bldg 192	0700-1900 dly 0700-1900 dly	C-86-5423/4 C-56-4326/30	
Bank/Exc	Bldg 436	0800-1430 M-F	C-86-5619 Also NAS I	
Hair Styles	Bldg 549 Bldg 192	0700-1900 M-Sa 0800-1700 Tu-F	C-86-5423 and C-56-4268 C-56-4337	
Laundry/DryC	Bldg 174	24 hrs dly	C-56-4346 Coin operated	
Medical	Bldg 201	24 hrs dly	C-42-5011 and C-56-4333	
Postal	Bldg 189	0900-1700 M-F	C-86-5242	
Valet/Dry C	Bldg 174	0600-2400	C-86-5423/4	
TML	Bldg 436 Bldg 545	24 hrs dly DV/VIP (06+)	C-86-5575 Limited availability C-86-5440-5439	
TRAVELERS AID ARC	Many support facilities on NAS NAS I	0800-1300 M-F	C-56-4382 Other hrs C-56-1110	
Chaplain	Bldg 180	Duty hrs	C-56-4295/6	
Emerg Relief	NAS I	0900-1300 M-F	C-56-4490	
Lost/Found	Bldg 436	24 hrs dly	C-86-5576 Pax Svc NCO	
Sec Police	Bldg 200	24 hrs dly	C-56-4201/2 Desk Sgt	
USO	NAS II (MWR)	0730-1600 M-F	C-86-5271	
ATTRACTIONS	Mount Etna (popular ski resort) - 20 mi N			

SCHEDULED FLIGHTS

DESTINATION	ROUTING	FREQ	EQ/CMTS
Athinai Arpt GR (ATH)	LGS-FRF-ATH-SIZ-ATH SIG-ATH WRI-LGS-FRF-TOJ-SIZ-ATH-ESB-ADA WRI-LGS-FRF-TOJ-SIZ-ATH-IGL-ADA	M Tu,W 1/2/3/W Sa	C-141B/M L-1011/P/CC C-141B/M C-141B/M

ITALY

Sigonella Arpt, Cont'd

Brindisi/Ca-sale Arpt IT (BDS)	SIZ-BDS-FRF	F	C009A/ME
Capodichino Arpt IT (NAP)	RTA-SIZ-NAP SIZ-NAP-RMS-FRF SIZ-NAP	M,W,F,Sa Tu W	C-141B/M C009A/ME C-141B/M
Diego Garcia Atoll IO (NKW)	NGU-TOJ-SIZ-NBO-NKW NGU-PHL-SIZ-ATH-NKW NGU-TOJ-SIZ-KRF-NBO-NKW	M,W,1/2/4F W 3/F	C-141B/C DC-8/P/CC C-141B/C
Jomo Kenyatta Intl KE (NBO)	NGU-TOJ-SIZ-NBO-NKW NGU-BGR-SIZ-NBO-NKW NGU-TOJ-SIZ-KRF-NBO-NKW	M,W,1/2/4/F Tu 3/F	C-141B/C DC-862/M/CC C-141B/C
Khartoum Arpt SU (KRT)	NGU-TOJ-SIZ-KRT-NBO-NKW	3/F	C-141B/
King Abdullah AB JO (AMM)	DOV-RMS-SIZ-AMM RMS-SIZ-AMM	1/3/Su M	C-141B/M C-141B/M
Norfolk NAS VA (NGU)	NKW-NBO-SIZ-TOJ-NGU NKW-BBE-NBO-SIZ-TOJ-NGU NKW-MGQ-NBO-SIZ-TOJ-NGU NKW-NBO-KRT-SIZ-TOJ-NGU NKW-NBO-SIZ-SNN-NGU	2/Su,W,F 2/M 4M 4M Th	C-141B/C C-141B/C C-141B/C C-141B/C DC-862/M/CC
Philadelphia Intl PA (PHL)	SIZ-SNN-PHL SIZ-RTA-PHL	Tu Th	L-1011/P/CC L-1011/P/CC
Ramstein AB GE (RMS)	SIZ-NAP-RMS-FRF	Tu	C009A/ME
Rhein Main AB GE (FRF)	SIZ-NAP-RMS-FRF SIZ-BDS-FRF	Tu F	C009A/ME C009A/ME
Rota NAS SP (RTA)	NAP-SIZ-RTA NAP-SIZ-RTA SIZ-RTA-PHL	M,W,F,Sa M,F,Sa Th	C-141B/M C-141B/C L-1011/P/CC
Shannon Arpt IR (SNN)	SIZ-SNN-PHL	Tu	L-1011/P/CC
Torrejon de Ardoz AB SP (TOJ)	NKW-NBO-SIZ-TOJ-NGU NKW-NBO-KRT-SIZ-TOJ-NGU NKW-MGQ-NBO-SIZ-TOJ-NGU	2/Su,W,F 4/M 4/M	C-141B/C C-141B/C C-141B/C

JAPAN

Atsugi Naval Air Facility (NJA)
Air Operations, Box 13
FPO Seattle 98767-1230

Comm: (81) 462-51-1520-EX
ATVN: 233-1101

LOCATION: In Central Japan off Tokyo Bay. Yokohama is 15 mi E and Tokyo is 28 mi NE. Camp Zama is 5 mi N. NMC: Tokyo, 28 mi NE.

JAPAN
Atsugi NAF, Cont'd

FACILITIES	LOCATION	HOURS	PHONE	COMMENTS
PAX TERM INFO	Bldg 202	0600-2200 dly	C-462-51-1530-EX-3801/3	A-228-3801/3 Main gate to traffic circle, turn L, 4 blks and turn R to Pax Term on L. No immigration facilities - persons not assigned in JA must acquire entry & exit stamps on passports at Yokohama within 24 hrs.
Pax Svc Ofc	Bldg 202	0730-1800 dly	C-462-51-1530-EX-3519	
Recording	Bldg 202	After 2200 dly	C-462-51-1530-EX-3801	
Pax Paging	Bldg 202	0600-2200 dly	EX-3801/3	
PAX LOUNGES General	No family lounge Bldg 202	24 hrs dly	EX-3801/3	A/C, Bag chk, Game rm, Tel L&A, TV, Rest-rms, Showers, O/S seats
DV/VIP	Bldg 202	0600-2200 dly	EX-3801/3	A/C, Bag check, Game rm, Rest-rms, O/S seats
Protocol Svc	Bldg 66	24 hrs dly	EX-3111	Officer of the day
FOOD SERVICE Enl Club	Many facilities on and off Base Bldg 55	Call for hrs.	EX-6233/3736	
NCO/CPO Club	Bldg 75	Call for hrs.	EX-3658	
OFC Club	Bldg 495	Call for hrs.	EX-3211	
Restaurants	Bldg 176	1000-2100 M-F, 0700 Sa-Su	EX-3572	"19th Hole"
Snack Bars	Bldg 187	0700-2100 dly	EX-6114	
Vending	Bldg 202	24 hrs	EX-3801/3	
TRANSPORTATION Air Tickets	Adequate on Base. Good off Base. Bldg 77	0830-1700 M-F	EX-3786	Tours office
Bus(Comm) (Shuttle)	Main gate Bldg 90	Call for hrs. 0800-1700 dly	EX-3519 EX-6248	On Base locations
Car Rentals	Bldg 77	0830-1700 M-F	EX-3786	Gas station
TAXI(Comm) (Gov)	Bldg 202 Bldg 90	0600-2200 dly 0730-1700 dly	C-462-74-0595 EX-6248	Off Base taxi Official on Base
Trains	Main gate	24 hrs dly		Branch-line connects to Tokyo at Zama
Parking	Bldg 202	24 hrs dly	EX-3801/3	Short term-in front, reserved; long term-across fm Terminal. Notify Security Police EX-3200/3500.
OTHER SERVICES Exchange	Many military services in Tokyo area Bldg 37	1000-1800 M-W,F-Sa	EX-3196	
Bank/Exc	Bldg 39	Call for hrs.	EX-3652	
Hair Styles	Bldg 77	Call for hrs.	EX-6201 Barber, EX-3746 Beauty	

JAPAN

Atsugi NAF, Cont'd

Laundry/DryC	Bldg 41	Call for hrs.	EX-3733
Medical	Bldg 21	24 hrs dly	EX-3311 Hospital at Camp Zama
Postal	Bldg 42	Call for hrs.	EX-3570
TML	Bldg 84	24 hrs dly	EX-3519 for NJA. Call Yokota AB A-225-7712 for TML and A-225-5901 for MWR taxi to TML. Commercial lodging is approximately $85.00 per night.
TRAVELERS AID ARC	Many in Tokyo area Camp Zama	0800-1630 M-F	A-233-4181/3166
Chaplain	Bldg 79	Duty hrs	EX-3202
Emerg Relief	Bldg 66	1030-1330 Tu-Th	EX-3691/23
Lost/Found	Bldg 202	0600-2200 dly	EX-3692
Sec Police	Bldg 28	24 hrs dly	EX-3200/3500
USO	Yokota AB	Bldg 403	C-425-52-2511 Call for svc hrs.
ATTRACTIONS	Tokyo, New Sanno US Forces Center, Tama Hills Rec area		

SCHEDULED FLIGHTS

DESTINATION	ROUTING	FREQ	EQ/CMTS
Agana NAS GU (NGM)	NJA-NGM	2 per mo	USN/M
Cubi Point NAS RP (CUA)	NJA-CUA	1-2 per wk	USN/M
Kadena AB JA (DNA)	NJA-DNA	1-2 per wk	USN/M
Osan AB RK (OSN)	NJA-OSN	2-3 per wk	USN/M

Note: Atsugi NAF JA (NJA) is used as alternate location for Yokota AB JA (OKO) during runway downtime. Flight into 24 hrs in advance only.

Fukuoka Airport (FUK)
OL-B, 316th APS/TRO, Box 12
FPO Seattle 98766-5000

Comm: (81) 092-451-2558
ATVN: 225-2438

LOCATION: On the NW corner of Island of Kyushu. NMC: Fukuoka, in the city.

FACILITIES	LOCATION	HOURS	PHONE	COMMENTS
PAX TERM INFO	Bldg 2518	0730-1600 M-F	C-451-2558, A-225-2438	On Itazuke AAF. Ask at west gate for directions to Pax Term.
PAX LOUNGES General	Bldg 2518	General Pax and small DV/VIP lounge A/C, O/S seats, Magazine racks, Rest-rms, Tel L&LD, Soda vending. No food service facilities.		

JAPAN
Fukuoka Arpt, Cont'd

TRANSPORTATION	Gov bus to Sasebo NB on flight days. Comm bus, taxi, trains, and car rental at airport on opposite side of runway.
OTHER SERVICES	No Gov TML. No US aid to travelers. Full support svcs at Sasebo NB, 50 mi SW. Advisable to have Japanese currency.

SCHEDULED FLIGHTS

DESTINATION	ROUTING	FREQ	EQ/CMTS
Clark AB RP (CRK)	OKO-FUK-DNA-CRK	W	C-141B/M
Kadena AB JA (DNA)	OKO-FUK-DNA-CRK	W	C-141B/M
Yokota AB JA (OKO)	OKO-MSJ-FUK-OKO	Th	C-130E/M

UNSCHEDULED FLIGHTS

Call for other destinations, routings, and schedules.

Futenma Marine Corps Air Station (NFO)
Air Operations Division
FPO Seattle 98772-5000

Comm: (81) 098-892-5111
ATVN: 640-1110

LOCATION: On southern part of Okinawa Island off JA-58. NMC: Naha, 10 mi SW.

FACILITIES	LOCATION	HOURS	PHONE	COMMENTS
PAX TERM INFO	Bldg 524	Duty hrs	C-892-3039, A-636-3041	Fm main gate to R at runway. Follow Perimeter Rd to Bldg 524 on L. All flights processed by Pax Terminal.
PAX LOUNGES General	Bldg 524	Pax Term hrs	C-636-3039	Each lounge has essential facilities.
DV/VIP	Bldg 510	Pax Term hrs	C-636-3220	
FOOD SERVICE	Enlisted Club EX-3438, NCO Club EX-3246/3769, Officers' Club EX-3432/3886, Snack bar EX-3896. Call for hours.			
OTHER SERVICES	BX EX-3296, Laundry/DryC EX-3391, Chaplain EX-3058.			

UNSCHEDULED FLIGHTS

Flights to: Agana NAS GU (NGM); Cubi Point NAS RP (CUA); Iwakuni MCAS JA (IWA); Misawa AB JA (MSJ); and Osan AB RK (OSN). Call for destinations, routings, and schedules.

Iwakuni Marine Corps Air Station (IWA)
Code 7ATD, MCAS
FPO Seattle 98764-5001

Comm: (81) 827-21-4171
ATVN: 253-3456
    236-XXXX

LOCATION: Facing the Inland Sea on the S portion of the island of Honshu, 450 mi SW of Tokyo, .5 mi off JA-188 on JA-189. NMC: Hiroshima, 25 mi N.

JAPAN

Iwakuni MCAS, Cont'd

FACILITIES	LOCATION	HOURS	PHONE	COMMENTS
PAX TERM INFO	Bldg 779	0600-2300 dly	C-4171-3570, A-236-3570	
	Main gate L to 2nd intersection, R to next intersection, L to flight line and Pax Term.			
Pax Svc Ofc	Bldg 779	0730-1630 dly	C-4171-3547/3570	NCO on duty
Pax Paging	Bldg 779	0600-2300 dly	C-4171-3570	See Pax Svc NCO.
PAX LOUNGES General	No family lounge			
	Bldg 779	0600-2300 dly	C-4171-3570	A/C, Bag chk/lks,
	Game rm, Tel L,LD&A, TV, Rest-rms, O/S seats			
DV/VIP	Bldg 779	0600-2300 dly	C-4171-3570	(O6+)
	A/C, TV, O/S seats. Located rear of building.			
Protocol Svc	Bldg 360	0800-1630 M-F	C-4171-4211	(O6+) Contact OD.
FOOD SERVICE Cafeteria	Many on Base	0600-2200 dly		Wendy's
	Bldg 401	0700-2300 dly	C-4171-4793	Next to BX
CONS Club	Bldg 1470	1600-2330 M-F,1100-0030 Sa-Su	C-4171-3825	"Club 19"
Enl Club	Bldg 175	1630-2300 M-F, 1300-0100 Sa-Su	C-4171-3506	
NCO/CPO Club	Bldg 439	1100-2300 M-F, 0900-0100 Sa-Su	C-4171-3363	
OFC Club	Bldg 601	0630-2230 M-F, 0900 Sa/Su	C-4171-3480/3803	
Restaurants	Bldg 702	0800-2100 dly	C-4171-4778/9	"Steak House"
Snack Bars	Bldg 779	During flight operations	C-4171-4787	
Vending	Bldg 779	0600-2300 dly	C-4171-3570	
TRANSPORTATION Air Tickets	Many means and facilities on and off Base			
	Bldg 210	0800-1630 M-F	C-4171-3541	Travel Bureau
Bus(Comm)	Bldg 779	0718-2100 dly	C-4171-3063	Every 30 min-IWA trains
Car Rentals	Bldg 139	0800-1600 M-F	C-4171-3186	Special Services
TAXI(Comm)	Bldg 779	24 hrs dly	C-4171-3366	
(Gov)	Bldg 170	0600-2200 dly	C-4171-3063	Duty Pax only
Trains	IWA	24 hrs dly		See Travel Bureau for schedules.
Parking	Bldg 779	24 hrs dly		Across fm Term. See Sec Police.
OTHER SERVICES Exchange	Full services on and off Base			
	Bldg 401	1000-1800 dly	C-4171-5641	
Bank/Exc	Bldg 201	0830-1530 M-F	C-4171-4794	NFCU
	Bldg 201	0900-1500 M-F	C-4171-3842	AMEXCO
Hair Styles	Bldg 408	1000-1730 M-Sa	C-4171-4728	Barber
	Bldg 408	0900-1730 M-Sa	C-4171-4708	Beauty

JAPAN
Iwakuni MCAS, Cont'd

Laundry/DryC	Bldg 348	0900-1730 M-F, 1500 Sa	C-4171-4710
Medical	Bldg 125	24 hrs dly	C-4171-3300
Postal	Bldg 261	0830-1500 M-F	C-4177-5435
TML	Bldg 603	24 hrs dly	C-4174-5541/3579,A-236-5541/3579
	Hostess House EX-3221 All Ranks.	DV/VIP (O6+) EX-4211.	
TRAVELERS AID ARC	Many agencies on Base		
	Bldg 210	0730-1600 M-F	C-4174-3252 Other hrs EX-4211
Chaplain	Bldg 360	0800-1630 M-F	C-4171-3414
Emerg Relief	Bldg 210	1000-1400 M-F	C-4171-5311 Navy Relief
Lost/Found	Bldg 610	24 hrs dly	C-4171-4590
Sec Police	Bldg 610	24 hrs dly	C-4171-3222/119 Desk Sgt
ATTRACTIONS	Parks, Hiroshima, castles, native festivals		

SCHEDULED FLIGHTS

DESTINATION	ROUTING	FREQ	EQ/CMTS
Clark AB RP (CRK)	IWA-DNA-CUA-CRK	M,F	C-141B/M
Cubi Point NAS RP (CUA)	IWA-DNA-CUA-CRK	M,F	C-141B/M
Kadena AB JA (DNA)	OKO-IWA-DNA IWA-DNA-CUA-CRK	Su,Th M,F	C-141B/M C-141B/M
Misawa AB JA (MSJ)	OKO-NAG-IWA-MSJ-OKO	Su,Th	CO09A/ME
Yokota AB JA (OKO)	OKO-NAG-IWA-MSJ-OKO DNA-IWA-OKO	Su,Th Tu,Th,Sa	CO09A/ME C-141B/M

UNSCHEDULED FLIGHTS

Flights to: CONUS, 1-2 per month (DC-8/10, B707/747); Futenma MCAS JA (NFO), 4 per month (C-130A/C-12A); Misawa AB JA (MSJ), 2 per month (C-130A/C-141A); Osan AB RK (OSN), 2 per month (C-130/C-141).

Japan (Mainland) Air Bases & Airports (Hokkaido Island) (JXP)

(Not listed separately in this book)

The bases listed below have Space-A air opportunities. Base support facilities area very limited. The Bases are located on Hokkaido Island (most northern major island). Tokyo is 600 mi south.

JAPAN

Japan (Mainland) AB's & Arpt's, Cont'd

CHITOSE AIRPORT, JA (CTS)
Resource Mgmt Group (AFE/GSS)
APO San Francisco 96292-5000
Location: South central part of
Hokkaido Island.
NMC: Tomakomai, 10 mi S.
Comm: (81) 01232-3-5131 EX-576
ATVN: 225-4761
Note: Flights also transit OBIHIRO
AIRPORT JA (OBO) located in South
central part of Hokkaido Island.

KUSHIRO AIRPORT, JA (KUH)
USCG Loran Station (MAC Rep)
APO Seattle 98763-5000
Location: Southeastern part of
Hokkaido Island.
NMC: Kushiro, 10 mi E.
Comm: (81) 015-576-2439
ATVN: 226-3515
Note: USCG Loran Station is 2.5
hours from airport.

SCHEDULED FLIGHTS

DESTINATION and ROUTING	FREQ	EQ/CMTS
KUH-CTS-MSJ-OKO	Tu	C-130E/M
OBO-CTS-MSJ-OKO	Tu	C-130E/M

Japan (Pacific Island) Air Bases & Airports (JAB)
(Not listed separately in this book)

The bases listed below have Space-A air opportunities. Base support facilities are very limited. The bases are located in the North Pacific, SE of mainland Japan.

IWO JIMA AIR BASE, JA (IWO)
USCG Loran Station
FPO Seattle 98781-5000
Location: In the North Pacific, 900
mi SE of Tokyo. World War II historical significance.
Comm: None
ATVN: None

MINAMI TORISHIMA AIRPORT, JA (MUS)
USCG Loran Station
FPO Seattle 98783-5000
Location: In the North Pacific,
1500 mi SE of Tokyo.
Comm: None
Atvn: None

SCHEDULED FLIGHTS

DESTINATION and ROUTING	FREQ	EQ/CMTS
IWO-OKO	W	C-130E/M
MUS-OKO	F	C-130E/M

Kadena Air Base (Okinawa) (DNA)
603rd APS/TROP
APO San Francisco 96239-5000

Comm: (81) 098-938-1111
ATVN: 630-1110

LOCATION: On central Okinawa, adjacent to JA-58, 27 and 16. NMC: Naha JA, 15 mi S.

FACILITIES	LOCATION	HOURS	PHONE	COMMENTS
PAX TERM INFO	Bldg 3409	24 hrs dly	C-938-634-4462/1281, A-634-4462/1281	Fm gate 1 on Douglas Blvd to L on Schreiber Avenue to Term R.

JAPAN
Kadena AB, Cont'd

Recording	Bldg 3409	24 hrs dly	C-634-4000	
	Hotline-schd flts,destinations,check-in times for next 48 hrs			
Pax Svc Ofc	Bldg 3409	0700-1630 M-F	C-634-4495/1273 Space-A counter	
Pax Paging	Bldg 3409	24 hrs dly	C-634-4462/1281 See Pax Svc NCO.	
PAX LOUNGES General	Bldg 3409	24 hrs dly	No separate family lounge	
	Bldg 3409	24 hrs dly	C-634-4462/1281 Center Bldg	
	A/C, Bag lks, Game rm, Rest-rms, TV, Video movies, O/S seats, Nursery. No food or sleeping overnight.			
DV/VIP	Bldg 3409	24 hrs dly	C-634-4462 At Gate 2	
	A/C, Bag chk, Rest-rms, Showers, TV, Sep read/write rms, Coffee/tea svc, O/S seats. Staffed as required. (06+)			
Protocol Svc	Bldg 3409	24 hrs dly	C-634-3548 313th Air Div	
FOOD SERVICE Cafeteria	Many facilities and locations on and off Base			
	Bldg 3409 2nd floor 24 hrs dly C-633-3183			
	Breakfast/Lunch-burgers and chicken "Flag room"			
Dining Hall	Bldg 3522	0600-2300 dly	C-634-1684 Call for svc hrs.	
Enl Club	Bldg 431	0600-2400 dly	C-634-0644 "Banyan Tree"	
NCO/CPO Club	Bldg 621	0630-2400 dly	C-634-0740 Call for svc hrs.	
OFC Club	Bldg 313	0630-2400 dly	C-634-0482 Call for svc hrs.	
Restaurants	Bldg 9950	1700-2200 W-Su	C-633-3220 "Skoshi Room"	
Snack Bars	Vincent Ave	1000-2300 dly	C-633-9150 Drive-in	
Vending	Bldg 3409	24 hrs dly	C-634-4370	
TRANSPORTATION Air Tickets	Many facilities and means on and off Base			
	Bldg 3409	0800-1500 dly	C-634-0519	
Bus(Comm)	Bldg 412	24 hrs dly	C-634-3383 Call for svc info.	
(Shuttle)	Bldg 3409	0530-0030 dly-every 30 min, C-634-4462 Base area		
Car Rentals	Bldg 219	0800-1730 dly	C-633-0007	
TAXI(Comm)	Bldg 3409	24 hrs dly C-633-1405 on Base, C-97-4002/97-2467		
(Gov)	Bldg 3409	24 hrs dly	C-634-1806/7 Duty Pax only	
Parking	Bldg 3409	24 hrs dly	C-634-2475 Short term-2 hrs	
	in front of Pax Term; long term-hill above Pax Term.			
OTHER SERVICES Exchange	Many on and off Base			
	Bldg 3409	24 hrs dly	C-634-4927	
	Main BX Bldg 413 1000-2000 M-Th, 2100 F, 0900-2000 Sa,			
	1000-1800 Su C-633-4570			
Bank/Exc	Bldg 409	0900-1500 Tu-Sa C-634-3347 Nat'l Bank		
Hair Styles	Bldg 3409	0900-1700 M-Sa	C-634-4927 Barber (Also clubs)	
	Bldg 409	0900-1800 dly	C-633-4176 Beauty	

JAPAN

Kadena AB, Cont'd

Laundry/DryC	Bldg 409	1000-1800 dly	C-633-1405	Svc mall
Medical	Bldg 703	24 hrs dly	C-634-3333	Emergency care
Postal	Bldg 403	0900-1700 Tu-F, 1200 Sa	C-634-2237	
TML	Bldg 332 C-634-1173.	24 hrs dly C-634-1700/3849 All Ranks. Navy Kuwae Lodge C-634-0214. DV/VIP C-634-1273 (06+).		
TRAVELERS AID ARC	Many agencies Bldg 99	"HELP" C-634-4357, Fam Svc C-634-3600 0730-1630 M-F C-634-1294 Other hrs C-634-3374		
Chaplain	Bldg 9800	Duty hrs	C-634-1288	Other hrs C-634-4274
Emerg Relief	Bldg 99	0730-1630 M-F	C-634-3366	AF Aid Society
Lost/Found	Bldg 3409	0730-1630	C-634-4221	
Sec Police	Main gate	24 hrs dly	C-633-3333	Desk Sgt
USO	Bldg 337	0900-2230 dly	C-634-0473/0438	
ATTRACTIONS	Naha JA, Okuma Rec Center, White Beach Rec Center			

SCHEDULED FLIGHTS

DESTINATION	ROUTING	FREQ	EQ/CMTS
Clark AB RP (CRK)	LAX-OAK-ANC-DNA-CRK DNA-CRK DNA-CUA-CRK STL-LAX-ANC-DNA-CRK DNA-CRK	M M-Sa M-Sa Th Sa	B747/P/CC C-141B/M C-141B/M B747/P/CC C-130E/M
Cubi Point NAS RP (CUA)	DNA-CUA-CRK	M,W,F	C-141B/M
Hickham AFB HI (HIK)	DNA-HIK-SUU	M	C-141B/C
Iwakuni MCAS JA (IWA)	DNA-IWA-OKO	Tu,Th,Sa	C-141B/M
Kimhae IAP RK (KHE)	DNA-KHE-TAE-KUZ-OSN	2/4/W	C-130E/M
Kunsan AB RK (KUZ)	DNA-TAE-KUZ-OSN DNA-KWJ-KUZ-OSN-TAE-OKO DNA-KHE-TAE-KUZ-OSN DNA-KUZ-OSN-TAE-OKO DNA-KUZ-TAE-OKO	M,1/3/W,F Tu 2/4/W Th,3/4/Sa 1/Sa	C-130E/M C-141B/M C-130E/M C-141B/M C-141B/M
Kwang Ju ROK AFB RK (KWJ)	DNA-KWJ-KUZ-OSN-TAE-OKO	Tu	C-141B/M

JAPAN

Kadena AB, Cont'd

Lambert St Louis Intl MO (STL)	CRK-DNA-ANC-LAX-STL	Tu	B747/P/CC
Los Angeles Intl CA (LAX)	CRK-DNA-ANC-OAK-LAX	F	B747/P/CC
Osan AB RK (OSN)	DNA-OSN-OKO DNA-TAE-KUZ-OSN DNA-KWJ-KUZ-OSN-TAE-OKO DNA-KHE-TAE-KUZ-OSN DNA-KUZ-OSN-TAE-OKO DNA-OSN-TAE-OKO	Su M,1/3/W,F Tu 2/4/W Th,Sa 2/Sa	C-141B/M C-130E/M C-141B/M C-130E/M C-141B/M C-141B/M
Oakland IAP CA (OAK)	CRK-DNA-ANC-OAK-STL CRK-DNA-ANC-OAK-LAX	T F	B747/P/CC B747/P/CC
Taegu AB RK (TAE)	DNA-TAE-KUZ-OSN DNA-KWJ-KUZ-OSN-TAE-OKO DNA-KHE-TAE-KUZ-OSN DNA-KUZ-OSN-TAE-OKO DNA-KUZ-TAE-OKO DNA-OSN-TAE-OKO	M,1/3/W,F Tu 2/4/W Th,3/4/Sa 1/Sa 2/Sa	C-130E/M C-141B/M C-130E/M C-141B/M C-141B/M C-141B/M
Travis AFB CA (SUU)	DNA-OKO-SUU DNA-HIK-SUU	M M	C005A/C C-141B/C
Yokota AB JA (OKO)	DNA-OKO-CRK DNA-OSN-OKO DNA-OKO-SUU DNA-KWJ-KUZ-OSN-TAE-OKO DNA-IWA-OKO DNA-KUZ-TAE-OKO DNA-OSN-TAE-OKO DNA-OKO DNA-KUZ-OSN-TAE-OKO	Dly 1/Su M Tu Tu,Th,Sa 1/Sa 2/Sa 2/4/Sa Th,3/4/Sa	C-141B/M C-141B/M C005A/C C-141B/M C-141B/M C-141B/M C-141B/M C-130E/M C-141B/M

Misawa Air Base (MSJ)

Det 1, 316th APS
APO San Francisco, 96519-5000

Comm: (81) 176-53-5181
ATVN: 226-1110 and
221-5623

LOCATION: On the NE portion of the Island of Honshu, 400 mi N of Tokyo.
NMC: Hachinohe City, 17 mi SE.

FACILITIES	LOCATION	HOURS	PHONE	COMMENTS
PAX TERM INFO	Bldg 738 0730-1630 Tu-Su, 0700-1630 M C-53-5181-3300/4455, A-226-3300/4455. Fm main gate (Misawa City) straight to 5th St L. Term is .25 mi W of Base Ops Bldg 998.			
Pax Svc Ofc	Bldg 738 US Navy Ops	Pax Term hrs C-53-5181-4670	C-53-5181-3300/4455	
Pax Paging	Bldg 738	Pax Term hrs	C-53-5181-4031	

JAPAN

Misawa AB, Cont'd

PAX LOUNGES General	Small DV/VIP lounge and nursery for families Bdlg 738 Pax Term hrs C-53-5181-3300 Bag chk/lks, Coffee/tea srvd, Tel L&ATVN, TV, Rest-rms, P/C & O/S seats
Protocol Svc	Bldg 504 24 hrs dly C-53-5181-SDO 432nd TFW
FOOD SERVICE	Cafeteria C-53-5181-4513/5671, Dining Hall C-53-5181-3889 (Menu EX-3997), Ofc Mess C-53-5181-4724, CONS Club C-53-5181-4408, Burger King C-53-5181-5905
TRANSPORTATION	Air Tickets C-53-5181-5279, Bus(Shuttle) C-53-5181-4062, Car Rentals C-53-5181-6722, Taxi(Comm) C-53-5181-5438 (Gov) C-53-5181-4062, Parking (no long term or overnight)
OTHER SERVICES	Exchange C-53-5181-3354/6085, Bank/Exc C-53-5181-3380/5412, Barber C-53-5181-6186, Beauty C-53-5181-5755, Laundry/DryC C-53-5181-5521, Medical C-53-5181-3676/119, Postal C-53-5181-3492/3173
TML	Bldg 10 24 hrs dly C-53-5181-3526/4294 All Ranks. DV/VIP C-53-5181-3526/4294.
TRAVELERS AID	ARC C-53-5181-3772/225-9901, Chaplain C-53-5181-4630/3676, Emerg Relief(CBPO) C-53-5181-3721, Lost/Found C-53-5181-3145, Sec Police C-53-5181-4358/116
ATTRACTIONS	Ski area and lodge on Base

SCHEDULED FLIGHTS

DESTINATION	ROUTING	FREQ	EQ/CMTS
Atsugi NAF JA (NJA)	MSJ-IWA-NJA-OKO	Tu,F	C009A/ME
Fukuoka/Itaz Arpt JA (FUK)	MSJ-FUK-OKO	Th	C-130B/M
Iwakuni MCAS JA (IWA)	MSJ-IWA-NJA-OKO	Tu,F	C009A/ME
Yokota AB JA (OKO)	MSJ-OKO MSJ-IWA-NJA-OKO MSJ-OKO	M,W,F Tu,F Tu,Sa	C-141B/M C009A/ME C-130E/M

Yokota Air Base (OKO)
316th APS
APO San Francisco 96328-5000

Comm: (81) 425-225-1101
ATVN: 248-1101

LOCATION: Take JA-16 S fm Tokyo. AB is 1 mi W of Fussa JA. Clearly marked. NMC: Tokyo JA, 35 mi NE.

FACILITIES	LOCATION	HOURS	PHONE	COMMENTS
PAX TERM INFO	Bldg 80	24 hrs dly	C-255-9547/9839, A-248-9547/9839 Fm Gate #5 straight on Bobzien Ave to Terminal on R.	
Recording	Bldg 80	24 hrs dly	C-225-4677	Far East TV broadcast flts & Space-A backlog at 1758 & 2158 dly

JAPAN
Yokota AB, Cont'd

Service	Location	Hours	Phone	Notes
Pax Svc Ofc	Bldg 80	0730-1630 dly	C-225-7572/9526	NCO on duty
Pax Paging	Bldg 80	24 hrs dly	C-255-7119	Pax Svc NCO
PAX LOUNGES General	Bldg 80 Bldg 80	24 hrs dly 24 hrs dly	 C-225-9547	No separate family lounge A/C, Bag chk/lks, Coffee/tea srvd, Game rm, Rest-rms, Showers, TV, P/C seats. No sleeping in the Terminal overnight.
DV/VIP	Bldg 80	24 hrs dly	C-225-9547	(O6+) A/C, Rest-rms, Read/write rms, TV, O/S seats. Not staffed.
Protocol Svc	Bldg 403	24 hrs dly	C-225-1101	475th ABW
FOOD SERVICE Cafeteria	Many facilities on and off Base Bldg 80	24 hrs dly	C-225-7146	
Dining Hall	Bldg 427	0530-2200 dly	C-225-1101	Call for svc hrs.
Enl Club	Bldg 336	0600-2200 dly	C-225-8692	Call for svc hrs.
NCO/CPO Club	Bldg 2066	0900-0100 dly	C-225-2337	Call for svc hrs.
OFC Club	Bldg 31	0900-2400 dly	C-225-8341	Call for svc hrs.
Restaurants	Bldg 442	0900-2300 dly	C-225-1101	Drive-In
Snack Bars	Bldg 3	0800-2000 dly	C-225-7677	
Vending	Bldg 80	24 hrs dly	C-225-9547	
TRANSPORTATION Air Tickets	Many facilities and means on and off Base Bldg 80	0800-1800 M-F, 1700 Sa	C-225-8051	
Bus (Comm) (Gov) (Shuttle)	Bldg 80 Bldg 80 Bldg 529	0730-1630 dly Call for hrs. 24 hrs dly	C-225-8051 C-225-7750/0519 C-225-9547	Local area Svc to New Sanno and Narita - adults $6/24, children $4/12 Schedule at Space-A counter
Car Rentals	Bldg 119	0730-1630 dly	C-225-5901	
TAXI (Comm) (Gov)	Bldg 1296 Bldg 409	24 hrs dly 24 hrs dly	C-224-3421 C-225-9121	
Trains	Gate 2	24 hrs dly		Higashi-Fusa station OKO-Tokyo
Parking	Bldg 80	24 hrs dly		Short term-at Pax Term; long term-across JA-16. Notify Security Police.
OTHER SERVICES Exchange	Many on and off Base Bldg 80	0800-1700 M-Sa	C-225-7236	
Bank/Exc	Bldg 1297	0900-1500 M-Sa	C-225-7703	
Hair Styles	Bldg 416	0900-1700 M-Sa	C-225-7236	Barber & Beauty
Laundry/DryC	Bldg 114	0800-1800 dly	C-225-1101	
Medical	Bldg 4408	24 hrs dly	C-225-119	Emergency

JAPAN

Yokota AB, Cont'd

Postal	Bldg 538	0800-1600 M-F	C-225-1101	
WIRE Svc	Bldg 424	0800-2400 dly	C-225-1101	Rec Ctr overseas
TML	Bldg 10 DV/VIP C-225-7326	24 hrs dly (06+).	C-225-7712	All ranks.
TRAVELERS AID ARC	Bldg 432 Bldg 530	Duty hrs 0730-1630 M-F	C-225-8730 C-225-7522	AF Family Services O/hrs C-225-9901
Chaplain	Bldg 345	0800-1630 M-F	C-225-7009/8009	
Emerg Relief	Bldg 4	0730-1630 M-F	C-225-7953	AF Aide
Lost/Found	Bldg 80	24 hrs dly	C-225-9547	Pax Svc NCO
Sec Police	Bldg 555	24 hrs dly	C-225-116	Desk Sgt
USO	Bldg 403	24 hrs dly	C-225-2095	
ATTRACTIONS	Tokyo, Mount Fuji, New Sanno US Forces Center			

SCHEDULED FLIGHTS

DESTINATION	ROUTING	FREQ	EQ/CMTS
Clark AB RP (CRK)	DNA-OKO-CRK OKO-CRK	Tu,W,Th,F,Sa,Su Sa	C-141B/M C-141B/M
Elmendorf AFB AK (EDF)	OSN-OKO-EDF-TCM CRK-OKO-EDF-SUU OSN-OKO-EDF-SUU	W F F	C-141B/C C-141B/C C-141B/C
Fukuoka/Itazuke JA (FUK)	OKO-FUK-DNA	Tu	C-141B/M
Iwakuni MCAS JA (IWA)	OKO-IWA-DNA	Su,Th	C-141B/M
Iwo Jima AB JA (IWO)	OKO-IWO	W	C-130E/M
Kadena AB JA (DNA)	OKO-IWA-DNA OKO-KUZ-TAE-OSN-DNA OKO-DNA OKO-KUZ-TAE-OSN-KWJ-DNA OKO-FUK-DNA OKO-OSN-DNA SBD-SUU-HIK-UAM-OKO-DNA	Su,Th Su,Th 2/4/Su Tu Tu F Sa	C-141B/M C-141B/M C-130E C-141B/M C-141B/M C-141B/M C-141B/M
Kunsan AB RK (KUZ)	OKO-KUZ-TAE-OSN-DNA OKO-KUZ-TAE-OSN-KWJ-DNA	Su,Th Tu	C-141B/M C-141B/M
Kwang Ju ROK AFB RK (KWJ)	OKO-KUZ-TAE-OSN-KWJ-DNA	Tu	C-141B/M
Lambert St Louis Intl MO (STL)	OSN-OKO-OAK-STL	W,F	B747/P/CC

JAPAN
Yokota AB, Cont'd

Minami Tori-shima Arpt JA (MUS)	OKO-MUS	Th	C-130E/M
McChord AFB WA (TCM)	OSN-OKO-EDF-TCM	W	C-141B/C
Misawa AB JA (MSJ)	OKO-MSJ OKO-MSJ	M,W,F W,Sa	C-141B/M C-130E/M
Obihiro Arpt JA (OBO)	OKO-OBO	W	C-130E/M
Osan AB RK (OSN)	OKO-OSN OKO-KUZ-TAE-OSN-DNA OKO-OSN SUU-HIK-OKO-OSN OKO-KUZ-TAE-OSN-KWJ-DNA STL-OAK-OKO-OSN OKO-OSN OKO-OSN-DNA	Su Su,Th M M Tu Tu,Th Tu,F F	C-130E/M C-141B/M C-141B/M C005A/C C-141B/M B747/P/CC C-141B/C C-141B/M
Oakland CA (OAK)	OSN-OKO-OAK-STL	W,F	B747/P/CC
Taegu AB RK (TAE)	OKO-KUZ-TAE-OSN-DNA OKO-KUZ-TAE-OSN-KWJ-DNA	Su,Th Tu	C-141B/M C-141B/M
Travis AFB CA (SUU)	CRK-OKO-SUU DNA-OKO-SUU OSN-OKO-SUU OSN-OKO-SUU CRK-OKO-EDF-SUU OSN-OKO-EDF-SUU CUA-OKO-SUU	4/Su,Tu M Tu Th F F 1/3/Sa	C005A/C C005A/C C-141B/M C005A/C C-141B/C C-141B/C C005A/C

JORDAN

King Abdullah Air Base (AMM)
MAP Jordan, US Embassy
APO New York 09892-5000

Comm: 644371-EX-263
ATVN: None

LOCATION: In Amman, Jordan, capital city of Hashemite Kingdom of Jordan. Tel Aviv, Israel, 70 mi W of Amman. NMC: Amman, 3 mi W.

FACILITIES	LOCATION	HOURS	PHONE	COMMENTS
PAX TERM INFO	Pax Term During flt processing C-644371-EX-263/265/268 Contact MAC/Amer Embassy personnel for Pax processing. No US Base support facilities. $21 departure tax for out-bound pax.			

SCHEDULED FLIGHTS

DESTINATION	ROUTING	FREQ	EQ/CMTS
Ramstein AB GE (RMS)	AMM-RMS	4/Tu	C-141B/M

KENYA

Jomo Kenyatta International Airport (NBO) Comm: (254) 2-822328 or
PANAM Station Manager   2-822213
Nairobi, Kenya   ATVN: None

LOCATION: On the East Coast of Africa, 30 mi W of Indian Ocean and 175 mi E
of Lake Victoria. Airport is 6 mi SE of Nairobi. NMC: Nairobi, 6 mi NW.

FACILITIES	LOCATION	HOURS	PHONE	COMMENTS
PAX TERM INFO	Pax Term During flt processing C-822328 or 822213 Pax Svc provided by PANAM contractor. LIMITED ACCESS. See appendix for personal entry requirements. No US Base spt fac. US Embassy in Kenya, PO Box 30137, Moi/Haile Selassie Ave, Nairobi Kenya. Tel (254) 334141. Public hrs 0730-1630. Essential services of an international airport available.			

SCHEDULED FLIGHTS

DESTINATION	ROUTING	FREQ	EQ/CMTS
Diego Garcia Atoll IO (NKW)	NGU-TOJ-SIZ-NBO-NKW NGU-TOJ-SIZ-KRT-NBO-NKW	M,W,1/2/4/F 3/F	C-141B/C C-141B/C
Khartoum Arpt SU (KRT)	NKW-NBO-KRT-SIZ-TOJ-NGU NGU-BGU-SIZ-NBO-NKW	4/M 1/2/3/Tu	C-141B/C DC-862/M/C
Norfolk NAS VA (NGU)	NKW-NBO-SIZ-TOJ-NGU NKW-BBE-NBO-SIZ-TOJ-NGU NKW-NBO-KRI-SIZ-TOJ-NGU NKW-NBO-SIZ-SNN-NGU NKW-MGQ-NBO-SIZ-TOJ-NGU NKW-NBO-SIZ-SNN-NGU	2/Su,W,F 3/M 4/M Th Th 1/2/3/Th	C-141B/C C-141B/G C-141B/C DC-862/P/CC C-141B/C DC-862/M/CC
Shannon Arpt IR (SNN)	NKW-NBO-SIZ-SNN-NGU NKW-NBO-SIZ-SNN-NGU	Th 1/2/3/Th	DC-862/P/CC DC-862/M/CC
Sigonella Arpt IT (SIZ)	NKW-NBO-SIZ-TOJ-NGU NKW-BBE-NBO-SIZ-TOJ-NGU NKW-NBO-KRT-SIZ-TOJ-NGU NKW-NBO-SIZ-SNN-NGU NKW-MGQ-NBO-SIZ-TOJ-NGU NKW-NBO-SIZ-SNN-NGU	2/Su,W,F 3/M 4/M Th Th 1/2/3/Th	C-141B/C C-141B/C C-141B/C DC-862/P/CC C-141B/C DC-862/M/CC
Torrejon de Ardoz AB SP (TOJ)	NKW-NBO-SIZ-TOJ-NGU NKW-BBE-NBO-SIZ-TOJ-NGU NKW-NBO-KRI-SIZ-TOJ-NGU NKW-MGQ-NBO-SIZ-TOJ-NGU	2/Su,W,F 3/M 4/M Th	C-141B/C C-141B/C C-141B/C C-141B/C

KOREA (SOUTH)

Korean Stations (KOE)
(Not listed separately in this book)

The stations listed below have Space-A air opportunities. US Base support facilities are limited. Essential facilities are available.

KOREA (SOUTH)
Korean Sta's, Cont'd

CHEJU DO IAP, RK (CJU)
Cheju Do R&R Center
APO San Francisco 96220-5000
Location: On Cheju Do Island, 60 mi SW of RK. IAP is 4 mi SW of Cheju City.
Comm: (82) 641-2472
ATVN: 262-1101 Ask for Cheju Do.

KIMHAE INTL ARPT, RK (KHE)
OL-D, 611th MASS/TROP
APO San Francisco 96259-5000
Location: Southeast sector of RK.
NMC: Pusan, 15 mi SE.
Comm: (82) 51-3279
ATVN: 262-3279

KWANG JU ROKAFB, RK (KWJ)
OL-A, 611th MASS/TROP
APO San Francisco 96324-5000
Location: Southwest sector of RK.
NMC: Kwang Ju, in the city.
Comm: (82) 62-4811/4890
ATVN: 272-2345-EX-4811/4890

SCHEDULED FLIGHTS

DESTINATION and ROUTING	FREQ	EQ/CMTS
OSN-CJU	M	C-130E/M
OKO-KUZ-TAE-OSN-KWJ-DNA	Tu	C-141B/M
DNA-KWJ-KUZ-OSN-TAE-OKO	Tu	C-141B/M
DNA-KHE-TAE-KUZ-OSN	1/3/4/W	C-130E/M
OSN-KUZ-TAE-KHE-DNA	1/3/4/Th	C-130E/M

Kunsan Air Base (KUZ)
OL-B, 611th APS/TROP
APO San Francisco 96264-5000

Comm: (82) 654-7-3596
ATVN: 272-5403

LOCATION: On the SW coast of the Korean peninsula at the terminus of RK-26.
NMC: Kunsan, 10 mi W.

FACILITIES	LOCATION	HOURS	PHONE	COMMENTS
PAX TERM INFO	Bldg 2858	0900-1630 M-Sa	C-7-3596-5403/4024, A-272-5403	Three mi fm main gate on Ave B, W. Adjacent to weather tower.
Pax Svc Ofc	Bldg 2858	0700-1630 M-Sa	C-7-3596-5403/4901, A-272-5403	
Pax Paging	Bldg 2858	0700-1630 M-Sa	C-7-3596-5403, A-272-5403	
PAX LOUNGES General	One lounge Bldg 2858 A/C, Rest-rms, O/S seats	DV/VIP 0700-1630 dly	C-7-3596-5403/4901 C-7-3596-5403, A-272-5403/4024	
FOOD SERVICE Cafeteria	Adequate on and off Base Bldg 1004	0800-1800 dly	C-7-3596-4736	
Dining Hall	Bldg 1360	0530-1745 dly	C-7-3596-5104/4736	
NCO/CPO Club	Bldg 1004	0600-2100 dly	C-7-3596-4312/4575	"Seabreeze"
OFC Club	Bldg 387	0600-2100 dly	C-7-3596-4494/5/4425	
Restaurants	Bldg 1004	0600-2100 dly	C-7-3596-4100/4102	"Oriental House"

KOREA (SOUTH)

Kunsan AB, Cont'd

Snack Bars	Bldg 2858 0800-1530 M-F, 1300 Sa C-7-3596-4912
TRANSPORTATION Air Tickets	Limited and off Base Bldg 1012 1130-1700 M-F C-7-3596-4027
TAXI(Comm) (Gov)	Bldg 638 24 hrs dly C-7-3596-4537/4318 Bldg 804 24 hrs dly C-7-3596-4597/5317
Parking	Bldg 2858 24 hrs dly C-7-3596-5403 Front/rear of Term
OTHER SERVICES Exchange	Adequate on and off Base Bldg 1004 1100-1800 Tu-Sa, 1700 Su C-7-3596-4578 Also Fed Credit Union, Hair styles, Laundry/DryC in Bldg 1004
Medical	Bldg 405 24 hrs dly C-7-3596-4333/4571
Postal	Bldg 1058 0900-1500 M-F C-7-3596-5514
TML	Bldg 309 24 hrs dly C-7-3596-4604/4743, A-272-4604/4743 All Ranks. No DV/VIP facilities.
TRAVELERS AID ARC	Limited facilities. Full support Seoul area. Bldg 1051 0800-1600 M-F C-7-3596-4601/4680
Chaplain	Bldg 301 0800-1600 M-F C-7-3596-4300/4511
Lost/Found	Bldg 2858 0800-1600 M-Sa C-7-3596-5403
Sec Police	Bldg 4765 24 hrs dly C-7-3596-4291/4944
ATTRACTIONS	Yellow Sea

SCHEDULED FLIGHTS

DESTINATION	ROUTING	FREQ	EQ/CMTS
Kadena AB JA (DNA)	OKO-KUZ-TAE-OSN-DNA OKO-KUZ-TAE-OSN-KWJ-DNA OSN-KUZ-TAE-DNA OSN-KUZ-TAE-KHE-DNA	M,1/2/3/Th W Tu,2/4/Th,F 1/2/4/Th	C-141B/M C-141B/M C-130E/M C-130E/M
Kimhae Intl RK (KHE)	OSN-KUZ-TAE-KHE-DNA	1/2/4/Th	C-130E/M
Kwang Ju ROK AFB RK (KWJ)	OKO-KUZ-TAE-OSN-KWJ-DNA	W	C-141B/M
Osan AB RK (OSN)	OKO-KUZ-TAE-OSN-DNA DNA-TAE-KUZ-OSN OKO-KUZ-TAE-OSN-KWJ-DNA DNA-KWJ-KUZ-OSN-TAE-OKO DNA-KHE-TAE-KUZ-OSN DNA-KUZ-OSN-TAE-OKO	M,1/2/3/Th M,2/4/W,2/4/F W Tu 1/3/4/W,1/3/4/F Th,3/4/Sa	C-141B/M C-130E/M C-141B/M C-141B/M C-130E/M C-141B/M

KOREA (SOUTH)
Kunsan AB, Cont'd

Taegu AB RK (TAE)	OKO-KUZ-TAE-OSN-DNA DNA-KWJ-KUZ-OSN-TAE-OKO OKO-KUZ-TAE-OSN-KWJ-DNA OSN-KUZ-TAE-DNA DNA-KUZ-OSN-TAE-OKO OSN-KUZ-TAE-KHE-DNA DNA-KUZ-TAE-OKO	1/2/3/Th Tu Tu Tu,2/4/Th,F Th,3/4/Sa 4/Th 1/Sa	C-141B/M C-141B/M C-141B/M C-130E/M C-141B/M C-130E/M C-141B/M
Yokota AB JA (OKO)	DNA-KWJ-KUZ-OSN-TAE-OKO DNA-KUZ-OSN-TAE-OKO DNA-KUZ-TAE-OKO	Tu Th,3/4/Sa 1/Sa	C-141B/M C-141B/M C-141B/M

Osan Air Base (OSN)
611th MASS/TROP
APO San Francisco 96570-5000

Comm: (82) 332-284-113
ATVN: 284-4110

LOCATION: At Song Tan city, 6 mi W of Seoul-Pusan North/South Expressway. Directions to AB fm expressway are marked. NMC: Seoul RK, 38 mi N.

FACILITIES	LOCATION	HOURS	PHONE	COMMENTS
PAX TERM INFO	Bldg 884	0630-2100 dly	C-284-1854/6809, A-284-1854/6809	
	Fm main gate straight on Texas St to dead end at flight line, Pax Term L.			
Recording	Bldg 884	0630-2100 dly	C-284-1854/6809	
	AFKN Broadcast + next days schedule at 1800 and 2200 hrs dly			
Pax Svc Ofc	Bldg 884	0700-1700 M-F	C-284-5571/5563	Space-A desk
Pax Paging	Bldg 884	0630-2100 dly	C-284-1854/6809	Pax Svc NCO
PAX LOUNGES General	Bldg 884	No family lounge		
	Bldg 884	0630-2100 dly	C-284-1854/6809	A/C, Bag chk, Tel L&ATVN,TV,Rest-rms,O/S seats,Flt monitors. No smoking.
DV/VIP	Bldg 884	0630-2000 dly	C-284-1854/6809	A/C, Coffee/tea svc, Tel L&ATVN, TV, Rest-rms, Showers, O/S seats
Protocol Svc	Hq 314 AD	Duty hrs	C-284-4110	See Pax Svc NCO.
FOOD SERVICE Cafeteria	Many facilities on and off Base			
	Bldg 884	24 hrs dly	C-284-3137	Small facility
Dining Hall	Bldg 1343	0530-2200 dly	C-284-5632	Call for svc hrs.
NCO/CPO Club	Bldg 342	0600-2300 dly	C-284-6665	Call for svc hrs.
OFC Club	Bldg 782	0600-2200 dly	C-284-6749	Call for svc hrs.
Snack Bars	Bldg 948	24 hrs dly	C-284-4711	Rec Center
Vending	Bldg 848	24 hrs dly	C-284-3137	
TRANSPORTATION Air Tickets	Many facilities and means available			
	Bldg 884	1000-1700 M-F, Sa 1500	C-284-3043/3236	

KOREA (SOUTH)

Osan AB, Cont'd

Bus(Comm) (Shuttle)	Bldg 884 0700-2100 hrly OSN-Yongsan $1.50,Kunsan 1600 dly $3. Bldg 884 0630-0900 dly, 1600-1730 dly C-284-1843 OSN Base. 0600-2300 dly OSN main gate.
Car Rentals	Kimpo IAP arrival lobby. Major rent-a-car companies.
TAXI(Comm) (Gov)	Bldg 884 24 hrs dly C-284-4121/2/3 AAFES Bldg 1310 24 hrs dly C-284-5841 Duty Pax only
Trains	TMO Bldg Duty hrs C-284-4997
Parking	Bldg 884 24 hrs dly C-284-5515 Short term-24 hrs at Term; long term-72 hrs at main gate. Notify Sec Police.
OTHER SERVICES Exchange	Many on and off Base Bldg 920 1030-1730 Tu-Su C-284-3371
Bank/Exc	Bldg 952 1000-1630 M-Sa C-284-4185 AMEXCO
Hair Styles	Bldg 953 0900-1800 Tu-Su C-284-3133 Barber Bldg 957 1030-1700 Tu-Sa C-284-3285 Beauty
Laundry/DryC	Bldg 958 1030-1700 Tu-Su C-284-3144
Medical	Bldg 76B 24 hrs dly C-284-4732
Postal	Bldg 959 1000-1800 Tu-Sa C-284-4394/4658
TML	Bldg 771 24 hrs dly C-284-1844/4096, C-794-4448 Limited space on AB. See Yongsan (Seoul) C-7914-4448/5026.
TRAVELERS AID ARC	Many agencies available Bldg 944 0730-1630 M-F C-284-4140/1855
Chaplain	Bldg 779 24 hrs dly C-284-4184
Emerg Relief	Bldg 936 Duty hrs C-284-5826 AF Aid
Lost/Found	Bldg 884 0700-1700 dly C-284-4720 Pax Svc NCO
Sec Police	Bldg 363 24 hrs dly C-284-5515
USO	Yongsan 0800-2200 dly C-793-3478
ATTRACTIONS	DMZ, Korean customs & culture, Seoul, Inchon

SCHEDULED FLIGHTS

DESTINATION	ROUTING	FREQ	EQ/CMTS
Cheju Do IAP RD (CJU)	OSN-CJU	M	C-130E/M
Elmendorf AFB AK (EDF)	OSN-OKO-EDF-TCM OSN-OKO-EDF-SUU	W F	C-141B/C C-141B/C
Kadena AB JA (DNA)	OKO-KUZ-TAE-OSN-DNA OKO-KUZ-TAE-OSN-KWJ-DNA OSN-KUZ-TAE-DNA OKO-OSN-DNA	Su,Th Tu Tu,1/3/Th,F F	C-141B/M C-141B/M C-130E/M C-141B/M

KOREA (SOUTH)
Osan AB, Cont'd

Kimhae Intl RK (KHE)	OSN-KUZ-TAE-KHE-DNA	2/4/Th	C-130E/M
Kunsan AB RK (KUZ)	OSN-KUZ-TAE-DNA OSN-KUZ-TAE-KHE-DNA	Tu,1/3/Th,F 2/4/Th	C-130E/M C-130E/M
Kwang Ju ROK AFB RK (KWJ)	OKO-KUZ-TAE-OSN-KWJ-DNA	Tu	C-141B/M
Lambert St Louis Intl MO (STL)	OSN-OKO-OAK-STL	W,1/2/4/F	B747/P/CC
McChord AFB WA (TCM)	OSN-OKO-EDF-TCM	W	C-141B/C
Taegu AB RK (TAE)	DNA-KWJ-KUZ-OSN-TAE-OKO OSN-KUZ-TAE-DNA DNA-KUZ-OSN-TAE-OKO OSN-KUZ-TAE-KHE-DNA DNA-OSN-TAE-OKO	Tu Tu,1/3/Th,F Th,2/3/Sa 2/4/Th 1/Sa	C-141B/M C-130E/M C-141B/M C-130E/M C-141B/M
Travis AFB CA (SUU)	OSN-OKO-SUU OSN-OKO-SUU OSN-OKO-EDF-SUU	M Th F	C-141B/M C005A/C C-141B/C
Yokota AB JA (OKO)	DNA-OSN-OKO OSN-OKO-SUU DNA-KWJ-KUZ-OSN-TAE-OKO OSN-OKO OSN-OKO-EDF-TCM OSN-OKO-SFO-STL OSN-OKO-SUU DNA-KUZ-OSN-TAE-OKO OSN-OKO-EDF-SUU DNA-OSN-TAE-OKO	Su M Tu Tu W W,1/2/4/F Th Th,2/3/Sa F 1/2/Sa	C-141B/M C-141B/M C-141B/M C-130E/M C-141B/C B747/P/CC C005A/C C-141B/M C-141B/C C-141B/M

Taegu Air Base (TAE)
OL-C, 611 MASS/TROP
APO San Francisco 96213-5000

Comm: (82) 53-7814-1110
ATVN: 284-4110
Ask for Taegu AB

LOCATION: South central section of peninsula of South Korea, 80 mi NW of Pusan and 180 mi SE of Seoul on the Seoul-Pusan Expressway (toll road). NMC: Taegu, 4 mi SW.

FACILITIES	LOCATION	HOURS	PHONE	COMMENTS
PAX TERM INFO	Bldg S-118 0730-1630 dly C-7814-4424, A-266-4424 After entering main gate, along Perimeter Rd 1.5 mi L.			
Pax Svc Ofc	Bldg S-118 0730-1630 dly C-7814-4424/4313			
PAX LOUNGES General	General svc lounge only. DV/VIP, see Pax Svc NCO. Bldg S-118 0730-1630 dly C-7814-4313 Game rm, TV, Rest-rms, P/C seats			

KOREA (SOUTH)

Taegu AB, Cont'd

FOOD SERVICE			
Cafeteria	Adequate facilities on and off Base		
	Bldg B-555	0630-2245 dly	C-7814-4319/4875
Consol Club	Bldg B-555	0630-2245 dly	C-7814-4319/4875
Restaurants	Bldg B-490	1100-2400 M-Th, 1100-0100 F-Su	C-7814-4460/4309
TRANSPORTATION			
Air Tickets	Car rental service in Taegu		
	Camp Henry	1100-1800 Tu-Su	C-7618-7646
Bus Shuttle	Base motor pool	0700-1730 M-F	C-7814-4462
TAXI(Comm)	Bldg S-118	0730-2300 dly	C-7814-4544
(Gov)	Bldg S-118	0700-1730 dly	C-7814-4462
Trains	Main station 24 hrs dly	Blue (fast train) Pusan-Seoul	
Parking	Bldg 485	24 hrs dly	Across from Base gym
OTHER SERVICES			
Exchange	Full services at air Base and in Taegu area		
	Bldg 320	1000-1700 M-F	C-7814-4823
Bank/Exc	Camp Henry	0900-1600 M-F	C-7618-7469
Hair Styles	Bldg 453	0930-1800 M-F, 1600 Sa	C-7814-4823 Barber
	Camp Walker	0900-1700 M, Th, Sa	No phone Beauty
Laundry/DryC	Bldg 453	1000-1800 M-F, 1600 Sa	C-7814-4823
Medical	Bldg 449	24 hrs dly	C-7814-4789
Postal	Bldg 447	0730-1700 M-F, 1200 Sa	C-7814-4338
TML	Camp Walker	24 hrs dly C-7618-4562	All Ranks. No DV/VIP.
TRAVELERS AID			
ARC	Camp Henry	Duty hours	C-7618-7993
Chaplain	Bldg 440	0700-1730 M-F	C-7814-4800
Emerg Relief	Camp Henry	Duty hours	C-7618-7993
Lost/Found	Bldg 460	24 hrs dly	C-7814-4433
Sec Police	Bldg 460	24 hrs dly	C-7814-4433

SCHEDULED FLIGHTS

DESTINATION	ROUTING	FREQ	EQ/CMTS
Kadena AB JA (DNA)	OKO-KUZ-TAE-OSN-DNA	M,F	C-141B/M
	OSN-KUZ-TAE-DNA	1/2/4/Tu, 2/4/Th,1/2/4/Sa	C-130E/M
	OKO-KUZ-TAE-OSN-KWJ-DNA	W	C-141B/M
	OSN-KUZ-TAE-KHE-DNA	1/Th	C-130E/M
Kimhae Intl RK (KHE)	OSN-KUZ-TAE-KHE-DNA	Every other Th	C-130E/M

KOREA (SOUTH)
Taegu AB, Cont'd

Kunsan AB RK (KUZ)	DNA-TAE-KUZ-OSN	1/4/M,2/4/W, 1/2/4/F	C-130E/M
	DNA-KHE-TAE-KUZ-OSN	1/W	C-130E/M
Kwang Ju ROK AFB RK (KWJ)	OKO-KUZ-TAE-OSN-KWJ-DNA	Every other W, Th	C-141B/M
Osan AB RK (OSN)	OKO-KUZ-TAE-OSN-DNA DNA-TAE-KUZ-OSN	M,W,F 1/4/M,2/4/W 1/2/4/F	C-141B/M C-130E/M
	OKO-KUZ-TAE-OSN-KWJ-DNA DNA-KHE-TAE-OSN	W 1/W	C-141B/M C-130E/M
Yokota AB JA (OKO)	DNA-KUZ-OSN-TAE-OKO	Tu,Th,3/4/Sa	C-141B/M

Note: Seating is very limited on all C-130 missions out of Taegu.

LIBERIA

Monrovia Roberts International Airport (ROB)
USDAO, American Embassy
APO New York 09155-5000
Comm: (231)-222991-EX-240/1/2/3/4
ATVN: None

LOCATION: On the W coast of Africa. The airport is 27 mi NE of the city.
NMC: Monrovia, 27 mi SW.

FACILITIES	LOCATION	HOURS	PHONE	COMMENTS
PAX TERM INFO	Pax Term	During flt processing C-222991-EX-240/1/2/3/4 Contact Amer Embassy personnel for Pax processing. No US Base support facilities. Essential facilities of an IAP available		

SCHEDULED FLIGHTS

DESTINATION	ROUTING	FREQ	EQ/CMTS
Charleston AFB Intl SC (CHS)	FIH-ROB-LGS-CHS	2/Th,4/F	C005A/M
Kinshasa N'Djili Arpt ZA (FIH)	CHS-LGS-ROB-FIH	2/4/W	C005A/M
Lajes Fld PO LGS)	FIH-ROB-LGS-CHS	2/Th,4/F	C005A/M

NEW ZEALAND

Christchurch International Airport (CHC)
Detachment 2, 619 MASS
FPO San Francisco 96690-3000
Comm: (64) 03-583-079-EX-8062
ATVN: None

LOCATION: At Christchurch IAP. NMC: Christchurch, 5 mi SE.

NEW ZEALAND

Christchurch Intl Arpt, Cont'd

FACILITIES	LOCATION HOURS PHONE COMMENTS
PAX TERM INFO	Pax Term 0900-1600 M-F, 1000-1500 Sa, 1200-1800 Su C-03-583-079-EX-8062/3. After hrs and Sa-Su C-584-985. Sign-up at USAF hangar Gate 2 Orchard Rd. Counter-Gate 9 to process departure flights only.
Pax Svc Ofc	Gate 2 Orchard Rd Same as Pax Term C-03-583-079-EX-8061
Pax Paging	Gate 2 Orchard Rd or Gate 9 IAP Term C-03-583-079-EX-8061
PAX LOUNGES General	CHC IAP No DV/VIP or family lounges Pax Term 24 hrs dly A/C, Bag check/lockers, Game rm, TV, Tel L&LD, Rest-rms, O/S seats. Pax Term has spt fac: Bank, Restaurant, Caf, Rent-A-Car, Barber/Beauty, Book/Gift shops.
FOOD SERVICE Enl Club	US Navy Oct-Mar 0600-2400, Apr-Sept 1100-1300 C-03-583-079 Ask for EX. Only US fac (except FPO) avail to Space-A Pax.
TRANSPORTATION Bus(Comm)	Pax Term 0600-2200 dly CHC IAP to CHC and return
TAXI(Comm)	Pax Term 24 hrs dly C-03-795-795/799-799
OTHER SERVICES Postal	US Navy C-03-583-079 Letters & post cards ONLY
ATTRACTIONS	Christchurch, sheep ranches, thermal region

SCHEDULED FLIGHTS

DESTINATION	ROUTING	FREQ	EQ/CMTS
Alice Springs Arpt AU (ASP)	SBD-HIK-PPG-CHC-RCM-ASP	M	C-141B/C
Hickam AFB HI (HIK)	LEA-RCM-CHC-PPG-HIK-SBD	Sa	C-141B/C
Norton AFB CA (SBD)	LEA-RCM-CHC-PPG-HIK-SBD	Sa	C-141B/C
Pago Pago Intl AS (PPG)	LEA-RCM-CHC-PPG-HIK-SBD	Sa	C-141B/C
Richmond RAAFB AU (RCM)	SBD-HIK-PPG-CHC-RCM-ASP	M	C-141B/C

Note: If you are on the Space-A list for PPG, HIK, & SBD, call at 1400 local time on a Friday for seat availability and check-in instructions. For RCM & ASP seat availability & instructions, call at 1600 local time on Saturday.

NORWAY

Fornebu Airport (OSL)
7240th ABS/LGTR
APO New York 09085-5270

Comm: (47) 2-24-30-30
ATVN: None

LOCATION: Osterndalen 13, Osteras. Fm Oslo take 168 N for 7 mi. NMC: Oslo, 7 mi S.

FACILITIES	LOCATION	HOURS	PHONE	COMMENTS
PAX TERM INFO	Hangar 7240 ABS During flt processing C-24-30-30-EX-173/174 Joint use - US and Norway. Pax processed by USAF personnel.			
PAX LOUNGES	Hangar 7240 ABS As required C-24-30-30-EX-173/174 General & DV/VIP lounge. Bag chk, Cof/tea, Tel C, Rest-rms, P/C seats.			
OTHER SERVICES	All spt fac at comm arpt. Medical C-24-30-30-EX-168, Chaplain C-24-30-30, BX, and other US Base spt at Fornebu Arpt.			

SCHEDULED FLIGHTS

DESTINATION	ROUTING	FREQ	EQ/CMTS
Ramstein AB GE (RMS)	OSL-RMS	W	C-130E/C

UNSCHEDULED FLIGHTS

Flights to: RAF Mildenhall UK (MHZ); Ramstein AB GE (RMS); Rhein Main AB GE (FRF).

Note: Flights operate out of two airports, Gardermoen AB & Fornebu Airport. Sign up for Space-A at Aircraft Services Office in industrial area (see location above). Bus departs office for airport on the day of the flight. Call for destinations, routings, and schedules.

OMAN

Masirah Oman Air Force Base (MRH)
USDAO, AMEMB, PO Box 966
Muscat, Oman

Comm: 745-231/3 or 745-006
ATVN: None

LOCATION: On the gulf of Oman & Arabian Sea. 700 mi W of Karachi, Pakistan. NMC: Muscat OM, in the city.

FACILITIES	LOCATION	HOURS	PHONE	COMMENTS
PAX TERM INFO	Pax Term During flt processing C-745-1-231/3 Pax processed by Amer Embassy or contractor personnel. No US Base support facilities. Essential facilities of IAP avail.			

SCHEDULED FLIGHTS

DESTINATION	ROUTING	FREQ	EQ/CMTS
Diego Garcia Atoll IO (NKW)	NKW-MRH-NKW	Tu,Sa	C-141B/M

PANAMA

Howard Air Force Base (HOW)
1300th MAS/TROP
APO Miami 34001-5000

Comm: (507) 284-6110
ATVN: 285-6110

LOCATION: Adjacent to Thatcher Hwy(K-2) on the Pacific side of the Republic of Panama. RM: p-119, I/25. NMC: Panama City, 10 mi West.

FACILITIES	LOCATION	HOURS	PHONE	COMMENTS
PAX TERM INFO	Bldg 228 Main gate to 1st intersection. Terminal on right.	0500-2100 dly	C-284-4306/4857, A-284-3608/5758	
Recording	Bldg 228	0500-2100 dly	C-284-4306/3608	
Pax Svc Ofc	Bldg 228	0715-1615 dly	C-284-4306/5117	NCO on duty
Pax Paging	Bldg 228	0500-2100 dly	C-284-4306/3608	See Pax NCO.
PAX LOUNGES General	Bldg 228 Family Svc & Nursery on inbound side of Pax Term Bldg 228 A/C, Bag lockers, Rest-rms, O/S seats, TV	0500-2100 dly	C-284-4306/3608	
DV/VIP	Bldg 228 A/C, Separate read/write rms, O/S seats, TV.	0500-2100 dly	C-284-4306/3608	No staff.
Protocol Svc	Quarry Hts	Duty hrs	A-221-3456	C/S USSOUTHCOM
FOOD SERVICE Cafeteria	On Base facilities and off Base restaurants Bldg 709	0630-2130 dly	C-284-3927	AAFES,.25 mi fm Term
NCO/CPO Club	Bldg 710	0600-2300 dly	C-284-7189/2111	C/for svc hrs.
OFC Club	Bldg 113	0600-2300 dly	C-284-4105	Call for svc hrs.
Snack Bars	Bldg 5004	1200-1700 dly	C-284-3395	At Fort Kobbe/HOW
Vending	Bldg 228 Military public phones avail for Pax in Term (main lobby)	0500-2100 dly	C-284-4306	
TRANSPORTATION Air Tickets	Means and facilities available at HOW and Panama City, PN Albrook AFS	1000-1700 M-F	C-286-3180	SATO
Bus(Comm)	Bldg 228	0500-2400 dly		No shuttle bus/limo svc on HOW
Car Rentals	Bldg 228	0800-1700 dly	C-284-4931/3476	Also at AAFES
TAXI(Comm) (Gov)	Bldg 228 Bldg 6	24 hrs dly 24 hrs dly	C-80-52-5348/5677 C-284-5285	Exp on HOW Duty Pax only
Parking	Bldg 228 Short term-in front of Term; long term-across from Term.	24 hrs dly	C-284-3608	
OTHER SERVICES Exchange	Avail at HOW & other Mil Installations in Panama City area Bldg 707	1100-1800 M-Sa	C-284-3944/4731	Many Exc's in PN
Hair Styles	Bldg 707 Bldg 707	0800-1700 M-Sa 0900-1800 M-Sa	C-284-4880 C-284-3719	Barber Beauty
Laundry/DryC	Bldg 707	1000-1800 M-Sa	C-284-3182	C/for one-day svc.

PANAMA
Howard AFB, Cont'd

Medical	Bldg 192	24 hrs dly	C-284-3092, C-284-3562 Appoint
Postal	Bldg 711	0900-1600 M-F	C-284-6110 Call for svc hrs.
TML	Bldg 708 All Ranks.	24 hrs dly C-312-84-6411/5306, A-285-6411/5306 DV/VIP Bldg 119 C-EX-84-4601	
TRAVELERS AID ARC	Spt for HOW & other Pacific side Installations C-287-5261 Fort Clayton 0730-1600 M-F C-287-5647 O/hrs C-284-6110		
Chaplain	Bldg 500	Duty hrs	C-284-3220 O/hrs C-284-6110
Lost/Found	Bldg 228	0500-2100 dly	C-284-4306/3608 See Pax NCO.
Sec Police	Bldg 726	24 hrs dly	C-284-6110 Ask for desk Sgt.
USO	792X La Boca Road, Panama City PN C-52-5972/2617 C/for hrs.		
ATTRACTIONS	Panama Canal, Panama City, beaches		

SCHEDULED FLIGHTS

DESTINATION	ROUTING	FREQ	EQ/CMTS
Alex Hamilton VI (STX)	HOW-PAP-SDQ-NRR-STX	3/Tu	C-130E/C
Andrews AFB MD (ADW)	HOW-BDA-ADW-CHS	Th	C-141B/ME
A Merinobeni- tez CH (SCL)	HOW-BSB-RIO-BUE-SCL-LIM-HOW HOW-LIM-SCL-BUE-RIO-BSB-HOW	1/Tu 3/Tu	C-141B/M C-141B/M
A C Sandino Intl NI (MGA)	HOW-MGA	3/Th	C-130H/C
Belize Intl BZ (BZE)	HOW-BZE	4/W	C-130H/C
Bermuda NAS BM (BDA)	HOW-BDA-ADW-CHS	Th	C-141B/ME
Brasilia Arpt BR (BSB)	HOW-BSB-RIO-BUE-SCL-LIM-HOW HOW-LIM-SCL-BUE-RIO-BSB-HOW	1/Tu 3/Tu	C-141B/M C-141B/M
Carrasco Intl UG (MVD)	HOW-ASU-MVD-LPB-HOW HOW-LPB-MVD-ASU-HOW	2/W 4/W	C-141B/M C-141B/M
Charleston AFB Intl SC (CHS)	HOW-PLA-CHS HOW-PLA-CHS HOW-BDA-ADW-CHS HOW-CHS HOW-PLA-CHS	M M,W,F Th M,Th F	C-141B/C/CC C-100/C/CC C-141B/ME B727/P/CC C-141B/C
El Dorado Intl CL (BOG)	HOW-BOG	1/3/M	C-130H/C
Ezeiza AG (BUE)	HOW-BSB-RIO-BUE-SCL-LIM-HOW HOW-LIM-SCL-BUE-RIO-BSB-HOW	1/Tu 3/Tu	C-141B/M C-141B/M

PANAMA

Howard AFB, Cont'd

F Duvalier Intl HA (PAP)	HOW-PAP-SDQ-NRR-STX	3/Tu	C-130E/C
I Lopango Intl ES (SAL)	HOW-SAL	Tu	C-130H/C
J Chavez Intl PE (LIM)	HOW-BSB-RIO-BUE-SCL-LIM-HOW HOW-LIM-SCL-BUE-RIO-BSB-HOW	1/Tu 1/Tu	C-141B/M C-141B/M
J F Kennedy Intl BO (LPB)	HOW-ASU-MVD-LPB-HOW HOW-LPB-MVD-ASU-HOW	2/W 4/W	C-141B/M C-141B/M
Mariscal Sucre EC (UIO)	HOW-UIO	4/M	C-130H/C
Palmerola Arpt HO (PLA)	HOW-PLA-CHS HOW-PLA-CHS HOW-PLA-HOW	M,W,F M,F F	L-100/C C-141B/C C-130H/M
P Stroessner Arpt PG (ASU)	HOW-ASU-MVD-LPB-HOW HOW-LPB-MVD-ASU-HOW	2/W 4/W	C-141B/M C-141B/M
Rio de Janeiro BR (RIO)	HOW-BSB-RIO-BUE-SCL-LIM-HOW HOW-LIM-SCL-BUE-RIO-BSB-HOW	1/Tu 3/Tu	C-141B/M C-141B/M
Roosevelt Rds NAS PR (NRR)	HOW-PAP-SDQ-NRR-STX HOW-NRR	3/Tu Sa	C-130E/C C-141B/M
San Isidro AB DR (SDQ)	HOW-PAP-SDQ-NRR-STX	3/Tu	C-130E/C
Simon Bolivar Intl VE (MIQ)	HOW-MIQ	3/Th	C-130E/C
Toncontin Intl HO (TGU)	HOW-TGU HOW-TGU-PLA	1/W F	C-130H/M C-130H/M

UNSCHEDULED FLIGHTS

Flights to Kelley AFB TX (SKF) via C005/A aircraft, CONUS destinations via C-130A aircraft.

PHILIPPINES

Clark Air Base (CRK)
374th APS/TROP
APO San Francisco 96274-5000

Comm: (63) 55-110
ATVN: 822-1201

LOCATION: On the island of Luzon, adjacent to Angeles city. Entrance to AB is on Hwy 3. NMC: Manila RP, 50 mi SE.

FACILITIES	LOCATION	HOURS	PHONE	COMMENTS
PAX TERM INFO	Bldg 7549	24 hrs dly	C-46215/33491, A-894-6215/5177	
	Main gate W on Mitchell Hwy to R Wagner Ave, 2 mi to Term R.			
Recording	Bldg 7549	24 hrs dly	C-55177, A-893-3491/6215	

PHILIPPINES
Clark AB, Cont'd

Pax Svc Ofc	Bldg 7549	24 hrs dly	C-33255/6/7	NCO on duty
Pax Paging	Bldg 7549	24 hrs dly	C-55177	See Pax Svc NCO.
PAX LOUNGES General	Bldg 7549 Bldg 7549 Rest-rms, Showers, TV, P/C seats. Inbound & outbound lounges.	24 hrs dly 24 hrs dly	C-55177 C-46215	A/C, Bag chk/lks,
DV/VIP	Bldg 7549 A/C, Rest-rms, O/S seats.	24 hrs dly No attendant.	C-21111	Outbound only
Protocol Svc	Bldg 2122	Duty hrs	C-21288	O/hrs C-44176 13th AF
Family	Bldg 7549	24 hrs dly	A/C, O/S seats, Nursery	
FOOD SERVICE Cafeteria	Many facilities on and off Base Bldg 7549	24 hrs dly	C-41226	
Dining Hall	Bldg 6478	0500-1800 dly	C-45180	Call for svc hrs.
Enl Club	Bldg 5721	0700-2400 dly	C-22279	Call for svc hrs.
NCO/CPO Club	Bldg 5100	0530-2400 dly	C-22181	Call for svc hrs.
OFC Club	Bldg 1978	0700-2400 dly	C-21246	Call for svc hrs.
Restaurants	Bldg 5414	Colony House	C-41135	Call for svc hrs.
Snack Bars	Bldg 6307	0900-2400 dly	C-22177	Bowling alley
Vending	Bldg 7547	24 hrs dly	C-55177	
TRANSPORTATION Air Tickets	Many facilities and means on and off Base Bldg 6316	0700-1700 dly	C-24184	Silver Wing Svc Club
Bus(Comm) (Gov)	Bldg 7549 Bldg 7549 Bldg 7549 and Camp O'Donnell.	0430-2400 dly 0700-1500 dly Svc to Subic NB, Wallace AS, John Hay AB, Ask Pax svc for details.	On Base $.13 C-41272 CRK to MNL $5 one-way C-41274	
Car Rentals	Bldg 6124	0700-2100 dly	C-22228	MWR
Limo Service	Bldg 6128	0700-1600	C-47209/41116 MWR	
TAXI(Comm) (Gov)	Bldg 6444 Bldg 7549	24 hrs dly 24 hrs dly	C-33021 C-33756	Duty Pax only
Trains	Main gate	0810 F,Sa,Su to MNL		
Parking	Bldg 7549	24 hrs dly	C-33484	No restrictions
OTHER SERVICES Exchange	Many facilities and services on and off Base Bldg 5415 1000-1800 dly C-33015 Retirees call merchandise control C-55100/33407 for access			
Bank/Exc	Bldg 5402	0830-1500 M-F	C-22223	AMEXCO
Hair Styles	Bldg 7549 Bldg 5429	0600-2000 dly 0800-1800 dly	C-46215 C-42249	Barber Beauty Shop

PHILIPPINES

Clark AB, Cont'd

Laundry/DryC	Bldg 7394	0630-1700 M-Sa	C-46251	
Medical	Bldg 3700	24 hrs dly	C-23333	
Postal	Bldg 5427	0730-1600 M-F, Sa 1200	C-33777	
Tel Svc	Bldg 7549	24 hrs dly	Globe McKay C-41286, Overseas C-22231	
TML	Bldg 6048 24 hrs dly C-41174 All Ranks. Airmen Bldg 5187 C-55648. DV/VIP (06+) C-21288. VOQ C-55333.			
TRAVELERS AID ARC	Many agencies Bldg 2043	Duty hrs	C-33981	Other hrs C-61408
Chaplain	Bldg 5788	Duty hrs C-33687		Other hrs C-55110
Emerg Relief	Bldg 6003	0600-1500 M-F	C-33718	
Lost/Found	Bldg 7549	24 hrs dly	C-33255/6/7	See Pax Svc.
Sec Police	Bldg 7235	24 hrs dly	C-33484	Desk Sgt
USO	Roxas Blvd	0800-2400 dly	C-581-143	C/for activities.
ATTRACTIONS	Baguio City, Manila, sports, beaches			

SCHEDULED FLIGHTS

DESTINATION	ROUTING	FREQ	EQ/CMTS
Andersen AFB GU (UAM)	CRK-UAM CRK-UAM-HIK-SUU	Daily Tu,W,Th,Sa	C-141B/M C-141B/M
Cubi Point NAS RP (CUA)	CRK-CUA-DNA	Tu,Sa	C-141B/M
Diego Garcia Atoll IO (NKW)	CRK-NKW CRK-SGP-NKW CRK-VBU-NKW	Su,M,Tu,Th 1/2/4/Sa Tu,F 2/3/Sa	C-141B/M C-141B/M C-141B/M
Don Muang TH (BKK)	CRK-BKK	Th,Sa	C-130E/M
Halim Perdana-kusuma IE(DJK)	CRK-DJK	1/3/Tu	C-130E/M
Hickam AFB HI (HIK)	CRK-UAM-HIK-SUU	W,Sa	C-141B/ME
Kadena AB JA (DNA)	CRK-DNA-ANC-LAX-STL CRK-CUA-DNA CRK-DNA-ANC-LAX	1/2/4/F Tu,Sa 1/2/4/F	B747/P/CC C-141B/M B747/P/CC
Los Angeles Intl CA (LAX)	CRK-DNA-ANC-LAX	1/2/4/F	B747/P/CC

PHILIPPINES
Clark AB, Cont'd

RSAF Paya Lebar SG (SGP)	CRK-SGP-NKW	M,Th	C-141B/M
Lambert St Louis Intl MO (STL)	CRK-DNA-ANC-LAX-STL	1/2/4/Tu	B747/P/CC
Travis AFB CA (SUU)	CRK-UAM-HIK-SUU	W,Sa	C-141B/ME
U-Tapao RTN TH (VBU)	CRK-VBU-NKW	2/3/Sa	C-141B/M

Cubi Point Naval Air Station (CUA)
Air Terminal Div, Box 21
FPO San Francisco 96654-1210

Comm: (63) 89-885-3211
ATVN: 882-3011

LOCATION: On the SW side of Luzon Island, on Subic Bay. Manila is 50 mi SE and Clark Air Base is 25 mi NE. NMC: Olongapo City, outside main gate.

FACILITIES	LOCATION	HOURS	PHONE	COMMENTS
PAX TERM INFO	Bldg 8052	24 hrs dly	C-885-3441, A-882-3441	
	From main gate of Subic Bay NS fol signs to NAS on Rizal Hwy to R on Argonaut Hwy to Pax Term on R. Gate to Term is 5 mi.			
Pax Svc Ofc	Bldg 8052	0800-1700 M-F	C-885-3441/3211	NCO at Pax Svc
Pax Paging	Bldg 8052	24 hrs dly	C-885-3441/3749	See Pax Svc.
PAX LOUNGES General	No family lounge or nursery			
	Bldg 8052	24 hrs dly	C-885-3441/3749	
	A/C,Bag chk,Game rm,Read/write rm,Tel L,LD&A,TV,P/C&O/S seats			
DV/VIP	Ops Bldg #4	24 hrs dly	C-885-3175/3558	
	A/C, Rest-rms, Showers, O/S seats			
Protocol Svc	Ops Bldg	24 hrs dly	C-885-3175	See Pax Svc OIC.
FOOD SERVICE Cafeteria	Many on NAS, Subic Bay NS, and Olongapo City			
	Bldg 8050	24 hrs dly	C-885-4276	
Dining Hall	NAS #9	0600-2400 dly	C-885-4101	Call for svc hrs.
Enl Club	NAS "E"	0900-0100 dly	C-885-4101	Call for svc hrs.
NCO/CPO Club	NAS "J"	0900-0200 dly	C-885-4107	Call for svc hrs.
OFC Club	NAS "H"	0900-0100 dly	C-885-4197	Call for svc hrs.
Restaurants	NS #2	1100-2100 M-F, 0600-2100 Sa-Su	C-882-9268	
Snack Bars	NAS #12	1000-1900 dly	C-885-4202	
Vending	Bldg 8052	24 hrs dly	C-885-4132	
TRANSPORTATION Air Tickets	NS #18	0800-1700 M-F, 1200 Sa	C-884-85/8663 SATO	

PHILIPPINES

Cubi Point NAS, Cont'd

Bus(Comm)	Bldg 8052	0600-2400 dly	C-855-3891	NAS&NS/Violago Bus Svc
(Shuttle)	Bldg 8052	0515-2215 dly	C-882-8294	NAS & NS-San Miguel
Car Rentals	NAS #12	0900-1700 M-Sa, 1000-1600 Su	C-884-8716	
TAXI(Comm)	Bldg 8052	24 hrs dly	C-882-8294	Casa de Meubles
Parking	No parking available.	Pick-up and discharge Pax only.		
OTHER SERVICES Exchange	Most services at NAS & NS or Clark Air Base NAS #12 1000-1700 M-Sa, 1600 Su C-885-4222			
Bank/Exc	NAS #12	0900-1630 M-F, 1530 Sa	C-885-4280	NFCU
Hair Styles	NAS #12	0830-1900 M-F, 1600 Sa/Su 0830-1700 M-Sa C-885-3576	C-885-4254 Barber Beauty	
Laundry/DryC	Bldg 8348	0700-1700 M-Sa, 1500 Su	C-885-4137/4112	
Medical	NS Hospital	24 hrs dly	C-885-118	
Postal	NS	0900-1600 M-F, 1200 Sa	C-884-6496	
Valet/Dry C	NAS	1000-1900 M-Sa	C-885-4206	
TML	NS #11 24 hrs dly C-884-8500/8845/8990 Navy Lodge Ofc C-884-9216/9585,Enl 884-9198,DV/VIP (05+) C-884-9813/9821			
TRAVELERS AID ARC	Many services at NS, NAS, and Clark Air Base NS "B" Duty hours C-884-3822			
Chaplain	NS "D"	Duty hours	C-885-3219	
Emerg Relief	NS "Q"	Duty hours	C-884-3822	Navy Relief
Lost/Found	Bldg 8052	24 hrs dly	C-885-3441	
Sec Police	Main Gate	24 hrs dly	C-885-3447	
USO	NS Call for hrs. C-884-8157/8209 Phil-Am Cultural Bldg			
ATTRACTIONS	Grande Island Rec Area, Camp John Hay AFRC, Manila			

SCHEDULED FLIGHTS

DESTINATION	ROUTING	FREQ	EQ/CMTS
Clark AB RP (CRK)	DNA-CUA-CRK CUA-CRK CUA-CRK	M,F M,W,1/2/4/Th F	C-141B/M C-141B/M C-141B/C
Kadena AB JA (DNA)	CRK-CUA-DNA	Tu,Sa	C-141B/M
Travis AFB CA (SUU)	CUA-OKO-SUU	1/3/Sa	C005A/C
Yokota AB JA (OKO)	CUA-OKO-SUU	1/3/Sa	C005A/C

PHILIPPINES
Cubi Point NAS, Cont'd

UNSCHEDULED FLIGHTS

Flights to: Andersen AFB GU (UAM); Clark AB RP (CRK) (C-12A/P aircraft); Diego Garcia Atoll IO (NKW); Hickam AFB HI (HIK); Kadena AB JA (DNA); Manila IAP RP (MNL) (C-12A/P aircraft); Travis AFB CA (SUU); and Yokota AB JA (OKO).

PORTUGAL

Lajes Field (Azores) (LGS)
1605th MASS/TROP
APO New York 09406-5000

Comm: (351) 95-52101
ATVN: 723-1410

LOCATION: On Terceira Island (Azores PO) 20 mi L & 12 mi W. Lajes Fld is 2 mi W of Praia da Vitoria PO, on Mason Hwy. NMC: Lisbon, 850 mi E.

FACILITIES	LOCATION	HOURS	PHONE	COMMENTS
PAX TERM INFO	Bldg T-612	0800-1700 M,W,F,Sa,Su 0500-1700 Tu,Th Other hrs as required C-95-52101-EX-23227/8, A-723-1401-EX-23227/8 Fm main gate straight for .5 mi. Pax Term on R.		
Pax Svc Ofc	Bldg T-612 A-723-1410-EX-23227	0745-1700 dly	C-95-52101-EX-23227, Located off Bldg T-715	
Pax Paging	Bldg T-612 A-723-1410-EX-23227	0745-1700 dly	C-95-52101-EX-23227,	
PAX LOUNGES General	Bldg T-612 Bldg T-612	DV/VIP lounge under construction 0800-1700 dly C-95-52101-EX-23227/8 1st floor. Tel L&ATVN, TV, Rest-rms, P/C seats.		
Protocol Svc	Base Ops	24 hrs dly	C-95-52101-EX-6201 (06+) MAC	
Family	Bldg T-612	0800-1700 dly	C-95-52101-EX-23227/8 L inside main door to R corner. Same fac as above + Nursery	
FOOD SERVICE Cafeteria	Many facilities on and off Base Bldg T-319 0700-2300 dly C-95-52101-22211			
Dining Hall	Bldg T-415	0600-1800 dly	C-95-52101-4156	
Enl Club	Bldg T-112	0630-2300 dly	C-95-52101-23265	
NCO/CPO Club	Bldg T-112	0630-2300 dly	C-95-52101-23265/23202	
OFC Club	Bldg T-121	0630-2300 dly	C-95-52101-23195/23100	
Snack Bars	Bldg T-629	0800-2300 dly	C-95-52101-2114 Roller rink	
Vending	Bldg T-612	0800-1700	C-95-52101-EX-23227	
TRANSPORTATION Air Tickets	Many facilities and means on and off Base C-Term 24 hrs dly C-95-52101-23295-TAP, C-95-52101-22189-SATO			
Bus (Comm) (Shuttle)	Bldg T-612 Bldg T-612	0600-2300 dly-every hr 0700-1730 dly-every .5 hr/Base	C-95-52101-23227 C-95-52101-23227	
Car Rentals	Comm Term	24 hrs dly	C-95-52373/52305 AcorAuto	

PORTUGAL

Lajes Fld, Cont'd

TAXI(Comm) (Gov)	Bldg T-612 24 hrs dly Call operator-ask for taxi or 3288. Bldg T-220 24 hrs dly C-95-52101-23151 Duty Pax only
Parking	Bldg T-612 24 hrs dly Short term & long term. No restrictions.
OTHER SERVICES Exchange	Many facilities and services on and off Base Bldg T-323 1000-1800 M-Sa C-95-52101-EX-23288/21290
Bank/Exc	Near Bldg T-612 Portugal banks 0830-1445 M-F & NCO/O'clubs
Hair Styles	Bldg T-121 0800-1700 Tu-Sa C-95-52101-21121 Barber Bldg T-307 0800-1700 Tu-Sa C-95-52101-22166 Beauty
Laundry/DryC	Bldg T-331 0800-1700 M-Sa C-95-52101-7230
Medical	Bldg T-241 24 hrs dly C-95-52101-23237
Postal	Bldg T-324 0800-1700 M-F C-95-52101-6173
WIRE	PO Term 0900-1730 M-F
TML	Bldg T-166 24 hrs dly C-95-52101-5178/6176 DV/VIP C-95-52101-operator
TRAVELERS AID ARC	Facilities and services on and off Base Bldg T-615 0800-1600 M-F C-95-52101-3263 Other hrs-oper
Chaplain	Bldg T-305 0800-1700 M-F C-95-52101-4211 Other hrs-oper
Lost/Found	Bldg T-815 24 hrs dly C-95-52101-23222
Sec Police	Bldg T-815 24 hrs dly C-95-52101-23222 Desk Sgt
ATTRACTIONS	Bull fights, caves, cliffs. CAUTION: DO NOT export scrimshaw (whale ivory) to USA.

SCHEDULED FLIGHTS

DESTINATION	ROUTING	FREQ	EQ/CMTS
Andrews AFB MD (ADW)	KEF-LGS-ADW-WRI	Sa	C-141B/M
Athinai Arpt GR (ATH)	WRI-LGS-FRF-TOJ-ATH LGS-FRF-ATH-SIZ-ATH WRI-LGS-FRF-TOJ-SIZ-ATH-ESB-ADA WRI-LGS-FRF-TOJ-SIZ-ATH-IGL-ADA	M M 1/2/3/W Sa	C-141B/M C-141B/M C-141B/M C-141B/M
Charleston AFB Intl SC (CHS)	FIH-ROB-LGS-CHS	2/Th,4/F	C-141B/M
Cigli TAB TU (IGL)	WRI-LGS-FRF-TOJ-SIZ-ATH-IGL-ADA	Sa	C-141B/M
Esenboga Arpt TU (ESB)	WRI-LGS-FRF-TOJ-SIZ-ATH-ESB-ADA	1/2/3/W	C-141B/M

PORTUGAL
Lajes Fld, Cont'd

Incirlik Arpt TU (ADA)	WRI-LGS-FRF-TOJ-SIZ-ATH-ESB-ADA WRI-LGS-FRF-TOJ-SIZ-ATH-IGL-ADA	1/2/3/W SA	C-141B/M C-141B/M
Kinshasa N'Djili Arpt ZA (FIH)	CHS-LGS-ROB-FIH	2/4/M	C-141B/M
McGuire AFB NJ (WRI)	ADA-FRF-LGS-WRI TOJ-LGS-WRI TOJ-LGS-WRI FRF-LGS-WRI LGS-WRI ADA-FRF-LGS-WRI LGS-WRI KEF-LGS-ADW-WRI	Su,Tu,Th 1/Tu 3/Tu W W 1/2/3/Th 2/F Sa	C-141B/M C-130H/C C-130B/M C-141B/M C-141B/C C-141B/M C-130E/C C-141B/M
Monrovia Roberts Intl LI (ROB)	CHS-LGS-ROB-FIH	2/3/Tu	C-141B/C
Rhein Main AB GE (FRF)	WRI-LGS-FRF-TOJ-ATH LGS-FRF-ATH-SIZ-ATH WRI-LGS-FRF WRI-LGS-FRF-TOJ-SIZ-ATH-ESB-ADA WRI-LGS-FRF-TOJ-SIZ-ATH-IGL-ADA	M M Tu,W,Th,Sa 1/2/3/W Sa	C-141B/M C-141B/M C-141B/M C-141B/M C-141B/M
Sigonella Arpt IT (SIZ)	LGS-FRF-ATH-SIZ-ATH WRI-LGS-FRF-TOJ-SIZ-ATH-ESB-ADA WRI-LGS-FRF-TOJ-SIZ-ATH-IGL-ADA	M 1/2/3/W Sa	C-141B/M C-141B/M C-141B/M
Torrejon de Ardoz AB SP (TOJ)	WRI-LGS-TOJ WRI-LGS-TOJ WRI-LGS-FRF-TOJ-ATH WRI-LGS-FRF-TOJ-SIZ-ATH-ESB-ADA WRI-LGS-FRF-TOJ-SIZ-ATH-IGL-ADA	1/Su 2/Su M 1/2/3/W Sa	C-130H/C C-130B/M C-141B/M C-141B/M C-141B/M

SAUDI ARABIA

Dhahran International Airport (DHA)
Det 2, 322nd ALD
APO New York 09616-5000

Comm: (966) 3-879-2281-
EX-1337/1338
ATVN: 550-1311-EX-1337/1338

LOCATION: On the Persian Gulf near the island of Bahrain. Arpt is 5 mi W of city. NMC: Dhahran, 5 mi E.

SAUDI ARABIA

Dhahran Intl Arpt, Cont'd

FACILITIES	LOCATION HOURS PHONE COMMENTS
PAX TERM INFO	Pax Term During flt processing C-891-5678 Processing at IAP. IAP has essential services. Very limited US facilities available. Access limited. See appendix for personal entry requirements.
OTHER SERVICES	TML C-EX-5136, ARC C-EX-7241, Sec Police C-EX-7121

SCHEDULED FLIGHTS

DESTINATION	ROUTING	FREQ	EQ/CMTS
Athinai Arpt GR (ATH)	DHA-ATH-FRF	Every other Th	C-130E/C
Jeddah Airfld SA (JED)	DHA-JED	3 ea week	C-141B/C
Ramstein AB GE (RMS)	DHA-RMS-DOV	Su	C-141B/C
Rhein Main AB GE (FRF)	DHA-ATH-FRF	Every other Th	C-130E/C

Jeddah Airfield (JED)
OL-H, 322nd ALD
APO New York 09697-5000

Comm: (966) 2-644-7368
ATVN: 550-1311 Ask for 021-2239.

LOCATION: On the Red Sea. Mecca is 50 mi E. Airport is 5 mi E of city.
NMC: Jeddah, 5 mi W.

FACILITIES	LOCATION HOURS PHONE COMMENTS
PAX TERM INFO	Pax Term During flt processing C-644-7368 Pax processed at arpt. Essential support services at arpt. No US facilities available. Access limited. See appendix for personnel entry requirements.

UNSCHEDULED FLIGHTS

International flights no longer operate out of Jeddah Airfield. Call for destinations, routings, and schedules of other types of flights.

SINGAPORE

RSAF Paya Lebar (SGP)
MAC Terminal Office
FPO San Francisco 96699-5000

Comm: (65) 280-0624
ATVN: None

LOCATION: Tip of Malay Peninsula. Off Arpt Rd. NMC: Singapore SG, 5 mi SW.

FACILITIES	LOCATION	HOURS	PHONE	COMMENTS
PAX TERM INFO	Bldg 30	0800-1600 M-F	C-280-0624	MAC Term is off Arpt Rd on Paya Lebar Rd. On Arpt Rd, R at AMC sign to guard post, Terminal next to guard post. Limited US Base fac. No photos at RSAF.
Pax Svc Ofc	Bldg 30	0800-1600 M-F	C-280-0624	
PAX LOUNGES General	One consolidated lounge Bldg 47 A/C, Bag check, Tel L, Rest-rms, P/C seats	0800-1600 M-F	C-280-0624	
Protocol Svc	USDAO	0800-1600 M-F	C-338-0251	
FOOD SERVICE Cafeteria	Limited Arpt Rd	0800-1630 M-F		Breakfast, fast food
TRANSPORTATION TAXI(Comm)	Arpt Rd	24 hrs dly		SGP-Singapore $5 US
OTHER SERVICES Medical	Limited at SGP. Many in Singapore. Amer Embassy 30 Hill St	24 hrs dly	C-338-0251	Very limited
Postal	Amer Embassy 30 Hill St	0800-1600 M-F	C-338-0251	AD only
TRAVELERS AID Emerg Relief	Consulate sec Amer Embassy 30 Hill St	0730-1615 M-F	C-338-0251	
Sec Police	Bldg 30	24 hrs dly	C-280-0624	

SCHEDULED FLIGHTS

DESTINATION	ROUTING	FREQ	EQ/CMTS
Clark AB RP (CRK)	NKW-SGP-CRK	W	C-141B/M
Diego Garcia Atoll IO (NKW)	CRK-SGP-NKW	Tu,F	C-141B/M

SOUTH AFRICA

Jan Smuts Airport
(Johannesburg) (JNB)

USDAO Pretoria, State Dept Pouch Rm
Washington, DC 20520-5000

Comm: (27) 12-28-4266-EX-251
      Ask for USDAO Rep.
      (27) 12-65346 US Tracking
      Station Pretoria
ATVN: None

LOCATION: In NE South Africa, 300 air mi fm Indian Ocean. Pretoria is 30 mi NE. NMC: Johannesburg, 14 mi SW.

FACILITIES	LOCATION	HOURS	PHONE	COMMENTS
PAX TERM INFO	IAP Lower level	24 hrs dly	C-28-975-3170	Flights met by PAA contractor personnel, directions & assistance provided. Full facilities of an IAP. After hrs, call PAA Sr Rep C-28-73-2740. No US mil fac avail. Access limited. See appendix for personnel entry requirements.
PAX LOUNGES General	DV/VIP facilities for Intl Pax only. Not for mil visitors. IAP Lower level 24 hrs dly C-28-975-3170 A/C, Bag check/lockers, Tel L&LD, Rest-rms, P/C seats			
Family	IAP Upper level	24 hrs dly	C-28-975-3170	Same as Gen Pax
TRANSPORTATION Bus(Comm)	IAP Domestic arrivals 0615-2400 dly Johannesburg, 30 min and $1.35 US. Pretoria, 45 min and $2.00 US.			
Car Rentals	IAP	0600-2300 dly	Hertz=C-970-1363, Avis=C-975-3354	
TAXI(Comm)	IAP	24 hrs dly	Metered, 1-4 persons Johannesburg $15 US	
Parking	IAP	24 hrs dly		Underground level
OTHER SERVICES Bank/Exc	IAP Lower level	24 hrs dly		Two banks in Terminal
Medical	IAP	24 hrs	C-975-3170	
TRAVELERS AID Sec Police	South Africa's veterans' organization, "MOTHS", welcomes US veterans in Johannesburg. Call C-11-834-1681. IAP 24 hrs dly Police desk			
ATTRACTIONS	Kruger Natl Park, African wildlife & "Blue Train," transcontinental fm Johannesburg to Capetown, 900 mi.			

UNSCHEDULED FLIGHTS

U.S. Embassy in Pretoria operates C-12A/P aircraft. Space-A possible. Call USDAO C-28-4266-EX-251 for information. NOTE: the round-trip flight from Patrick AFB to Coolidge Arpt to Ascension Aux AF to Jan Smuts has been indefinitely cancelled. Updated information about flights to and from Jan Smuts will be published in Military Living's R&R report as it becomes available.

SPAIN

Rota Naval Air Station (RTA)
Air Term Dept, Box 29
FPO New York 09540-5000

Comm: (34) 56-86-4580
EX-2411/2171
ATVN: 727-2411/2171

LOCATION: On Spain's S Atlantic Coast. Accessible from E-25 S and SP-342 W.
HE: map p-61, C-5. **NMC:** Cadiz, 22 miles S.

FACILITIES	LOCATION	HOURS	PHONE	COMMENTS
PAX TERM INFO	Bldg 2 main floor 24 hrs dly C-86-4580-EX-2411, A-727-2411 Fm main gate, straight on 3rd St for 6 blks to Pax Term on R. Get 2 day Base pass fm Pax rep. Ask about longer pass if req.			
Pax Svc Ofc	Bldg 2 (top floor)	0800-1700 M-F Secretary on duty	C-86-4580-EX-2803, A-727-2803	
Pax Paging	Bldg 2	24 hrs dly	C-86-4560-EX-2411	See Pax rep.
PAX LOUNGES General	In Pax Term Bldg 2 main floor. No family lounge. Bldg 2 24 hrs dly C-86-4580-EX-2411, A-727-2411 A/C,Bag chk/lks,Game rm,Tel L&A,TV,Rest-rm,P/C seats,Nursery			
DV/VIP	Bldg 2 24 hrs dly C-86-4560-EX-2411/2803, A-727-2411 (06+) Bag chk/lks,Tel L,TV,Rest-rms,O/S seats. Key at Pax counter.			
Protocol Svc	Bldg 1	0800-1700 M-F	C-86-4560-EX-2744, A-727-2744 (06+)	
FOOD SERVICE Cafeteria	Many facilities on and off Base Bldg 2 24 hrs dly C-86-4580-EX-2331 "Teakwood" (closed 1400-1600 dly)			
Dining Hall	Bldg 38	0600-1830 dly	C-86-4580-EX-2317	C/for svc hrs.
Enl Club	Bldg 1631	1100-2200 dly	C-86-4580-EX-2591	"Windjam'r"
NCO/CPO Club	Bldg 49	1100-2200 dly	C-86-4580-EX-2433	(E6+) C/f svc hrs.
OFC Club	Bldg 50	0600-2230 dly	C-86-4580-EX-2509	Call for svc hrs.
Snack Bars	Bldg 593 1100-2000 dly C-86-4580-EX-5137 Pool hous'g drive-in. Bldg 321 1100-2300 dly C-86-4580-EX-7213 Pizza Villa.			
Vending	Bldg 2	24 hrs dly	C-86-4580-EX-2411	Lounge area
TRANSPORTATION Air Tickets	Many means and facilities on and off Base Bldg 1 24 hrs dly C-86-4580-EX-2913 SATO Bldg 2 0900-1700 M-F C-86-4580-EX-2429 Marsans Tvl Agency			
Bus(Comm) (Shuttle)	Bldg 197 Bldg 197	0645-2030 M-F 0600-1800 M-F	C-86-4580-EX-2720 C-86-4580-EX-2720	C/for sched. (every .5 hr)

SPAIN

Rota NAS, Cont'd

Car Rentals	Bldg 2 0900-1700 M-F, 1300 Sa C-86-4580-EX-2675 BX Major rental car companies in Rota
TAXI(Comm) (Gov)	Front m/gate 24 hrs dly C-86-4580-EX-2929 RTA-Rota 30 P Bldg 149 0600-2400 dly C-86-4580-EX-2403 Duty Pax only
Trains	Puerto 24 hrs dly Puerto-Sevilla-Madrid Express & Rapid
Parking	Bldg 2 24 hrs dly C-86-4580-EX-2688 Long & short term avail
OTHER SERVICES Exchange	Many facilities on and off Base Bldg 40 1000-1700 Tu-F, 1200-1500 Sa-Su Retirees, DAVs,& unaccompanied dep are auth use only of PO, Banks, Clubs, Hospital, Air Terminal, & Rec fac due to SOFA.
Bank/Exc	Bldg 1 0900-1500 M-F, 0900-1200 Sa C-86-4580-EX-2913 Comm Bank 0830-1400 M-F, 0900-1200 Sa C-86-4580-EX-2827 Money exchange also available at clubs and NEX
Hair Styles	Bldg 40 0900-1700 Tu-Su C-86-4580-EX-2507 Barber Bldg 134 0900-1700 Tu-Su C-86-4580-EX-4034 Beauty
Laundry/DryC	Bldg 41 0800-1700 M-F, 0900-1700 Sa C-86-4580-EX-2559
Medical	Bldg 36 & 52 24 hrs dly C-86-4580-EX-2225/2303
Postal	Bldg 210 0900-1700 M-F C-86-4580-EX-2518
TML	Bldg 1610 24 hrs dly C-86-4580-EX-2567/8 All Ranks. Bldg 1674 Navy lodge C-86-4580-EX-2643. DV/VIP C-86-4580-EX-2744.
TRAVELERS AID ARC	Many agencies on Base Bldg 29 0800-1630 M-F C-86-4580-EX-2333
Chaplain	Bldg 42 0800-1700 M-F, 0900-1400 Su C-86-4580-EX-2161
Emerg Relief	Bldg 268 1000-1500 M-F C-86-4580-EX-2805
Lost/Found	Bldg 2 0600-1400 M-F C-86-4580-EX-2816 O/hrs EX-2411
Sec Police	Bldg 207 24 hrs dly C-86-4580-EX-2688/2000 Desk Sgt
USO	Bldg 48 1100-1400 dly C-86-4580-EX-7105 Pax Term AR area
ATTRACTIONS	Andalusia area, sherry, flamenco dancing, bull fighting, and Don Quixote

SCHEDULED FLIGHTS

DESTINATION	ROUTING	FREQ	EQ/CMTS
Bahrain Intl BA (BAH)	NGU-RTA-BHA NGU-RTA-BAH	Tu Sa	C-141B/C C005A/M

SPAIN
Rota NAS, Cont'd

Capodichino Arpt IT (NAP)	RTA-SIZ-NAP PHL-RTA-NAP-SIZ	M,W,F,Sa Th	C-141B/M DC-863/P/CC
Dover AFB DE (DOV)	BAH-RTA-DOV	Sa,Su	C005A/M
Norfolk NAS VA (NGU)	RTA-NGU BAH-RTA-NGU	Su,M,W,F W	C-141B/M C-141B/C
Philadelphia Intl PA (PHL)	SIZ-RTA-PHL NAP-SIZ-RTA-PHL	Tu F	DC-863/P/CC L-1011/P/CC
Ramstein AB GE (RMS)	RTA-TOJ-RMS-FRF	Tu	C009A/ME
Rhein Main AB GE (FRF)	RTA-TOJ-RMS-FRF RTA-ZAZ-FRF	Tu F	C009A/ME C009A/ME
Sigonella Arpt IT (SIZ)	RTA-SIZ-NAP NGU-RTA-SIZ PHL-RTA-NAP-SIZ	M,W,F,Sa Tu W	C-141B/M C-141B/M L-1011/P/CC
Torrejon de Ardoz AB SP (TOJ)	RTA-TOJ-RMS-FRF RTA-TOJ RTA-TOJ RTA-TOJ	Tu 1/Tu 3/Tu 2/Th,4/F	C009A/ME C-130H/C C-130B/C C-130E/C
Zaragoza AB SP (ZAZ)	RTA-ZAZ-FRF	F	C009A/ME

Torrejon de Ardoz Air Base (TOJ)
625th MASS/TROP
APO New York 09283-5000

Comm: (34) 1-205-7777
ATVN: 723-1110

LOCATION: Take Hwy N-11(A2) NE toward Zaragoza SP, pass the IAP at Barajas on the L. AB is on L and clearly marked. HE map: p-59, D/2. NMC: Madrid, 11 miles SW.

FACILITIES	LOCATION	HOURS	PHONE	COMMENTS
PAX TERM INFO	Bldg 403	24 hrs dly	C-205-1854/7601, A-723-1854/7601 Main gate to L on 2nd St to Pax Term at flt line. Obtain gate pass and "Entrada Visa" letter fm MAX Pax Svc before leaving Base or re-entry will be denied.	
Recording	Bldg 403	24 hrs dly	C-205-7664/5/6, A-723-7664/5/6	
Pax Svc Ofc	Bldg 403	0800-1700 dly	C-205-1854/7601 NCO on duty	
Pax Paging	Bldg 403	24 hrs dly	C-205-1854/7601 See Pax Svc NCO.	
PAX LOUNGES General	No family or DV/VIP lounges Bldg 403 24 hrs dly C-205-1854/7601 A/C, Bag check, Rest-rms, P/C seats			
Protocol Svc	Bldg 105	Duty hrs	C-205-7432	Hq 16th AF USAFE

SPAIN

Torrejon de Ardoz AB, Cont'd

FOOD SERVICE	Many Facilites on and off Base		
Cafeteria	Bldg 304	1530-2100 M-F, 1200-2200 Sa-Su	C-650-0643
Dining Hall	Bldg 205	0600-0100 dly	C-205-7394/3317 C/for svc hrs.
NCO/CPO Club	Bldg 116	0630-0100 dly	C-205-5165/6386 C/for svc hrs.
OFC Club	Bldg 122	0630-2400 dly	C-205-5104/6526 C/for svc hrs.
Restaurants	Bldg 237	1800-0100 dly	C-205-7777 ROAKS Club
Snack Bars	Bldg 236	1100-2330 dly	C-205-7340 Rec Center
Vending	Bldg 403	24 hrs dly	C-205-1854/7601 Depart lounge
TRANSPORTATION	Many facilities and means available		
Air Tickets	Bldg 236	0930-1700 M-F, 1230 Sa	C-250-7199 Davis Travel
Bus(Gov)	Bldg 403	M-F	C-205-1854/7601 TOJ to ZAZ
(Shuttle)	Bldg 403	0710-1810 dly	C-250-7209/7439 3 Rts on TOJ
Car Rentals	Bldg 406	0800-2300 M-Sa	C-250-7725
TAXI(Gov)	Bldg 406	0800-2300 M-Sa	C-250-1843/7280 Duty Pax only
Parking	Bldg 403	24 hrs dly	C-250-5400 Check with SP.
OTHER SERVICES	Full support services on Base and in Madrid SP		
Exchange	Bldg 110	1000-1800 Tu-Sa	C-250-7777-EX-462
Bank/Exc	Bldg 300	0900-1400 M-Sa	C-205-7777-EX-719
Hair Styles	Bldg 110	0900-1700 M-Sa	C-205-6530 Barber
	Bldg 123	0900-1800 Tu-Sa	C-205-7777-EX-706 Beauty
Laundry/DryC	Bldg 270	0800-1800 M-Sa	C-250-7777-EX-522
Medical	Bldg 108	24 hrs dly	C-205-5515/6116, C-205-1847/7746
Postal	Bldg 110	0900-1700 M-F, 1400 Sa	C-205-6619
TML	Bldg 121	24 hrs dly C-205-1844/7675	DV/VIP C-205-7432
TRAVELERS AID	Bldg 300	1000-1500 Tu,W,F	C-205-7234 AF Family Svc
ARC	Bldg 105	0900-1500 M-F	C-250-1855 O/hrs C-205-7782
Chaplain	Bldg 115	0730-1630 M-F	C-205-5161/3174 O/hrs C-205-6140
Lost/Found	Bldg 403	24 hrs dly	C-205-1854/7601 Pax Svc NCO
Sec Police	Bldg 300	24 hrs dly	C-205-5400/6119 Desk Sgt
ATTRACTIONS	Madrid, museums, bull fights, great food & wine		

SPAIN
Torrejon de Ardoz AB, Cont'd

SCHEDULED FLIGHTS

DESTINATION	ROUTING	FREQ	EQ/CMTS
Athinai Arpt GR (ATH)	FRF-TOJ-ATH-IGL-ADA DOV-TOJ-ATH WRI-LGS-FRF-TOJ-ATH TOJ-ATH WRI-LGS-FRF-TOJ-SIZ-ATH-ESB-ADA FRF-TOJ-ATH-ESB-ADA WRI-LGS-FRF-TOJ-SIZ-ATH-IGL-ADA	Su 2/3/4/Su M 2/M 1/2/3/W Th Sa	C-141B/M C-141B/C C-141B/M C-141B/C C-141B/M C-141B/M C-141B/M
Aviano AB IT (AVB)	DOV-TOJ-AVB TOJ-AVB-RMS-MHZ	Su 1/2/3/Th	C-141B/C C-141B/M
Charleston AFB Intl SC (CHS)	AVB-PSA-TOJ-CHS ATH-TOJ-CHS	M 2/3/4/M	C-141B/C C-141B/C
Cigli TAB TU (IGL)	FRF-TOJ-ATH-IGL-ADA WRI-LGS-FRF-TOJ-SIZ-ATH-IGL-ADA	Su Sa	C-141B/M C-141B/M
Dhahran Intl SA (DHA)	DOV-TOJ-DHA-JED	Th	C-141B/C
Diego Garcia Atoll IO (NKW)	NGU-TOJ-SIZ-NBO-NKW NGU-TOJ-SIZ-KRT-NBO-NKW	M,W,1/2/4/F 3/F	C-141B/C C-141B/C
Dover AFB DE (DOV)	TOJ-LGS-DOV TOJ-LGS-DOV TOJ-DOV DHA-TOJ-DOV	1/Tu 3/Tu F Sa	C-130H/C C-130B/M C005A/M C005A/C
Esenboga Arpt TU (ESB)	WRI-LGS-FRF-TOJ-SIZ-ATH-ESB-ADA FRF-TOJ-ATH-ESB-ADA	1/2/3/W Th	C-141B/M C-141B/M
Incirlik Arpt TU (ADA)	FRF-TOJ-ATH-IGL-ADA WRI-LGS-FRF-TOJ-SIZ-ATH-ESB-ADA FRF-TOJ-ATH-ESB-ADA DOV-TOJ-ADA TOJ-ADA WRI-LGS-FRF-TOJ-SIZ-ATH-IGL-ADA	Su 1/2/3/W Th 2/Th /3/4/F Sa	C-141B/M C-141B/M C-141B/M C-141B/M C-141B/C C-141B/M
Jomo Kenyatta Intl KE (NBO)	NGU-TOJ-SIZ-NBO-NKW NGU-TOJ-SIZ-KRT-NBO-NKW	M,W,1/2/4/F 3/F	C-141B/C C-141B/C
Khartoum Arpt SD (KRT)	NGU-TOJ-SIZ-KRT-NBO-NKW	3/F	C-141B/C
Jeddah Airfld SA (JED)	DOV-TOJ-DHA-JED	Th	C-141B/C
Lajes Fld PO (LGS)	TOJ-LGS-DOV TOJ-LGS-DOV	1/Tu 3/Tu	C-130H/C C-130B/M

SPAIN

Torrejon de Ardoz AB, Cont'd

McGuire AFB NJ (WRI)	ADA-ESB-ATH-SIZ-TOJ-WRI TOJ-WRI	4/M 2/Tu	C-141B/M C-141B/C
RAF Mildenhall UK (MHZ)	TOJ-ZAZ-RMS-MHZ TOJ-AVB-RMS-MHZ TOJ-ZAZ-RMS-MHZ	1/2/3/Tu 1/2/3/Th Sa	C-141B/M C-141B/M C-141B/M
Norfolk NAS VA (NGU)	NFW-NBO-SIZ-TOJ-NGU NKW-BBE-NBO-SIZ-TOJ-NGU NKW-MGQ-NBO-SIZ-TOJ-NGU NKW-NBO-KRT-SIZ-TOJ-NGU	2/Su,W,F 3/M 4/M 3F	C-141B/C C-141B/C C-141B/C C-141B/C
Palma de Mallorca Arpt SP (PMI)	TOJ-PMI TOJ-PMI	1/2/W,4/Th 3/W	C-130E&H C-130B/M
Ramstein AB GE (RMS)	RTA-TOJ-RMS-FRF TOJ-ZAZ-RMS-MHZ TOJ-AVB-RMS-MHZ TOJ-ZAZ-RMS-MHZ	Tu 1/2/3/Tu 1/2/3/Th Sa	C009A/ME C-141B/M C-141B/M C-130E/M
Rhein Main AB GE (FRF)	ADA-ESB-ATH-TOJ-FRF ADA-ESB-ATH-SIZ-TOJ-FRF RTA-TOJ-RMS-FRF ADA-IGL-ATH-TOJ-FRF ADA-IGL-ATH-SIZ-TOJ-FRF ADA-ATH-TOJ-FRF ADA-ATH-SIZ-TOJ-FRF TOJ-FRF	M M Tu W W F,Sa 1/2/3/F,Sa 2/F,4/Sa	C-141B/M C-141B/M C009A/ME C-141B/M C-141B/M C-141B/M C-141B/M C-130E/C
Rota NAS SP (RTA)	TOJ-RTA FRF-RMS-TOJ-RTA	1/3/Tu,2/Th,4/F F	C-130E&H/C C009A/ME
Sigonella Arpt IT (SIZ)	NGU-TOJ-SIZ-NBO-NKW WRI-LGS-FRF-TOJ-SIZ-ATH-ESB-ADA NGU-TOJ-SIZ-KRT-NBO-NKW WRI-LGS-FRF-TOJ-SIZ-ATH-IGL-ADA	M,W,1/2/4F 1/2/3/W 3/F Sa	C-141B/C C-141B/M C-141B/C C-141B/M
Zaragoza AB SP (ZAZ)	TOJ-ZAZ TOJ-ZAZ TOJ-ZAZ-RMS-MHZ TOJ-ZAZ-RMS-MHZ	1/Tu,2/Th,4/F 3/Tu 1/2/3/Tu Sa	C-130E&H/C C-130B/M C-141B/M C-130E/M

Zaragoza Air Base (ZAZ)
406th TFW/LGTT
APO New York 09286-5000

Comm: (34) 76-214600-EX
ATVN: 724-1110

LOCATION: Accessible from A-68 S and E-4 N. HE: map, p-56, 5/H. NMC: Zaragoza, 10 mi NW.

FACILITIES	LOCATION	HOURS	PHONE	COMMENTS
PAX TERM INFO	Bldg 686 A-724-2517	0800-1700 M-F (flt hrs) C-76-214600-2517, Main gate on I St to L on 1st St to L on B St to Pax Term on right.		

SPAIN
Zaragoza AB, Cont'd

Pax Svc Ofc	Bldg 686 0800-1700 M-F C-76-214600-2284 NCO on duty
Pax Paging	Bldg 686 0800-1700-M-F C-76-214600-2517 See Pax svc NCO
PAX LOUNGES General	No DV/VIP or family lounges Bldg 686 0800-1700 M-F C-76-214600-2517 A/C, Bag lks, Rest-rms, P/C seats
Protocol Svc	Bldg 612 Duty hrs C-76-214600-EX Ask for Chief of Staff.(06+)
FOOD SERVICE	Cafeteria C-76-214600-2795, Dining Hall C-76-214600-1110, NCO/CPO Club C-76-214600-2763/2164, O'Club C-76-214600-2646/ 2636, Snack Bars C-76-214600-2727/2388
TRANSPORTATION	SATO C-76-214600-2698, Car Rentals C-76-214600-2793, Taxi (Comm) C-76-214600-2793 (Gov) C-76-214600-2070, Parking C-76-214600-2517
OTHER SERVICES	Exchange C-76-214600-2081, Bank/Exc (AF finance) C-76-214600-2475, Hair Styles C-76-214600-2081, Laundry/DryC C-76-214600-2684, Medical C-76-214600-2035, Postal C-76-214600-2198
TML	Bldg 900 24 hrs dly C-76-214600-2141/2715 All Ranks. DV/VIP - Call Protocol Services.
TRAVELERS AID	ARC C-76-214600-2363, Chaplain C-76-214600-2122, Lost/Found (Pax Svc NCO) C-76-214600-2517, Sec Police C-76-214600-2114
ATTRACTIONS	International ski and beach resorts an easy drive away

SCHEDULED FLIGHTS

DESTINATION	ROUTING	FREQ	EQ/CMTS
RAF Mildenhall UK (MHZ)	TOJ-ZAZ-RMS-MHZ TOJ-ZAZ-RMS-MHZ	1/2/3/Tu Sa	C-141B/M C-130E/M
Ramstein AB GE (RMS)	TOJ-ZAZ-RMS-MHZ TOJ-ZAZ-RMS-MHZ	1/2/3/Tu Sa	C-141B/M C-130E/M
Rhein Main AB GE (FRF)	RTA-ZAZ-FRF	F	C009A/ME
Rota NAS SP (RTA)	FRF-ZAZ-RTA	Tu	C009A/ME
Torrejon de Ardoz AB SP (TOJ)	MHZ-RMS-ZAZ-TOJ ZAZ-TOJ ZAZ-TOJ	1/2/3/M 1/Tu,2/Th,4/F 3/Tu	C-141B/M C-130E&H/C C-130B/M

THAILAND

Don Muang Airport (BKK)
Ch-JUSMAGTHAI   ATTN: MAGTRM-SMS
APO SAN FRANCISCO   96346-5000

Comm: (66) 2-287-1036-
EX-333
ATVN: None

LOCATION: Bangkok is on Chao Phraya R, 20 mi N of gulf of Thailand. Arpt is 10 mi NE of Bangkok. NMC: Bangkok, 10 mi SW.

THAILAND

Don Muang Arpt, Cont'd

FACILITIES	LOCATION HOURS PHONE COMMENTS
PAX TERM INFO	JUSMAGITHAI Bldg A Rm 210 0700-1600 M-F C-287-1027 or C-287-1036-EX-333. Check-in here & use comm bus (100 Baht) to military arpt. No comm taxi at arpt. Limited US fac.
PAX LOUNGES	Bldg A Rm 210 0700-1600 M-F Tel C, Rest-rms, P/C seats
OTHER SERVICES	Bldg A-106 JUSMAG Breakfast,fast food & in-flt meals EX-2740; Bldg C-129 Barber 0800-1500 M-F; Bldg D-109 APO 1200-1600 M-F; and Marine Guard 24 hrs dly C-252-5040-EX-2470.

SCHEDULED FLIGHTS

DESTINATION	ROUTING	FREQ	EQ/CMTS
Clark AB RP (CRK)	BKK-CRK	2/4/F	C-130E/M
Diego Garcia Atoll IO (NKW)	CRK-VBU-NKW	3/Sa	C-141B/M

Note: VBU is U-Tapao TH, 75 mi SE of Bangkok TH.

TURKEY

Cigli Turkey Air Base (IGL)
7241st ABG, Izmir Air Station
APO New York 09224-5000

Comm: (90) 51-25-4420
ATVN: 675-1110

LOCATION: In Western Turkey on Aegean Sea. Fm Izmir take E-24 N for 12 mi to W exit for Camalti & Air Base on R. HE: p-84, E/1. NMC: Izmir, 15 mi SE.

FACILITIES	LOCATION HOURS PHONE COMMENTS
PAX TERM INFO	Pax Term 0800-1630 dly C-3-9690-EX-3442, A-675-3442 No US facilities at TAFB. US MAC rep meets all flts with free bus outside Customs Bldg for transport directly to Kordon Hotel, Izmir,TML fac (on Base Map #13).Also has dining hall, TV rm, Restaurant, Cons Open Mess, Barber shop & Cashier.
FOOD SERVICE Cafeteria	Map #8 Operated by AAFES Pizza & Baskin Robbins Map #13 0600-2400 dly C-31-044 Kordon Hotel
TRANSPORTATION	Generous & cheap public trans: taxi, buses, & horse carriages. Most US spt fac easy walk from each other.
OTHER SERVICES	Map #6 - BX C-13-2347 Shopette & Commissary; Map #7 - S&S Bookstore, Family Services, Dry cleaners, Class VI Store; Map #8 - Security Police C-3-3222, Rec Center; Map #9 - APO, Barber/Beauty shops; Map #11 - USAF Clinic 24 hrs dly C-3-9680-EX-3523; Map #12 - Chaplain's office.
ATTRACTIONS	Ancient Bible/historic sites, Aegean Sea

TURKEY
Cigli Turkey AB, Cont'd

SCHEDULED FLIGHTS

DESTINATION	ROUTING	FREQ	EQ/CMTS
Athinai Arpt GR (ATH)	ADA-ESB-IGL-ATH-RMS-FRF ADA-ESB-IGL-ATH	Th Sa	C009A/ME C-130E/M
Balikesir Arpt TU (BZI)	ADA-IGL-BZI-ESB-ADA ADA-IGL-ESK-ESB-ADA ADA-IGL-BZI-YES-ADA	M W Th	C-130E/M C-130E/M C-130E/M
Esenboga Arpt TU (ESB)	ADA-IGL-BZI-ESB-ADA ADA-IGL-ESK-ESB-ADA	M W	C-130E/M C-130E/M
Eskisehir TUAF TU (ESK)	ADA-IGL-ESK-ESB-ADA	W	C-130E/M
Incirlik Arpt TU (ADA)	ADA-IGL-BZI-ESB-ADA ADA-IGL-ESK-ESB-ADA ADA-IGL-BZI-YES-ADA	M W Th	C-130E/M C-130E/M C-130E/M
Ramstein AB GE (RMS)	ADA-IGL-SIZ-RMS-FRF ADA-ESB-IGL-ATH-RMS-FRF	Su Th	C009A/ME C009A/ME
Rhein Main AB GE (FRF)	ADA-IGL-FRF ADA-IGL-SIZ-RMS-FRF ADA-ESB-IGL-ATH-RMS-FRF	Su Su Th	C-141B/M C009A/ME C009A/ME
Sigonella Arpt IT (SIZ)	ADA-IGL-SIZ-RMS-FRF	Su	C009A/ME
Yesilkoy Arpt TU (YES)	ADA-IGL-BZI-YES-ADA	Th	C-130E/M

Esenboga Airport (ESB)
7217th ABG/RMQA, Ankara Air Station
APO New York 09254-5000

Comm: (90) 41-33-7080
ATVN: 672-4118
ATVN: 672-2206 (Air Sta)

LOCATION: In the N center of the country, 125 mi S of the Black Sea.
NMC: Ankara, 16 mi SW.

PAX TERM INFO	Bldg 2018 0800-1600 M-F C-41-33-2206, A-672-2206 Lobby of Intl Terminal. For MEDEVAC flt info, call C-33-3108. All services of International Airport.
Pax Svc Ofc	Bldg 2018 0730-1630 M-F C-33-2154/3266
FOOD SERVICE Cafeteria	Bldg 2001 0700-1700 M-Sa C-33-7080
NCO/CPO Club	Bldg 2009 0730-0200 Sa, 0900-2300 Su C-33-3296
OFC Club	Off Base 1400-0100 dly C-33-3272
TRANSPORTATION Air Tickets	Bldg 2424 0730-1630 M-F C-33-3266
Bus(Shuttle)	Bldg 2088 0600-2400 dly C-33-2220-EX-255

TURKEY

Esenboga Arpt, Cont'd

OTHER SERVICES Exchange	Bldg 2263	1000-1700 dly	C-33-3275	
Hair Styles	Bldg 2263	0800-1700 M-Sa	C-33-287	
Medical	Bldg 2001	24 hrs dly	C-33-3279	
Postal	Bldg 2124	0800-1700 M-F, 1200 Sa	C-33-292	
TML	Kirk Pinar, Off Base, Cankaya EX-3128. 24 hrs dly.			
TRAVELERS AID Chaplain	Air Station Air Station	Duty hrs Duty hrs	C-33-3124 C-33-2192	AF Family Svcs
Sec Police	Air Station	24 hrs dly	C-33-2241	
ATTRACTIONS	Attaturk and Hittite museums			

SCHEDULED FLIGHTS

DESTINATION	ROUTING	FREQ	1	EQ/CMTS
Athinai Arpt GR (ATH)	ESB-ADA-FRF ADA-ESB-IGL-ATH-RMS-FRF ADA-ESB-IGL-ATH	M Th Sa		C-130B/M C009A/ME C-130E/M
Cigli TAFB TU (IGL)	ADA-ESB-IGL-ATH-RMS-FRF ADA-ESB-IGL-SIZ-RMS-FRF	Th Sa		C009A/ME C-130E/ME
Eskisehir TUAF TU (ESK)	ADA-ESB-YES-ESK-ADA	F		C-130E/M
Incirlik Arpt TU (ADA)	ADA-IGL-BAL-ESB-ADA ESB-ADA-FRF ADA-IGL-ESK-ESB-ADA ADA-ESB-YES-ESK-ADA ESB-ADA-FRF-TOJ ESB-ADA-IGL-SIZ-RMS-FRF	M M W F F Sa		C-130E/M C-141B/M C-130E/M C-130E/M C-141B/M C-130E/M
Ramstein AB GE (RMS)	ADA-ESB-IGL-ATH-RMS-FRF ESB-ADA-IGL-SIZ-RMS-FRF	Th Sa		C009A/ME C009A/ME
Rhein Main AB GE (FRF)	ADA-ESB-IGL-ATH-RMS-FRF ESB-ADA-FRF-TOJ ESB-ADA-IGL-SIZ-RMS-FRF	Th F Sa		C009A/ME C-141B/M C009A/ME
Sigonella Arpt IT (SIZ)	ESB-ADA-IGL-SIZ-RMS-FRF	Sa		C009A/ME
Torrejon de Ardoz SP (TOJ)	ESB-ADA-FRF-TOJ	F		C-141B/M
Yesilkoy Arpt TU (YES)	ADA-ESB-YES-ESK-ADA	F		C-130E/M

TURKEY

Incirlik Airport (Adana) (ADA)
628th MASS/TROP
APO New York 09289-5000

Comm: (90) 711-14228
ATVN: 676-1110

LOCATION: Fm Adana (in SE Turkey, 30 mi N of Mediterranean Sea), E on E-5 for 3 mi, L at sign for Incirlik AB. Base clearly marked. NMC: Adana, 3 mi W.

FACILITIES	LOCATION	HOURS	PHONE	COMMENTS
PAX TERM INFO	Bldg 500	0600-2200 dly	C-711-6424/5, A-676-6424/5	
	Fm main gate on 1st st to R on "A" St to Pax Term on L.			
Recording	Bldg 500	0700 dly on local Armed Forces Network radio		
Pax Svc Ofc	Bldg 500	0730-1700 dly	C-711-3162	NCO on duty
Pax Paging	Bldg 500	0600-2200 dly	C-711-6424/5	
PAX LOUNGES	Bldg 500	No family lounge at this time		
General	Bldg 500	0600-2200 dly	C-711-6424/5	
	A/C, Bag chk/lks, Tel L,LD&ATVN, TV,Rest-rms, O/S & Wood seats			
DV/VIP	Bldg 500	0600-2200 dly	C-711-6424/5	L side of Term
	A/C, Bag check, Tel L,LD,&ATVN, TV, O/S & Wood seats			
Protocol Svc	Bldg 480	0730-1630 M-F	C-711-6347	O/hrs EX-6376 (06+)
FOOD SERVICE	Many facilities on Base. Call for service hrs.			
Cafeteria	Bldg 957	0600-2200 dly	C-711-6993	
Enl Club	Bldg 884	0500-1800 dly	C-711-3194	"Willows Dining Hall"
NCO/CPO Club	Bldg 864	0630-2100 M-F, 0830-1330 Sa-Su	C-711-6775	
OFC Club	Bldg 950	1100-2030 M-Th, 2100 F-Sa, 1000-1300 Su	C-711-6967	
Restaurants	Bldg 970	1100-2300 dly	C-711-3269	Pizza parlor
Snack Bars	Bldg 6	0800-1900 Tu-Su	C-711-6249	Golf course
Vending	Bldg 500	0630-2130 dly	C-711-6424/5	Term Cafeteria
TRANSPORTATION	Many facilities & means			
Air Tickets	Bldg 974	1030-1500 M-F	C-711-6038	SATO
Bus(Comm)	Bldg 500	0610-2400 dly C-711-6424/5 15 min/ADA-Incir $.60		
(Shuttle)	Bldg 500	Limited service - Base area		
Car Rentals	Off Base	0800-1900 dly	AJAX-Incirlik	
TAXI(Comm)	Main gate	0600-2200 dly	C-711-6461	Give your location.
(Gov)	Bldg 492	24 hrs dly	C-711-6756/6284	Duty Pax only
Parking	Bldg 500	24 hrs dly C-711-6424 Short term-front of Pax Term, no overnight;long term-R side of Pax Term. No restrict.		
OTHER SERVICES	Many services on and off Base			
Exchange	Bldg 912	0930-1730 M-F, 1000-1630 Sa-Su	C-711-6937	
Bank/Exc	Bldg 480	0800-1500 M-F	C-711-6696	Finance office

TURKEY

Incirlik Arpt, Cont'd

Hair Styles	Bldg 957/8	0730-1730 M-Sa	C-711-6093	
Laundry	Bldg 958	24 hrs dly	Self-serve	
Medical	Bldg 3850	24 hrs dly	C-711-6666	
Postal	Bldg 870	0800-1530 dly	C-711-6301	
TML	Bld 952 All Ranks.	24 hrs dly	C-711-6786, A-676-6786 DV/VIP (06+) C-711-6347.	
TRAVELERS AID ARC	Bldg 1022 Bldg 978	Duty hrs 0730-1630 M-F	C-711-6755 C-711-6927	Family Spt Center O/hrs C-362-6376
Chaplain	Bldg 945	0730-1630 M-F	C-711-6441	
Emerg Relief	Bldg 924	0730-1630 dly	C-711-6201	AF Aid
Lost/Found	Bldg 500	0600-2200 dly	C-711-6424/5	
Sec Police	Bldg 649	24 hrs dly	C-711-6826	Desk Sgt
ATTRACTIONS	Snow skiing, beaches, mountain climbing, fishing			

SCHEDULED FLIGHTS

DESTINATION	ROUTING	FREQ	EQ/CMTS
Athinai Arpt GR (ATH)	ADA-ATH-TOJ-FRF	M	C-141B/M
	ADA-ATH-FRF	Tu	C-141B/M
	ADA-ATH-TOJ-FRF	W	C-141B/M
	ADA-ESB-IGL-ATH-RMS-FRF	Th	C009A/ME
	ADA-ATH-TOJ-FRF	F	C-141B/M
	ADA-ATH-TOJ-FRF	Sa	C-141B/M
	ADA-ESB-IGL-ATH	Sa	C-130E/M
Balikesir Arpt TU (BZI)	ADA-IGL-BZI-ESB-ADA	M	C-130E/C
	ADA-ESK-BZI-YES-ADA	Tu	C-130E/C
	ADA-IGL-BZI-YES-ADA	Th	C-130E/C
Cigli TAFB TU (IGL)	ADA-IGL-SIZ-RMS-FRF	Su	C009A/ME
	FRF-TOJ-ATH-ADA-IGL-FRF	Su	C-141B/M
	ADA-IGL-BZI-ESB-ADA	M	C-130E/C
	ADA-IGL-ESK-ESB-ADA	W	C-130E/M
	ADA-IGL-BZI-YES-ADA	Th	C-130E/C
	ADA-ESB-IGL-ATH-RMS-FRF	Th	C009A/ME
	ADA-ESB-IGL-ATH	Sa	C-130E/C
Diyarbakir Arpt TU (DIY)	ADA-EHC-DIY-ERZ-ADA	Tu	C-130E/C
	ADA-DIY-EHC-ADA	Th	C-130E/C
	ADA-DIY-ERZ-SIO-ADA	F	C-130E/C
Dover AFB DE (DOV)	ADA-RMS-DOV	W	C005A/M
	ADA-FRF-MHZ	F	C005A/M

TURKEY

Incirlik Arpt, Cont'd

Esenboga Arpt TU (ESB)	ADA-IGL-BZI-ESB-ADA ADA-IGL-ESK-ESB-ADA ADA-ESB-FRF ADA-ESB-IGL-ATH-RMS-FRF ADA-ESB-YES-ESK-ADA ADA-ESB-IGL-ATH	M W Th Th F Sa	C-130E/C C-130E/M C-141B/M C009A/ME C-130E/C C-130E/M
Eskisehir TUAF TU (ESK)	ADA-ESK-BZI-YES-ADA ADA-IGL-ESK-ESB-ADA ADA-ESB-YES-ESK-ADA	Tu W F	C-130E/C C-130E/C C-130E/C
Erhac TUAF TU (EHC)	ADA-EHC-SIO-ADA ADA-EHC-DIY-ERZ-ADA ADA-DIY-EHC-ADA	M Tu Th	C-130E/C C-130E/C C-130E/C
Erzurum Arpt TU (ERZ)	ADA-EHC-DIY-ERZ-ADA ADA-ERZ-SIO-ADA ADA-DIY-ERZ-SIO-ADA	Tu W F	C-130E/C C-130E/M C-130E/C
McGuire AFB NJ (WRI)	ADA-FRF-WRI	M	C009A/ME
RAF Mildenhall UK (MHZ)	ADA-FRF-MHZ-DOV	F	C005A/M
Ramstein AB GE (RMS)	ADA-IGL-SIZ-RMS-FRF ADA-RMS-DOV ADA-ESB-IGL-ATH-RMS-FRF	Su W Th	C009A/ME C005A/M C009A/ME
Rhein Main AB GE (FRF)	ADA-IGL-FRF ADA-IGL-SIZ-RMS-FRF ADA-FRF-WRI ADA-ATH-TOJ-FRF ADA-ATH-FRF ADA-ESB-FRF ADA-ESB-IGL-ATH-RMS-FRF ADA-FRF-MHZ-DOV	Su Su M M,W,F,Sa Tu Th Th F	C-141B/M C009A/ME C009A/ME C-141B/M C-141B/M C-141B/M C009A/ME C005A/M
Sigonella Arpt IT (SIZ)	ADA-IGL-SIZ-RMS-FRF	Su	C009A/ME
Sinop AAF TU (SIO)	ADA-EHC-SIO-ADA ADA-ERZ-SIO-ADA ADA-DIY-ERZ-SIO-ADA	M W F	C-130E/M C-130E/M C-130E/M
Torrejon de Ardoz AB SP (TOJ)	ADA-ATH-TOJ-FRF	M,W,F,Sa	C-141B/M
Yesilkoy Arpt TU (YES)	ADA-ESK-BZI-YES-ADA ADA-IGL-BZI-YES-ADA ADA-ESB-YES-ESK-ADA	Tu Th F	C-130E/M C-130E/M C-130E/M

Turkey Air Bases & Airports (TUR)
(Not listed separately in this book)

The bases listed below have Space-A air opportunities. Base support facilities at most stations are very limited.

TURKEY

Turkey AB's & Arpt's, Cont'd

BALIKESIR AIRPORT, TU (BZI)
7391 MUNSS/LGST
APO New York 09040-5000
Location: In NW Turkey, 60 mi S of the Marmara Denizi.
NMC: Balikesir, 5 mi NW.
Comm: None
ATVN: 672-1110-EX-227

DIYARBAKIR AIRPORT, TU (DIY)
7022 ABS/LGTT
APO New York 09294-5000
Location: In SE Turkey, 60 mi N of Syrian border.
NMC: Diyarbakir, 2 mi E.
Comm: 90-11913
ATVN: 679-1110-EX-3360

ERHAC TURKEY AIR FORCE, TU (EHC)
Det 93/CC, TUSLOG
APO New York 09051-5000
Location: In east central Turkey, 100 mi N of Syrian border.
NMC: Malatya, 3 mi SE.
Comm: None
ATVN: 676-1110-EX-358

ERZURUM AIRPORT, TU (ERZ)
Det 98/CC, TUSLOG
APO New York 09117-5000
Location: In east central Turkey, 90 mi S of the Black Sea.
NMC: Erzuram, 5 mi SE.
Comm: None
ATVN: 676-1110-EX-3287

ESKISEHIR TURKEY AIR FORCE, TU (ESK)
Det 100/CC, TUSLOG
APO New York 09338-5000
Location: In NW Turkey, 100 mi S of the Black Sea.
NMC: Eskisehir, in the city.
Comm: None
ATVN: 672-1110-EX-844

SINOP ARMY AIRFIELD, TU (SIO)
Sinop Army Field Station
APO New York 09133-5000
Location: In north central Turkey on the Black Sea, 190 mi NE of Ankara.
NMC: Sinop, in the city.
Comm: (90) 41-337080-99
ATVN: 672-1110-Flight Operations

SCHEDULED FLIGHTS

DESTINATION and ROUTING	FREQ	EQ/CMTS
ADA-IGL-BZI-ESB-ADA	M	C-130E/M
ADA-EHC-SIO-ADA	M	C-130E/M
ADA-ESK-BZI-YES-ADA	Tu	C-130E/M
ADA-EHC-DIY-ERZ-ADA	Tu	C-130E/M
ADA-IGL-ESK-ESB-ADA	W	C-130E/M
ADA-ERZ-SIO-ADA	W	C-130E/M
ADA-IGL-BZI-YES-ADA	Th	C-130E/M
ADA-DIY-EHC-ADA	Th	C-130E/M
ADA-ESB-YES-ESK-ADA	F	C-130E/M
ADA-DIY-ERZ-SIO-ADA	F	C-130E/M
ADA-ESB-IGL-ATH	Sa	C-130E/M

Yesilkoy Airport (Istanbul) (YES)
OL-B/LGTT, 7217th ABG
APO New York 09380-5000

Comm: (90) 1-573-9435
ATVN: 672-1110 *

LOCATION: On the European side of the Bosphorus and the Marmara Denizi. Take TU-1 fm Istanbul SW. HE: p-80, H/6. NMC: Istanbul, 9 mi NE.

FACILITIES	LOCATION	HOURS	PHONE	COMMENTS
PAX TERM INFO	Swiss Air Cargo 2nd floor 0730-1630 dly & during flight processing C-573-9435, A-672-9435 Ask for TUSLOG office. All the services of an International Airport. Most US support facilities located at US Consulate downtown Istanbul on Cakmakli Army Post 20 km distant.			

TURKEY

Yesilkoy Arpt, Cont'd

FOOD SERVICE	AAFES and Dining Hall available
TRANSPORTATION	Adequate public transportation. Official taxi C-573-2315.
TML	None. TMO has listing of discounted hotels.
ATTRACTIONS	Istanbul, Bazaar, Yalova Resort Island

SCHEDULED FLIGHTS

DESTINATION	ROUTING	FREQ	EQ/CMTS
Incirlik Arpt TU (ADA)	ADA-ESK-BZI-YES-ADA ADA-IGL-BZI-YES-ADA ADA-ESB-YES-ESK-ADA	Tu Th F	C-130E/C C-130E/C C-130E/M

UNSCHEDULED FLIGHTS

Many unscheduled flights via C-12 aircraft to various points in Italy. Call for destinations, routings, and schedules.

Note: * Ask for 1st Consulate, then ask for Traffic Management Office.

UNITED KINGDOM

Ascension Auxiliary Air Field (ASI)
Base Commander/Manager
PO Box 4608, Ascension Island
Patrick AFB, FL 32925-5100

Comm: 63-5747
ATVN: 854-1110 Ask for Ascension
EX-200/201

LOCATION: In the South Atlantic Ocean approx halfway between Recife, BR, and Luanda, Angola. A United Kingdom possession. NMC: Georgetown, .5 mi.

FACILITIES	LOCATION	HOURS	PHONE	COMMENTS
PAX TERM INFO	Base Ops	During flight processing		C-63-5747
	Very limited support facilities. Prior permission required to visit/transit ASI and JNB from ESMC/FA, Patrick AFB, FL. See appendix for personal entry requirements.			

SCHEDULED FLIGHTS

DESTINATION	ROUTING	FREQ	EQ/CMTS
Coolidge Arpt AN (SJH)	ASI-SJH-COF	3/4/Su,W,F	C-141B/M
Patrick AFB FL (COF)	ASI-SJH-COF	3/4/Su,W,F	C-141B/M

UNITED KINGDOM

RAF Bentwaters (BWY)
81st TFW
APO New York 09755-5000

Comm: (44) 3943-3737
ATVN: 225-1110

LOCATION: Take A-12 N from Ipswich to exit signs E on B-1069 for twin bases of RAF Bentwaters/Woodbridge. HE: p-13, F/1. NMC: Ipswich, 12 mi SW.

FACILITIES	LOCATION	HOURS	PHONE	COMMENTS
PAX TERM INFO	Bldg 60 0600-1600 dly C-3737-2328/2663, A-225-2328/2663 Enter flight line side of Base to Pax Term between Hangar 45 and Post Office (Bldg 59) on ramp area.			
Pax Svc Ofc	Bldg 60 0600-1600 dly C-3737-2328/2663, A-225-2328			
PAX LOUNGES General	No DV/VIP or family lounge Bldg 60 0600-1600 dly C-3737-2663 Rear of Bldg Bag check, Coffee srvd, Tel ATVN, Rest-rms, P/C seats			
Protocol Svc	Bldg 116 0730-1630 M-F C-3737-2105			
FOOD SERVICE	Cafeteria C-3942-0223, NCO/CPO Club C-3942-2659, O'Club C-3942-2256, Snack Bars C-3942-2725			
TRANSPORTATION	Bus(Shuttle) C-3737-2725, Car Rentals C-3737-2968, Taxi (Comm) C-3737-2909 (Gov) C-3737-2725, Train (Ipswich to Liverpool Station in London - 1.5 hrs)			
OTHER SERVICES	Exchange C-3737-2867, Bank/Exc C-3737-2662, Barber C-3737-6570, Beauty C-3737-2680, Laundry C-3742-0365, Medical C-3737-2574, Postal C-3737-2959, Valet/Dry C C-3742-0212			
TML	Bldg 629 24 hrs dly C-3737-2281/2837, A-225-2281/2837 All Ranks. DV/VIP C-3737-2281.			
TRAVELERS AID	ARC C-3737-2120, Chaplain C-3737-2710, Lost/Found C-3737-2204, Sec Police C-3737-2204			
ATTRACTIONS	Ipswich, coastline, London			

SCHEDULED FLIGHTS

DESTINATION	ROUTING	FREQ	EQ/CMTS
Ahlhorn GAFB GE (LHN)	MHZ-BWY-SEX-LPH-LHN MHZ-BWY-LHN-NRV-SEX	M Th	C-130E/C C-130E/C
Leipheim GAFB GE (LPH)	MHZ-BWY-SEX-LPH-LHN BWY-NRV-SEX-LPH BWY-LPH-LHN-NRV	M Tu F	C-130E/C C-130E/C C-130E/C
RAF Mildenhall UK (MHZ)	SEX-BWY-MHZ LPH-LHN-NRV-BWY-MHZ	Tu F	C-130E/C C-130E/C
Norvenich GAFB GE (NRV)	BWY-NRV-SEX-LPH MHZ-BWY-LHN-NRV-SEX	Tu Th	C-130E/C C-130E/C
Sembach AB GE (SEX)	MHZ-BWY-SEX-LPH-LHN BWY-NRV-SEX-LPH MHZ-BWY-LHN-NRV-SEX	M Tu Th	C-130E/C C-130E/C C-130E/C

UNITED KINGDOM

RAF Fairford (FFD)
7020 TRANS/LGTT
APO New York 09125-5000

Comm: (44) 285-714000
ATVN: 247-1110

LOCATION: Eighty mi W of London & 10 mi E of Cirencester. Take A-417 Rd fm Circencester to Fairford. HE: p-13, B/12. NMC: Oxford, 18 mi E.

FACILITIES	LOCATION	HOURS	PHONE	COMMENTS
PAX TERM INFO	Bldg 29	0730-1630 M-F & during flt processing C-285-714000-EX-4864, A-247-4864 Straight, near Base fire dept		
Pax Svc Ofc	Bldg 29	0730-1630 M-F	C-EX-4864	NCO on duty
PAX LOUNGES General	No DV/VIP or family lounges Bldg 29 0730-1630 M-F Tel-A, Rest-rms, P/C seats		C-EX-4864	Limited facilities
FOOD SERVICE Dining Hall	On and off Base facilities Bldg 581	0600-0100	C-EX-4218	4th meal Call for svc hrs.
Enl Club	Bldg 173	1630-0100 M-Sa	C-EX-4495	Lounge only
NCO/CPO Club	Bldg 179	1630-2400 M-F	C-EX-4445	Lounge only
OFC Club	Bldg 179	1700-2100 M-F	C-EX-4485	Lounge only
Cons Mess	Bldg 179	1100-2130 M-Sa	C-EX-4495	Call for svc hrs.
Snack Bars	Bldg 490	0700-1700 M-Sa, 1500 Su	C-EX-4367	
TRANSPORTATION Air Tickets	No transportation services on Base Bldg 157 0930-1630		C-EX-4358	AMEXCO
Bus(Comm)	Bldg 662	Limited hrs posted in lot near Base chapel		
Car Rentals	Near Bldg 662 Swindon-C-38833	0900-1700 M-F	C-EX-4107	RUMSHALL 24 hr
TAXI(Comm)	Near Bldg 662	24 hrs dly	C-EX-FFD-714015	
Parking	Gate 7	24 hrs dly	C-EX-4226	Notify Sec Police.
OTHER SERVICES Exchange	Many on and off Base Bldg 156	1030-1730 M-F, 1500 Sa		C-EX-4114
Bank/Exc	Bldg 157	0900-1500 M-F, 1200 Sa	C-EX-4913	AMEXCO
Hair Styles	Bldg 490	0900-1700 M-F, 1300 Sa	C-EX-4102 Barber C-EX-4166 Beauty	
Laundry/DryC	Bldg 490	1000-1730 M-F	C-EX-None	
Medical	Bldg 546	24 hrs dly	C-EX-4101	Ambulance EX-999
Postal	Bldg 66	1000-1730 M-F	C-EX-4403	
TML	Bldg 584 All Ranks.	24 hrs dly	C-EX-4419 DV/VIP (06+)	Limited facilities. Call operator.

UNITED KINGDOM

RAF Fairford, Cont'd

TRAVELERS AID ARC	Bldg 157	0930-1500 M-F	C-EX-4188/4857
Chaplain	Bldg 662	000-1500 M-F, 1200 Sa	C-EX-4216
Lost/Found	Bldg 478	24 hrs dly	C-EX-4226
Sec Police	Bldg 478	24 hrs dly	C-EX-4226
ATTRACTIONS	Oxford, London		

SCHEDULED FLIGHTS

DESTINATION	ROUTING	FREQ	EQ/CMTS
Pease AFB NH (PSM)	FFD-PSM	1-2 per wk	KC-135 *
Lajes Fld PO (LGS)	FFD-LGS	1-2 per mo	KC-135 *

* Note: KC-135 air-to-air refueling mission. Aircraft are on 2-3 wk rotation status between Europe and CONUS. Good Space-A opportunity.

UNSCHEDULED FLIGHTS

Unscheduled flights to many major SAC Bases in CONUS. Very limited customs facilities and customs personnel for servicing passengers.

RAF Mildenhall (MHZ)
313 APS
APO New York 09127-5000

Comm: *(44) 512248
ATVN: 238-1110
*If outside, dial (STD) 0638 then 512248. In area, dial direct.

LOCATION: Twenty-seven mi from Cambridge in eastern UK. Follow the A-11(M) to Newmarket, then to Barton Mills. Take the A-1101 for 2.5 miles through Mildenhall Town to Beck Row Village to RAF Mildenhall. HE: p-13, E/1. NMC: Cambridge, 24 mi SW.

FACILITIES	LOCATION	HOURS	PHONE	COMMENTS
PAX TERM INFO	Bldg 598 A-238-2248/2526	24 hrs dly	C-712511-EX-2248/2526, 1/4 mi inside Gate 1.	
Pax Svc Ofc	Bldg 598	0800-1700 M-F	EX-2248/2250	
Pax Paging	Bldg 598	24 hrs dly	EX-2248	
PAX LOUNGES General	Lounges for all categories of travelers Bldg 598 24 hrs dly EX-2248 TV, Rest-rms, Lockers, Game rm, P/C seats, Tel C&A			
DV/VIP	Bldg 598 24 hrs dly EX-2248 Ground floor-L of Gate 1 Game rm,Lks,TV,Tel C&A,Rest-rms,O/S seats. Not staffed. (06+)			
Protocol Svc	Bldg 239	0800-1700 M-F	EX-2132	(Q7+) 3rd AF

UNITED KINGDOM
RAF Mildenhall, Cont'd

Family	Bldg 598 24 hrs dly EX-2248 Upstairs-left. No restrict. Game rm,Lks, Tel C&A, TV, Rest-rms,O/S seats,Playroom,Nursery
FOOD SERVICE Cafeteria	Many good restaurants off Base Bldg 423 0700-2200 M-F,0900-1530 Sa-Su EX-2488 "Starlifter"
Dining Hall	Bldg 436 0600-0030 dly 4th meal & Officers' Breakfast EX-2689
Enl Club	Bldg 449 1100-2300 dly EX-2683 Call for svc hrs.
NCO/CPO Club	Bldg 449 1100-2300 dly EX-2683 "Galaxy" C/for svc hrs.
OFC Club	Bldg 464 0630-2200 dly EX-2615 Call for svc hrs.
Restaurants	Bldg 433 0800-2200 dly EX-2795 "Pizza Cove"
Snack Bars	Bldg 423 0900-2200 dly EX-2488, Bowling Center EX-2348
Vending	Bldg 598 24 hrs dly EX-2248/2526
TRANSPORTATION Air Tickets	Bldg 404 0800-1800 M-F C-712083 John Hilary Travel
Bus(Comm)	To Lakenheath Billeting - M-F, LKZ-Heathrow routing. Bury St Edmonds C-(98) 66171 and Cambridge C-(92) 343418. To London - near Gate 2, schedule in Bldg 598. Book early.
(Shuttle)	Bldg 598 0630-1730 dly MHZ to LKZ, hourly
Car Rentals	Barton Mills 0800-1800 M-Sa C-712080
TAXI(Comm) (Gov)	Bldg 461 24 hrs dly EX-2984 Base Cab Stand Bldg 611 24 hrs dly EX-2339
Trains	Bury St Edmonds 0745-2138 M-Sa, 0924-0256 Su C-(98) 3947 Cambridge C-(92) 311999. Schedule avail,Bldg 598, London,etc.
Parking	Short term-in front of Bldg 598, 24 hr limit; long term-in Sec Police compound Bldg 645, 24 hrs dly, EX-2667.
OTHER SERVICES Exchange	Main BX in RAF Lakenheath Bldg 598 2nd floor Mini Exchange, hrs vary. Main BX Bldg 998 1000-1800 M-F,1000-1700 Sa,1100-1600 Su C-7-2996.
Bank/Exc	Bldg 436 0900-1500 M-F Exc at clubs AMEXCO EX-2850
Hair Styles	Bldg 442 0830-1700 M-F, 0830-1200 Sa EX-2676 Barber Bldg 442 0900-1700 M-Sa EX-2977 Beauty
Laundry/DryC	Bldg 123 24 hrs dly C-712067
Valet/Dry C	Bldg 123 0900-1600 M-Sa EX-2404
Medical	Bldg 444 24 hrs dly EX-2765
Postal	Bldg 442 0800-1700 M-Sa EX-2151
TML	Bldg 123 24 hrs dly EX-2407 Enlisted Billeting Bldg 464 24 hrs dly EX-2568 Officer Billeting DV/VIP available, ATVN 238-2777/2568 Lakenheath EX-7-3770 B&B list at Pax Svc

UNITED KINGDOM

RAF Mildenhall, Cont'd

TRAVELERS AID ARC	Bldg 442 Bldg 598	0800-1600 M-F 0800-1600 M-F	EX-2032 EX-2113	AF Family Services Other hrs EX-2667
Chaplain	Bldg 474	Duty hrs	EX-2822	
Emerg Relief	Bldg 436	0730-1730 M-F	EX-2084	AF Aid Society
Lost/Found	Bldg 598	0800-1700 M-F	Weekends, ask Shift Supervisor.	
Sec Police	Bldg 645	24 hrs dly	EX-2667	
ATTRACTIONS	New Market-13 mi S, Cambridge-24 mi SW, London			

SCHEDULED FLIGHTS

DESTINATION	ROUTING	FREQ	EQ/CMTS
Aviano AB IT (AVB)	MHZ-AVB MHZ-RMS-AVB-TOJ	Tu 1/2/3/W	C-130E/C C-141B/M
RAF Bentwaters UK (BWY)	MHZ-BWY-LPH-SEX MHZ-BWY-NRV-SEX	M Th	C-130E/C C-130E/C
Capodichino Arpt IT (NAP)	MHZ-NAP	Su	C-130E/C
Charleston AFB Intl SC (CHS)	PIK-MHZ-YYR-CHS MHZ-PIK-CHS MHZ-YYR-CHS	1/3/4/Su,3/M, 2/4/Tu,1/3/W, 1/3/4/F 1/Tu 1/2/3/F	C-141B/C DC-863/P/CC C-141B/C
Decimomanna ITAB IT (DCU)	MHZ-RMS-DCU-TOJ	F	C-130E/M
Dover AFB * DE (DOV)	MHZ-DOV-TIK-SUU MHZ-DOV	W,Th,Sa 2/Sa	C005A/C K-010/C
Goose AB CN (YYR)	PIK-MHZ-YYR-CHS MHZ-YYR-CHS	1/3/4/Su,3/M, 2/4/Tu,1/3/W, 1/3/4/F 1/2/3/F	C-141B/C C-141B/C
Leipheim GAFB GE (LPH)	MHZ-BWY-LPH-SEX	M	C-130E/C
Norvenich GAFB GE (NRV)	MHZ-BWY-NRV-SEX	Th	C-130E/C
Philadelphia Intl PA (PHL)	MHZ-PHL	Th	DC-863/P/CC
Ramstein AB GE (RMS)	MHZ-RMS-ZAZ-TOJ MHZ-RMS-AVB-TOJ MHZ-RMS-DCU-TOJ MHZ-RMS	1/2/3/M 1/2/3/W F Sa	C-141B/M C-141B/M C-130E/M C-130E/C
Rhein Main AB GE (FRF)	WRI-MHZ-FRF MHZ-FRF MHZ-FRF	Su Tu,Th,F Th	C-141B/M C-141B/M DC-10

UNITED KINGDOM

RAF Mildenhall, Cont'd

Sembach AB GE (SEX)	MHZ-BWY-LPX-SEX MHZ-BWY-NRV-SEX	M Th	C-130E/C C-130E/C
Tinker AFB OK (TIK)	MHZ-DOV-TIK-SUU	M,Sa	C005A/C
Torrejon de Ardoz AB SP (TOJ)	MHZ-RMS-ZAZ-TOJ MHZ-RMS-AVB-TOJ MHZ-RMS-DCU-TOJ	1/2/3/M 1/2/3/W F	C-141B/M C-141B/M C-130E/M
Travis AFB CA (SUU)	MHZ-DOV-TIK-SUU	M,Sa	C005A/C
Zaragoza AB SP (ZAZ)	MHZ-RMS-ZAZ-TOJ	1/2/3/M	C-141B/M

* Note: 6-7 flights per week. Also, Space-A flts frequently operate out of NAF Mildenhall to numerous European cities via UC-12B aircraft. Call ahead.

Prestwick Airport (Scotland) (PIK)
OL-P, 313 APS/MAC
APO New York 09049-5364

Comm: (44) 292-79866
ATVN: 238-1110
Ask for PIK.

LOCATION: On the W coast of Scotland. Take A-77 S from Glasgow, exit at Ayr, N to airport. HE: p-8, C/4. NMC: Glasgow, 30 mi NE.

FACILITIES	LOCATION	HOURS	PHONE	COMMENTS
PAX TERM INFO	Main concourse 0730-1630 dly C-292-79866, A-238-1110-EX-PIK All support facilities at Intl Arpt. No US military fac in Prestwick area. US Navy Holy Loch C-(44) 0369-5555, A-221-8689, is near Dunoon UK, 2 hrs N. US Navy Security Group Act, Edzell C-(44)-03564-431,A-229-1110, near Brechin UK,5 hrs NE.			
Pax Svc Ofc	Main concourse 0730-1630 dly C-292-79866 Attendant on duty			
Pax Paging	Main concourse 0730-1630 dly A-238-1110-EX-PIK			
PAX LOUNGES General	Main concourse 24 hrs dly A-292-79822 Nursery, O/S Seats			
DV/VIP	Gateway Lounge at entrance to departure lounge when required. A-238-1110-EX-PIK Rest-rms, Cof/tea srvd. Provided by Gateway Scotland.			
FOOD SERVICE Cafeteria	Mezzanine Summer 0600-1800 dly C-292-79822/78326 Winter 0800-1600 dly EX-3082			
Restaurants	Mezzanine Summer 1030-1800 dly C-292-79822/78326 Winter 1030-1500 dly EX-3082			
Snack Bars	Roof top Summer 1030-1800 dly C-292-79822/78326 Open May to Oct EX-3082			
TRANSPORTATION Air Tickets	Main concourse 0630-1700 M,W,F 0530 Tu,Th 0500-1600 Sa,Su Northwest Orient C-292-79822-EX-2013			

UNITED KINGDOM

Prestwick Arpt, Cont'd

Bus(Gov)	US Navy Dunoon 0800-1630 M-F A-221-8689
Car Rentals	Avis 0600-1700 M-F, 0600-1300 Sa-Su C-292-77218 Europcar 0600-1700 M-F, 0600-1300 Sa-Su C-292-70566 Hertz 0600-1700 M-F, 0600-1300 Sa-Su C-292-79822 Swan Natl 0600-1700 M-F, 0600-1300 Sa-Su C-292-76517
TAXI(Comm)	Taxi rank 24 hours daily C-292-79822-EX-2013 or thru British Airports Authority information desk.
Parking (Comm)	Opposite center main concourse 24 hrs dly 50 ft from main door. 50 pound fine for parking in front of main Terminal. All cars must be in paying car parking lot. Hourly rates unless arranged with parking lot attendant.
OTHER SERVICES Skyshop	Main concourse Summer 24 hrs dly if req/dependent on flt ops Winter 0800-1300 C-292-78681
Money Exch	Main concourse Same as Skyshop C-292-79822-EX-2049
Postal	Main concourse Same as Skyshop C-292-79822
TRAVELERS AID ARC	RAF Mildenhall A-238-1110
ATTRACTIONS	Culzean Castle, Edinburgh, Glasgow (45 min-2 hrs by train)

SCHEDULED FLIGHTS

DESTINATION	ROUTING	FREQ	EQ/CMTS
Charleston AFB IAP SC (CHS)	PIK-MHZ-YYR-CHS	Varies/frequent	C-141B/C
Goose Bay AB CN (YYR)	PIK-MHZ-YYR-CHS	Varies/frequent	C-141B/C
RAF Mildenhall UK (MHZ)	PIK-MHZ-YYR-CHS	Varies/frequent	C-141B/C

UNSCHEDULED FLIGHTS

Frequent unscheduled flights to: Bradley IAP CT (BDL); Charleston AFB/IAP SC (CHS); and Goose AB CN (YYR) via B707, DC-8, and C-141 aircraft.

ZAIRE

Kinshasa N'Djili Airport (FIH)
US Military Mission to Zaire (ZAMISH)
APO New York 09662-0006

Comm: (243) 12-22336/25881
ATVN: None

LOCATION: In Central Africa near W Coast. Kinshasa, capital city is on Zaire River, 225 NE of Atlantic Ocean. Arpt is 15 mi SE of city. NMC: Kinshasa, 15 mi NW.

ZAIRE

Kinshasa N'Djili Arpt, Cont'd

FACILITIES	LOCATION	HOURS	PHONE	COMMENTS
PAX TERM INFO	Pax Term	10 hrs dly	C-22336	Pax processed by USMM personnel. Essential fac at arpt. Small US military fac. Access limited. See appendix for personal entry requirements.

SCHEDULED FLIGHTS

DESTINATION	ROUTING	FREQ	EQ/CMTS
Charleston AFB Intl SC (CHS)	FIH-ROB-LGS-CHS FIH-ROB-LGS-DOV	2/4/Th,4/F 2/4/Th,4/F	C-141B/M C005A/M
Lajes Fld PO (LGS)	FIH-ROB-LGS-CHS FIH-ROB-LGS-DOV	2/4/Th,4/F 2/4/Th,4/F	C-141B/M C005A/M
Monrovia Rbts Intl LI (ROB)	FIH-ROB-LGS-CHS FIH-ROB-LGS-DOV	2/4/Th,4/F 2/4/Th,4/F	C-141B/M C005A/M
N'Djamena Intl Arpt CD (NDJ)	FIH-NDJ-FIH	2/Th every other month	C-141B/M

Note: Flts inbound to Africa may change routing and frequency once in Africa. Outbound flts may also transit TOJ and/or RTA in route to LGS & CHS.

-NOTES-

APPENDIX A

NOTE: See Page iii for Space-A Passenger Regulation Update.

This appendix (chapter 4) contains references to chapters in DOD 4515.13-R (draft) not published here because of space limitations. A copy of the entire regulation can be found at most military Space-A departure locations and military personnel offices.

SPACE AVAILABLE PASSENGER REGULATIONS
CHAPTER 4 - DOD 4515.13-R (DRAFT)

SECTION A - SPACE AVAILABLE POLICY

4-1. Required Documentation. Uniform service members on ordinary leave are required to have a valid leave authorization as prescribed by the services concerned. Uniformed service members must be on leave to register for Space-A travel, remain in a leave status while awaiting travel, and be in a leave status for the entire period of travel. The member's leave form, and leave documentation for DOD civilians on EML, will be stamped with the date and time of sign up when they register for space available travel. (See Chapter 10 for EML travel.) Required documentation for active status Reserve members is contained in paragraphs 4-5d(5)(a)(b), 4-6d(3)(a)(b), and 4-7e(3)(a)(c). Retired service members are required to present identification listed in paragraph 2-4x. Bona fide dependents accompanying active and retired members present only their DD Form 1173, Uniformed Services Identification and Privilege Card. Active duty members in pass status without orders, the provisions of paragraphs 4-6b(1) and 4-7c(2)(a), may travel upon the presentation of a DD Form 2 (green) "Armed Forces Identification Card" Form 2 NOAA (green), "Uniformed Services Identification Card," or PHS 1866-1 (green), and necessary border clearance documentation when required. For foreign exchange personnel, the required documentation for the sponsor is the DD Form 1173, the appropriate uniformed service leave authorization, and a copy of attachment orders to a uniformed service activity. All other individuals must present travel orders or a transportation authorization which contains reference to the applicable paragraph of this regulation under which an authenticating officer has authorized travel.

4-2. Registration for Space Available Travel. Space available registers are maintained for travel to those locations served by each terminal. To compete for space available travel, eligible personnel must sign-up in person with all documentation, as indicated in paragraph 4-1 above. Passengers may register for a maximum of five countries. Passengers may choose not to compete for all seats offered without jeopardizing their position on the space available register. However, passengers must revalidate their intent to travel every 15 days. If passengers fail to revalidate, their name will be removed from the space available register space available passengers will be removed from the space available register after remaining on the list for 30 consecutive days, except for Category 4 passengers. Category 4 passengers will be purged after 45 days on the register. All space available passengers dropped from the list will be allowed to register again with a new date and time of sign up within their respective categories.

4-3. Eligibility. The categories of passengers listed in Sections B through D may be permitted space available transportation. The order in which these categories are listed will be the normal precedence of movement. The listing within each of the categories is not intended to indicate a precedence within categories. Eligible personnel in each category will be furnished space available transportation on a first-in first-out basis. The installation commander may change the precedence of any categories of space available movement for emergency or extreme humanitarian reasons when requested by the sponsoring uniformed service, and the facts provided fully support such exception. The installation commander may delegate the authority to make changes to the

Appendix A, Cont'd

terminal reservation section (TRS). Where MAC units are tenants, the local MAC commander should advise the installation commander of this authority and offer technical assistance as needed. When a movement priority is changed, the passengers will be moved no higher than the bottom of the Category One Space-A list. Reservations will not be made for any category of space available passenger, and there is no guaranteed space for such passengers. The DOD is not obligated to continue an individual's travel or return him or her to point of origin. Eligible personnel must be physically capable of caring for themselves while enplaning and deplaning and in flight. An exception to this is permitted when the disabled individual is accompanied by a sponsor or dependent who is eligible for space available transportation and who can provide the assistance required.

NOTE: Except as otherwise noted, transportation as authorized by this chapter may be between oversea stations or between overseas and CONUS terminals where adequate border clearance facilities exist or can be made readily available. Travel may be on transport aircraft operated under the control of MAC or other military aircraft. Aircraft may carry dependents only if apppropriately equipped to accommodate their needs. Except as otherwise noted in this regulation, dependents are not authorized military air-travel within the CONUS.

4-4. Not used.

SECTION B - TRANSPORTATION OF PASSENGERS BETWEEN THE CONUS AND OVERSEAS BY DOD-OWNED OR -CONTROLLED AIRCRAFT

4-5. Eligible Passengers.

   a. **Category 1.** This authority applies in bona fide emergencies, as determined by the uniformed service regulations, involving the immediate family members of the following. OPTIONS TO UTILIZE SPACE REQUIRED TRAVEL IS AUTHORIZED IN PARAGRAPH 3-3b(3).
   (1) US citizen civilian employees of the DOD stationed overseas.
   (2) Members and dependents of the American Red Cross when the member is serving with the US military departments overseas on a full-time paid basis.
   (3) Command-sponsored dependents of US citizen civilian employees of the DOD paid from either appropriated or nonappropriated funds.
   (4) Foreign exchange officers and enlisted personnel filling DOD positions, and their dependents.
   (5) US citizen civilian employees of nonappropriated fund activities whose travel from the CONUS, Alaska or Hawaii to overseas was incident to a PCS assignment at nonappropriated fund expense.
   (6) Dependents of uniformed service members stationed in the CONUS or dependents of members who are serving an unaccompanied tour overseas from the CONUS APOE to the oversea APOD and return in a bona fide family emergency in connection with the serious illness, death, or impending death of a member of their immediate family who resides in an oversea areas. (For command sponsored dependents stationed overseas, see paragraph 3-3a(3).

NOTE: Individually sponsored dependents of uniformed service members stationed outside CONUS are permitted transportation under the provisions of this paragraph from overseas to the CONUS APOD, and Alaska, or Hawaii only; space available or space-required transportation to return individually sponsored dependents to overseas area where sponsor is stationed is not authorized.

   b. **Category 2.**
   (1) Category 2A. Sponsors on Environmental and Morale Leave (EML), or dependents who travel with their sponsors in an EML status from an approved origination site to the approved destination designated in accordance with

Appendix A, Cont'd

Chapter 10, and return. This provision applies to Department of Defense Dependent Schools (DODDS) teachers and their accompanied dependents in an EML status only during school year holiday/vacation periods.

(2) Category 2B.

(a) Members of the uniformed services, foreign exchange officers and enlisted personnel filling DOD positions, when in a leave status other than emergency, and uniformed service patients on convalescent leave.

(b) Close blood or affinitive relatives who are permanent members of the household and dependent upon a member of the uniformed services, a civilian employee of the DOD, or American Red Cross personnel stationed with the DOD overseas, when such member or employee is authorized transportation of legal dependents at Government expense. Travel must be performed in conjunction with the sponsor's, or his or her dependent's, PCS move and is permitted for only the transocean portion of the journey. The option to use space required transportation is authorized in paragraph 3-3b(5).

(c) Foreign born dependent spouse and accompanied dependent children of military personnel officially reported in a missing status as defined in paragraph 551, Title 37, United States Code, who reside overseas are authorized space available travel to the CONUS, Alaska, or Hawaii and return overseas, and those who reside in the CONUS, Alaska, or Hawaii are authorized to travel to oversea areas and return on ASIF missions for humanitarian reasons upon approval of the Chief of Staff, United States Army; Chief of Staff, United States Air Force; Chief of Naval Operations; Commandant of the Marine Corps; or their designated representatives. Travel identification will be by DD Form 1173, and a letter of approval from the appropriate military department.

(d) When accompanied by their sponsor who is in an authorized leave status, bona fide dependents of uniformed service members (to include college students up to 23 years of age), foreign exchange officers and enlisted personnel filling DOD positions. This privilege is not applicable to travel of dependents to or from a sponsor's restricted or "all other" (unaccompanied) tour location. It will not be used to establish a home for dependents in an oversea area or the CONUS. When members are authorized leave in conjunction with TDY/TAD, members and their dependents may not travel between the permanent duty station and the TDY/TAD location in a leave status; however, upon arrival at the temporary duty location, dependents are authorized space available travel with the member under the following conditions:

1. When the member's permanent duty station and TDY/TAD location is within the CONUS, travel to an oversea area and return is authorized.

2. When the member's permanent duty station and TDY/TAD location are in different countries within the oversea area, travel from the TDY/TAD location to the CONUS or within the oversea area and return to a country other than the country in which the member is permanently assigned is authorized.

3. When the member's permanent duty station and TDY/TAD location are within the same country, travel within the oversea area is authorized from and return to the TDY/TAD point or to a location other than the member's permanent duty station.

(e) Oversea commanders authorized to publish circuitous travel orders for members under current policy of their military departments, where extenuating circumstances prevail, may approve requests for space available travel of their dependents (see paragraph 2-41) between the oversea APOE and APOD in CONUS, Alaska or Hawaii incident to approved circuitous travel of the member. Option to use space required travel is authorized. See paragraph 3b(6).

(f) Cadets and midshipmen of the US military and Coast Guard academies, and foreign military cadets and midshipmen attending these academies, when in a leave status. Foreign cadets' and midshipmen's native countries must be identified in the leave authorization, and the transportation is authorized from the CONUS APOE to the oversea APOD and return.

(g) Civilian US Armed Forces patients as identified in paragraphs 11-21(3) and 11-4c(3) who have recovered after treatment in medical facilities and their accompanying nonmedical attendants. Travel is permitted to return the

Appendix A, Cont'd
recovered patient and the nonmedical attendant to the oversea post of assignment from a CONUS APOE to an oversea APOD. In the event of death or extended hospitalization of the patient, the nonmedical attendant retains the space available travel authority to return to the patient's oversea post of assignment.
  (h) Medal of Honor holders and accompanied dependents. Dependents must present DD Form 1173, "Dependent Identification Card." Sponsor must possess a Medal of Honor Identification and Travel Card.
  (3) Category 2C.
    (a) Unaccompanied EML dependents 17 years of age or older. EML dependents under 17 must be accompanied by an adult EML eligible family member (see Chapter 10).
    (b) DODDS teachers or dependents (accompanied or unaccompanied) in an EML status during the summer break.

  c. Category 3.
    (1) Secondary school student dependents (children) of members of the uniformed services, US citizen civilian employees of the DOD paid from either appropriated or nonappropriated funds, and American Red Cross personnel serving an accompanied tour overseas may travel between APOEs serving their sponsor's oversea duty station and the US only when there is no DOD oversea dependent accredited school at a nearer oversea location. The following provisions apply.

NOTE: The provisions of this subparagraph do not apply to an unmarried dependent student attending a secondary school in the United States, Alaska, or Hawaii for the purpose of obtaining a secondary education if the student is eligible to attend a secondary school under the Defense Department's Education Act of 1978.
      (a) Students must present written authorization from an approving authority.
      (b) Transportation between the US and a school in an oversea area or between points to attend foreign schools is not permitted.
      (c) Only one round trip per year is authorized. Trips may not be accumulated from school year to school year.
      (d) This provision does not apply to dependents authorized space required travel under paragraph 3-3b(9).
    (2) Dependents (students) of members of the uniformed services, US citizen civilian employees of the DOD paid from either appropriated or nonappropriated funds, and American Red Cross personnel serving an accompanied tour outside the US while engaged in trade school or undergraduate college study in the US for travel between the APOE serving their sponsor's oversea duty station and US points of entry. The following provisions apply:
      (a) Students must present written authorization from an approving authority.
      (b) Travel may originate in the US or oversea area.
      (c) Only one round trip per year is authorized. Trips may not be accumulated from school year to school year.
      (d) Transportation from the US to attend school in an oversea area is not permitted.
      (e) Students shall not be permitted space available transportation to the oversea area of their sponsor when:
        1. Sponsor has received a port call in conjunction with PCS reassignment to the US that is within 30 days of the anticipated date of student's departure to the oversea area; and
        2. US citizen civilian employees of DOD paid from either appropriated or nonappropriated funds (sponsor) has port call for transfer to the US or authorizing travel from home leave and such port call is within 30 days of the anticipated date of the student's departure for the oversea area.
        3. Authorized space required travel under paragraph 3-3b(9).

Appendix A, Cont'd

NOTE: The space available privilege cited in paragraph 4-5c(2) also applies to students who are 21 years of age or older at the time of the sponsor's PCS to the oversea area. This privilege will terminate on the sponsor's PCS to the US or the student's 23rd birthday, whichever is earlier.

(3) Dependents of active duty US military personnel, who at the time of PCS, were not entitled to transportation at Government expense to accompany or join their sponsor at his or her duty station. Transportation is limited to travel from the APOE in the CONUS, Alaska or Hawaii to the oversea APOD serving the sponsor's duty station. Prior to travel, approval of the oversea major commander for entrance of these dependents is required. They may provide DD Form 1056, Authorization to Apply for a No-Fee Passport and/or Request for Visa. This privilege may be afforded to dependents of members who:
    (a) After arrival at their oversea station, attained eligibility for transportation of dependents at Government expense upon subsequent reassignment; or
    (b) Acquire bona fide dependents after the effective date of PCS orders and desire that dependents accompany or join them at their oversea duty station.
    (c) Option to utilize space required travel as authorized. See paragraph 3-3b(8).
(4) Military personnel traveling on permissive TDY. Military personnel traveling on permissive temporary duty orders published under applicable military department regulations.
(5) Individually sponsored dependents acquired in an oversea area during the course of a member's current tour of assigned duty in that area who are not otherwise entitled to transportation at government expense are eligible for transportation from the overseas to an APOD in CONUS, Alaska or Hawaii in conjunction with the members PCS from the oversea area provided:
    (a) Command regulations pertaining to their acquisition are complied with.
    (b) For foreign nationals, requirements of the US Immigration and Naturalization Service for entry into the US have been completed.
    (c) The option to utilize space required travel as authorized in paragraph 3-3b(4)(c).

d. Category 4.
(1) Unaccompanied retired military members as defined in paragraph 2-4x (note paragraph 2-12b).
(2) Dependents of retired members when accompanied by their sponsor. (Note paragraph 2-12b).
(3) Dependents of active duty uniformed services personnel and US citizen civilian employees of the DOD paid from either appropriated or nonappropriated funds with transportation agreements and of American Red Cross personnel, who are stationed overseas with their sponsor, who desire to return to the US for the purpose of enlisting in one of the uniformed services when local enlistment in the oversea area is not authorized.
(4) Dependents of active duty uniformed service personnel and US citizen civilian employees of the DOD paid from either appropriated or nonappropriated funds with transportation agreements, and American Red Cross personnel who are stationed overseas with their sponsor, may travel to and from the nearest overseas military academy testing site to take scheduled entrance examinations for entry to any of the uniformed service academies.
(5) Members of the reserve components of the uniformed services traveling between Alaska, Hawaii, Puerto Rico, the Virgin Islands, American Samoa and Guam (Guam and American Samoan travelers may transit Hawaii) and CONUS in the following categories:

Appendix A, Cont'd

(a) Active status members in uniform, upon presentation of a DD Form 2 (red) and authentication of their current reserve status with a completed Form DD 1853.

(b) Members of the reserve components who have received official notification of retirement age (60), upon presentation of DD Form 2 (red) and a notice of retirement eligibility as described by DOD Directive 1200.15, 16 Feb 73, "Assignment to and Transfer Between Reserve Categories, Discharge from Reserve Status, Transfer to the Retired Reserve and Notification of Eligibility for Retired Pay." Wearing of the uniform is not required.

SECTION C - TRANSPORTATION OF PASSENGERS WITHIN THE CONUS BY DOD-OWNED OR -CONTROLLED AIRCRAFT

4-6. Eligible Passengers.

a. **Category 1.** Active duty uniformed services personnel on emergency leave (emergency status must be indicated in the leave orders).

b. **Category 2.**

(1) Active duty military uniformed services personnel and foreign exchange officers and enlisted personnel on duty within the DOD in a leave or pass status other than emergency.

(2) Dependent spouse, accompanying dependent children, and dependent parents of military personnel reported missing or captured. Travel must be for humanitarian purposes and is authorized only on transport-type aircraft appropriately equipped to accommodate the needs of dependent travelers. Travel must be approved by the Chief of Staff, US Army; Chief of Staff, US Air Force; Chief of Naval Operations; or the Commandant of the Marine Corps. Travel authority is DD Form 1173 and a letter of approval from the appropriate military service.

(3) Medal of Honor holders possessing a Medal of Honor Identification and Travel Card.

c. **Category 3.**

(1) Military personnel traveling on permissive temporary duty orders published under applicable military department regulations.

d. **Category 4.**

(1) Unaccompanied retired members as defined in paragraph 2-4x. (Note paragraph 2-12b.)

(2) ROTC students of the Army, Navy and Air Force receiving financial assistance, and those enrolled in advanced training, in uniform, during authorized absences from school upon presenting a document bearing the signature of the senior commissioned officer, who is the professor in charge of the ROTC program at the civilian educational institution. The document will identify the individual by name as being in the advanced course or enrolled under the Financial Assistance Program.

(3) Unaccompanied members of the reserve components of the Uniformed Services in the following categories:

(a) Active status members of the reserve components in uniform and upon presentation of DD Form 2 (red) and authentication of their current active status in the reserve components with a completed Form DD 1853.

(b) Members of the reserve components who have received official notification of retirement eligibility, but have not reached the mandatory retirement age (60), upon presentation of DD Form 2 (red) and a notice of retirement eligibility as described by DOD Directive 1200.15, 16 Feb 73. Wearing of the uniform is not required.

Appendix A, Cont'd
SECTION D - TRANSPORTATION OF PASSENGERS WITHIN AND BETWEEN OVERSEA AREAS BY DOD-OWNED OR -CONTROLLED AIRCRAFT

4-7. Eligible Passengers.

a. Category 1. Transportation to the nearest oversea aerial port and return to obtain transportation to the CONUS, Alaska, or Hawaii under the provision of paragraph 4-5a, or between oversea aerial ports in bona fide emergencies, as determined by the applicable uniformed services regulations, involving an immediate family member of the following. OPTION TO USE SPACE REQUIRED TRAVEL IS AUTHORIZED IN PARAGRAPH 3-3b(3).
   (1) US citizen civilian employee of the DOD when stationed overseas.
   (2) Command-sponsored dependents of uniformed service members and dependents of US citizen civilian employees of the DOD paid from either appropriated or nonappropriated funds when both sponsor and dependents are stationed overseas.
   (3) US citizen civilian employees of nonappropriated fund activities whose travel from the CONUS, Alaska or Hawaii to overseas was incident to a PCS assignment at nonappropriated fund expense.
   (4) Full-time paid personnel of the American Red Cross serving with the US military departments overseas and their dependents.
   (5) Personnel of nationally recognized welfare agencies when serving with the US military departments overseas.
   (6) Foreign exchange officers and enlisted personnel filling DOD positions, and their dependents.

NOTE: Individually sponsored dependents of members of the uniformed services stationed outside CONUS are eligible for transportation to terminal nearest the overseas location of the verified emergency in their immediate family. Space available or space required transportation to return individually sponsored dependents to oversea location where sponsor is stationed is not authorized.

   (7) Third Country Nationals (TCN) personnel who are employees of the DOD (appropriated or nonappropriated funds) who are not citizens of the United States or citizens or permanent residents of the host country in which the US Forces activity is located, from their duty assignment to their home country and return.

b. Category 1-HIATUS. Military personnel in a leave status under the EML program who travel from installations designated to EML origination sites in designated hostile fire areas to EML destination sites (specified in compliance with Chapter 10), and return.

c. Category 2.
   (1) Category 2A. Sponsors on EML or dependents who travel with their sponsors in an EML status from an approved origination site to the approved destination (specified in compliance with Chapter 10), and return. This provision applies to DODDS teachers and their accompanied dependents in an EML status only during school year holiday/vacation periods.
   (2) Category 2B.
      (a) Active duty uniformed service members, foreign exchange officers and enlisted personnel filling DOD positions in leave or pass status other than emergency, and uniformed service patients on convalescent leave.
      (b) When accompanied by their sponsor who is in an authorized leave status, bona fide dependents of uniformed service members (to include college students up to 23 years of age), foreign exchange officers and enlisted personnel on duty with the DOD. This privilege is not applicable to travel of dependents to or from a sponsor's restricted or all others (unaccompanied) tour area, or to travel in a leave status in conjunction with TDY or TAD. This privilege is intended only for a visit to an oversea area or the CONUS on a round-

Appendix A. Cont'd
trip basis with the sponsor. It will not be used to establish a home for dependents in an oversea area or the CONUS. Flights will not be scheduled for any of the above travel.

(c) Civilian US Armed Forces patients, as identified in paragraph 11-21(3) and (4), who have recovered after treatment in medical facilities and their accompanying non-medical attendants. Travel is permitted to return the recovered patient and non-medical attendant from an oversea APOE to the oversea post of assignment. In the event of the death or extended hospitalization of the patient, the non-medical attendant retains the space available travel authority to return to the patient's oversea port of assignment.

(d) Medal of Honor Holders. Presentation of the Medal of Honor Identification and Travel Card is required, if not active or retired military.

(e) Dependents of Medal of Honor Holders when accompanied by their sponsor. Dependents must present DD Form 1173, "Dependent Identification Card."

(3) Category 2C.

(a) Unaccompanied EML dependents 17 years of age or older. EML dependents under 17 must be accompanied by an adult, EML eligible family member (see Chapter 10).

(b) DODDS teachers or dependents (accompanied or unaccompanied) in an EML status during the summer break.

d. **Category 3.**

(1) Dependents of active duty uniformed service personnel and US citizen civilian employees of the DOD paid from either appropriated or nonappropriated funds with transportation agreements and American Red Cross personnel, who are stationed overseas with their sponsor, may travel to and from the nearest oversea military academy testing site to take scheduled entrance examinations for entry into any of the US service academies.

(2) Student dependents of members of the uniformed services and US citizen civilian employees of the DOD paid from either appropriated or nonappropriated funds and American Red Cross personnel serving an accompanied tour overseas, including secondary school students (grade 7 through 12 or equivalent) and college or trade school students, engaged in undergraduate study as follows:

(a) When studying in the US, for travel to and from the nearest oversea MAC terminal for onward travel from the oversea APOE to the US. Dependents of uniformed service members, and of US citizen civilian employees traveling under the Foreign Service Act of 1980, are given space required transportation under paragraph 3-3b(9), and as such are not entitled to space available travel under this paragraph.

(b) When traveling between their sponsor's oversea duty station when attending, in residence, an oversea branch of an American (US) university located in the same oversea area. In addition, during periods of extended school vacation when boarding facilities of a branch of an American university in the oversea area normally are closed, round-trip transportation between oversea schools and sponsor's oversea station is authorized.

1. Students must present written authorization from an approving authority.

2. Transportation from the US to attend school in an oversea area is not permitted.

NOTE: The space available privilege cited in paragraph 4-7d(2) also applies to students who are 21 years of age or older at the time of the sponsor's PCS to the overseas area. This privilege will terminate on the sponsor's PCS to the US or the student's 23rd birthday, whichever is earlier.

(3) On dedicated ambassadorial support flights only, employees of US Government agencies and their accompanying dependents traveling in a leave status. Employees and their dependents traveling for medical treatment or consultation (accompanied or unaccompanied) when medical treatment or consultaion is inadequate at the home stations.

Appendix A, Cont'd

(4) Military personnel traveling on permissive temporary duty orders published under applicable military department regulation.

e. Category 4.
(1) Unaccompanied retired uniformed services members as defined in paragraph 2-4x. (Note paragraph 2-12b.)
(2) Retired uniformed services members accompanied by dependents. (Note paragraph 2-12b.)
(3) Members of reserve components of the Armed Forces traveling within Alaska, Hawaii, Puerto Rico or the Virgin Islands only or between Hawaii, Guam and American Samoa in the following categories:

(a) Active status members in uniform upon presentation of DD Form 2 (red) and authentication of their current active status with a completed DD Form 1853.

(b) Members of the reserve components who have received official notification of retirement eligibility, but have not reached the mandatory retirement age (60), upon presentation of DD Form 2 (red) and a notice of retirement eligibility as described in DOD Directive 1200.15, 16 Feb 73. Wearing of the uniform is not required.

(c) Active Reserve members in a pass status who are on active duty in an oversea area for any length of time are eligible for space available travel. Required documentation is DD Form 2 (red), Armed Forces Identification Card, and active duty orders authorizing the reservist to be in the assigned oversea area during the period travel is requested.

APPENDIX B

PERSONAL ENTRY REQUIREMENTS

The information contained in this appendix is synthesized (to specifically meet Space-A travelers' needs) from the US Air Force Foreign Clearance Guides, corrected to 5 April 1986. The information for some countries is from the International Flight Information Manual, DOT, April 1985, Vol 33 with corrections. The publisher, DOD and DOT are not responsible for the currency of data in this appendix because it is subject to change on an infrequent basis. Space-A travelers, when in doubt about personal entry requirements to foreign countries, should call or write to the anticipated departure location or military personnel office (which issues official duty orders) for current entry information.

NOTE: For regional (NSA, EUR, AF and PAC) vaccination requirements see the end of this appendix.

ANTIGUA (AN)

PASSPORT: Not required.
VISA: Not required.
VACCINATION: NSA, + yellow fever if arriving from infected areas.
OTHER: ID card (All). AD, orders. Embarkation and debarkation cards are required for civilians arriving on civil aircraft.

ARGENTINA (AG)

PASSPORT: Required (All).
VISA: Required (All).
VACCINATION: NSA, + yellow fever.
OTHER: AD, ID card and orders. No uniforms. AD notify USDAO (Comm: 774-7611) of planned travel, name, rank, dates & points of departure.

Appendix B, Cont'd
ASCENSION ISLAND (AS)
PASSPORT: Not required.
VISA: Not required.
VACCINATION: NSA.
OTHER: AD, ID card and orders.

AUSTRALIA (AU)
PASSPORT: Required (All).
VISA: Required (All).
VACCINATION: All arriving from infected areas require smallpox, DPT, polio (oral), influenza (vol for non-military) and yellow fever.
OTHER: AD, ID card and orders. All Space-A Pax, $20 departure fee. AD, civilian clothing will be worn to and from UMR & ASP. AD must advise USDAO in Canberra (Comm:(062) 73-3711), of length of stay and leave address. Follow with letter & orders.

AZORES (See Portugal, PO)

BAHAMAS (BH)
PASSPORT: Not required. ID or POC.
VISA: Not required.
VACCINATION: NSA, + yellow fever and cholera if arriving from infected areas.
OTHER: AD, ID card and orders.

BAHRAIN (BA)
PASSPORT: Required (All).
VISA: Required (All). Landing visa valid for 72 hrs. Available at arpt.
VACCINATION: AF, + yellow fever if arriving from infected areas.
OTHER: No uniforms.

BARBADOS (BB)
PASSPORT: Not required. ID or POC.
VISA: Not required for up to 6 mos.
VACCINATION: NSA, + yellow fever if arriving from infected areas.
OTHER: Customs and immigration if leaving airport.

BARBUDA (BD)
PASSPORT: Not required.
VISA: Not required.
VACCINATION: NSA, + yellow fever if arriving from infected areas.
OTHER: ID card (All). AD, orders.

BELGIUM (BE)
PASSPORT: Required (AD exempt).
VISA: Not required for 90 days.
VACCINATION: EUR.
OTHER: AD, ID card and orders. Civilian clothing recommended. Registration with police required within 8 days of arrival.

BELIZE (BZ)
PASSPORT: Not required. POC. ID card is unacceptable.
VISA: Not required.
VACCINATION: NSA, + yellow fever and cholera if arriving from infected areas.
OTHER: AD, ID card and orders.

BERMUDA (BM)
PASSPORT: Not required. POC.
VISA: Not required for 6 mos.
VACCINATION: NSA.
OTHER: AD, ID card and orders.

BOLIVIA (BO)
PASSPORT: Required (All).
VISA: Required, except transient Pax. AD, tourist card (good for 90 days) or visa.
VACCINATION: NSA, + yellow fever.
OTHER: No uniforms in public places. Show entry stamp in passport or tourist card when departing.

BRAZIL (BR)
PASSPORT: Required (All).
VISA: Required (All).
VACCINATION: NSA, + yellow fever.
OTHER: AD, ID card and orders. AD, uniforms at airport only and while transiting to/from airports.

CANADA (CN)
PASSPORT: Not required.
VISA: Not required.
VACCINATION: NSA.
OTHER: AD, ID card and orders. No uniforms.

CHAD (CD)
PASSPORT: Required (All).
VISA: Required (All).
VACCINATION: AF, + yellow fever,

Appendix B, Cont'd

cholera and smallpox. Gamma globulin recommended.
OTHER: AD must notify USDAO N'Djamena (Comm: 32-69) upon arrival. ID card (All). AD, orders. No photography allowed.

CHILE (CH)

PASSPORT: Required (All).
VISA: Not req for up to 90 days.
VACCINATION: NSA, + yellow fever.
OTHER: AD, ID card and orders.

COLUMBIA (CL)

PASSPORT: Required (All).
VISA: Required (All) or 90-day tourist card with 2 photos.
VACCINATION: NSA, + yellow fever.
OTHER: AD, ID card and orders. AD, contact USDAO (Comm: 285-1300/1688) upon arrival for briefing on current security situation. No uniforms.

COSTA RICA (CS)

PASSPORT: Required (All).
VISA: Required (All). Exit permit required and available at airport.
VACCINATION: NSA, + yellow fever.
OTHER: AD, ID card and orders. AD, contact USDAO (Comm: 33-0482) on 1st working day after arrival. AD, no uniforms without AMEM permit.

CRETE (CR)
(Same as Greece.)

CUBA (CU)
(Guantanamo Bay, NAS)

PASSPORT: Not required.
VISA: Not required.
VACCINATION: NSA, + yellow fever.
OTHER: ID card (All). AD, orders. AD, Class "A" uniforms on arrival and departure.

CYPRUS (CY)

PASSPORT: Required (All).
VISA: Not required.
VACCINATION: EUR, + yellow fever and cholera if arriving from infected areas.
OTHER: ID card (All). AD, orders. Entry permit for predetermined period is entered in passport at port of entry based on info given by Pax. It may be extended if more than 90 days are needed. Prior clearance fm USDAO (Comm: 33-11-55) required for group leave travel. Inform USDAO, in person or by phone, of arrival, duration of stay and address. No uniforms.

DENMARK (DN)

PASSPORT: Required (AD exempt).
VISA: Not required. Residence permit over 3 months.
VACCINATION: EUR.
OTHER: AD, ID card and orders.

DIEGO GARCIA (See INDIAN OCEAN, IO)

DOMINICAN REPUBLIC (DR)

PASSPORT: Not required.
VISA: Not required if tourist card is used to enter. Tourist card available in country with birth certificate or passport.
VACCINATION: NSA, + yellow fever if arriving from infected areas.
OTHER: No uniforms.

ECUADOR (EC)

PASSPORT: Required (All).
VISA: Required after 30 days.
VACCINATION: NSA, + yellow fever.
OTHER: AD, ID card and orders.

UNITED ARAB REPUBLIC OF EGYPT (EG)

PASSPORT: Required (All).
VISA: Required (All).
VACCINATION: AF, + yellow fever and cholera.
OTHER: ID card (All). Anyone with tourist passports may obtain visas at Cairo Intl upon arrival; however, expect a 1 to 2 hr delay and a cost of $2-$6 US. Tourists need in-country sponsor prior to arrival. Must coordinate with Office of Military Cooperation, American Embassy (Comm: 3548211-EX-486/487). No uniforms.

EL SALVADOR (ES)

PASSPORT: Required for over 48 hrs.
VISA: Required for over 48 hrs and good for 3 mos. Exit permits req.
VACCINATION: NSA, + yellow fever.
OTHER: AD, passport, visa, ID card, exit permit, orders and clearance from USDAO San Salvador, APO Miami 34023 (Comm: 26-7100). No uniforms.

Appendix B, Cont'd

GERMANY (WEST) & BERLIN (GE)

PASSPORT: Required (AD exempt).
VISA: Not required under 90 days.
VACCINATION: EUR.
OTHER: AD, ID card and orders. Resident permit from Bonn is required if stay exceeds 3 mos. Civilian clothing recommended.

GREECE (GR)

PASSPORT: Not required.
VISA: Not required up to 60 days.
VACCINATION: EUR, + yellow fever from endemic areas and smallpox if arriving from Israel.
OTHER: AD, passport or ID card and orders. Over 60 days must obtain alien resident permit or police ID card. Four photos req with application. Civilian clothing recommended.

GREENLAND (GL)

PASSPORT: Required if landing at other than US bases.
VISA: Not required, but clearance required from Commander, Thule AB, APO New York 09023.
VACCINATION: NSA. A medical statement dated the day before departure is required. It must be certified by Danish Consul and must contain statement from local health authority certifying that no malignant epidemic disease has been reported at point of departure.
OTHER: AD, ID card and orders. Off-base activity is restricted. Must get permission from Danish Liaison Officer, thru Base Commander, to travel to villages and settlements off base. Confirmation of quarters is required before arrival.

GUAM (GU)

PASSPORT: Not required.
VISA: Not required.
VACCINATION: PAC, + yellow fever if arriving from endemic areas.
OTHER: AD, ID card and orders.

GUATEMALA (GT)

PASSPORT: Required (AD, see below).
VISA: Required (AD, see below).
VACCINATION: NSA, + yellow fever.
OTHER: ID card (All). AD, orders.

AD may use tourist card plus birth certificate in lieu of passport and visa. Obtain tourist card before entry fm Guatemala Consulate, travel agency, or civil airlines. It is good for 30 days. AD, notify USDAO (Comm: 31-15-41) on arrival.

HAITI (HA)

PASSPORT: Required (All).
VISA: Required; or tourist card good for 90 days.
VACCINATION: NSA, + yellow fever if arriving from infected areas.
OTHER: AD on leave for 90 days or less require only POC and a tourist card (available at aerodrome for $2 US). POC and tourist card may be used in lieu of passport and visa. US citizen tourist who stays 1 mo or less and US dependents on leave or in transit, arriving by commercial aircraft, may use tourist card and POC in lieu of passport and visa. Haitian citizens serving in the US military will be permitted to enter but must have no-fee passport and exit permit to depart. Unless traveling by military aircraft, a $5 US departure tax is required. AD should inform USDAO upon arrival (Comm: 2-0200, 2-0368, EX 228/230, country code 509, city code 1).

HONDURAS (HO)

PASSPORT: Required (All).
VISA: Required (see below).
VACCINATION: NSA, + yellow fever. Preventive dosages of gamma globulin (to minimize hepatitis risk) are required.
OTHER: Space-A Pax may enter at any of the 4 airports. AD may depart fm any of the 4 airports for any destination in CONUS. However, space-A dependents and retired military Pax may only depart these airports for CONUS destinations that are serviced by civilian customs and immigration officers. AD on leave require a tourist passport valid for at least 6 mos. Tourist visas can be obtained at Honduran diplomatic offices in US. Valid for 30 days and one entry, but can be renewed for up to 6 mos while in Honduras. AD may enter with tourist passport and no visa. However, they will be required to pur-

Appendix B, Cont'd

chase a tourist card for 4.00 lempira at the airport of entry. It is valid for 30 days, but may be renewed for up to 6 mos. All Pax departing on commercial airlines must pay a 20.00 lempira exit tax (2 lempiras/$1 US). No uniforms.

ICELAND (IC)

PASSPORT: Required (AD exempt).
VISA: Not required under 90 days.
VACCINATION: EUR, + meningococcal and adenovirus vaccine.
OTHER: AD, ID card and orders. No uniforms off military installations.

INDIAN OCEAN (IO)
DIEGO GARCIA
(CHAGOS ARCHIPELAGO)

PASSPORT: Not required.
VISA: Not required.
VACCINATION: PAC.
OTHER: Clearance is required from: Commander, NAVSUPPFAC DEIGO GARCIA, FPO San Francisco 96685-1200. Must have sponsor or confirmation of local accomodations. Publisher has been informally advised that space-A Pax may transit Diego Garcia provided advance clearance is obtained from the above.

INDONESIA (IE)

PASSPORT: Required (All).
VISA: Required (All). Can be obtained in country, good for 60 days.
VACCINATION: PAC.
OTHER: ID card (All). AD, orders. AD must advise USDAO Jakarta (Comm: 34 0001-9). Permission is required to travel to Irian Jaya and Timor. Civilian clothing recommended.

IRELAND (IR)

PASSPORT: Required (AD exempt).
VISA: Required (AD exempt).
VACCINATION: EUR.
OTHER: ID card (All). AD, orders.
No uniforms.

ISRAEL (IS)

PASSPORT: Required (All).
VISA: Required (All).
VACCINATION: AF.
OTHER: ID cards (All). AD, orders.
AD inform USDAO Tel Aviv by phone (Comm: (03)654338) immediately upon arrival of presence & travel plans. Civilian clothing recommended.

ITALY (IT)

PASSPORT: Required (AD exempt).
VISA: Not required for up to 90 days.
VACCINATION: EUR, + cholera if arriving from infected areas.
OTHER: AD, ID card and orders. Civilian clothing recommended.

JAMAICA (JM)

PASSPORT: Not required.
VISA: Not required up to 6 mos.
VACCINATION: NSA, + yellow fever if arriving from infected areas.
OTHER: ID card (All). AD, orders. Civilian clothing recommended.

JAPAN (JA)

PASSPORT: Required (AD exempt with Japan destination).
VISA: Required (AD exempt).
VACCINATION: PAC.
OTHER: Space-A Pax should have confirmed lodging. AD, ID card & orders.

JOHNSTON ATOLL (JO)

PASSPORT: Not required.
VISA: Not required.
VACCINATION: PAC.
OTHER: Clearance required: MAC RAP/FCDNA, Terminal Operations, APO San Francisco 96305-5000. AD, ID card, orders and copy of entrance approval required.

JORDAN (JR)

PASSPORT: Required (All).
VISA: Required (All).
VACCINATION: AF.
OTHER: ID card (All). AD, orders.
Visas available on entry at aerodrome. No uniforms.

KENYA (KE)

PASSPORT: Required (All).
VISA: Required. Transit visas available for 8 days.
VACCINATION: AF, + yellow fever and cholera.
OTHER: Entry & exit passes required + visa for next destination. Space-

Appendix B, Cont'd

A to or from Kenya is not authorized except emergency leave & those residing/stationed in East Africa, Sudan, Madagascar, Mauritius or the Seychelles. Space-A Pax must have documentation of above. Travelers who are not AD or Civ on orders may be required to show proof of means of departure from Kenya or make a deposit in cash or travelers checks until departure. No uniforms. AMEM Kenya, PO Box 30137, Moi/Haile Selassie Ave, Nairobi, Kenya. Comm: 334141.

LIBERIA (LI)

PASSPORT: Required (All).
VISA: Required & valid for 90 days.
VACCINATION: AF.
OTHER: All Pax entering Liberia must report to immigration headquarters Monrovia within 48 hrs of arrival to obtain permit to stay for duration of their planned visit. (AMEM in Liberia, PO Box 98, 111 United Nations Dr, Monrovia, Liberia. Comm: 222991.) The maximum stay is 3 mos. US State Dept strongly advises that Pax maintain permits in good order; failure to do so can result in a heavy fine. Pax are required to obtain an exit permit from immigration headquarters before departing Liberia. There is a 7-day delay in issuing exit visas. AMEM recommends Americans who plan to spend a week or more in Liberia register at the Consular Section and obtain an info packet for newcomers.

MARIANA (MR)
(See Trust Territories)

MIDWAY ISLANDS (MW)

PASSPORT: Not required.
VISA: Not required.
VACCINATION: None.
OTHER: Clearance required. Address: COMTHIRDFLT, Pearl Harbor, HI 96860. Clearance can be assumed unless otherwise advised. Include following statement in request: "Concurrence will be assumed unless otherwise advised within ten days."

NETHERLANDS (NT)

PASSPORT: Required (AD exempt).
VISA: Not required.
VACCINATION: EUR.
OTHER: AD, ID card and orders.
No uniforms.

NEW ZEALAND (NZ)

PASSPORT: Required (All).
VISA: Required except for US citizens remaining less than 30 days.
VACCINATION: PAC.
OTHER: ID card (All). AD, orders. US citizens traveling space-A who are unintentionally delayed beyond 30 days because of lack of available trans must request an extension thru New Zealand immigration officials.

NICARAGUA (NI)

PASSPORT: Required (All).
VISA: Required (All).
VACCINATION: NSA, + yellow fever.
OTHER: Pax arriving and departing on the same aircraft require passport but not visa. AD arriving and departing on same aircraft will be required to complete entry and exit cards. No uniforms. Uniforms should not be carried as part of luggage. All US-naturalized former Nicaraguan citizens serving in US Armed Forces and their dependents should use a US passport to avoid departure delays.

NORWAY (NO)

PASSPORT: Required (All).
VISA: Required (All).
VACCINATION: EUR.
OTHER: AD, ID card and orders.
No uniforms.

OMAN (OM)

PASSPORT: Required (All).
VISA: Required (All).
VACCINATION: AF, + yellow fever if arriving from infected areas.
OTHER: No uniforms.

PARAGUAY (PG)

PASSPORT: Required (All).
VISA: Not required up to 90 days.
VACCINATION: NSA, + yellow fever.
OTHER: ID card (All). AD, orders, immunization records and passport with necessary visas. Visas not available at airport. AD do not require prior clearance but should contact USDAO upon arrival (Comm:

Appendix B, Cont'd

201-041, EX 265). All persons holding regular passports and intending to visit more than 24 hrs and less than 90 days are required to obtain a tourist card. Card is available from commercial carriers serving Paraguay or at port of entry. Cost is $3 US. One half of card is handed over to immigration officials at time of entry; remaining half is handed over at time of departure.

PERU (PE)

PASSPORT: Required (All).
VISA: Required (All).
VACCINATION: NSA, + yellow fever.
OTHER: ID cards (All). AD, orders. AD, require tourist card if using Official passport. Tourist card (Cedula C) is issued at no charge at, or inbound to, Jorge Chavez Intl to all persons with Official passports in tourist status and all persons with regular passports staying 2 to 90 days. AF AD must contact USAIRA office (Comm: 286000) for an area briefing. All other AD must register with diplomatic officials designated by pilot.

PORTUGAL (AZORES) (PO)

PASSPORT: Required (All).
VISA: Not required.
VACCINATION: EUR, + yellow fever if arriving from infected areas.
OTHER: AD on leave to Lajes require a passport or bilingual orders in Portuguese and English or French and English. Dependents are required to have individual passports. Dependents of AD must personally clear thru Portuguese immigration authorities immediately upon arrival in and prior to departure from Azores. When passports are required, Pax receives a free 60-day visa upon entry. Visa must be renewed every 60 days (for a small fee) unless marked "good born" by US authorities in the Azores. Civilians on MAC aircraft transiting Lajes as through-flights are not required to clear immigration unless delayed for longer than 24 hrs after arrival.

PUERTO RICO (PR)

PASSPORT: Not required.
VISA: Not required.

VACCINATION: NSA, + yellow fever if arriving from infected areas.
OTHER: ID card (All). AD, orders & POC. Passports required for civilian personnel if entering fm other than North, South or Central America, or adjacent islands. Check local regulations for off-limit restrictions.

REPUBLIC OF KOREA (RK)

PASSPORT: Required (AD exempt).
VISA: Required for over 15 days (AD exempt).
VACCINATION: PAC, + cholera if arriving from infected areas.
OTHER: ID card (All). AD, orders. Korean nationals, who are dependents of US personnel, holding Korean Resident Abroad Passport or a Korean Immigrant Passport, must obtain consular approval and passport validation (stamp) prior to their temporary return to Korea. Article 9 of Korean passport law states that a passport will be canceled upon the holder's return to Korea unless the person returns to Korea with a temporary Home Coming Permit given in adv by Ministry of Foreign Affairs. Transit visas are available for visits of 15 days or less. Tourist visas are valid for one entry within 6 mos of issue for 30-day stay (cannot change status). Entry and exit permits are required for civilians. Non-US citizens, including dependents, must have passports and visas if staying more than five days.

REPUBLIC OF PANAMA (PN)

PASSPORT: Required (All).
VISA: Required (All).
VACCINATION: NSA, + yellow fever & and cholera if arriving from infected areas.
OTHER: AD and civ personnel entering Panama on leave must have valid US passport with visa or tourist card for Panama. Not available at Panama airports. All AD outbound fm Howard AFB on DOD aircraft bound for CONUS, Alaska, Hawaii or Puerto Rico are required to clear military customs prior to departure. Absolutely no uniforms.

Appendix B, Cont'd
REPUBLIC OF PHILIPPINES (RP)

PASSPORT: Required (All).
VISA: Required (All).
VACCINATION: PAC.
OTHER: AD may enter thru Clark AB, Cubi Point NAS and Subic Bay Naval Base, in uniform, with ID card and orders. May stay up to 30 days, which may be extended, and will be allowed to exit thru a commercial airport if so desired. No immigration fee will be levied for either the initial period of stay or any extension. **Note:** Orders should include the Philippines as a leave location/destination even if the member does not intend to remain in the Philippines. Failure to do so will result in stay being limited to 72 hrs by Philippines immigration officials. If 72-hr limit is exceeded, the member is subject to immigration fees or fines. Do not use APO/FPO numbers to satisfy this requirement. All dependents, military retirees & other civilian personnel entering the Philippines thru US facilities for the purpose of leave are req to possess a passport and a 9a visa. Philippine immigration regs allow all tourists to enter the country via an international commercial airport with a valid passport and no visa requirement for stays up to 21 days, extendable to 59 days, if the traveler is in possession of onward ticket. Pax who enter Philippines thru commercial airports without visas may not exit via the US facilities. Philippine nationals in the US Armed Forces may enter Philippines for purposes of leave upon presentation of the same documentation as other US military members, i.e., ID card and orders, when in uniform.

SAUDI ARABIA (SA)

PASSPORT: Required (All).
VISA: Required (All).
VACCINATION: AF, + yellow fever if arriving from infected areas.
OTHER: It is highly unlikely that AD would be permitted to conduct leave travel in Saudi Arabia. Such travel requires a visa granted by the Saudi govt and visas are not normally issued except for official business and for matters of interest to the SAG. Although it is extremely unlikely that such a situation might develop, AD should inform both USDAO Jidda (Comm: 464-0012) and CHUSMTM/MR Dhahran if leave occurs in Saudi Arabia. No uniforms.
   ID card (All). AD, orders. All space-A Pax attempting thru passage must have a valid transit visa in case they are removed for duty passengers. Transit visas are required for all arriving via commercial air to depart via MAC Channel Flight or arriving MAC Channel Flight for departure via commercial flight. Visas are valid for 87 days (three Saudi months). Personnel arriving without a valid passport and Saudi Arabian visa will be denied entry to the country and are subject to deportation, at personal expense, on the next available flight.

SINGAPORE (SG)

PASSPORT: Required (All).
VISA: Not required.
VACCINATION: PAC. Physician must sign and authenticate with stamp in the space provided on International Certificate of Vaccination. Unless record is annotated in this manner and immunizations are up-to-date, Pax will be detained at airport for reimmunization. Singapore health authorities are uncompromising on this matter.
OTHER: Entry permits are stamped in passports on entry and are valid for one entry and up to 14 days. All US citizens planning to remain beyond expiration of entry permit will require visas. Visas are obtained thru consular section of AMEM, 30 Hill Street, Singapore 0617 (Comm: 338-0251). All personnel who arrive via Paya Lebor Airport but who depart from another airport must notify immigation authorities so documents can be ammended to reflect such. There is a $12 airport tax when departing Seletar or Changi Intl ($5 to Maylasia). No uniforms.

SOMALI DEMOCRATIC REPUBLIC (SM) (SOMALIA)

PASSPORT: Required (All).
VISA: Required (All).
VACCINATION: AF, + yellow fever. Cholera, arriving fm infected areas.

Appendix B, Cont'd
OTHER: AD, ID card and orders. AD must give prior notice to AMEM: USDAO Mogadishu, Somalia, State Dept Pouch Room, Washington, DC 20520 (Comm: 28011). Uniform or civilian clothing is acceptable.

SOUTH AFRICA (SF)
PASSPORT: Required (All).
VISA: Required (All).
VACCINATION: AF.
OTHER: ID card (All). AD, orders & shot records. AD should advise USDAO (Comm: (012)28-4266) upon arrival & provide a contact point in case of recall/emergency. No uniforms.

SPAIN (SP)
PASSPORT: Required. (AD exempt with ID card and orders. See below.)
VISA: Not required.
VACCINATION: EUR. Yellow fever going to Canary Islands fm infected areas.
OTHER: AD, leave authorization should contain the following statement: "La persona a quien esta orden pertenezca esta authorizada por las autoridades militares competentes de los Estados Unidos de America para entrar o salir de Espana en mision oficial vestido de civil o militar." No uniforms.

SUDAN (SU)
PASSPORT: Required (All).
VISA: Required (All).
VACCINATION: AF, + yellow fever and cholera, arriving fm infected areas. AMEM recommends all Pax begin taking malaria suppressants (500mg of chloroquine) two weeks prior to arrival.
OTHER: No uniforms. AD should contact USDAO (Comm: 74700) upon arrival.

THAILAND (TH)
PASSPORT: Required (All).
VISA: Req for more than 15 days.
VACCINATION: PAC.
OTHER: All persons who depart Thailand must have a valid passport bearing an unexpired Thai entry stamp or resident permit. Personnel and dependents with passports may enter Thailand for 15 days without a visa. This period may not be extended. If there is any possibility the visit may exceed 15 days, Pax must obtain non-immigrant or tourist visas, depending on purpose of visit. A stamp in lieu of a visa is given at the aerodrome or border if a visa has not been previously obtained. This is good for 15 days & cannot be renewed. A tourist visa, which must be obtained before arrival from a Thai embassy or consulate abroad, is good for 60 days. Not renewable (except for 30 days in some cases by posting a bond of $1000 US per person).

TRUST TERRITORY OF THE PACIFIC ISLANDS (TT)
(Includes Western Caroline Islands: Palau and Yap Islands; Eastern Caroline Islands: Truk, Ponape & Kosrae Islands; Marshall Islands: which include Majuro, Kwajalein, Enewetak, etc. Mariana Islands, which include Saipan, Tinian and Rota but not Guam, are no longer Trust Territories but the following data still applies.)

PASSPORT: Not required.
VISA: Not required.
VACCINATION: PAC.
OTHER: POC and ID cards (All). AD, orders. All Pax must have round trip or onward ticket and, if required, a valid visa the next destination.

TURKEY (TU)
PASSPORT: Required (AD exempt).
VISA: Required after 90 days.
VACCINATION: EUR, + yellow fever if arriving from endemic areas.
OTHER: AD, ID card and orders. AD will inform USDAO Ankara (Comm: 26-54-70) with info copy to CJUSMMAT/TDAI, 110 Ataturk Blvd, Ankara, Turkey, of their arrival & place of residence while in Turkey. Stays in excess of 90 days require a resident permit. Private US citizens should apply for ID card/residence permit directly fm appropriate GOT authorities in their area of residence. Pax entering Turkey should always get individual copy of orders or passports stamped by customs/immigration upon arrival, and be prepared to present such documentation to customs/immigration officials

Appendix B, Cont'd

upon departure fm Turkey regardless of length of stay. AD are required to wear civilian clothes in city of Istanbul. Personnel traveling to, from, or within Turkey on board military aircraft whose embarkation or debarkation point is Esenboga Airport (Ankara), Ataturk (Istanbul), or Cigli AB (Ismir) will wear civilian clothing unless otherwise directed. Military members will wear the appropriate service uniform unless directed as above.

UNITED KINGDOM (UK)

PASSPORT: Required (AD, except attaches, exempt).
VISA: Not required.
VACCINATION: EUR.
OTHER: AD, ID card and orders. Civilian clothes at all times in N Ireland; uniforms elsewhere only when specified by host.

URUGUAY (UG)

PASSPORT: Required (All).
VISA: Not required.
VACCINATION: NSA, + yellow fever.
OTHER: ID card (All). AD, orders. No uniforms.

VENEZUELA (VE)

PASSPORT: Required (All).
VISA: Required (All).
VACCINATION: NSA, + yellow fever.
OTHER: Registration with authorities required for stay over 3 days. Passport with visa and a tourist card or "carte de tourismo" in hand required. General/Flag officers, notify USDAO (Comm: 284-6111/7111) of leave travel.

VIRGIN ISLANDS (VI)

PASSPORT: Not required.
VISA: Not required for up to 6 mos.
VACCINATION: NSA, + yellow fever if arriving from infected areas.
OTHER: ID card (All). AD, orders. Non-US citizens are required to complete Form I-151 (Alien Registration Card).

WAKE ISLAND (WK)

PASSPORT: Not required.
VISA: Not required.
VACCINATION: None.
OTHER: Clearance required. Call thru Honolulu, HI, Small Island Operator, and ask for Wake Island EX 428 or 210/483. Address: Det 4, 15ABW, San Francisco 96501-5000. Clearance can be assumed unless otherwise advised. Include following statement in request: "Concurrence will be assumed unless otherwise advised within ten days."

WEST CAROLINE ISLANDS (WC)
(See Trust Territories)

ZAIRE (ZA)

PASSPORT: Required (All).
VISA: Required (All).
VACCINATION: AF.
OTHER: ID card (All). AD, ID card and orders. Must enter country at Kinshasa. Visas must be obtained prior to arrival. Visas for other than official business require approval from Foreign Ministry, Kinshasa, with probable three weeks delay. Multiple entry visas should be obtained for period well in excess of planned stay to cover any changes requiring overstay. Travel on leave status is highly discouraged by USDAO. Clearance is required from USDAO (Comm: 25881/6) prior to entry. US military space-A travel is highly discouraged and must be approved in advance by the Chief, US Military Mission to Zaire (ZAMISH). Uniforms will not be worn when on leave or liberty.

IMMUNIZATION REQUIREMENTS

The following are the immunization requirements for areas designated as North and South America (NSA); Europe (EUR); Africa and Southwest Asia (AF); and Pacific, South Asia, and Indian Ocean (PAC). In addition, individual countries may have their own requirements. This information is synthesized from the US Air Force Foreign Clearance Guide, current as of 17 April 1986. This publisher, DOD and the Air Force are not responsible for the accuracy or currency of the information as it is subject to change without notice.

Appendix B, Cont'd

NOTE: The International Certificates of Vaccination, Form PHS-731, are issued by the Public Health Service. These yellow shot records are available at your local military medical facility and/or passport offices.

NORTH AND SOUTH AMERICA (NSA)

1. Immunization requirements for travel to the Caribbean and South American area are as follows: DPT, polio (oral) and influenza (voluntary for non-military).

2. Immunization requirements for travel from North America to the South American area are as follows (voluntary for non-military personnel): DPT, polio (oral), influenza, meningococcal and adenovirus.

3. Smallpox immunization required for all active duty and reserve personnel but not for DOD civilians (including dependents).

EUROPE (EUR)

1. Immunizations required (voluntary for non-military personnel) for travel to the European area: DPT, polio (oral) and influenza.

2. Smallpox immunization required for all active duty and reserve personnel but not for DOD civilians (including dependents).

AFRICA AND SOUTHWEST ASIA (AF)

DOD personnel traveling to this area require the following immunizations: DPT, polio (oral) and influenza (voluntary for non-military personnel). Yellow fever is also required for travel to or thru yellow fever endemic or receptive areas. Smallpox is required for all active duty and reserve military personnel but not for DOD civilians (including dependents).

PACIFIC, SOUTH ASIA, AND INDIAN OCEAN (PAC)

1. Immunization required (voluntary for non-military personnel) for travel to the Pacific area: DPT, polio (oral) influenza and meningococcal.

2. Yellow fever immunization required for all travel to or thru a yellow fever endemic area.

3. Smallpox immunization required for all active duty and reserve personnel but not for DOD civilians (including dependents).

PROOF OF US CITIZENSHIP (POC)

The following documents are considered valid proof of US citizenship:
    a. US Passport.
    b. Birth or baptismal certificate.
    c. State identification card.
    d. Naturalization certificate.
    e. Voter identification card.
    f. US military identification card (regardless of true citizenship of military member).
    g. US military dependent identification card (regardless of true citizenship of military member).

APPENDIX C

PASSPORTS AND OTHER DOCUMENTS

The required personal entry documents vary from country to country, but you probably will require one or more of the following: passport or other proof of citizenship, visa, or tourist card. A few countries also require evidence that you have enough money for your trip and/or your ongoing transportation tickets. To find out what you need, consult this appendix, Appendix D: Visa Information, Appendix B: Personal Entry Requirements, and embassies or nearest consulates of the countries you plan to visit. These official institutions representing foreign governments in the United States are located in major US cities and have the most up-to-date information. They are, therefore, your best source.

Who Needs A Passport

To enter most foreign countries and to depart from and enter the US, US citizens will need a passport. Exceptions include short-term travel between the US and Mexico or Canada. Many Caribbean countries only require proof of US citizenship, such as a birth certificate. (Check Appendix B.) However, a valid US passport is the best travel document available and, with appropriate visas, is acceptable in all countries.

When To Apply

Demand for passports becomes heavy in January each year and begins to decline in June. But even in the months of July through December there are periods of high demand. It is therefore suggested that you apply several months in advance of your planned departure. If you need visas, allow additional time.

How To Apply

For your first passport, you must present, in person, a completed Passport Application, Form DSP-11, at one of the passport agencies listed in this appendix or at one of several thousand Federal or State courts or US Post Offices that accept passport applications.

Parents or guardians may execute applications for children under the age of 13.

If you have had a previous passport and wish to obtain another, you may be eligible to apply by mail, using Form DSP-82. Check the qualifications listed below under "When To Apply By Mail." If you do not qualify you must apply in person at one of the authorized offices previously mentioned.

What You Need To Obtain A Passport

You must have (1) a properly completed Passport Application (Form DSP-11), (2) proof of US citizenship, (3) proof of identity, (4) two photographs and (5) fees. Each is explained below.

(1) Passport Application - Form DSP-11 is issued by the US Department of State and is available at any place that issues passports.

(2) Proof of US Citizenship - This can be a previously owned passport or one in which you were included. If you are applying for your first passport or cannot submit a previous passport, you must submit other evidence of citizenship as described below.

a. If you were born in the US you may use a birth certificate or secondary evidence of birth. The birth certificate must show that the birth record was filed shortly after birth and must be certified with the registrar's signature and raised, impressed, embossed or multi-colored seal. A delayed birth certificate (filed more than one year after the date of birth) is acceptable if it is accompanied by secondary evidence of birth as described below. If a primary birth certificate is unobtainable, submit a notice from a state registrar stating no birth records exist and include the best possible secondary evidence of birth. This may be a baptismal certificate, a hospital birth record, or other documents such as school, family Bible rec-

Appendix C, Cont'd

ords, newspaper files, or insurance papers.

b. If you were born abroad you will need a Certificate of Naturalization, a Certificate of Citizenship and a Report of Birth Abroad of a Citizen of the USA (Form FS-240) or a Certification of Birth (Form FS-545 or DS-1350).

(3) Proof of Identity - You must establish your identity to the satisfaction of the person executing your application. The following are generally accepted documents of identity if they contain your signature and if they readily identify you by physical description or by photograph.
  a. Previous US passport.
  b. A Certificate of Naturalization or Citizenship.
  c. Driver's license.
  d. A government (federal, state or municipal) identification card or pass.

If you are unable to present one of the above documents to establish your identity, you must be accompanied by a person who has known you for at least two years and who is a US citizen or permanent resident alien of the US. That person must sign an affidavit in the presence of the same person who executes the passport application. The witness will be required to establish his or her own identity.

(4) Two Photographs - Present two identical photographs of yourself which are sufficiently recent (normally taken within the past six months) to be a good likeness. They must be signed on the reverse, with the signature agreeing with that on the application. They must be 2 x 2 inches in size, and the image size measured from the bottom of the chin to the top of the head (including hair) must not be less than 1 nor more than 1-3/8 inches. Passport photos are acceptable in either color or black and white. They should be portrait-type prints taken in normal street attire without a hat and should include no more than the head and shoulders or upper torso. Dark glasses are not acceptable unless for medical reasons.

They should be clear, front view, fullface and printed on thin paper with a plain, light (white or off-white) background. Only active duty personnel on official business may submit photos in uniform. Passport Services of the Dept of State welcomes photos in which the applicant is relaxed - so smile! Vending machine, newspaper and magazine prints are not acceptable.

(5) Fees (and Validity) - US passports for persons over 18 years old are valid for 10 years. Applicants under 18 are isssued 5-year passports, since their appearance changes more quickly. The fee for the 10-year passport is $35. The fee for the 5-year passport is $20. In addition, a $7 execution fee is charged if the application is made in person. This fee is waived if you are mailing in your application. The following forms of payment are acceptable.
  a. Bank draft or cashier's check.
  b. Check: certified, personal or traveler's.
  c. Money order: US Postal, international, currency exchange or bank.
  d. Cash (should not be sent through the mail).

When To Apply By Mail
You may apply by mail if (1) you have been the bearer of a passport issued within 8 years prior to the date of a new application, and (2) you are able to submit your most recent US passport with your new application, and (3) your previous passport was not issued before your 18th birthday.

Eligibility To Apply By Mail
If you are eligible to apply by mail, obtain Form DSP-82, "Application for Passport by Mail," from one of the offices accepting applications and complete the information requested. Sign and date the application. Attach your previous passport. Send two identical photos, which are sufficiently recent (normally taken within the past six months) to be a good likeness, signed on the reverse with a signature that agrees with that on the application. Include the fee: $35 if 18 years of age or older, $20 if

Appendix C, Cont'd

under 18. Mail the completed application and attachments for processing to one of the passport agencies listed in this appendix. An improperly prepared application will delay issuance of your passport.

When You Receive Your Passport
Be sure to sign your passport and fill in the personal notification data.

Additional Visa Pages
If you obtain a passport and thereafter require additional visa pages before your passport expires, you can obtain them by submitting your passport to a passport agency listed in this appendix. Be sure to order a 48-page passport at the time of application if you are planning to travel abroad extensively.

Mutilated or Altered Passports
If you mutilate or alter your US passport in any way other than changing the address and personal notification data, you may render it invalid, cause yourself much inconvenience and expose yourself to possible prosecution under the law (Section 1543 of Title 22 of the US Code). Mutilated or altered passports should be turned in to passport agents, clerks of court, authorized postal employees, or US consular offices abroad.

Loss or Theft of US Passport
If your passport is lost or stolen in the United States, report the loss or theft immediately to Passport Services, Department of State, Washington, DC 20524, or to the nearest passport agency. The loss or theft also should be reported to local police authorities. Should your passport be lost or stolen abroad, report the loss immediately to the nearest Foreign Service post and to local police authorities. If you can provide the consular officer with the information contained in the passport, it will facilitate issuance of a new passport. Therefore, we suggest you photocopy the data page and keep it in a separate place.

Tourist Card
Some countries (Mexico, for example) allow you to enter and remain without a passport or visa. If a country you plan to visit requires a tourist card, you can obtain one from that country's embassy or consulate, from an airline serving that country, or at the port of entry. A fee is required for some tourist cards. Check required. Check entry requirements before you leave the United States.

Proof of Citizenship
If the country you plan to visit requires only proof of US citizenship, you may need a birth certificate, a naturalization certificate, or other document. Check with appropriate embassy or consulate for requirements.

Vaccinations
Under the International Health Regulations adopted by the World Health Organization, a country may require International Certificates of Vaccination against cholera and yellow fever and some countries may require certain other immunizations. Specific information may be obtained from:
   a. Appendix B: Personal Entry Requirements.
   b. Your local or state health department.
   c. Your physician.
   d. A private or public agency that advises international travelers.
   e. The embassy or consulate of each country you plan to visit.
If you do need vaccinations, they must be recorded on approved forms such as the yellow booklet, Form PHS-731, International Certificates of Vaccination. This can be obtained from a military medical facility, any office that issues passports or from Superintendent of Documents, US Government Printing Office, Washington, DC 20402. Keep it with your passport. Double check requirements before you leave.

"Your Trip Abroad"
The State Department Bureau of Consular Affairs issues a complete booklet called "Your Trip Abroad." It is available at Passport Agencies listed below. It can be purchased from the Government Printing Office, Washington, DC 20402. Ask for Dept of State Publication 8872.

Appendix C, Cont'd
PASSPORT AGENCIES

Boston Passport Agency
Room E123, John F Kennedy Bldg
Government Center
Boston, MA 02203
*Recording: (617) 223-3831
**Public Inquiries: (617) 223-2946

Chicago Passport Agency
Suite 380, Kluczynski Federal Bldg
230 South Dearborn St
Chicago, IL 60604
*Recording: (312) 353-5426
**Public Inquiries: (312) 353-7155

Honolulu Passport Agency
Room C-106, New Federal Bldg
300 Ala Moana Blvd
PO Box 50185
Honolulu, HI 96850
*Recording: (808) 546-2131
**Public Inquiries: (808) 546-2130

Houston Passport Agency
One Allen Center
500 Dallas St
Houston, TX 77002
*Recording: (713) 229-3607
**Public Inquiries: (713) 229-3600

Los Angeles Passport Agency
Room 13100, 11000 Wilshire Blvd
Los Angeles, CA 90024
*Recording: (213) 209-7070
**Public Inquiries: (213) 209-7075

Miami Passport Agency
16th Floor, Federal Office Bldg
51 Southwest Ave
Miami, FL 33130
*Recording: (305) 350-5395
**Public Inquiries: (305) 350-4681

New Orleans Passport Agency
Room T-12005, Postal Services Bldg
701 Loyola Ave
New Orleans, LA 70013
*Recording: (504) 589-6728
**Public Inquiries: (504) 589-6161

New York Passport Agency
Room 270, Rockefeller Center
630 Fifth Avenue
New York, NY 10111
*Recording: (212) 541-7700
**Public Inquiries: (212) 541-7710

Philadelphia Passport Agency
Room 4426, Federal Bldg
600 Arch Street
Philadelphia, PA 19106
*Recording: (215) 597-7482
**Public Inquiries: (215) 597-7480

San Francisco Passport Agency
Suite 200, 525 Market Street
San Francisco, CA 94105
*Recording: (415) 974-7972
**Public Inquiries: (415) 974-9941

Seattle Passport Agency
Room 992, Federal Bldg
915 Second Avenue
Seattle, WA 98174
*Recording: (206) 442-7941
**Public Inquiries: (206) 442-7942

Stamford Passport Agency
One Landmark Square
Broad and Atlantic Streets
Stamford, CT 06901
*Recording: (203) 325-4401
**Public Inquiries: (203) 325-3538

Washington Passport Agency
1425 K Street, NW
Washington, DC 20524
*Recording: (202) 523-1673
**Public Inquiries: (202) 523-1355

---

*Twenty-four hour recording includes general passport information, passport agency location and hours of operation.

**For other questions, call Public Inquiries number.

APPENDIX D
VISA INFORMATION

OBTAINING A FOREIGN VISA

A visa is a permit to enter and leave the country to be visited. It is a stamp of endorsement placed in a passport by a consular official of the country to which entry is requested. Nearly all countries require visitors from other na-

Appendix D, Cont'd

tions to have in their possession a valid visa obtained before departing from their home country. A visa may be obtained from foreign embassies or consulates located in the U.S. (Visas are not always obtainable at the airport of entry of the foreign location and verification of visa issuance must be made in advance of departure.) Various types of visas are issued depending upon the nature of the visit and the intended length of stay. Passport services of the Department of State cannot help you obtain visas.

A valid passport must be submitted when applying for a visa of any type. Because the visa is usually stamped directly onto one of the blank pages in your passport, you will need to fill out a form and give your passport to an official of each foreign embassy or consulate. The process may take several weeks for each visa, so apply well in advance. We have listed the visa requirements of each country in **Appendix B**, **"Personal Entry Requirements."**

Some visas require a fee. You may need one or more photographs when submitting your visa applications. They should be full face, on white background and should not be larger than 3 x 3 inches nor smaller than 2.5 x 2.5 inches.

Several countries do not require U.S. citizens to obtain passports and visas for certain types of travel, mostly tourist. Instead, they issue a simple tourist card which can be obtained from the nearest consulate of the country in question (presentation of a birth certificate or similar documentary proof of citizenship may be required.) In some countries, the transportation company is authorized to grant tourist cards. A fee is required for some tourist cards.

The official institutions (embassies or consulates) representing foreign governments in the United States are located in major US cities and have the most up-to-date information. They are, therefore, your best source. Double check visa requirements before you leave. (The Congressional Directory, available at most public libraries, lists their addresses and phone numbers.)

For your convenience, we have listed below the names, addresses and phone numbers of embassies in the countries where stations are frequently used by DOD-owned or controlled aircraft. United States Trust Territories and possessions overseas have the same requirements as the United States has for US citizens upon return from a foreign country. If you wish to travel to a country not listed below, visa and other personal entry requirements can be obtained from the **"U.S. Air Force Foreign Clearance Guide"** available at most MAC (USAF) and other service passenger counters or at many military personnel offices.

NOTE: Embassies may close on their respective national holidays. Call before going to be sure they are open.

ANTIGUA AND BARBUDA (AN - BD)
Embassy of Antigua and Barbuda
2000 N Street NW, Suite 601
Washington, DC 20036
Comm: (202) 296-6310/1/2

ARGENTINA (AG)
Embassy of the Argentine Republic
1600 New Hampshire Ave, NW
Washington, DC 20009
Comm: (202) 939-6400

AUSTRALIA (AU)
Embassy of Australia
1601 Massachusetts Avenue NW
Washington, DC 20036
Comm: (202) 797-3000

AZORES (PO)
(See Portugal (PO).)

BAHAMAS (BH)
Embassy of The Commonwealth of
The Bahamas
600 New Hampshire Ave NW, Suite 865
Washington, DC 20037
Comm: (202) 338-3940

BAHRAIN (BA)
Embassy of the State of Bahrain
3502 International Drive NW
Washington, DC 20008
Comm: (202) 342-0741/2

Appendix D, Cont'd

BARBADOS (BB)
Embassy of Barbados
2144 Wyoming Avenue NW
Washington, DC 20008
Comm: (202) 939-9200

BARBUDA (BD)
(See Antigua (AN).)

BELGIUM (BE)
Embassy of Belgium
3330 Garfield Street NW
Washington, DC 20008
Comm: (202) 333-6900

BELIZE (BZ)
Embassy of Belize
1575 Eye Street NW, Suite 695
Washington, DC 20005
Comm: (202) 289-1416

BERMUDA (BM)
(See United Kingdom.)

BOLIVIA (BO)
Embassy of Bolivia
3014 Massachusetts Avenue NW
Washington, DC 20008
Comm: (202) 483-4410/1/2

BRAZIL (BR)
Brazilian Embassy
3006 Massachusetts Avenue NW
Washington, DC 20008
Comm: (202) 797-0100

CANADA (CN)
Embassy of Canada
1746 Massachusetts Avenue NW
Washington, DC 20036
Comm: (202) 785-1400

CHAD (CD)
Embassy of the Republic of Chad
2002 R Street NW
Washington, DC 20009
Comm: (202) 462-4009

CHILE (CH)
Embassy of Chile
1732 Massachusetts Avenue NW
Washington, DC 20036
Comm: (202) 785-1746

COLOMBIA (CL)
Embassy of Colombia
2118 Leroy Place NW
Washington, DC 20008
Comm: (202) 387-8338

COSTA RICA (CS)
Embassy of Costa Rica
2112 S Street NW
Washington, DC 20008
Comm: (202) 234-2945/6/7

CUBA (CU)
Cuban Interests Section
Embassy of Czechoslovak Socialist
  Republic
2630 16th Street NW
Washington, DC 20009
Comm: (202) 797-8518/8609

CYPRUS (CY)
Embassy of the Republic of Cyprus
2211 R Street NW
Washington, DC 20008
Comm: (202) 462-5772

DENMARK (DN)
Royal Danish Embassy
3200 Whitehaven Street NW
Washington, DC 20008
Comm: (202) 234-4300

DOMINICAN REPUBLIC (DR)
Embassy of the Dominican Republic
1715 22nd Street NW
Washington, DC 20008
Comm: (202) 332-6280

ECUADOR (EC)
Embassy of Ecuador
2535 15th Street NW
Washington, DC 20009
Comm: (202) 234-7200

EGYPT (EG)
Embassy of the Arab Republic of Egypt
3210 Decatur Place NW
Washington, DC 20008
Comm: (202) 232-5400

EL SALVADOR (ES)
Embassy of El Salvador
2308 California Street NW
Washington, DC 20008
Comm: (202) 265-3480/1/2

WEST GERMANY (and West Berlin) (GE)
Embassy of the Federal Republic of
  Germany
4645 Reservoir Road NW
Washington, DC 20007
Comm: (202) 298-4000

GREECE (GR)
Embassy of Greece
2221 Massachusetts Avenue NW
Washington, DC 20008
Comm: (202) 667-3168/3094

Appendix D, Cont'd

GREENLAND (GL)
(See Denmark (DN).)

GUATEMALA (GT)
Embassy of Guatemala
2220 R Street NW
Washington, DC 20008
Comm: (202) 745-4952

HAITI (HA)
Embassy of Haiti
2311 Massachusetts Avenue NW
Washington, DC 20008
Comm: (202) 332-4090/1/2

HONDURAS (HO)
Embassy of Honduras
4301 Connecticut Avenue NW, Suite 100
Washington, DC 20008
Comm: (202) 966-7700/1/2

ICELAND (IC)
Embassy of Iceland
2022 Connecticut Avenue NW
Washington, DC 20008
Comm: (202) 265-6653/4/5

INDONESIA (IE)
Embassy of the Republic of Indonesia
2020 Massachusetts Avenue NW
Washington, DC 20036
Comm: (202) 293-1745

IRELAND (IR)
Embassy of Ireland
2234 Massachusetts Avenue NW
Washington, DC 20008
Comm: (202) 462-3939

ISRAEL (IS)
Embassy of Israel
3514 International Drive NW
Washington, DC 20008
Comm: (202) 364-5500

ITALY (IT)
Embassy of Italy
1601 Fuller Street NW
Washington, DC 20009
Comm: (202) 328-5500

JAMAICA (JM)
Embassy of Jamaica
1850 K Street NW, Suite 355
Washington, DC 20006
Comm: (202) 452-0660

JAPAN (JA)
Embassy of Japan
2520 Massachusetts Avenue NW
Washington, DC 20008
Comm: (202) 234-2266

JORDAN (JR)
Embassy of the Hashemite Kingdom of Jordan
3504 International Dr, NW
Washington, DC 20008
Tel: (202) 966-2664

KENYA (KE)
Embassy of Kenya
2249 R Street NW
Washington, DC 20008
Comm: (202) 387-6101

KOREA (RK)
Embassy of Korea
2370 Massachusetts Avenue NW
Washington, DC 20008
Comm: (202) 483-7383

LIBERIA (LI)
Embassy of the Republic of Liberia
5201 16th Street NW
Washington, DC 20011
Comm: (202) 723-0437

NETHERLANDS (NT)
Embassy of the Netherlands
4200 Linnean Avenue NW
Washington, DC 20008
Comm: (202) 244-5300

NEW ZEALAND (NZ)
Embassy of New Zealand
37 Observatory Circle NW
Washington, DC 20008
Comm: (202) 328-4800

NICARAGUA (NI)
Embassy of Nicaragua
1627 New Hampshire Avenue NW
Washington, DC 20009
Comm: (202) 387-4371

NORWAY (NO)
Royal Norwegian Embassy
2720 34th Street NW
Washington, DC 20008
Comm: (202) 333-6000

OMAN (OM)
Embassy of the Sultanate of Oman
2342 Massachusetts Avenue NW
Washington, DC 20008
Comm: (202) 387-1980

PANAMA (PN)
Embassy of Panama
2862 McGill Terrace NW
Washington, DC 20008
Comm: (202) 483-1407

Appendix D, Cont'd

PARAGUAY (PG)
Embassy of Paraguay
2400 Massachusetts Avenue NW
Washington, DC 20008
Comm: (202) 483-6960

PERU (PE)
Embassy of Peru
1700 Massachusetts Avenue NW
Washington, DC 20036
Comm: (202) 833-9860

PHILIPPINES (RP)
Embassy of the Philippines
1617 Massachusetts Avenue NW
Washington, DC 20036
Comm: (202) 483-1414

PORTUGAL (PO)
Embassy of Portugal
2125 Kalorama Road NW
Washington, DC 20008
Comm: (202) 328-8610

SAUDI ARABIA (SA)
Embassy of Saudi Arabia
601 New Hampshire Avenue NW
Washington, DC 20037
Comm: (202) 342-3800

SINGAPORE (SG)
Embassy of the Rupublic of Singapore
1824 R Street NW
Washington, DC 20009-1691
Comm: (202) 667-7555

SOMALIA (SM)
Embassy of the Somali Democratic
  Republic
600 New Hampshire Avenue NW, Suite 710
Washington, DC 20037
Comm: (202) 342-1575

SOUTH AFRICA (SF)
Embassy of South Africa
3051 Massachusetts Avenue NW
Washington, DC 20008
Comm: (202) 232-4400

SPAIN (SP)
Embassy of Spain
2700 15th Street NW
Washington, DC 20009
Comm: (202) 265-0190

SUDAN (SU)
Embassy of the Democratic Republic of
  the Sudan
2210 Massachusetts Avenue NW
Washington, DC 20008

THAILAND (TH)
Embassy of Thailand
2300 Kalorama Road NW
Washington, DC 20008
Comm: (202) 483-7200

TURKEY (TU)
Embassy of the Republic of Turkey
1606 23rd Street NW
Washington, DC 20008
Comm: (202) 667-6400

UNITED KINGDOM (UK)
British Embassy
3100 Massachusetts Avenue NW
Washington, DC 20008
Comm: (202) 462-1340

URUGUAY (UG)
Embassy of Uruguay
1918 F Street NW
Washington, DC 20006
Comm: (202) 331-1313

VENEZUELA (VE)
Embassy of Venezuela
2445 Massachusetts Avenue NW
Washington, DC 20008
Comm: (202) 797-3800

VIRGIN ISLANDS (VI)
(See United Kingdom (UK).)

ZAIRE (ZA)
Embassy of the Republic of Zaire
1800 New Hampshire Avenue NW
Washington, DC 20009
Comm: (202) 234-7690

APPENDIX E
CUSTOMS AND DUTY

DECLARATIONS: ALL articles acquired abroad and in your possession at the time of your return must be declared. This can be done in any of the three forms described below.

Oral Declaration - Customs declaration forms are distributed on planes and should be prepared in advance of arrival for presentation to the immigration and customs inspectors. Fill out the identification portion of the declaration form. You may declare orally to the customs inspector the articles you acquired abroad if the articles are accompanying you and you have not exceeded the duty-free exemption allowed. A customs officer may, however, ask you to prepare a written list if it is necessary.

Written Declaration - A written declaration will be necessary when:
   a. The total fair retail value of articles acquired abroad exceeds your personal exemption.
   b. More than one liter (33.8 fl oz) of alcoholic beverages, 200 cigarettes (one carton), or 100 cigars are included.
   c. Some of the items are not intended for your personal or household use, such as commercial samples, items for sale or use in your business, or articles you are bringing home for another person.
   d. Articles acquired in the US Virgin Islands, American Samoa, or Guam are being sent to the US.
   e. A customs duty or internal revenue tax is collectible on any article in your possession.

Family Declaration - The head of a family may make a joint declaration for all members residing in the same household and returning together to the United States. Example: A family of four may bring in articles of duty valued up to $1,600 retail value on one declaration, even if the articles acquired by one member of the family exceeds the personal exemptions allowed. Infants and children returning to the US are entitled to the same exemptions as adults (except for alcoholic beverages). Children born abroad, who have never resided in the US, are entitled to the customs exemptions granted nonresidents.

YOUR EXEMPTIONS: In clearing US Customs, a traveler is considered either a "returning resident of the US" or a "nonresident." Generally speaking, if you leave the US for purposes of traveling, working or studying abroad and return to resume residency in the US, you are considered a returning resident by Customs. Residents of American Samoa, Guam or the US Virgin Islands, who are American citizens, are also considered as returning US residents. Articles acquired abroad and brought into the US are subject to applicable duty and internal revenue tax, but as a returning resident you are allowed certain exemption from paying duty on items acquired while abroad.

$400 Exemption - Articles totaling $400 (based on the fair value of each item in the country where acquired) may be entered free of duty, subject to the limitations of liquors, cigarettes and cigars, if:
   a. Articles were acquired as an incident of your trip for your personal or household use.
   b. You bring the articles with you at the time of your return to the US and they are properly declared to Customs. Articles purchased and left for alterations or other purposes cannot be applied to your $400 exemption when shipped to follow at a later date. Duty is assessed when received.
   c. You are returning from a stay abroad of at least 48 hours. (Example: A resident who leaves US territory at 1:30 p.m. on June 1st would complete the required 48-hour period at 1:30 p.m. on June 3rd.) This time limitation does not apply if you are returning from Mexico or the US Virgin Islands.
   d. You have not used this $400 exemption, or any part of it, within the

Appendix E, Cont'd
preceding 30-day period. Also, your exemption is not cumulative. If you use a portion of your exemption on entering the US, then you must wait for 30 days before you are entitled to another exemption other than a $25 exemption.
   e. Articles are not prohibited or restricted.

Cigars and Cigarettes - Not more than 100 cigars and 200 cigarettes (one carton) may be included in your exemption. Products of Cuban tobacco may be included if purchased in Cuba. This exemption is available to each person regardless of age. Your cigarettes, however, may be subject to a tax imposed by state and local authorities.

Liquor - One liter (33.8 fl oz) of alcoholic beverages may be included in this exemption if you are 21 years of age or older, if it is for your own use or for use as a gift, and if it is not in violation of the laws of the state in which you arrive. Information about state restrictions and taxes should be obtained from the state government as laws vary from state to state. Alcoholic beverages in excess of the one liter limitation are subject to duty and internal revenue tax. Shipping of alcoholic beverages by mail is prohibited by US postal laws.

$800 Exemption - If you return directly or indirectly from the US Virgin Islands, American Samoa or Guam, you may receive a customs exemption of $800 (based on the fair retail value of the articles in the country where acquired). Not more than $400 of this exemption may be applied to merchandise obtained elsewhere than in these islands. Residents, 21 years of age or older, may enter four liters (135.2 fl oz) of alcoholic beverages free of duty and tax, provided not more than one liter of this amount is acquired elsewhere than in these islands. Note: 1.75 liter bottle contains 59.2 fl oz. Articles acquired in and sent from these islands to the US may be claimed under your duty-free personal exemption if properly declared. Other provisions under the $400 exemption apply.

$50 Exemption - If you cannot claim the $400 or $800 exemption because of the 30-day or 48-hour minimum limitations, you may bring in free of duty and tax articles acquired abroad for your personal or household use if the total fair retail value does not exceed $50. This is an individual exemption and may not be grouped with other members of a family on one customs declaration. You may include any of the following: 50 cigarettes, 10 cigars, 4 ounces of alcoholic beverages or 4 ounces of alcoholic perfume. If any article brought with you is subject to duty or tax, or if the total value of all dutiable articles exceeds $50, no article may be exempted from duty or tax.

Bona fide gifts of not more than $50 in fair retail value where shipped can be received by friends and relations in the US free of duty and tax if the same person does not receive more than $50 in gift shipments in one day. The "day" in reference is the day in which the parcel(s) are received for customs processing. This amount is increased to $100 if shipped from the US Virgin Islands, American Samoa or Guam. These gifts are not declared by you upon your return to the US. Perfume containing alcohol valued at more than $5 retail, tobacco products, and alcoholic beverages are excluded from the gift provision. Gifts intended for more than one person may be consolidated in the same package provided they are individually wrapped and labeled with the name of the recipient. Be sure the outer wrapping of the package is marked (1) unsolicited gift, (2) nature of the gift, and (3) its fair retail value. In addition, a consolidated gift parcel should be marked as such on the outside with the names of the recipients listed and the value of each gift. This will facilitate customs clearance of your package. If any article imported in the gift parcel is subject to duty and tax, or if the total value of all articles exceeds the bona fide gift allowance, no article may be exempt from duty or tax. If a parcel is subject to duty, the US Postal Service will collect the duty plus a handling charge in the form of Postage Due stamps. Duty cannot be

Appendix E, Cont'd

prepaid. You, as a traveler, cannot send a "gift" parcel to yourself nor can persons traveling together send "gifts" to each other. Gifts ordered by mail from the US do not qualify under this duty-free gift provision and are subject to duty. **Gifts accompanying you** are considered to be for your personal use and may be included with your exemption. This includes gifts given to you by others while abroad and those you intend to give to others after you return. Gifts intended for business or promotional purposes may not be included.

Personal belongings of US origin are entitled to entry free of duty. Personal belongings taken abroad, such as worn clothing, etc., may be sent home by mail before you return and receive free entry provided they have not been altered or repaired while abroad. These packages should be marked "American Goods Returned." When a claim of US origin is made, marking on the article to so indicate facilitates customs processing.

Foreign-made personal articles taken abroad are dutiable each time they are brought into our country unless you have acceptable proof of prior possession. Documents which fully describe the article, such as a bill of sale, insurance policy, jeweler's appraisal, or receipt for purchase, may be considered reasonable proof of prior possession. Items, such as watches, cameras, tape recorders, or other articles which may be readily identified by serial number or permanently affixed markings, may be taken to the Customs office nearest you and registered before your departure. The Certificate of Registration provided will expedite free entry of these items when you return. Keep the certificate as it is valid for any future trips. Registration cannot be accomplished by telephone nor can blank registration forms be given or mailed to you to be filled out at a later time.

Articles imported in excess of your customs exemption will be subject to duty unless the items are entitled to free entry or prohibited. The inspector will place the items having the highest rate of duty under your exemption and duty will be assessed upon the lower rated items. After deducting your exemptions and the value of any duty-free articles, a flat rate of duty will be applied to the next $800 worth (fair retail value) of merchandise. Any dollar amount of an article or articles over $800 will be dutiable at the various rates of duty applicable to the articles. Articles of which the flat rate of duty is applied must be for your personal use or for use as gifts and you cannot receive this flat rate provision more than once every 30 days, excluding the day of your last arrival. The flat rate of duty is 10% based on fair retail value in the country of acquisition including Communist block countries, and articles must accompany you. The flat rate of duty is 5% for articles purchased in the US Virgin Islands, American Samoa or Guam, whether the articles accompany you or are shipped.

Payment of duty, required at the time of your arrival on articles accompanying you, may be made by any of the following ways:
   a. US currency (foreign currency not acceptable).
   b. Personal check in the exact amount of duty, drawn on a national or state bank or trust company of the US, made payable to the "US Customs Service."
   c. Government check, money order or traveler's checks are acceptable if they do not exceed the amount of the duty by more than $50. (Second endorsements are not acceptable.) Identification must be presented, i.e., traveler's passport or Social Security card.

A complete booklet of customs hints for returning US citizens, "Know Before You Go," is free by writing Department of Treasury, US Customs Service, Washington, DC 20229. Ask for Customs Publication No. 512.

APPENDIX F

LOCATIONS REPORTING LIMITED OR NO SPACE-A

The following locations have reported limited or no Space-A air opportunities. This list contains Reserve and Guard bases and commercial airports on which Reserve and Guard flights are located in addition to active military installations. These locations have not been fully described in this edition in order to conserve space, but they are listed here for your use. More information may be provided about these locations in future editions of Military Living's "Military Space-A Air Opportunities Around the World." Watch for updated information about these locations in Military Living's travel newsletter, the "R&R Report." This appendix is organized alphabetically by departure location.

LOCATION IDENTIFIER	DEPARTURE LOCATION	COMM	ATVN/FTS
AYH	RAF Alconbury APO/NY 09238-5000	44-048052131	223-1110
DCA	Arlington CGAS DC 20001-5000	202-267-2380	267-2380
AST	Astoria CGAS OR 97146-9693	503-861-2243	420-9272
ACY	Atlantic City Arpt NJ 08405-5199	609-645-6000	445-6000
BAF	Barnes Munic Arpt MA 01085-5000	413-568-9151	636-1210
BTL	Battle Creek MI 49015-1291	616-963-1596	580-3210
BYS	Bicycle Lake AAF CA 92310-5000	619-386-4111	470-4111
BBJ	Bitburg AB GE APO/NY 09132-5000	49-06561-61-1110	453-1110
BKT	Blackstone AAF VA 23824-5000	804-292-8261	438-8261
BOI	Boise Air Term ID 83707-5000	208-385-5001	941-5001
NOP	Brooklyn CGAS NY 11234-7097	718-664-0403	664-0410
BTV	Burlington IAP VT 05401-5000	802-658-0770	689-4310
AGS	Bush Field GA 30905-5000	404-791-0110	780-0110
RIC	Byrd IAP VA 23150-5000	804-222-8884	274-8210
N/A	Camp New Amsterdam NT APO/NY 09292-5226	31-03404-34222	496-1110
CUS	Cannon AFB NM 88103-5000	505-784-2801	681-2801
NMK	Cape May CGAS NJ 08204-5000	609-884-6980	234-3896
SPI	Capitol Arpt IL 62707-5000	217-753-8850	631-8210
NBU	Chicago CGAS IL 60026-5000	312-657-2145	932-2145
CBM	Columbus AFB MS 39701-5000	601-434-7611	742-7611
TAX	Dane City Reg Arpt WI 53704-2591	608-241-6200	273-8210
MGM	Dannelly Field Arpt AL 36196-5000	205-284-7210	742-9210
DSM	Des Moines Munic Arpt IA 50321-5000	515-285-7182	939-8210
DLH	Duluth IAP MN 55811-5000	218-727-6886	825-7210
FAF	Felker AAF VA 23604-5015	804-878-5251	927-5251
FSM	Fort Smith Munic Arpt AR 72906-5000	501-646-1601	962-8210
FWA	Fort Wayne Munic Arpt IN 46809-5000	219-478-3210	786-1210
FEW	Francis E Warren AFB WI 82005-5000	307-775-1110	481-1110
FAT	Fresno Air Term CA 93727-2199	209-454-5100	949-9210
FTF	Great Falls IAP MT 59401-5000	406-727-4650	279-2301
PIA	Greater Peoria Arpt IL 61607-5000	309-697-6400	724-9210
EWY	RAF Greenham Common APO/NY 09150-5000	44-0635-46263	266-1110
GSP	Greenville/Spartanburg Arpt SC 29301-5000	N/A	N/A
GPT	Gulfport-Biloxi Reg Arpt LA 39501-5000	601-868-6200	363-8200
HHN	Hahn AB GE APO/NY 09109-5000	49-06543-5-EX-1110	223-1110
SYR	Hancock Field NY 13211-7099	315-458-5500	587-9110

Appendix F, Cont'd

FAR	Hector Field ND 58105-5536	701-237-6030	362-8110
HMN	Holloman AFB NM 88330-5000	505-479-6511	867-4411
HUF	Hulman Reg Arpt IN 47803-5000	812-877-5210	724-1210
ACV	Humboldt Bay CGAS CA 95521-5000	707-839-3241	896-3600
HGT	Hunter-Liggett AHP 93928-5000	408-385-2544	949-2544
JAX	Jacksonville IAP FL 32229-5000	904-757-1360	460-7210
FSD	Joe Foss Field SD 57104-5000	605-336--670	939-7210
JFK	John F. Kennedy IAP NY 11430-5000	718-630-4234	232-4234
NGF	Kaneohe MCAS HI 96615-5000	808-257-2170	430-2170
MEI	Key Field MS 39302-1825	601-693-5031	694-9210
LMT	Kingsley Field Arpt OR 97603-0400	503-883-6350	830-6350
NQI	Kingsville NAS TX 78363-5000	512-595-6136	861-6136
LSF	Lawson AAF GA 31905-5065	404-545-2857	784-2857
FHU	Libby AAF AZ 85613-6000	602-538-2373	879-2373
LNK	Lincoln Munic Arpt 68524-1897	402-473-1326	720-1210
LAX	Los Angeles CGAS CA 90045-6378	213-215-2112	983-2112
MNL	Manila IAP RP APO/SF 96274-5000	63-598-011-EX-2553	N/A
RNO	May ANGB NV 89502-5000	702-788-4500	830-4500
8A4	McCollum Arpt GA 30144-5000	404-422-2500	925-2474
CMY	McCoy AAF WI 54656-5000	608-388-2222	280-2222
NMT	McEntire ANGB SC 29044-5000	803-776-5121	583-8201
OPF	Miami CGAS FL 33054-5000	305-681-3591	894-1190
DPG	Michael AAF UT 84022-5000	801-831-3545	789-3545
MUI	Muir AAF PA 17003-5011	717-273-2151	235-2151
SJU	Muniz ANGB PR 00914-5000	809-728-5450	860-9210
MYR	Myrtle Beach AFB SC 29579-5000	803-238-7144	748-7144
NBG	New Orleans CGAS LA 70143-6001	504-589-2150	363-2155
OTG	North Bend CGAS OR 97459-5000	502-269-3215	891-1451
ONT	Ontario IAP CA 91761-5000	714-984-2705	898-1895
PTB	Petersburg Munic Arpt VA 23801-5000	804-734-1011	687-0111
APN	Phelps Collins ANGB MI 49707-5000	517-354-4141	722-3760
NOW	Port Angeles WA 986-362-0519	206-457-4401	744-6431
GVW	Richards-Gebaur AFB MO 64030-5000	816-348-3132	463-3132
FWI	Roslyn ANG Station NY 11576-5000	516-299-5201	456-5201
SFO	San Francisco CGAS CA 94128-5000	415-876-2900	859-6900
SFO	San Francisco IAP CA 94128-1002	415-877-0311	837-5558
SVN	Savannah CGAS GA 31409-5000	912-352-2908	434-1690
SUX	Sioux City Munic Arpt IA 51110-5000	712-255-3511	939-6210
SPM	Spandahlem GE APO/NY 09405-5000	N/A	225-1110
SGH	Springfield-Beckley Munic Arpt OH 45501-1780	513-323-8653	346-2311
TOL	Toledo Express Arpt OH 43558-5000	419-866-2078	580-2078
TVC	Traverse City CGAS MI 49684-5000	616-922-8214	722-3470
TUL	Tulsa IAP OK 74115-5000	918-832-5208	956-5297
TUS	Tuscon IAP AZ 85734-5000	602-573-2210	631-8210
PAM	Tyndall AFB FL 32403-5000	904-863-4244	970-4244
END	Vance AFB OK 73705-5000	405-237-2121	962-7110
UHF	RAF Upper Heyford APO/NY 09194-5000	44-08692-2331	263-1110
HHI	Wheeler AFB HI 96854-5000	808-655-1414	455-1414
WSD	White Sands Ms'l Rng NM 88002-5047	505-678-2121	258-2121
SZL	Whiteman AFB MO 65305	816-687-3101	975-3101
NSE	Whiting Field NAS FL 32570-5000	904-623-7437	868-7437
CHD	Williams AFB AZ 85240-5000	602-988-5361	474-5361
WOB	RAF Woodbridge APO/NY 09405-5000	N/A	225-1110

APPENDIX G
BRIEF DESCRIPTIONS OF AIRCRAFT ON WHICH MOST SPACE-A TRAVEL OCCURS

The following transport and tanker aircraft are used by many of the uniformed services for missions having Space-A opportunities.

C-5 Galaxy

The free world's largest aircraft, the C-5 is a long-range air-refuelable heavy transport. It has four GE TF39-GE-1C turbofan engines, each with 41,000 lbs of thrust. It flies at a maximum speed of 571 miles per hour at 25,000 feet, with a ceiling of 35,750 feet and a range of 2,700 miles with a payload of 200,000 lbs. The C-5 carries a crew of five with a rest area accommodating 15. It has room for 75 troops and 36 standard 463L pallets or assorted vehicles, or an additional 270 troops. The C-5 weighs 374,000 lbs empty, has a wing span of 222 feet 8 1/2 inches, is 247 feet 10 inches long and 65 feet 1 1/2 inches high.

C009A Nightingale

The C009A is a modified DC-9 generally used as an aeromedical airlift transport. It has two Pratt & Whitney JT8D-9 turbofan engines, each with 14,500 lbs of thrust. It flies at a maximum speed of 565 miles per hour at 25,000 feet, with a ceiling of 35,000 feet and a range of more than 2,000 miles. The C-9 carries a crew of three, 40 patients, and a medical staff of five. It weighs 108,000 lbs gross, has a wing span of 93 feet 3 inches, is 119 feet 3 inches long and 27 feet 6 inches high.

C-12A Huron

The C-12A is a modified Beechcraft Super King Air 200. Its role is to support attache and military assistance advisory missions around the world. It is powered by two Pratt & Whitney Canada PT6A-38 turboprop engines and flies at a maximum speed of 301 miles per hours with a ceiling of 31,000 feet and a range of 1,824 miles. The C-12A carries a crew of two, up to eight passengers or 4,764 lbs of cargo. The C-12A weighs 12,500 lbs gross, has a wing span of 54 feet 6 inches, is 43 feet 9 inches long and 15 feet high.

C-21A

The C-21A is a modified Learjet 35A used by the AF to provide operational support airlift from 16 bases in the US and the Pacific and European theaters. It is powered by two Garrett TFE731-2A turbofan engines, each having 3,500 lbs of thrust. It flies at a maximum speed of Mach .81 with a ceiling of 45,000 feet and a range of 2,420 miles for passengers or 1,653 miles for cargo. The C-21A carries a crew of two and up to eight passengers. It weighs 18,500 lbs, has a wing span of 39 feet 6 inches, is 48 feet 8 inches long and 12 feet 4 inches high.

C-130 Hercules

The C-130 is used worldwide in a variety of roles ranging from airlift support to Arctic ice cap resupply. It has four Allison T56-A-15 turboprop engines and flies at a maximum speed of 345 miles per hour with a ceiling of 23,000 feet and a range with max payload of 840 miles. The C-130 carries a crew of five, up to 92 troops, 64 paratroops, 74 litter patients, or five 463L standard freight pallets. It has a gross weight of 175,000 lbs, a wing span of 132 feet 7 inches, is 97 feet 9 inches long and 38 feet 3 inches high.

Appendix G, Cont'd

C-141 Starlifter

The C-141 cargo transport has four Pratt & Whitney TF33-P-7 turbofan engines, each with 21,000 lbs of thrust. It flies at a maximum speed of 566 miles per hour with a range of 2,293 miles with maximum payload. It carries a crew of five, and can also accommodate 200 fully-equipped troops, 155 paratroops, or 103 litter patients and attendants. The C-141 weighs 343,000 lbs gross, has a wing span of 159 feet 11 inches, is 168 feet 3 1/2 inches long and 39 feet 3 inches high.

KC-10A Extender

Based on the commericial DC-10, the KC-10A combines the tasks of cargo and tanker aircraft by refueling fighter aircraft in flight and simultaneously carrying the fighters' support equipment and support personnel on overseas missions. It has three GE CF6-50C2 turbofan engines, each with 52,500 lbs of thrust. It flies at a maximum speed of 528 miles per hour with a service ceiling of 42,000 feet and a range with maximum cargo of 4,370 miles. It can also deliver 200,000 lbs of fuel 2,200 miles from its home base and return. The KC-10A carries a crew of three on the flight deck with seating for a limited number of essential support personnel and a maximum of 27 cargo pallets. The KC-10A has a gross weight of 590,000 lbs, a wing span of 165 feet 4.4 inches, is 181 feet 7 inches long and 58 feet 1 inch high.

KC-135 Stratotanker

The KC-135 is similar in appearance to the commercial B-707. It is powered by four Pratt & Whitney J57-P-59W turbojet engines, each with 13,750 lbs of thrust. It flies at a maximum speed of 585 miles per hour at 30,000 feet, with a ceiling of 50,000 feet and a ferry-mission range of 9,200 miles. The KC-135 carries a crew of four or five and up to 80 passengers. It weighs 98,466 lbs empty, has a wing span of 130 feet 10 inches, is 136 feet three inches long and 38 feet 4 inches high.

APPENDIX H
COUNTRY AND STATE ABBREVIATIONS
(used in this book)

We could not find standard two-letter country abbreviations. The state two-letter abbreviations are those used by the US Postal Service.

COUNTRY ABBREVIATIONS

AG-ARGENTINA
AN-ANTIGUA
AS-ASCENSION ISLAND
AU-AUSTRALIA
BA-BAHRAIN
BB-BARBADOS
BD-BARBUDA
BE-BELGIUM
BH-BAHAMAS
BM-BERMUDA
BO-BOLIVIA
BR-BRAZIL
BZ-BELIZE
CD-CHAD

CH-CHILE
CL-COLUMBIA
CN-CANADA
CR-CRETE*
CS-COSTA RICA
CU-CUBA
CY-CYPRUS
DN-DENMARK
DR-DOMINICAN REPUBLIC
EC-ECUADOR
EG-ARAB REPUBLIC OF EGYPT
ES-EL SALVADOR
GE-WEST GERMANY (and WEST BERLIN)
GL-GREENLAND*

Appendix H, Cont'd

GR-GREECE
GT-GUATEMALA
GU-GUAM**
HA-HAITI
HO-HONDURAS
HK-HONG KONG
IC-ICELAND
IE-INDONESIA
IO-INDIAN OCEAN (DIEGO GARCIA)
IR-IRELAND
IS-ISRAEL
IT-ITALY
JA-JAPAN
JM-JAMAICA
JO-JOHNSTON ISLAND**
JR-JORDAN
KE-KENYA
LI-LIBERIA
MR-MARIANA**
MW-MIDWAY ISLAND
NI-NICARAGUA
NO-NORWAY
NT-NETHERLANDS
NZ-NEW ZEALAND
OM-OMAN
PE-PERU
PG-PARAGUAY

PN-REPUBLIC OF PANAMA
PO-PORTUGAL (AZORES)
PR-PUERTO RICO**
RK-REPUBLIC OF KOREA
RP-REPUBLIC OF PHILIPPINES
SA-SAUDI ARABIA
SF-SOUTH AFRICA
SG-SINGAPORE
SM-SOMALIA
SP-SPAIN
SU-SUDAN
TH-THAILAND
TT-US TRUST TERRITORIES**
TU-TURKEY
UG-URUGUAY
UK-UNITED KINGDOM
US-UNITED STATES
VE-VENEZUELA
VI-VIRGIN ISLANDS**
WC-WEST CAROLINE ISLANDS**
WK-WAKE ISLAND
ZA-ZAIRE

*-Not a Separate Country
**-US Possession or Protectorate

STATE ABBREVIATIONS

AK-ALASKA
AL-ALABAMA
AR-ARKANSAS
AZ-ARIZONA
CA-CALIFORNIA
CO-COLORADO
CT-CONNECTICUT
DC-DISTRICT OF COLUMBIA
DE-DELAWARE
FL-FLORIDA
GA-GEORGIA
HI-HAWAII
IA-IOWA
ID-IDAHO
IL-ILLINOIS
IN-INDIANA
KS-KANSAS
KY-KENTUCKY
LA-LOUISIANA
MA-MASSACHUSETTS
MD-MARYLAND
ME-MAINE
MI-MICHIGAN
MN-MINNESOTA
MO-MISSOURI
MS-MISSISSIPPI

MT-MONTANA
NE-NEBRASKA
NC-NORTH CAROLINA
ND-NORTH DAKOTA
NH-NEW HAMPSHIRE
NJ-NEW JERSEY
NM-NEW MEXICO
NV-NEVADA
NY-NEW YORK
OH-OHIO
OK-OKLAHOMA
OR-OREGON
PA-PENNSYLVANIA
RI-RHODE ISLAND
SC-SOUTH CAROLINA
SD-SOUTH DAKOTA
TN-TENNESSEE
TX-TEXAS
UT-UTAH
VA-VIRGINIA
VT-VERMONT
WA-WASHINGTON
WI-WISCONSIN
WV-WEST VIRGINIA
WY-WYOMING

APPENDIX I

General Abbreviations

This appendix contains general abbreviations used in this book. Commonly understood abbreviations, such as M-F for Monday through Friday, have not been included. Abbreviations found in addresses are not included because they have proven to be accurate if used as stated in this book.

1/M - i.e., First Monday of month
1/2/3/Tu - i.e., First, second and third Tuesday of the month
2 monthly - two flights monthly; call for dates
3 weekly - three flights weekly; call for dates

AAF - Army Air Field
AAFES - Army Air Force Exchange System
AB - Air Base
A/C - Air Conditioning
Acf - Aircraft
Acft - Aircraft
AD - Active Duty
Add'l - Additional
Adm - Administration
Adv - Advance
AF - Air Force
AFB - Air Force Base
AFN - Armed Forces Network
AFRC - Air Force Reserve Center
AFRES - Air Force Reserve
AFS - Air Force Station
AFSC - Air Force Systems Command
Amb - Ambulance
AMEM - American Embassy
AMEXCO - American Express Company
ANG - Air National Guard
APO - Army Post Office
APOD - Aeroport of Debarkation
APOE - Aeroport of Embarkation
Appoint - Appointment
Approx - Approximately
ARC - American Red Cross
Arpt - Airport
AS - Air Station
ATC - Air Traffic Control
ATCO - Air Traffic Coordinating Organization
ATVN - Automatic Voice Network (AUTOVON)
Aux - Auxiliary
Avail - Available
Avn - Aviation

BART - Bay Area Rapid Transit
BEQ - Bachelor Enlisted Quarters
Bks - Barracks
Bldg - Building
Blks - Blocks
BOQ - Bachelor Officers Quarters
BW - Bomb Wing
BX - Base Exchange

C - Cargo
C/for - Call for
CAC - Combined Arms Center
Cat - Categories
CC - Commercial Carrier
CG - Coast Guard
CG - Commanding General
CGAS - Coast Guard Air Station
CGLS - Coast Guard Loran Station
Chg - Change
Chk - Check
Chld - Child(ren)
Civ - Civilian
Cmd - Command
Cmts - Comments
Comm - Commercial
Comm - Commercial Telephone System
Cons - Consolidated
Consol - Consolidated
CONUS - Continental United States
Cp - Camp
CPO - Chief Petty Officer
Ctr - Center

DAV - Disabled American Veteran
Dep - Dependent
Destn - Destination
Dly - Daily
DOD - Department of Defense
DOT - Department of Transportation
DV - Distinguished Visitor

ECI - East Caroline Islands
EM - Enlisted Member
EML - Environmental & Morale Leave
Enl - Enlisted
EX - Telephone Extension
Exc - Exchange (money)

Fac - Facilities
Fam - Family
Fam Svc - Family Services
FCU - Federal Credit Union
Fm - From
FPO - Fleet Post Office
Flt - Flight(s)
Freq - Frequency
Ft - Fort
FTS - Federal Telephone System

GAFB - German Air Force Base
GH - Greyhound Bus
GMT - Greenwich Meridian Time
Gov - Government

Appendix I, Cont'd

Gp - Group
GTR - Government Travel Request

Helo - Helicopter
HE:p - Hallwag Europe Atlas:page
Hol - Holiday(s)
Hq - Headquarters
Hrs - Hours

I - Interstate
IAP - International Arpt
Info - Information
Int - Intersection
Intl - International

Km - Kilometer

LI - Location Identifier
Lks - Lockers
Loc - Located/location
LSD - Local Standard Time

M - Mixed Mission
MAC - Military Airlift Command
MAP - Military Assistance Program
MARS - Military Affiliated Radio Station
MATCU - Military Air Traffic Coordinating Unit
Max - Maximum
MC - Marine Corps
MCAS - Marine Corps Air Station
MCLB - Marine Corps Logistical Base
ME - Medical Evacuation
Med - Medical
Mi - Miles
Mil - Military
MILGP - Military Group
Min - Minimum
Mo - Monthly
MOH - Medal of Honor
MTA - Military Transportation Authorization
Munic - Municipal

N/A - Not Applicable
N/A - Not Available
NAEC - Naval Air Engineering Center
NAF - Naval Air Facility
NAS - Naval Air Station
Natl - National
NB - Naval Base
NCO - Noncommissioned Officer
NCU - Naval Communication Unit
NMC - Nearest Major City
NMI - Nearest Military Installation
Nr - Near
NS - Naval Station
NSA - Naval Support Activity

O/hrs - Other hours
OAFB - Oman Air Force Base

OCONUS - Outside the Continental United States
OD - Officer of the Day
OOD - Officer of the Day
Ofc - Office(r)
OIC - Officer in Charge
Ops - Operations
O/S - Overstuffed
Oth - Other

P - Passenger
Pax - Passenger(s)
P/C - Plastic Contour
PCS - Permanent Change of Station
Pers - Person/Personnel
PO - Post Office
POC - Proof of Citizenship
Pol - Police
POV - Privately Owned Vehicle
PX - Post Exchange

Qtrs - Quarters

RAAF - Royal Australian Air Force
RAF - Royal Air Force
Rd - Reading
Rep - Representative
Req - Required
Resv - Reservation
Ret - Retired
RM:p - Rand McNally Atlas:page
Rm - Room
ROKAFB - Republic of Korea Air Force Base
RSAF - Royal Singapore Air Force

SAC - Strategic Air Command
SATO - Scheduled Airline Ticket Office
Sched - Schedule
SDO - Staff Duty Officer
Sec - Security
SOFA - Status of Forces Agreement
SP - Security Police
Space-A - Space Available
Spon - Sponsor(s)
Srvd - Served
Sta - Station
Sts - Seats
Sumr - Summer
Supv - Supervisor
Svc - Service
Svd - Served

TAD - Temporary Attached Duty
TAFB - Turkish Air Force Base
TDY - Temporary Duty
Tel - Telephone:L-Local; LD-Long distance; A-AUTOVON; C-Commercial
Term - Terminal
TLF - Transient Lodging Facility
TML - Temporary Military Lodging
Tng - Training

Appendix I, Cont'd

TOQ - Temporary Officers Quarters
Trans - Transient
TUAF - Turkish Air Force
TV - Television
Tvl - Travel
TVOQ - Transient Visiting Officers Qtrs
TW - Trailways Bus

Unk - Unknown
US - United States
USA - United States Army
USAF - United States Air Force
USDAO - United States Defense Attache Office
USMAAG - United States Military Assistance Advisory Group

USMC - United States Marine Corps
USN - United States Navy
USO - United Service Organizations

Veh - Vehicle
VEQ - Visiting Enlisted Quarters
VIP - Very Important Person
VOQ - Visiting Officer Quarters

W/Seats - Wood Seats
WCI - West Caroline Islands
Wd - Wood
Wk - Week
Wkend - Weekend
Wknd - Weekend
Wkly - Weekly

APPENDIX J

LOCATION IDENTIFIERS AND CROSS-REFERENCED INDEX

The location identifiers (LIs) used in this book are the Federal Aviation Administration coordinated three-letter LIs for the United States, its possessions, and Canada. Foreign country LIs have been coordinated by the Department of Defense. An LI represents the name/location of an airport/ airbase. They are considered permanent (changes are made for air safety only) and cannot be transferred. The original LI remains in effect even if it becomes necessary to change the name of a given facility. This appendix has been cross referenced so that each LI is followed by the page number on which the LI appears as the destination of a scheduled and/or unscheduled flight. The number in **bold face** indicates the page number of the main base listing for the given LI.

ABQ Kirtland AFB NM: 45, **113**, 134, 154
ADA Incirlik Arpt (Adana) TU: 48, 212, 225, 229, 236, 237, 286, 294, 298, 299, **300**, 304
ADK Adak NAS AK: 176, **181**, 182, 186, 189
ADQ Kodiak CGAS AK: **187**, 189
ADW Andrews AFB MD: 3, 28, 31, 37, 40, 45, 52, 57, 59, 70, 80, 83, **83**, 90, 97, 105, 109, 114, 115, 123, 129, 134, 140, 161, 168, 220, 228, 240, 278, 285
AEX England AFB LA: **78**, 149, 158
AFR Africa Stations: **207**
AGS Bush Field Arpt GA: 85, 97
AIS Alaska Isolated Stations AK: **182**
AKN King Salmon Arpt AK (AIS): **182**
AKT Akrotiri Arpt CY: **220**, 235
AMM King Abdullah AB JO: 48, 226, 253, **266**
ANC Anchorage IAP AK: 41, 182, **182**,
APG Phillips AAF MD: **88**, 168
ASI Ascension Auxiliary Airfield UK: 59, 208, **304**
ASP Alice Springs Arpt AU: 33, 190, 197, **208**, 211, 275

ASU Pres Stroessner Arpt PG (CAB): **218**, 279
ATH Athinai Arpt GR: 138, 221, 228, **234**, 237, 238, 243, 244, 246, 252, 285, 287, 294, 298, 299, 301
ATU Attu CGS AK: 188, 189
AVB Aviano AB IT: 138, 225, 228, 235, 238, **243**, 246, 249, 294, 309
AWK Wake Island AFB WK: **200**
AYE Moore AAF MA: **90**
AYH RAF Alconbury UK: 249
BAB Beale AFB CA: **13**
BAD Barksdale AFB LA: 45, 76, 78, 105, 129, 134, 152, 158
BAH Bahrain IAP BA: 138, 170, **212**, 291
BBE Berbera Arpt SM (AFR): **207**, 241
BBJ Bitburg AB GE: 249
BDA Bermuda NAS BM: 55, 83, 121, 140, **214**, 240, 278
BDL Bradley IAP CT: **46**, 311
BDS Brindisi/Casale Arpt IT: 221, 229, 235, 238, 244, **245**, 248, 253
BED Hanscom Field Arpt MA: **89**, 168
BFS Florennes AB BE: **213**

Appendix J, Cont'd

BGI	Grantley Adams Intl BB (CAB): 170, 204, **218**	CRK	Clark AB RP: 22, 35, 39, 102, 193, 198, 200, 241, 242, 256, 258, 261, 265, **279**, 283, 288, 297
BGR	Bangor IAP ME: **81**, 169		
BHM	Birmingham Munic Arpt AL: **1**, 97, 100, 149	CRW	Yeager Arpt WV: **178**
BIF	Biggs AAF TX: 6, 7, 43, 75, **150**	CTS	Chitose Arpt JA: **259**
BIG	Allen AAF AK (AIS): **182**	CUA	Cubi Point NAS RP: 37, 39, 191, 193, 195, 198, 255, 256, 258, 261, 281, **282**
BIX	Keesler AFB MS: 52, 53, 57, 59, 63, 71, 85, **96**, 149, 158		
BKF	Buckley ANG Base CC: **42**, 40, 66, 70, 100, 125, 126, 147, 149, 154, 165, 173, 179	CYS	Cheyenne Munic Arpt WY: **179**
		DAA	Davison AAF VA: 2, 75, 113, **166**, 168
BKK	Don Muang Arpt TH: 281, **296**	DAG	Barstow-Daggett Arpt CA: 19, 43
BLV	Scott AFB IL: 3, 6, 8, 26, 40, 42, 46, 52, 57, 63, 66, 68, **69**, 78, 86, 93, 95, 99, 100, 103, 105, 114, 123, 125, 126, 130, 134, 144, 147, 149, 150, 152, 159, 163, 165, 174	DCU	Decimomannu AB IT: 225, 244, **248**, 309
		DHA	Dhahran IAP SA: 48, 212, 225, 229, **286**, 294
		DIY	Diyarbakir Arpt TU: 301, **303**
		DJK	Halim Perdanakusuma IAP IE: **242**, 281
BNA	Nashville Metro Arpt TN: **150**		
BOG	El Dorado Arpt CL (CAB): **218**, 278	DLF	Laughlin AFB TX: **160**
		DMA	Davis-Monthan AFB AZ: **5**, 7, 114, 149, 158
BQN	Borinquen CGAS PR: 121, **201**		
BSB	Brasilia Arpt BR (CAB): **218**, 278	DNA	Kadena AB JA: 15, 18, 22, 33, 35, 37, 40, 101, 121, 159, 185, 191, 193, 198, 199, 255, 256, 258, **259**, 265, 269, 271, 273, 281, 283
BSM	Bergstrom AFB TX: 45, 129, **150**		
BUE	Ezeiza Arpt AG (CAB): **218**, 278		
BWY	RAF Bentwaters UK: 231, **305**, 309		
BYH	Eaker AFB AR: **9**	DOV	Dover AFB DE: 39, **46**, 57, 107, 112, 123, 132, 134, 159, 212, 225, 229, 292, 294, 301, 309
BZE	Belize Intl BZ (CAB): **218**, 278		
BZI	Balikesir Arpt TU: 298, 301, **303**		
CAB	Caribbean, Central & S America: 143, **217**	DYS	Dyess AFB TX: 123, **155**, 158
		ECG	Elizabeth City CGAS NC: **121**, 201
CAE	Columbia Metro Arpt SC: **145**, 149, 168	EDF	Elmendorf AFB AK: 10, 29, 39, 149, 176, 182, 184, **185**, 188, 189, 195, 265, 271
CAI	Cairo IAP EG: 48, **223**, 225		
CBM	Columbus AFB MS: 149	EDW	Edwards AFB CA: **15**
CCS	Caracas Arpt VE (CAB): **218**	EFD	Houston CGAS TX: 80, 154, **156**
CDV	Cordova CGS AK: 188	EHC	Erhac TUAF TU: 302, **303**
CEF	Westover AFB MA: **91**	EIL	Eielson AFB AK: 15, 39, 152, 173, 176, **183**, 186
CHC	Christchurch IAP NZ: 33, 37, 190, 198, 210, 211, **274**		
		ELP	El Paso IAP TX: 154, 158
CHE	Chievres AB BE: **212**	ERZ	Erzurum Arpt TU: 302, **303**
CHS	Charleston AFB/IAP SC: 11, 28, 49, 50, 53, 55, 57, 59, 63, 70, 85, 98, 112, 123, 132, 134, 138, **141**, **144**, 159, 170, 171, 203, 215, 216, 220, 225, 229, 233, 244, 274, 278, 285, 294, 309, 311, 312	ESB	Esenboga Arpt TU: 229, 236, 285, 294, 298, **298**, 302
		ESK	Eskisehir TUAF TU: 298, 299, 302, **303**
		FBG	Simmons AAF SC: 168
		FCS	Butts AAF CO: **43**
		FEL	Fuerstenfeldbrueck GAFB GE (WGS): **233**, 245
CJU	Cheju Do IAP RK: **268**, 271		
CLF	Clear AFS AK (AIS): **182**	FFD	RAF Fairford UK: 10, 11, 77, 95, 109, 115, 124, 126, 132, 152, 156, 173, **306**
CLT	Charlotte/Douglas IAP NC: **119**, 178		
CLW	Clearwater Air Park Arpt FL: 121	FFO	Wright-Patterson AFB OH: 4, 5, 16, 26, 46, 52, 57, 68, 71, 106, 114, 116, **128**, 134, 159, 162, 168
CNA	Camp New Amsterdam NT: 249		
COF	Patrick AFB FL: 11, **58**, 98, 112, 123, 128, 144, 208, 304		
COS	Peterson AFB CO: 26, **43**, 105, 130, 134	FIH	Kinshasa N'Djili Arpt ZA: 144, 274, **286**, **311**
CPD	Otis ANG Base MA: **90**	FLV	Sherman AAF KS: 43, **74**

Appendix J, Cont'd

FME	Tipton AAF MD: **88**		JAN	Jackson Munic Arpt MS: **96**
FOE	Forbes Field ANG Base KS: **72**		JED	Jeddah Airfield SA: 287, **287**, 294
FOK	Suffolk County ANG Base NY: **118**		JNB	Jan Smuts Arpt SF: **289**
FRF	Rhein Main AB GE: 48, 102, 112, 134, 139, 145, 170, 226, **226**, 233, 236, 237, 243, 245, 246, 248, 251, 253, 276, 286, 287, 292, 295, 296, 298, 299, 302, 309		JNU	Juneau CGS AK: 188
			JON	Johnston Island JO (PIS): **199**
			JXP	Japan (Mainland) AB & Arpts: **258**
			KEF	Keflavik Arpt IC: 112, 138, 170, **238**
FRI	Marshall AAF KS: 43, **73**		KHE	Kimhae IAP RK: 261, **268**, 269, 272, 273
FSI	Henry Post AAF OK: **132**			
FTK	Godman AAF KY: **75**, 168		KIN	Norman Manley Intl JM (CAB): 203, 204, **218**, 220
FTY	Fulton County Aprt GA: 168			
FUK	Fukuoka Arpt JA: **255**, 263, 265		KOE	Korean Stations RK: **267**
FWH	Carswell AFB TX: 78, **151**, 158		KPC	Port Clarence CGS AK: 188
GAL	Galena Arpt AK (AIS): **182**		KRT	Khartoum Arpt SU (AFR): 170, **207**, 241, 253, 267, 294
GAO	Guantanamo Bay NS CU: 55, 70, 121, 170, 171, 203, 204, **219**			
			KSA	Kosrae Arpt WCI/TT (PIS): 193, **199**
GBI	Grand Bahama Aux AF BH (CAB): 59, **218**			
			KTN	Ketchikan Intl AK: 188
GFA	Malmstrom AFB MT: 66, **103**, 165, 173		KUH	Kushiro Arpt JA: **259**
			KUZ	Kunsan AB RK: 261, 265, **268**, 272, 274
GMF	General Billy Mitchell Field WI: **178**			
			KWA	Kwajalein, Marshall Is/TT (PIS): **199**, 201
GRF	Gray AAF WA: **174**			
GRK	Robert Gray AAF TX: 43, 78, **163**		KWJ	Kwang Ju ROKAFB RK: 261, 265, **268**, 269, 272, 274
GSB	Seymour Johnson AFB NC: **123**			
GSP	Greenville/Spartanburg Arpt SC: 63, 123, 143		LAW	Lawton Munic Arpt OK (LAW): 158
			LAX	Los Angeles IAP CA: **20**, 35, 42, 45, 102, 171, 262, 281
GTB	Wheeler-Sack AAF NY: **118**			
GUA	La Aurora Arpt GT (CAB): **218**		LCA	Larnaca Arpt CY: **221**
GUS	Grissom AFB IN: **71**		LCK	Rickenbacker ANG Base OH: **127**, 149
GVW	Richards-Gebaur AFB MO: 149			
HIF	Hill AFB UT: 16, 26, 66, 114, 125, 147, **164**, 159, 173		LEA	Learmonth RAAFB AU: 33, 190, 198, **209**, 211, 212
HIK	Hickam AFB HI: 15, 23, 24, 26, 29, 33, 40, 127, 152, 159, 190, 193, **196**, 199, 200, 209, 210, 211, 261, 275, 281, 284		LFI	Langley AFB VA: 2, 52, 57, 130, **167**
			LGS	Lajes Fld PO: 112, 140, 144, 159, 217, 229, 236, 274, **284**, 294, 307, 312
HNL	Honolulu IAP HI: 22, 41			
HOP	Campbell AAF KY: **75**		LHN	Ahlhorn GAFB GE (WGS): 231, **233** 305
HOW	Howard AB PN: 72, 143, 145, 158, 159, 203, 204, 215, **277**			
			LIM	Jorge Chavez Intl PE (CAB): **218**, 279
HST	Homestead AFB FL: **52**, 55, 56, 57, 95, 98, 130, 143			
			LIZ	Loring AFB ME: **83**, 85
HSV	Huntsville-Madison Co Arpt AL: 98, 158		LPB	J F Kennedy Intl BO (CAB): **218**, 279
HUA	Redstone Arsenal AL: **4**, 168		LPH	Leipheim GAFB GE (WGS): **233**, 305, 309
IAB	McConnell AFB KS: **73**			
IAG	Niagara Falls IAP NY: **116**		LRF	Little Rock AFB AR: **10**, 123, 132, 156
IGL	Cigli TAFB TU: 229, 236, 285, 294, **297**			
			LSF	Lawson AAF GA: 85, 98, 100
ILE	Killeen Munic Arpt TX: 43		LSV	Nellis AFB NV: 8, 31, 107, **107**
ILG	Greater Wilmington Arpt DE: **49**, 299, 301		LTS	Altus AFB OK: **130**,
			LUF	Luke AFB AZ: **6** 107, 158
ILH	Illishiem AAF GE: 234		MCC	McClellan AFB CA: **25**, 45, 105, 159, 185
IWA	Iwakuni MCAS JA: 121, 256, **256**, 261, 263, 265			
			MCF	MacDill AFB FL: 53, 55, 56, **56**, 95, 98, 123, 126, 127, 144
IWO	Iwo Jima AB JA: **259**, 265			
JAB	Japan (Pacific Island) AB & Arpts: **259**		MCI	Kansas City IAP MO: 5, 100
			MCO	Orlando IAP FL: 61, 98

Appendix J, Cont'd

MDT	Harrisburg IAP PA: **137**		NDO	Nordholz GAFB GE (WGS): **233**
MDY	Midway Island NAS MW: 29, 191, 195, **198**		NEL	Lakehurst NAEC NJ: **110**
			NFL	Fallon NAS NV: 13, 20, 32, **106**, 171, 177
MEM	Memphis IAP TN: **148**		NFO	Futenma MCAS JA: **256**, 258
MER	Castle AFB CA: **15**		NGM	Agana NAS GU: 37, **191**, 195, 255, 256
MFD	Mansfield Lahm Arpt OH: **126**			
MGA	Augusto C Sandino Intl NI (CAB): **217**, 278		NGP	Corpus Christi NAS TX: 61, **153**
MGE	Dobbins AFB GA: 61, **61**, 98, 123, 127, 129, 143, 149		NGU	Norfolk NAS VA: 13, 31, 48, 50, 55, 61, 80, 83, 85, 88, 89, 91, 98, 107, 112, 121, 138, 140, 144, 149, **168**, 203, 212, 215, 220, 236, 240, 241, 253, 267, 292, 295
MGQ	Mogadishu IAP SM (AFR): **207**, 241			
MHR	Mather AFB CA: **23**, 162			
MHZ	RAF Mildenhall UK: 15, 40, 46, 48, 74, 95, 109, 124, 134, 138, 144, 152, 159, 170, 173, 213, 226, 229, 233, 240, 245, 248, 276, 296, 302, 305, **307**		NGZ	Alameda NAS CA: **12**, 20, 28, 31, 80, 106, 149, 177, 195
			NHK	Patuxent River NAS MD: 28, 29, 55, 83, **86**, 149
MIA	Miami IAP FL: 201, 220, 311		NHZ	Brunswick NAS ME: 29, 50, 55, 81, 85, 88, 89, 91, 140, 149
MIB	Minot AFB ND: 125, 147, **125**			
MIQ	Simon Bolivar Intl VE (CAB): 279		NID	China Lake NWC Arpt CA: 20, 32, 107
MKC	Kansas City Downtown Arpt MO: 5			
MMU	Morristown Munic Arpt NJ: **112**		NIP	Jacksonville NAS FL: 13, 29, 31, 50, 53, **53**, 57, 59, 61, 80, 83, 88, 89, 91, 98, 107, 140, 144, 149, 171, 195, 215
MNL	Manila IAP RP: 284			
MOB	Mobile CG Avn Tng Ctr AL: **4**, 201			
MRB	Eastern WV Regional Arpt WV: **177**		NIR	Chase Field NAS TX: 107, 149, **152**
MRH	Masirah OAFB OM: 241, **276**			
MSJ	Misawa AB JA: 258, **262**, 266		NJA	Atsugi NAF JA: 195, **253**, 263
MSP	Minneapolis-St Paul IAP MI: 68, **95**		NJK	El Centro NAF CA: **16**
			NKT	Cherry Point MCAS NC: 9, 89, 98, 107, **119**, 149
MTC	Selfridge ANG Base MI: **93**, 149			
MTN	Martin State Arpt MD: **86**		NKW	Diego Garcia Atoll IO: 81, 138, 170, 236, **240**, 253, 267, 281, 284, 288, 297
MUO	Mountain Home AFB ID: **65**, 165, 173			
MUS	Minami Torishima Arpt JA: **259**, 266		NKX	Miramar NAS CA: 20, **27**, 85, 107, 149, 154, 159
MVC	Monroe County Arpt AL: 100		NLC	Lemoore NAS CA: 13, **19**, 32, 107, 149, 177
MVD	Carrasco Intl UG (CAB): **218**, 278			
MXF	Maxwell AFB AL: **2**, 45, 57, 98, 162, 168		NMM	Meridian NAS MS: **99**, 107
			NOU	Sitka CGAS AK (AIS): **182**, 188
NAP	Capodichino Arpt (Naples) IT: 138, 229, 235, 238, 244, 246, **246**, 249, 250, 253, 292, 309		NPA	Pensacola NAS FL: 28, 52, **60**, 80, 89, 99, 107, 149, 154, 171
			NQA	Memphis NAS TN: 13, 28, 29, 61, 80, 89, **148**
NAS	Nassau IAP BH: 220			
NAX	Barbers Point NAS HI: 18, 29, 31, 107, 191, **194**, 199		NQI	Kingsville NAS TX: 149, 154
			NQX	Key West NAS FL: **55**, 98, 149, 171
NBC	Beaufort MCAS SC: 9, 28, 121, **141**			
NBE	Dallas NAS TX: 13, 28, 80, 88, 89, 134, 149, **153**, 195		NRR	Roosevelt Roads NAS PR: 55, 71, 144, 159, 170, 171, 201, **201**, 204, 208, 220, 279
NBG	New Orleans NAS LA: 31, 61, **78**, 89, 107, 140, 149, 154, 159		NRV	Norvenich GAFB GE (WGS): **233**, 305, 309
NBO	Jomo Kenyatta Intl KE: 81, 170, 241, **267**		NSF	Washington NAF MD: 61, **88**, 91, 121, 149
NBU	Glenview NAS IL: 13, 29, 31, 67, 80, 89, 149, 177, 195		NTD	Point Mugu NAS CA: 28, 29, 32, 36, 107, 149, 195
NCA	New River MCAS NC: 39		NTU	Oceana NAS VA: 32, 107, 149, **171**
NCQ	Atlanta NAS GA: 80			
NDI	Kadena NAF JA: 195		NUE	Nurnberg Arpt GE (WGS): 233, **233**
NDJ	N'Djamena IAP CD (AFR): **207**, 312		NUQ	Moffett Field NAS CA: **28**, 31, 89, 149, 195

Appendix J, Cont'd

NUW	Whidbey Island NAS WA: 13, 20, 28, 29, 31, 107, 149, 154, **176**, 195		PPG	Pago Pago IAP AS: 34, **189**, 198, 209, 210, 211, 275
NXP	29 Palms MCAS CA: 9		PSA	San Guisto Arpt, (Pisa) IT: 230, 245, **250**
NXX	Willow Grove NAS PA: 13, 28, 88, 89, 91, **139**		PSM	Pease AFB NH: 10, 11, 57, 74, 77, 85, 95, **108**, 116, 124, 126, 132, 152, 156, 307
NZC	Cecil Field NAS FL: 28, **49**, 107, 149		PZU	Port Sudan Arpt SU (AFR): **207**, 230
NZJ	El Toro MCAS CA: 9, **17**, 107, 121, 195		RCA	Ellsworth AFB SD: 125, 126, **146**
NZW	South Weymouth NAS MA: 88, 89, 90		RCM	Richmond RAAFB AU: 34, 191, 198, 209, 210, **210**, 212, 275
NZY	North Island NAS CA: 18, 20, 29, 30, 80, 107, 149, 154, 171, 177, 195		RDR	Grand Forks AFB ND: **124**, 147
			REE	Reese AFB TX: **162**
			REG	Reggio Calabria ITAF IT: 246
N68	Chambersburg Munic Arpt PA: **136**		RIO	Rio de Janeiro Intl BR (CAB): **218**, 279
OAK	Oakland Metro IAP CA: 22, **34**, 102, 262, 266		RIV	March AFB CA: 19, **22**, 42, 45, 126, 152
OAR	Fritzsche AAF CA: **18**			
OBO	Obihiro Arpt JA: 266		RME	Griffiss AFB NY: 85, **114**
OCO	Santamaria Intl CS (CAB): **218**		RMS	Ramstein AB GE: 40, 48, 134, 159, 213, 223, **223**, 230, 233, 236, 237, 238, 243, 248, 249, 251, 253, 266, 276, 287, 292, 295, 296, 298, 302, 309
OFF	Offutt AFB NE: 26, 45, 71, **104**, 114, 125, 130, 132, 134			
OKC	Will Rogers ANG Base OK: **135**			
OKO	Yokota AB JA: 34, 36, 37, 40, 102, 176, 187, 193, 195, 198, 256, 258, 262, 263, **263**, 270, 272, 274, 283		RND	Randolph AFB TX: 3, 24, 45, 105, 114, 130, 134, **160**, 168
			ROB	Monrovia Roberts IAP LI: 144, **274**, 286, 312
OLB	Olbia/Costa Smeralda IT: 248		ROR	Babelthuap Arpt WCI/TT (PIS): 193, **199**
OPF	Opa Locka Arpt FL: 201			
OQU	Quonset State Arpt RI: **140**			
ORD	O'Hare Air Res Forces Fac IL: 68		RTA	Rota NAS SP: 37, 139, 140, 170, 212, 230, 248, 253, **290**, 295, 296
ORL	Orlando Executive Arpt FL: 149			
OSC	Wurtsmith AFB MI: **94**			
OSL	Fornebu Arpt NO: 226, **276**		SAL	I Lopango Intl ES (CAB): **218**, 279
OSN	Osan AB RK: 36, 40, 102, 159, 198, 255, 256, 258, 262, 266, 269, **270**, 274		SAN	San Diego CGAS CA: 13, **37**
			SAV	Savannah IAP GA: **64**
OUN	Westheimer Airpark Arpt OK: **134**		SAW	K I Sawyer AFB MI: **92**
OZR	Cairns AAF AL: **1**, 100, 168		SBD	Norton AFB CA: 8, 26, **32**, 40, 45, 105, 107, 114, 123, 132, 134, 159, 176, 185, 190, 193, 198, 209, 210, 211, 275
PAM	Tyndall AFB FL: 99, 159			
PAP	Francois Duvalier Intl HA (CAB): 203, 204, **218**, 279			
PBG	Plattsburgh AFB NY: **116**		SCH	Schenectady County Arpt NY: **117**
PDX	Portland IAP OR: **135**, 177		SCL	Art Merinobenitez Arpt CH (CAB): **217**, 278
PHL	Philadelphia IAP PA: 46, 102, **137**, 145, 217, 236, 240, 245, 253, 292, 309		SDF	Standiford Field (ANG) KY: **76**
			SDQ	San Isidro AB DR (CAB): 203, 204, **218**, 279
PHX	Sky Harbor IAP AZ: **8**			
PIE	Clearwater CGAS FL: **50**, 201		SEX	Sembach AB GE: **230**, 305, 310
PIK	Prestwick Arpt UK: 46, 144, **310**		SFJ	Sondrestrom AB (Greenland) DN: 112, 216, **221**, 223
PIS	Pacific Islands TT: **199**			
PIT	Greater Pittsburgh IAP PA: **136**		SFO	San Francisco IAP CA: 19
PLA	Palmerola Arpt HO (CAB): 144, **218**, 279		SGP	RSAF Paya Lebar SG: 242, 282, **288**
PMI	Palma de Mallorca Arpt SP: 295		SIG	Isla Grande Arpt (San Juan) PR: 204
PNI	Ponape ECI/TT (PIS): 193, **199**			
POB	Pope AFB NC: 57, 59, 63, 85, 98, 112, **122**, 144, 156		SIO	Sinop AAF TU: 302, **303**
POE	Polk AAF LA: **80**			

Appendix J, Cont'd

SIZ	Sigonella Arpt (Sicily) IT: 37, 48, 81, 139, 170, 221, 226, 230, 236, 242, 243, 246, 248, **251**, 267, 286, 292, 295, 298, 299, 302	TIK	Tinker AFB OK: 26, 40, 48, 78, 130, **132**, 154, 159, 226, 310
		TKK	Truk ECI/TT (PIS): 193, **199**
		TLV	Ben Gurion IAP (Tel Aviv) IS: 235, **242**
SJH	Coolidge Arpt AN: 59, 203, **207**, 304	TOJ	Torrejon de Ardoz AB SP: 49, 171, 226, 230, 236, 242, 245, 249, 251, 253, 267, 286, 292, **292**, 296, 299, 302, 310
SKA	Fairchild AFB WA: 66, 165, **172**, 177		
SKF	Kelly AFB TX: 6, 7, 40, 45, 52, 63, 71, 78, 85, 98, 105, 114, 130, 134, 152, 154, **156**, 163	TUL	Tulsa IAP OK: 154
		TUR	Turkey AB's & Arpts TU: **302**
		TXK	Muni Webb Field Arpt TX: **160**
SLC	Salt Lake City IAP UT: 13, **166**	TYS	McGhee Tyson Arpt TN: **147**
SLI	Alamitos AAF CA: 19	UAM	Andersen AFB GU: 10, 21, 23, 33, 39, **191**, 197, 281, 284
SNN	Shannon Arpt IR: 241, 253, 267		
SNP	St. Paul Island CGS AK: 188	UIO	Mariscal Sucre Arpt EC (CAB): 218, 279
SOC	Souda Bay NAF (Crete) GR: 226, 236, **238**, 248		
		UMR	Woomera Airfield AU: 34, 191, 198, 211, **211**
SPN	Saipan, Mariana Islands (PIS): **199**		
		VAD	Moody AFB GA: **63**, 98
SPS	Sheppard AFB TX: 78, 159, **163**	VBG	Vandenberg AFB CA: **41**
SSC	Shaw AFB SC: 86, 99, 130, **146**	VBU	U-Tapao RTN TH: 282
STJ	Rosecrans Memorial Arpt MO: **102**	VCV	George AFB CA: **19**
STL	Lambert St Louis IAP MO: 5, 35, 101, 138, 229, 262, 265, 272, 282	VEN	Venezia/Tessera Arpt IT: 230, 245
		VIO2	St. Thomas Heliport VI: 203
STR	Echterdingen AAF GE (WGS): **233**, 234, 244	VKS	Vicksburg Munic Arpt MS: **100**
		VNY	Van Nuys ANG Base CA: **40**, 180
STT	Cyril E. King Arpt VI: 204	VOK	Volk Field ANG Base WI: **179**
STX	Alexander Hamilton Arpt VI: 169, 203, **204**, 278,	VPS	Eglin AFB FL: 45, **50**, 57, 63, 70, 94, 98, 129, 159, 168
SUU	Travis AFB CA: 6, 8, 11, 19, 28, 34, **37**, 42, 43, 46, 49, 66, 71, 86, 103, 108, 114, 123, 134, 151, 156, 159, 165, 174, 176, 185, 187, 193, 198, 226, 262, 266, 272, 282, 283, 310	VWH	Iraklion AS (Crete) GR: 221, 229, 236, **237**
		WGS	West Germany Stations: **233**
		WRB	Robins AFB GA: **64**, 98, 128
		WRI	McGuire AFB NJ: 59, 71, 85, 110, 123, 132, 144, 170, 216, 222, 223, 226, 229, 236, 240, 286, 295, 302
SVN	Hunter AAF GA: 65		
SWF	Stewart IAP NY: **117**,		
SYA	Shemya AFB AK: 182, 187, 188, **188**,	YAP	Yap Island WCI/TT (PIS): 191, 193, **199**
TAE	Taegu AB RK: 262, 266, 270, 272, **272**	YES	Yesilkoy Arpt (Istanbul) TU: 298, 299, 302, **303**
TBN	Forney AAF MO: **100**	YNG	Youngstown Munic Arpt OH: **130**
TCL	Tuscaloosa Munic Arpt AL: 100	YQX	Gander Intl Fld CN: 121
TCM	McChord AFB WA: 13, 31, 34, 40, 45, 57, 66, 71, 107, 123, 132, 165, 173, **174**, 177, 182, 184, 186, 189, 266, 272	YUM	Yuma MCAS AZ: **8**, 18, 107, 171
		YYR	Goose Bay AB (Newfoundland) CN: 112, **215**, 222, 225, 309, 311
TGU	Toncontin Intl HO (CAB): **218**, 279	YYT	St John's Arpt (Newfoundland) CN: 112, **216**
THF	Tempelhof Central Arpt GE: 230, **231**	ZAZ	Zaragoza AB SP: 226, 230, 292, 295, **295**, 310
THU	Thule AB (Greenland) DN: 112, 216, 222, **222**		

APPENDIX K

SPACE-A Questions and Answers

One of the biggest fringe benefits, dollar-wise, for uniformed personnel and their family members is space-available travel on US military aircraft. While there are some old pros who know all the ropes, having learned the hard way by flying Space-A, there are those who are a bit afraid to jump into the unknown. This book is especially for those who want to know more about Space-A. Soon, you can be a Space-A expert and will be ready to save thousands of dollars on R&R trips on US military aircraft.

Answers are based on information available to us at press time. Due to the fact that policies can change or be interpreted differently, these general answers must be regarded only as guides....not rules. Specific questions should be directed to military officials who are the final authority on the subject.

1. What is Space-A?
Hundreds of military flights are made daily, performing our country's military missions. If flights are suitable for passengers and if there are seats unoccupied and not required for the mission, there is a possibility that excess seats will be offered to active duty military service members and retirees. Family members may also travel space available but only when accompanied by their military sponsor on flights going outside the continental US. Family members may not accompany their sponsors on flights from point to point within the continental US. They may fly on flights departing the continental US for overseas locations. A new rule allows family members to take flights which make stops in the US before the final destination (see Space-A rules change info on page iii). This Space-A fringe benefit is a privilege, not a right.

2. What is the current status of the $10.00 Space-A passenger processing fee?
A $10.00 Space-A passenger processing fee was established by the Air Force (other services have complied) in response to a Congressional reduction of the Air Force FY-78 budget. The stated intent of the fee was to make the Space-A system self-supporting pending further study of the Space-A transportation category by DOD. Terminals manifesting more than 1,000 international or intertheater Space-A passengers each year must collect the $10.00 fee for each Space-A passenger. This is a one-time charge for a one-way trip, regardless of en route stops, as long as the traveler is proceeding to a specific destination, even if this travel involves changing airplanes.

A passenger failing to register within six hours after arrival at an enroute station, or who changes the specified destination, will be reassessed the $10.00 charge for onward travel. However, passengers originating at a non-paying terminal may transit paying terminals without paying the $10.00 charge, provided they are proceeding to their specified destination.

3. Must I pay $10.00 for each leg of a Space-A trip?
When paying the $10.00 processing fee for a Space-A air flight, be sure to state your FINAL destination. If, for example, you plan a Space-A flight to Berlin and no flight is listed to Berlin from your departure location, but there is a flight listed to Frankfurt, write in Berlin, not Frankfurt, as your final destination. If you re-sign up in Frankfurt for a Berlin flight within six hours, you will not have to pay again. If you arrive in Frankfurt, however, and find that you now want to go to Spain instead of Berlin, you will have to repay the $10.00 processing fee. Please ask at your Space-A counter for more info when signing up for your trip.

4. Must we pay the $10.00 fee for our small baby?
Yes, infants flying Space-A must have a seat allocation and pay the $10.00 processing fee. The US Federal Aviation Administration (FAA) requires that infants have a seat for flight safety purposes.

5. Who has priority on these Space-A flights?
Active duty personnal have first priority. Retirees may travel but have a lower priority. There are numerous rules and exceptions which are spelled out in detail in Appendix A of this book. If you believe you need more information

Appendix K, Cont'd
to better understand the detailed rules, visit the Space-A desk at any MAC or other Service terminal or departure location and discuss the regulations governing space available air travel with passenger service personnel. The name, location identifier code, address and telephone numbers of over 300 departure locations worldwide are listed in this book.

6. What does it mean to be "bumped?"
You can be removed from a flight after you have been manifested and en route if there are mission requirements for space-required passengers or cargo.

7. Can I be "bumped" by other Space-A passengers?
If you are traveling Space-A, you will not be "bumped" by other Space-A passengers except persons traveling in connection with a serious illness or the impending death of a family member. These passengers have priority over ordinary leave passengers.

8. Can all uniformed service personnel fly Space-A?
Yes, all seven uniformed services, both active and retired, as follows: US Army, US Navy, US Marine Corps, US Air Force, US Coast Guard, US Public Health Service Corps, and the National Oceanic and Atmospheric Administration Corps.

9. I am an enlisted man, new to the Service and am married. Can my spouse and I take a trip to Europe on Space-A?
Happily, the answer is now YES. Formerly, one had to be an E-4 with more than two years of service to qualify, but the new rule allows all uniformed service members to travel regardless of rank. Remember, you must be in a financial position to get yourself back to your duty station should you not be able to return by Space-A.

10. Can Reservists and Guard members fly Space-A?
Reservists and National Guard members can fly anywhere in CONUS, Alaska, Hawaii, Puerto Rico, Guam and US Virgin Islands. Reserve and Guard personnel must have the red ID Card (DD Form 2), DD Form 1853 (Authentication of Reserve Status for Travel Eligibility), and be in uniform. The same is true of Reserve and Guard personnel who have received official notification of retirement eligibility but have not reached retirement age (60). This retirement eligible group must present their ID cards and retirement eligibility notices. A uniform is not required.

11. When can Reservists and Guard family members fly Space-A?
When the sponsor retires and receives full benefits at age 60, eligible family members may then fly Space-A. These family members must be accompanied by their sponsor.

12. Can I fly on Reserve and Guard flights?
It depends on the mission. Sometimes the Guard and the Reserve have some of the best flights available. The catch is that they are not generally scheduled flights. Many different types of flight missions are given to reserve/guard members, therefore, one can often find some very special flights to places not normally seen on flight schedules. Most Reserve and Guard departure locations are listed in this book. See our travel newsletter, Military Living's R&R Report, for details on more locations as they become available to us.

13. I know that active duty personnel have priority over retirees for getting a flight and that dependents can only fly on flights going overseas or in an overseas area, but I need more specific information. We want to take our daughter, age 22, to Europe over her Spring college break. She has a dependent ID card, what else will we need?
Rules have changed on this subject since our first few printings of the first edition of the Space-A Air Opportunities book. Previously, all dependent children lost the Space-A privilege at age 21. A recent rule change allows active duty and retired personnel's dependent children up to age 23, who are full-time undergraduate college students, to fly Space-A with their sponsor on ordinary leave. In addition, the active duty student dependents up to age 23 may fly Space-A alone when joining their active duty parents stationed overseas. A valid military ID card is needed for students wishing to travel.

14. Is there any difference in Space-A rules regarding eligibility for active duty personnel versus retirees?
Yes. First of all, active duty personnel have priority on Space-A flights at

Appendix K, Cont'd
all times. Other differences include the fact that active duty personnel may take their dependent mothers and fathers with them on Space-A trips. (Dependent in-laws are NOT included in this privilege.) Retirees do not have this privilege at all. Also, dependent children of active duty and retired personnel may now fly Space-A up to age 23. (This rule was recently changed. For a time, retiree's children were not eligible for this privilege to age 23.)

15. My husband was killed in Vietnam and is buried in the Punch Bowl Military Cemetery in Hawaii. The children and I would like to take a trip to Hawaii to visit his grave. Can we fly Space-A?
Sorry, but widows are not afforded the privilege of Space-A air travel. The rules state that family members must be accompanied by their military sponsor, so naturally this is impossible. We have not heard of any proposal to grant this privilege to widows of service personnel. Read Military Living's R&R Report for news on this subject and info about air travel discounts for widows/widowers.

16. Can I use Space-A to take my dependents to my unaccompanied duty station overseas or back to the CONUS after the tour is completed?
No. Family members may use Space-A travel only when they are with the sponsor on an accompanied tour (on military orders) overseas. The Space-A privilege is intended only for a visit to an overseas or CONUS area on a round-trip basis with the sponsor. Space-A cannot be used to establish a home for dependents overseas or in CONUS.

17. I am a 100% disabled American veteran. I've heard that some of us can fly Space-A and some can't. Could you give me more information on this?
Disabled veterans must be RETIRED from a uniformed service to qualify for Space-A travel. Those who were separated in lieu of being retired are not eligible. Here's an easy way to check your eligibility. If your monthly retired check is paid by a uniformed services finance center, e.g., DOD, and your ID card is DD Form 2 (old ones are grey in color; new cards are blue), you can fly Space-A. If you are paid by the Veterans Administration and your ID card is a Form 1173 (butterscotch in color), you cannot fly Space-A. The color of these cards is the key to being allowed to sign up for a Space-A flight. DD Form 1173 is the same ID form used by dependents. In any case, dependents are not generally allowed to fly Space-A without their sponsors, so this butterscotch color card is a red flag alerting the officials at the Space-A desk that the carrier of the DD Form 1173 is not eligible to fly.

18. Can 100% disabled veterans (DAV) who are "retired" travel Space-A?
Yes, if they are retired by a uniformed service and are able to care for themselves or if they have a companion who is eligible for Space-A in their own right who can safely move the 100% disabled retired veteran.

19. May a military retiree, who relies on a guide dog because of vision deficiency, travel with the animal aboard military aircraft Space-A?
Yes. This is allowed when the dog is properly harnessed and muzzled, and the animal does not obstruct the aisle. Also, the dog may not occupy a seat in the aircraft.

20. May pets be transported Space-A?
Active duty may now move pets Space-A on military contract flights when traveling on a permanent change of station.

21. My husband has a wonderful TDY (government business) trip planned to Europe from Washington, DC. Can I go with him Space-A? Also, see Q38.
No. Family members may not fly space available in conjunction with an official trip by their sponsor. The only exception we know of is in the case of those authorized Environmental and Morale Leave (EML), in which case it would be possible to end up on the same flight. Eligible family members are allowed to take Space-A trips without their sponsor on EML. There is no EML leave authorized from the United States.

22. How often must I revalidate to stay on the Space-A list?
Because of a change in Space-A regulations, revalidation is no longer necessary. See page iii for details on this and other changes.

23. What is the best time for me to travel Space-A?
The best time is a function of departure locations, arrival locations and

Appendix K, Cont'd
space-required mission needs. Generally the best times to travel Space-A are autumn, late winter, early spring and after 15 July. It is best to avoid trying to travel between 1 May-15 July, 15-30 November and 10-25 December when traffic is the heaviest.

24. What documents must I have to travel?
If active duty, you need your leave papers. All personnel will need a valid military or dependent ID card. If traveling overseas, you will need a valid passport, visas where necessary, and in some cases, immunization records. See the appendices in this book for details on travel documentation.

25. I am retired. When I was on active duty my personnel officer issued me travel and leave orders which specified requirements for visiting foreign countries. Where can I now get that information?
The appendices in this book provide details on travel documentation and requirements to enter foreign countries listed in the book. Pay particular attention to Appendix B - Personal Entry Requirements. You may also check the latest changes to the US Air Force Foreign Clearance Guide at local personnel offices and MAC or other Service Space-A counters.

26. How much luggage can Space-A passengers take with them?
The maximum amount allowed on Military Airlift Command flights is two pieces of luggage, but they may not exceed a combined weight of 66 pounds. On other military missions, the allowance may be less, according to the aircraft. As an example, the C-21A aircraft baggage limit is 30 pounds.

27. As a Space-A passenger, can I carry and pay for baggage in excess of the allowed 66 pounds?
Space-A passengers do not have the option of paying for excess baggage. Space-A passengers may check oversize baggage if it is the only piece to be checked and meets weight requirements of 66 pounds total. (Families may pool their luggage.) Oversized baggage is described in the regulation as items such as duffle bags, garment bags, golf clubs, skis, bicycles, fishing equipment, backpacks and musical instruments. A carry-on bag is allowed. It cannot exceed 45 linear inches and must fit under the passenger's aircraft seat.

28. Are meals served to Space-A passengers on flights?
Yes, but only on MAC contract and some special-mission flights. On flights of more than three hours, you can purchase a box meal from the in-flight kitchen for $1.85. This is usually done at the time of seat assignment or manifesting. You may, of course, bring your own snack aboard.

29. Are specialized meals available to Space-A passengers?
Specialized meals are made available for duty passengers only for medical or religious reasons. If you need special food, we suggest you bring your own to maintain flexibility. While you can make your requirements known to passenger processing personnel at the time of seat assignments, the chance of having additional specialized meals available at the last minute for Space-A passengers might be slim, indeed.

30. How about alcoholic beverages?
They are not served on military aircraft. Some commercial contract flights which frequently carry Space-A passengers offer full beverage service. You cannot consume alcoholic beverages from your own supplies on a military aircraft- or for that matter on any commercial aircraft.

31. As a uniformed service member, eligible for Space-A, must I wear the uniform when traveling Space-A?
Yes. Duty, leave, Reservist and National Guard personnel must wear the uniform when traveling Space-A on DOD/DOT owned or controlled aircraft. Exceptions are when civilian clothing is required by the US Air Force Foreign Clearance Guide, of if member's orders or military specialty authorize or require civilian attire. This policy may be waived for reasons beyond the Service member's control provided the local representative of the member's Service concurs.

32. I am active duty. May I sign out on leave, sign up for Space-A, and, if there is a wait for the flight, go back to work?
The US Air Force policy is as follows: When registering for Space-A travel, the member must have an approved leave authorization effective on or before the date of registration. The "three-day before and after effective date window" is

Appendix K, Cont'd
not accepted for Space-A registration. If a member registers for Space-A travel but voluntarily returns to work during intervening days before actual flight departure, leave will be charged for those days. The Air Force states that past audits in this area have shown this to be a prime area for abuse of the leave system. Although these procedures are not in Air Force Regulations 35-9, Military Personnel Leave and Administrative Absence Policy, "they are still in effect," according to Air Force officials. The Army in Europe charged over 100 personnel with violating this rule in 1987. You must be on leave to sign up and stay on leave until the time of departure.

33. As a Space-A passenger, will I be subjected to security screening prior to boarding a flight?
Yes, in most cases you and your baggage will receive electronic and/or personal security screening prior to boarding flight or entering a secure area.

34. I am going on business to Japan and would like to take a Space-A flight to get there. Any problem?
You bet there's a problem. Don't do it. When you sign on for a Space-A flight you certify that neither you nor accompanying family members are traveling for private gain. Space-A is for leave travel only. Such use of Space-A would be deemed fraudulent.

35. What improvements or changes in Space-A service can I expect?
In the past few years, MAC has made a concentrated effort to improve its service to active duty personnel and their families traveling with them. Some examples we have noticed include: sponsors may now take all of the family paperwork to the passenger terminal instead of having all the family members present to check documents related to overseas travel; dependents' flight schedules have been improved, avoiding the 2400-0500 hours whenever possible; passengers are being asked if they would prefer smoking or no-smoking sections; baggage inspection at key continental US stations has been speeded up with the installation of X-Ray devices; personnel are reflecting the results of more intensive training for staffers; and commanders at various terminals have initiated many improvements for all concerned, especially family member comforts like nurseries and snack bars.

Baggage handling systems are being redesigned by experts to improve service in MAC terminals. MAC is repainting all its C-5 Galaxy and C-141 Starlifter aircraft from the present gray-and-white color scheme to the European I camouflage pattern.

The new MAC appears to be a more caring outfit. Naturally, while these improvements are aimed at active duty military personnel and their family members traveling on duty or permanent change of station, those traveling on Space-A also benefit!

36. What is EML leave?
EML means Environmental and Morale Leave Program. It is an effort to provide environmental relief from a duty station which has some "drawbacks" and to offer a source of affordable recreation otherwise not available. In simple terms, it boils down to allowing active duty military personnel and their dependents to fly space available on military aircraft. There are, however, a couple of big differences in EML leave and regular Space-A leave.

First, dependents are permitted to travel either accompanied or UNACCOMPANIED by their sponsors. They may utilize "suitably equipped DOD logistic type aircraft" as well as MAC channel aircraft. Secondly, EML leave has a Category 2 classification which is higher than regular Space-A leave given to retirees. EML leave is the same travel category afforded active duty on leave.

A good bit of EML travel is utilized in the Far East. This means that others traveling Space-A in a lower category must watch out and carry even more extra funds than usual when traveling Space-A in the Far East. Because of the EML leave travel, many military families have found it necessary to pay their children's travel to and from the Far East because the student category is lower than EML leave and chances of travel in a short period of time can be very difficult. The EML program is a tremendous morale booster to those assigned in far-off places and is very popular. There are, therefore, fewer available seat for other Space-A passengers with a lower category.

Appendix K, Cont'd

37. What should I wear aboard a Space-A flight?
"Appropriate attire" is required to fly on military aircraft. While this is not spelled out, you can be sure you will be denied Space-A travel if you are shoeless, in tank tops, halters or shorts. If you want to take a Space-A flight, don't gamble - dress in good taste. We know that our readers would not turn up at a terminal in an unkempt condition, but sometimes it happens. Slacks are a good idea for women because of the type of military aircraft used (ladders to climb, changing cabin temperatures, unusual seating, etc.) See our reader letters in Military Living's R&R Report for more inside information on this subject.

38. In the old days, I always carried my shot records. Should I carry them today?
Please see the Personal Entry Requirements, Appendix B, Immunization Requirements, in this book. If you have been traveling through or to an "infected area," you will need your shot records. Some of the more popular travel destinations do not normally require the records. If in doubt you will need to consult the immunization requirements and also ask questions. (Ask the departure personnel, or call the Embassy of the country you want to visit.)
It is the opinion of the Publishers that it is always best to be prepared. For flexibilty in your Space-A travels, we recommend that you carry your shot records and that you get visas for as many countries as possible. For example, if you are trying to get out of Germany to the US and having difficulty, you might be able to get a flight to Turkey and then leave from there. This would be difficult if you did not have a visa. The question of shot records could always arise.

39. What can I do if I get extremely ill overseas and need to get back to the United States?
Air evacuation through the Military Airlift Command (MAC) is available for active duty, retired, and their family members. One must get in touch with a U.S. military medical facility, preferably a hospital, or the American Embassy or Consulate to be considered for this service. On the other hand, if death occurs overseas, a retiree's or their family member's body may not be shipped by MAC. Active duty personnel fall under different regulations.

40. Should we expect any additional fees to be levied when flying Space-A?
It is always possible that new fees may be added. As an example, since our first Space-A book was published, there has been a $10.00 fee added to many flights for customs inspection. This is also required at civilian airports. On some commercial contract flights, there may be a $3.00 US airport departure tax, depending on the location. Some foreign countries may also levy a departure tax. Watch the R&R Report travel newsletter for the latest information.

41. I keep seeing references to Military Living's R&R Report. What is it?
It is a six-times yearly travel newsletter for all ranks which gives updated information on military Space-A air travel, temporary military lodging around the world, discounts in civilian hotels, travel discounts, news on military recreation areas and serves as a reader clearinghouse for info on their trips. Ordering information is contained in the back of this book. If the coupon is missing, write to Military Living R&R, P.O. Box 2347, Falls Church, VA 22042, or call (703) 237-0203.

42. Do you pay for articles in the R&R report which are about Space-A air travel or places visited as a result of Space-A travel?
No. To do so would put our writers in violation of Space-A regulations (see Appendix M, Space-A Passenger Booking Card). In addition, our readers freely share with each other and others are encouraged to share with them. R&R serves as a clearinghouse for information about military travel.

43. Any last bits of advice for the Space-A traveler?
Space available air travel is one of the most sought after fringe benefits enjoyed by US uniformed personnel, but don't go unless you can afford to lose.
It's a bit like gambling: You can win big, e.g., a Space-A flight to Europe for you, your spouse and the children; but you can also "lose" by being unable to return Space-A on a military aircraft. We emphasize the fact that you MUST be prepared to pay for your return from whatever destination you reach.

Appendix K, Cont'd
Although thousands of military families do travel Space-A without a problem, you may be the one out of the whole group who runs into a problem! Keep smiling and don't turn into a grouch if things don't go your way. Sometimes a little psychology and common sense can help you out of a tight spot. Keep "cool" and check out the possibilities of flying home by alternate and indirect routes. The way home may not necessarily be in a straight line, but the flights are almost free!

Please send your Space-A questions to Military Living R&R, P.O. Box 2347, Falls Church, VA 22042. We will attempt to get an answer to share with all our readers in the R&R Report. If you would like a reply, kindly enclose a self-addressed, stamped envelope. Thank you.

-NOTES-

APPENDIX L
SPACE-A PASSENGER BOOKING CARD

(THIS FORM IS SUBJECT TO THE PRIVACY ACT OF 1974 - See Reverse)

MAC FORM 53 SEP 84 PREVIOUS EDITIONS ARE OBSOLETE   **APPLICATION FOR AIR TRAVEL**

PLEASE READ BEFORE YOU SIGN
SPACE AVAILABLE PASSENGER CERTIFICATION

I CERTIFY THAT I AM ON LEAVE OR PASS STATUS AT THE TIME I REGISTER FOR SPACE AVAILABLE TRAVEL AND WILL REMAIN IN SUCH STATUS WHEN AWAITING AND/OR HAVE BEEN ACCEPTED FOR SPACE AVAILABLE TRAVEL. If accompanied by dependents, I further certify that my travel is not in conjunction with TDY/TAD and that I am not using space available travel to transport my dependents to or from my restricted duty station or all others (unaccompanied) tour location/station. I certify that my request for, and acceptance of, transportation via military aircraft is not for personal gain, nor for, nor in connection, with business of any nature and that this trip will not result in any form of remuneration to myself or to my family. I understand violation of any of the above could result in billing and/or punitive action.

DATE	PASSENGER'S SIGNATURE

	BORDER CLEARANCE/IDENTIFICATION VALIDATION
DATE	SIGNATURE BORDER CLEARANCE REPRESENTATIVE

PRIVACY ACT STATEMENT

AUTHORITY: 10 U.S.C. 8012; Executive Order 9397 - 22 November 1943.
PRINCIPAL PURPOSES: To apply for air travel. SSN is for positive identification.
ROUTINE USES: For preparing passenger manifests and publishing the space required and space available roster on military aircraft. Disclosure of SSN is voluntary.
DISCLOSURE IS VOLUNTARY: Failure to provide the information may result in member not being accepted for travel on military aircraft. Disclosure of SSN is voluntary.

MAC FORM 53, SEP 84 REVERSE   ☆ U S GPO 1986-0-652-037/20127

APPENDIX M

AUTHENTICATION OF RESERVE STATUS FOR TRAVEL ELIGIBILITY

AUTHENTICATION OF RESERVE STATUS FOR TRAVEL ELIGIBILITY

1. DATE PREPARED (YYMMDD)

PRIVACY ACT STATEMENT
AUTHORITY: 10 USC 8102, 44 USC. 3101 and EO 9397.
PRINCIPAL PURPOSE: Use of your SSN is necessary to positively identify you.
ROUTINE USE: Used by Reserve personnel for space available on DoD-owned or controlled aircraft.
DISCLOSURE IS VOLUNTARY: However, failure to disclose it will prevent you from traveling on a DoD-owned or controlled aircraft.

PART A. TO BE COMPLETED BY APPLICANT

2. NAME (Last, First, MI)	3. PAY GRADE	4. BRANCH OF SERVICE	5. SSN

6. UNIT/COMMAND NAME	7. UNIT/COMMAND ADDRESS

I hereby certify that my space-available travel on military aircraft is not for personal gain, or in connection with business enterprise or employment, or to establish a home either overseas or in the United States.

8. SIGNATURE	9. DATE SIGNED (YYMMDD)

PART B. TO BE COMPLETED BY RESERVE ORGANIZATION COMMANDER

The Reservist named above is an active reserve component member and is eligible for space-available transportation on DoD-owned or controlled aircraft in accordance with DoD Regulation 4515.13-R, and is authorized to so travel from _____ to _____ (Not to exceed 30 days.)

		10. Date (YYMMDD)	11. Date (YYMMDD)
12. NAME (Last First, MI)	13. PAY GRADE	14. SIGNATURE	15. DATE SIGNED (YYMMDD)

DD Form 1853, 84 APR   *Previous editions are obsolete.*   ☆U.S. Government Printing Office: 1984—460-962/23346

MAC - BOARDING PASS/TICKET/RECEIPT

PASSENGER'S NAME (Last, First, Middle Initial)		FLIGHT NUMBER	GATE	SEAT NUMBER	SMOKING	SPACE AVAILABLE CHARGE TAX $
ORIGIN	DESTINATION	VIA	DEPARTURE DATE		BOARDING TIME	MEAL COST
BAGGAGE WEIGHT PIECES	EXCESS WEIGHT	OTHER WEIGHT	MEAL PURCHASE (KIND - TYPE - QUANTITY)			BAGGAGE COST
REFUND						OTHER COSTS
To get a refund, the Passenger Service Officer or a designated representative must complete the following						
DATE	REASON FOR REFUND					TOTAL COSTS $
SIGNATURE (Passenger Service Representative)		SIGNATURE (Passenger)				SPACE AVAILABLE CHARGE PAID TO SPECIFIED DESTINATION:

MAC FORM AUG 79 **124a**   PREVIOUS EDITION IS OBSOLETE   **PASSENGER COPY**

BAGGAGE IDENTIFICATION

NAME (Last, First, M.I.)

STREET ADDRESS (Home or Unit/APO)

CITY, STATE AND ZIP CODE

DD FORM 80 SEP **1839** USE PREVIOUS EDITION.

APPENDIX N
SPECIAL TRAVEL AIDS

1. **American Society of Travel Agents**
   Public Relations Department
   4400 MacArthur Blvd, NW
   Washington, DC 20007   Comm: (202) 965-7520
   Write for the following free brochures (include a stamped, self-addressed, #10 envelope): Packing Tips for Him; Packing Tips for Her; What Every Overseas Traveler Should Know; and Cruise Safety.

2. **Consumer Information Center**
   Department 165-P
   Pueblo, CO 81009
   The Department of Transportation offers a pamphlet for air travelers. They state, "With our advice, we hope you can become your own consumer advocate." Send $1.00 and ask for "Fly Rights, A Guide to Air Travel in the U.S."

3. **International Association for Medical Assistance to Travelers (IAMAT)**
   736 Center Street
   Lewiston, NY 14092-1796
   This is a no membership fee organization that publishes a directory of English-speaking physicians at IAMAT Centers in hundreds of cities all over the world (including some very remote places). For a tax deductible (we think) contribution of your choice they will provide you with the directory, a passport-size medical record to be completed by your physician before departure, world immunization charts, and world climate charts. The centers will have daily lists of approved doctors available on a 24-hour basis. The schedule of fees (as of Aug 31, 1983) agreed to be charged is: office call-$20; house/hotel call-$30; night, Sunday and local holiday-$35. These fees do not apply to consultations, hospital or laboratory fees.

4. **The International Directory of Access Guides**
   Rehabilitation International USA Inc.
   20 West 40th Street
   New York, NY 10018
   Publishes a directory of Access Guides as aids for disabled and elderly travelers. The directory is free and has been developed as a result of a joint grant from the American Express Foundation and the Fireman's Fund Insurance Company Foundation.

5. **United Service Organization (USO)**
   World Headquarters
   601 Indiana Ave, NW
   Washington, DC 20004   Comm: (202) 783-8211
   Write for a free directory of USO's worldwide. The USO is a civilian, non-profit organization, supported by the contributions of the American public through the United Way, Combined Federal Campaign, and individual donations.

6. **Visa Requirements to Foreign Governments**
   US Department of State
   Bureau of Consular Affairs
   2201 C Street NW, Room 683
   Washington, DC 20520
   "Visa Requirements to Foreign Governments" is free information from the above address or any passport office.

APPENDIX O
LI-ICAO CONVERSION TABLE

The table below converts standard three-character location identifiers to the sometimes-used four-character international location identifiers found at military departure locations.

UNCLASSIFIED
STATION CHARACTERISTICS

LI	ICAO	LI	ICAO	LI	ICAO	LI	ICAO	LI	ICAO	LI	ICAO
ADA	LTAG	BUE	SAEZ	ENT	PKMA	JON	PJON	MHZ	EGUN	ORF	KORF
ADC	LTAF	BWY	EGVJ	ERZ	LTCE	KAI	OEKM	MIA	KMIA	OSL	ENFB
ADK	PADK	BZE	MZBZ	ESB	LTAC	KEF	BIKF	MIO	MVMI	OSN	RKSO
ADL	AAAD	BZI	LTBF	ESK	LTBI	KHE	RKPK	MKK	WMKK	OTZ	PAOT
ADW	KADW	CAI	HECA	FAI	PAFA	KIN	MKJP	MRB	KMRB	PAL	SADP
AKN	PAKN	CDB	PACD	FEL	EDSF	KRT	HSSS	MRH	OOMA	PAP	MTPP
AKT	LCRA	CGY	RPWL	FIH	FZAA	KSA	PTSA	MRU	FIMP	PHL	KPHL
ALA	LPAR	CHC	NZCH	FRA	EDDF	KUH	RJCK	MSJ	RJSM	PIK	EGPK
AMM	OJAF	CHS	KCHS	FRF	EDAF	KUZ	RKJK	MSP	KMSP	PLA	MHCG
ANC	PANC	CJU	RKPC	FUK	RJFF	KWA	PKWA	MTN	KMTN	PMI	LESJ
ASI	FHAW	CLT	KCLT	FYU	PAFY	KWJ	RKJJ	MUS	RJAM	PNI	PTPN
ASP	ASAS	COF	KCOF	GAL	PAGA	LAX	KLAX	MVD	SUMU	POB	KPOB
ASU	SGAS	CRK	RPMK	GAO	MUGM	LCA	LCLK	NAP	LIRN	PPG	NSTU
ATH	LGAT	CRW	KCRW	GBI	MYGM	LCE	MHLC	NBE	KNBE	PSA	LIRP
AVB	LIPA	CTG	MCCG	GDT	MKJT	LEA	APLM	NBO	HKNA	PVD	KPVD
AWK	PWAK	CTS	RJCC	GUA	MGGT	LEM	EGXE	NDJ	FTTJ	PZU	HSSP
BAD	KBAD	CUA	RPMB	HAJ	EDVV	LFI	KLFI	NDO	EDCN	RCM	ASRI
BAH	OBBI	CYS	KCYS	HAM	EDDH	LGS	LPLA	NGU	KNGU	REG	LICR
BBE	HCMI	CZF	PACZ	HIK	PHIK	LHN	EDNA	NIM	DRRN	RIO	SBGL
BDA	MXKF	DCA	KDCA	HLV	RKSW	LIM	SPIM	NJA	RJTA	RIV	KRIV
BDL	KBDL	DCU	LIED	HNL	PHNL	LPB	SLLP	NKW	FJDG	RMS	EDAR
BDS	LIBR	DHA	OEDR	HOW	MPHO	LPH	EDSD	NQA	KNQA	ROB	GLRB
BGI	MKPB	DIY	LTCC	IGL	LTBL	LRF	KLRF	NRR	MJNR	ROR	PTRO
BGR	KBGR	DJK	WIIH	ILG	KILG	LTS	KLTS	NRV	EDNN	RTA	LERT
BKK	VTBD	DNA	RODN	IWA	RJOI	LUR	PALU	NUE	EDDN	RUH	OERY
BLV	KBLV	DOV	KDOV	IWO	RJAW	MAH	LEMH	OAK	KOAK	SAL	MSSS
BNA	KBNA	DYS	KDYS	JAN	KJAN	MDY	PMDY	OBO	RJCB	SAP	MHLM
BOG	MCBO	EDF	PAED	JDW	OEJN	MEM	KMEN	OCO	MROC	SAV	KSAV
BRU	EBBR	EHC	LTAT	JED	OEJD	MFD	KMFD	OKC	KOKC	SBD	KSBD
BRW	PABR	EHM	PAEH	JFK	KJFK	MGA	MNMG	OKO	RJTY	SCH	KSCH
BSB	SBBR	EIL	PAEI	JNB	FAJS	MGQ	HCMM	OLB	LIEO	SCL	SCEL

LI	ICAO	LI	ICAO
SDQ	MDSI	TIK	KTIK
SEA	KSEA	TKK	PTKK
SEB	OOMS	TLJ	PATL
SEL	RKSS	TLV	LLBG
SEX	EDAS	TNC	PATC
SFJ	BGSF	TOJ	LETO
SFO	KSFO	TRJ	MHTJ
SGP	WSAP	TUU	OETB
SIO	LTSI	TXL	EDBT
SIZ	LICZ	TYA	LTBP
SJC	KSJC	UAM	PGUA
SJH	MKPA	UIO	SEQU
SNN	EINN	UMR	AAWR
SOC	LGSA	UTO	PAIM
SPN	PGSN	VBU	VTBU
SSS	EHSB	VCE	LIPT
STJ	KSTJ	VEN	LIPZ
STL	KSTL	VNY	KVNY
STR	EDOC	VTK	WSSS
STX	MISX	VWH	LGIR
SUU	KSUU	WRI	KWRI
SVW	PASV	YAP	PTYA
SYA	PASY	YAW	CYAW
SYD	ASSY	YES	LTBA
TAE	RKTN	YQX	CYQX
TCM	KTCM	YYR	CYYR
TGA	WSAT	YYT	CYYT
TGU	MHTG	ZAZ	LEZA
THF	EDBB		
THU	BGTL		
TIF	OETF		

APPENDIX P   Military Airlift Command

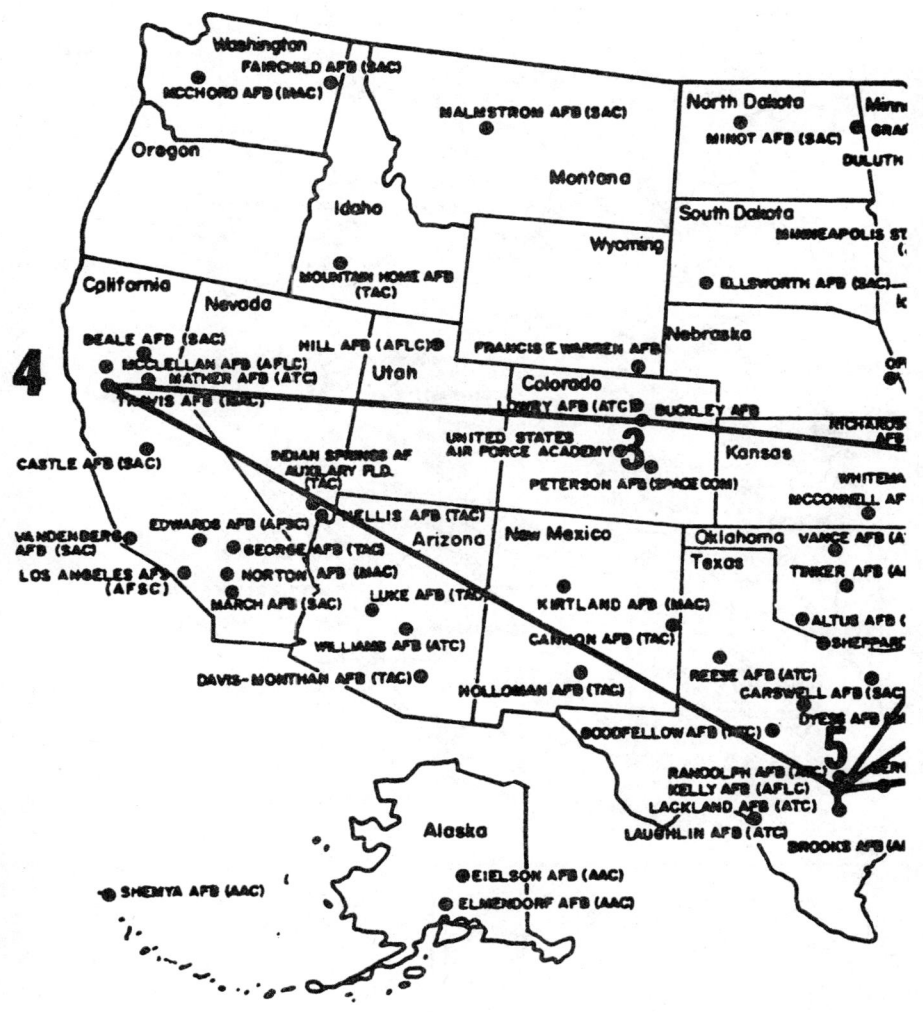

KEY TO SCHEDULED FLIGHTS (C9's)

1	ANDREWS	1 TO 2	MON THU		2 TO 1	WED SUN
2	KEESLER	1 TO 4	THU SAT		2 TO 5	WED SAT
3	BUCKLEY	1 TO 6	MON		3 TO 4	WED SAT
4	TRAVIS		WED		3 TO 6	TUE THU FRI
5	KELLY		THU			
6	SCOTT		SAT			
			SUN			

(MAC) MEDEVAC Flights

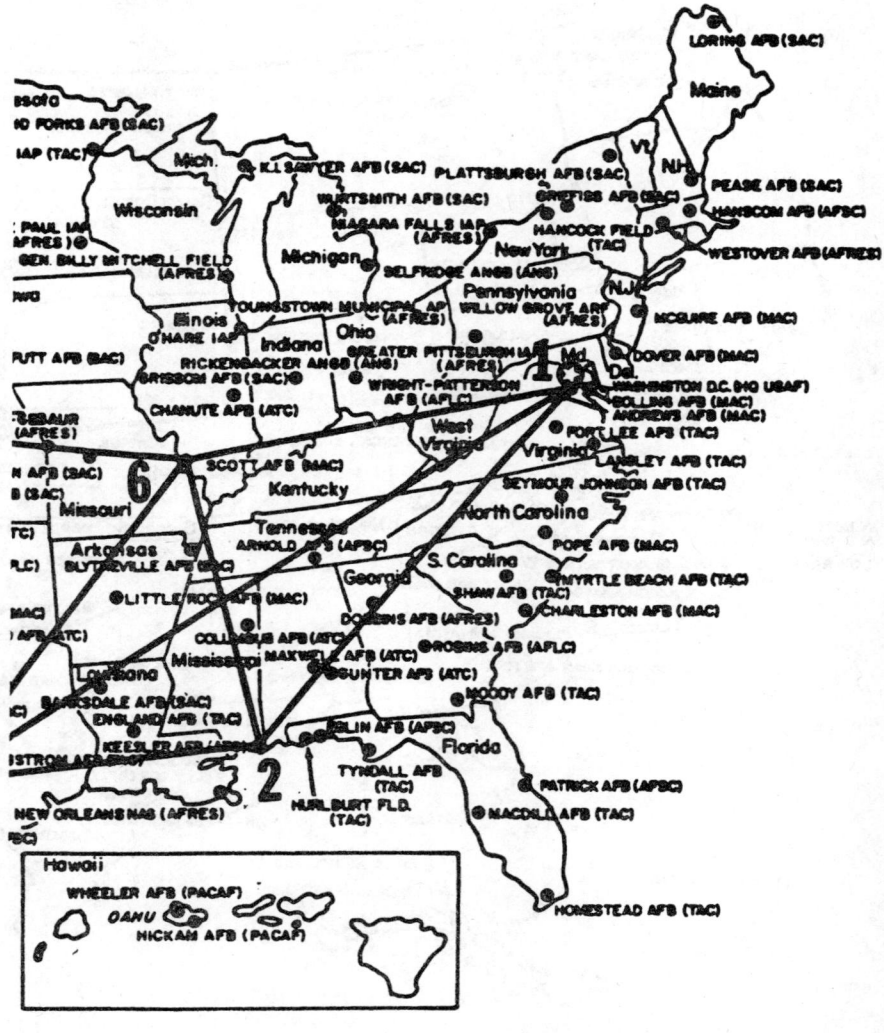

4 TO 1	THU SUN	5 TO 2	FRI	6 TO 1	MON WED THU FRI SAT SUN
4 TO 3	FRI	5 TO 4	MON WED	6 TO 2	MON TUE WED FRI SUN
4 TO 5	TUE	5 TO 6	TUE	6 TO 3	MON TUE WED THU FRI SA
4 TO 6	TUE		WED	6 TO 4	MON WED THU SAT
	THU		FRI	6 TO 5	MON TUE WED THU SAT
	FRI		SAT		
	SUN		SUN		

APPENDIX Q

STANDARD TIME CONVERSION TABLE

-12	-11	-10	-9	-8	-7	-6	-5	-4	GMT	+1	+2	+3	+5	+5:30	+7	+8	+9	+9:30	+10	+12
ISLA-LEIA	MIDWAY PAGO PAGO CANTON	NOMI 11, SHEMYA	ELMEN-DORF	PACIFIC TIME (US)	MOUNTAIN TIME (US)	CENTRAL TIME (US) SCOTT AFB	EASTERN TIME (US) PANAMA CUBA	BERMUDA PUERTO RICO GREEN-LAND	ICELAND ASCEN-SION AZORES ENGLAND SCOTLAND	GERMANY ITALY, SPAIN	GREECE, EGYPT, JOHAN-NESBURG	DHAHRAN TURKEY	KARACHI (PAKI-STAN)	NEW DELHI (INDIA)	THAILAND	PHILIP-PINES, TAIWAN S. VIETNAM	OKINAWA JAPAN, KOREA	ALICE SPRINGS (AUS) NORTH (AUS)	GUAM, RICHMOND (AUS)	WAKE, NEW ZEALAND
0600	0700	0800	0900	1000	1100	1200	1300	1400	1800	1900	2000	2100	2300	2330	0100	0200	0300	0330	0400	0600
0700	0800	0900	1000	1100	1200	1300	1400	1500	1900	2000	2100	2200	2400	0030	0200	0300	0400	0430	0500	0700
0800	0900	1000	1100	1200	1300	1400	1500	1600	2000	2100	2200	2300	0100	0130	0300	0400	0500	0530	0600	0800
0900	1000	1100	1200	1300	1400	1500	1600	1700	2100	2200	2300	2400	0200	0230	0400	0500	0600	0630	0700	0900
1000	1100	1200	1300	1400	1500	1600	1700	1800	2200	2300	2400	0100	0300	0330	0500	0600	0700	0730	0800	1000
1100	1200	1300	1400	1500	1600	1700	1800	1900	2300	2400	0100	0200	0400	0430	0600	0700	0800	0830	0900	1100
1200	1300	1400	1500	1600	1700	1800	1900	2000	2400	0100	0200	0300	0500	0530	0700	0800	0900	0930	1000	1200
1300	1400	1500	1600	1700	1800	1900	2000	2100	0100	0200	0300	0400	0600	0630	0800	0900	1000	1030	1100	1300
1400	1500	1600	1700	1800	1900	2000	2100	2200	0200	0300	0400	0500	0700	0730	0900	1000	1100	1130	1200	1400
1500	1600	1700	1800	1900	2000	2100	2200	2300	0300	0400	0500	0600	0800	0830	1000	1100	1200	1230	1300	1500
1600	1700	1800	1900	2000	2100	2200	2300	2400	0400	0500	0600	0700	0900	0930	1100	1200	1300	1330	1400	1600
1700	1800	1900	2000	2100	2200	2300	2400	0100	0500	0600	0700	0800	1000	1030	1200	1300	1400	1430	1500	1700
1800	1900	2000	2100	2200	2300	2400	0100	0200	0600	0700	0800	0900	1100	1130	1300	1400	1500	1530	1600	1800
1900	2000	2100	2200	2300	2400	0100	0200	0300	0700	0800	0900	1000	1200	1230	1400	1500	1600	1630	1700	1900
2000	2100	2200	2300	2400	0100	0200	0300	0400	0800	0900	1000	1100	1300	1330	1500	1600	1700	1730	1800	2000
2100	2200	2300	2400	0100	0200	0300	0400	0500	0900	1000	1100	1200	1400	1430	1600	1700	1800	1830	1900	2100
2200	2300	2400	0100	0200	0300	0400	0500	0600	1000	1100	1200	1300	1500	1530	1700	1800	1900	1930	2000	2200
2300	2400	0100	0200	0300	0400	0500	0600	0700	1100	1200	1300	1400	1600	1630	1800	1900	2000	2030	2100	2300
2400	0100	0200	0300	0400	0500	0600	0700	0800	1200	1300	1400	1500	1700	1730	1900	2000	2100	2130	2200	2400
0100	0200	0300	0400	0500	0600	0700	0800	0900	1300	1400	1500	1600	1800	1830	2000	2100	2200	2230	2300	0100
0200	0300	0400	0500	0600	0700	0800	0900	1000	1400	1500	1600	1700	1900	1930	2100	2200	2300	2330	2400	0200
0300	0400	0500	0600	0700	0800	0900	1000	1100	1500	1600	1700	1800	2000	2030	2200	2300	2400	0030	0100	0300
0400	0500	0600	0700	0800	0900	1000	1100	1200	1600	1700	1800	1900	2100	2130	2300	2400	0100	0130	0200	0400
0500	0600	0700	0800	0900	1000	1100	1200	1300	1700	1800	1900	2000	2200	2230	2400	0100	0200	0230	0300	0500

NOTE: This chart is for planning purposes only, as local times may vary from the above due to local conditions, such as daylight savings time, etc. For exact local times, consult current Foreign Clearance Guide, DOD Flight Information Publication, or Air Almanac.

-NOTES-

Space-A Travel Newsletter
(Space-A Air ... Space-A RV & Camping ... Space-A Temporary Military Lodging)

FREE COPIES FOR PURCHASERS of THIS BOOK

"TRAVEL ON LESS PER DAY.... THE MILITARY WAY"

We'd like to acquaint you with our travel newsletter, Military Living's R&R Report. It gives late breaking info on Space-A air travel, new info on military camping and rec areas, and temporary military lodging plus informative and helpful reader trip reports.

We'll send you two free copies (a $4.00 value) if you will send $1.00 to cover the cost of postage and handling.

To get your copies, send your name and address and $1.00 to:
Military Living R&R (Dept. SA)
Box 2347
Falls Church, VA 22042

Note: We regret that this must be a one-time offer and may not be used to extend a current R&R Report subscription or combined with any other discount.

Coming Soon!

U.S. Forces Travel Guide: Europe Plus Near East / Atlantic Areas

by Roy & Ann Crawford

For information send a stamped, self-addressed envelope to:

Military Living Publications
P. O. Box 2347
Falls Church, Virginia 22042

MOVING TO WASHINGTON COUPON

MILITARY Living Magazine's "One Shot" Help

MOVING TO WASHINGTON?
Make one call or send this coupon & help will be on its way. As a military wife, one of my chief goals is to boost military family morale... so mail this coupon today & help will be on its way.

Hope to hear from you soon.

Ann Crawford, Publisher
Military Living Magazine

Have you sent your One Shot?
No, but I'm stepping on it!

TO: Mrs. Ann Crawford, Publisher, Military Living
P.O. Box 2347, Falls Church, VA 22042
Phone: (703) 237-0203

Our Family Is:
- [ ] Army
- [ ] Navy
- [ ] Air Force
- [ ] Marine
- [ ] Coast Guard
- [ ] P.H.S.
- [ ] NOAA
- [ ] Other
- [ ] Active
- [ ] Retired
- [ ] 100% DAV

Grade/Rank of military member in family _____
Name: _____
Address: _____
City/State/Zip: _____
Tel: _____
Number in family: _____
Number of children: _____

Assigned to: _____
We expect to arrive: _____

We would like info, if possible, on the following:
- [ ] House
- [ ] Apt.
- [ ] Condo
- [ ] Renting
- [ ] Buying
- [ ] Car
- [ ] Doctor
- [ ] Furniture
- [ ] Dentist
- [ ] Major Appliances
- [ ] Short Term Housing
- [ ] Military B&B
- [ ] Hotel/Motel
- [ ] Short Term Apt.
- [ ] Banking/Checking Accounts
- [ ] Employment Opportunities for spouse
- [ ] Real Estate Career Opportunities
- [ ] Legal Services/Settlement Atty.
- [ ] College Opportunities
- [ ] Investment Opportunities
- [ ] Travel in nearby areas
- [ ] Back Issues of Military Living
- [ ] Window Treatments

Other things we need: _____

Space-A Travel Newsletter
(Space-A Air . . . Space-A RV & Camping . . . Space-A Temporary Military Lodging)

FREE COPIES FOR PURCHASERS of THIS BOOK

"TRAVEL ON LESS PER DAY. . . . THE MILITARY WAY"

We'd like to acquaint you with our travel newsletter, Military Living's R&R Report. It gives late breaking info on Space-A air travel, new info on military camping and rec areas, and temporary military lodging plus informative and helpful reader trip reports.

We'll send you two free copies (a $4.00 value) if you will send $1.00 to cover the cost of postage and handling.

To get your copies, send your name and address and $1.00 to:
Military Living R&R (Dept. SA)
Box 2347
Falls Church, VA 22042

Note: We regret that this must be a one-time offer and may not be used to extend a current R&R Report subscription or combined with any other discount.

CENTRAL ORDER COUPON

MILITARY Living™

MILITARY LIVING PUBLICATIONS
P.O. Box 2347, Falls Church, VA 22042
Telephone: (703) 237-0203.

Publications	Qty.	Publications	Qty/Yrs.
The One Everyone is Talking About **Military Space-A Air Opportunities Around the World°** $15.45 ea.		Assignment Washington A Guide to Washington Area Military Installations $7.45 ea.	
You Can Have Fun With This Book! **Military RV, Camping & Rec Areas Around the World°** $9.45 ea.		The World-Wide Travel Newsletter **Military Living's R&R Report** 5 yrs. - $42.00 2 yrs. - $20.00 3 yrs. - $27.00 1 yr. - $12.00 (6 issues)	
Our All Time Best Seller! **Temporary Military Lodging Around the World°** $11.45 ea.		Local Washington Area Magazine **Military Living** 3 yrs. - $16.00 1 yr. - $7.00 (12 issues) 2 yrs. - $12.00	
U.S. Forces Travel Guide U.S.A. & Caribbean Areas° $9.45 ea.			
Subtotal: $		Subtotal: $	

*If you are an R&R subscriber, you may deduct $1.00 per book. (No discount on R&R Report itself.)

For 1st Class Mail, add $1.00 per book

Mail Order Prices are for the U.S., APO & FPO addresses. Please consult Publisher for International Mail Price. Sorry, no billing. GREAT FUND RAISERS! Please write for wholesale rates.

Total: $ _____

VA addresees
add 4½% sales tax $ _____
(Books only)

Total Amount $ _____
Enclosed

We're as close as your telephone. . .by using our Telephone Ordering Service. We honor Visa, American Express, Choice or Mastercard. Call us at **(703) 237-0203** and order today! Sorry, no collect calls. Or. . . fill out the info in the mail order coupon below.

Name: _____
Street: _____
City/State: _____
Phone: _____
(with area code)
Signature: _____

☐ Active Duty
☐ Retired
☐ Widower
☐ 100% Disabled Veteran
☐ Guard
☐ Reservist
☐ Other _____

Rank: _____ or Rank of Sponsor: _____

Branch of Service: _____

Please mail check or money order to: Military Living, P.O. Box 2347, Falls Church, VA 22042.

Family Of Publications

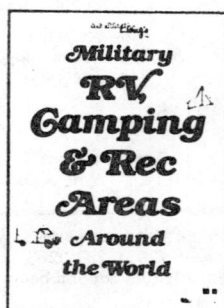

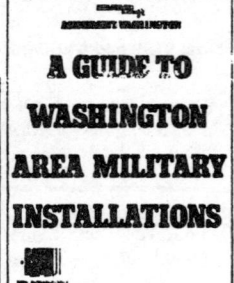

Phone orders are accepted with Visa, American Express and Mastercard.

 **Call (703) 237-0203
Sorry, no collect calls.**

CENTRAL ORDER COUPON
MILITARY LIVING PUBLICATIONS
P.O. Box 2347, Falls Church, VA 22042
Telephone: (703) 237-0203.

Publications	Qty	Publications	Qty/Yrs
The One Everyone is Talking About Military Space-A Air Opportunities Around the World* $15.45 ea.		Assignment Washington A Guide to Washington Area Military Installations $7.45 ea.	
You Can Have Fun With This Book! Military RV, Camping & Rec Areas Around the World* $9.45 ea.		*The World-Wide Travel Newsletter* Military Living's R&R Report 5 yrs. - $42.00 2 yrs. - $20.00 3 yrs. - $27.00 1 yr. - $12.00 (6 issues)	
Our All Time Best Seller! Temporary Military Lodging Around the World* $11.45 ea.		*Local Washington Area Magazine* Military Living 3 yrs. - $16.00 1 yr. - $7.00 (12 issues) 2 yrs. - $12.00	
U.S. Forces Travel Guide U.S.A. & Caribbean Areas* $9.45 ea.			
Subtotal: $		Subtotal: $	

*If you are an R&R subscriber, you may deduct $1.00 per book. (No discount on R&R Report itself.)

For 1st Class Mail, add $1.00 per book

Mail Order Prices are for the U.S., APO & FPO addresses. Please consult Publisher for International Mail Price. Sorry, no billing. GREAT FUND RAISERS! Please write for wholesale rates.

Total: $ _____
VA addressees
add 4½% sales tax $ _____
(Books only)

Total Amount $ _____
Enclosed

We're as close as your telephone. . .by using our Telephone Ordering Service. We honor Visa, American Express, Choice or Mastercard. Call us at (703) 237-0203 and order today! Sorry, no collect calls. Or. . . fill out the info in the mail order coupon below.

Name: _____

Street: _____

City/State: _____

Phone: _____
(with area code)

Signature: _____

☐ Active Duty
☐ Retired
☐ Widower
☐ 100% Disabled Veteran
☐ Guard
☐ Reservist
☐ Other _____

Rank _____ or Rank of Sponsor: _____

Branch of Service _____

Please mail check or money order to: Military Living, P.O. Box 2347, Falls Church, VA 22042.

NOTES